15622

810.9
SMA
C. 1
$30.00

MICHIGAN AUTHORS

by the Michigan Association of Media in Education

Third Edition

1993

—— All entries new or revised ——

Carol Smallwood, editor
Media Director, Pellston Public Schools
Pellston, Michigan

Judy Evers
Project Coordinator for M.A.M.E.

Cover design and production assistance by
David B. McConnell

Published by Hillsdale Educational Publishers in cooperation
with the Michigan Association for Media in Education

ISBN 0-910726-28-0

Printed in Michigan using soy based ink and acid free paper

Additional copies may be purchased through
Hillsdale Educational Publishers
P.O. Box 245, 39 North Street, Hillsdale, Michigan 49424
phone   517-437-3179

Library of Congress Cataloging in Publication Data

Michigan authors / by the Michigan Association for Media in Education
 ; Carol Smallwood, editor. — 3rd ed.
      p.   cm.
    "All entries new or revised."
    Includes bibliographical references and indexes.
    ISBN 0-910726-28-0 : $39.95
    1. Authors, American—Michigan—Biography—Dictionaries.
 2. American literature—Michigan—Bio-bibliography. I. Smallwood,
 Carol, 1939- . II. Michigan Association for Media in Education.
 PS283.M5M54 1993
 810.9'9774'03—dc20   93-30097
                                                        CIP

Michigan Association for Media in Education

MICHIGAN AUTHORS Committee

Judy Evers, Vice-President of Special Interest Groups, Chairperson

Mary Adrion, President MAME

Burton Brooks, Past President, MAME; Executive Director MAME

Ricki Chowning, Past President, MAME

Barbara Wallace, Past President, MAME

Peg Sanford, Past President, MAME

Della Wilder, Chairperson- Awards and Citations

"Every people is polarized in some locality, which is home, the homeland. Different places on the face of the earth have different vital influence, different vibration, different chemical exhalation, different polarity with different stars: call it what you like. But the spirit of place is a great reality."

D. H. Lawrence, *Studies on Classic American Literature*, 1923

Dedication

To Rachel M. Hilbert, Livonia, Michigan, High School Librarian, editor of the first edition of *Michigan Authors,* 1960 for The Michigan Association of School Librarians; editor, *Michigan Poets with Supplement to Michigan Authors,* 1964, for the Michigan Association of School Librarians.

To Donna Taylor, Publisher, Green Oak Press, Brighton, Michigan, chairperson for the editorial committee of the Michigan Association for Media in Education, second edition of *Michigan Authors* published by Michigan Association for Media in Education, Ann Arbor, Michigan, 1980.

To all past and present Michigan authors, and especially to those in our schools now.

Table of Contents

Foreword

The Michigan Association for Media in Education (MAME) is the professional organization for library media personnel in this state. Our award-winning journal, *Media Spectrum*, and our newsletter provide professional updates and inform us. Our conferences, August Academy, and our regional meetings provide inservice training. Our 1,400 members provide support to each other through networking. We have valid reasons to be proud MAME members.

MAME is sponsoring the third edition of *Michigan Authors*. We have had a groundswell of requests for an updated reference and also for more copies of the second edition. Although there are no second edition copies available, many of those authors are covered retrospectively in the third edition, (1993). This is our first indexed, hard-cover edition and it will fill the reference need you have had.

This book would not have been possible without the support of a number of people. In addition to the names already listed are other MAME members. Some of you met with committes; some sent references, clippings, or researched material to Carol Smallwood or me; some of you gave encouragement to us to complete the project and showed your strong interest throughout the three-and-a-half years. You are greatly appreciated. Thank you.

Judy Evers
MICHIGAN AUTHORS project chairperson
Hillsdale, Michigan
1993

Preface

Editing the third edition of *Michigan Authors* has been a unique privilege filled with much learning, enjoyment, challenge, and awe. Just a brief sampling of authors encountered included wives of Michigan governors, construction workers, medical doctors, retired executives, farmers, judges, housewives, national park interpreters, a beekeeper, rock group singer, nun, circus performer, animal shelter manager, and a masseuse.

Questionnaires have been returned from authors born 1890's-1960's, in several states and foreign countries. Most writers responding to questionnaires have careers other than writing but some combine careers like illustrator-author. Many have written over a life-time, others upon retiring. You will notice that their aims and goals are as diverse as their writing and that they live in isolated woods, inner cities, on lake shores, in apartments and renovated churches. Michigan authors provide information, pleasure, cultural identity, challenge to the status quo, beauty, guidance, encouragement and inspire beginning authors to find their own voices and continue the tradition of diversity. These writers of many races add to the rich texture of Michigan's literary fabric first begun by tales told over Indian camp fires.

It is hoped this new edition may also encourage the younger generation to pursue Michigan History with renewed interest since, as noted by Andrew J. Green when reviewing *A Centennial History of Michigan* over fifty years ago: "Literature, which must always derive its universals from an understanding of the immediate, is in the last analysis merely a phenomenon of general history; and, like history, a healthy literature must have its specific, local origins."

Carol Smallwood
MICHIGAN AUTHORS Editor
Cheboygan, Michigan
1993

Introduction

The third edition of *Michigan Authors* includes almost 50% more authors than the second edition and added these new features: biographical books in which the author appears, locations of colleges attended, if the writer may be contacted for workshops/readings and two types of indexing.

It does not pretend to cover all of Michigan's authors- a list of authors for the next edition has already begun and with the help of readers (see Call to Readers page), a more extensive coverage will be realized. The term authors includes: poets, screen writers, short story writers, journalists, novelists, playwrights, nonfiction writers, and other genre.

Inclusion criteria:

(1) The author was born in Michigan

(2) The author was presently residing year-around in Michigan

(3) The author had at least one book completely set in Michigan

Most of the entries were based on questionnaires completed by the authors. If the author could not be located, nor help provided by publishers or agents, local libraries or museums, or by other means, secondary information was used.

Arrangement:

Authors are arranged alphabetically by last name with cross references to authors using pseudonyms. The following format was used:

Name: Name, birth/death dates if dead

Address: An address is included if supplied by author

Pseudonym: pen name, if used

Date of Birth: month, date, year. **Place of Birth:** city, state

Name of father; mother: including **(maiden)** name if known

Children: first name(s)

Education: Name of school, degree, city/state of location, dates

Career: Position, organization, city/state of location, dates

Writings: Title, publisher, date. Work in Progress-current work

Awards or inclusion in other biographical books: Name of book, edition if supplied. Title, source, date of award. If in over 12 biographical books, "others" was indicated; in over 18, "several others" was indicated

What is the aim or goal of your writing? Quote supplied by author

May inquiries be sent to you about doing workshops, readings? Yes, No. With comments

Quotes by the author or others from the second edition of *Michigan Authors* if author was unable to be contacted or deceased

The aim for consistency in content was not always realized because of information supplied or available. The name of spouse was not requested but some added it. When the author was prolific, their first, middle, last works, those relating to Michigan, their best known, were included, number of books, if provided. "Others" indicates more. Information was taken from questionnaires, and awards, biographical books were not added if not supplied by the author with the exception of *Michigan Authors,* 1st and 2nd editions and *Michigan Poets with Supplement to Michigan Authors 1960.* In a few entries inclusion into Michigan Women's Hall of Fame was also indicated if not provided.

Indexes:1) Alphabetical by author's last name 2) Geographical by either city of Michigan residence, birthplace, or locations used in settings if neither of the first two apply or are available.

Call to readers and authors

Please send names and addresses of authors you would like to see in the next edition. If you are an author, please request an author questionnaire. News clippings, author conference flyers, other leads, comments, would be most helpful.

The Fourth edition will tentatively be published in 1998 and *with your help* it will continue to provide an indispensable, ongoing reference on Michigan authors.

Send author information or questionnaire requests to:
MAME Headquarters, Michigan Authors Committee, 6810 South Cedar Street, Suite 8, Lansing, Michigan 48911.

Acknowledgements

Many authors in the 3rd edition provided help in locating fellow authors and to all of these, a sincere thanks. Appreciation is also expressed to the following for the important aid each kindly extended:

Proofreaders:
Pat Charlton, Ricki Chowning, Judy Evers, David McConnell, Stella McConnell, Terri Nicola, Carol Smallwood, Randal Smith, Barbara Wallace, and Della Wilder

Alcona County Library. Harrisville, Michigan.

Alcona County Review. Harrisville, Michigan.

Alpena County Library. Staff. Alpena, Michigan.

Ambrogio, Anthony. Publisher, Corridors Press, Southfield, Michigan.

Anderson, Gay. Librarian, Mancelona Township Library, Mancelona, Michigan.

Andrews, Shirley. Media Specialist, Edwardsburg, Michigan.

Bahr, Nancy. Media Center, Brighton High School, Brighton, Michigan.

Baker Book House. Grand Rapids, Michigan.

Beasecker, Robert. Archivist, Grand Valley State University, Allendale, Michigan.

Bellezza-Dziurda, Jane. Media Director, Madison High School, Madison Heights, Michigan.

Benson, Virginia. Spring Lake Junior/Senior High School, Spring Lake, Michigan.

Bentley, Margaret. Adult Services Librarian, Owosso Public Library, Owosso, Michigan.

Billings, Shirley. Burt Lake, Michigan.

Bondy, Doris. Marketing and Publications, Glendon Publishing, Las Vegas, Nevada.

Borland, Janet Kaufman. Adrian Public Library, Adrian, Michigan.

Bowen, Tammy. White Pine Library, Stanton, Michigan.

Biuletyn. Grand Rapids Polish Heritage Society.

Burns, Virginia. Laingsburg, Michigan.

Callard, Don. Reference Librarian, Ann Arbor Public Library, Ann Arbor, Michigan.

Charles A. Ransom District Library. Plainwell, Michigan.

Christensen, Pamela R. Director, Peter White Public Library, Marquette, Michigan.

Clark, Thomas. Wood Artist. Traverse City, Michigan.

Clement, Cindy. Media Center, Farmington High School, Farmington, Michigan.

Cohen, Martin. Professor Emeritus, School of Librarianship, Western Michigan University, Kalamazoo, Michigan.

Curtis, Jim. Information Services Librarian, Northland Library Cooperative, Alpena, Michigan.

Dawson, Lawrence R. Mt. Pleasant, Michigan.

DeFields, Victoria. Bridgman High School Media Center, Bridgman, Michigan.

Delaney, Lisa. Library Assistant, Central Michigan University, Mt. Pleasant, Michigan.

Detroit Women Writers.

Devine, Iola M. Indian River, Michigan.

DeVinney, CoraEllen. Library Director, Troy Public Library, Troy, Michigan.

DeWaard, Jeanne Elders. Publicity Manager, Wm. B. Eerdmans Publishing Company, Grand Rapids, Michigan.

Dion, Cyndi. Work Study Student, Alpena Community College Library, Alpena, Michigan.

Duncan, Arlene. Secretary, Associate Director for Human Resources, Detroit Public Library, Detroit, Michigan.

Edsel Ford High School. Media Center, Dearborn, Michigan.

Eisenhauer, Jane. Director, Surrey Township Public Library, Farwell, Michigan.

England, H. Elaine. Spring Arbor, Michigan.

Evers, Judy. Media Specialist, Hillsdale Public Schools, Hillsdale, Michigan.

Feltner, Jeri. Seajay Publication, Dearborn, Michigan.

Ferriby, Martha. Executive Director of Library Services, Veterans Memorial Library, Mt. Pleasant, Michigan.

Fortushniak, Jane M. Librarian, Deckerville Community Schools, Deckerville, Michigan.

Fosbender, Jule. Director, Adrian Public Library, Adrian, Michigan.

Foster, Carmen. Librarian, Three Oaks Township Library, Three Oaks, Michigan.

Gemini Publications. Editor, Grand Rapids, Michigan.

Gobles Middle/High School Library. Gobles, Michigan.

Greenville Public Library. Greenville, Michigan.

Grueneberg, Mark D. Media Specialist, St. Johns High School, St. Johns, Michigan.

Hall, Grace. President, Upper Peninsula of Michigan Writers' Association, Crystal Falls, Michigan.

Hammerstein, Mary Jo. Instructional Media Assistant, Washtenaw Community College, Ann Arbor, Michigan.

Hampton, Eva. L. Lansing, Michigan.

Handy, Virginia. Log Cabin Society, Sodus, Michigan.

Hartman, Leigh. Sales and Promotion, Xpressway Publishing, Detroit, Michigan.

Heinonen, Claire. Union City High School, Union City, Michigan.

Helwig, Ruth. Interlibrary Loan Specialist, Central Michigan University, Mt. Pleasant, Michigan.

Hill, Tom. East Lansing, Michigan.

Hillsdale Public Schools. Graphics, Printing Department. Hillsdale, Michigan.

Hirsimaki, B. Mileposts Publishing Company, North Olmsted, Ohio.

Holly Township Library. Holly, Michigan.

Howell, Clare. Coordinator of Educational Media & Technology, Livonia Public Schools, Livonia, Michigan.

Howes, Theresa. Work Study Student, Alpena Community College Library, Alpena, Michigan.

Huddleston, Eugene L. Professor, Michigan State University, East Lansing, Michigan.

Hutchins, Mary J. Director, and Staff, Bement Public Library, St. Johns, Michigan.

Hutchins, Richard G. St. Johns, Michigan.

Irvine, Aline. Treasurer, Reference Publications, Inc., Algonac, Michigan.

Isaacson, David. Humanities Librarian, Western Michigan University, Kalamazoo, Michigan.

Jackson District Library. Jackson, Michigan.

Johnson, Christine E. Reference Assistant, Northland Library Cooperative, Alpena, Michigan.

Joint Archives of Holland. Holland, Michigan.

Jones, Thomas L. Executive Director, Historical Society of Michigan, Ann Arbor, Michigan.

Kalinka, Deb. Education Director, Holland Area Arts Council, Holland, Michigan.

Kerman, Judith B. Dean, College of Arts & Behavioral Sciences, Saginaw Valley State University, University Center, Michigan.

Kiefer, Marilyn. MAME 17 Regional Representative, Novi Schools, Novi, Michigan.

Klein, Clayton. Wilderness Adventure Books, Fowlerville, Michigan.

Kohler, Jeri. Publisher, Editor, *The Parma News,* Parma, Michigan.

Krawczak, Joyce. Interlibrary Loan, Cheboygan Public Library, Cheboygan, Michigan.

Lake Linden Hubbell Public School Library. Lake Linden, Michigan.

Larson, Catherine A. Local History Specialist, Kalamazoo Public Library, Kalamazoo, Michigan.

Lavin, Helen S. Library/Media Specialist, Midland High School, Midland, Michigan.

Leasher, Evelyn. Public Services Librarian, Clark Historical Library, Central Michigan University, Mount Pleasant, Michigan.

Lengnick, Marcia. Siena Heights College, Adrian, Michigan.

Lewis, Barbara. Birmingham, Michigan.

Lindsey, Elizabeth. Volunteer Librarian, Michigan Women's Studies Association, Inc., Lansing, Michigan.

Lintz Funeral Home. Indian River, Michigan.

Little Traverse Historical Society. Petoskey, Michigan.

Lowe, Kenneth S. Editor, *Michigan Out-of-Doors,* Lansing, Michigan.

Lowell, Virginia. Director, Jackson District Library, Jackson, Michigan.

Lynch, Rosemary. Youth Librarian, City of Rochester Hills Public Library, Rochester, Michigan.

Mackinac State Historic Parks. Lansing, Michigan.

Malott, Kathy. Volunteer, Bacon Memorial Library, Wyandotte, Michigan.

Marshall Public Library. Marshall, Michigan.

McBroom, Kathleen. Fordson High School, Dearborn, Michigan.

McConnell, David B. Editor, Hillsdale Educational Publishers, Hillsdale, Michigan.

McManman, Mary. Head of Reference Services, Bay City Branch Library, Bay City, Michigan.

Melancon, Beverlee. MAME Region 16 Representative, Hartland Consolidated School, Ann Arbor, Michigan.

Meloche-Chang, Sylvia. St. Mary's College, Orchard Lake, Michigan.

Michigan Association for Media in Education.

Michigan Historical Collections. Bentley Historical Library, University of Michigan, Ann Arbor, Michigan.

Michigan Nature Association. Avoca, Michigan.

Miles, William. Reference Librarian, Central Michigan University, Mt. Pleasant, Michigan.

Nearing, Susan E. Director of Public Services, Library of Michigan, Lansing, Michigan.

Neveu, Ruth. Kenneth J. Shouldice Library, Lake Superior State University, Sault Ste. Marie, Michigan.

Nicola, Terri D. Word processing operator, Hillsdale Educational Publishers, Hillsdale, Michigan.

Nordin, Elizabeth. Librarian, Hesperia Public Library and Civic Center, Hesperia, Michigan.

Nordman Funeral Home. Cheboygan, Michigan.

Palicki, Walter. Media Specialist, Bedford Junior High, Temperance, Michigan.

Papai, Beverly D. Director, Farmington Community Library, Farmington Hills, Michigan.

Passic, Frank. Curator of Local History, Albion Historical Society, Gardner House Museum, Albion, Michigan.

Pellston High School Library. Pellston Public Schools, Pellston, Michigan.

Perkins, Stan. Broadblade Press, Swartz Creek, Michigan.

Petoskey Public Library. Staff, Petoskey, Michigan.

Plymouth District Library. Plymouth, Michigan.

Quinn, Sister Lucy Ann, O.P. Bishop Baraga School, Cheboygan, Michigan.

Richards, Freda. Wylie E. Groves High School, Beverly Hills, Michigan.

Roberts, Sherry. Youth Librarian, Ann Arbor Public Library, Ann Arbor, Michigan.

Robinson, Christopher. Assistant Sales Manager, McFarland & Company, Inc., Jefferson, North Carolina.

Roscommon County Herald News. Roscommon, Michigan.

Roscommon School & Public Library. Roscommon, Michigan.

Royal Oak Public Library. Royal Oak, Michigan.

Rudden, Rick. Editor, *Daily Press,* Escanaba, Michigan.

Ryan, Pat. Bayliss Public Library, Sault Ste. Marie, Michigan.

Saranac Public Library. Saranac, Michigan.

Scott, Kyle. Senior Editor, Altwerger & Mandel Publishing Company (A & M), West Bloomfield, Michigan.

Shaffer, Patricia. Hubbard Lake, Michigan.

Sherwood, Robert L. Director, Herrick Public Library, Holland, Michigan.

Sinclair, Ann. Board Member, Lawrence Memorial Library, Climax, Michigan.

Smallwood, Ann. Medical Records, Munson Hospital, Traverse City, Michigan.

Smallwood, Michael. Student, University of Arizona, Tucson, Arizona.

Smith, Joan. Reference Desk, Library of Michigan, Lansing, Michigan.

Spence, Theresa Sanderson. Access Services Coordinator and University Archivist, Michigan Technological University, Houghton, Michigan.

Stella, Elizabeth. Director, Stair Public Library, Morenci, Michigan.

Stephenson High School. Library, Stephenson, Michigan.

Strader, Dick. Director, Media and Technology, Battle Creek Public Schools, Battle Creek, Michigan.

Tabacchi, Sandy. Library/Media Specialist, Avondale High School, Auburn Hills, Michigan.

Tanis, Beryl Bosca. Office Manager, Milkweed Editions, Minneapolis, Minnesota

Taylor, James E. Publisher, Green Oak Press, Brighton, Michigan.

Torres, Deborah. Director, Saugatuck-Douglas District Library, Douglas, Michigan.

Town, Wallace P. Sunday Editor, *The Bay City Times*, Bay City, Michigan.

Turner, Gordon. News Editor, *Cheboygan Daily Tribune*, Cheboygan, Michigan.

Valleywood Media Center. Kentwood Public Schools, Kentwood, Michigan.

Verwys, Sue. Director, Cheboygan Public Library, Cheboygan, Michigan.

Vest, Hilda. Publisher/Editor, Broadside Press, Detroit, Michigan.

Wadman, Linda J. Library Director, Ontonagon Township Library, Ontonagon, Michigan.

Wallace, Barbara. Director of Library Services, Wyandotte Public Schools, Wyandotte, Michigan.

Walling, Regis. Director of Archives, Bishop Baraga Association, Marquette, Michigan.

Warner, Joann. Library Assistant, Central Michigan University, Mt. Pleasant, Michigan.

Washington, Naomi. Shanghai, People's Republic of China.

Weber, Ginny. Lowell Senior High School Library, Lowell, Michigan.

Weber, Shelley. Assistant Director, McKune Memorial Library, Chelsea, Michigan.

Wilder, Della. Media Specialist, Heritage High School, Saginaw, Michigan.

Willard Library. Battle Creek, Michigan.

Woods, Elaine. Elementary Librarian, Livonia, Michigan.

Wright, Jan. Media Specialist, Vicksburg High School, Learning Resources Center, Vicksburg, Michigan.

A

AARDEMA, VERNA
Address: 784 Via Del Sol, N. Ft. Myers, Florida 33903
Born: June 6, 1911; New Era, Michigan
Parents: Alfred E. Norberg, Dora (Vander Ven) Norberg
Children: Austin, Paula
Education: Michigan State College, A.B., major in composition & journalism, East Lansing, Michigan, 1929-1934
Career: Teacher, Pentwater, Michigan, 1934-1935. Teacher, Muskegon, Michigan, 1935-1936. Teacher, Mona Shores Schools, Muskegon, Michgan, 1951-1973. City staff correspondent, *The Muskegon Chronicle* daily paper, 1949-1971

Writings: *Anansi Finds a Fool* Dial l992. *Borreguita and the Coyote* Knopf 1991. *Pedro and the Padre* Dial 1991. *Traveling to Tondo* Knopf 1991. *Rabbit Makes a Monkey of Lion* Dial 1989. *Princess Gorilla and a New Kind of Water* Dial 1988. *Bimwili and the Zimwi* Dial 1985. *Oh, Kojo! How Could You!* Dial 1984. *The Vingananee and the Tree Toad* Viking 1983. *What's So Funny, Ketu?* Viking 1982. *Bringing the Rain to Kapiti Plain* Dial 1981. *Who's in Rabbit's House?* Dial 1977. *Why Mosquitoes Buzz in People's Ears* Dial 1975. *Behind the Back of the Mountain* Dial 1973. *Tales From the Third Ear* E.P. Dutton 1969. *More Tales From the Story Hat* Coward McCann 1966. *The Sky God Stories* Coward McCann 1960. *Otwe* Coward McCann 1960. *The Na of Wa* Coward McCann 1960. *Tales From the Story Hat* Coward McCann 1960.
Work in Progress: *Misoso: Once Upon a Time Tales of Africa* Knopf 1994. *Sebgugugu the Glutton* Eerdmans. *A Bookworm Who Hatched* Owen 1993. *This for That* Dial.
Awards or inclusion in other biographical books: *Michigan Authors,* 2nd ed.; *Something About the Author* Autobiography Series, Vol. 8. *Borreguita and the Coyote* will be a Reading Rainbow Selection. *Traveling to Tondo,* ALA Notable Book, 1992. *Why Mosquitoes Buzz in People's Ears* Caldecott winner, 1975
What is the aim or goal of your writing? "My aim is to select the best tales which anthropologists and missionaries in the field have collected, and get them into the hands of children. I believe that an appreciation of the folk lore of other cultures promotes respect and understanding. And if the stories teach a lesson children ought to learn, that is a plus. I want my stories to be fun for children to read, and exciting but not scary enough to give them nightmares."
May inquiries be sent to you about doing workshops, readings? Yes. I do not do workshops. I tell how I became an author and some of my stories.

ABBOTT, MARGARET EVANS (1896-1976)
Born: October 6, 1896; Galesburg, Illinois
Parents: Edward J. Evans, Mary Josephine (Betrand) Evans
Children: Helen, Jane, John
Education: University of Northern Iowa, B.A., Cedar Falls, Iowa, 1924
Career: Teacher, writer. President of Lansing Poetry Club for one year, editorial consultant for *Peninsula Poets* published by the Poetry Society for ten years

Writings: *Matched Pair* (with Lawrence Abbott) Candor Press 1963. *Beyond Now* (with Lawrence Abbott) Candor Press 1968. Poems published in the *Diplomat, Chicago Tribune, Denver Post*

Awards or inclusion in other biographical books: *Michigan Poets; Michigan Authors,* 2nd ed., First Prize in Kentucky State Poetry Contest and many others from Poetry Society of Michigan.

ABRAMOWSKI, DWAIN M.
Address: P.O. Box 184, Belmont, Michigan 49306
Born: Muskegon, Michigan; March 22, 1956
Parents: Raymond J. Abramowski, Lorraine (Zynda) Abramowski
Children: Nathan
Education: Central Michigan University, Bachelor of Science in Education, Mt. Pleasant, Michigan, 1977-1979. Grand Rapids Junior College, Associate in Arts, Grand Rapids, Michigan, 1974-1976. The Institute of Children's Literature, Western Michigan University
Career: Freelance Writer, "In Flight Creations", Belmont, Michigan, last 7 years. Interim Executive Director of the Council of Performing Arts for Children, Grand Rapids, Michigan, Spring and Summer, 1989. Teacher, Grand Rapids Public Schools, Grand Rapids, Michigan, 1979-1984. Grand Rapids Recreation Department, Grand Rapids, Michigan. Cannonsburg Ski Area, Cannonsburg, Michigan. Skampt Shop, Grand Rapids, Michigan. Co-founder and President of Michigan Mountain Biking Association. Chair of the Department of Natural Resources Trails Advisory Committee

Writings: *Mountain Bike* Franklin Watts Press 1990. Dozens of published articles of publications including (but not limited to): *Skiing Magazine, Wind Surf Magazine, PSIAC Educational Newsletter, Great Lakes Boardsailing Magazine, West Michigan Running News, Home Mechanix Magazine, Michigan Sports Gazette, National Hardwoods Magazine, West Michigan Bride and Groom Magazine. Young Minds* column, *Advance News,* 1987-1991. Midwest Terrain Editor/Correspondent for *Bicycling's Mountain Bike Magazine.* Publisher/ Editor/ Writer/ Photographer of *Bent Rim Bugle.* Work in progress: *Michigan Mountain Biking Trails Guide,* and a novel called *Fifteen Minutes*
What is the aim or goal of your writing? "Sometimes I think writing is a disease, and its symptom is putting your thoughts down on paper. Other times, I think I write to better understand the world and my place in it. All in all, I think my main goal in writing is to celebrate life, and words let everyone join in on the celebration."

ADAMS, BETSY
Address: P.O. Box 296, Dexter, Michigan 48130
Born: May 1, 1942; Port Huron, Michigan
Parents: Lorne P. Adams, Dora B. Adams
Education: University of Michigan and others, B.S., Biology, Ann Arbor, Michigan,1960-1964. Western Michigan University, off and on, Kalamazoo, Michigan,1965-1969. Boston University, M.F.A., Boston, Massachusetts, 1975-1976
Career: Manager of home for stray, abandoned, wounded animals including wildlife, Chelsea Cats, 1984—. Chem Tech III, 1982—. Teaching/Biology, Creative Writing, K-12, Undergrad and Grad, and those in golden years, Western Michigan University, Michigan Council for the Arts. Research/Biology Writer 1966-1982

Writings: *The Dead Birth, Itself* Paul Green 1992. *Face at the Bottom of the World* Peg Lauber Rhiannon Press 1983. Work in Progress: Introductory volume to multiple volume series, *Child of the Light.* Poetry, fiction, nonfiction
Awards or inclusion in other biographical books: *Michigan Authors,* 2nd ed.
What is the aim or goal of your writing? "None."
May inquiries be sent to you about doing workshops, readings? Yes

ALGREN, NELSON (1909-1981)
Born: March 28, 1909; Detroit, Michigan
Education: University of Illinois, B.A., 1931
Career: Salesman. Migratory worker during the Depression. Worked in gas station, Rio Hondo, Texas, 1933. Writers' project, W.P.A. Chicago Board of Health. Co-edited*The New Anvil,*1939-1941. U.S. Army, 1942-1945. As journalist covered Vietnam War, 1969

Writings: *Somebody in Boots* Vanguard 1935; Berkley 1965. *Never Come Morning* Harper 1942; Berkley 1968. *The Neon Wilderness* Doubleday 1947, 1986. *The Man with the Golden Arm* Doubleday 1949, 1978. *Chicago: City on the Make* Doubleday 1951; McGraw 1983. *A Walk on the Wild Side* (also made into a play) Farrar, Straus 1956; Greenwood Press 1978. *Who Lost an American?* Macmillan 1963. *Notes from a Sea Diary: Hemingway All the Way* Putnam 1965. *The Last Carousel* Putnam 1973. *The Devil's Stocking* Arbor House (1981 in German translation),1983. Also contributor to anthologies, book forewords. Short stories, articles, reviews, essays in such periodicals as *Saturday Evening Post, Rolling Stone, Atlantic, Life, Nation, American Mercury.* Movies made of two novels
Awards or inclusion in other biographical books: *American Authors and Books; American Novelists of Today; Cassell's Encyclopaedia of World Literature; Contemporary Authors; Contemporary Novelists; Dictionary of Literary Biography; A Directory of American Fiction Writers; Modern American Literature; Oxford Companion to American Literature; Who's Who in America; Who's Who in Twentieth Century Literature; Who's Who in the World,* others. National Institute of Arts and Letters Fellowship, 1947. Newberry Library Fellowship, 1950. National Book Award, 1950. National Institute of Arts and Letters Medal of Merit, 1974. Fiction contest established in his name by *Chicago Magazine,* 1982. P.E.N./Nelson Algren Fiction Award begun in his memory by P.E.N. American Center 1983

ALLEN, DURWARD L.
Address: 2627 Calvin Court, West Lafayette, Indiana 47906
Born: October 11, 1910; Uniondale, Indiana
Parents: Harley J. Allen and Jennie M. (LaTurner) Allen
Children: Harley, Susan
Education: North Side High School, Fort Wayne, Indiana 1929-1932. University of Michigan, Ann Arbor, Michigan, A.B. Zoology. Michigan State University, Ph.D. Two honorary doctorates: Northern Michigan University, LHD (Humane Letters). Purdue University DA (Doctor of Agriculture)
Career: Swan Creek Wildlife Experimental Station, Michigan Conservation Department, Allegan, Michigan, Biologist in Charge, 1937-1939. Rose Lake Wildlife Experimental Station, Michigan Conservation Department, East Lansing, Michigan, Biologist in Charge, 1939-1946. Armed Services, Med. Dept., Paris, France, 1943-1945. Research Biologist U.S. Dept. of the Interior, Fish & Wildlife Service, Laurel, Maryland 1946-1950. Assistant Chief, Branch of Wildlife Research, Fish & Wildlife Service, Washington, DC,

1950-1954. Assoc. Professor of Wildlife Ecology, Purdue University, West Lafayette, Indiana 1954-1976; Emeritus, to present

Writings: *Wolves of Minong* Houghton Mifflin 1979. *The Life of Prairies and Plains* McGraw Hill 1967. *Land Use and Wildlife Resources* National Acad. Sciences 1970. *Our Wildlife Legacy* Funk & Wagnalls 1954, 1960. *Pheasants in North America* Wildlife Management Institute 1956. *Pheasants Afield* Stackpole 1953. *Michigan Fox Squirrel Management* Michigan Department of Conservation 1943. Total published titles 239-see *Audubon Magazine* March 1985

Awards or inclusion in other biographical books:
American Men of Science 1938; *Michigan Authors,* 2nd ed.; *Who's Who* (many years; last edition 1988);*Who's Who in Science* Richard H. Stroud 1985; *National Leaders of American Conservation* Smithsonian Institution 1985

What is the aim or goal of your writing? "Public education in the natural sciences, conservation."

May inquiries be sent to you about doing workshops, readings? Yes

ALLEN, ELIZABETH (1914-1984)
Born: 1914; Syracuse, New York
Parents: S.W. Allen, Helen (Brown) Allen
Children: Patricia, James Jr., Robert
Education: University of Michigan, A.B., Ann Arbor, Michigan, 1936; M.A. 1938. Poetry workshop, Women's Concerns Center
Career: Several years in medical case work, writer

Writings: *The In-Between* Dutton 1959.*The Loser* Dutton 1963.*The Forest House* Dutton 1967.*You Can't Say What You Think, and Other Stories* Dutton 1968. *Margie* Dutton 1969.*Younger's Race* Grosset 1972. Stories and poems in a variety of publications. Weekly column for *Sister Advocate*

Awards or inclusion in other biographical books: *Michigan Authors,* 1st ed., 2nd ed. University of Michigan, Hopwood winner, 1932, 1936

What is the aim or goal of your writing? In the previous edition of *Michigan Authors* she is credited with saying: "It seems strange that my publications have been, at least as far as books are concerned, in the field of 'literature for young people,' and all but one of these books have been novels. The fact that I got very involved with my children's concerns prompted these books. Now that my children are grown, I find that I am returning to short stories and poems. I am very interested in writing some truly honest stories about women, and do have a group of stories in progress."

ALLYN, DOUG L.
Address: 325 E. State Street, Montrose, Michigan 48457
Born: October 10, 1942; Bay City, Michigan
Parents: Ronald B. Allyn, Bonnie Allyn
Children: Doug
Education: Alpena High School, 1956-1960. Alpena Community College, Indiana University, University of Michigan
Career: USAF Intelligence, translator/interpreter (Mandarin Chinese) 1963-1967, Nationalist China, Japan, Philippines. Co-leader, singer/guitarist with the rock group Devil's Triangle playing in Midwest. Creative writing teacher, Mott Community College, Flint, Michigan. Author. Radio/television/newspaper interviews/speaking dates

Writings:*The Cheerio Killings* St. Martin's Press 1989. Published some 25 short stories such as: "Final Rites", *Alfred Hitchcock's Mystery Magazine,* December 1985; "A Death in Heaven", *Ellery Queen's Mystery Magazine,* December 1988. Several short stories have been translated into foreign languages. Four appear in anthologies. "A Death in Heaven" has been optioned as a potential film. Work in Progress: *Motown Underground* St. Martin's Press 1993

Awards or inclusion in other biographical books: Robert L. Fish Award Winner, Mystery Writers of America, Best First Short Story, 1985. Edgar Award Finalist, 1986, 1988, 1991. *Ellery Queen Mystery Magazine* Reader's Award Finalist, 1990. International Crime Reader's Award Winner, 1988

May inquiries be sent to you about doing workshops, readings? Yes

ALTROCCHI, JULIA COOLEY (1893-1972)

Born: July 4, 1893; Seymour, Connecticut. Summers spent at family cottage in Harbert, Michigan

Parents: Harland Ward Cooley, Nellie (Wooster) Cooley

Children: John, Paul

Education: Vassar, A.B., Poughkeepsie, New York, 1914

Career: Writer and lecturer

Writings: *Poems of a Child; Being Poems Written between the Ages of Six and Ten* R.H. Russell 1904. *Dance of Youth & Other Poems* Sherman French 1917. *Snow Covered Mountains: A Pioneer Epic* Macmillan 1936. *Wolves Against the Moon* Macmillan 1940; others such as Pageant Book Company 1957. *The Old California Trail* Caxton Printers 1945. *The Spectacular San Franciscans* E.P Dutton 1949. *Girl with Ocelot, & Other Poems* Bruce Humphries 1964. Contributor, *Atlantic, Yale Review, Harper's* and others

Awards or inclusion in other biographical books: *American Authors and Books; Childhood in Poetry; Contemporary Authors; Michigan Authors,* 1st ed., 2nd ed.;*Who Was Who in America; Who Was Who among North American Authors*

AMIDON, RICK E.

Address: 1216 N. Washington, Owosso, Michigan 48867

Born: October 9, 1959; Owosso, Michigan

Parents: Charles R. Amidon, Patricia M. (Bruckman) Amidon

Children: Charles L., Russell R.

Education: Northern Michigan University, B.S., Marquette, Michigan. Michigan State University, M.A., Ph.D., East Lansing, Michigan

Career: President, Baker College of Owosso, Owosso, Michigan, 1990—. Dean, Baker College of Owosso, Owosso, Michigan, 1987-1990

Writings: *Selling Yourself Raw* Slipstream Publishers 1991. *The Fat Boy With No Imagination From Down the Block* Slipstream Publishers 1989

Awards or inclusion in other biographical books: Michigan New Voice in Poetry, Poetry Resource Center Award, 1986

May inquiries be sent to you about doing workshops, readings? Yes

AMOS, WINSOM

Address: P.O. Box 416, 673 Omar Circle, Yellow Springs, Ohio 45387-1419

Born: May 10, 1921; Lansing, Michigan

Parents: Charles E. Amos, Inez E. (Kinnebrew) Amos

Children: Patsy
Education: Lansing J.W. Sexton High School. Ferris State University, B.S. in Commerce, Big Rapids, Michigan, 1947-1951. Ohio State University, M.A. in Education, Columbus, Ohio, 1969-1970. Michigan State University, Graduate School, Guidance, summer 1952, East Lansing, Michigan. Virginia State University, Army Specialist School, Topographic Drafting, 1943, Petersburg, Virginia.
Career: Technical Writer, Defense Construction Supply Center (DCSC), Columbus, Ohio, 1971 until retirement in 1984. Counselor on-the-job training, DCSC, Columbus, Ohio 1969-1970. Supply Cataloger, DCSC, Columbus, Ohio, 1955-1968. Public School Teacher, Martinsville, Virginia, 1951-1953. Public Accountant in Virginia, 1951-1955. Public Accountant in Ohio 1955-1990. Athletic Director and Boys' Worker, Lansing Departments of Recreation and Education at Lincoln Community Center, Lansing, Michigan, 1948-1949 and summer 1952

Writings: *Surprise!* Soma Press 1987. *Youth Poems* Soma Press 1983. *Oriole to Black Mood* Soma Press 1973. *Like a Dream* Soma Press 1971. Poems have appeared in various periodicals from 1944-1991. Work in progress: a romantic novel approximately 275 pages
Awards or inclusion in other biographical books: *Michigan Authors,* 2nd ed. Editor's Choice Award, *On the Threshold of a Dream.* The National Library of Poetry, 1988. *Ohioana Quarterly,* Ohioana Library Association, Autumn 1987 and 1984. *Our Western World's Great Poems,* World of Poetry Press, 1983. *American Poetry Anthology,* American Poetry Association, 1983
What is the aim or goal of your writing? "My aim is to express myself creatively with tenderness and force through various forms of communication."
May inquiries be sent to you about doing workshops, readings? No

ANDERSEN, LINDA G.
Address: 1150 48th Ave., Hudsonville, Michigan 49426
Born: November 20, 1940; Lawton, Oklahoma
Parents: Bruce Palmer and Goldie F. (Hitchcock) Palmer
Children: Dean, Kelly, Dawn
Education: Bob Jones University, Business Degree, Greenville, South Carolina 1961-1962
Career: Freelance Writer/Author last 20 years, Montague, Marne, Hudsonville. Andersen Writing Services (Writing business), Hudsonville, Michigan, 1981-1985. Beauty Consultant, Hudsonville, Michigan, 1990-1991. Secretary through Temporary Services, 1980-1990

Writings: *Irresistable Wifestyles* David C. Cook 1990. *Slices of Life* Baker Book House 1985. *Love Adds the Chocolate* Baker Book House 1981. Three hundred articles published in magazines. Freelance writing business, writing for local businesses, colleges, businessmen. Columnist for 12 years, *Women's World*, Radio Bible Class, Grand Rapids. Beginning work on *Picture Windows from the Empty Nest*
What is the aim or goal of your writing? "To inspire and uplift women of all ages....to encourage them to turn their lemons into lemonade....to turn their hearts toward God as their reliable resource in every situation. I take current issues as they relate to women, look at them through the eyes of a Christian, and encourage them to relate to their world in a positive, constructive way. Women have said I speak directly to their hearts."
May inquiries be sent to you about doing workshops, readings? Yes

ANDERSON, WILLIAM T.
Address: P. O. Box 423, Davison, Michigan 48423
Born: February 5, 1952; Flint, Michigan
Parents: Thomas D. Anderson, Wilma S. Anderson
Education: Albion College, B.A., Albion, Michigan, 1974. South Dakota State University, M.A., Brookings, South Dakota, 1982
Career: Instructor, Lapeer Community Schools, Lapeer, Michigan, 1977—. Editor, *Laura Ingalls Wilder Lore*, newsletter, 1975—.

Writings: *Laura Ingalls Wilder: A Biography* Harper Collins 1992. *Laura Ingalls Wilder Country* Harper Collins 1990. *A Little House Sampler* Harper Collins 1989; University of Nebraska Press 1988. *Little House Country* Kyrudo Publishers (Japan), 1988. *Michigan's Marguerite De Angeli* Lapeer County Library 1987. Wilder Series: *A Wilder in the West, The Story of the Ingalls, The Story of the Wilders, Laura Wilder of Mansfield, The Ingalls Family Album, Laura's Rose: The Story of Rose Wilder Lane. Laura Ingalls Wilder: Pioneer and Author* Kipling Press 1987. Contributor to *The Horn Book, The Saturday Evening Post, Travel and Leisure, Kid's Club, Highlights, Jack and Jill, American History Illustrated, Family Life Today, Home and Away, Language Arts, Elementary English, Cobblestone, Diversion, Grit, Christian Science Monitor, Americana Magazine, The Catholic Digest, Modern Maturity*, and others. Text-writer, historic markers, State of South Dakota. Scripting, tourism audio guides. Literary sketches for *Something About the Author* Series. *Leaders in South Dakota History*, 1989. Work in Progress: Several untitled manuscripts
Awards or inclusion in other biographical books: National Endowment for the Humanities scholar, 1983, 1984, 1986, 1987. Western History Association, Billington Award for Historical Writing, 1984. Robinson Award for Historical Writing, South Dakota State Historical Society, 1984, 1987. Herbert Hoover Library Association Award, Best Article of the Year, 1985. Hoover Presidential Library Scholar, 1986, 1987. Achievements in Children's Literature Award, Central Missouri State University, 1986
What is the aim or goal of your writing? "To collect history that may be lost to the future and to preserve it in readable, descriptive prose for young and old readers."
May inquiries be sent to you about doing workshops, readings? Yes

ANDREWS, CLARENCE A.
Address: 108 Pearl Street, Iowa City, Iowa 52245
Born: October 24, 1912; Waterloo, Iowa
Parents: Harry Leon Andrews, June Jennie (Jones) Andrews
Children: Linda, Terry, Stephen
Education: Sheldon Junior College, Iowa, 1951. University of Iowa, B.A., M.A., Ph.D., Iowa City, Iowa, 1951-1953, 1958-1963
Career: Writer, lecturer, Iowa City, Iowa, 1975—. Publisher, Midwest Heritage Publishing Company, Iowa City, Iowa, 1975-1990. Director of Technical Communications, Professor, Michigan Tech University, Houghton, Michigan, 1971-1975. Writer, self-employed, Tucson, Arizona, 1969-1971. Professor of English, Journalism, Engineering, University of Iowa, 1963-1969. Taught writing courses

Writings: *Michigan in Literature* Wayne State University Press 1992. *Chicago in Story* MW Heritage Publishing l982. *A Literary History of Iowa* University of Iowa Press 1972. *Writing* Glenco Press 1972. *Technical and Business Writing* Houghton Mifflin 1975. Edited/written introductions to some twenty other books. Articles on the Michigan

Upper Peninsula in *Michigan History, Milwaukee Journal, Des Moines Register,* and the Tucson *Citizen.* Numerous articles in newspapers, magazines, journals including the *Great Lakes Review* such as *A Bibliography of the Literature and Lore, Together With Historical Materials, of the Upper Peninsula of Michigan* and *A Bibliography of Fiction and Drama By Women from Iowa and Michigan*

Awards or inclusion in other biographical books: *Contemporary Authors; Who's Who in the Midwest; Who's Who in America; Directory of American Scholars; Directory of International Biography; Who's Who in the World.* Phi Beta Kappa. Mid-America Award for Distinguished contributions to the Study of Midwestern Literature. Kappa Tau Alpha

What is the Aim or Goal of Your Writing? "To preserve information about midwest literature and its creators."

May inquiries be sent to you about doing workshops, readings? Yes

ANDREWS, TOM C.

Address: 1161 Parkview Dr., Lancaster, Ohio 43130

Born: April 30, 1961; Charleston, West Virginia

Parents: Raymond Andews, Alice A. Andrews

Education: Hope College, B.A. in Philosophy, Holland, Michigan, 1980-1984. University of Virginia, M.F.A. in Creative Writing, 1985-1987

Career: Assistant Professor, Creative Writing, Ohio University, Athens, Ohio, 1991— Copy Editor, *Mathematical Reviews*, 1987-1990

Writings: *The Brother's Country* Persea Books 1990. *Hymning the Kanawha* Haw River Books, Ltd. 1989. Work in Progress: *On William Stafford: What the River Says*, editing a collection of essays and reviews on Stafford's work-forthcoming with the University of Michigan Press

Awards or inclusion in other biographical books: Winner of the 1989 National Poetry Series Open competition for *The Brother's Country.* Included in *My Poor Elephant: 27 Male Writers at Work*, edited by Eve Shelnutt, Longstreet Press, 1992; essays by 27 male writers on why they write. Winner of the Academy of American Poets Prize, 1984

What is the aim or goal of your writing? "I suppose the best, or most accurate, response I can offer in such a brief space is to say that I write to recover a sense of the mystery of existence-mystery being that which is so often leached out of our experience. I write to allow the world to be present to me, to enter more fully into the complexity and unpredictability of the world's presence."

May inquiries be sent to you about doing workshops, readings? Yes

ANGELO, FRANK

Born: September 6, 1914; Detroit, Michigan

Parents: Nicolo Angelo, Ida (Carini) Angelo

Children: Frank, Andrew

Education: Wayne State University, B.A., Detroit, Michigan, 1934

Career: *Detroit News*, 1934-1941. Columnist, editor, *Detroit Free Press*, Detroit, Michigan, beginning 1941

Writings: *For the Children: A History of the Old Newsboys Goodfellows* The Old Newsboys Goodfellow Fund of Detroit 1989. *On Guard, a History of the Detroit Free Press* Detroit Free Press 1981. *Yesterday's Detroit* E.A. Seeman 1974. *Yesterday's Michigan* E.A. Seeman 1976

Awards or inclusion in other biographical books: *Contemporary Authors; Michigan Authors,* 2nd ed.; *Who's Who in America*

ANKER, ROY M.
Address: Burning Tree SE, Grand Rapids Michigan 49546
Born: January 10, 1945; Harvey, Illinois
Parents: John A. Anker, Alice H. Anker
Children: Elizabeth, David, Christina
Education: Hope College, B.A., Holland, Michigan, 1962-1966. University of Illinois, M.A., Michigan State University, East Lansing, Michigan, Ph.D., 1968-1973
Career: Professor, Calvin College, Grand Rapids, Michigan, 1989—. Associate Professor, Northwestern College, Orange City, Iowa, 1975-1989. Instructor, Michigan State University, East Lansing, Michigan, 1971-1975

Writings: *Dancing in the Dark: Youth, Popular Culture, and Electronic Media* Eerdmans 1991. Work in Progress: Books on self-help, religion, film
Awards or inclusion in other biographical books: Published book received second place in *Christianity Today's* annual book awards
What is the aim or goal of your writing? "To provide 1. Insight into the working of American culture 2. Insight and appreciation of films as a medium 3. Illuminate religious stories in American culture".
May inquiries be sent to you about doing workshops, readings? Yes

ANNEBERG, LISA M.
Address: 3123 Roosevelt, Dearborn, Michigan 48124
Born: August 9, 1957; West Germany
Parents: Allen D. Anneberg, Joan A. Anneberg
Children: Ken (Erwood), Evelyn Anneberg
Education: University of Michigan, B.S. in Industrial Engineering, Ann Arbor, Michigan, 1975-1979. University of Michigan, M.S., Ph.D., Ann Arbor, Michigan, 1982-1991. Wayne State University, Detroit.
Career: Assistant Professor, Lawrence Technological University, Southfield, Michigan 1991—. Neighborhood Column Writer, *Dearborn Press and Guide,* Dearborn, Michigan, 1987—. Reliability Engineer, General Motors, Pontiac, Michigan, 1978-1982. Graduate Teaching Assistant, Wayne State University, Detroit, Michigan, 1988-1990

Writings: Inclusion in *Encyclopedia of Computers* with entry entitled "Parallel Computing", coauthored by H. Singh, E. Yaprak, D. Kaur, MacMillan, 1992. Technical articles about computer engineering. Biweekly column for *Dearborn Press and Guide.* Work in Progress: Non-fiction
What is the aim or goal of your writing? "Presently, I concentrate in non-fiction, but hope to expand to fiction, as time and interest permit. My biggest satisfaction comes from making complicated matters accessible and interesting, and to promote critical reading of non-fiction material and articles."
May inquiries be sent to you about doing workshops, readings? Yes

APPLE, MAX
Born: October 22, 1941; Grand Rapids, Michigan
Parents: Samuel Apple, Betty (Goodstein) Apple
Children: Jessica, Sam

Education: University of Michigan, A.B., Ann Arbor, Michigan, 1963; Ph.D., 1970. Stanford University, 1964

Career: Assistant Professor, Reed College, Portland, Oregon, 1970-1971. Assistant Professor, Rice University, Houston, Texas, 1972—

Writings: *The Oranging of America and Other Stories* Grossman 1976. *Zip: A Novel of the Left and the Right* Viking 1978. Contributor to *Nathanial West: The Cheaters and the Cheated* Everett/Edwards 1972. *Studies in English* (with others) Rice University 1975. *Mom, the Flag, and Apple Pie: Great American Writers on Great American Things* Doubleday 1976. *Free Agents* Harper & Row 1984. *The Propheteers: a Novel* Harper & Row 1987

Awards or inclusion in other biographical books:*Contemporary Authors; Contemporary Literary Criticism.* National Endowment for the Humanities Younger Humanities Fellowship, 1971. Jesse Jones Award, Texas Institute of Letters, 1976

ARMOUR, DAVID A.

Address: 2330 Northwest Avenue, Lansing, Michigan 48906
Born: July 12, 1937; Grove City, Pennyslvania
Parents: Arthur S. Armour and Marian (Bowie) Armour
Children: Marian, Arthur, David J., Anneke
Education: Grove City High School, Diploma, 1951-1955. Calvin College, Grand Rapids, Michigan, B.A., 1955-1959. Northwestern University, Evanston, Illinois, M.A., 1960, Ph.D, 1965
Career: Deputy Director, Mackinac State Historic Parks, Mackinac Island, Michigan 1967—. Asst. Professor, University of Wisconsin-Milwaukee, Milwaukee, Wisconsin, 1965-1967. Instructor, University of Wisconsin-Milwaukee, Milwaukee, Wisconsin, 1963-1965

Writings: *The Merchants of Albany, New York: 1686-1760* Garland 1986. *Michilimackinac: A Handbook to the Site* (with Keith R. Widder) Mackinac Island State Park Commission 1980. *At the Crossroads: Michilimackinac During the American Revolution* (with Keith R. Widder) Mackinac Island State Park Commission 1978. *Attack at Michilimackinac* Mackinac Island State Park Commission 1971. *Treason at Michilimackinac* Mackinac Island State Park Commission 1967. Articles in *Dictionary of Canadian Biography* Vol. III, IV, V, VI, VII, University of Toronto 1974, 1979, 1983, 1985, 1987, 1988
Awards or inclusion in other biographical books: *Michigan Authors,* 2nd ed.
May inquiries be sent to you about doing workshops, readings? Yes

ARMSTRONG, CHARLOTTE (1905-1969)

Pseudonym: Jo Valentine
Born: May 2, 1905; Vulcan, Michigan
Parents: Frank H. Armstrong, Clara (Pascoe) Armstrong
Children: Jeremy, Jacquelin, Peter
Education: Ferry Hall, Lake Forest, Illinois, 1922. University of Wisconsin, 1922-1924. Barnard College, A.B., New York. Columbia University, New York, 1925
Career: Housewife, Writer

Writings: *The Innocent Flower* Coward-McCann 1945. *The Unsuspected, a Novel* Coward-McCann 1946. *Mischief* Coward-McCann 1950. *Catch-as-Catch-Can* Coward-

McCann 1952. *The Dream Walker* Coward-McCann 1955. *The Trouble in Thor* 1953, 1971.*The Better to Eat You* Coward-McCann 1954. *A Dram of Poison* Coward-McCann 1956; Fawcett 1964. *Duo: The Girl with a Secret; Incident at a Corner* Coward-McCann 1959. *The Seventeen Widows of Sans Souci* Coward-McCann 1959. *The Turret Room* Coward-McCann 1965. *The Witch's House* Coward-McCann 1963. *The Gift Shop* Coward-McCann 1966. *I See You* Coward-McCann 1966. *Lemon in the Basket* Coward-McCann 1967. *The Balloon Man* Coward-McCann 1968. *Seven Seats to the Moon* Coward-McCann 1969. Several others. Plays, movie and television scripts
Awards or inclusion in other biographical books: *American Authors and Books; American Women Writers; Contemporary Authors; Corpus Delicti of Mystery Fiction; Encyclopedia of Mystery and Detectiion; Who Was Who in America; World Authors.* Edgar Allen Poe Award, Mystery Writers of America, 1956

ARMSTRONG, HAROLD HUNTER (1884-?)
Pseudonym: Henry G. Aikman
Born: April 9, 1884; Morenci, Michigan
Parents: Oscar S. Armstrong, Clara (Allen) Armstrong
Children: Elizabeth
Education: University of Michigan, A.B., Ann Arbor, Michigan, 1905. Detroit College of Law, Law Degree, 1907
Career: Admitted to Michigan Bar, 1907; became member of the firm, Carey, Armstrong & Weadock, 1909. Secretary/Director, Brown-McLaren Mfg. Company beginning in 1942, others. Resigned, Detroit Bar Association, 1973

Writings: *The Groper* 1919. *For Richer, for Poorer* Knopf 1922. *The Red-Blood; A Novel* Harper 1923. *Zell: A Novel* Knopf 1921
Awards or inclusion in other biographical books: *American Authors and Books; Who Was Who in America*

ARNDT, LESLIE E.
Address: 932 S. Huron Road, Linwood, MI 48634
Born: August 22, 1915; Ironwood, Michigan
Parents: William A. Arndt, Julia G. (Clark) Arndt
Children: Linda, Dale, Donald, Mava
Education: Luther L. Wright High School, Ironwood, Michigan, 1933. University of Wisconsin, Madison, Wisconsin, Journalism-Education 1934-1938
Career: Reporter-Columnist-Copy Editor, *Bay City Times* Newspaper, 1950-1980. Copy Desk, *Milwaukee Sentinel*, Milwaukee, Wisconsin, 1949-1950. Magazine Editor, *Lafayette Journal & Courier*, Lafayette, Indiana, 1944-1949. Reporter, *Elkhart Daily Truth,* Elkhart, Indiana, 1941-1944. Sports Editor, *Neenah Daily News-Times,* Neenah, Wisconsin, 1938-1941. *Wisconsin State Journal,* newspaper, Madison, Wisconsin, 1936-1938. "Sophomore Willie" Campus Columnist, Sports Writer while attending University of Wisconsin. Has led workshops in writing

Writings: *Mutual Savings and Loan Association, F.A.* Harlo Printing 1987. *Coonskin Capers*, Harlo Printing 1985. *The Bay County Story* Harlo Printing 1976. *By These Waters* Harlo Printing 1976. "Memory Lane", Column, senior citizens newspaper, last 10 years. Work in Progress: Bay County regional history
Awards or inclusion in other biographical books: General Eisenhower National Award, 1966 and Michigan Minuteman Award, 1967 for founding Bay City chapter of

People-to-People International. Recognized in 1978 as the national volunteer of the year by Sister Cities International. Recepient of Bay Area Chamber of Commerce's Golden Frog Award in 1983. Received wide recognition for 20 years as Davy Crockett entertaining through 29 states, Canada, Europe. Inducted into Chippewa tribe as "Scout Strongheart" 1958 near Tawas City

What is the aim or goal of your writing? "Mostly updating and expanding on Bay County history since the pioneers."

May inquiries be sent to you about doing workshops, readings? Yes

ARNETT, CARROLL

Born: November 9, 1927; Oklahoma City, Oklahoma

Education: Beloit College, B.A., magna cum laude, Beloit, Wisconsin, 1951. University of Texas, M.A., 1958

Career: Military Service, 1946-1947. Instructor, Knox College, Galesburg, Illinois, 1958-1960. Stephens College, Columbia, Missouri, 1960-1964. Assistant Professor, Wittenberg University, Springfield, Ohio, 1964-1968. Associate Professor, Nasson College, Springvale, Maine, 1968-1970. Professor, Central Michigan University, Mt. Pleasant, Michigan, beginning in 1970. Journal editor

Writings: *Earlier* Elizabeth Press 1972. *Like a Wall* Elizabeth Press 1969. *South Line: Poems* Elizabeth Press 1979. *Then: Poems* Elizabeth Press, 1965, 1969. *Through the Woods* Elizabeth Press 1971. *Tsalagi: Poems* Elizabeth Press 1976. *Rounds* Cross-Cultural Communications 1982. Others

Awards or inclusion in other biographical books: *Contemporary Authors; A Directory of Americn Poets; Who's Who in Writers, Editors & Poets.* NEA Fellowship, 1974

ARNOLD, EDMUND C.

Address: 3208 Hawthorne Ave., Richmond,Virginia 23222

Born: June 25, 1913; Bay City, Michigan

Parents: Ferdinand M. Arnold, Anne J. Arnold

Children: Kathleen, Bethany, Bruce Robert

Education: Arthur Hill High School, Saginaw, Michigan. Bay City Junior College, 1933-1934. Cité Université, Paris, France, 1945. Michigan State University, East Lansing, Michigan, A.B., 1953-1954, summa cum laude

Career: President, ETAOIN Inc., consultants to publications, 1985—. Distinguished Professor of Journalism, Virginia Commonwealth University, 1975-1983. Department of Journalism, Syracuse University, 1960-1975. Editor, *Linotype News,* New York City, 1954-1966. Director of Trade Relations, Mergenthaler Linotype Co., Brooklyn, New York, 1954-1960. Night Editor, *The State Journal*, Lansing, Michigan, 1953-1954. Picture Editor, *Saginaw News,* 1946-1953. Editor and Publisher, *Frankenmuth News,* 1946-1966. Combat correspondent, 70th Infantry Division and *Stars & Stripes,* Nancy Edition, 1943-1945. Conducted workshops and seminars in every state except Hawaii and every Canadian province except the Northwest Territory, and in various other countries. As consultant to publications, designed and re-designed over two hundred publications.

Writings: *The Trailblazers: The Story of the 70th Infantry Division* 1989. *34 Distinguished Organizational Publications* 1986. *Improving Your Publication* 1985. *F, F & P: Producing Flyers and Brochures* 1984. *Editing the Organizational Publication* 1982. *Designing the Total Newspaper* 1981. *Arnold's Ancient Axioms* 1978. *Handbook of*

Student Journalism (with Hillier Krieghbaum)1976. *Editing the Yearbook* 1974. *Ink on Paper 2* 1972. *Modern Newspaper Design* 1969. *Random House Dictionary* (Section Editor) 1968. *Layout for Advertising* 1966. *Processes of Printing and Engraving* (International Correspondence Schools) 1966. *The Student Editor and The Yearbook* 1966. *Tipografia y Diagramado para Periodicos* 1965. *Ink on Paper: A Handbook of the Graphic Arts* 1963. *Japanese Newspaper Advertising* 1963. *Feature Photos That Sell* 1960. *Profitable Newspaper Advertising* 1960. *The Student Journalist* (with Hillier Krieghbaum) 1960. *Functional Newspaper Design* 1956. More than 2,000 articles in professional journals. Editor, *The Trailblazer Magazine* 1982. Contributing editor, *Publishers' Auxiliary, Editor & Publisher, The Ragan Report, Print & Graphics, Canadian Printer and Publisher, Typographic Pursuits, Editors Workshop, Corporate Annual Reports Newsletter.* Work in Progress: *My Piece of History*

Awards or inclusion in other biographical books: *Michigan Authors,* 2nd ed. Bronze Star, Army Commendation Medal, Croix de Guerre, France Libre Medal. Academic Honors: 1963, L.H.D., Hartwick College; 1980, L.H.D., Wagner College; 1983, Gold Key Award, Columbia University; 1981, Arts and Sciences Lecturer Award (initial); Virginia Commonwealth University; 1971, The Friars' Award, St. Bonaventure University; Phi Kappa Phi, Michigan State University; Kappa Tau Alpha, Virginia Commonwealth University; Phi Theta Kappa, Bay City Junior College; American Academy of Advertising. Professional Honors: 1990, Army Distinguished Civilian Service Medal; 1988, American Press Institute Award for Service to Journalism; 1987, Michigan Journalism Hall of Fame; 1986, Virginia Communications Hall of Fame (Initial Class); 1984, Photo-Journalism Award, United States Navy; 1983, Distinguished Alumnus, School of Journalism, Michigan State University; 1983, Honorary Life Membership, Virginia Press Association; 1979, Army Outstanding Civilian Service Medal; 1978, Journalism Pioneer Medal, the Newspaper Fund; 1973, The John Fields Memorial Award, Central Michigan University; 1968, The Carl Towley Memorial Award, Journalism Education Association; 1960, U.S. Army Certificate of Appreciation; 1958, Award of Appreciation, National Editorial Association; 1957, George Polk Memorial Award, The Overseas Press Club

What is the aim or goal of your writing? "The written language is the greatest gift the human race has ever received. I want to keep the language vital, growing and clear both in the written content and the way it is packaged through the printing processes. I want to reinforce the truism that the printed (or written) word is the best way to transmit information accurately and permanently, that we cannot rely on the fragmented messages that broadcast media provide. I want to preserve the visual beauty of the characters of the Latin alphabet—indeed of <u>all</u> alphabets, syllabaries and ideograms."

May inquiries be sent to you about doing workshops, readings? Yes

ARNOLD, JACLYN SMITH

Address: P.O. Box 7, Peck, Michigan 48466
Born: October 3, 1932; Bessemer, Alabama
Parents: Bill F. Smith, Lillian (McDougal) Smith
Children: David Batts, Charles Batts, Thomas Batts
Education: Macomb Community College, Legal Assistant, Warren Michigan. Writers Digest School of Writing; Institute for Children's Literature
Career: Managing Director, Detroit & Wayne County Tuberculosis Foundation, Detroit, Michigan, 1977—. Burnett Studios, 1976, Consulting, Detroit, Michigan. Overseas

Advisory Associates, Inc., Assistant to Treasurer, Detroit, Michigan, 1972-1977. William Arnold Associates, Vice-President, ongoing consulting firm, Peck, Michigan. Speaker at writers conferences and workshops. Regional reporter for St. Clair County Community College, Port Huron, Michigan. Editor/feature writer for *McKenzie Monitor*

Writings: *Kinship: It's All Relative II* Genealogical Publishing 1993. *Kinship: It's All Relative* Genealogical Publishing 1990. *Kinship is a Relative Thing* (booklet, recommended by Ann Landers to her readers) William Arnold Associates 1985. Co-author of *Fermi I: New Age for Nuclear Power* by the American Nuclear Society. Short stories, poems, articles, essays published in: *Byline Magazine, Detroit Free Press, McCalls, Intimacy Magazine, Detroit News, Woman's Day* and in genealogical publications. Work in Progress: *Yesterday's Memories. Kinship: Legally Speaking*
Awards or inclusion in other biographical books: *Who's Who in Writers, Editors, and Poets.* First place in poetry contest, *Christian Outlook.* Third place in essay contest, Clairol "Not Just Any Woman"
May inquiries be sent to you about doing workshops, readings? Yes

ARNOW, HARRIETTE SIMPSON (1908-1986)
Born: July 7, 1908; Wayne County, Kentucky
Parents: Elias Thomas Simpson, Mollie Jane (Denney) Simpson
Children: Marcella Jane, Thomas Louis
Education: Berea College, Berea, Kentucky, 1924-1926. University of Louisville, B.S., Louisville, Kentucky, 1931
Career: Teacher, housewife, author. Became acquainted with a newspaper reporter in Petoskey, Michigan who became husband. Moved to Detroit mid 1940's-a setting she used to begin writing *The Dollmaker,* Ann Arbor 1951

Writings: *Mountain Path* Covici-Friede 1936. *Hunter's Horn* Macmillan 1949. *The Doll Maker* Macmillan 1954; television movie 1984. *Seedtime on the Cumberland* Macmillan 1960.*The Flowering of the Cumberland* Macmillan 1963. *The Weedkiller's Daughter* Knopf 1970. *The Kentucky Trace* Knopf 1973. *Old Burnside* University of Kentucky Press 1977
Awards or inclusion in other biographical books: *American Authors and Books; American Novelists of Today; American Women Writers; Contemporary Authors; Contemporary Literary Criticism; Contemporary Novelists; Current Biography; Index to Women; International Authors and Writers Who's Who; Michigan Authors,* 1st ed., 2nd ed.; *Who's Who of American Women; World Authors; The Writers Directory.* Inducted into Michigan Women's Hall of Fame 1983 when living in Ann Arbor. Friends of American Writers Award, 1955. Honorary Degree, Albion College, 1955. Berea College Sentinel Award, 1955. Runner up, National Book Award, 1955. *Women's Home Companion* Silver Distaff Award, 1955. Commendation from Tennessee Historical Commission, 1961. Award of Merit of American Association for State and Local History, 1961. *Tennessee Historical Quarterly* prize for the best article of the year, 1962. Cranbrook Writers Guild Award, 1975. Mid America Award for Distinguished Contributions to Midwestern Literature. Mark Twain Award, Michigan State University, 1984

ARTEN, LEE H.
Address: 107 N. Pewabic Street, Laurium, Michigan 49913
Born: June 23, 1951; Minneapolis, Minnesota
Parents: Oliver M. Arten, Shirley H. Arten

Children: Isaac, Linnea, Ethan
Education: Calumet High School, Calumet, Michigan,1965-1969. Northern Michigan University, B.S., English, Marquette, Michigan, 1972-1975. Michigan Technological University, Houghton, Michigan, 1969-1970
Career: Writer, self-employed, 1975—. Reporter, *Daily Mining Gazette,* Houghton, Michigan. Other writing jobs, dishwasher, sawmill worker, groundskeeper, 1968-1975

Writings: *Who Cares What You Want? I'm the Cat!* Chunkabunka Press 1985. Work in Progress: Essays, fiction, and a cartoon book
What is the aim or goal of your writing? "To observe, then to report what I see as well as I can."
May inquiries be sent to you about doing workshops, readings? Yes

B

BAILEY, LIBERTY HYDE (1858-1954)
Born: March 15, 1858; South Haven; Michigan
Parents: Liberty Hyde Bailey, Sarah (Harrison) Bailey
Children: Sara May, Ethel Zoe
Education: Michigan Agricultural College, B.S., East Lansing, Michigan; M.S., 1886. University of Wisconsin, LL.D, 1907. Alfred University, 1908. University of Vermont, Litt.D., 1919. University of Puerto Rico, D. Sc., l932
Career: Assistant to Asa Gray, Harvard University, 1882-1883. Professor, Michigan Agricultural College, 1885-1888. Professor, Cornell University, 1888-1903. Founded and organized the New York Agricultural College, at Cornell. Appointed by President Roosevelt Chairman, Commission on Country Life, 1908. Director and Dean, College of Agriculture, 1903-1913. President, American Academy of Arts and Science, 1926

Writings: *Survival of the Unlike* 1896. *The Nature-Study Idea; Being an Interpretation of the New School-Movement to Put the Child in Sympathy with Nature* Doubleday, Page 1903. *Beginners' Botany* Macmillan 1909. *The Training of Farmers* Century 1909. *The Country-Life Movement in the United States* Macmillan 1911. *Outlook to Nature* 1915. *Plant-breeding* Macmillan 1915. *The Holy Earth* Charles Scribner's Sons 1915. *Wind and Weather* Macmillan 1916. *What is Democracy?* Comstock 1918. *Universal Service, the Hope of Humanity* Sturgis and Walton 1918. *R.U.S. Rural Uplook Service: A Preliminary Attempt to Register the Rural Leadership in the United States and Canada* 1918. *Cyclopedia of Farm Animals* Macmillan 1922. *The Cultivated Evergreens; A Handbook of the Coniferous and Most Important Broad-Leaved Evergreens Planted for Ornament in the United States and Canada* Macmillan 1923. *The Garden Lover* Macmillan 1928. *Cyclopedia of American Agriculture; A Popular Survey of Agricultural Conditions, Practices and Ideals in the United States and Canada* (editor) 4 volumes Macmillan 1907-1909. *The Standard Cyclopedia of Horticulture* 3 volumes Macmillan 1925.*The Cultivated Conifers in North America, Comprising the Pine Family and the Taxads; Successor to the Cultivated Evergreens* Macmillan 1933. Others. Some manuals have gone into 12 editions
Awards or inclusion in other biographical books: *American Literary Yearbook; Appleton's Cyclopaedia of American Biography; Biographical Dictionary of American Educators; Dictionary of American Biography; Dictionary of Scientific Biography; Lincoln Library of Social Studies; National Cyclopaedia of American Biography; Twentieth Century Biographical Dictionary of Notable Americans; Webster's American Biographies; Who Was Who among North American Authors; Who Was Who in America; American Authors and Books 1640 to Present Day.* Veitchian Gold Medal, 1927. George Robert White Medal, 1927. Gold Medal National Institute Social Science. Grande Medaille, Societe Nationale d'Acclimatation de France, 1928. Gold Medal of Honor, Garden Club of America, 1931. Distinguished Service Award, American Association of Nurserymen, 1931. Several others. The frame house in which he was born in South Haven was dedicated in 1964 with a Michigan Historical Marker

BAILEY, WILLIAM "BILL" L.
Address: 2015 Arthur Street, Saginaw, Michigan 48602
Born: March 23, 1952; Bay City, Michigan
Parents: Benjamin E. Bailey, Kathryn A. Bailey
Children: Michael, Ryan
Education: Western Michigan University, B.A., Kalamazoo, Michigan
Career: Assistant to City Manager, City of Saginaw, Saginaw, Michigan, 1977—. Journalist, Booth Newspapers, Lansing, Michigan, 1976-1982. Reporter. Media relations and marketing consulting under the name of Bailey & Associates, specializing in travel and education

Writings: *Michigan's Only Antique and Flea Market Guidebook* Glovebox Guidebooks 1992. *Michigan Zoos and Animal Attractions* Glovebox Guidebooks 1992. Others no longer in print. Work in Progress: *Guide to Ohio State Parks. Guide to Family Attractions in Michigan*
What is the aim or goal of your writing? "Travel writing, objective reviews and information about travel and visitor destinations, also humor as it relates to travel. Information driven guidebooks for auto travelers."
May inquiries be sent to you about doing workshops, readings? Yes

BAKER, RAY STANNARD (1870-1946)
Pseudonym: David Grayson
Born: April 17, 1870; Lansing, Michigan
Parents: Joseph Stannard Baker, Alice (Potter) Baker
Children: James, Roger, Rachel, Alice
Education: Michigan State University, B.S., East Lansing, Michigan, 1889. University of Michigan, Law and Literature
Career: Author, historian. Reporter, *Chicago Daily Record* 1892-1897. Manager, McClure Syndicate 1898-1905. Editor and part owner, *American Magazine* 1906-1915. Special commissioner, State Department, 1918

Writings: *Seen in Germany* McClure, Phillips 1901. *Boy's Second Book of Inventions* Doubleday, Page 1903. *Following the Color Line; an Account of Negro Citizenship in the American Democracy* Doubleday, Page 1908; 1922; Harper & Row 1964; Corner House 1973. *The Spiritual Unrest* Frederick A. Stokes 1910. *Adventures in Friendship* Doubleday Page 1910. *The Friendly Road: New Adventures in Contentment* Grosset & Dunlap 1913. *Hempfield; a Novel* Doubleday, Page 1915. *Great Possessions, a New Series of Adventures* Doubleday, Page 1917. *What Wilson Did in Paris* Doubleday, Page 1919. *The New Industrial Unrest* Doubleday, Page 1920. *Woodrow Wilson and World Settlement* Doubleday, Page 1922. *Adventures in Contentment* Garden City 1907; Doubleday, Page 1910. *A Day of Pleasant Bread* Doubleday, Doran 1910. *Adventures in Understanding* Doubleday, Page 1925. *The Adventures of David Grayson* Doubleday, Doran 1925. *The Public Papers of Woodrow Wilson* (authorized edition, co-editor) Harper 1925-1927. *The Countryman's Year* Doubleday, Doran 1936. *Native American* Charles Scribner's & Sons 1941. *Under My Elm, Country Discoveries and Reflections* Doubleday, Doran 1942. *American Chronicle* Charles Scribner's & Sons 1945. Others
Awards or inclusion in other biographical books: *American Literary Yearbook; Appleton's Cyclopaedia of American Biography; Contemporary American Literature; Current Biography; Dictionary of American Authors; Michigan Authors*, 1st ed., 2nd ed.; *National Cyclopaedia of American Biography; Reader's Encyclopedia of American*

Literature; Twentieth Century Authors; Twentieth Century Writing; Webster's American Biographies; Who Was Who among North American Authors; Who Was Who in America, others. Pulitzer Prize for Biography, 1940

In the 2nd edition of *Michigan Authors* appears: "He believed, 'When men come really to understand one another-if that time ever comes-war will end, poverty will end, tyranny will end, and this under almost any sort of government, almost any economic system.' *The Detroit News*, December 22, 1941."

BALD, F. CLEVER (1897-1970)

Born: August 12, 1897; Baltimore, Maryland
Parents: Frederick William Bald, Elizabeth (Krise) Bald
Children: Robert
Education: Franklin and Marshall College, Lancaster, Pennsylvania, 1914-1917. University of Aix-Marseille, 1919. University of Michigan, A.B., Ann Arbor, Michigan, 1920, Ph.D., 1943. Wayne State University, M.A., Detroit, Michigan, 1937
Career: Served overseas in the army during World War I. History teacher, Hudson School (private school for boys), Detroit, Michigan, 1922-1929, Headmaster, 1929-1932. Professor, Detroit Institute of Technology, 1932-1943. Instructor, University of Michigan, 1943-1947. Assistant Director, Michigan Historical Collections, University of Michigan, 1943-1960. Member, Michigan Civil War Centennial Observance Commission. Professor of History, Director of Michigan Historical Collections, 1960-1967

Writings: *De Bonne-De Repentigny Seigniory at Sault Ste. Marie, 1750-1867* 1936. *Detroit's First American Decade, 1796-1805* University of Michigan Press 1948. *Michigan in Four Centuries* Harper, 1954, 1961. Articles in historical periodicals
Awards or inclusion in other biographical books: *Contemporary Authors; Michigan Authors,* 1st ed., 2nd ed.

BALDUCCI, CAROLYN F.

Address: 624 Fifth Street, Ann Arbor, Michigan 48103.
Literary Agent: Barbara S. Kouts, P.O. Box 558; Bellport, New York 10019
Born: February 13, 1946; Pelham, New York
Parents: Ernest J. Feleppa, Rosaria (Pignone) Feleppa
Children: Sirad, Victoria
Education: Manhattanville College of the Sacred Heart, B.A., Purchase, New York, 1963-1967. Others: New York University, Goddard, The New School, The University of Michigan
Career: Freelance author, dramatist, screen writer, poet, editor, translator, self employed, Ann Arbor, Michigan,1969—. Lecturer in Creative Writing, The University of Michigan

Writings: *Margaret Fuller, A Life of Passion & Defiance* Bantam 1991. *A Self-Made Woman: The Life of Nobel Prize Winner Grazia Deledda* Houghton Mifflin 1975. *Earway* Houghton Mifflin 1972. *Is There Life after Graduation, Henry Birnbaum?* Houghton Mifflin 1971, Dell 1972; French Translation,*Y'a-t'-il une Vie Apres Le Bac?* Medium, 1992, Poche, 1992. Work in Progress: Plays: translation. Aristophanes' *Lysistrata* performed by RC Players, University of Michigan, 1991. *Giovanni the Fearless* scheduled for May 1992 Young Peoples Theatre. *La Veniexiana* scheduled May 1992, University of Michigan
Awards or inclusion in other biographical books: ALA Notable Book Award, 1991.

Mademoiselle Guest Editor, 1966
What is the aim or goal of your writing? "To learn."
May inquiries be sent to you about doing workshops, readings? Yes. Written inquiries only

BALMER, EDWIN (1883-1959)

Born: July 26, 1883; Chicago, Illinois
Parents: Thomas Balmer, Helen (Pratt) Balmer
Children: Caroline, Thomas, Katherine
Education: Northwestern University, A.B., Evanston, Illinois, 1902. Harvard University, A.M., Cambridge, Massachusetts, 1903
Career: Reporter, *Chicago Tribune*, 1903. Editor, *Red Book*, 1927-1949; Associate Publisher, 1949-1953, retired. Editorial adviser, *Hampton's Magazine*. Workshop leader. Leadership positions in writing, magazine associations, book clubs

Writings: *Waylaid by Wireless,* 1909. *The Blind Man's Eyes* Little, Brown 1916. *Resurrection Rock* Grosset & Dunlap 1920. *The Indian Drum* (with William MacHarg) Grosset & Dunlap 1917.*The Breath of Scandal* 1922. *Keeban* Grosset & Dunlap 1923. *That Royle Girl* Dodd 1925. *Dangerous Business* Dodd, Mead 1927. *Five Fatal Words* 1932. *When Worlds Collide* (with Philip Wylie) 1933; made into film 1951.
The Golden Hoard Frederick A. Stokes 1934. *The Shield of Silence* 1936. Others. Works appeared in foreign languages. Short stories, some made into plays, films, television. In *Hampton's Magazine,* others
Awards or inclusion in other biographical books: *American Authors and Books; Contemporary Authors; Encyclopedia of Mystery and Detection; Encyclopedia of Science Fiction; Reader's Encyclopedia of American Literature; Science Fiction and Fantasy Literature; Twentieth-Century Crime and Mystery Writers; Who Was Who among North American Authors; Who Was Who in America*

BANNON, LAURA (1894-1963)

Born: July 25, 1894; Acme, Michigan
Parents: James William Bannon, Carrie (Freeman) Bannon
Education: Western Michigan State College, 2 year course. School of the Art Institute of Chicago, 4 year course, post-graduate work
Career: Teacher, Battle Creek, Michigan. Supervisor, public school art, Mt. Clemens, Port Huron, Michigan; Racine, Wisconsin. Instructor and Director, Art Institute of Chicago Junior School. Author, illustrator

Writings: *Manuela's Birthday* A. Whitman 1939, 1972. *Gregorio and the White Llama* A. Whitman 1944. *Red Mittens* Houghton Mifflin 1946. *Baby Roo* Houghton Mifflin 1947. *Billy and the Bear* Houghton Mifflin 1949. *The Best House in the World* Houghton Mifflin 1952. *Mind Your Child's Art; a Guide for Parents and Teachers* Pellegrini & Cudahy 1952. *The Wonderful Fashion Doll* Houghton Mifflin 1953. *When the Moon was New* A. Whitman 1953. *Burro Boy and His Big Trouble* Abington 1955. *The Little Doll Sister* A. Whitman 1955. *The Scary Thing* Houghton 1956. *Jo-Jo, the Talking Crow* Houghton Mifflin 1958. *Katy Comes Next* A. Whitman 1959.*Whistle for a Pilot* A. Whitman 1959. *The Other Side of the World* Houghton Mifflin 1960. *Hop-High, the Goat* Bobbs-Merrill 1960. *Who Walks the Attic?* A. Whitman 1962. *Little People of the Night* Houghton 1963. *Make Room for Rags* Houghton 1964. *Twirlup on the Moon* A. Whitman 1964. Many other children's books, illustrated children's books by other authors

Awards or inclusion in other biographical books: *Authors of Books for Young People; Contemporary Authors; Illustrators of Children's Books; Michigan Authors,* 2nd ed.; *More Junior Authors; Something about the Author; Who's Who of American Women.* Chicago Society of Typographic Arts Award, 1944. *New York Herald Tribune* Spring Book Festival Honor Award, 1953. Friends of American Writers Award, 1960. Children's Reading Round Table of Chicago Annual Award, 1962

BARAGA, FREDERIC (1797-1868)
Born: June 29, 1797; Dobernig, Slovenia (Austria)
Parents: Johann Nepomuc Baraga, Maria Katharin Josefa (Jencic) Baraga
Education: Gymnasium, Laibach, 1809. University of Vienna, law course, 1821. Ordained a priest, Laibach, 1823
Career: Parish priest, seven years, then assigned as Roman Catholic missionary to Ottawa village of Arbre Croche, now Harbor Springs, Michigan, 1831. Began mission at site of what is now Grand Rapids, 1833. Transferred 1835 to shores of Lake Superior, went to Europe for funds 1836 and built church. Added Indian languages to several European languages he already knew. Began mission in L'Anse, Michigan, 1843. Became bishop 1853 with headquarters at Sault Ste. Marie, Michigan, 1853-1866; Marquette, Michigan, 1868

Writings: Several in Chippewa such as: *Abinodjiiag Omasinaiganiwan* (Children's Reading-Book) Buffalo 1837; Bagg and Harmon, printers, Detroit 1845. The next two are still used: *Theoretical and Practical Grammar of the Otchipwe Language* J. Fox, printer, Detroit 1850; 2nd edition, Beauchemin & Valois (Montreal) 1878. *A Short Compendium of the Catechism for the Indians: with Approbation of the Rt. Rev. Frederic Baraga, Bishop of Sault Sainte Marie, 1864* C. Wieckmann, Buffalo,1869. *Dictionary of the Otchipwe Language* Printed by Joseph A. Hemann Cincinnati 1853. *Pastoral Letter to the English-Speaking Clergy and People of Upper Michigan* Cincinnati 1853; *Ninidjajanis-sidog Saiagiinagog*—pastoral letter to the Ojibwe of Lake Superior, the only pastoral letter written in a tribal language in the United States. In French: *Arbege de l'Histoire des Indiens de l'Amerique Septentrionale* (A Short History of the North American Indians) A la Societe des Bons Livres (Paris) 1837. In German: *Tagebuch* (Diary) 3 vols. 1852-1863) published as *The Diary of Bishop Frederic Baraga, First Bishop of Marquette, Michigan* Wayne State University Press 1990. In Latin: *Statuta Dioecesa Sanctae Mariae* (Statutes) C. Clark, Cincinnati 1856; Detroit 1863. In Ottawa: *Ottawa Anamie-Misinaigan* (Prayerbook) Detroit 1832; Paris 1837; Detroit 1842, 1846; Cincinnati 1855, 1858. Several in Slovenian such as: *Popis Navad in Sadershanja Indijanov Polnozhne Amerike* (Description of Customs and Manners of Indians in Midnight America) Ljubljana 1837. Others
Awards or inclusion in other biographical books: *American Biographies; Appleton's Cyclopaedia of American Biography; Dictionary of American Biography; Drake: Dictionary of American Biography; Dictionary of American Authors; Dictionary of North American Authors; National Cyclopaedia of American Biography; Reader's Encyclopedia of the American West; Twentieth Century Biographical Dictionary of Notable Americans.* Monument, in church at Dobernig; state park, village, schools, statue, archives in Michigan bear his name. Site of his first church, north of Manistique in Schoolcraft County was dedicated August 10, 1958 as a Registered State Historic Site, by the State of Michigan

BARFKNECHT, GARY

Born: Virginia, Minnesota
Children: Amy, Heidi
Education: University of Minnesota, B.S., 1967. University of Washington, Seattle, Washington, 1969
Career: Paint Chemist, E. I. DuPont & deMemours Company, Flint, Michigan. Freelance writer. Hockey Director, Genesee County, 1977-1981. Owner, managing editor, Friede Publications, Davison, Michigan

Writings: *33 Hikes From Flint* Friede Publications 1975. *Michillaneous* Friede Publications 1982. *Murder, Michigan* Friede Publications 1983. *Mich-Again's Day* Friede Publications 1984. *Michillaneous II* Friede Publications 1985. *Ultimate Michigan Adventures* Friede Publications 1989

BARNES, HALLY "AL"

Born: December 8, 1904; Madison, South Dakota
Parents: Rubin Perry Barnes; Sadie Dessie (Smith) Barnes
Children: Dennis, JoAnn, Vickie
Education: Athens, Michigan, one year of high school. Pathfinder School, high school diploma, Traverse City, Michigan, 1977. Self-taught
Career: Writer, photographer, *Traverse City Record-Eagle,* Traverse City, Michigan, 30 years, retired. Lectured throughout Michigan

Writings: *One Hundred Years from the Old Mission in Grand Traverse County, Michigan* Henderson Print Shop (Traverse City) 1939. *Vinegar Pie and Other Tales of the Grand Traverse Region* Wayne State University 1959; dedication reads: "to Alice, my wife, and to Jay P. Smith" (one of the editors of the *Traverse City Record-Eagle*). *Supper in the Evening* Dorrance 1967; Horizon Books (Traverse City) 1985. *Let's Fly Backward* Harlo Press 1976
Awards or inclusion in other biographical books: *Michigan Authors,* 2nd ed.
In the second edition of *Michigan Authors* appears: "He says: 'I am a nut about writing the truth and researching my projects. My errors in writing have been very few and I apologize for them. I am sick in the gut with half-truth-writing and sensationalism. One of my lectures is "You can't believe everything you read." The Media is a rabble-rousing mess despite the fact that I gave it so much of my life. My philosophy? It can be found, beginning with the book of Genesis and on through the book of Jude and as much of Revelations as I understand'."

BARTLEY, JACQUELINE S.

Address: 646 Pinecrest, Holland, Michigan 49424
Born: April 4, 1951; Pittsburgh, Pennsylvania
Parents: Clarence R. Salamon, Helen H. Salamon
Education: Western Michigan University, M.F.A., Kalamazoo, Michigan, 1984-1988. Clarion University of Pennsylvania, B.S., 1969-1973. Mercy Hospital School of Medical Technology, B.S., MT(ASCP) 1973-1974. Additional coursework: Hope College, English, 1982-1984. Michigan State University, Clinical Laboratory Science, 1980-1981
Career: Visiting Assistant Professor, Advisor/counselor for FOCUS and SOAR Programs, Hope College, Holland Michigan, 1991—. Lecturer, Hope College, Holland, Michigan, 1989-1991. Instructor, Western Michigan University, Kalamazoo, Michigan, 1989. Medical Technologist, various hospitals in Michigan, Oklahoma, Pennsylvania,

1974-1988. Holland Area Arts Council poetry classes for ages 8-14 as instructor. Visiting Writer, Workshop Leader.

Writings: Published in: *Journal of the American Medical Association, Dominion Review, Plainsong, Permafrost, Gulfstream, M U S E, Hubbub, Riverwind, The Sow's Ear Poetry Review, Whetstone, Birmingham Poetry Review, West Branch, Jeopardy, Roanoke Review, Black Fly Review, Oxford Magazine, Red Cedar Review, Yarrow, Sunrust, Green River Review, Trial Balloon, Currents.* Work in Progress: full length manuscript: *Explaining the Differential.* Chapbooks: *Meditation on the Statue of Mary Next Door, Lost Language, Terrible Boundaries of the Body*

Awards or inclusion in other biographical books: Sow's Ear Poetry Contest, second prize, 1990. Richard Benvento Poetry Award, *Red Cedar Review,* 1989. All-University Graduate Research and Creative Scholars Award, Western Michigan University, 1989. Best Poem, *Trial Balloon,* Western Michigan University, 1987. Snowbound Writers Competition, first prize, 1986; honorable mention, 1989. Honorable Mention, Poetry, *OPUS,* Hope College, 1983

What is the aim or goal of your writing? "To explore and respect the differences; to find the connections; to be real."

May inquiries be sent to you about doing workshops, readings? Yes

BATES, MARSTON (1906-1974)
Born: July 23, 1906; Grand Rapids, Michigan
Parents: Glenn F. Bates, Amy M. (Button) Bates
Children: Marian, Glenn, Sally, Barbara
Education: University of Florida, B.S., Gainesville, Florida, 1927. Harvard University, Cambridge, Massachusetts: M.A., 1933; Ph.D., 1934
Career: Entomologist, Director, United Fruit Company, Honduras, Guatemala, 1928-1931. Sheldon Traveling Fellow, 1934-1935. Research Assistant, Museum of Comparative Zoology, 1935-1937. Staff, International Health Division, 1937-1950. Professor, University of Michigan, Ann Arbor, Michigan, 1952-1972. On Editorial Board, *American Scholar,* various administrative positions with Guggenheim Foundation, Cranbrook Institute of Science, National Science Foundation

Writings: *The Natural History of Mosquitoes* Macmillan 1949. *The Prevalence of People* Scribner 1955. *The Forest and the Sea* Random House 1960. *Men in Nature* Prentice-Hall 1961, 1964. *Animal Worlds* Random House 1963, 1975. *The Land and Wildlife of South America* Time/Life Books 1964, 1968. *Gluttons and Libertines: Human Problems of Being Natural* Random House 1967. *A Jungle in the House: Essays in Natural and Unnatural History* Walker 1970. Others. In various periodicals

Awards or inclusion in other biographical books: *American Authors and Books; American Men and Women of Science; Current Biography, Contemporary Authors; New York Times Biographical Service; Who Was Who in America; Who's Who in the World.* Sc.D., Kalamazoo College, 1955. Phi Beta Kappa Writing Award, 1960. Fellow, Center for Advanced Studies, 1961. Phi Beta Kappa Visiting Scholar, 1962-1963, 1968-1969. Medal, American Geographic Society, 1967. Distinguished Faculty Achievement Award, University of Michigan, 1968

BAUMAN, MICHAEL
Address: 4202 W. Hallett Rd., Hillsdale, Michigan 49242
Born: February 14, 1950; Moline, Illinois
Parents: Edward P. Bauman, Edith J. (Pulver) Bauman
Education: Fordham University, Ph.D. in Historical Theology & English Literature, Bronx, New York, 1980-1983. McCormick Theological Seminary, M.A., New Testament/Church History, 1979. Trinity College, B.A., Biblical Studies, 1977
Career: Hillsdale College, Associate Professor of Theology and Culture; Director of Christian Studies, Hillsdale, Michigan, 1988—. Centre for Medieval & Renaissance Studies, Associate Dean of the Summer School, Lecturer in Renaissance Literature and Theology, Oxford, England, 1990—. Northeastern Bible College, Chairman, Division of General Education; Assistant Professor of History and Church History, Essex Fells, New Jersey, 1983-1988. Fordham University, Associate Professor of History of Christianity (adjunct), Bronx, New York, 1986-1987. Regional Seminary of the Northeast, Lecturer in Church History, Basking Ridge, New Jersey, 1985-1986. Pastor, Chicago, Illinois, 1975-1976. Assistant Pastor, Roselle Park, New Jersey, 1979-1980. Youth Pastor, Illinois and New Jersey, 1977-1982. Book Review Editor, *Journal of the Evangelical Theological Society*, 1987—. Editorial Assistant, *Newsweek*, 1982-1984

Writings: *Pilgrim Theology: Taking the Path of Theological Discovery* Zondervan 1992. *Are You Politically Correct?: Debating America's Cultural Standards* Prometheus 1992. *Man and Marxism: Religion and the Communist Retreat* Hillsdale College Press 1991. *Roundtable: Conversations with European Theologians* Baker 1990. *The Best of the Manion Forum: A Conservative and Free Market Sourcebook* Mellen Research University Press 1991. *A Scripture Index to John Milton's De Doctrina Christiana* MRTS 1989. *Milton's Arianism* Verlag Peter Lang 1987. Numerous articles, papers, book reviews, political editorials. Work in Progress:*The Broadman Handbook of Church Historians* (with Martin Klauber).*The Apostles' Creed: An Evangelical Exposition of the Historic Christian Faith. Southey's Christian Doctrine: The Religion of the Poet Laureate. Lexical Scholasticism: Why Pastor Can't Read.* Various articles
Awards or inclusion in other biographical books: *Who's Who in Religion; Who's Who in the Midwest; Who's Who in Theology and Science.* Professor of the Year, 1992. AMY Foundation Writing Award, 1991. National Endowment for the Humanities Visiting Research Fellow, Department of English, Princeton University, 1988. University Teaching Fellowship, Fordham University, 1982-1983. Graduate Assistantship (library acquisition, faculty research) Fordham University, 1980-1982
What is the aim or goal of your writing? "To integrate Christian orthodoxy into other fields of knowledge, such as political theory, economics, literary criticism, and history."
May inquiries be sent to you about doing workshops, readings? Yes

BAXTER, CHARLES M.
Address: 1585 Woodland Drive, Ann Arbor, Michigan 48103
Born: May 13, 1947; Minneapolis, Minnesota
Parents: John T. Baxter, Mary B. (Eaton) Baxter
Children: Daniel
Education: Macalester College, B.A., St. Paul, Minnesota, 1965-1969. State University of New York at Buffalo, Ph.D., Buffalo, New York, 1970-1974
Career: Professor of English, University of Michigan, Ann Arbor, Michigan, 1989—. Professor of English, Wayne State University, Detroit, Michigan, 1974-1988

Writings: *Shadow Play* W.W Norton 1993. *A Relative Stranger* W.W. Norton 1990. *Imaginary Paintings* Paris Review Editions 1990. *First Light* Viking/Penguin 1987. *Through the Safety Net* Viking/Penguin 1985. *History of the World* University of Missouri Press 1984

May inquiries be sent to you about doing workshops, readings? Yes

BEACH, REX (ELLINGWOOD) (1877-1949)
Born: September 1, 1877; Atwood, Michigan
Parents: Henry Walter Beach, Eva Eunice (Canfield) Beach
Education: Rollins College, Winter Park, Florida, 1891-1896. College of Law, Chicago, Illinois, one year. Kent College of Law, 1899-1900
Career: Joined Chicago Athletic Association to play football but transferred to swimming team. Left in 1900 to join Klondike Gold Rush. Tried zinc mining in Missouri, other jobs. President of the Author's League of America, 1917-1921; required movie rights in his own publishing contracts

Writings: *Pardners* Doubleday 1905. *The Spoilers* Burt 1906. *The Barrier* Harper, 1908. *The Silver Horde* Burt 1909. *Going Some* Burt 1910. *The Ne'er-Do-Well* Burt 1911. *The Net; A Novel* Harper & Brothers 1912. *The Iron Trail; An Alaskan Romance* Harper & Brothers 1913. *The Auction Block* Harper & Brothers 1914. *Heart of the Sunset* Burt 1915. *Rainbow's End* Burt 1916. *The Crimson Gardenia* Burt 1916. *Laughing Bill Hyde and Other Stories* Harper & Brothers 1917. *The Winds of Chance* Burt 1918. *Too Fat to Fight* Harper 1921. *Oh, Shoot* Garden City 1921. *Flowing Gold* Burt 1922. *Big Brother* Harper 1923. *Four in One Adventures* Garden City 1923. *North of Fifty-three* Garden City 1924. *The Goose Woman* Burt 1925. *The Miracle of Coral Gables* Baird-Ward 1926. *Padlocked: A Novel* Burt 1926. *The Mating Call* Harper & Brothers 1927. *Don Careless* Harper 1928. *Son of the Gods* Harper 1929. *Money Mad* Cosmopolitan 1931. *Men of the Outer Islands* Farrar 1932. *Beyond Control* Farrar 1932. *Alaskan Adventures: The Spoilers* Burt 1932. *The Hands of Dr. Locke* Farrar 1934. *Masked Women* Farrar & Rinehart 1934. *Wild Pastures* Farrar 1935. *Jungle Gold* Farrar 1935. *Valley of Thunder* Farrar l939. *Personal Exposures* (autobiography) Harper 1941. *The World in His Arms* Putnam 1946. *Woman in Ambush* (unfinished) Putnam 1951. Others. Films have been made of his books-*The Spoilers* had the honor of being the first six-reel movie. Included in collected works

Awards or inclusion in other biographical books: *American Authors and Books; Cyclopedia of World Authors; Dictionary of American Biography; Dictionary of Literature in the English Language; Dictionary of North American Authors; Everyman's Dictionary of Literary Biography, English and American; Michigan Authors,* 1st ed., 2nd ed.; *National Cyclopaedia of American Biography; Oxford Companion to American Literature; Twentieth Century Authors; Twentieth Century Writing; Who Was Who in America; Who Was Who among North American Authors,* others. Dubbed the "Victor Hugo of the North".

BEASECKER, ROBERT
Address: 1641 Jefferson, Muskegon, Michigan 49441
Born: February 3, 1946; Detroit, Michigan
Education: Hillsdale College, A.B., Hillsdale, Michigan, 1964-1969. University of Michigan, A.M.L.S., Ann Arbor, Michigan 1969-1970.
Career: Librarian/Archivist, Grand Valley State University, Allendale, Michigan 1970-

Writings: Book Reviews of Michigan fiction and non-fiction appearing in the Historical Society of Michigan's publication, *Chronicle.* Work in Progress: *Bibliography of Michigan Novels*
Awards or inclusion in other biographical books: Mid America Award, Society for the Study of Midwestern Literature, 1984
May inquiries be sent to you about doing workshops, readings? Yes

BECK, EARL CLIFTON (1891-1977)
Pseudonym: Doc Beck
Born: April 7, 1891; Hickman, Nebraska
Parents: Cornelius Porter Beck, Louisa (Theade) Beck
Children: Margymae, Jane Louise
Education: Peru Teachers College, Peru, Nebraska. University of Nebraska, B.A., M.A. Harvard University, M.A. George Peabody College, Ph.D.
Career: Teacher and administrator in Nebraska public schools, college training school in Dillon, Montana. College teacher in Florida; Stillman College, Alabama; head of English Department at Central Michigan University, Mt. Pleasant, Michigan

Writings: *Songs of the Michigan Lumberjacks* University of Michigan Press 1941, 1942. *Lore of the Lumber Camps* University of Michigan Press 1948. *They Knew Paul Bunyan* University of Michigan Press 1956. *Sounds of the Lake and the Forest* Hillsdale 1959. Wrote the Foreword for Louise Jean Walker's *Legends of Green Sky Hill.* The second edition of *Michigan Authors* includes this by Arlies G. Fairman: "My father-in-law, Earl C. Beck, died on March 21, 1977, in Farmington Hills, Michigan. My brief comments do not do justice to the man, his literary efforts, or his contribution to the education of thousands of young people of every race and creed over a period of nearly sixty years. He taught the meek and the mighty, and he entertained many audiences with his lumberjack tales, songs, and perfomers. He was many things-farmer, cowpuncher, miner, sportsman, athlete, husband, father-and a friend to all who extended a hand of welcome."
Awards or inclusion in other biographical books: *Michigan Authors,* 1st ed., 2nd ed.

BECKER, THERESE J.
Address: P.O. Box 2401, Eaton Gate Rd., Lake Orion, Michigan 48360
Born: December 2, 1940; Detroit, Michigan
Parents: Jacob R. Kloeckner, Blanche E. (DeGriselles) Kloeckner
Children: Jeanette, Michael, Christopher
Education: Oakland University, Bachelor of Arts, Rochester, Michigan, 1978-1984. Warren Wilson College, Master of Fine Arts, Swannanoa, North Carolina, 1989-1991
Career: Writer, Michigan Council for the Arts Creative Writers in the Schools program, Detroit, Michigan, 1986—. Reporter, *Oxford Leader,* Oxford, Michigan, 1984-1985. Public Relations Director, Artrain, Detroit, Michigan, 1982-1983. Photojournalist and journalist for *The Detroit Free Press, The Detroit News, The Oakland Press, Heritage Magazine,* and others.

Writings: Poetry published in: *The Midwest Poetry Review, The Bellingham Review, The Beloit Poetry Journal, Poetry Now, Passages North, The Greenfield Review, The Laurel Review, The New York Quarterly, Moving Out, Milkweed Chronicle, The Louisville Review, Witness,* and others. Anthologies: *Woman Poet-The Midwest, The Third Coast: Michigan Contemporary Poetry,* 1986/1987 *Anthology of Magazine Verse & Yearbook of*

American Poetry, and others. Personal Essays in: *Milkweed Chronicle, Detroit Free Press.* Work in Progress: Working to complete three chapbooks of poetry and one full-length poetry manuscript. Also on a book of experiences while teaching creative writing to school children and compiling their poems for a book called *Listen to the Children*

Awards or inclusion in other biographical books: Scholarships to the Cranbrook summer writing program, 1979, 1980, 1982, 1983. Fellowship to Oakland Writers' Conference, 1980.

What is the aim or goal of your writing? "My goal is to witness the world and to write the best poetry I'm capable of. As regards the children's work, I believe the world needs to hear from them, since we are rapidly destroying their world as if they didn't exist. I'm hoping my book, on how to teach the creative process to students, will enable teachers to incorporate the creative process into the learning process, as I believe they are one. I also hope I will be able to raise some money, through the sale of the book of the children's poems, to provide assistance to homeless children."

May inquiries be sent to you about doing workshops, readings? Yes

BEDFORD, JAMES W.
Address: 1804 Wood Street, Lansing, Michigan 48912
Born: December 3, 1942; Colfax, Washington
Parents: Clifford L. Bedford, Dorothy S. Bedford
Children: Allan, Terri
Education: Michigan State University, B.S., East Lansing, Michigan, 1961-1965; M.S., Ph. D., 1965-1970
Career: Environmental Health Ombudsman, Michigan Department of Public Health, Lansing, Michigan, 1990—. Senior Toxicologist, Toxic Substance Control Commission, Lansing, Michigan, 1984-1989. Organic Analyses Unit, Michigan Department of Natural Resources, Lansing, Michigan, 1975-1984. Instructor, Lansing Community College, Lansing, Michigan, 1980—. Field Editor*Michigan Hunting & Fishing Magazine* 1982–.
Writings: Over 200 feature articles in *Field and Stream, Outdoor Life, Trout, Fishing Journal, Salmon Trout Steelheader, Michigan Out-Of-Doors, Great Lakes Fisherman, Michigan Fisherman, Michigan Natural Resources, Striper, Tuebor Terra, Ontario Fisherman.* Work in Progress: Book on Steelhead fishing
Awards or inclusion in other biographical books: *Who's Who in the Midwest; Who's Who in the Environment.* Michigan Outdoor Writer's Association awards in features, conservation, black and white and color photography
What is the aim or goal of your writing? "Entertain and inform fishermen (and women). Increase public awareness of water quality and other conservation issues. Increase public appreciation of rivers and the fish that inhabit them."
May inquiries be sent to you about doing workshops, readings? Yes

BELLAIRS, JOHN A. (1938-1991)
Born: January 17, 1938; Marshall, Michigan
Parents: Frank E. Bellairs, Virginia (Monk) Bellairs
Children: Frank
Education: University of Notre Dame, A.B., English, Notre Dame, Indiana, 1959. He credited his mentor at Notre Dame, Professor Frank O'Malley, with teaching him to write. University of Chicago, M.A., Chicago, Illinois, 1960
Career: Instructor, College of St. Teresa, Winona, Minnesota, 1963-1965. Faculty, Shimer College, Mount Carroll, Illinois, 1966-1967. Instructor, Emmanuel College,

Boston, Massachusetts, 1968-1969. Faculty, Merrimack College, North Andover, Massachusetts, 1969-1971

Writings: *St. Fidgeta and Other Parodies* Macmillan 1966. *The Pedant and the Shuffly* Macmillan 1968. *The Face in the Frost* Macmillan 1969. *The House with a Clock in Its Walls* Dial 1973; Listening Library 1991. *The Figure in the Shadows* Dial 1975. *The Letter, the Witch, and the Ring* Dial Press 1976. *The Treasure of Alpheus Winterborn* Harcourt 1978. *The Curse of the Blue Figurine* Dial 1983. *The Mummy, the Will, and the Crypt* Dial 1983. *The Dark Secret of the Weatherend* Dial 1984. *The Revenge of the Wizard's Ghost* Dial Books for Young Readers 1985. *The Eyes of the Killer Robot* Dial 1986. *The Lamp from the Warlock's Tomb* Dial Books for Young Readers 1988. *The Chessmen of Doom* Dial Books for Young Readers 1989. *The Trolley to Yesterday* Dial Books for Young Readers 1989. *The Face in the Frost* Collier Books; Maxwell Macmillan Canada; Maxwell Macmillan International 1991. *The Mansion in the Mist* Dial Books for Young Readers 1992. Others
Awards or inclusion in other biographical books: *Contemporary Authors; Science Fiction and Fantasy Literature; Something about the Author; Writers Directory.* Outstanding Book Citation, *New York Times,* 1973. Woodrow Wilson Fellowship. Utah Childrens Book Award, 1981

BENEDICT, ELINOR D.
Address: 2610 Washington Mill Road, Bellbrook, Ohio 45305
Born: June 4, 1931; Chattanooga, Tennessee
Parents: Thomas M. Divine, Mary H. Divine
Children: Samuel, Jonathan, Kathleen
Education: Dobyn S. Bennett High School. Duke University, B.A., Durham, North Carolina, 1949-1953. Wright State University, M.A., Dayton, Ohio, 1976-1977. Vermont College, M.F.A., Montpelier, Vermont, 1981-1983
Career: Freelance poet, fiction writer. Editor, *Passages North Magazine,* Escanaba, Michigan, 1979-1989. Instructor of English, Bay de Noc Community College, Escanaba, Michigan, 1977-1986. Staff Writer, Times Publications, Kettering, Ohio, 1969-1976. Public Information Consultant, Centerville Public Schools, Centerville, Ohio, 1975-1976

Writings: *Landfarer* Hardwood Books 1978. *A Bridge to China* Hardwood Books 1983. Work in Progress: Poetry collection, *The Green Heart*
Awards or inclusion in other biographical books: *Who's Who in American Writers and Editors,* 1990. *Mademoiselle* Fiction Prize, 1953. Ohio Press Association, First Prize for Community Service, 1972. National Mental Health Bell Award for Media, 1972. AAUW Individual Project Award, 1982. Michigan Council for the Arts Creative Arts Award, 1985. Coordinating Council for Literary Magazines (CCLM) Editors Award, 1986
What is the aim or goal of your writing? "To create writing of value out of experience and imagination."
May inquiries be sent to you about doing workshops, readings? Yes

BENJAMIN, STANLEY L. (1895-1979)
Born: September 19, 1895; Constantine, Michigan
Parents: William H. Benjamin, Cora Belle (Langton) Benjamin
Children: Robert, Edward, William, Dorothy, Norma, Helen
Education: Albion College, A.B., Albion, Michigan, 1924. University of Michigan, M.A.,

Ann Arbor, Michigan. Eden Seminary, 1958
Career: U.S. Army, 2nd Lieutenant, 1917-1918. Superintendent of Schools in various cities such as Carsonville, Michigan; Galesburg-Augusta, Michigan. Minister, First Congregational Church, Cheboygan, Michigan

Writings: *Through the Years: the Poems* Harlo Press 1971
In the Second Edition he is credited with saying: "My poems were written 'just for fun' over a period of more than fifty years. I was ordained into the Ministry past the age when most Ministers have retired. After serving thirty-eight years as a school superintendent, I served the Cheboygan Church for nine years."
Awards or inclusion in other biographical books: *Michigan Authors,* 2nd ed.

BERNHARDT, DEBRA E.

Address: 233 Bernhardt Rd., Iron River, Michigan 49935
Born: May 9, 1953; Nurnberg, Germany
Parents: Harold O. Bernhardt, Marcia A. Bernhardt
Children: Alexander
Education: University of Michigan, B.A., Ann Arbor, Michigan, 1971-1975. Wayne State University, M.A., Detroit, Michigan, 1977. New York University, Ph.D., New York City, 1980-1987
Career: Head Archivist, New York University, Elmer Bobst Library, New York City, 1989—. Archivist, New York University, Elmer Bobst Library, 1979—. Co-Director of research project on labor history, State of Ohio, Columbus, Ohio, 1978-1979. Student Librarian, Wayne State University, Labor Archives, 1976-1977

Writings: *New Yorkers at Work: Oral Histories of Life, Labor and Industry,* Curriculum Units growing out of documentary radio series, done for Public Radio broadcasts in 1981, New York University 1985. *Oral History Manual-Twentieth Century Trade Women Union: Vehicle for Social Change* New York University 1982. *We Knew Different--The Michigan Timber Workers' Strike of 1937* Mid-Peninsula Library Cooperative 1978. *Spring Valley Series*, a series of short stories. Over the past 10 years numerous articles and book reviews for professional magazines. Work in Progress: Poetry, short stories
Awards or inclusion in other biographical books: *Michigan Authors,* 2nd ed. Hopwood Award for Short Stories, University of Michigan, 1974. Award of Merit, Historical Society of Michigan, 1976. Regents Cultural Education Committee Award for Program Excellence, 1991
What is the aim or goal of your writing? "*Black Rock and Roses* grew out of over a hundred oral history interviews with miners, muckers, union men, management, boarding house matrons-the inhabitants of an Upper Peninsula iron mining town as the mining reality was rapidly fading away. I sought out the old timers, many of them immigrants, to understand myself through the community I grew up in, believing as William Faulkner said that 'No Man is himself; he is the sum of his past'. What I heard revealed so much of importance in language and imagery that the poet in me envied, that I knew it must be shared. I came to see myself as an instrument through which these people, many of whom had never been heard, could speak."
May inquiries be sent to you about doing workshops, readings? Yes

BERNHARDT, MARCIA A.

Address: 233 Bernhardt Rd., Iron River, Michigan 49935
Born: July 12, 1926; Ingham County, Michigan
Parents: Glen S. Webster, E. Hilda (Eifert) Webster
Children: Debra E., Andra E.
Education: Michigan State University, B.A., East Lansing, Michigan, 1944-1947. University of Wisconsin, Madison, Wisconsin, summer 1951. Handelskoskolen, Copenhagen, Denmark, summer 1953. Northern Michigan University, Marquette, Michigan, M.A., 1967
Career: Iron County Museum Curator, Iron County Museum, Caspian, Michigan, 1968—. Senior High English Teacher, West Iron County Public Schools, 1962-1984. Amasa High School English Teacher, 1961-1962. Teacher in Army Education Centers in Germany, 1952-1954. Psychiatric Social Worker, State of Michigan, 1947-1950

Writings: *A Celebration of Chocolate, Ed.* Iron County Museum 1990. *Iron County Historical Sites and Landmarks* Iron County Museum 1985. *More Than Just a Farmer, Beechwood, Michigan 1882-1982, Editor, Photographer* Iron County Museum 1982. *The Jewel of Iron County (A Photographic Essay)* Iron County Museum 1976. *Frames for the Future-Iron River Area* Taylor Publishing Co. 1981. *They Came...to Iron County, Michigan* Dickinson-Iron Intermediate School District 1975. *Carrie Jacobs-Bond, As Unpretentious as a Wild Rose* Iron County Museum 1978. Several other publications have been edited which have been published by the Historical Society such as: *As Time Goes By, Iron River, Michigan* 1981-1972. *The Rum Rebellion Tabloid,* 1970. *The Blend of the Century Cookbook*, 1981. *A Visitors' Handbook and Guide to the Iron County Museum*, 1988, revised 1990, 1992. Work in Progress: Two oral history projects, one on Service people from World War II, the other, the History of Caspian on its Diamond Jubilee.
Awards or inclusion in other biographical books: *Michigan Authors,* 2nd ed. Charles Follo Award for Upper Peninsula Historians, 1980. Commendation from the American Association for State and Local History, 1983.
What is the aim or goal of your writing? "My writing, secondary and often editorial, is supplemented by a strong sense for the need of historical preservation. After several years of continuous writing of press releases, I began to write feature articles for the *Green Bay Press-Gazette* and occasionally for the *Milwaukee Sentinal.* I also worked with students on publications for the Junior Historical Society, co-advising *The Rum Rebellion*, supervised the writing and production of four vaudeville type shows in the historical vein, and edited their cookbook. I have also written the newsletter of the Historical Society for the past 25 years. It has ranged from 4 to 10 pages in length. My early goal was to assemble and edit much of the material that we have gathered into the archival files of the Museum. My present goal is to put the archival collections in order, appropriately indexed, so that they will be of use to other writers. For pleasure, I write poetry and short animal tales for my grandchildren."
May inquiries be sent to you about doing workshops, readings? Yes

BETZOLD, MICHAEL J.

Address: 20025 Renfrew, Detroit, Michigan 48221
Born: June 26, 1950; Detroit, Michigan
Parents: Eugene G. Betzold, Inez M. (Ruwart) Betzold
Children: Patrick, Bridget
Education: Sacred Heart Seminary High School, Detroit, Michigan, 1964-1968. Michigan State University, B.A. in Psychology, East Lansing, Michigan, 1968-1972. Wayne

State University, M.A., in Linguistics, Detroit, Michigan, 1976-1978
Career: Reporter, *Detroit Free Press,* Detroit, Michigan, 1988—; Copy editor 1985-1988. Freelance writer, 1980-1985. Reporter, *Health Care News* Detroit, Michigan, 1979-1980

Writings: *Queen of Diamonds: The Tiger Stadium Story* (with Ethan Casey) A & M Publishing 1992. *End of the Line: Autoworkers and the American Dream* (with Richard Feldman) Weidenfeld & Nicholson 1988. *Tiger Stadium: Where Baseball Belongs* Tiger Stadium Fan Club 1988. *Mal Sillars' Detroit Weather Book* (with Mal Sillars) Weather Enterprise 1986. *Sexual Scarcity: The Marital Mistake and the Communal Alternative* Human Press 1978
What is the aim or goal of your writing? "To raise consciousness and spread information on vital issues."
May inquiries be sent to you about doing workshops, readings? Yes

BEZINE, CHING YUN
Address: 1226 Old Hwy. 2 and 41, Bark River, Michigan 49807
Born: June 9, 1937; Chingdou, China
Parents: Wei-yu Yun, Show-mei Shih Yun
Children: Julia, Everett
Education: China, Law, B.L. 1960. Western Kentucky University, Art. George Peabody College, M.A. Art Education, Nashville Tennessee, completed 1973
Career: Teacher in Public Schools, Kentucky, Tennessee, Hawaii, 1963-1974

Writings: *Children of the Pearl* NAL/Dutton 1991. *Temple of the Moon* NAL/Dutton 1992. Fourteen novels in Chinese, published in China. Work in Progress: *On Wings of Destiny* will be published in October, 1992. Two more books untitled sold to NAL/Dutton will be published in 1993, 1994
What is the aim or goal of your writing? "Share my feelings with my readers"
May inquiries be sent to you about doing workshops, readings? Yes

BINGAY, MALCOLM WALLACE (1884-1953)
Born: Sandwich, Ontario, Canada; December 16, 1884
Parents: George Bingay, Isabella (McIntyre) Bingay
Education: Y.M.C.A. night classes, private instruction after grammar school, Detroit Michigan. University of Michigan, Ann Arbor, Michigan.
Children: Sybil
Career: Reporter, *Detroit News,* Detroit, Michigan; editorial positions, 1906 until becoming Director, 1930.

Writings: *He Who Went About Doing Good* Press of the Round Circle 1939. *A Radio Discussion of What Do You Mean—Americanism?* University of Chicago 1939. *What I Saw in Europe and What We Must Do About It* Knight Newspapers, Inc. 1945. *Detroit Is My Own Home Town* Bobbs Merrill 1946. *Of Me I Sing* Bobbs-Merrill 1949.
"Good Morning" Column, *Detroit Free Press*
Awards or inclusion in other biographical books: *Dictionary of American Biography; Who Was Who in America.* Honorary D. Litt., Wayne State University, 1932; LL.D., Olivet College, 1946. Honorary Member, Wayne County Medical Society, 1933.

BINKOWSKI, DON
Address: 11939 E. 13 Mile, Warren, Michigan 48093
Born: October 26, 1929; Detroit, Michigan
Parents: Alexander A. Binkowski; Helen (Wojtowicz) Binkowski
Children: Donna F., Beth Ann, Alex
Education: John J. Pershing High School, Detroit, Michigan, 1947. University of Michigan, A.B., Ann Arbor, Michigan, 1947-1951. University of Detroit Evening Law School, Wayne State University Law School, J.D., 1956
Career: District Judge, 37th District Court, Warren, Michigan, 1969-1986. Councilman/Mayor Pro Tem, Warren, Michigan, 1965-1969. Private Practice, Detroit/Warren, 1963-1969. Attorney, Wayne County Circuit Court, Detroit, 1960-1962. Delegate, Michigan Constitutional Convention, 1961-1962. Assistant Michigan Attorney General, 1957-1959

Writings: *Ethnic Politics in Urban America* (with Thaddeus C. Razialowski) Polish Historical Association 1978. Published in *Michigan Challenge.* Contributor to *Enduring Poles* Masspac Publishing 1977. Work in Progress: *Polish American Officials of Michigan-A Personal Declaration of Independence.* "Norris' Contributions to Michigan". Research completed for *History of Warren.* Completed manuscript *Norris of Yellowstone: America's First Environmental Martyr*
Awards or inclusion in other biographical books: *Who's Who in the Midwest* 1972-1980; *Who's Who in the Law* 1973. Macomb County Historical Society, in recognition of contribution of about 5,000 volumes of Michigan histories, pamphlets, to the Warren Public Library, 1975. National Citizens Award, 1979. Wayne State University Law School Recognition, 1980. Polish Government-In-Exile, 1980. Polish Central Citizens Committee, 1981
What is the aim or goal of your writing? "Primarily, I am interested in Michigan and ethnic history, especially local history. After the publication of the *Michigan Pioneer and Historical Collections,* it appears that Michigan lost its zest for history and particularly local history. Tragically, most of our large, rich ethnic contributions have never been recorded."
May inquiries be sent to you about doing workshops, readings? Yes

BITTNER, ROSANNE
Address: 6013 N. Coloma Rd., Coloma, Michigan 49038
Born: January 14, 1945; LaPorte, Indiana
Parents: Frank L. Reris, Ethel A. Reris
Children: Brock, Brian
Education: Coloma High School, Coloma, Michigan, High School Graduation 1963. Lake Michigan College, Night Classes, 1963-1964
Career: Writer 1984—. Executive Secretary, D.C. Cook Nuclear Plant, Bridgman, Michigan, 1982-1984. Executive Secretary, Indiana/Michigan Electric Company, St. Joseph, Michigan, 1972-1982. Legal Secretary, Ryan, McQuillan and Vanderplogh, St. Joseph, Michigan, 1970-1972. Secretary to Personnel Manager, Gast Mfg. Corp., Benton Harbor, Michigan, 1966-1969

Writings: Zebra Books: (Savage Destiny Series 1983-1986): *Sweet Prairie Passion, Ride the Free Wind, River of Love, Embrace the Wild Land, Climb the Highest Mountain, Meet the New Dawn* ; (Single Titles-1985-1991)-*Arizona Bride, Lawless Love, Rapture's Gold, Prairie Embrace, Heart's Surrender, Ecstasy's Chains, Arizona Ecstasy, Sweet Mountain*

Magic, Sioux Splendor, Comanche Sunset, Caress. Blue Hawk Series, 1987: *Savage Horizons, Frontier Fires, Destiny's Dawn. This Time Forever,* 1989. Bantam 1990-1992: *Montana Woman, Embers of the Heart, In the Shadow of the Mountains, Song of the Wolf. Outlaw Hearts* coming out1993. Doubleday and Bantam: *Thunder on the Plains* 1992. Work in Progress: Civil War novel for Bantam Books. Some books have been printed in several foreign languages.

Awards or inclusion in other biographical books: Nominated by *Romantic Times* Magazine for a career Achievement Award and for Best Western Saga for *In the Shadow of the Mountains.* Silver Pen Award, 1987, 1989. Golden Certificate, 1989, 1990. Awards for Best Fictionalized Biography, 1990 and Best Post-Civil War Romance, 1991. Bookstores that Care Award (third place) for Outstanding Historical Romance Author,1990

What is the aim or goal of your writing? "To show the history of our American West in an entertaining format. All my stories are heavily researched and based on historical fact. I also strive to tell the truth about what happened with our Native Americans."

May inquiries be sent to you about doing workshops, readings? Yes. I do charge a fee.

BLACKBIRD, ANDREW JACKSON (1820?-1908)

(Pe-ness-wi-qua-am Mack-a-te-be-nessy)

Born: 1815-1825 near Lake Michigan

Parents: Mack-a-te-pe-nessy (Black Hawk), Ottawa Indian chieftain, mother's name unknown

Children: Three sons, one daughter

Education: Mission school at New Arbre Croche. Twinburg Institute, Ohio, four years. Michigan State Normal School, Ypsilanti, Michigan, 1856-1858

Career: Various jobs before being elected to local government positions such as probate judge, Little Traverse (Harbor Springs, Michigan). Promoted loyalty to the Government during the Civil War. United States Interpreter, Mackinac Indian Agency, 1861-1869. Supervisor, Little Traverse Township and Chairman of the Board of Supervisors, 1870-1872. Postmaster for Little Traverse, 11 years. Looked after soldiers' claims for widows and orphans, for whites and Indians

Writings: *History of the Ottawa and Chippewa Indians of Michigan; A Grammar of their Language, and Personal and Family History of the Author* The Ypsilantian Job Printing House 1887; Little Traverse Regional Historical Society 1967 (1500 copies); 1977 (2500 copies). *The Indian Problem from the Indian's Standpoint* circulated by National Indian Association of Philadelphia, Pennsylvania, 1900

Awards or inclusion in other biographical books: *Allibone: A Critical Dictionary of English Literature; Dictionary of North American Authors.* Harbor Springs school bears his name. His house is a museum for Ottawa Indians in Harbor Springs

BLACKHAWK, TERRY M.

Address: 16215 Warwick, Detroit, Michigan 48219

Born: February 5, 1945; Glendale, California

Parents: Ben A. Bohnhorst, Marie W. Bohnhorst

Children: Ned

Education: Antioch College, B.A., Yellow Springs, Ohio, 1962-1968. Oakland University, Ph.D. Candidate, Rochester, Michigan, 1986—.

Career: Teacher, Detroit Public Schools, Detroit, Michigan, 1968—.

Writings: Over 30 poems have appeared in various journals including *America, Passages North, Iris, Louisville Review, Wayne Review,* others. Articles on teaching writing published by Christopher-Gordon, Inc., *Language Arts Journal of Michigan.* Work in Progress: Manuscript: *Even Ordinary Ground*

Awards or inclusion in other biographical books: Distinguished Merit Award for Poetry, Poetry Atlanta Chapbook Competition 1990. Foley Poetry Award, *America* Magazine, 1990. Michigan Poet Hunt, Honorable Mention, 1989. First Place Poetry Award, *Moving Out* 1992. Poetry Honorarium, *MacGuffin* New Decade, New Writers, Special Issue

What is the aim or goal of your writing? "Discovery; comfort; to bear witness."

May inquiries be sent to you about doing workshops, readings? Yes

BLAIN, ALEXANDER

Address: 8 Stratford Place, Grosse Pointe, Michigan 48230

Born: March 9, 1918; Detroit, Michigan

Parents: Alexander W. Blain, Ruby J. Blain

Children: Helen, Alexander, Bruce, Josephine

Education: Detroit University School, Grosse Pointe, 1923-1935. Washington and Lee University, Lexington, Virginia, 1935-1937. Wayne State University, B.A.,1937-1940, Detroit, Michigan. Wayne State University, Medical School, M.D., Detroit, Michigan, 1939-1943. University of Michigan, M.S., Ann Arbor, Michigan

Career: Medical Adjudicator and Consultant, Veterans Administration, 1990—. Chief Surgeon, Alexander Blain Hospital, Detroit, Michigan 1958-1978. Assistant Resident, Resident in Surgery, Instructor, University Hospital, Ann Arbor, Michigan 1946-1957. House Officer and William Steward Halstead Fellow in Surgery, Johns Hopkins, Baltimore, Maryland, 1943-1946. Assistant Professor of Surgery, Wayne State University, 1960-1990. Consulting Surgeon, St. Joseph, (Detroit) and Highland Park Hospitals. Associate Surgeon, Harper and St. John Hospitals, 1963-1990. Chief Surgeon, U.S. Army Hospital in West Germany, 1955-1957

Writings: *Clackshant* Sylvan Press 1982. *Partridge Springs Anthology* Grosse Pointe Press 1984. *Shu Shu Ga* Grosse Pointe Press 1980. *Remembered Voices* Grosse Pointe Press 1972. *Prismatic Papers and an Ode* Cranbrook 1968. *Indications for Results of Splenectomy* Charles C. Thomas, St. Louis 1950. Over 40 papers appearing in surgical and medical journals, 1945-1965. Editorial Board, Review of Surgery, 1952-1977. Work in Progress: unpublished poems

Awards or inclusion in other biographical books: *Directory of Medical Specialists; Who's Who in America.* Fellowship, New York Academy of Sciences, for published research on the effect of penicillin in experimental intestinal obstruction, 1946

What is the aim or goal of your writing? "Surgical papers related to career in surgery. Prose and poems related to career essentially serious poetry. Goal now is personal pleasure in critiqued poetry and creative writing."

May inquiries be sent to you about doing workshops, readings? Yes

BLAIN, DIANE

Address: 7725 Noffke Drive, Caledonia, Michigan 49316

Born: March 2, 1950; Grand Rapids, Michigan

Parents: Bryce E. Smith; Mary E. Smith

Children: Jody, Jessica

Education: Western Michigan University, Kalamazoo, Michigan, B.A., 1968-1971; M.A., 1974-1979. Michigan State University, Elementary Teaching Certificate, East Lansing, Michigan, 1984-1985
Career: Teacher, Caledonia Public Schools, Caledonia, Michigan, 1972—.

Writings: *The Boxcar Children Cookbook* Albert Whitman 1991
What is the aim or goal of your writing? "To make doing by reading an enjoyable experience by children."
May inquiries be sent to you about doing workshops, readings? Yes

BLOCKSMA, MARY
Address: P.O. Box 728, Douglas, Michigan 49406
Born: January 19, 1942; Chicago, Illinois
Parents: Ralph Blocksma, Ruth N. Blocksma
Children: Dylan Kuhn
Education: Wheaton College, Wheaton, Illinois, B.A., 1959-1963. Johns Hopkins University, Baltimore, Maryland, M.A., 1963-1964. University of Michigan, Ann Arbor, M.L.S., 1968
Career: Head of Periodicals, DePaul University, Chicago, Illinois, 1968-1970. Peace Corps Volunteer, Ministry of Education, School Library Administrator, Enugu, Eastern Nigeria, 1965-1967. Director, Albany County Public Library, Laramie, Wyoming, 1970-1976. Staff Writer, Addison-Wesley Reading Program, Boston, Massachusetts and Menlo Park, California, 1977-1980. Freelance Writer of Children's Fiction and Nonfiction and Adult Nonfiction Books, 1980—.

Writings: Nonfiction for Older Children: *Amazing Mouths and Menus* Prentice-Hall 1986. *The Marvelous Music Machine* Prentice-Hall 1984. *Ticket to the Twenties* Joy Street, Little Brown 1993. Co-authored with brother, Dewey Blocksma: *Action Contraptions* S & S 1987. *Easy-to-Make-Spaceships that Really Fly* S & S 1985. *Easy-to-Make Water Toys* S & S 1988. *Space-Crafting* S & S 1986. Fiction for Younger Children: *All My Toys Are on the Floor* Children's Press 1986. *Apple Tree, Apple Tree* Children's Press 1983. *The Best-Dressed Bear* Children's Press 1984. *Did You Hear That?* Children's Press 1983. *Grandma Dragon's Birthday* Children's Press 1983. *The Pup Went Up* Children's Press 1983. *Rub-a-Dub-Dub, What's in the Tub?* Children's Press 1984. *Where's that Duck* Children's Press 1985. *Yoo Hoo Moon!* Bantam (Bank Str.) 1992. Nonfiction for Adults: *Reading the Numbers* Viking Penguin 1989. *Naming Nature* Penguin 1992. Several have translations in Spanish, Dutch, Japanese. Work in Progress: Books for adults and children
Awards or inclusion in other biographical books: Reading Rainbow selection: *Easy-to-Make Spaceships That Really Fly*. Junior Literary Guild selection: *The Marvelous Music Machine*. Quality Paperback Book Club, Best Science Books of 1989 (ALA List): *Reading the Numbers*.
What is the aim or goal of your writing? "To entertain and educate myself and my readers."
May inquiries be sent to you about doing workshops, readings? Yes-with reservations. I really have to limit my time and energy.

BLOS, JOAN W.
Address: c/o K. Balkun, Children's Publicity, Morrow Jr. Books, 1350 Avenue of the Americas, New York, NY 10019
Education: Vassar College, Poughkeepsie, New York, B.A., 1946-1949. CCNY, New York, 1950-1951, M.A., 1956
Career: Lecturer, University of Michigan, Ann Arbor, Michigan, 1973-1980. Research Assistant, University of Michigan, Ann Arbor, 1970-1973. Publications Division and Graduate Faculty, Bank Street College, New York, New York, 1958-1970

Writings: *A Seed, a Flower, a Minute, an Hour* Simon & Schuster 1992. *The Heroine of the Titanic* Morrow Jr. Books 1991. *The Grandpa Days* Simon & Schuster 1990. *One Very Best Valentines Day* Simon & Schuster 1990. *Lottie's Circus* Morrow Jr. Books 1986. *Old Henry* Morrow Jr. Books 1987. *Brothers of the Heart* Charles Scribners 1985. *A Gathering of Days* Charles Scribners 1979. *Just Think!* (with B. Miles) Knopf 1970. *It's Spring, She Said* Knopf 1968
Work in Progress: Picture books and historical fiction for children
Awards or inclusion in other biographical books: John Newbery Medal, American Book Award (Children's Fiction),1980 for *A Gathering of Days*. Globe-Horn Book Honor Award for *Old Henry*, 1987. *Booklist* Editor's Choice for *Old Henry*. Midland Society of Authors (juvenile non-fiction) for *Heroine of the Titanic* 1992. Biographical books: *Junior Book of Authors* (5th Ed.) Gale Research Inc. *Something about the Author,* Autobiographical Series, etc. Who's who, etc.
What is the aim or goal of your writing? "Have stated somewhere that I believe that children's books in the aggregate are among the ways in which literate societies cherish and inform their young. I am glad to be part of that process."
May inquiries be sent to you about doing workshops, readings? Yes

BLOUGH, GLENN ORLANDO
Born: September 5, 1907; Edmore, Michigan
Parents: Levi Blough, Catherine (Thomas) Blough
Education: Central Michigan University, Mt. Pleasant, Michigan, Teaching Certificate, 1926. University of Michigan, Ann Arbor, Michigan, B. A., 1929; M.A., 1932. Graduate study at University of Chicago, Columbia University
Career: Eastern Michigan University, Ypsilanti, Michigan, 1932-1936. Colorado State University, 1937-1938. University of Chicago, 1939-1942. Served in World War II. U.S. Office of Education, 1946-1954. University of Maryland, 1956-1972. President, National Science Teachers Association, 1957-1958. President, National Council for Elementary Science, 1952-1953

Writings: *Doing Work* Harper 1943. *Animals that Live Together* Harper 1945. *Methods and Activities in Elementary-School Science* Dryden Press 1951. *How the Sun Helps Us* Harper 1952. *The Tree on the Road to Turntown* McGraw Hill 1953. *Not Only for Ducks* McGraw Hill 1953. *Lookout for the Forest* McGraw Hill 1955. *After the Sun Goes Down* McGraw Hill 1956. *Who Lives in This House?* McGraw Hill 1957. *Young People's Book of Science* Whittlesey House 1958. *Who Lives at the Seashore?* McGraw Hill 1962. *Bird Watchers and Bird Feeders* McGraw Hill 1962. *Elementary School Science and How to Teach It* (with Julius Schwartz) Winston 1967, other editions 1978, 1984. Several others including a series of textbooks. Contributed to many magazines
Awards or inclusion in other biographical books: *American Authors and Books; Authors of Books for Young People; Contemporary Authors; Michigan Authors,* 2nd ed.;

More Junior Authors; Something about the Author; Who's Who in America. Phil Delta Kappa. Phi Sigma. Diamond Award, University of Maryland. Honorary Doctorate, Central Michigan University. Award, American Nature Study Society, 1980. Books selected for Junior Literary Guild

In the 2nd edition of *Michigan Authors* he is credited with "My initial feeling about natural science developed when I was a small boy living in Montcalm, Michigan. *The Tree on the Road to Turntown* is a Michigan oak. I am an environmentalist and ecologist, and these had their beginning when I attended college and the University of Michigan. My personal and professional roots are in Michigan."

BOLOGNA, GIACOMO J.

Address: 150 N. Main St., Plymouth, Michigan 48170
Pseudonym: Jack Bologna
Born: January 1, 1929; Detroit, Michigan
Parents: Salvatore J. Bologna, Cristina M. Bologna
Children: James, Michael, Anne, Mary, Paul, Janine
Education: Detroit Institute of Technology, B.B.A.-Acctg., Detroit, Michigan, 1947-1951. University of Detroit, Law School, J.D., Detroit, Michigan, 1952-1957
Career: Associate Prof. of Mgt., Siena Heights College, Adrian, Michigan, 1984—. President, Computer Protection Sys., Plymouth, Michigan, 1980-1984. President, Geo. Odiorne Assoc., Plymouth, Michigan, 1973-1980. Vice-President, International Intelligence, Inc., Washington, DC, 1970-1973. U.S. Government Agencies for 15 years, IRS Criminal Division, Department of Labor, Senate Antitrust Subcommittee, Food and Drug Adminstration

Writings: *Handbook of Fraud and Commercial Crime* John Wiley and Sons 1992. *Handbook on Corporate Fraud* Butterworth Pub. 1992. *Fraud Auditing and Forensic Accounting* John Wiley and Sons 1987. *Corporate Fraud: Prevention, Detection* Butterworth 1984. Co-author, *Fraud Examiner's Manual, Forensic Accounting Handbook.* Work in Progress: *Ethical Issues in Information Technologies*
What is the aim or goal of your writing? "To train accountants in detecting fraud in corporate books of account."
May inquiries be sent to you about doing workshops, readings? Yes

BORDIN, RUTH B.

Born: November 11, 1917; Litchfield, Minnesota
Parents: Emil W. Anderson, Martha (Linner) Anderson
Children: Martha, Charlotte
Education: University of Minnesota, B.S., 1938
Career: Research Assistant, University of Minnesota, Minneapolis, Minnesota, 1945-1946. Research Associate, Washington State University, Pullman, Washington, 1946-1948. Research Associate, University of Michigan, Ann Arbor, Michigan, 1956-1957; Assistant Curator, 1957-1960; Curator, Michigan Historical Collections, 1960-1965; Research Associate, 1965-1967. Research Affiliate, University of Michigan, Bentley Historical Library, beginning in 1978

Writings: *Hear Me, My Chiefs! Nez Perce History and Legend* (editor) Caxton 1952. *Andrew Dickson White, Teacher of History* University of Michigan 1958. *The Michigan Historical Collections: the Vander Velde Years; Twenty-Five Years of Leadership* Univer-

sity of Michigan 1961.*The Modern Manuscript Library* (with Robert M. Warner) Scarecrow 1966. *The University of Michigan: A Pictorial History* University of Michigan Press 1967. *A Michigan Lumbering Family* Tawas Herald 1967. *Woman and Temperance* Temple University Press 1981. *Michigan: Promise & Performance* University of Michigan 1985. *Frances Willard: A Biography* University of North Carolina Press 1986. *Washtenaw County: An Illustrated History* Windsor Publications 1988. Others
Awards or inclusion in other biographical books: *Contemporary Authors; Michigan Authors,* 2nd ed.

BORLAND, KATHRYN KILBY
Pseudonym: Jane Land, Alice Abbott
Born: August 14, 1916; Pullman, Michigan
Parents: Paul M. Borland; Vinnie (Bensinger) Kilby
Children: James Barton, Susan Lee
Education: Butler University, B.S., Indianapolis, Indiana, 1937
Career: Editor, *North Side Tropics,* Indianapolis, Indiana, 1939-1942. Freelance writer

Writings: *Southern Yankees* Bobbs-Merrill 1960. *Allan Pinkerton* Bobbs-Merrill 1962. *Miles and the Big Black Hat* E.C. Seale 1964. *Everybody Laughed and Laughed* E.C. Seale 1964. *Eugene Field, Young Poet* Bobbs-Merrill 1964. *Phillis Wheatley: Young Colonial Poet* Bobbs-Merrill 1968. *Harry Houdini, Young Magician* Bobbs-Merrill 1969; Macmillan, Maxwell Macmillan 1991. *Clocks, From Shadow to Atom* Follett 1969; World's Work 1970. *The Third Tower* Ace Books 1974. *Stranger in the Mirror* Ballantine 1974. *Goodbye to Stony Crick* McGraw-Hill 1974, 1975. *Goodbye Julie Scott* Ace Books 1975. *To Walk the Night* Ballantine 1976.*These Tigers' Hearts* Doubleday 1978; Hale 1979. *Irena* Doubleday 1979; Hale 1980
Awards or inclusion in other biographical books: *Biography Index; Contemporary Authors; Indiana Authors and Their Books; Michigan Authors,* 2nd ed.; *Something about the Author; Who's Who in America; Writers Directory.* Co-recipient, award for most distinguished children's book by an Indiana author, Indiana University, 1970. National Gothic Novel contest, second prize.
In the 2nd edition of *Michigan Authors* appears: "She says: 'Everything I have written has been done with Helen Ross Speicher of Indianapolis as co-author. Friends since childhood, we live 40 miles apart and commute to write together two days a week'."

BOTTOM, RAYMOND P.
Address: 120 Ruff Drive, Monroe, Michigan 48161
Born: May 23, 1927; Cincinnati, Ohio
Parents: Robert B. Bottom, Tressie (Anderson) Bottom
Children: Sandra, Cheri
Education: Western Kentucky University, B.A., Bowling Green, Kentucky, 1947-1951. Eastern Michigan University, M.S., Ypsilanti, Michigan, 1958-1960. Wayne State University, Educ. Specialist, Detroit, Michigan, 1963-1966
Career: Retired, Monroe Public Schools, Monroe, Michigan, 1985—. Superintendent of Schools, Monroe Public Schools, Monroe, Michigan, 1979-1985. Assistant Supt. of Schools, Monroe Public Schools, Monroe, Michigan, 1973-1979. Principal, Monroe Public Schools, Monroe, Michigan, 1962-1973. History/English Teacher, Monroe Public Schools, Monroe, Michigan, 1952-1962

Writings: *The Education of Disadvantaged Children* Parker Publishing Company, Inc. 1970. *Hardwood Hero* Abingdon Press 1971. *Monroe (Michigan) County's Other Generals* Monroe County Library System 1991. Over 300 articles, short stories and children's stories published in magazines and journals in the United States and several foreign countries. Work in Progress: Book of story problems for Junior High School students
Awards or inclusion in other biographical books: *Michigan Authors,* 2nd ed.
What is the aim or goal of your writing? "My work is based on those matters I know best-my experiences based on responses and reactions to my world."
May inquiries be sent to you about doing workshops, readings? No

BOWMAN, JAMES CLOYD (1880-1961)
Born: January 18, 1880; Leipsic, Ohio
Parents: Martin Van Buren Bowman, Anne (Hull) Bowman
Children: Jeanne
Education: Ohio Northern University, B.S., Ada, Ohio, 1905; B. Litt., 1908. Harvard University, A.M., Cambridge, Massachusetts, 1910
Career: Professor, Iowa State College, 1910-1921. Chairman of English Department, Northern State Teachers College, Marquette, Michigan, 1921-1939

Writings: *Into the Depths* University Press 1905. *Essays for College English* Heath 1915, 1918. *Contemporary American Criticism* Henry Holt 1926. *The Adventures of Paul Bunyan* Century 1927. *Tales From a Finnish Tupa* (with Margery Bianco) Whitman (Junior Literary Guild Selection) 1936. *Pecos Bill: The Greatest Cowboy of All Time* Whitman (Junior Literary Guild Selection) 1937, 1972. *Winabojo: Master of Life* (Junior Literary Guild Selection) Whitman 1941. *Seven Silly Wise Men* Whitman 1965. *Who Was Tricked?* Whitman 1966. Several others. In *Michigan History*
Awards or inclusion in other biographical books: *American Authors and Books; Anthology of Children's Literature; Authors of Books for Young People; Contemporary Authors; Junior Book of Authors; Story and Verse for Children; Who Was Who in America; Who Was Who in North American Authors.* Litt. D., Ohio Northern University, 1923

BRADLEY, RICHARD E.
Address: 4158 Woodcreek Lane, Lansing, Michigan 48911
Born: June 1, 1933; Battle Creek, Michigan
Parents: Charles A. Bradley, Margaret M. Bradley
Children: James, Kay
Education: Western Michigan University, Kalamazoo, Michigan: B.B.A., B.A., 1951-1954, 1957-1959. Michigan State University, M.B.A., East Lansing, Michigan, 1962-1965
Career: Freelance writer, Lansing, Michigan, 1987—. Teacher, Waverly Community Schools, Lansing, Michigan, 1963-1987. Teacher, Lansing Public Schools, Lansing, Michigan, 1962-1963. Teacher, St. Johns Public Schools, St. Johns, Michigan, 1959-1962

Writings: *Alaskan Adventure* Millbrook Printing 1989
What is the aim or goal of your writing? "To foster enjoyment of the outdoors and responsibility for the environment."
May inquiries be sent to you about doing workshops, readings? Yes

BRAUN, RICHARD EMIL
Address: P.O. Box 178, Errington, British Columbia,VOR 1VO Canada
Born: November 22, 1934; Detroit, Michigan
Children: Nicolas
Education: University of Michigan, A.B., A.M., Ann Arbor, Michigan, 1952-1957, 1956-1957. University of Texas, Ph.D., Austin, Texas, 1960-1962
Career: Lecturer, University of Alberta, Edmonton, Alberta, 1962-1964. Assistant Professor, University of Alberta, Edmonton, Alberta, 1964-1969. Associate Professor, University of Alberta, Edmonton, Alberta, 1969-1976. Professor, University of Alberta, Edmonton, Alberta, 1976—.

Writings: *Last Man In* The Jargon Society 1990 (verse novel). *Persius' Satires* Coronado Press 1984 (translations with introduction and notes). *Euripides' Rhesas* Oxford University Press 1978 (translations with introduction and notes). Others earlier. Inclusion of original verse and of translations, *Penguin Book of American Verse, Penguin Roman Poets of the Early Empire.* Work in Progress: Three books of verse
Awards or inclusion in other biographical books: *Contemporary Authors; Contemporary Poets; Michigan Authors,* 2nd ed.
What is the aim or goal of your writing? "Harmony".
May inquiries be sent to you about doing workshops, readings? Yes

BRAUN-HASS, LINDA A.
Address: 5722 Brown's Lake Rd., Jackson, Michigan 49203
Born: August 31, 1953; Jackson, Michigan
Parents: Charles E. Braun, Ann (Suda) Braun
Children: Jason Hass
Education: Parkside High School, Jackson, Michigan. Western Michigan University, B.A., double major in English and French and Teaching Certificate in Secondary Education, Kalamazoo, Michigan. Michigan State University, M.A. in Journalism, East Lansing, Michigan, 1985-1988
Career: Freelance Writer, main client: *The Jackson Citizen Patriot* newspaper, 1981—

Writings: *Jackson-Birthplace of the Republican Party: A History of the Early Party and the Man Who Helped Found It* Vantage Press 1991
Awards or inclusion in other biographical books: Two national awards in journalism from the National Federation of Press Women, 1986, 1987. Fifty-three State Awards in Journalism from the Michigan Press Women, 1984-1991. Award in journalism, Michigan Press Association Better Newspaper Contest, Lifestyle/Family Section, 1990
What is the aim or goal of your writing? "The goals of my book are: 1) to preserve an important slice of Jackson's history for posterity, 2) to add to documentation establishing Jackson as the 'birthplace' of the Republican Party, and 3) to showcase the contributions of Jackson pioneer Col. Charles DeLand towards the Party's founding in Jackson."
May inquiries be sent to you about doing workshops, readings? Yes

BREISACH, ERNST A.
Address: 228 W. Ridge Circle, Kalamazoo, Michigan 49009
Born: October 8, 1923; Schwanberg, Austria
Parents: Otto Breisach, Maria Breisach
Children: Nora, Sylvia, Eric, Ernst

Education: University of Vienna, Ph.D., History, Austria, 1941-1946. Wirtscharts Universitat, Vienna, Austria, 1946-1950
Career: Realgymnasium, Vienna XIV, Vienna, Austria, 1946-1952. Olivet College, Olivet, Michigan, 1953-1957. Western Michigan University, Kalamazoo, Michigan, 1957—

Writings: *Historiography: Ancient, Medieval, and Modern* University of Chicago 1983. *Renaissance Europe, 1300-1517* Macmillan 1973. *Caterina Sforza: A Renaissance Virago* University of Chicago 1967. *Introduction to Modern Existentialism* Grove 1962. *Classic Rhetoric and Medieval Historiography* Medieval Institute, Western Michigan University 1985. Work in Progress: *American Progressive History*
Awards or inclusion in other biographical books: Fellowship, National Foundation for the Humanities, 1989-1990. Distinguished Faculty Scholar, Western Michigan University, 1983. Higher Education Award, Michigan Association of Governing Boards (15 state universities) 1988
What is the aim or goal of your writing? "To gain knowledge about the past and make it available to a wider public."
May inquiries be sent to you about doing workshops, readings? Yes

BRINKS, HERBERT J.
Born: May 25, 1935; South Holland, Illinois
Children: Timothy, Steven, Marie, John
Education: Calvin College, A.B., Grand Rapids, Michigan, 1957. University of Michigan, Ann Arbor, Michigan, M.A., 1962; Ph.D., 1965
Career: Teacher, Allendale, Michigan, 1957-1960. Instructor, Associate Professor, Curator of Colonial Origins Collection, 1965-1969; Curator of Manuscripts, 1972—. Director, Historical Society of Michigan, 1970-1971.. Editor, Historical Society of Michigan *Chronicle,* 1969-1971. Teacher, Extension Courses at Grand Rapids, Flint, Dearborn

Writings: *Guide to the Dutch-American Historical Collections of Western Michigan* Dutch American Historical Commission 1967. *Peter White* Eerdmans 1970. *A Michigan Reader:11,000 B.C. to A.D. 1865* (co-editor) Eerdmans 1974. *Schrijf Spoedig Terug! Brieven Van Immigranten in Amerika, 1847-1920* Boekencentrum (Netherlands) 1978. *Pine Rest Christian Hospital, 75 Years: 1910-1985* The Hospital 1985. *Write Back Soon: Letters From Immigrants in America* CRC Publications 1986. Contributor to history journals, books
Awards or inclusion in other biographical books: *Contemporary Authors; Michigan Authors,* 2nd ed.; *Directory of American Scholars*

BROWN, ELIZABETH L.
Address: 9161 Kenowa, S.W., Grand Rapids, Michigan 49504
Born: October 12, 1924; Kent County, Michigan
Parents: Charles W. Brown, Mabel F. (Whitney) Brown
Education: Grand Rapids Junior College, Associate of Arts, Grand Rapids, Michigan, 1950's to 1960. Grand Rapids Baptist Evening School, part time to 1960
Career: Retired now. Executive Secretary, Zondervan Publishing House, Grand Rapids, Michigan, 1960-1989. State of Michigan, Michigan Crippled Children Commission, typist/secretarial, 1950's. American Seating Company, before college

Writings: *The Candle of the Wicked* Zondervan 1972. Issued in Spanish in 1978, by CLIE, under the title, *La Lampara de los Impios.* A poem "Summer Night", published in 1950 by Twentieth Century Press, Los Angeles, California. Several poems published in *Faith & Inspiration* Magazine over a period of time. *The Message of the Bells,* a complete Christmas program, published late 1950's by Moody Press, Chicago. Work in Progress: a mystery
Awards or inclusion in other biographical books: In a who's who, not sure of title
What is the aim or goal of your writing? "To write a well-written, captivating story which will also be God-honoring and potentially carry an evangelical message to its readers."
May inquiries be sent to you about doing workshops, readings? "No? Inquiries could be sent-I have done a few of this kind of thing, a few years back. The book has been out 20 years, and I would not anticipate that this would be a problem. I do not care to drive all over, anymore."
Awards or inclusion in other biographical books: *Michigan Authors,* 2nd ed.

BROWN, GERALD S.
Address: 1720 Hanover Rd., Ann Arbor, Michigan 48103
Born: February 25, 1911; Port Maitland, Nova Scotia, Canada
Parents: George E. Brown, Catherine E. (Nickerson) Brown
Children: Catherine
Education: Acadia University, Wolfville, Nova Scotia, Canada, B.A. 1932. University of Minnesota, M.A., 1937. University of Minnesota, Ph.D., 1948
Career: Teaching Fellow, University of Minnesota and University of Michigan. Assistant, Associate, Full Professor, Emeritus, University of Michigan, Ann Arbor

Writings: *Canada and the U.S.* (with H. L. Keenleyside) Knopf 1952. *The American Secretary* University of Michigan Press 1963. *The American Past,* 2 vols., (Ed. with Sidney Fine) Macmillan 4 editions. Articles in professional journals.
Awards or inclusion in other biographical books: *Michigan Authors,* 2nd ed.

BROWN, PRENTISS MARSH (1889-1973)
Born: June 18, 1889; St. Ignace, Michigan
Parents: James John Brown, Minnie (Gagnon) Brown
Children: Mariana, Ruth, James, Barbara, Patricia, Prentiss M., Paul
Education: Albion College, A.B., Albion, Michigan, 1911. University of Illlinois, 1911-1912, graduate courses
Career: Michigan bar admission, 1914. Lawyer, St. Ignace, Michigan. City Attorney, St. Ignace, Michigan, 1914-1933. Prosecuting Attorney, Mackinac County, 1914-1926. Michigan Representative, 1933-1937. Appointed to fill unexpired term of late James Couzens, U.S. Senate and then elected 1937-1943. Member, War Production Board, 1943. Member of Brown, Lund and Fitzgerald, Washington, DC, a partnership beginning 1943. Chairman of the Board, Detroit Edison Company, beginning 1944. President, 1st National Bank of St. Ignace, Essex County Light & Power Company, Peninsular Electric Light Company, others. Ran for Congress, 1924; Michigan Supreme Court, 1928. Chairman, Democratic State Convention in Michigan five times. Member, Michigan Board of Law Examiners, 1930-1941. Official, Edison Illuminating Company of Detroit; St. Clair Edison Company, others. Chairman, Mackinac Bridge Authority

Writings: *Taking Life Easy* 1911. *Increasing the Debt Limit of the United States and Providing for Federal Taxation of Future Issues of Obligations of the United States and its Instrumentalities* U.S. Government Printing Office 1941. *Alex Dow, 1862-1942, for 28 Years the President of Detroit Edison* Newcomen Society in North America 1951. *The Mackinac Bridge Story* Wayne University Press 1956. *The Civil War in the Religious Perspective* 1959

Awards or inclusion in other biographical books: *Biographical Dictionary of the American Congress 1774-1971; Current Biography; The New York Times Biographical Edition; Michigan through the Centuries: Family and Personal History* Vol. 3; *Standard and Poor's Register of Corporations, Directors and Executives; Who Was Who in America; Who's Who in American Politics.* LL.D., Albion College, 1937. LL.D., University of Michigan, 1952

BRUCKER, CLARA H. (1900-1980)
Born: December 22, 1900; St. Ausger, Iowa
Parents: Emil Hantel, Regina (Stroebel) Hantel
Children: Wilber
Education: Drexel Institute, Philadelphia, Pennyslvania, 1918. Columbia University, A.B., New York, New York; M.A., 1930
Career: Statistician for General Motors Corporation, New York. Active in International YMCA, Rainbow Division Veterans auxiliary, others.

Writings: *To Have Your Cake and Eat It* Vantage 1968. Several magazine articles
Awards or inclusion in other biographical books: *Contemporary Authors.* Honored by Northwood Institute (Midland) as one of the distinguished women in 1972
What is the aim or goal of your writing? In the second edition of *Michigan Authors* she is credited with: "Because of my busy life collecting my husband's papers for U. of M. Bentley Library in Ann Arbor, and collecting his memorabilia for the Wilber M. Brucker Hall at Ft. Myers, Virginia, I have had little time for writing, but hope soon to continue working on my experiences while Governor's wife of Michigan. I have organized a School of government in Detroit-was first president and founder, and am still coordinator for programs. *To Have Your Cake and Eat It* is about our Washington experiences."
(Mrs. Brucker's husband, Wilber M. Brucker, was Governor of Michigan 1931-1932. In Washington DC he served as General Counsel for the Department of Defense, Secretary of the Army 1961-1966, under President Eisenhower)
Awards or inclusion in other biographical books: *Michigan Authors,* 2nd ed.

BRUINS, ELTON J.
Address: 633 Appletree Dr., Holland, Michigan 49423
Born: July 29, 1927; Fairwater, Wisconsin
Parents: Clarence R. Bruins, Angeline T. Bruins
Children: Mary Elain, David Lewis (wife: Elaine A. Bruins)
Education: Hope College, B.A., Holland Michigan, 1946-1950.
Western Theological Seminary, B.D., Holland, Michigan, 1950-1953. Union Theological Seminary, S.T.M., 1953-1954. Princeton Theological Seminary, Princeton, New Jersey, 1954-1955. New York University, Ph.D., New York, 1956-1962
Career: Minister, Reformed Church in America, Elmsford, New York. Minister, Reformed Church in America, Flushing, New York, 1961-1966. Assistant Professor, Hope College, 1966-1970. Associate Professor, Hope College, 1970-1973. Professor, Hope College, Holland, Michigan , 1973-1980. Blekkink Professor of Religion, 1980—.

Writings: *Unto the Sixth Generation: The Descendants of Derk & Cynthia Bruins, 1865-1990* Hope College 1990. *Isaac Cappon: Holland's 'Foremost Citizen'* Hope College 1987. Compiler: *The Dutch in America*, papers presented at the Fourth Biennial Conference of the Association for the Advancement of Dutch-American Studies, Holland, Michigan, Hope College 1987. Editor: *The Bruins Family of Alto, Wisconsin* Historical and Genealogical Data relating to the family of Hendrik and Hendrika Van Wechel Bruins and their descendants, 1750 to 1980, Hope College 1980.*The Manuscript and Archival Holdings of Beardslee Library, Western Theological Seminary, Holland, Michigan* Western Theol. Seminary 1978. *The Americanization of a Congregation* Eerdmans 1970. Several essays published in various books edited by others. Work in Progress: Second edition of *The Americanization of a Congregation*
Awards or inclusion in other biographical books: Current editions of: *Who's Who in the Midwest; Who's Who in Religion; Who's Who in Education; Who's Who in the World*
What is the aim or goal of your writing? "Local history, family history, Reformed Church in America history."
May inquiries be sent to you about doing workshops, readings? Yes

BRUNO, MARIA F.
Address: Route 5, St. Johns Michigan 48879
Born: August 14, 1948; Highland Park, Michigan
Parents: Philip P. Bruno, Mary C. Bruno
Children: Emily, Rebecca
Education: Michigan State University, Ph.D., East Lansing, Michigan, 1981-1986
Career: Assistant Professor, Michigan State University, East Lansing, Michigan, 1986—.

Writings: Book chapters: "Tie a Yellow Ribbon" in *The Gulf War: A Broader Perspective* Vergen Press 1993. "Teaching Women in America: Some Notes on Pedagogy and Charlotte Perkins Gilman" in *Charlotte Perkins Gilman: The Woman and Her Work* UMI Press 1989. Others forthcoming. Articles: "Madonnas, Whores, and Wars" *New Directions For Women* (May-June 1992), others. Short stories: "The Man Who Made Teeth", *Korone: Women's Voices* 1992; *Red Cedar Review* (Spring, 1988). "A Matter of Disguise", *Ms.* (October, 1984). "Clippings", *Midway Review* (September, 1984); *The Red Cedar Review* (1984). "Bad Endings"*Cranbrook Institute of Arts* (Summer, 1983). Others. Also book reviews. Work in Progress: *The Wild Heart* (novel) and untitled novel
Awards or inclusion in other biographical books: Finalist, The Writer's Open Voice Fiction Competition, 1992. First Prize, *Korone* Fiction Award, Womanspace Center, 1992. First Prize, Midwestern Literature Conference Fiction, 1991. Finalist, Roberts Writing Awards, 1991. Finalist, PEN Syndicated Fiction Project, 1990. Finalist, *Story Quarterly* Fiction Contest, 1985. Finalist, Nelson Algren Awards, *Chicago Magazine* , 1985. Third Prize, Detroit Women Writers Fiction Competition, 1985. First Prize, *Ms.* College Fiction Contest, 1984. Second Prize, *Midway Review,* 1984. Women's Studies Fiction Contest, Michigan State University, 1984. Runner-up, *Ms.* College Fiction Contest, 1983. Full Fellowship, Cranbrook Writers' Conference, 1982-1983. Fiction Prize, *Red Cedar Review,* 1981, 1982, 1984
May inquiries be sent to you about doing workshops, readings? Yes

BRUSSO, CLIFTON J.
Address: 109 N. Iroquois Street, Laurium, Michigan 49913
Born: November 20, 1934; Laurium, Michigan
Parents: Lawrence A. Brusso, Leona M. (Gamache) Brusso
Children: Carmaleta, Robin, Clifton, Shawn, Courtney
Education: Michigan Technological University, M.E., Houghton, Michigan, 1958-1962. U.S. Army Corp Engr., Engineering, 1962-1968.
Career: Administrator, Houghton County Medical Care Facility, Hancock, Michigan, 1962-1991

Writings: *Breakthru* Vantage Press 1991. *Tales From the U.P.'s Copper Country* Iroquois Press 1992. Work in Progress: Sequel to *Breakthru*
Awards or inclusion in other biographical books: Golden Poet Award, World of Poetry Press, 1989
What is the aim or goal of your writing? "National distribution and recognition."
May inquiries be sent to you about doing workshops, readings? Yes

BUNGE, NANCY L.
Address: 401 Rampart Way, Apt. 304, East Lansing, Michigan 48823
Born: May 13, 1942; La Crosse, Wisconsin
Parents: Jonathan C. Bunge, Anne G. Bunge
Education: Radcliffe, A.B., Cambridge, Massachusetts, 1960-1964. University of Chicago, M.A., 1965-1966. University of Wisconsin-Madison, Ph.D., 1970
Career: Professor, Dept. of American Thought and Language, Michigan State University, East Lansing, Michigan, 1973—.

Writings: *Finding the Words: Conversations with Writers Who Teach* Swallow/Ohio University Press 1985. Work in Progress: *Nathaniel Hawthorne: A Study of the Short Fiction* forthcoming from Twayne. *How Writers Work*
Awards or inclusion in other biographical books: *Contemporary Authors; Who's Who in the Midwest*
What is the aim or goal of your writing? "To enjoy myself while doing work that may benefit others."
May inquiries be sent to you about doing workshops, readings? Yes

BURGESS, BARBARA A.
Address: 9929 Auburndale, Livonia, Michigan 48150
Born: April 20, 1926; Detroit, Michigan
Parents: Leland D. Hood, Alma M. (Westphal) Hood
Children: Lee, Christopher, Deborah, Eric
Education: Cooley High School, Detroit, Michigan. Wayne State University, B.A., Detroit, Michigan
Career: Mother and grandmother for 44 years filling in with clerical jobs along the way

Writings: *Oren Bell* Dell/Bantam/Doubleday Delecarte Book for Young Readers 10-16, 1991. Work in Progress: *Fred Lightfoot Memorial Ball Field*
Awards or inclusion in other biographical books: Judith Siegel Pearson Award, for work on early American Puritan dissenter, Anne Hutchinson, Wayne State Univ., 1983
What is the aim or goal of your writing? "To write books that young people will enjoy reading."
May inquiries be sent to you about doing workshops, readings? Yes

BURGETT, DONALD R.

Address: 4848 Vines Rd., Howell, Michigan 48843
Born: April 5, 1925; Detroit, Michigan
Parents: Elmer W. Burgett, Lillian M. (Bruce) Burgett
Children: Kenneth, Rene, Mark, Gary, Jeffrey
Education: Mackenzie High School, Detroit, Michigan, Brighton High School, Brighton, Michigan
Career: Residential Builder, Howell, Michigan 1967—. Residential Builder, Taylor, Michigan, 1952-1967. Carpenter, Michigan and California, 1948-1951. Various places, 1946-1948. Military paratrooper

Writings: *Currahee* Houghton Mifflin 1967. *As Eagles Scream* Bantam Books 1967. Work in Progress: *Seven Roads to Hell*
Awards or inclusion in other biographical books: *Michigan Authors,* 2nd ed. Written endorsement for *Currahee* in Reader's Digest condensed books 1967 by General of the Army, Dwight D. Eisenhower, the only book on WWII that he endorsed. My interview on WWII and my photo appear in Richard Collier's *Freedom Road: 1944-1945.* My photo is miscaptioned as (B), it should be (C). The name Lt. Col. Saul K. Padover apears under my photo. The picture was taken at Mourmelon Le Petit, France, I was nineteen, just out of battle, in Bastogne. I represented the American Airborne in BBC's film documentary "Soldiers", a thirteen hour filmed documentary.
What is the aim or goal of your writing? "To complete my experiences in war. Once completed to continue writing in another direction, about hunting, fishing, and adventures in the wilds."
May inquiries be sent to you about doing workshops, readings? Yes

BURGTORF, FRANCES D.

Address: 2671 Tryban Rd., Cheboygan, Michigan 49721
Born: June 10, 1916; Cleveland, Ohio
Parents: James, Genevieve Donoghue
Education: Cleveland High School, University of Michigan

Writings: *Chief Wawatam, Story of a Hand-Bomber* Fowler 1975
Awards or inclusion in other biographical books: *Michigan Authors,* 2nd ed.
What is the aim or goal of your writing? "Historical subjects-Great Lakes oriented."
May inquiries be sent to you about doing workshops, readings? No

BURKLUND, CARL EDWIN (1897-1964)

Born: March 15, 1897; White Cloud, Michigan
Children: Ingrid, Carl
Education: Western Michigan University, A.B., Kalamazoo, Michigan, 1922. University of Michigan, M.A., Ann Arbor, Michigan, 1925; Ph.D., 1928
Career: English Instructor, College of Engineering, The University of Michigan, 1925; Assistant Professor, 1929; Associate Professor, 1935; Professor, 1940. A founder, first president, The Poetry Society of Michigan

Writings: *The Moment of Time: Collected Poems of Carl Edwin Burklund* Memorial Edition 1973. *New Michigan Verse* (editor) University of Michigan Press 1940. *Patterns and Perspectives, Essays for College Use* F. S. Crofts 1942. *President as Poet: a Note on the Life of Henry Philip Tappan, D.D.* University of Michigan Press 1952

BURNS, VIRGINIA LAW
Address: 8600 S. Fenner Rd., Laingsburg, Michigan 48848
Born: May 23, 1925; Redford, Michigan
Parents: Alvin J. Law, Leola M. (Wadley) Law
Children: James Richie, Jr., Duncan L. Richie, Meg M. Richie
Education: Cranbrook Academy of Art, Bloomfield Michigan, 1943. University of Michigan, 1943-1947, Ann Arbor, Michigan. Michigan State University, East Lansing, graduated 1956
Career: Elementary Reading Teacher, various Michigan Public Schools,1953-1987

Writings: *Tall Annie* Enterprise Press 1987. *First Frontiers* Enterprise Press 1985. *Lewis Cass-Frontier Soldier* Enterprise Press 1980.*William Beaumont-Frontier Soldier* Enterprise Press 1978. *The House at the End of the Lane* (poetry) edited. Work in Progress: Just completed: *The Searcher: Alice Evans-Bacteriologist*
Awards or inclusion in other biographical books: *Who's Who of American Women*, currently. Award of Merit-Historical Society of Michigan, 1990. First Lady of Literature-Nominee, State of Michigan, 1987
What is the aim or goal of your writing? "To provide young readers with excellence in historical non-fiction; give them heroines and heroes."
May inquiries be sent to you about doing workshops, readings? Yes

BURROWS, EDWIN GLADDING
Born: July 23, 1917; Dallas, Texas
Parents: Millar Burrows, Irene (Gladding) Burrows
Children: Edwin, Daniel, David
Education: Yale University, B.A., New Haven, Connecticut, 1938. University of Michigan, M.A., Ann Arbor, Michigan, 1940
Career: Served in U.S. Navy, 1944-1946. Manager and Executive Producer, WUOM/WVGR, Ann Arbor, Michigan, 1950-1977; Executive producer, 1973. Director of National Center for Audio Experimentation, University of Wisconsin, Madison, 1970-1973

Writings: *The Artic Tern, and other Poems* Grove Press 1957. *Man Fishing* Sumac Press 1969. *The Crossing* New Moon/Humble Hills 1976. *Kiva* Ithaca House 1976. *On the Road to Bailey's* Fallen Angel Press 1979. *The Cup & the Unicorn: Episodes from a Life, Millar Burrows, 1889-1980* E.G. Burrows 1981. *The House of August* Ithaca House 1985. In anthologies. Poems in *Paris Review, Poetry Northwest, Atlantic Monthly, Poetry Now, Michigan Review, Poetry, Epoch,* others. Verse plays broadcasted by Radio Nederland, Earplay, others
Awards or inclusion in other biographical books:*Contemporary Authors; International Who's Who in Poetry; Michigan Authors,* 2nd ed. John Masefield Poetry Award, 1938. Hopwood Award, University of Michigan, 1940. Ohio State Award, 1953, 1954, 1955, 1956, 1971, 1974. Fellow, Yaddo Foundation, 1963, 1966. Borestone Mountain Poetry Award, 1964. Runner-up, National Book Award

BURTON, CLARENCE MONROE (1853-1932)
Born: November 18, 1853; Whiskey Diggins, California
Parents: Charles S. Burton, Ann Eliza (Monroe) Burton
Children: Agnes, Charles, Clarence, Louise, Fred, Frank, Ralph, Harriet, Elizabeth (three marriages)

Education: Hastings, Michigan Public Schools. University of Michigan, Law, Ann Arbor, Michigan, 1874
Career: Law Clerk, Ward & Palmer. Partner, Ward & Skinner, 1883; owner, year later. Organized C. M. Burton Abstract Company, 1891. Director, Official, Guaranty Trust Company, Michigan Investment Company, Wayne County & Home Savings Bank, and others. Traveled widely gathering local history until had several thousand books, documents, maps, papers, photographs, reports, transcripts, and other historical material which he presented to Detroit Library Commission, 1914 along with library building. This collection (called the Burton Collection) included copies of several Detroit church records from 1701. Member, Detroit Charter Commission, 1913. Member, Michigan State Constitutional Convention, 1908. President, Michigan Pioneer and Historical Society, many years; held offices in Michigan Society of Colonial Wards and Detroit Chapter of Sons of the American Revolution. Detroit Board of Education, 1902-1913. Honorary city (Detroit) historiographer, 1908-1932

Writings: *A Sketch of the Life of Antoine de la Mothe Cadillac, Founder of Detroit* Wilton-Smith Company 1895. *Cadillac's Village, or Detroit under Cadillac* Detroit 1896. *Historical Memoranda of the Territory of Michigan* C.M. Burton 1904. *Compendium of History and Biography of the City of Detroit and Wayne County, Michigan* H. Taylor & Company 1909. *In the Footsteps of Cadillac* Wolverine Printing 1899. *City of Detroit* Clarke 1922. *Detroit in Earlier Days* Burton Abstract & Title Company 1914. *Detroit in 1849* Speaker-Hines Press 1910? *Journal of Pontiac's Conspiracy* Speaker-Hines Printing 1912. *Historical Papers Delivered Before the Society of Colonial Wars of the State of Michigan* The Wilton-Smith Company 1895; Winn & Hammond 1908. *History of Wayne County and the City of Detroit, Michigan* S.J. Clarke 1930. *When Detroit Was Young: Historical Studies* Burton Abstract and Title 1951? Others. Contributor, historical periodicals. Numerous book introductions, chapters
Awards or inclusion in other biographical books: *Appleton's Cyclopaedia of American Biography; Dictionary of American Biography; Dictionary of North American Authors; Michigan: A Centennial History of the State and its People* Michigan Biography Vol 4; *National Cyclopaedia of American Biography; Who Was Who in America; Who Was Who among North American Authors.* Honorary Degree, Master of Arts, University of Michigan, 1905. Doctor of Letters, Detroit City Colleges, 1931

BURTON, GABRIELLE B.
Address: 211 LeBrun Rd., Eggertsville, New York 14226
Born: February 21, 1939; Lansing, Michigan
Parents: Clifford J. Baker, Helen M. Baker
Children: Maria, Jennifer, Ursula, Gabrielle, Charity
Education: Marygrove College, B.A., Detroit, Michigan, 1956-1960
Career: Freelance writer, Washington DC, 1972-1974. Freelance writer, Buffalo, New York, 1974—.

Writings: *Heartbreak Hotel* Charles Scribner's Sons 1986, Penguin, England & U.K. 1987, Trevi (Denmark)1988, Viking Penguin, U.S. 1988. *I'm Running Away from Home But I'm Not Allowed to Cross the Street* Know 1972, Avon 1975. Numerous essays and book reviews. Two one act plays. Work in Progress: Novel
Awards or inclusion in other biographical books: *Michigan Authors,* 2nd ed. Maxwell Perkins Prize, 1987, for exceptional first novel. Great Lakes Colleges Assoc. New Writers Award for Fiction, 1987

What is the aim or goal of your writing? "To communicate my concerns/to tell stories."
May inquiries be sent to you about doing workshops, readings? Yes

BUSH, MAX R.
Address: 5372 132nd Avenue, Hamilton, Michigan 49419
Born: February 6, 1950; Holland, Michigan
Parents: Raymond R. Bush, Myra B. Bush
Education: Grand Valley State University, B.A., Allendale, Michigan, 1968-1973. Michigan State University, M.F.A., East Lansing, Michigan, 1982-1985
Career: Freelance playwright/Director, Hamilton, Michigan, 1985—. Teaching Assistant, Michigan State University, East Lansing, Michigan, 1982-1985. Adjunct Professor, Grand Valley State University, Allendale, Michigan, 1978-1979. High School Teacher, Marshall, Michigan, 1973-1976

Writings: *Rockway Cafe* New Plays, Inc. 1992. *Voyage of the Dragonfly* Anchorage Press 1990. *Puss in Boots* New Plays, Inc. 1989. *Rapunzel* New Plays, Inc. 1987. *Boglewood* Anchorage Press 1986. *Troll and the Elephant Prince* Anchorage Press 1985. Work in Progress: *The Emerald Circle. The Crystal. Simple Man* (screenplay)
Awards or inclusion in other biographical books: Distinguished Play Award, American Alliance of Theatre and Education, 1990
May inquiries be sent to you about doing workshops, readings? Yes

BUZZELLI, ELIZABETH K.
Address: 60185 Lamplight Ct., Washington, Michigan 48094
Born: March 5, 1937; Detroit, Michigan
Parents: John A. Kane, Dorothy L. (Deveines) Kane
Children: Kathryn, Patricia, Nino, David, Cynthia
Education: B.A. 1 and 1/2 year of graduate studies, University of Michigan, Ann Arbor, Michigan
Career: Writer, 1982—. Reporter, *Observer,* 1976-1982. Teacher, Utica, Michigan, 1974-1976

Writings: *Voices on Writing Fiction* Writers Digest Books 1989. *Gift of Evil* Bantam 1984. *A History of the Rural Schools* Edward 1976. Short stories, articles, criticism. Work in Progress: Two novels
Awards or inclusion in other biographical books: *Who's Who's in American Writers.* Awards, Michigan History Division, Michigan Department of State
What is the aim or goal of your writing? "To be as clear, as perfect a novelist as it is possible to be"
May inquiries be sent to you about doing workshops, readings? Yes

C

CAMPBELL, NANCY A.
Address: 306 N. Huron, Mackinaw City, Michigan 49701
Born: December 11, 1930; Charlevoix, Michigan
Parents: Elton C. Dagwell, Genevieve M. (Weber) Dagwell
Children: Steven, Eric
Education: Eastern Michigan University, 1948-1949, Ypsilanti, Michigan. Central Michigan University, B.S., Mt. Pleasant, Michigan, 1949-1952. Graduate work: Wayne State University, Detroit, Michigan; Michigan State University, East Lansing, Michigan; University of Michigan, Ann Arbor, Michigan
Career: Teacher/Librarian, Mackinaw City Public Schools, Mackinaw City, Michigan, 1960-1990. Elementary Teacher, Farmington Public Schools, Farmington, Michigan, 1952-1954. Librarian, Mackinaw Woman's Club Library

Writings: *Memories of Mackinaw* Little Traverse Printing 1976.
Work in Progress: A supplement to *Memories of Mackinaw,* a major portion to contain maritime history of the area
Awards or inclusion in other biographical books: *Michigan Authors,* 2nd ed.
May inquiries be sent to you about doing workshops, readings? No

CANDLER, JULIE J.
Address: 19400 W. Ten Mile, #217, Southfield, Michigan 48075
Born: December 28, 1919; Springfield, Illinois
Parents: Frank Jennings, Edith (Rickey) Jennings
Children: Carolyn, William, Rickey
Education: Wayne State University, Detroit, Michigan, 1940-1942. University of Michigan, Ann Arbor, Michigan 1942-1943.
Career: Operates the public relations firm, Julie Candler and Associates, Bloomfield Hills, Michigan, 1960—. Member of National Motor Vehicle Safety Advisory Council, a 25-member group meeting in Washington to advise the Secretary of Transporation on safety, 1973-1977. Writer, Dodge News Bureau, 1954. Reporter-photographer-editor, *Birmingham Eccentric,* Michigan, 1955-1960. Has appeared on such television programs as "The Today Show". Director of Cranbrook Writers' Guild and Camp Oakland Youth Programs, Inc. Color photographs have appeared in many travel and boating magazines.

Writings: *Woman at the Wheel* Paperback Library 1967. First and only automotive column to appear in major women's magazine, "Woman at the Wheel", running 12 times a year for 18 years in *Woman's Day Magazine.* Byline has appeared in *Mechanix Illustrated, McCall's, Consumer's Digest, Nation's Business, Working Woman, MS, Redbook, Sea, Rudder* and others
Awards or inclusion in other biographical books: *Michigan Authors,* 2nd ed. National Safety Council Public Service Award, 1967. Recreational Vehicle Industry Association, Award. Outdoor Writers Association of American, Deep Woods Award, 1974. Women in Communication, Headliner of the Year Award, 1967. Evinrude Writing Awards Contest, 1974

CANTONI, LOUIS JOSEPH
Address: 2591 Woodstock Drive, Detroit, Michigan 48203
Born: May 22, 1919; Detroit, Michigan
Parents: Pietro Cantoni, Stella (Puricelli) Cantoni
Children: Christopher Louis, Sylvia Therese. Wife is a retired social work administrator, author of professional books and articles
Education: University of California at Berkeley, A.B., 1946. University of Michigan, M.S.W., Ann Arbor, Michigan, 1949. University of Michigan, Ph.D., Ann Arbor, Michigan, 1953
Career: Professor Emeritus, Wayne State University, Detroit, Michigan, 1989—. Professor and Coordinator of Rehabilitation Counseling, Wayne State University, Detroit, Michigan, 1956-1989. Conference Leader, Psychology Teacher, and Counselor, General Motors Institute, Flint, Michigan, 1951-1956. Rehabilitation Counselor, Michigan Department of Education, Detroit, Michigan, 1949-1950. Social Caseworker, City of Detroit, Detroit Michigan, 1946-1949

Writings: *Essays, Theses, and Projects in Rehabilitation Counseling* Oklahoma State University. *Supervised Practice in Rehabilitation Counseling* Oklahoma State University 1986. *Golden Song: Fiftieth Anniversary Anthology* Poetry Society 1985. *Writings of Louis J. Cantoni* Wayne State University 1981. *Gradually the Dreams Change* (75 poems) South and West 1979.*With Joy I Called to You* (75 poems) South and West 1969. *Counseling Your Friends* (with Mrs. Cantoni) William Frederick 1961. *Preparation of Rehabilitation Counselors Through Field Instruction* (Co-editor) Vocational Guidance and Rehab. Svcs. 1958. *Placement of the Handicapped in Competitive Employment* (Editor) Wayne State University 1957. *Marriage and Community Relations* General Motors Institute 1954.*The 1939-1943 Flint, Michigan Guidance Demonstration* University Microfilms 1953. Poems published in many publications, journals and anthologies. Many articles, essays, reviews, abstracts, drawings have appeared in journals. Bibliography, books, reprints, and other materials have been placed in Wayne State University's Walter P. Reuther Library for Urban, Labor, and Metro Affairs. Work in Progress: *A Gathering of Lanternes* (100 poems)
Awards or inclusion in other biographical books: *International Authors and Writers Who's Who; Michigan Authors,* 2nd ed.*; Michigan Poets; Who's Who in America; Who's Who in Poetry; Who's Who in Rehabilitation; Who's Who in Science and Engineering; Who's Who in the World.* South and West Annual Poetry Award 1970. Outstanding Service Award, Poetry Society of Michigan 1984. Edwin Falkowski Memorial Award, World Poetry Society 1990. Award for Leadership and Service, Michigan Rehabilitation Association 1964. Award from the Michigan Rehabilitation Counseling Association 1988. Outstanding Service Award, Michigan State Board of Education 1989
What is the aim or goal of your writing? "Perhaps my best response is an excerpt from the 'Epilogue' of *Gradually the Dreams Change:* His destination, when he set out, was pure poetry, although he did not recognize it. He came to cherish the gifts of sun, rain, a walk in the woods, a brightening smile. His wife radiates the clear beauty of mature women. His children, albeit circuitously, took on his values. He feels near to man and God and views death as another beginning. He has reached his destination many times and welcomes sunset as well as sunrise, conflict as well as calm. He knows now that much of his life has been pure poetry."
May inquiries be sent to you about doing workshops, readings? Workshops, no. Readings, yes

CAREY, VALERIE B.
Address: Contact through publishers
Pseudonym: Valerie Scho Carey
Born: August 6, 1949; Pittsburgh, Pennsylvania
Parents: Ira C. Scho, Zelda (Markowitz) Scho
Children: Kimberly, Allison, Jeffrey
Education: University of Michigan, M.A. in History, Ann Arbor, Michigan, 1971-1973. University of Michigan, B.A., Ann Arbor, Michigan, 1967-1971. Northwestern High School, 1964-1967, Flint, Michigan
Career: Instructor, Institute of Children's Literature, West Redding, Connecticut, 1988—. Student Curator, Michigan Historical Division, Walker Tavern Historic Site, Brooklyn, Michigan, 1974. Substitute Teacher, Flint Public Schools, Flint, Michigan, 1968-1972

Writings: *Maggie Mab and the Bogie Beast* Arcade 1992. *Quail Song* G.P. Putnam/Whitebird, 1990. *The Devil and Mother Crump* Harper Collins 1987. *Harriet and William and the Terrible Creature* E.P. Dutton/Viking-Penguin 1985. Work in Progress: *Tsugele's Broom. Two Lumps of Coal*
Awards or inclusion in other biographical books: *Something About the Author.* The Child Study Association of America Book of the Year 1986. Parents' Choice Award Winner 1987. Children's Choice for 1988 by joint committee of the International Reading Association and Children's Book Council. Golden Kite Award 1987, Society of Children's Book Writers for picture book illustration
What is the aim or goal of your writing? "To fulfill my own desire to write and work with words, and with luck-to please readers. Writing is a way to share thoughts, feelings, ideas. I hope people will read what I have written and will enjoy the language and think about the tales."
May inquiries be sent to you about doing workshops, readings? Yes

CARLETON, WILL (1845-1912)
Born: October 21, 1845; Hudson, Michigan
Parents: John Hancock Carleton, Celestia (Smith) Carleton
Education: Hillsdale College, Hillsdale, Michigan, 1869
Career: Newspaper reporter, part owner. Editor, *Detroit Weekly Tribune.* Founder and publisher of *Everywhere* magazine, 1894-1912. Poet and lecturer, Hillsdale College, 1887-1912. Toured United States, England, Canada, reading his poetry

Writings: *Poems* Lakeside 1871. *Farm Ballads* Harper 1873. *Farm Legends* Harper 1875. *Young Folks' Centennial Rhymes* Harper 1876. *Farm Festivals* Harper 1881. *City Ballads* Harper 1885. *Country Ballads* Dillingham 1887. *An Ancient Spell* Clark, Maynard 1887. *City Legends* Harper 1890. *City Festivals* Harper 1892. *Rhymes of Our Planet* Harper 1895. *The Life of William Carleton: Being His Autobiography and Letters; and an Account of His Life and Writings, from the Point at which the Autobiography Breaks Off* Downey & Company 1896. *Old Infant and Similar Stories* Harper 1896. *Songs of Two Centuries* Harper 1902. *Poems for Young Americans* Harper 1906. *In Old School Days* Moffat, Yard 1907. *The Duke and the King* Loeb Literary Bureau 1908. *Drifted In* Everywhere Publishing 1908. *A Thousand Thoughts from Will Carleton* Everywhere Publishing 1908. *The Burglar-Bracelets: a Farce in One Act* Loeb Literary Bureau 1909. *Arnold and Talleyrand* Loeb Literary Bureau 1909. *Tainted Money* Loeb Literary Bureau 1909. *A Thousand More Verses* Everywhere Publishing 1912. *Over the*

Hill to the Poor House and Other Poems Century 1913. "Over the Hill to the Poorhouse" was his most famous poem

Awards or inclusion in other biographical books: *Allibone: A Critical Dictionary of English Literature; American Authors 1600-1900; American Authors and Books; American Biographies; Appleton's Cyclopaedia of American Biography; Bibliophile Dictionary; Dictionary of American Biography; Everyman's Dictionary of Literary Biography, English and American; Michigan Authors,* 2nd ed.; *Michigan Poets; National Cyclopaedia of American Biography; Oxford Companion to American Literature; Twentieth Century Biographical Dictionary of Notable Americans; Who Was Who in America,* others. Carleton, Michigan was named after him. October 21 was desigated Will Carleton Day by the Michigan State Legislature. Carleton Highway (Adrian, Hudson, Hillsdale, Michigan) and Will Carleton Road West (Flat Rock, Michigan)

CARLI, AUDREY M.
Address: P.O. Box 158, Stambaugh, Michigan 49964
Born: March 14, 1932; Bessemer, Michigan
Parents: Henry P. Johnson, Helen K. Johnson
Children: Debbie, Glenn, Lynn, Lori
Education: Wakefield High School, Wakefield, Michigan, 1946-1950. Creative Writing Courses, Iron County Community School, Iron River, Michigan, 1963
Career: Writer.

Writings: Columnist by mail *House of White Birches,* women's household magazine, 1989—. Columnist, *Our Sunday Visitor,* parish family digest. Free lance writer in numerous publications in U.S. and elsewhere.*When Jesus Holds Our Hand* AMC Publishing 1987. *Jimmy's Happy Day* T.S. Denisen Publishing 1967. Contributed numerous booklets to the National Research Bureau in the early 1980's. Work in Progress: Various articles and short stories. One book outline

Awards or inclusion in other biographical books: *International Authors and Writers Who's Who* 1979; *Michigan Authors,* 2nd ed.; *Who's Who in Writers, Editors and Poets: United States and Canada* 1989, 1992

What is the aim or goal of your writing? "Aim: to share with readers ways God eased my grief when my husband died from cancer at age 54. To share with readers researched and personal experiences that will ease various family and life problems. To help ease others' hurts—to sum it up."

May inquiries be sent to you about doing workshops, readings? Yes

CARLSON, BERNICE WELLS
Address: Route 2, Box 332d, Skillmans La., Somerset, New Jersey 08873
Born: July 21, 1910; Clare, Michigan
Parents: George B. Wells, Bernice (Cook) Wells
Children: Christine, Philip, Marta
Education: Ripon College, A.B., Ripon, Wisconsin, 1928-1932
Career: Substitute teacher, Franklin Twp. New Jersey, 1948-1970. Reporter, *State Journal,* Lansing, Michigan, 1936-1944. Feature Writer, *Detroit News,* 1935. Feature Writer, *Milwaukee Journal* 1935

Writings: *My Very Own Pet* Harcourt Brace Jovanovich 1990. *What's the Big Idea?* Abingdon Press 1982. *Quick Wits Add Nimble Fingers* Abingdon Press 1978. *Picture That!* Abingdon Press 1977. *Funny Bone Dramatics* Abingdon Press 1974. *Let's Pretend*

It Happened to You Abingdon Press 1973. *Play a Part* Abingdon Press 1970. *You Know What? I Like Animals* Abingdon Press 1967. *Listen! And Help Tell the Story* Abingdon Press 1965. *The Party Book for Boys and Girls* Abingdon Press 1963. *Mary Had a Baby* Abingdon Press 1975. *The Right Play for You* Abingdon Press 1960. *Make It and Use It* Abingdon Press 1958. *Act It Out* Abingdon Press 1956. *Fun for One or Two* Abingdon Press 1958. *Do It Yourself* Abingdon Press 1952. *Make It Yourself* Abingdon Press 1950. *The Junior Party Book* Abingdon Press, 1939, 1948. Co-authored: *We Want Sunshine in Our Houses, Water Fit to Use, Masks and Mask Makers, Ready to Work, Recreation for Retarded Teenagers and Young Adults, Play Activities for the Retarded Child*. Selections appear in anthologies, elementary school reading series. Work in Progress: *It's Your Play*-simple skits and plays for children to put on with puppets or live actors

Awards or inclusion in other biographical books: *Contemporary Authors; Dictionary of International Biography; Michigan Authors,* 2nd ed.; *Something about the Author; World Who's Who of Authors; Writers' Dictionary*. Member, New Jersey Hall of Fame, 1979

What is the aim or goal of your writing? "To give children books they can read and enjoy and in many cases use with little or no adult help. I'd like to bring children and books together with my writing and also with several community activities."

May inquiries be sent to you about doing workshops, readings? No

CARLSON, LEWIS H.

Address: 3530 Meadowcroft Dr., Kalamazoo, Michigan 49004

Born: August 1, 1934; Muskegon, Michigan

Parents: Robert Lavine, Margaret H. (Carlson) Lavine

Children: Ann, Linda

Education: Muskegon High School. University of Michigan, B.A., Ann Arbor, Michigan 1957; M.A., 1962. Michigan State University, Ph.D., East Lansing, Michigan, 1967

Career: Assistant Professor of English, Ferris State College, Big Rapids, Michigan, 1965-1968. Professor of History, Western Michigan University, Kalamazoo, Michigan, 1968—.

Writings: *Tales of Gold: Olympic Stories as Told by Those Who Lived Them* (with John J. Fogarty) Contemporary Books 1987. *In Their Place: White America Defines Her Authorities* (with George A. Colburn) John Wiley & Sons 1981. Work in Progress: An oral history of German and American prisoners of war who were incarcerated in each other's country during World War II

Awards or inclusion in other biographical books: *Michigan Authors,* 2nd ed. *Tales of Gold* won the U.S. Olympic committee's 1988 Olympic Book of the Year Award

What is the aim or goal of your writing? "To make readers understand how individual and national values dictate many of our historical decisions."

May inquiries be sent to you about doing workshops, readings? Yes

CARR, HARRIETT HELEN

Born: January 1, 1899; Ann Arbor, Michigan

Parents: Paul Carr, Nellie (Loomis) Carr

Education: Ann Arbor High School. Michigan State Normal College, East Lansing, Michigan. University of Michigan, Ann Arbor, Michigan. New York University, New York, New York

Career: At age 11, became published with a poem in national magazine. Reporter and

News Editor,*Ypsilanti Daily Press*, 1920-1935-the first woman editor of a daily newspaper in Michigan. Feature writer, *The Detroit News*, 1935-1939. Staff writer, *Michigan Education Journal*, 1939-1940. Associate Editor, *Michigan Vocational Outlook,* 1940-1945. Assistant Director of Field Services, *Scholastic Magazine*, 1945-1963. Editorial Assistant, *American Vocational Journal*. Full-time fiction writer beginning 1963

Writings: *Gravel Gold* Farrar, Straus 1953. *Borghild of Brooklyn* (a Junior Literary Guild selection) Farrar, Straus 1955. *Where the Turnpike Starts* Macmillan 1955. *Against the Wind* Macmillan 1955. *Miami Towers* Macmillan 1956. *Sharon* Hastings House 1956. *Wheels for Conquest* Macmillan 1957. *Valley of Defiance* Macmillan 1957. *Confidential Secretary* Macmillan 1958. *The Mystery of the Aztec Idol* Macmillan 1959. *Young Viking of Brooklyn* Viking 1961. *Mystery of Ghost Valley* Macmillan 1962. *Rod's Girl* Hastings House 1963. *Bold Beginnings* Hastings House 1964, others.

The 2nd edition of *Michigan Authors* includes: "The Carr family did not come to America on the Mayflower, but by 1670 they were established in Massachusetts. And almost from that time on they have followed the frontier, from Massachusetts to New York State, on to Michigan, Colorado, North Dakota; to the Pacific coast and back again. Generation after generation they wrote letters...they told stories to their children...they made friends with the Indians, established trading posts, broke the soil of the plain states, mined gold."

Awards and inclusion in other biographical books: *The Author's and Writer's Who's Who; Authors of Books for Young People; Contemporary Authors; Foremost Women in Communications; Michigan Authors,* 1st ed., 2nd ed.; *More Junior Authors; Something about the Author; Who's Who of American Women*

CARR, WILLAM H.

Address: 8197 Springwood Lake Road, Harrison, Michigan 48625
Pseudonym: Bill Carr
Born: September 12, 1922; Cedarville, Michigan
Parents: Otto Carr, Thelma (Loomis) Carr
Children: Karen, Meri, Dawn, Tina, Kitti
Education: Pickford High School, Academic Diploma,1927
Career: Ford Motor Company, Dearborn, Michigan, 1948-1973, retired. U.S. Army, Combat Infantry, Overseas, Pacific, 1942-1945

Writings: *The Best of My Roses* Midway Press 1990, 1991, 1992. *The Last Rose* Midway Press 1985. *Everything's Roses* Midway Press 1983. *Roses With Love* Midway Press 1981. *Roses in Rhyme* Midway Press 1980. *Roses in the Snow* Midway Press 1979
Awards or inclusion in other biographical books: Poetry has been included in the yearly hard cover edition of *The Salesian Collection*
What is the aim or goal of your writing? "My aim is to continue to write poetry that will give a spiritual uplift to those who read it leaving them with a feeling of well-being for having read it."
May inquiries be sent to you about doing workshops, readings? Yes

CARSON, ADA L.

Address: 229 Starr Building, Ferris State University, Big Rapids, Michigan 49307
Born: March 6, 1932; Pittsburgh, Pennsylvania
Parents: Morris M. Siegel, Mary C. Siegel
Children: William, Rosalyn, Bryan

Education: University of Pittsburg, B.A., magna cum laude, Pittsburgh, Pennsylvania, 1951-1953. Columbia University, M.A., New York, New York, 1953-1955. University of Minnesota, Ph.D., Minneapolis, Minnesota, 1955-1985
Career: Professor, Ferris State University, Big Rapids, Michigan, 1961—. Teaching Assistant, University of Minnesota, Minneapolis, Minnesota, 1955-1959. Teacher, Hillsdale, New Jersey, 1954-1955

Writings: All with Dr. H. Carson: *The Image of the West* Kendall-Hunt 1989. *Domestic Tragedy in English* University of Salzburg 1982. *Royall Tyler* Twayne/G.K. Hall 1979. *The Impact of Fiction* Cummings 1970. *Voices from Antiquity* Ferris State University 1989. *Mindsearch* Ferris State University 1986. More than twenty book reviews for *The Grand Rapids Press*. Various articles and classroom anthologies. Work in Progress: Critical biography of Frank Lloyd Wright, and biography of Mary Palmer Tyler
Awards or inclusion in other biographical books: *Contemporary Authors; Michigan Authors,* 2nd ed. Phi Beta Kappa and Omicron Delta Kappa. Teaching Excellence Award, Ferris State University and Michigan legislature 1990. Distingished Teacher of the Year, Ferris State University 1986. Distinguished Teaching Award, Michigan Association of Governing Boards, 1985
What is the aim or goal of your writing? "My goals are (1) to do research until I thoroughly understand a topic and (2) to communicate that knowledge to my readers in a clear and interesting manner."
May inquiries be sent to you about doing workshops, readings? Yes

CARSON, HERBERT L.
Address: 823 Cherry Ave., Big Rapids, Michigan 49307
Born: October 3, 1929; Philadelphia, Pennsylvania
Parents: Saul P. Carson, Bryna Carson
Children: William, Rosalyn, Bryan
Education: University of Pittsburgh, Pennsylvania, B.A., 1951-1953. Columbia University, M.A., New York, New York, 1953-1955. University of Minnesota, Ph.D., Minneapolis, Minnesota, 1955-1959
Career: Instructor, University of Minnesota, Minneapolis, Minnesota,1955-1959. Instructor, University of Nebraska, Lincoln, Nebraska, 1959-1960. Professor, Ferris State University, Big Rapids,1960—. Visiting Professor, Youngstown State, 1969. Copy, *Metro Advtg.,* New York, 1950. *Philadelphia Inquirer,* 1946

Writings: Co-author with Dr. A. Carson: *The Image of the West* Kendall-Hunt 1989. *Domestic Tragedy in English* (two volumes), University of Salzburg 1982. *Mindsearch* Ferris State University 1986. *Royall Tyler* Twayne 1979. Author: *Steps in Successful Speaking* Van Nostrand 1967. Editor: *Convergence* Anniversary volume, Poetry Society of Michigan 1980. Co-editor:*Voices from Antiquity* Ferris State University 1989. *The Impact of Fiction* Cummings 1970. More than 935 publications: including books, poetry, fiction, essays, scholarly articles, and book reviews. My writings have appeared in such journals as *The Cresset, Classical Outlook, Classical Bulletin, Western Review* and others. Reviews for *Quarterly Journal of Communication, Journal of Aesthetics and Art Criticism, Grand Rapids Press*. Work in Progress: *In Pursuit of Frank Lloyd Wright. Mindsearch: A Perilous Journey through Philosophy*
Awards or inclusion in other biographical books: *Michigan Authors,* 2nd ed.; *Michigan Poets,* others
May inquiries be sent to you about doing workshops, readings? Yes

CARTER, JAMES L.
Address: 320 Green Garden Road, Marquette, Michigan 49855
Born: October 17, 1935; Marquette, Michigan
Parents: Forest L. Carter, Cecille L. Carter
Children: Emily, Catherine
Education: Grand Marais High School, 1953. Aquinas College, Bachelor of Arts/History, Grand Rapids, Michigan, 1961. Northern Michigan University, Master of Arts/History, Marquette, Michigan, 1966-1967. University of Michigan, Grand Rapids Center, Graduate School,1962-1964
Career: Assistant Director Research & Development, Northern Michigan University, Marquette, Michigan, 1968-1975. News Director/Director-University Press, Northern Michigan University, 1975—. Journalist/reporter, *Mining Journal,* Marquette, Michigan 1964-1968. Teacher, Spring Lake Public Schools, Spring Lake, Michigan, 1963-1964. Teacher, Sacred Heart School, Grand Rapids, Michigan,1961-1963. Publisher and founder *Grand Marais Pilot & Pictured Rocks Review*, Grand Marais, Michigan, 1970-1975

Writings: *Superior-A State for the North Country* The Pilot Press 1980. *The Grand Island Story* John M. Longyear Research Library 1974. *North to Lake Superior-The Journal of Charles W. Penny, 1840* editor with Ernest H. Rankin, John M. Longyear Research Library 1970. *American Voyager: The Journal of David Bates Douglass* editor with Sydney W. Jackman, et al. Northern Michigan University Press 1969. *Grand Marais: Voyageurs' Harbor* The Pilot Press 1967. Book reviews for *Michigan History* magazine, feature articles in *The Detroit Free Press, Grand Rapids Press, Christian Science Monitor* and others. Introduction, Chapters, Series in various publications. Work in Progress: Article: *The Story of Caribou Island, Lake Superior.* Book: Revision (Third Edition) of *Voyageurs' Harbor*
Awards or inclusion in other biographical books: *Michigan Authors,* 2nd ed. Award of Merit, Historical Society of Michigan, 1978. Helel Longyear Paul Memorial Award, Marquette County Historical Society, 1991. Charles Follo Award, Historical Society of Michigan, 1991
What is the aim or goal of your writing? "Regional history."
May inquiries be sent to you about doing workshops, readings? No

CARTER, KEITH A.
Address: 25 E. Palmer, Apt. 35, Detroit, Michigan 48202
Pseudonym: Keith Sterling
Born: July 10, 1954; Detroit, Michigan
Parents: Joseph T. Carter, Genevieve Carter
Education: Cass Techical High, Diploma, Detroit, Michigan, 1972. Kalamazoo College, B.A. Fine Arts, 1972-1976, Kalamazoo, Michigan. Cornell University, M.A., Ithaca, New York, 1980-1982
Career: Freelance Writer, Sterling Unlimited, Detroit, Michigan, 1983—. Documentation supervisor, CANC, Detroit, Michigan,1990-1991. Documentation specialist, Blue Cross Blue Shield, Detroit, Michigan 1985-1986. Planner/Technical Writer, City of Cleveland, Cleveland, Ohio, 1982-1983. Community Arts Workshop Leader in Writing and Art for Sterling Unlimited. Some performance credits: The Warehouse, Burts Place, Majestic Theatre in Detroit. Host, narrator, dramatic reader on WDET Radio, WDTR Radio, and Barden Cablevision. Instructor and conductor of community arts classes, listed in Michigan Writers Guidelines.

Writings: *Poetry Detroit* Broken Twig Press1989. *Hipology! Anthology* Broadside Press1990. *The Wayne Review* Wayne State Press1989, 1988.*Voices in Poetics* 1987. *Once Upon a Poet* 1987. *Baby Fish Lost His Mama* 1986. *I Never Meant to Take Your Space* Cornell University Press 1986. *Arteur* Wayne State University Press 1985. *Demimonde of the Dwarfs: A Collection of Essays* 1992. Has written poetry, prose, short fiction, fiction, nonfiction, essays. Freelance reporter and frequent contributor for *The Michigan Chronicle, Thedamu Arts Magazine, The City Arts Quarterly,* others. Work in Progress: *To Dance with Fire*, a nonfiction novel

Awards or inclusion in other biographical books: Kellogg Fellowship, Kalamazoo College, 1972

What is the aim or goal of your writing? "To convert many of my literary works into 'performance art', i.e., song, video, motion picture and live performance. To continue with experiments involving literature and dance as well as combinations of literature and visual art. To evolve to a voice and intrepetation of style that is universal, unique and truly my own."

May inquiries be sent to you about doing workshops, readings? Yes

CARTHEW, ANNICK

Address: 807 Medinah, Rochester Hills, Michigan 48309
Pseudonym: Annick Hivert-Carthew
Born: May 10, 1947; Paris, France
Parents: Maurice Hivert, Emilienne (Bachelier) Hivert
Children: Paul, Jessica
Education: Ste. Genevieve High School, Paris, France. Musee du Louvre, Paris, France; Sorbonne, Paris, France, 1967-1968. Cambridge, England, English, Diploma in translation and interpretation, 1969-1970. Teachers in-training
Career: Corporate writer/speaker, Omega Productive Service, Rochester Hills, Michigan, 1988—. Presentations adapted to all audiences on Detroit's early founding brought to life by its first pioneer lady, Marie-Therese Guyon Cadillac-includes exhibits. Freelance writer, Rochester Hills, Michigan, 1980—. Realtor, Cranbrook Realtor, Bloomfield Hills, Michigan, 1976-1977. Teacher of French, M. Technical College, Maidstone-Kent, England, 1970-1975

Writings: *The Bells of Chartres* Trogan Press 1989. Monthly column on early Michigan, 1988—. Work in Progress: Everyday life in French Colonial Detroit. Biography of A. Cadillac, founder of Detroit. Cassette: Madame Cadillac speaks of early Detroit

What is the aim or goal of your writing? "Michigan-settled by ordinary people with a dream-Detroit-founded by a Frenchman's vision-Antoine de Lamothe Cadillac-both would fall upon some hard times, but like a cat with nine lives, always overcame. From the glory and strength of Michigan's past, I bring hope for its future."

May inquiries be sent to you about doing workshops, readings? Yes

CASTEL, ALBERT E.

Address: 66 Westwood Drive, Hillsdale, Michigan 49242
Born: November 11, 1928; Wichita, Kansas
Parents: Albert E. Castel, Jr., Dorothy W. Castel
Children: Ann, Charles
Education: Wichita University, B.A., Wichita, Kansas 1950. Wichita University, M.A., Wichita, Kansas 1951. University of Chicago, Ph.D. in History and Political Science, 1951-1955

Career: Currently a professional writer and lecturer. Professor of History, Western Michigan University, Kalamazoo, Michigan, 1960-1991. Assistant Professor of History and Political Science, Waynesburg College, Waynesburg, Pennsylvania, 1958-1960. Instructor in History, University of California at Los Angeles, 1957-1958. Special Agent, Counter Intelligence Corps, U.S. Army, Baltimore, Chicago, Kansas City, 1956-1957. Visiting Professor, City College of New York, Summers, 1960, 1962. Eugene C. Eppley Chairholder in History, Culver Military Academy, Culver, Indiana

Writings: *Decision in the West: The Atlanta Campaign* University Press of Kansas 1992. *Three Years with Quantrill* (co-editor, by John McCorkle) University of Oklahoma Press 1992. *Presidency of Andrew Johnson* Regents Press of Kansas 1979. *The Yeas and Nays: Key Congressional Votes, 1774-1945* (co-author) New Issues Press 1975. *General Sterling Price and the Civil War in the West* Louisiana State University Press 1968. *William Clarke Quantrill: His Life and Times* Frederick Fell, Inc. 1962. *A Frontier State at War: Kansas, 1861-1865* Cornell University Press 1958. Articles in *Civil War Times Illustrated*. Work in Progress: Various articles

Awards or inclusion in other biographical books: Honorable Mention, Albert J. Beveridge Award of American Historical Association, for *A Frontier State at War: Kansas, 1861-1865*, 1957. American Council of Learned Societies Research Grant, 1977. Best Author Award, *Civil War Times Illustrated,* 1979, for three-part article on W.T. Sherman. *General Sterling Price and the Civil War in the West* selected as one of the hundred best Civil War books by *Civil War Times Illustrated* in 1985 and by the Society of Civil War Historians in 1986. Distinguished Faculty Scholar Award, Western Michigan University, 1985 (resigned it 1991 in protest of the university's hiring policy). Eastern National Parks Association Award for Best Article in Military History, 1989

What is the aim or goal of your writing? "To inform, stimulate, and entertain".

May inquiries be sent to you about doing workshops, readings? Yes

CATHERWOOD, MARY HARTWELL (1847-1902)
Born: December 16, 1847; Luray, Ohio
Parents: Marcus Hartwell, Phoebe (Thompson) Hartwell
Children: one
Education: Female College, Grandville, Ohio, 1868
Career: Teacher, Danville, Illinois and Newburgh, New York. Lived in Maine, Canada. Editor, *Graphic,* Chicago weekly, beginning 1891

Writings: *Cracque-o'-Doom,* 1881. *Rocky Fork* 1882. *Old Caravan Days* 1884. *The Secrets of Roseladies,* 1888. *The Romance of Dollard* Century 1889. *The Bells of Ste. Anne* 1889. *The Story of Tonty* A.C. McClurg 1890. *The Lady of Fort St. John* 1891. *Old Kaskaskia* Houghton, Mifflin 1893. *The White Islander* Century 1893. *The Chase of St. Castin and Other Stories of the French in the New World* Mifflin 1894. *The Days of Jeanne d'Arc* Century 1897. *Heroes of the Middle West: The French* Ginn 1898. *Mackinac and Lake Stories* Harper 1899; Garrett Press 1969. *Lazarre* Bowen-Merrill 1901. *Rocky Fork* Lothrop, Lee & Shepard 1911. *The Queen of the Swamp and Other Plain Americans* Garrett Press 1969. *Lower Illinois Valley: Local Sketches of Long Ago of Mrs. Mary Hartwell Catherwood* Umphress Printing 1975. Other books and short stories. *The Romance of Dollard* appeared as a serial in *Century*

Awards or inclusion in other biographical books: *Allibone: A Critical Dictionary of English Literature; American Authors 1600-1900; American Authors and Books; American Biographies; American Women; American Women Writers; Appleton's Cyclo-*

paedia of American Biography; Bibliophile Dictionary; Dictionary of American Authors; Index to Women; Twentieth Century Biographical Dictionary of Notable Americans; Who Was Who in America, others. Prize from *Wood's Household Magazine*

CATLIN, GEORGE BYRON (1857-1934)
Born: August 10, 1857; Rushville, New York
Parents: S. Stanley Catlin, Elizabeth (Redout) Catlin
Children: George B. Catlin, Jr., Mrs. Frank Wachter
Education: Fort Edward Institute, on Hudson River, 1872-1873
Career: After various odd jobs, newspaper career began, 1884. City Editor, *Herald,* Grand Rapids, Michigan. Staff, *The Detroit News,* 1892; Editorial writer, 1896-1917; Commissioned to collect books, data for newspaper reference library, to become one of the leading newspaper libraries in the country, headed until 1934.

Writings: *Landmarks of Wayne County and Detroit* The Evening News Association 1898. *A Brief History of Detroit in the Golden Days of '49* Detroit Savings Bank 1921. *Historic Michigan, Land of the Great Lakes: Its Life, Resources, Industries, People, Politics, Government, Wars, Institutions, Achievements, the Press, School and Churches, Legendary and Prehistoric Lore* National Historical Association 1928. *The Story of Detroit* Detroit News 1923
Awards or inclusion in other biographical books: *Dictionary of North American Authors; National Cyclopaedia of American Biography.* Library he organized was dedicated, George B. Catlin Memorial Library, upon his death. On Cass Avenue side of the Detroit Public Library, elm tree was planted in his memory, 1934

CATTON, BRUCE (1899-1978)
Born: October 9, 1899; Petoskey, Michigan
Parents: George R. Catton, Adella M. (Patten) Catton
Children: William Bruce
Education: Oberlin College, Oberlin, Ohio, 1917-1920
Career: Reporter on Boston and Cleveland newspapers, 1920-1926. Newspaper Enterprise Association, Washington DC; special writer and Washington correspondent, 1926-1941. War Production Board, Associate Director of Information, 1942; Director of Information, 1943. Department of Commerce, Director of Information, 1945-1946. Special Assistant to Secretary of Commerce, 1948. Founded *American Heritage,* Editor, Senior Editor, 1954-1978. Charter member of the faculty, one of the founders of Famous Writers course published in Westport, Connecticut

Writings: *War Lords of Washington* Harcourt 1948. *Mr. Lincoln's Army* Doubleday 1951. *Glory Road* Doubleday 1952. *A Stillness at Appomattox* Doubleday 1953. *U.S. Grant and the American Military Tradition* Little, Brown 1954. *Banners at Shenandoah* Doubleday 1955. Editor of *American Heritage Reader* Dell 1956. *This Hallowed Ground* Doubleday 1956. *America Goes to War* Wesleyan University Press 1958. Editor of *The Battle of Gettysburg* by Franklin Haskell, Houghton 1958. Editor of *American Heritage Picture History of the Civil War* American Heritage Publishing 1960. *Grant Moves South* Little, Brown 1960. *The Coming Fury* Doubleday 1961. *The Army of the Potomac* (consolidation of three books) Doubleday 1962. *This Hallowed Ground* (juvenile) Doubleday 1962. *American Heritage Short History of the Civil War* Dell 1963. With William Catton *Two Roads to Sumter* McGraw 1963. *Terrible Swift Sword* Doubleday 1963. *Never Call Retreat* Doubleday 1965. *Grant Takes Command* Little, Brown 1969. *Waiting for the*

Morning Train: An American Boyhood Doubleday 1972. *Gettysburg: The Final Fury* 1974. *Michigan: A Bicentennial History* (with W.B. Catton) Norton and American Association of Local History 1976. *The Bold and Magnificent Dream: America's Founding Years, 1492-1815* 1978. *Bruce Catton's America* (edited by Oliver Jensen) 1980. *Reflections on the Civil War* (edited by John Leekley) 1981. Various book introductions
Awards or inclusion in other biographical books: *Allibone: A Critical Dictionary of English Literature; American Authors and Books; Authors in the News; Contemporary Authors; Current Biography; International Authors and Writers Who's Who; Michigan Authors,* 2nd ed.; *Oxford Companion to American Literature; Reader's Encyclopedia; Something about the Author; Who's Who in America; Who's Who in the World; Writers Directory,* several others. Pulitzer Prize for History; National Book Award, 1954. Received over 26 honorary degrees such as: Litt.D., University of Maryland, 1955, Wesleyan University, 1955, Dickinson College, 1955, Olivet College, 1957, Western Michigan College, 1958. LL.D., Knox College, 1958. D.L.C., Union College, 1956. Ohioana Book Award from Martha Kinney Cooper Ohioana Library Association. Special Pulitzer citation, 1961. Fletcher Pratt Award from The Civil War Round Table of New York, 1957. Award from Harry S Truman, 1959. Christopher Book Award, 1961. Presidential Medal of Freedom, 1976. Lifetime honorary membership, Little Traverse Historical Society and helped curator of its new museum arrange his exhibit. "Bruce Catton Days" celebrated in Petoskey, Michigan, July 30-31, 1965; in Benzie County, Michigan, 1972. Plaque with his likeness by Petoskey sculptor, Stanley Kellogg, is set in a stone on the front lawn of Petoskey Public Library. When awarded the National Book Award for *Stillness at Appomattox,* the author said: "What both the reporter and the historian are really looking at is people on the march.... What we see, if we look closely, is that the sum of many small victories won by individual human beings... is... a victory for all of us.... Out of sight, somewhere, something great is moving." Catton credited his Michigan background with: "When I was growing up in Northern Michigan, all the old men in town were Civil War veterans. We boys used to sit around and listen to their yarns, and see them parading in the Fourth of July celebrations."

CHAPPEL, BERNICE M.
Address: 5946 Alan Dr. #43, Brighton, Michigan 48116
Born: June 4, 1910; Fowlerville, Michigan
Parents: George L. Klein, Gertrude E. (Avery) Klein
Children: Kenneth Jr.
Education: University of Michigan, Masters, Ann Arbor, Michigan. Eastern Michigan University, Masters, Ypsilanti, Michigan, 1950-1955
Career: Rural teacher, Shiawassee County, Perry, Michigan, 1929-1931. Teacher, Brighton Area Schools, Brighton, Michigan, 1944-1960. School Social Worker, Farmington Schools, Farmington, Michigan,1960-1970

Writings: *Blowing in the Wind* Wilderness Adventure Books 1990. *Reap the Whirlwind* Wilderness Adventure Books 1987. *Bittersweet Trail* Great Lakes Books 1984. *Lure of the Artic* Wilderness Adventure Books 1983. *In the Palm of the Mitten* Great Lakes Books 1981. *Listening and Learning* Fearon Publishers 1983. *A Time for Learning* Ann Arbor Publishers 1974. *Rudolph the Rooster* Bethany Press 1969. *Harvey Hopper* T.S. Denison 1966. *Happy Hopper Tales* Comet Press 1955. *Happy Hopper* Comet Press 1954. Work in Progress: *Frontier Furry,* Wilderness Adventure Books

What is the aim or goal of your writing? "I have written juvenile, educational and historical material. For the past several years I have concentrated on the historical narrative type of fiction with strictly authentic background material."

May inquiries be sent to you about doing workshops, readings? No

CHAPUT, DONALD

Born: December 19, 1933; Houghton County, Michigan
Parents: Arthur Chaput, Mamie-Louis (Remillard) Chaput
Children: Ben, Ed
Education: Suomi College, Hancock, Michigan, 1953. Michigan State University, M.A., East Lansing, Michigan, 1958
Career: Instructor, Elgin Community College, Elgin, Illinois, 1964-1966. Research director, editor, Michigan Historical Commission, 1966-1971. Senior curator of history, Natural History Museum, Los Angeles, California, beginning 1972

Writings: *Le Pesant Affair of 1706: French Struggle to Control the Upper Great Lakes* 1968? *Hubbell: A Copper Country Village* privately printed (Lansing)1969; John H. Forster Press (Hancock) 1986. *Michigan Indians: A Way of Life Changes* Hillsdale Educational Publishers 1970. *The Cliff: America's First Great Copper Mine* Sequoia Press 1971. *Chaput Mining Research Collection* Michigan State Archives 1972. *Francois X. Aubry: Trader, Trailmaker, and Voyageur in the Southwest, 1846-1854* Arthur Clark 1975

Awards or inclusion in other biographical books: *Contemporary Authors; Directory of American Scholars; Michigan Authors,* 2nd ed.

CHORZEMPA, ROSEMARY A.

Address: 7904 Jackman Road, Temperance, Michigan 48182
Born: February 27, 1951; Toledo, Ohio
Parents: David S. Dembinski, Irene R. (Boczkowski) Dembinski
Children: Rebecca, Nancy, Timothy, Andrew
Education: Central Catholic High School, Toledo, Ohio, 1965-1969. University of Toledo, B.A. Chemistry, Toledo, Ohio, 1969-1974
Career: Lecturer/Teacher, Pisanki (Polish Egg Decorating); Genealogy; Polish Culture. Member, Compagnie Franche de la Marine du Detroit, a re-enactment group portraying the French at Detroit, 1750. Member, Board of Directors, Polish Genealogical Society of America

Writings: *Korzenie Polskie / Polish Roots* Genealogical Publishing 1993. *Morbus: Why and How Our Ancestors Died* P.G.S.A. 1992. *Design Your Own Coat of Arms: An Introduction to Heraldry* Dover 1987. *What's My Heritage?* (Folder designed for Statue of Liberty Centennial) Nestle Company 1984. *My Family Tree Workbook: Genealogy for Beginners* Dover 1982. Magazine articles, others. Work in Progress: Book about Polish-style egg decorating for children

What is the aim or goal of your writing? "To teach people, especially children, about topics not usually found in books, in a way that they become actively involved in the book, (i.e., workbooks and work as you read)."

May inquiries be sent to you about doing workshops, readings? Yes

CINTRON, ESPERANZ M.
Address: P.O. Box 7202, Albany, New York 12224
Born: October 31; Detroit, Michigan
Parents: Luis, Julia
Children: Lena
Education: Wayne State University, B.S., Detroit, Michigan, 1974. Memphis State University, graduate study, Memphis, Tennessee, 1975-1977. Wayne State University, Master of Art, Detroit, Michigan, 1982. State University of New York at Albany, doctoral study in English, 1990-.
Career: Regents Fellow, New York State Education Department, 1988-1990. Michigan Council for the Arts, Individual Artists' Grant. Administrative Assistant, City-County Building, Detroit,Michigan, 1984-1987. Special Events Coordinator, Detroit Educational Television Foundation, 1982-1984. Teacher, Highland Park Continuing Education, 1981-1985. Program coordinator, The University of Michigan, Department of Continuing Education,1980-1981. Various teaching positions in Detroit Public Schools, Detroit Institute of Technology. Lecturer, instructor in college, university in Albany and Loudonville, New York. Various community involvements such as teaching workshops on radio scriptwriting, founding member of The Sisters of Color, a women's writers collective founded in 1988, active in political campaigns, many performances of creative work such as at the Cranbrook Writers Guild Benefit in Birmingham, Michigan

Writings: Editor/Writer, *Eberhard Reports*, quarterly informational newsletter, 1986-1987. Editor/Writer, *Insights,* quarterly magazine, 1989-1990. Editor and creator, *Seeds,*1991-1992. Poems in such publications as: *Wayne Review, Feminist Women's Anthology, The Journal of The Sisters of Color,* Beacon Press. Work in Progress: Novel, *Shades* and collection of short works, *Shards*
Awards or inclusion in other biographical books: Agascha Publishing House Scholarship for fiction, 1971. Cranbrook Writers Guild Scholarship in 1986 for fiction, 1987 for poetry. National Judith Siegel Pearson Award for poetry, 1987. Poetry exhibited in traveling exhibit of the New York State Museum. 1988-1989. Awarded certificate for outstanding community service by the Albany Social Justice Center for work with Sisters of Color, 1991. Full fellowship and tuition scholarships to earn a Doctor of Arts in English at the State University of New York at Albany
May inquiries be sent to you about doing workshops, readings? Yes

CLARK, KELLY JAMES
Address: 1955 Griggs SE, Grand Rapids, Michigan 49506
Born: March 3, 1956; Muncie, Indiana
Parents: Jack L. Clark, Phyllis A. Clark
Children: William, Emily
Education: University of Notre Dame, Doctorate and Master Degrees, Notre Dame, Indiana, 1980-1985. Western Kentucky University, Master Degree, Bowling Green, Kentucky, 1979-1980. Michigan State University, Bachelor Degree, East Lansing, Michigan, 1974-1978
Career: Associate Professor, Calvin College, Grand Rapids, Michigan, 1989—. Assistant Professor, Gordon College, Boston, Massachusetts, 1985-1989. Teaching Assistant, University of Notre Dame, Notre Dame, Indiana, 1980-1985

Writings: *Our Knowledge of God: Essays on Natural and Philosophical Theology* Kluwer Academic Publishers 1992. *Return to Reason* Eerdmans 1990. *Quiet Times for*

Christian Growth Inter Varsity Press 1980. Work in Progress: *Confession & Apology: Philosopher's Testament of Grace. The Authentic Christian: Character and Commitment in the Post-Modern World*
What is the aim or goal of your writing? "Religious and philosophically informed thought for scholars and educated lay persons."
May inquiries be sent to you about doing workshops, readings? Yes

CLARK, PATRICIA F.
Address: 1426 Johnson SE, Grand Rapids, Michigan 49507
Born: February 8, 1951; Tacoma, Washington
Parents: Cecil D. Clark, Norma Clark
Education: University of Washington, B.A., Seattle, Washington, 1969-1974. University of Montana, M.F.A., Missoula, Montana, 1978-1980. University of Houston, Ph.D., Houston, Texas, 1981-1986
Career: Assistant Professor, Grand Valley State University, Allendale, Michigan, 1989—. Instructor, University of Tennessee, Knoxville, Tennessee, 1986-1989

Writings: Poems have appeared in *Poetry, The New Criterion, New England Review, North American Review, Missouri Review, Pennsylvania Review, Seattle Review.* Work in Progress: Manuscript of poems, *Commencement*
Awards or inclusion in other biographical books: Co-winner, Lucille Medwick Memorial Award, Poetry Society of America, 1989. Alan Collins Scholar in Poetry, Bread Loaf Writers' Conference, 1984. Resident Fellow, MacDowell Colony, 1984
What is the aim or goal of your writing? "To explore ideas, feelings, and emotions in poetry."
May inquiries be sent to you about doing workshops, readings? Yes

CLARY, JAMES G.
Address: 201 N. Riverside, St. Clair, Michigan 48079
Pseudonym: J. Clary
Born: August 20, 1939; Burlington, Iowa
Parents: Donald M. Clary, Francis (Lewauski) Clary
Children: Pamela, Donald, Todd, Jimmy, Robin
Education: St. Augustine High School, 1953-1957
Career: Artist, author, historian, gallery owner, 1975—. Department of Defense, Quality Assurance, 1967-1975, St. Clair Shores, Michigan. Military U.S. Air Force, 1959-1967, Texas, Oklahoma, Thailand, Illinois. Sign Painting, Michigan, 1957-1959

Writings: *Ladies of the Lakes II* A & M 1992. *Ladies of the Lakes* Michigan Department of Natural Resources 1981. *Great Lakes Childrens Coloring Book* Maritime History in Art 1980. Work in Progress: *Ladies of the Sea, Superstitions of the Sea*
Awards or inclusion in other biographical books: Michigan Natural Resources, 1981. First place in a special publications category, the Association for Conservation Information
What is the aim or goal of your writing? "As I had great difficulty in finding the hidden data and facts associated with our Great Lakes and national maritime heritage, it is my hope to be able to bring to the public, especially the younger generation, the fascinating and compelling factual treasures that are not accessible to most people."
May inquiries be sent to you about doing workshops, readings? Yes

CLELAND, CHARLES E.

Address: 2250 Haslett Rd., Williamston, Michigan 48895
Born: February 2, 1936; Kane, Pennsylvania
Parents: Charles E. Cleland, Margaret E. Cleland
Children: Elizabeth, Joshua, Elena, Katherine
Education: Denison University, B.A., Grandville, Ohio 1954-1958. University of Kansas, M.S,. Lawrence, Kansas, 1958-1960. University of Michigan, M.A., Ann Arbor, Michigan, 1960. University of Michigan, Ph.D., Ann Arbor, Michigan 1965
Career: Professor of Anthropology, Michigan State University, 1964—.

Writings: *Rites of Conquest: The Culture and History of Michigan's Native People* University of Michigan Press 1992. Numerous articles of Michigan prehistoric and historic archaeology and native people of the Great Lakes region
Awards or inclusion in other biographical books: *Michigan Authors,* 2nd ed.
What is the aim or goal of your writing? "To make the details of the historic past interesting and accessible to the sophisticated lay public."
May inquiries be sent to you about doing workshops, readings? Yes

COMFORT, WILL LEVINGTON (1878-1932)

Born: January 17, 1878; Kalamazoo, Michigan
Parents: Silas H. Comfort, Jane (Levington) Comfort
Children: Jane, John, Tom
Education: Detroit Public Schools
Career: 5th U.S. Cavalry, Spanish-American War, 1898. War Correspondent, Philippines and China, *Detroit Journal,* 1899. Reporter, Russia and Japan, 1904. Baseball player, writer

Writings: *Trooper Tales: a Series of Sketches of the Real American Private Soldier* Street & Smith 1899. *Lady of Fallen Star Island* Street & Smith 1902. *Routledge Rides Alone* Lippincott 1910. *She Buildeth Her House* Lippincott 1911. *Fate Knocks at the Door* Lippincott 1912. *The Road of Living Men* Lippincott 1913. *Lot & Company* Doran 1915. *Child and Country; a Book of the Younger Generation* George H. Doran 1915. *The Last Ditch* George H. Doran 1916. *The Hive* George H. Doran 1918. *The Yellow Lord* George H. Doran 1919. *This Man's World* Doubleday, Page 1921.*The Public Square* Appleton 1923.*Somewhere South in Sonora* Houghton Mifflin 1925. *Samadhi* Houghton 1927. *Apache* Dutton 1931.*The Pilot Comes Aboard* Dutton 1932. Others
Awards or inclusion in other biographical books: *American Authors and Books; Contemporary American Literature; Dictionary of American Biography; Dictionary of North American Authors; Michigan Authors,* 2nd ed.*; National Cyclopaedia of American Biography; Reader's Encyclopedia of American Literature; Science Fiction and Fantasy Literature; Twentieth Century Authors; Who Was Who in America; Who Was Who among North American Authors*

CONBOY, JAMES C., JR.

Address: P.O. Box 405, Cheboygan, Michigan 49721
Born: October 31, 1947; Detroit, Michigan
Parents: James C. Conboy, Marjorie J. Conboy
Children: J. Ryan, Rebecca, Brendan
Education: Oakland University, B.A., Rochester, Michigan, 1965-1968. Wayne State University, J.D., Detroit, Michigan, 1969-1972

Career: Partner, Attorney, Bodman, Longley & Dahling, Cheboygan, Michigan, 1990—
Principal, Compliance Consultants, Inc., Kalamazoo and Cheboygan, Michigan, 1988-
1991. Partner, Attorney, Conboy, Fell, Stack, Lieder & Hanson, Cheboygan, Michigan,
1990. Partner, Attorney, Simpson & Moran, Cheboygan and Birmingham, Michigan,
1982-1990. Attorney, In-house Counsel and Compliance Officer, Citizens National Bank
of Cheboygan

Writings: *Law and Banking: Principles* American Bankers Association 1982, revised
1986,1989. Articles in publications such as the *State Bar of Michigan Journal*
May inquiries be sent to you about doing workshops, readings? Yes

CONRAD, LAWRENCE HENRY (1898-?)
Born: March 6, 1898; Royal Oak, Michigan
Parents: Joseph Conrad, Frances (Meininger) Conrad
Children: son
Education: Royal Oak High School, 1917. University of Michigan, A.B., Ann Arbor,
Michigan, 1923; A.M., 1926
Career: Ford Motor Company, Factory work, Royal Oak, Michigan, 1918-1921. Faculty,
University of Michigan, upon graduation. State Teachers College, Montclair, New
Jersey. President, Michigan Authors Association

Writings: *Temper* Dodd, Mead 1924. *The Author's Mind; An Analysis from the Author's
Point of View, of the Faculties and Processes Concerned in Literary Invention* The Editor
Council 1925. *Descriptive and Narrative Writing* Houghton Mifflin 1927.*Teaching
Creative Writing* D. Appleton-Century 1937. Others. Introduction to *Poems*, Herbert
Bitterman Conrad Group 1945. In *The Forum, Century, Saturday Review of Literature,*
others
Awards and inclusion in other biographical books:*Childhood in Poetry; Who Was
Who Among North American Authors*

COOK, BERNADINE F.
Address: 10625 E. Garrison Rd., Durand, Michigan 48429
Born: September 6, 1924; Saginaw, Michigan
Parents: Luke C. Smith, Evelyn E. (Rands) Smith
Children: George, Joan, Marcie, Lise, Brian
Education: Bay City Central High, Diploma 1942. Classes at Saginaw Valley State
College, Delta College
Career: Public Information Officer, Volunteer Coordinator, Saginaw County Mental
Health, Saginaw, Michigan, 1973-1978. Office Manager, WNBY Radio, Newberry,
Michigan, 1980. Correspondent, reporter, feature writer, *Owosso Argus Press,* Owosso,
Michigan 1960-1962, freelanced 1962-1972. Various secretarial positions, audio-visual
presentations

Writings: *Little Fish That Got Away* Wm. R. Scott 1956, currently with Scholastic.
Curious Little Kitten Wm. R. Scott 1956, currently with Fukuinkan Shoten (Japan).
Looking for Susie Wm. R. Scott 1959; Shoe String Press 1991. *If I Were* Little People's
Press 1980. Articles such as *The Durand Depot Stands, For Now.* Short stories,
brochures, radio and television commercials. Work in Progress: two juvenile books
Awards or inclusion in other biographical books: *Michigan Authors,* 1st ed., 2nd
ed.; *Who's Who in American Women*
May inquiries be sent to you about doing workshops, readings? Yes

COOK, WILLIAM WALLACE (1867-1933)
Pseudonym: John Milton Edwards
Born: April 11, 1867; Marshall, Michigan
Parents: Charles R. Cook, Jane E. (Bull) Cook
Education: Schools in Ottawa, Kansas; Lafayette, Indiana; Cleveland Ohio
Career: Journalist, court reporter, author

Writings: Popular novels for Street & Smith Publishing Company such as *Diamond Dick, Jr's Call Down* 1896. *His Friend the Enemy* Dillingham 1903. *Wilby's Dan* Dodd, Mead 1904. *A Quarter to Four* Dillingham 1909. *The Fiction Factory* The Editor Company 1912. *Around the World in Eighty Hours* Chelsea House 1925. *Plotto: A New Method of Plot Suggestion for Writers of Creative Fiction* Ellis 1928. Screenplays, hundreds of stories, regular contributor to *Rough Rider Weekly*. In *Detroit Free Press, Puck, Truth*
Awards or inclusion in other biographical books: *American Authors and Books; Contemporary Authors; Dictionary of North American Authors; Encyclopedia of Science Fiction; Michigan Authors,* 2nd ed.; *Science Fiction and Fantasy Literature; Who Was Who in America*

COOLEY, JOHN R.
Address: 2504 Crescent Dr., Kalamazoo, Michigan 49001
Born: Oneonta, New York
Children: Carolyn, Meredith (wife: Barbara Cooley)
Education: Syracuse University, B.A, M.A., Syracuse, New York. University of Massachusetts, Ph.D., Amherst, Massachusetts
Career: Professor of English, Western Michigan University, Kalamazoo, Michigan, 1970—

Writings: *Mark Twain's Aquarium: The Samuel Clemens-Angelfish Correspondence* University of Georgia Press 1991. *The Great Unknown: the Journals of the First Exploration of the Colorado River* Northland Press 1988. *Savages and Naturals: Black Portraits by White American Writers* University of Delaware Press 1980. Work in Progress: *Earthly Words: Essays on Contemporary American Nature and Environmental Writers* University of Michigan Press
Awards or inclusion in other biographical books: *Directory of American Scholars 1988; Who's Who in American Education* 1990
What is the aim or goal of your writing? "To challenge myself, my readers and the status quo, and perhaps to inform and entertain, in the process."
May inquiries be sent to you about doing workshops, readings? Yes

COOPER, JAMES FENIMORE (1789-1851)
Born: (as James Cooper) September 15, 1789; Burlington, New Jersey
Parents: William Cooper, Elizabeth (Fenimore) Cooper
Children: seven
Education: Village school, Cooperstown, New York. Household of a rector, Albany, New York, 1800-1802. Yale University, 1803-1805
Career: Prepared for the navy, 1806; served as midshipman 1808. Married at 21, settled as country squire after resigning commission in the navy, 1811, began writing as challenge from his wife. Founder, Bread and Cheese Club, New York. Lived in Europe, 1826-1833, returned to Cooperstown

Writings: *Precaution* A.T. Goodrich & Company 1820. *The Spy* Wiley & Halstead 1821. *The Pioneers; or the Sources of the Susquehanna: a Descriptive Tale* Charles Wiley 1823. *The Pilot; a Tale of the Sea* C. Wiley 1823. *Lionel Lincoln: or, the Leaguer of Boston* C. Willey 1825. *The Last of the Mohicans* H.C. Carey & I. Lea 1826. *The Prairie* Carey, Lea 1827. *The Red Rover* Carey, Lea & Carey 1828. *The Borderers; or, The Wept of Wish-ton-Wish* Carey, Lea & Carey 1829. *The Water-Witch, or, the Skimmer of the Seas: a Tale* Carey & Lea 1831. *Gleanings in Europe* Carey, Lea & Blanchard 1837. *The Chronicles of Cooperstown* H. & E. Phinney 1838. *Eve Effingham: or, Home* R. Bentley (London) 1838. *The History of the Navy of the United States of America* 2 Vols. 1839. *The Bravo: a Tale* Lea & Blanchard 1839. *The Pathfinder, or, the Inland Sea* Lea and Blanchard 1840. *The Deerslayer, or, the First War-Path: a Tale* Lea & Blanchard 1841. *Afloat and Ashore: a Sea Tale* Hurd and Houghton 1844. *The Crater, or, Vulcan's Peak: a Tale of the Pacific* Burgess Stringer 1847. *The Oak Openings, or the Bee-Hunter* Burgess, Stringer 1848. Several others. Many editions, including foreign translations

Awards or inclusion in other biographical books: *American Authors 1600-1900; American Authors and Books; American Biographies; American Writers; Dictionary of American Authors; Dictionary of American Biography; Dictionary of English Authors; National Cyclopaedia of American Biography; Reader's Adviser; Reader's Encyclopedia; Who Was Who in America; Who Was Who of Children's Literature,* others. Honorary degree, Columbia College

CORBETT, RUTH
Address: 25681 Sun City Blvd., Sun City, California 92586
Born: January 24, 1912; Northville, Michigan
Parents: Howard J. Corbett, Rhoda A. (Fuller) Corbett
Children: Jana Loi (Janczarek Paton)
Education: Pontiac High School, Pontiac, Michigan. Cranbrook Adademy, 1932. Meinzinger Found. Art School, 1935-1936. Famous Writer's School, 1967-1969
Career: Illustrator, Simons-Michelson Advertising Co., Detroit, Michigan 1935-1937. Bass-Luckoff, Inc., Detroit, 1937-1939. *Detroit Times,* 1939-1940. Canfield Assocs., Detroit, Michigan 1947-1953. Dow Chemical Company, Midland, Michigan, 1950-1953. Creative Services, Detroit, Michigan, 1953-1956; other various companies in Michigan. Illustrator for Universal Pictures in Universal City, California, 1956-1974. Columnist, cartoonist, *Sun City Times,* Sun City, California. One woman show, Freeman Gallery, Montrose, California, 1964. Private art tutor, also taught adult art classes in Pontiac, Michigan, High School. Lecturer, freelance artist and writer

Writings: *Daddy Danced the Charleston* 1970. *Dying for a Cigarette?* 1976. *Some Doctors Make Me Sick* 1980. *Diary of a Hill Hugger* 1982. *Some of My Best Friends Can Fly* 1983. *Art as a Living* 1984. *How to be a Professional Line Artist* 1987. *Film City* 1988. Contributor to numerous magazines, newspapers, illustrates many of her writings.
Work in Progress: Book manuscript: *Going Places with an Amateur.*
Fiction: *Episodes*
Awards or inclusion in other biographical books: *Contemporary Authors; Michigan Authors,* 2nd ed.; *Who's Who in California; Who's Who of American Women; World Who's Who of Women.* Soroptimist Club Award,"Women Helping Women". Nonfiction Book Award, National Writers Club 1976, 1982. Grand Prize, numerous first prizes 1935-1964. First, Second, Third Prizes, San Fernando Valley Club, 1961-1963. Two Awards from Canyon Lake Art Association

What is the aim or goal of your writing? "My goal is to entertain, inform, help people, keep alive our recent history of this century. I love to make people laugh too, as a medicine we could all find beneficial."

May inquiries be sent to you about doing workshops, readings? Possibly

CORBETT, SIDNEY (1891-1961)

Born: 1891; Detroit, Michigan
Parents: Sidney Corbett,Jr.; Katherine Ellener Mabley
Children: Sidney Boynton, Katherine
Career: Veteran, World War I. Executive, General Motors

Writings: *The Cruise of the Gull-Flight* Longmans, Green 1937. *The Gull-Flight Sails Again* Longmans, Green 1939. *Pot Shots From a Grosse Ile Kitchen* (with Lucy Corbett) Harper 1947. *Long Windows Being More Pot Shots From a Grosse Ile Kitchen* (with Lucy Corbett) Harper 1948. *French Cooking in Old Detroit Since 1701* (with Lucy Corbett) Wayne University Press 1951. Food column, *Detroit Sunday News,* beginning 1946

CORDIER, MARY HURLBUT

Address: 1115 Cherry Street, Kalamazoo, Michigan 49008
Born: December 24, 1930; Davenport, Iowa
Parents: Irving W. Hurlbut; Evelyn H. (Bolte) Hurlbut
Children: Gail, Ann
Education: Western Michigan University, Ed.S., Kalamazoo, Michigan, 1972. Michigan State University, M.A., East Lansing, Michigan, 1958. University of Northern Iowa, Cedar Falls, Iowa, B.A., 1955; Two Year Elementary Certificate, 1950
Career: Researcher, Author, Lecturer in Women's History and Children's Literature, 1982—. Associate Professor, Emerita and Adjunct, Education and Professional Development, Western Michigan University, Kalamazoo, Michigan, 1990—. Associate Professor, Education and Professional Development, Western Michigan University, Teaching Inservice and Preservice Teachers, Elementary Education. Assistant Professor, University Campus School, Western Michigan University, Kalamazoo, Michigan, 1958-1960. Teacher, public schools, Iowa, Michigan, 1950-1958

Writings: *Schoolwomen of the Prairies and Plains: Personal Narratives from Iowa, Kansas, and Nebraska, 1860's-1920's* University of New Mexico Press 1992. *Peoples of the American West: Historical Perspectives Through Children's Literature* (with Maria Perez-Stable) Scarecrow Press 1989. Nine articles, 36 reviews, 12 other publications-many relating to elementary education, women's history, career education, and community resources. Work in Progress: *America's Story Through Children's Literature: Children's Books and Activities to Enrich the K-8 Curriculum* (with Maria Perez-Stable) Oryx Press

Awards or inclusion in other biographical books: *Who's Who in the Midwest*, 23rd, 24th Edition;*Who's Who of American Women*, 13th Edition

What is the aim or goal of your writing? "The goal of my historical research and publications is to bring women's history to general readers, to educators, and to scholars in women's history and the history of education. My publications about historical literature for children are aimed at teachers, librarians and parents for the purpose of utilizing this rich literature to enhance children's understanding of the history of the United States."

May inquiries be sent to you about doing workshops, readings? Yes

COTTON, PHEBE E.
Address: 5958 Tyler Road S.E., Kalkaska, Michigan 49646
Born: January 15, 1911; Pittsburgh, Pennsylvania
Parents: Adopted at 3 weeks of age at Lupton, Michigan, A.L. Dunlap, Elizabeth T. Dunlap
Children: Donald, Glenn, Margaret, Elizabeth, Jane
Education: Central Michigan College, Mt. Pleasant, Michigan and Marion College, Marion, Indiana, Life Degree, 1928-1931
Career: Elementary school teacher, Haslett, Michigan, 1931-1934. After married in 1935, worked as husband's partner and bookkeeper, general secretary

Writings: *Phebe in Wonderland* Quick Print 1983. *Historical Atlas of Kalkaska County* Johnson & Clark 1974. *Excelsior Township, Kalkaska County* Leader & Kalkaskian 1968. *Orange Township, Kalkaska County* Leader & Kalkaskian 1971
Awards or inclusion in other biographical books: *Michigan Authors,* 2nd ed. Michigan Historical Society Award of Merit
What is the aim or goal of your writing? "In my writings, I succeeded to collect and publish authentic material which would have otherwise been lost. In fact, much of the sources I used are not now available."
May inquiries be sent to you about doing workshops, readings? No

COUGHLIN, WILLIAM JEREMIAH (1929-1992)
Pseudonym: Sean A. Key, for early titles
Children: six
Career: Defense attorney, prosecutor, senior United States administrative law judge, Detroit, Michigan

Writings: *The Mark of Cain. Cain's Chinese Adventure. The Widow Wondered Why. The Dividend Was Death. The Destruction Committee. The Grinding Mill. The Stalking Man* (1979) Delacorte. *Day of Wrath* (1980) Delacorte. *No More Dreams* (1982) A&W Publishers. *The Twelve Apostles* (1984) G.P. Putnam. *Her Father's Daughter* (1986) G.P. Putnam. *Her Honor* (1987) American Library. *In the Presence of Enemies. Shadow of Doubt* (1991) St. Martin's. *Death Penalty* (1992) Harper Collins.

COX, DENNIS E.
Address: 22111 Cleveland, Apt. 211, Dearborn, Michigan 48124
Pseudonym: D. E. Cox
Born: November 15, 1946; Greencastle, Indiana
Parents: Paul E. Cox, Mildred L. Cox
Children: Alicia, Colin
Education: Greencastle, Indiana, High School, 1960-1964. Western Michigan University, B.S., Kalamazoo, Michigan, 1964-1968
Career: Photographer, D.E. Cox Photography, Dearborn, Michigan, 1978—. Director, China Photo Workshop Tours, Dearborn, Michigan, 1981—. Social Worker, State of Michigan, Detroit, Michigan, 1970-1983

Writings: *Detroit Today* A & M Publishing 1991. Work in Progress: *The Michigan Coast* A & M Publishing 1993/1994. Untitled book on Mackinac Island 1993. Photography book, *Michigan* Graphic Arts Center Publishing 1993
What is the aim or goal of your writing? "To compliment the photography in my books."

May inquiries be sent to you about doing workshops, readings? Yes

CRAWFORD, LYNN E.
Address: 10034 Talbot, Huntington Woods, Michigan 48070
Born: November 13, 1959; Ann Arbor, Michigan
Parents: Richard A. Crawford, Sophie S. Crawford
Education: New York University, Masters Social Work, 1988-1990. University of Michigan, Bachelor Degree., Ann Arbor, Michigan, 1977-1981
Career: Editor, News/Literary Quarterly, St. Mark's Poetry Project, 1991—. Associate Editor, *Lacanian Ink,* New York, New York, 1990—. Social Worker, Post Graduate, Center for Mental Health, New York City, 1989—. Vocational Counselor, Fountain House, New York City, 1988-1989

Writings: Published in journals: *Talisman, Long News in the Short Century, The World, Lacanian Ink.* Co-editing, with author Harry Mathews, an issue of the journal *New Observation.* Work in Progress: novel, *Soap Reign*
What is the aim or goal of your writing? "To experiment with language with in a narrative, prose, format".
May inquiries be sent to you about doing workshops, readings? Yes

CROSS, GILBERT B.
Address: 1244 Ferdon Rd., Ann Arbor, Michigan 48104
Born: May 2, 1939; Nr. Manchester, England
Parents: Gilbert E. Cross, Doris (Gregory) Cross
Children: John, Robert
Education: University of Louisville, M.A. in English, Louisville, Kentucky, 1963-1965. University of Michigan, Ph.D. in English, Ann Arbor, Michigan, 1966-1971
Career: Professor of English, Eastern Michigan University, Ypsilanti, Michigan, 1966—

Writings: *A Witch Across Time* Atheneum 1990. *Terror Train* Atheneum 1987. *Mystery at Loon Lake* Atheneum 1986. *A Hanging at Tyburn* Atheneum 1983. Adult and scholarly books. Work in Progress: *Something Wicked* (young adult)
What is the aim or goal of your writing? "To please a wide audience."
May inquiries be sent to you about doing workshops, readings? Yes

CROWLEY, MARY CATHERINE (1869-1920)
Pseudonym: Janet Grant
Born: Boston, Massachusetts
Parents: John C. Crowley, Mary J. (Cameron) Crowley
Education: Sacred Heart College, New York graduate
Career: Editor, *Catholic Missions Magazine, The Annals,* 1907-1912. Worked with others on *Memorial History of Detroit.* Lived in Detroit 1893-1903 and researched local resources on French history

Writings: *The City of Wonders: A Souvenir of the Worlds Fair* William Graham 1894. *Merry Hearts and True* 1889. *A Daughter of New France: With Some Account of the Gallant Sieur Cadillac and His Colony on the Detroit* Little, Brown 1901. *The Heroine of the Straits* Little, Brown 1902. *Love Thrives in War: A Romance of the Frontier in 1812* Little, Brown 1903. *In Treaty with Honor: A Romance of Old Quebec* Little, Brown 1906.

Others. Poems, short stories, in *Wide Awake, St. Nicholas, Ladies' Home Journal, Pilot, Boston Globe*, syndicates
Awards or inclusion in other biographical books: *Childhood in Poetry; Dictionary of American Authors; Dictionary of North American Authors; Index to Women; Who Was Who in America; Women's Who's Who of America*

CRUM, HOWARD A.
Address: 735 Dartmoor Road, Ann Arbor, Michigan 48103
Born: July 14, 1922; Mishawaka, Indiana
Parents: Earl E. Crum, Eunice E. Crum
Children: Mary, Roger
Education: Western Michigan College, B.S., Kalamazoo, Michigan, 1940-1947. University of Michigan, M.S., Ph.D., Ann Arbor, Michigan, 1947-1951
Career: Professor, University of Michigan, Ann Arbor, Michigan, 1965—. Curator, National Museum of Canada, Ottawa, Canada, 1954-1965. Assistant Professor, University of Louisville, 1953-1954. Post doctoral fellow, Standford University, Stanford, California, 1951-1954

Writings: *Liverworts and Hornworts of Southern Michigan* University of Michigan 1991. *A Focus of Peatlands and Peat Mosses* University of Michigan 1989. *Mosses of the Great Lakes Forest* University of Michigan 1983. *Mosses of Eastern North America* Columbia University Press 1981. Work in Progress: *Mosses of Mexico* (co-editor)
Awards or inclusion in other biographical books: *Michigan Authors,* 2nd ed. Gleason Award for Excellence in Scientific Writing, 1981
What is the aim or goal of your writing? "Scientific (botanical)".
May inquiries be sent to you about doing workshops, readings? No

CULPEPPER, MARILYN MAYER
Address: 2000 Moores River Drive, Lansing, Michigan 48910
Born: August 20, 1922; Flint, Michigan
Parents: (Samuel) Glenn Mayer, Florence (Tressler) Mayer
Education: University of Michigan, A.B., Ann Arbor, Michigan, 1940-1944; Ph.D., 1956. Columbia University, M.A., New York, New York, 1945-1946
Career: Instructor to full professor, 1946-1989

Writings: *Trials and Triumphs: The Women of the American Civil War* Michigan State University Press 1992. *Writing for Life: A Writer's Reader* (co-authored with Perry E. Gianakos) Macmillan 1988. Work in Progress: Southern women and Reconstruction
What is the aim or goal of your writing? "To reveal the myriad contributions of women during the Civil War."
May inquiries be sent to you about doing workshops, readings? Yes

CUMMING, JOHN
Address: 465 Hiawatha Drive, Mount Pleasant, Michigan 48858
Born: September 24, 1915; Shewsbury, Massachusetts
Parents: George H. Cumming, Isabel M. Cumming
Children: Robert, John
Education: Eastern Michigan University, B.A., Ypsilanti, Michigan, 1935-1940. University of Michigan, M.A., Ann Arbor, Michigan, 1940-1945

Career: Director, Clarke Historical Library, Mount Pleasant, Michigan, 1961-1983. Teacher, counselor, Detroit Public Schools, Detroit, Michigan, 1945-1961

Writings: *This Place Mount Pleasant* City of Mount Pleasant 1989. *Runners and Walkers: A Nineteenth Century Sports Chronicle* Regnery Gateway 1981. *A Guide for the Writing of Local History* Michigan Historical Commission 1974, 1976. *Little Jake of Saginaw* Rivercrest House 1978. Work in Progress: *A Centennial History of Central Michigan University*
May inquiries be sent to you about doing workshops, readings? Yes

CURWOOD, JAMES OLIVER (1878-1927)
Born: June 12, 1878; Owosso, Michigan
Parents: James Moran Curwood, Abigail (Griffen) Curwood
Children: Viola, Carolotta, James
Education: University of Michigan, Ann Arbor, Michigan, 1898-1900
Career: Reporter and editor, *Detroit News-Tribune*. Freelance writer, Canadian Government, explored Hudson Bay. Founded the first conservation movement in Michigan, January 1, 1927; named Chairman, Game, Fish & Wildlife Committee of the Conservation Department, State of Michigan. Head of Izaak Walton League

Writings: *Courage of Captain Plum* Bobbs-Merrill 1908. *The Wolf Hunters* Bobbs-Merrill 1908. *The Gold Hunters* Bobbs-Merrill 1909. *The Great Lakes; the Vessels that Plough Them* Putnam 1909. *The Danger Trail* Bobbs-Merrill 1910. *God's Country* Doubleday, Page 1915. *Philip Steel of the Royal Northwest Mounted Police* Bobbs-Merrill 1911. *The Honor of the Big Snows* Bobbs-Merrill 1911. *Flower of the North* Grosset & Dunlap 1912. *Isobel, a Romance of the Northern Trail* Harper & Brothers 1913. *Kazan* Grosset & Dunlap 1914. *The Hunted Woman* Doubleday, Page 1916. *Baree, Son of Kazan* Doubleday, Page 1917. *The Beloved Murderer* Winthrop Press 1914. *The Grizzly King, a Romance of the Wild* Grosset & Dunlap 1918. *The Courage of Marge O'Doone* Doubleday, Page 1918. *The River's End; a New Story of God's Country* Grosset & Dunlap 1919. *The Valley of Silent Men: a Story of the Three River Country* Grosset & Dunlap 1920. *Back to God's Country* Grosset & Dunlap 1920. *The Flaming Forest* Grosset & Dunlap 1921. *Nomads of the North; a Story of Romance and Adventure Under the Open Stars* Doubleday Page 1922. *The Country Beyond; a Romance of the Wilderness* Cosmopolitan Book Corporation 1922. *The Alaskan* Grosset & Dunlap 1923. *The Glory of Living* (autobiography) Hodder & Stoughton 1928. *The North-Country Omnibus* Grosset & Dunlap 1936. Many others. *Green Timber* and *Son of the Forests,* unfinished at the time of his death, was completed by others. Novels appeared in many editions, in several foreign languages
Awards or inclusion in other biographical books: *American Authors and Books; American Biographies; Appleton's Cyclopaedia of American Biography; Dictionary of American Biography; Dictionary of North American Authors; Lincoln Library of Language Arts; Longman Companion to Twentieth Century Literature; Michigan Authors,* 1st ed., 2nd ed.; *Oxford Companion to American Literature; Reader's Encyclopedia of American Literature; Twentieth Century Authors; Who Was Who in America; Who Was Who among North American Authors.* Curwood's studio was made a public memorial in Owosso, Michigan. Located on the banks of the Shiawassee River, its architecture was Norman in style

CZUCHNA-CURL, ARDYCE E.
Address: P.O. Box 19127, Kalamazoo, Michigan 49019
Born: March 23, 1934; Ashley, Michigan
Parents: Hermon K. Hoffer, Grace A. (Fehr) Hoffer
Children: Bruce, Marcia, Jodi
Education: Huntington College, A.B., Huntington, Indiana, 1951-1955. Michigan State University, M.A. in English, East Lansing, Michigan, 1956-1960. Graduate of Famous Writer's School, non-fiction correspondence, 1965-1967. Journalism class at Western Michigan University, 1990
Career: Writer, photo-journalist, newsletter editor, Kalamazoo, Michigan, 1967—. Substitute teacher, Climax-Scotts Community Schools, Climax, Michigan. Teacher, Lakeview Community Schools, Lakeview, Michigan, 1956-1959. Teacher, Long Beach City Schools, Long Beach, California, 1955-1956. Teacher, Hamilton Public Schools, Hamilton, Ohio, 1959-1960

Writings: *Mountains and Rainbows* Oak Woods Media 1989. Write, edit, and do photography and layout for company newsletters. Numerous articles in such publications as: *Michigan Farmer, Kalamazoo Gazette, Grand Rapids Press, Family Digest, The Woman* and others. Work in Progress: correspondence course from The Institute of Children's Literature
Awards or inclusion in other biographical books: Named State Friend of Extension, National Honorary Extension Fraternity, 1987. Communicator of the Year, Kalamazoo County Farm Bureau, 1978, 1983. Communicator of the Year, Van Buren County Farm Bureau, 1984. Communicator of Achievement, Michigan Press Women, 1990. Alumnus of the Year, Huntington College, 1990
What is the aim or goal of your writing? "To inform and to inspire readers to have dreams and to work to achieve them."
May inquiries be sent to you about doing workshops, readings? Yes

D

DAIN, FLOYD RUSSELL

Address: 565 Hiawatha, Mount Pleasant, Michigan 48858
Born: November 20, 1910; Hamburg, New York
Parents: Burton Roy Dain, Effie Alzada (Wolfe) Dain
Children: Kathleen Ann
Education: Wayne State University, B.A., Detroit, Michigan, 1929-1934. Wayne State University, M.A., Detroit, Michigan, 1943. Additional studies at the University of Michigan
Career: Professor, Central Michigan University, Mount Pleasant, Michigan, 1966-1981. Teacher, Detroit Public Schools, Detroit, Michigan, 1937-1966. Assistant Purchasing Agent, Michigan Mutual Liability Co., 1935-1937. Lieutenant, United States Navy Reserve, 1943-1947

Writings: *A Silver Spire* Enterprise Press 1971. *Education in the Wilderness* Michigan Historical Commission 1968. *Every House a Frontier* Wayne State University Press 1956. *Detroit: The Story of Water Transportation* Wayne State University Press 1951. *Detroit and the Western Movement* Wayne State University Press 1951. A number of articles, book reviews, etc., in various Michigan publications. Work in Progress: *Princess in Blue*-based on the life of a Vermont girl
Awards or inclusion in other biographical books: *Michigan Authors,* 2nd ed.; *Who's Who in the Midwest,* 1970-1971. The American Association for State and Local History Award of Merit, 1957. National Society Daughters of Colonial Wars, Teacher Award, 1980
What is the aim or goal of your writing? "I am now retired—Professor Emeritus—after more than forty years of teaching. I am now 81 years of age—but I hope to live long enough to write two more volumes relating to the life of the Vermont girl and her adventures in two more wars."
May inquiries be sent to you about doing workshops, readings? Yes

DALRYMPLE, DOROTHY E.

Address: 808 Riverview Dr., Plainwell, Michigan 49080
Born: December 13, l910; Otsego, Michigan
Parents: Charles Carroll, Lottie M. (Wilson) Carroll
Education: Otsego High School, Otsego, Michigan, 1924-1928
Career: Retailing Store-Self employed, Otsego, Michigan, 1932-1957. Office-Shoe Factory, 1930-1932. Telephone Operator, Otsego, Michigan, 1928-1930

Writings: *Memories of Pine Creek* self published 1983. *As It Was In Otsego* Archie Nevins & self 1975. *As the Automobile Came to Otsego* self published 1965. *History of the First 125 Years of the Otsego Congregational Church* self published 1962
Awards or inclusion in other biographical books: *Michigan Authors,* 2nd ed.
What is the aim or goal of your writing? "Enjoyment of local history and as a tribute to my father who was born and raised in the area."
May inquiries be sent to you about doing workshops, readings? No

DANIELS, JIM
Address: 3419 Parkview Ave., Pittsburgh, Pennsylvania 15213
Born: June 6, 1956; Detroit, Michigan
Parents: Raymond J. Daniels, Mary T. Daniels
Education: Alma College, B.A., English, Spanish, Alma, Michigan, 1974-1978. Bowling Green State University, Bowling Green, Ohio, 1978-1980
Career: Associate Professor of English, Carnegie Mellon University, Pittsburgh, Pennyslvania, 1981—.

Writings: *Hacking It* Ridgeway Press 1992. *Punching Out* Wayne State University Press 1990. *Digger's Territory* Adastra Press 1989. *The Long Ball* Pig-In-A-Poke Press 1988. *Places Everyone* University of Wisconsin Press 1985. *On the Line* Signpost Press 1980. *Factory Poems* Jack-In-The-Box Press 1978. Poems published in many literary journals and magazines. Work in Progress: A new collection of poems.
Awards or inclusion in other biographical books: Pennsylvania Arts Council Fellowships, 1987, 1990. National Endowment for the Arts Fellowship, 1985. Brittingham Prize for Poetry, 1985
May inquiries be sent to you about doing workshops, readings? Yes

DANNER, MARGARET ESSE (1915-1984)
Born: 1915; Chicago, Illinois
Parents: Caleb Danner, Naomi Danner
Children: Naomi Washington
Education: Chicago YMCA, 1943. Roosevelt College, 1944. Northwestern University, Evanston, Illinois,1945. Loyola University, Chicago, Illinois, 1946
Career: Staff Member, Art Cetner, Chicago, Illinois. Assistant Editor, *Poetry Magazine,* 1956. Poet-in-Residence, Wayne State University, 1959-1960. Founder, Director, Boone House Cultural Center, Detroit, Michigan. Virginia Union University, Richmond, Virginia, 1968-1972. Poet-in-Residence, LeMoyne-Owen College, 1972-1976. Has read her poetry in colleges and universities in the United States, England, France, West Africa

Writings: *To Flower* Hemphill 1963. *Poem Counterpoem* (co-author) Broadside 1966. *Impressions of African Art* Broadside 1968. *Iron Lace* Poets Press 1970. *The Down of the Thistle* Country Beautiful 1976. Poems in *Negro Story, Chicago Magazine, Poetry Magazine, Quicksilver, Talisman, Voices, Negro Digest, Negro History Bulletin,* others. Poems in anthologies such as: *Broadsides: Broadside #22* Broadside 1968; *The Poetry of Black America* Harper & Row 1973
Awards or inclusion in other biographical books: *Michigan Authors,* 2nd ed. John Hay Whitney Fellowship. American Writers Award. Harriet Tubman Award. Native Chicagoan Literary Award. American Society for African Culture Fellowship. Midwestern Writers Award
In the 2nd edition of *Michigan Authors* appears her statement: "I believe that creativity is one of the gifts from the force for Good. Attempting to develop my individual expression of this force is my activity."

DATSKO, TINA
Address: 550 Orange Avenue, Apt. 339, Long Beach, California 90802
Born: January 23, 1960; Ann Arbor, Michigan
Parents: Joseph Datsko, Doris Mae (Ross) Datsko

Education: Ann Arbor Pioneer High School, Ann Arbor, Michigan, 1974-1978. University of Michigan, B.A., M.F.A., Creative Writing, Ann Arbor, Michigan, 1978-1985. University of Southern California, Master of Professional Writing (Drama/Screenplay), Los Angeles, California, 1987-1989

Career: Lecturer Radio/Television/Film/Dance, English Departments, California State University, 1989—. Produced plays *Hattie's Earring,* University of Michigan. Produced documentary film *Rudolf Arnheim: Theories of Art*

Writings: Narrative, writer, producer of play *La Paz*, University of Southern California. Writer, producer of documentary film *Yo No Entiendo a la Gente Grande*. Work in Progress: Novels: *The Flesh Wedding. Women Under Glass.* Poetry books: *The Strength of Eggs. The Delirium.* Feature film, *La Paz*

Awards or inclusion in other biographical books: Los Angeles Arts Council Award, 1989. Phi Kappa Phi Awards, 1988, 1989. Michigan Council for the Arts Grant, 1985. Fourteen Hopwood Awards, 1979-1985. Two Virginia Voss Awards, 1982. Cowden Fellowships, 1979, 1980. Bain-Swiggert Award, 1980

What is the aim or goal of your writing? "The goal of my writing is the search for meaning—to examine human life in its complexity and contradiction and to glean from amid the darkness, ugliness, and brutality a glimpse of the transforming power which signals a spark of divinity within us."

May inquiries be sent to you about doing workshops, readings? Yes

DAVIS, LEILA E.

Address: 5824 E. HJ Ave., Kalamazoo, Michigan 49004

Born: May 21, 1936; Scobey, Montana

Parents: Clyde L. Wheeler, Thelma L. (Kestin) Wheeler

Children: Diana, Dana, Virginia, Steven

Education: Eastern Washington College, B.A. in Education, Cheney, Washington, 1954-1958. Graduate classes at Western Michigan University, Kalamazoo, Michigan

Career: Substitute teacher, Comstock High School, Comstock, Michigan, 1969—. Spanish teacher, Regina Catholic High School, Midland, Michigan, 1967-1968. Spanish teacher, Bellevue Junior High, Bellevue, Washington, 1958-1959. Frequent speaker at writing conferences, workshops, schools, including elementary schools

Writings: *Lover Boy* Avon Flare 1989, Cora Verlag reprinted in Germany, 1990. Cora Verlag has purchased two more teen novels, *Shining Through, Suddenly a Single.* American correspondent for British magazine *Writer's Monthly*. Columnist on marketing for *Romance Writers Report*. Work has appeared in such publications as *Woman's World, True Love, Secrets, Ford Times, The Writer, Kalamazoo Magazine, West Michigan Magazine, Working Mother, True Romance,* and magazines in Scotland, England, Norway and *Fourth Womansleuth Anthology*. Work in Progress: Three mysteries, one teen novel. Has published magazine articles since 1972, magazine fiction since 1983

Awards or inclusion in other biographical books: Golden Heart from Romance Writers of America. Best published Young Adult novel. Finalist for Rita (RWA), best published novel, 1990

What is the aim or goal of your writing? "Teen novels-to provide insight into ways of dealing with problems, show teens they're not alone in facing different kinds of problems. Mysteries (adult) offer escape and entertainment."

May inquiries be sent to you about doing workshops, readings? Yes

DAWSON, JOHN HARPER
Address: 715 Alexander Drive, Adrian, Michigan 49221
Born: September 10, 1914; Erie, Pennsylvania
Parents: John A. Dawson, Julia A. Dawson
Children: Marsha E., John R.
Education: Adrian College, A.B., Adrian, Michigan, 1935-1938. University of Pittsburgh, Ph.D., Pittsburgh, Pennsylvania, 1944-1954. Wesley Seminary, 1938-1941
Career: President of Adrian College, Adrian, Michigan, 1955-1978. Pastor of United Methodist Churches, Pittsburgh, Pennsylvania, 1941-1955. University of Pittsburgh, Lecturer, 1944-1946

Writings: *Wildcat Cavalry* Morningside Press 1982. *A Biography of Ray W. Herrerk* Morningside Press 1984

DE ANGELI, MARGUERITE (1889-1987)
Born: March 14, 1889; Lapeer, Michigan
Parents: Shadrach George Lofft, Ruby A. (Tuttle) Lofft
Children: John, Arthur, Harry, Nina, Maurice
Education: Public Schools, Lapeer Michigan and Philadelphia, Pennsylvania
Career: Concert and Church soloist, 1906-1920's. Studied drawing with an illustrator neighbor when her children were small, began illustrating stories she had written. Illustrated Sunday school papers beginning in 1922

Writings: *Ted and Nina Go to the Grocery Store* Doubleday 1935. *Ted and Nina Have a Happy Rainy Day* Doubleday 1936. *Henner's Lydia* Doubleday 1936. *Petite Suzanne* Doubleday 1937. *Copper-Toed Boots* Doubleday 1938. *Skippack School* Doubleday 1939. *A Summer Day with Ted and Nina* Doubleday 1940. *Thee, Hannah!* Doubleday 1940. *Elin's Amerika* Doubleday 1941. *Up the Hill* 1942. *Yonie Wondernose* Doubleday 1944. *Turkey for Christmas* Westminster 1944. *Bright April* Doubleday 1946. *Jared's Island* Doubleday 1947. *The Door in the Wall* Doubleday 1949. *Just Like David* Doubleday 1951. *Book of Nursery and Mother Goose Rhymes* Doubleday 1954. *The Black Fox of Lorne* Doubleday 1956. *The Old Testament* Doubleday 1960, 1967. *A Pocket Full of Posies* 1961. *Marguerite de Angeli's Favorite Hymns* Doubleday 1963. *The Goose Girl* Doubleday 1964. *Butter at the Old Price* (autobiography) Doubleday 1971. *Fiddlestrings* 1974. *The Lion in the Box* 1975. *Whistle for the Crossing* 1977. *Friendship and Other Poems* 1981
Awards or inclusion in other biographical books: *American Authors and Books; American Women Writers; Childhood in Poetry; Contemporary Authors; Current Biography; Junior Book of Authors; Michigan Authors,* 2nd ed.; *Something about the Author; Twentieth Century Children's Writers; Who's Who in America; Who's Who in American Art; Who's Who of American Women; Writers Directory,* others. Inducted into Michigan Women's Hall of Fame 1984. In 1979 Governor Milliken declared her 90th birthday "Marguerite de Angeli Day". The Lapeer City Branch Library was renamed the Marguerite De Angeli Branch Library. Book selected as an Honor Book by *New York Herald Tribune,* 1946. Junior Literary Guild Selection, 1946. John Newbery Award, 1950. Distinguished Daughter of Pennsylvania, 1958. Lewis Carroll Shelf Award, 1961. Lit Brothers Good Neighbor Community Service Award, 1963. Citation from Graduate School of Library Science, Drexel Institute of Technology, 1963. Regina Medal, Catholic Library Association, 1968

DE KRUIF, PAUL HENRY (1890-1971)
Born: March 2, 1890; Zeeland, Michigan
Parents: Hendrik de Kruif, Hendrika J. (Kremer) de Kruif
Children: Hendrik, David
Education: University of Michigan, B.S., Ann Arbor, Michigan, 1912, Ph.D., 1916
Career: Assistant Professor, University of Michigan, 1916-1917. Researcher, Pasteur Institute, Paris, 1918. Associate in Pathology, Rockefeller Institute, New York, 1920-1922. Consultant to Chicago Board of Health, Michigan State Health Department. Freelance Writer, 1922-1971. Contributing editor, *Reader's Digest,* 1940-1971

Writings: *Civilization in the United States: an Inquiry by Thirty Americans* (contributor) Harcourt 1922. *Our Medicine Men* Century 1922. *Microbe Hunters* Harcourt, Brace 1926; has appeared in many languages, editions. *Hunger Fighters* Harcourt 1928. *Seven Iron Men* Harcourt 1929. *Men Against Death* Harcourt 1932. *Yellow Jack* (with Sidney Howard) Harcourt 1933. *Why Keep Them Alive?* (with wife, Rhea de Kruif) Harcourt 1936. *Toward a Healthy America* Public Affairs Committee 1939. *Kaiser Wakes the Doctors* Harcourt 1943. *The Male Hormone* Harcourt 1945. *Life Among the Doctors* (with Rhea de Kruif) Harcourt 1949. *A Man Against Insanity* Harcourt 1957. *The Sweeping Wind, a Memoir* Harcourt 1962. Others. Collaborator on medical background for Sinclair Lewis' *Arrowsmith.* Regular contributor to *Country Gentlemen, Reader's Digest, Ladies' Home Journal* and others. Writings appeared on films, radio
Awards or inclusion in other biographical books: *American Authors and Books; Current Biography; Junior Book of Authors; Lincoln Library of Language Arts; Longman Companion to Twentieth Century Literature; Michigan Authors,* 1st ed., 2nd ed.; *Oxford Companion to American Literature; Reader's Encyclopedia; Reader's Encyclopedia of American Literature; Something about the Author; Twentieth Century Authors; Who Was Who in America*

DEJONG, DAVID CORNEL (1905-1967)
Born: June 9, 1905; Blija, Friesland, The Netherlands. Came with parents to Grand Rapids, Michigan, 1913
Parents: Remmeren R. DeJong, Jentje (DeJong-Cornel) DeJong
Education: Calvin College, A.B., Grand Rapids, Michigan, 1929. Duke University, M.A., Durham, North Carolina, 1932. Also attended University of Michigan, others
Career: Taught creative writing, Brown University, Providence, Rhode Island; University of Rhode Island, Kingston, Rhode Island, and others. Novelist-poet in residence, freelance writer, conductor of writers' workshops, translator

Writings: *Belly Fulla Straw* Knopf 1934. *Old Harlem* Houghton 1939. *Light Sons and Dark* Harper 1940. *Day of the Trumpet* Harper 1941. *Benefit Street* Harper 1942. *Across the Board* Harper 1943. *With a Dutch Accent* (autobiography) Harper 1945. *Domination in June* Harper 1946. *Somewhat Angels* Reynal 1947. *Snow on the Mountain* Reynal 1949. *Two Sofas in the Parlor* Doubleday 1951. *The Desperate Children* Doubleday 1952. *The Unfairness of Easter* Talisman 1959. *The Sayings of Mr. Jefferson* Parnassus 1959. *The Happy Birthday Umbrella* Atlantic-Little, Brown 1960. *The Birthday Egg* Atlantic-Little, Brown 1962. *Outside the Four Walls of Everything* Linden 1962. *Looking for Alexander* Atlantic-Little, Brown 1963, *The Squirrel and the Harp* Macmillan 1966. Other poetry books, juvenile and adult novels, stories. Contributor to magazines such as *Esquire, Harper's Bazaar, Poetry: A Magazine of Verse, The New Republic, The Virginia Quarterly Review,* newspapers. Editor of poetry journal, *Smoke*

Awards or inclusion in other biographical books: *American Authors and Books; American Novelists of Today; Authors of Books for Young People; Contemporary Authors; Lincoln Library of Language Arts; Oxford Companion to American Literature; Reader's Encyclopedia; Reader's Encyclopedia of American Literature; Something about the Author; Twentieth Century Authors; Who Was Who in America.* Houghton Mifflin fellowship, 1938. University of Minnesota, Rhode Island College, Ford Foundation fellowships. Stories recognized by O. Henry Memorial Prize Award, 1937, 1939, 1941

DEJONG, MEINDERT
Born: March 4, 1906; Wierum, Netherlands
Parents: Raymond DeJong, Jennie (DeJong) DeJong
Education: Calvin College, A.B., Grand Rapids, Michigan, 1928
Career: Author. Served in World War II

Writings: *The Big Goose and the Little White Duck* Harper 1938, 1963. *Dirk's Dog, Bello* Harper 1939. *The Cat that Walked a Week* Harper 1943. *Shadrach* Harper 1953. *Hurry Home, Candy* Harper 1953, 1965. *The House of Sixty Fathers* Harper 1956. *Along Came a Dog* Haprer 1958. *Far Out the Long Canal* Harper 1964. *Puppy Summer* Harper 1966. *Journey From Peppermint Street* Harper 1968. *The Almost All-White Rabbity Cat* Macmillan 1972. Others
Awards or inclusion in other biographical books: *Anthology of Children's Literature; Authors and Illustrators of Children's Books; Author's and Writer's Who's Who; Authors of Books for Young People; Book of Children's Literature; Contemporary Authors; Michigan Authors,* 2nd ed.; *More Junior Authors; Sense of Story; Something about the Author; Twentieth-Century Children's Writers; Who's Who in America; Writers Directory,* others. John Newbery Medal, American Library Association, 1954, Children's Book Award, Child Study Association of America, 1956, Aurianne Award, American Library Association, 1960. Hans Christian Andersen Award, 1962. National Book Award in Children Literature, 1969. National Catholic Regina Award, 1972

DEJONGE, JOANNE E.
Address: 6629 Leisure Way Drive, Caledonia, Michigan 49316
Born: May 18, 1943; Paterson, New Jersey
Parents: Andrew J. Haan, Johanna (DeHaan) Haan
Education: University of Michigan, B. Mus, Ann Arbor, Michigan, 1963-1965. Calvin College, M.A.T. Science Studies, Grand Rapids, Michigan, 1978
Career: Interpretive Ranger, National Park Service, Sleeping Bear Dunes National Lakeshore, Empire, Michigan, 1991—. Teacher, Grand Rapids Christian School Association, Grand Rapids, Michigan, 1968—. Freelance Writer, Grand Rapids, Michigan, 1975—. Volunteer Teacher, U.S. Peace Corps, Sarawak, Malaysia, 1965-1968

Writings: *More Object Lessons from Nature* Baker Book House 1991. *Sexuality and the Young Christian* Baker Book House 1985, 1991. *All Nature Sings* Eerdmans 1985, 1992. *My Listening Ears* Eerdmans 1985, 1992. *Of Skies and Seas* Eerdmans 1985, 1991. *The Rustling Grass* Eerdmans, 1985, 1991. *Object Lessons From Nature* Baker Book House 1989. *Hands Across Africa* Baker Book House 1988. *Skin and Bones* Baker Book House 1985. *Bats & Bugs & Snakes & Slugs* Baker Book House 1981. *Anaku, the True Story of a Wolf* Baker Book House 1979. *God's Wonderful World* CRC Publications 1978. *More About God's Wonderful World* Paedine Press 1979. Seven hundred-eight hundred articles in *The Banner* and *God's World.* Work in Progress: *The Trash Can Review*

What is the aim or goal of your writing? "To inform young people of the wonders of Creation."

May inquiries be sent to you about doing workshops, readings? Yes

DELBANCO, NICHOLAS FRANKLIN

Address: The Hopwood Room, The University of Michigan, 1006 Angell Hall, Ann Arbor, Michigan 48109-1003

Born: August 27, 1942; London, England

Education: Harvard College, B.A., magna cum laude in History and Literature, Cambridge, Massachusetts, 1959-1963. Columbia University, M.A. in English and Comparative Literature, New York, New York, 1964-1966

Career: The University of Michigan, Ann Arbor, Michigan, Professor of English, 1985— Bennington College, Bennington, Vermont, Faculty of Language and Literature, 1966-1985. Skidmore College, Saratoga Springs, New York, Professor of English, 1984-1985. Williams College, Williamstown, Massachusetts, Visiting Professor of English, 1982, 1985. Trinity College, Visiting Writer-in-Residence, 1980. Columbia University, New York, New York, Adjunct Professor In Graduate Faculty of Arts & Letters, Columbia Writers' Program, 1979. The University of Iowa, Iowa City, Iowa, Visiting Lecturer in Faculty of Arts & Letters, Iowa Writers' Program, 1979. Breadloaf Writers' Conference, Staff, 1984—. Bennington Writing Workshops, Founding Director, 1977-1985. Director of Hopwood Awards Program, 1988, and other university service positions. Visiting Fellow 1980—, Woodrow Wilson National Fellowship Foundation. Lila Wallace Readers' Digest Fellow, Visiting Writer, 1991—. Judge at PEN/Faulkner Contest, Fiction, New York State CAPS Program, and others. Panelist, National Endowment for the Arts, Literature Program. Many talks, readings, residencies such as The University of Alabama, Montevallo, Wesleyan University

Writings: *The Writer's Trade, and Other Stories* William Morrow & Co. 1990. *Running in Place: Scenes from the South of France* Atlantic Monthly Press 1989. *The Beaux Arts Trio: a Portrait* William Morrow & Co. 1985. *About My Table, & Other Stories* William Morrow & Co. 1983. *Group Portrait: Conrad, Crane, Ford, James and Wells* William Morrow & Co 1982. *Stillness* (novel) William Morrow & Co. 1980. *Sherbrookes* (novel) William Morrow & Co. 1978. *Possession* (novel) William Morrow & Co. 1977. *Small Rain* (novel) William Morrow & Co. 1975. *Fathering* (novel) William Morrow & Co. 1973. *In the Middle Distance* (novel) William Morrow & Co. 1971. *News* (novel) William Morrow & Co. 1970. *Consider Sappho Burning* (novel) William Morrow & Co. 1969. *Grasse 3/23/66* (novel) J.B. Lippincott & Co. 1968. *The Martlet's Tale* (novel) J.B. Lippincott & Co. 1966. Books edited: *Writers and Their Craft, Short Stories & Essays on the Narrative* (with Laurence Goldstein) Wayne State University Press 1991. *Speaking of Writing: Selected Hopwood Lectures* University of Michigan Press 1990. *Stillness & Shadows, two novels by John Gardner* Alfred A. Knopf 1986

Awards or inclusion in other biographical books: The University of Michigan, Undergraduate Excellence in Teaching Award, 1991. Faculty Recognition Award, University of Michigan, 1989. Rackham Fellowship Award, University of Michigan, 1987. Michigan Council for the Arts Award, 1986. National Endowment for the Arts/PEN Syndicated Fiction Award, 1983, 1985, 1989. National Endowment for the Arts Creative Writing Fellow, Fiction, 1973, 1982. National Endowment for the Arts Composer & Librettist Fellow, 1976. J.S. Guggenheim Memorial Foundation Fellow, 1980. New York State Creative Artists Public Service Award, 1978. Vermont Council on the Arts Individual Fellowship Award, 1972

DELP, MICHAEL W.

Born: December 21, 1948; Greenville, Michigan
Parents: William Delp, Francis (Kipp) Delp
Children: Jaimi
Education: Alma College, B.A., Alma, Michigan, 1971. Western Michigan University, Kalamazoo, Michigan, 1975. Central Michigan University, 1976
Career: Teacher, Grayling High School, Michigan, 1971-1984. Director, Creative Writing, Interlochen Arts Academy, Interlochen, Michigan, 1984—. Associate editor *Skywriting Magazine*

Writings: *A Dream of the Resurrection* Cold Mountain Press 1976. *A Short Guide to the Wilderness* 1976. *Languages* 1984. *Over the Graves of Horses* Wayne State University 1988. Editor/contributor, *Contemporary Michigan Poetry-Poems from the Third Coast* Wayne State University 1988. Contributed poems to *Southern Poetry Review,* and others including anthologies. Articles have appeared in *Detroit Magazine* and others
Awards or inclusion in other biographical books: *Contemporary Authors; Michigan Authors,* 2nd ed.; *Poets & Writers,* 1977 Supplement. Poem of the Year Award, *Passages North*, 1983. Creative Artist Grant, Michigan Council for the Arts, 1984
In the 2nd edition of *Michigan Authors* he is credited with "My writing draws its energy from the physical and spiritual environment of Michigan. I try to be aware that writing is more than a physical process, and is really the process of looking for and surprising yourself. To me writing is a conscious disordering of the senses, a fever, something you do because you have to."

DELP, WILLIAM J.D.

Address: 615 N. State Rd., Belding, Michigan 48809
Born: January 27, 1921; Lansing, Michigan
Parents: Guy E. Delp, Nelle L. (Eby) Delp
Children: Michael, Gretchen
Education: Lansing Central High School, Commercial Diploma, 1936-1939. Industrial Engineering, Scranton, Pennsylvania, Industrial Engineering Degree, 1946-1950
Career: Retired in 1981. Assistant Manager, Rayborn Hardware Company, Bending, Michigan 1973-1981. Plant Manager, Fedders Corporation, Greenville, Michigan, 1970-1973. Manager, Manufacturing Engineering, Gibson Division, White Consolidated Industries, Greenville, Michigan 1968-1970. Master Mechanic and Chief Tool Engineer, Gibson Refrigerator Company, Greenville, Michigan, 1939-1968. Master Sgt., U.S. Army, 1943-1946

Writings: *The Patriots-Montcalm County, Michigan, Men in the Civil War* TNT Publishing 1990. *The Patriots-Ionia County, Michigan, Men in the Civil War* TNT Publishing 1991. Various guest editorials published in *The Greenville Daily News,* 1980-1991. Work in Progress: Wartime History (1940-1953) of Gibson Refrigerator Company, Greenville, Michigan. Book of experiences in seven years as volunteer literacy tutor. History of the 339th Infantry Division (Russia in WWI)
What is the aim or goal of your writing? "Personal satisfaction; as well as providing a written record of my many lifetime experiences for future generations of my family."
May inquiries be sent to you about doing workshops, readings? Yes

DERRICOTTE, TOI

Address: 7958 Inverness Ridge Road, Potomac, Maryland 20854
Born: April 12, 1941; Detroit, Michigan
Parents: Benjamin Webster, Antonia (Cyrus) Webster
Children: Anthony
Education: Wayne State University, B.A., Detroit, Michigan, 1960-1965. New York University, M.A.,1974-1984
Career: Associate Professor, University of Pittsburgh, 1991—. Professor, George Mason University, Fairfax, Virginia, 1990-1991. Associate Professor, Old Dominion University, Norfolk, Virginia, 1988-1990. Member of Editorial Staff,*The New York Quarterly,* 1969-1974. Guest poet and lecturer at such colleges and universities as Barnard, Dartmouth, San Jose State College, Kent State University, Denison University and in over 100 theaters, museums, libraries. Visiting Professor, New York University, 1992. Poet, Squaw Valley Community of Writers, Olympic Valley, California, 1992. Poetry teacher, workshop leader, writer-in-residence, panelist, judge, master teacher, poet-in-the-schools, conference leader in numerous places. Educational Consultant, Columbia University, 1979-1982

Writings: *Captivity* University of Pittsburgh Press 1989. *National Birth* Crossing Press 1983. *Creative Writing: A Manual for Teachers* (with Madeline Bass) New Jersey State Council on the Arts 1985. *The Empress of the Death House* Lotus Press 1978. Two hundred poems in such publications and anthologies as *American Poetry Review, Paris Review, River Styx, 13th Moon, Chrysalis, Black American Literature Forum, Black Scholar, Massachusetts Review, Kenyon Review, Ploughshares, Woman Poet: East, Callaloo; An Introduction to Poetry, Adriadne's Thread, Early Ripening,* others. Work in Progress: *The Black Notebooks*, a book of autobiographical prose
Awards or inclusion in other biographical books: National Endowment for the Arts, Creative Writing Fellowships, 1985,1990. Pushcart Prize, 1989; nominated 1988, 1987, 1986. Maryland State Arts Council Grant, 1987, 1991. Lucille Medwick Memorial Award, Poetry Society of America, 1985. Poetry Committee Book Award, Folger Shakespeare Library, 1990. Nominated for Poets' Prize, Paragon, 1990, others
May inquiries be sent to you about doing workshops, readings? Yes

DETZER, CLARICE NISSLEY (1895-1982)

Born: December 11, 1895; Comanche, Iowa
Children: Karl Jr., Mary Jane
Education: Cornell College, Iowa. Columbia School of Journalism, New York, New York
Career: Chicago newspaper. After marriage, moved to Leland, Michigan, freelance writer

Writings: *True Tales, DCI* (with Karl Detzer) Bobbs Merrill 1925. *The Island Mail* Harcourt, Brace 1926. *The Marked Man* Bobbs Merrill 1927.*The Broken Three* (with Karl Detzer) Bobbs Merrill 1929. *Pirate of the Pine Lands* (with Karl Detzer) Bobbs Merrill 1929. *Contrabands* (with Karl Detzer) Bobbs Merrill 1936. *Carl Sandburg, Study in Personality* (with Karl Detzer) Harcourt Brace 1941. *The Mightiest Army* Readers' Digest 1945 (written with Karl while stationed with the army in Washington, DC). *Culture Under Canvas* (with Karl Detzer) Hastings House 1958. *Myself When Young* (with Karl Detzer) Funk & Wagnalls 1968. Short stories under both of their names

DETZER, KARL (1891-1987)
Pseudonym: Michel Costello, Wm. Henderson, Leland Woods
Born: September 4, 1891; Fort Wayne, Indiana
Parents: August Detzer, Laura (Goshorn) Detzer
Children: Karl, Jr., Mary Jane
Education: Fort Wayne High School, Fort Wayne, Indiana
Career: Newspaper Reporter, Photographer, Ft. Wayne, Indiana, 1909-1916. Indiana National Guard, Mexico Border, 1916-1917. Captain, Infantry, United States Army, World War I. Advertising Writer, Chicago, Illinois, 1920-1923. Screeplay writer, director, Hollywood, California, 1934-1936. Colonel, United States Army, 1944-1946. Roving Editor, *Readers' Digest,* 1938-1977. Publisher, *Enterprise-Tribune*, Leland, Michigan, 1947-1951. Chairman, Michigan Citizens Committee on Reorganization of State Government, 1950-1951. Special Adviser, Berlin, Germany, 1948

Writings:*True Tales, DCI* (with Clarice Nissley Detzer) Bobbs Merrill 1925. *The Marked Man* (with Clarice Nissley Detzer) Bobbs Merrill 1927. *The Broken Three* (with Clarice Nissley Detzer) Bobbs Merrill 1929. *Pirate of the Pine Lands* (with Clarice Nissley Detzer) Bobbs Merrill 1929. *Contrabands* (with Clarice Nissley Detzer) Bobbs Merrill 1936. *Carl Sandburg, Study in Personality* (with Clarice Nissley Detzer) Harcourt Brace 1941. *The Mightiest Army* (with Clarice Nissley Detzer) Readers' Digest 1945. *Army Reader* (edited with Clarice Nissley Detzer) Bobbs Merrill 1945. *Culture Under Canvas* (with Clarice Nissley Detzer) Hastings House 1958. *Myself When Young* (with Clarice Nissley Detzer) Funk & Wagnalls 1968. Included in several anthologies, numerous articles for *Readers' Digest*, others
Awards or inclusion in other biographical books: *American Authors & Books; Contemporary Authors; Michigan Authors,* 2nd ed.; *Who's Who in America, Indiana Authors and their Books; Who's Was Who among English and European Authors; Who Was Who among North American Authors; Who's Who in America.* Honorary Degree, Indiana University, 1979. Decorated, Distinguished Service Medal. Honorary member, Michigan State Police. Honorary life membership, Veterans of Foreign Wars

DEUR, LYNNE A.
Address: 830 East Savidge, Spring Lake, Michigan 49456
Born: March 14, 1941; Jamestown, New York
Parents: Milford L. Adams, Bessie H. Adams
Children: Vincent, Sara
Education: Hope College, B.A., Holland, Michigan, 1959-1963. Michigan State University, East Lansing, Michigan; M.A., doctoral program, 1989—.
Career: Publisher, River Road Publications, Inc., Spring Lake, Michigan, 1980—. Editor, Lerner Publications, Minneapolis, Minnesota, 1965-1967. Company Staff Writer, The Fideler Company, Grand Rapids, Michigan, 1963-1965

Writings: *Settling in Michigan* River Road Publications 1992. *Making of Michigan* River Road Publications 1987. *Explorers & Traders* River Road Publications 1985. *A Lumberjack's Story* River Road 1982. *Nishnawbe* River Road Publications 1981. *Before You Begin* Grand Haven Public Schools 1979. *Sixty-Five Years* Ottawa County 1976. *Political Cartoonists* Lerner Publications 1972. *Doers & Dreamers* Lerner Publications 1972. *Indian Chiefs* Lerner Publications 1972
Awards or inclusion in other biographical books: *Outstanding Young Women of America,* 1973

What is the aim or goal of your writing? "I am mainly interested in American history topics, attempting to combine the accuracy and skills of a historian with writing techniques that make it palatable to the student or general reader."
May inquiries be sent to you about doing workshops, readings? Yes

DEWITT, JIM CASSIUS

Address: 3922 Monte Carlo, Kentwood, Michigan 49512
Born: March 15, 1925; Grand Rapids, Michigan
Parents: George I. DeWitt; Marjorie (Dowling) DeWitt
Children: James, Cynthia, Christopher, Antony
Education: Montague High School. Michigan State University, B.A., East Lansing, Michigan, 1955-1959. University of Michigan, M.A.; A.B.D., Ann Arbor, Michigan, 1967. Calvin College, Grand Rapids, Michigan; Washington State, Bellingham; Bridgewater State, Massachusetts
Career: Fulltime writer, publishing books for schools, libraries, school libraries, working in home, 1983—. Teacher of language arts, 1952-1983. Taught at every level from elementary to adult education at East China Schools, Michigan. Marietta College, Ohio, Central Michigan University, Mt. Pleasant, Michigan. Ferris State University, Big Rapids, Michigan. Forest Hills High School, Grand Rapids, Michigan. Comstock Park High School, Michigan. Grandville Junior High, Michigan, others. Active in Michigan Council for the Arts, "Creative Writers in Schools" Program, Greater Grand Rapids. Writers/Poets Workshops

Writings: *Inventing From Me: How Writing Must Begin* Pen-Dec 1991. *Primer* Purple Peek Productions 1990. *The Zizzy Bird Connection* Pen-Dec 1989. *Fingernail Souffle* Pen-Dec Educational Publications 1988. *Collecting Shrillshadows* Purple Peek Productions 1987. *Night Balloon Fever Rising* Pen-Dec Educational Publications 1985. *Breath Etchings* Quality 1984. *Cloud Reflections in My Soup* Pen-Dec 1984. *Spelunkers Sideshow* Expedition Press l980. *Sprinting Into Sun* Pen-Dec 1979. *Just in Time* Fairmount Press 1972. *The En-Dec System* Pen-Dec 1972. Others-has 34 book titles, 21 titles for classroom use. Published poems and stories in about 350 small press publications, literary magazines, journals, anthologies and others, starting in 1976 such as *Peninsula Poets, Pegasus, Coffeehouse Poets Quarterly, Vegetarian Journal, Sisyphus, Michigan Natural Resources Magazine*. Work in Progress: Countless new poems and stories. Book, *Poetry Update-Newforms 1992*
Awards or inclusion in other biographical books: *Who's Who of Michigan Poets* 1982. Trophy, "Best Poet of the Year", Sarnia, 1976, 1978. Winner of Seminar 1977 Contest, Montgomery, Alabama. Poetry winner, Big Rapids "Pioneer's" Michigan Sesquicentennial Contest. Certificate, "Honorary Irish Poet"
What is the aim or goal of your writing? "To keep on writing/creating/inventing as long as I can do it (it's going so very well, just seems to get better and better)."
May inquiries be sent to you about doing workshops, readings? Yes

DICKERSON, ROBERT B.

Address: 2000 South Second St., Arlington, Virginia 22204. In summer: Accentor Lane, Hammond Bay, Cheboygan, Michigan 49721
Born: August 22, 1955; Detroit, Michigan
Parents: Robert B. Dickerson, Anna J. (Marlow) Dickerson
Education: Wayne State University, B.A., Detroit, Michigan, 1972-1974. Valencia, Spain, B.A., 1974-1979

Career: Director of Public Education, George Washington University Medical School, Washington DC, 1989—. President, Saville Books, Washington DC, 1988—. Senior Vice President, Rand Communication, Arlington, Virginia, 1983-1988. Editor, Reference Publications, Algonac, Michigan, 1979-1983. High school teacher, Ford of Spain, 1974--1979

Writings: Article in Vol. III *Encyclopaedia Africana* Reference 1992. Editor, *The Power of Prevention Cookbook* Saville 1991. Editor, *The Power of Prevention* Saville 1988. *Final Placement* Reference 1982. Index, *Concise Dictionary of Indian Tribes of North America* Reference 1980. Work in Progress: Novel loosely based on the fishing life of colorful Algonac, Michigan, Attorney Gerald M. Zamborowski. *Serpent in the Summer* Simon & Schuster to be out in 1993.

Awards or inclusion in other biographical books: Book of the Year (Children's), *Final Placement,* 1982. *Contemporary Authors* Vol. 104, and other who's who

What is the aim or goal of your writing? "To present historical and esoteric information in an amusing and entertaining manner."

May inquiries be sent to you about doing workshops, readings? Yes

DICKINSON-WASNER, ALINDA F. ALVAREZ
Address: 3627 Merritt Lake Drive, Metamora, Michigan 48455
Pseudonym: Alinda Alvarez; Melinda Redfeather
Born: October 22, 1945; Columbus, Ohio
Children: Erich, Lara, Jeremy
Education: Wittenberg University, B.A., Springfield, Ohio. Wayne State University, M.A.; Ph.D. Candidate, Detroit, Michigan
Career: Adjunct English Instructor, University of Detroit-Mercy, Detroit, Michigan, 1989—. Honors English Teacher, Detroit Public Schools, Detroit, Michigan, 1974-1989. Publicity Director, Detroit Adult and Community Education, Detroit, Michigan 1983-1985. Marketing Assistant, *Detroit Free Press,* 1973

Writings: *The Girl in the Red Sequin Hat* Paint Creek Press 1984. *Departures / Arrivals* Ridgeway Press 1985. *Anne Frank: Portals to Literature* (co-author). Included in *Tennessee Poets Anthology* 1989. Work in Progress: *The Best Way to Kill a Woman* Feminist Press 1993. *Holy Terror* (an ecclesiastical whodunit). Ain't No Gatsby-God's Little Bastard Child (memoirs). *The Church Lady From Dickens to Drieser: A Defense of the Mrs. Proudies in 19th Century Literature*

Awards or inclusion in other biographical books: Joanna Burgoyne Award, Amelia Press, 1989. Cranbrook Fellow, 1984. First Place Tompkins Awards, Fiction, Poetry, Essay; 1983, 1984, 1985. Lester Crowel Writing Awards, Wittenberg University, 1964, 1965. Wittenberg Review, First Place Poetry Award, 1967. Honorable Mention, Judith Siegel Pearson Awards, 1985

What is the aim or goal of your writing? "Purely selfish acts of self-discovery, or, I suppose, a search for intimacy—that momentary and fleeting sense of non-isolation/alienation."

May inquiries be sent to you about doing workshops, readings? Yes

DITCHOFF, PAMELA
Address: 605 Butterfield Drive, East Lansing, Michigan 48823
Born: September 21, 1950; Lansing, Michigan
Education: Michigan State University, Masters, East Lansing, Michigan, 1983-1985;

Bachelors, 1979-1982. Lansing Community College, Lansing, Michigan,1977-1979
Career: Instructor, Creative Writers in School, Michigan. Instructor, Quest Program for Gifted, Haslett, Michigan, 1985-1989. Graduate Teaching Assistant, Michigan State University, East Lansing, Michigan, 1986-1989. Copywriter/Creative Consultant, WFSL-TV, Lansing, Michigan, 1982-1984. Freelance copywriter, 1985-1987. Instructor, Lansing Community College, 1986-1987

Writings: *Poetry: One, Two, Three* Interact 1989. Stories appearing in *The Chicago Review, Vital Lines.* Poems in literary magazines such as *Negative Capability, Slipstream, Rhino, South Florida Poetry Review* and in anthology *The Tie That Binds.* Work in Progress: Teaching text, *Lexigram Learns America's Capitals.* Novel, *Prodigies*
Awards or inclusion in other biographical books: *Chicago Review,* Award for Fiction, 1991. John Ciardi Scholar, Bread Loaf conference, 1991. Bernice Jennings Traditional Poetry Prize, 1988. Scholar, Southampton Writers Conference, 1987. Michigan Addy Award for Excellence, 1984. Fellow, Virginia Center For the Creative Arts, Winter, 1981
What is the aim or goal of your writing? "The aim of my fiction and poetry is to urge the readers to examine their intentions. The aim of my nonfiction/creative nonfiction is to provide teaching materials in areas of study that lack creative approaches-to reach the imaginative spirit in children."
May inquiries be sent to you about doing workshops, readings? Yes

DODGE, MARY LOUISE
Address: 93 Vosper Street, Box 12, Saranac, Michigan 48881
Born: November 18, 1927; Montcalm County, Michigan
Parents: Harvey K. Dodge, Helen A. (Wallen) Dodge
Education: High School Education plus family library. First six years Grand Rapids Public Schools, final six years Saranac Public Schools
Career: Secretary/Bookkeeper, Saranac Tank and Coating, 1988-1991. Secretary/Bookkeeper/Phones, Advertiser Publishing, Saranac, Michigan, 1970-1988. Secretary/Bookkeeper, N.S. Johnson Insurance Agency, Saranac, Michigan, 1955-1968. Secretary/Bookkeeper, Forrest David Insurance Agency, Saranac, Michigan, 1947-1955. Employed in box office at Saranac Theatre from 1944 until it closed

Writings: *Tamara* Paperback Library 1969. *Sticks and Stones* Manor Books 1979. Star Trek short stories and short novels for *Delta Triad.* Newspaper columns on book reviews and travels in England for the local paper. Work in Progress: Mystery novel, *Stolen Grandmother*
What is the aim or goal of your writing? "Mostly it is for my own satisfaction (I like to tell stories), since most writers don't make enough to live on. Actually it's an obsession-some people drink, some people take drugs-I write!"
May inquiries be sent to you about doing workshops, readings? Yes

DODGE, ROY L. (1918-?)
Born: November 11, 1918, now deceased
Parents: Michigan pioneers

Writings: *History of the Dodge-Berry and Allied Families* Adams Press 1967. *Michigan Ghost Towns* Amateur Treasure Hunters Association 1970. *Michigan Ghost Towns, Volume 11* 1971. *Michigan Ghost Towns, Volume III* 1973. Vols. I, 11 reissued as: *Michigan Ghost Towns, Lower Peninsula* Glendon Publishing. *Ticket to Hell: a Saga of*

Michigan's Bad Men Northeastern Printers (Tawas City) 1975. *Michigan Ghost Towns of the Upper Peninsula* Glendon Publishing 1990. Started investigating Michigan ghost towns in 1954. Severely wounded in World War II but traveled to locations to meet with senior citizens who provided information. Wrote family history, series about northern Michigan towns published in *Bay City Times* 1968-1970, other volumes on particular periods and areas of Michigan; in other newspapers, magazines

DONAHUE, JAMES L.
Address: 41 E. Sanilac, Sandusky, Michigan 48471
Born: June 1, 1938; Harbor Beach, Michigan
Parents: Edwin G. Donahue, Velma L. Donahue
Children: Aaron, Ayn, Susan, Jennifer
Education: Harbor Beach High School, High School Diploma, 1952-1956. Central Michigan University, B.A. Degree-Journalism and English Literature, Mt. Pleasant, Michigan, 1956-1961
Career: Sanilac Bureau Reporter, *Times Herald,* Port Huron, Michigan, 1971—. Fine Arts and Religion Writer, *Kalamazoo Gazette*, Kalamazoo, Michigan, 1969-1971. Bureau Reporter, *News-Palladium,* Benton Harbor, Michigan, 1962-1969. Reporter, *Huron Daily Tribune,* Bad Axe, Michigan, 1961-1962

Writings: *Terrifying Steamboat Stories* A & M Publishing 1991. *Steaming Through Smoke and Fire-1871* Anchor Publications 1990. *Fiery Trial* (with Judge J. Lincoln) Historical Society of Michigan 1984. Work in Progress: *Steamers on Ice-1872.* Stories about schooners and sailing ships
What is the aim or goal of your writing? "Depict Michigan historical events-to tell stories of real events in an interesting style. Special interest in Great Lakes history."
May inquiries be sent to you about doing workshops, readings? Yes

DONER, MARY FRANCES
Born: July 29, 1893; Port Huron, Michigan
Parents: James Doner, Mary Jane (O'Rourke) Doner
Education: Holy Trinity Convent, Detroit, Michigan. Columbia University, New York University, College of the City of New York
Career: Staff writer, Dell Publishing, New York, New, York, 1924-1932. Reporter, *Herald-Traveller,* Boston, Massachusetts, 1928-1931. Writing teacher, Boston and West Shore Community College, Ludington, Michigan. Lecturer

Writings: *The Dancer in the Shadow* Chelsea House 1930. *The Dark Garden* Chelsea House 1930. *Let's Burn Our Bridges* Alfred H. King 1935. *Child of Conflict* Chelsea House 1936. *Gallant Traitor* Penn Publishing 1938. *Some Fell Among the Thorns* Penn Publishing 1939. *Chalice* Penn Publishing 1940. *Not By Bread Alone* Doubleday, Doran 1941. *Glass Mountain* Doubleday 1942. *O Distant Star!* Doubleday 1944. *Blue River* Doubleday 1946. *Cloud of Arrows* Doubleday 1950. *The Host Rock* Doubleday 1952. *The Salvager: the Life of Captain Tom Reid of the Great Lakes* Ross & Haines 1958. *The Shores of Home* Bouregy 1961. *While the River Flows* Bouregy 1962. *The Wind and the Fog* Bouregy 1963. *Cleavenger vs. Castle: A Case of Breach of Promise and Seduction* Dorrance 1968. *The Old House Remembers* Lakeside Printing 1968. *Pere Marquette: Soldier of the Cross* (booklet) Pere Marquette Society 1969. *Not By Appointment* Bouregy 1973. *The Darker Star* Bouregy 1974. Others. Nearly 300 short stories, novelettes. In *Charm, Toronto Daily Star, Woman's Home Companion, Chatelaine,* others.

Awards or inclusion in other biographical books: *American Authors & Books; American Novelists of Today; Authors' and Writers' Who's Who; Contemporary Authors; Foremost Women in Communications; Index to Women; Michigan Authors,* 1st ed., 2nd ed.; *Who's Who in America; Who's Who of American Women; Who's Who in the Midwest; Who's Who in the World; Writers Directory*

DORSON, RICHARD M. (1916-1981)
Born: March 12, 1916; New York, New York
Parents: Louis J. Dorson, Gertrude (Lester) Dorson
Children: Ronald, Roland, Jeffrey, Linda
Education: Harvard University, A.B., Cambridge, Massachusetts, 1937; M.A., 1940; Ph.D., 1943
Career: Instructor, Harvard University, Cambridge, Massachusetts, 1943-1944. Assistant Professor, Associate Professor, Professor, Michigan State University, East Lansing, Michigan, 1944-1957. Professor, Indiana University, Bloomington, Indiana, 1957-1971; Distinguished Professor, 1971-1981; Director of Folklore Institute, 1963-1981. Visiting Professor. Member of Smithsonian Institution Folklife Council, 1977-1981. Vice-President, International Society for Folk Narrative Research, 1959-1964, others. Founder, editor, *Journal of Folklore Institute,* 1963-1981. Book review editor of others

Writings: *Jonathan Draws the Long Bow: New England Popular Tales and Legends* Harvard University Press 1946; Russell 1970. *Bloodstoppers and Bearwalkers: Folk Traditions of the Upper Peninsula* Harvard University Press 1952, 1972. *America in Legend: Folklore From the Colonial Period to the Present* (Book-of-the-Month Club selection) Pantheon 1973. *Negro Folktales in Michigan* (editor) Harvard University Press 1956; Greenwood Press 1974. *Negro Tales From Pine Bluff, Arkansas, and Calvin, Michigan* Indiana Press 1958. *Folklore of the World* (editor) 38 vols. Arno 1980. Others. Contributor to *We Americans* National Geographic Society 1975, others. In *American Scholar, New Republic, Atlantic,* others
Awards or inclusion in other biographical books: *Contemporary Authors; Directory of American Scholars; Who's Who in America; Who's Who in the World.* Library of Congress fellowship, 1946. Chicago Folklore Prizes, 1947, 1965, 1969. Research grants: Smithsonian Institution, others. Fellowships: Guggenheim, American Council of Learned Societies, National Humanities Center

DOUGLAS, LLOYD CASSEL (1877-1951)
Born: August 27, 1877; Columbia City, Indiana
Parents: Alexander Jackson Douglas, Sarah Jane (Cassell) Douglas
Children: Bessie, Virginia
Education: Wittenberg College, B.A., Ohio, 1900; M.A., 1903. Hamma Divinity School, B.D., 1903. Fargo College, D.D., North Dakota, 1920
Career: Minister and lecturer, 1903-1933. Was pastor of the Congregational Church in Ann Arbor, Michigan for many years. Writer.

Writings: *Wanted- A Congregation* The Christian Century Press 1920. *An Affair of the Heart* Summit 1922. *Magnificent Obsession* Willett, Clark & Colby 1929. *Forgive Us Our Trespasses* Houghton Mifflin 1932. *Precious Jeopardy: A Christmas Story* Houghton Mifflin 1933. *Green Light* Grosset & Dunlap 1935. *White Banners* Houghton Mifflin 1936. *Home for Christmas* Houghton Mifflin 1937. *Disputed Passage* Houghton Mifflin 1939. *Doctor Hudson's Secret Journal* Houghton Mifflin 1939. *Invitation to Live* Grosset

and Dunlap 1940. *The Robe* Houghton Mifflin 1942. *The Big Fisherman* Houghton Mifflin 1948. *Time to Remember* Houghton Mifflin 1951. Others. Film versions.
Awards or inclusion in other biographical books: *American Authors & Books; American Novelists of Today; Cyclopedia of World Authors; Dictionary of American Biography; Everyman's Dictionary of Literary Biography, English and American; Lincoln Library of Language Arts; Michigan Authors,* 1st ed., 2nd ed.; *Oxford Companion to American Literature; Twentieth Century Authors; Twentieth Century Writing; Webster's American Biographies; Who Was Who among North American Authors; Who Was Who in America,* others

DRISCOLL, JACK
Born: March 7, 1946; Holyoke, Massachusetts
Parents: John Francis Driscoll, Teresa (Rheaume) Driscoll
Education: University of Massachusetts at Amherst, M.F.A., Amherst, Massachusetts, 1972
Career: Teacher, Interlochen Arts Academy, Interlochen, Michigan, 1975-1987

Writings: *Home Grown* Peaceweed Press 1972. *The Language of Bone: Poems* The Spring Valley Press 1979. *Fishing the Backwash* Ithaca House 1984. *Building the Cold From Memory* 1989. *Skylight: A Novel* Orchard Books 1991. *Wanting Only to be Heard* University of Massachusetts Press 1992. Poems in *North West Review, Poetry Northwest, Chelsea, Three Rivers Poetry Journal, Kansas Quarterly, Shenandoah,* others
Awards or inclusion in other biographical books: *Michigan Authors,* 2nd ed.; *Who's Who in Writers, Editors & Poets: United States & Canada.* NEA Fellow, 1982. In the 2nd Edition of *Michigan Authors* he is credited with: "Broadly speaking, my poems deal with the impossibility of maintaining human relationships. For example, in a series of poems ("Searching for Love") two people (let's call them husband and wife) are continually visited by a third who turns out to be the force that either pushes them apart or pulls them back together. In fact, this third person may not even be a separate identity but rather a part of each of them experiencing change. Sometimes we find a reconciliation, sometimes not. If not, we find characters in reclusion sorting out their lives. If so, we find a new set of rules by which to live, at least for a little while."

DUCEY, JEAN E.
Address: 1517 Hickory Street, Niles, Michigan 49120
Born: January 17, 1915; Berrien City, Michigan
Parents: L. J. Sparks, Verna M. (Young) Sparks
Children: John, Jay
Education: Lake Michigan Junior College, Benton Harbor, Michigan, 1969?-1971?
Career: Assistant Librarian, Niles Public Library, Niles, Michigan, 1950?-1959? Assistant in School Services/Children's, South Bend Public Library, South Bend, Indiana, 1960?-1962? Howard Community Schools, Elementary Library, Barron Lake, Michigan, 1962-1964? Central School, Niles, Michigan, 1964?-1968? Edwardsburg, Eagle Lake Library, 8 years until retirement.

Writings: *A Certain Slant of Light* Omnicomp 1991. *Out of This Nettle* Baker Book House 1983; Second Edition, Michiana News Service 1983. Poetry, essays, short fiction for adults and children, short nonfiction for adults and children. Work in Progress: *The Man With the Branded Hand, The Bitter-Sweet Time*
Awards or inclusion in other biographical books: *Out of This Nettle,* Juvenile

Award, University of Indiana Writer's Conference. *The Wind in His Fists*, Runner-up in National Contest, *Back Stage Magazine,* 1962; Runner-up in the National Contest, Broadway Theatre League, 1967

What is the aim or goal of your writing? "To improve in my writing each day; to learn more each day; to concentrate on more historical writing."

May inquiries be sent to you about doing workshops, readings? No

DUFRESNE, JIM F.

Address: P.O. Box 852, Clarkston, Michigan 48347

Born: August 15, 1955; Framingham, Massachusetts

Parents: Harris J. DuFresne, Eleanor N. DuFresne

Children: Jessica, Michael

Education: Grosse Ile High School, Michigan, 1970-1973. Michigan State University, B.A., Journalism, East Lansing, Michigan, 1973-1977

Career: Outdoor Writer, *Saginaw News,* 1986—. Feature writer for Booth Newspapers, a chain of eight major dailies in southern Michigan. Sports Information Director, University of Michigan-Dearborn, Michigan, 1983-1985. Outdoor Editor, *Juneau Empire,* Juneau, Alaska, 1978-1981. Sports Editor, *Port Lavaca Wave,* Port Lavaca, Texas, 1977-1978

Writings: *Trumping In New Zealand* Lonely Planet 1982. *Alaska: Travel Survival Kit* Lonely Planet 1983. *Isle Royale National Park: Foot Trails and Water Routes* Mountaineer-Books 1983. *Voyageurs National Park: Water Routes and Foot Paths* Mountaineer-Books 1985. *Glacier Bay National Park: A Backcountry Guide to the Glaciers and Beyond* Mountaineer-Books 1987. *Glaciers and Beyond* Mountaineer-Books 1987. *Michigan: Off the Beaten Path* Globe-Pequot 1988. *Michigan State Parks* Mountaineer-Books 1989. *Michigan's Best Outdoor Adventures for Children* Mountaineer-Books 1990. *50 Hikes in Lower Michigan* Backcountry Publications 1991. *Wild Michigan* Northwood Press 1992. *Lower Michigan's Best 75 Campgrounds* Glovebox Guidebooks 1992. Work in Progress: *Porcupine Mountains Wilderness Park*

Awards or inclusion in other biographical books: First Alaskan sportswriter in 1980 to win a national award from Associated Press, third place for best feature writing

May inquiries be sent to you about doing workshops, readings? Yes

DUKELOW, W. RICHARD

Address: 3801 Willoughby Road, Holt, Michigan 48824

Born: October 23, 1936; Princeton, Minnesota

Parents: William Robert Dukelow, Evelyn G. Dukelow

Children: Scott, Bruce, Kyle

Education: University of Minnesota, B.Sci., M. Sci., Ph.D, 1952-1962

Career: Professor and director, Michigan State University, East Lansing, Michigan, 1969—. Assistant Professor, University of Georgia, Athens, Georgia, 1964-1969. Assistant Professor, University of Minnesota, Grand Rapids, Minnesota, 1960-1964

Writings: *Reproduction and Development* Vol. 3 of *Comparative Primate Biology* Alan R. Liss 1986. *Nonhuman Primate Models for Human Diseases* CRC Press 1983. *Graduate Student Survival* Chas. Thomas 1980. About 200 full scientific research articles. Active as a free-lance outdoor writer. Work in Progress: *The Alpha Males,* a book on the early history and development of the U.S. Regional Primate Research Centers

What is the aim or goal of your writing? "Scientific writing to clarify science and

particularly the role of primates in research. Outdoor writing as a hobby, primarily oriented to fishing techniques, history and locations."
May inquiries be sent to you about doing workshops, readings? Yes

DUNBAR, WILLIS FREDERICK (1902-1970)
Born: June 9, 1902; Hartford, Michigan
Parents: Willis H. Dunbar, Nettie M. (Seabury) Dunbar
Children: Patricia, Robert
Education: Kalamazoo College, B.A., Kalamazoo, Michigan, 1924. University of Michigan, M.A., Ann Arbor, Michigan, 1932, Ph.D., 1939
Career: History Instructor and Instrumental Music Director, St. Joseph High School, 1924-1928. Professor, Kalamazoo College, 1928-1943. Dean, Kalamazoo College, 1938-1942. Program and Public Affairs Director, WKZO Kalamazoo and WJEF Grand Rapids, 1943-1951. Professor, Western Michigan University, 1951-1969. Chairman, History Department, Western Michigan University, 1960-1969. Writer, Lecturer. Adviser on Public Affairs to the Fetzer Broadcasting Company, with regular news commentaries and public affairs programs. Elected to Kalamazoo City Commission as Vice-Mayor 1951, 1953, 1955. Michigan State Historical Commissioner for 20 years, President of the Michigan Historical Society, and others

Writings: *Centennial History of Kalamazoo College* (co-author) Kalamazoo College Press 1933. *Michigan through the Centuries* 2 vols. Lewis 1955. *Kalamazoo and How it Grew* Western Michigan University Press1959. *Higher Education in Michigan's Constitution* The Commission 1961. *The Michigan Record in Higher Education* Wayne State University Press 1963. *A History of the Wolverine State* Eerdmans 1965. *All Aboard! History of Railroads in Michigan* Eerdmans 1965. *Life of Lewis Cass* Eerdmans 1965. *Michigan Historical Markers* (editor) Michigan Historical Commission 1967. *A Guide to Study Michigan* Michigan Department of Education 1967. *How it Was in Hartford: An Affectionate Account of a Michigan Small Town in the Early Years of the Twentieth Century* Eerdmans 1968. *A History of Education in Michigan* Michigan Historical Commission 1968. *Lewis Cass* Eerdmans 1970. Numerous articles in education and history journals such as *Michigan Alumnus Quarterly Review, Michigan History Magazine, School and Society, Social Education, Mississippi Valley Historical Review.* Contributor to *World Book Encyclopedia*
Awards or inclusion in other biographical books: *Contemporary Authors; Michigan Authors,* 1st ed., 2nd ed.; *Michigan Through the Centuries* (Family and Personal History: Vol. 4*); The National Cyclopaedia of American Biography.* Award of Merit, American Association for State and Local History, 1960. Kalamazoo, LL.D., 1965. Western Michigan University Alumni Association Distinguished Faculty Award, 1968

DUNLAP, CAROLINE M.
Address: 11949 Woods Court, R6, Gladwin, Michigan 48624
Born: September 28, 1940; Highland Park, Michigan
Parents: Orrin T. Seller, Pauline H. Seller
Children: Ingrid, Anna, Ellen, Sonja, Daniel
Education: Central Michigan University, Mt. Pleasant, Michigan, 1990-1992. Mid Michigan Community College, Associate of Arts, Harrison, Michigan, 1989-1990
Career: Secretary, Leelanau School, Glen Arbor, Michigan, 1987-1989. Secretary, Mid Michigan Community College, Harrison, Michigan, 1986-1987. Secretary, Clare-Gladwin Intermediate School District, Clare, Michigan, 1985-1986

Writings: *Gladwin: The Great Escape* Gladwin County Chamber of Commerce 1989. Published in *The Herald of Christian Science, Passages North, The Amaranth Review, Wellspring, Black River Review, The Gifted Child Today* and others. Work in Progress: Young Adult Novel
Awards or inclusion in other biographical books: Honorable Mention, *Black River Review Contest,* 1989. Norma Rhinehart Price Award, Mid Michigan Writers, 1988
What is the aim or goal of your writing? "To lift consciousness in an engrossing manner and to explore the human experience."
May inquiries be sent to you about doing workshops, readings? Yes

DUNNING, STEPHEN
Address: 517 Owego Street, Ann Arbor, Michigan 48104
Born: October 31, 1924; Duluth, Minnesota
Parents: Arthur S. Dunning, Julia H. Dunning
Children: Steven, Elizabeth, Julia, Sarah
Education: Carleton College, Northfield, Minnesota, 1945-1949. University of Minnesota, M.A., 1949-1951. Florida State University, Tallahassee, Florida, Ph.D., 1955-1959
Career: University of Michigan, Ann Arbor, Michigan, 1963-1988. Northwestern University, Evanston, Illinois, 1961-1963. Duke University, Durham, North Carolina, 1959-1961. High School Teaching, New Mexico, Minnesota, Florida, 1949-1959

Writings: 1959-1975, wrote, edited, co-edited about fifteen texts for junior and senior high school students: *Courage* Scholastic Books 1961. *Small World* Scholastic Books 1964. *Who I Am* Scholastic Books 1967. In 1975 began writing poetry, and in 1984, fiction: *Menominee* Years Press 1987. *Good Words* March Sheet Press 1992. *To the Beautiful Women* Samuel Russell 1991. Anthologies of poetry: *Reflections On a Gift of Watermelon Pickle* (co-edited) Scott, Foresman 1966. *Some Haystacks Don't Even Have Any Needle* (co-edited) Scott, Foresman 1969
Awards or inclusion in other biographical books: *Michigan Authors,* 2nd ed. Various Creative Artist Awards, Michigan Council for the Arts. Four Pen Syndicated Fiction Awards. "World's Best Short Short Story", Florida State, 1990. James B. Hall Short Fiction Award
What is the aim or goal of your writing? "I'm trying to discover my meanings by writing stories and poems. I trust memory and imagination equally."
May inquiries be sent to you about doing workshops, readings? Yes

DYBEK, STUART
Address: 320 Monroe, Kalamazoo, Michigan 49006
Born: April 10, 1942; Chicago, Illinois
Parents: Stanley Dybek, Adeline (Sala) Dybek
Children: Anne, Nicholas
Education: Loyola University, M.A., Chicago, Illinois, 1965-1967. University of Iowa, MFA, Iowa City, Iowa, 1970-1973
Career: Professor of English, Western Michigan University, Kalamazoo, Michigan, 1973—. Visiting Professor of Creative Writing, Princeton University, Princeton, New Jersey, 1990-1991. Creative Writing Fellow, University of Iowa, Iowa City, Iowa, 1970-1973. Junior High Teacher, Wayne Aspinal Junior High, St. Thomas, Virgin Islands, 1968-1970. Caseworker, Chicago, 1964-1966

Writings: *The Coast of Chicago* Knopf 1990. *Childhood and Other Neighborhoods* Ecco

1987. *Brass Knuckles* University of Pittsburgh Press 1979. Many magazine publications including: *The New Yorker, Atlantic, Harpers, Poetry, Paris Review* and others. Work in Progress: Collections of Poetry, Fiction, and a children's book

Awards or inclusion in other biographical books: Guggenheim Fellowship, NEA Fellowship, MCA Fellowships, Nelson Algren Award, Pushcart Prize, O. Henry First Prize, Three O' Henry Awards, Society of Midland Authors Prize in Fiction, Cliff Dweller Award, PEN Syndicated Fiction Prize, etc.

What is the aim or goal of your writing? "To make words sing."

May inquiries be sent to you about doing workshops, readings? Yes

DYER, WAYNE W.

Address: 1905 North Atlantic Blvd., Ft. Lauderdale Florida 33305

Born: May 10, 1940; Detroit, Michigan

Parents: Melvin Lyle, Hazel (Vollick) Dyer

Children: yes

Education: Wayne State University, B.S., Detroit, Michigan, 1965. Wayne State University, M.S. Detroit, Michigan 1966. Wayne State University, Ed.D., Detroit, Michigan 1970

Career: Resource Teacher/Counselor, Pershing High School, Detroit, 1965-1967. Director, Guidance & Counseling, Mercy High School, Farmington, Michigan, 1967-1971. Instructor, Wayne State University, 1969-1971 and summer school, 1970-1973. Staff Counsultant, Mental Health Association of Nassau County and Nassau County Department of Drug & Alcohol Addiction, 1973-1975. Assistant Professor, St. John's University, Jamaica, New York, 1971-1974. Various teaching positions, private counseling, therapy practice, speaker, guest on major radio and television shows-on talk shows in all fifty states and in foreign countries. Did various audiocassette albums.

Writings: *Real Magic: Creating Miracles in Your Everyday Life* Harper & Collins 1991. *You'll See It When You Believe It* William Morrow & Co. 1989. *Gifts from Eykis* Pocket Books 1983. *What Do You Really Want for Your Children?* William Morrow & Co. 1985. *Pulling Your Own Strings* Crowell 1978. *Your Erroneous Zones* Funk & Wagnalls 1976. *Counseling Techniques That Work: Applications to Individual and Group Counseling* (co-authored with John Vriend) American Personnel and Guidance Assoc. Press 1974. *Counseling Effectively in Groups* (Co-authored with John Vriend) Educational Technology 1973. Also: *The Sky's the Limit* and *Happy Holidays*. Magazine articles in such publications as: *Harper's Bazaar, Cosmopolitan, Family Circle* and professional journals

Awards or inclusion in other biographical books: *Michigan Authors,* 2nd ed.

E

EARNEY, FILLMORE C.F.
Address: 63 Elder Drive, Marquette, Michigan 49855
Born: October 25, 1931; Butts, Missouri
Parents: Patrick T. Earney; Grace V. (Wilderman) Earney
Children: Christopher, Peggy, Luanne
Education: Riverside Community College, Riverside, California, 1950-1951, 1954-1955. San Jose State University, San Jose, California, A.B., B.A., B.A., 1957; M.A., 1958. Michigan State University, Ph.D., East Lansing, Michigan, 1960-1965
Career: High School Teacher of Social and Biological Sciences, Chester, California, 1958-1960. Instructor/Assistant Professor of Geography, Castleton State College, Castleton, Vermont, 1961-1965. Associate Professor of Geography, Slippery Rock State College, Slippery Rock, Pennsylvania, 1965-1966. Assistant/Associate/Professor of Geography, Northern Michigan University, Marquette, Michigan, 1966—. Visiting Professor at the Geografisk Institutt, Universitetet i Bergen, 1982

Writings: *Marine Mineral Resources* Routledge 1990. *Ocean Mining: Geographic Perspectives* Geogrfisk Institutt (Norway) 1982. *Petroleum and Hard Minerals From the Sea* Edward Arnold 1980. *Proceedings: Twenty-First Annual Institute on Lake Superior Geology, April 30-May 4, 1975* Northern Michigan University 1975. *Researchers' Guide to Iron Ore* Libraries Unlimited 1974. Ten chapters in other books, 40 articles in refereed journals, 3 major monographs, 20 book reviews. Work in Progress: Chapter in a book, "United States Metallic Minerals: Conservation or Cornucopia?" *Conservation and Resource Management*
Awards or inclusion in other biographical books: *American Men and Women of Science; Community Leaders and Noteworthy Americans; Contemporary Authors; Dictionary of International Biography; Outstanding Educators of America; Who's Who Among Authors and Journalists.* Designated a Distinguished Professor, 1981. Michigan Association of Governing Boards Award for Extraordinary Contributions to Michigan Higher Education, 1982. Outstanding Faculty Award, 1991. Mortar Board Award for Excellence in Teaching and Advising, 1992
What is the aim or goal of your writing? "My goal is to further the knowledge of both the lay person and professional in industry and academia about the importance of mineral resources, especially as concerns the oceans."
May inquiries be sent to you about doing workshops, readings? Yes

EASTMAN, JOHN
Address: 4424 Moonlite, Kalamazoo, Michigan 49009
Born: April 23, 1935; Reed City, Michigan
Parents: Alva W. Eastman, Blanche M. Eastman
Education: University of Michigan, Ann Arbor, Michigan, 1962-1963. Western Michigan University, B.S., Kalamazoo, Michigan, 1963-1965
Career: Freelance Writer, Kalamazoo, Michigan, 1980—. Factoid Writer, TNT Cable Network, Atlanta, Georgia, 1991-1992. Copy Editor, Wadsworth Publishing Company, Belmont, California, 1978-1984. Wildlife biologist, Illinois Natural History Survey, Effingham, Illinois, 1966. Volunteer work with Kalamazoo Nature Center, Kalamazoo, Michigan, 1970's and 1986—.

Writings: *The Book of Forest and Thicket* Stackpole Books 1992. *Retakes: Behind the Scenes of 500 Classic Movies* Ballantine Books 1989. *Who Lived Where in Europe: A Biographical Guide to Homes and Museums* Facts on File Publications 1985. *Who Lived Where: A Biographical Guide to Homes and Museums* Facts on File Publications 1983; Bonanza Books 1987. *Kalama-Who? A Kalamazoo Quiz Book* (collaboration with Susan Woolley Stoddard-self-published) 1982. *Enjoying Birds in Michigan* (editor) Michigan Audubon Society 4th edition 1989. Contributed to *The Atlas of Breeding Birds of Michigan* Michigan State University Press 1991. Work in Progress: *The Book of Swamp and Bog* Stackpole Books scheduled 1994

Awards or inclusion in other biographical books: *Contemporary Authors,* Vol. 117

What is the aim or goal of your writing? "To write well in sharing my interests and to sell books."

May inquiries be sent to you about doing workshops, readings? Yes

EBERLY, CAROLE M.

Address: 1004 Michigan Avenue, East Lansing, Michigan 48823

Born: December 15, 1943; Detroit, Michigan

Parents: Paul W. Walaskay, Mary C. (Sintay) Walaskay

Children: Jessica

Education: Michigan State University, B.A., East Lansing, Michigan, 1962-1966; M.A., 1982-1985; Ph.D. 1989—.

Career: Instructor, Journalism, Michigan State University, East Lansing, Michigan, 1985—. Editor/publisher, Eberly Press, East Lansing, Michigan, 1977—. Capital Correspondent, Crain's Detroit Business, Detroit, Michigan, 1983-1984. Editor/publisher *Eberly's Michigan Journal* East Lansing, Michigan, 1979-1982. Legislative reporter, United Press International, Lansing, Michigan, 1968-1974. Reporter, *Charlevoix Courier,* Charlevoix, Michigan, 1966-1968

Writings: *Recipes of Americana: Potato Chip Cookies & Tomato Soup Cake* Eberly Press 1992. *Michigan Summers* Eberly Press 1990. *Christmas in Michigan* Eberly Press 1987. *101 Strawberry Recipes* Eberly Press 1986. *101 Cherry Recipes* Eberly Press 1984. *Brownie Recipes* Eberly Press 1983. *101 Fruit Recipes* Eberly Press 1983. *101 Vegetable Recipes* Eberly Press 1981. *More Michigan Cooking...and Other Things* Eberly Press 1981. *Our Michigan: Ethnic Tales & Recipes* Eberly Press 1979. *Wild Mushroom Recipes* Eberly Press 1979. *Michigan Puzzles* Eberly Press 1978. *101 Apple Recipes* Eberly Press 1977. *Michigan Cooking...and Other Things* Eberly Press 1977

Awards or inclusion in other biographical books: *Michigan Authors,* 2nd ed. Woman of Achievement, Michigan Press Women, 1981. Outstanding Alumni Award, College of Communication Arts & Sciences, Michigan State University, 1981. Second Place Non-fiction book, National Federation of Press Women, 1988. Numerous column writing and editing awards, National Federation of Press Women

What is the aim or goal of your writing? "My goal is to entertain readers and preserve part of Michigan's history by recording stories, letters and recipes around a central theme. Much of this material is overlooked for one reason or another. I'm unearthing these materials and presenting them in an entertaining manner, their value is highlighted and appreciated by a diverse readership."

May inquiries be sent to you about doing workshops, readings? Yes

EDDY, ARTHUR JEROME (1859-1920)
Born: November 5, 1859; Flint, Michigan
Parents: Jerome Eddy, Ellen Eddy
Education: Harvard University, Cambridge, Massachusetts, law degree
Career: Admitted to the Illinois bar, 1890, began practice in Chicago

Writings: *Delight, the Soul of Art* J.B. Lippincott 1902. *Tales of a Small Town, By One Who Lived There* J.B. Lippincott 1907. *Cubists, and Post-Impressionism* A.C. McClurg 1914. Others
Awards or inclusion in other biographical books: *Dictionary of North American Authors; Who Was Who in America*

ELLENS, JAY HAROLD
Address: 26705 Farmington Road, Farmington Hills, Michigan 48334
Born: July 16, 1932; McBain, Michigan
Parents: John S. Ellens, Grace (Kortman) Ellens
Children: Deborah Lynn, Jacqueline, Daniel Scott, Rebecca Jo, Harold Rocklan, Brenda Leigh
Education: Northern Michigan Christian High School, McBain, Michigan. Calvin College, B.A., Grand Rapids, Michigan, 1953. Calvin Seminary, BD, MDIV, Grand Rapids, Michigan, 1956. Princeton University, ThM., Princeton, New Jersey, 1963-1965. Wayne State University, Ph.D., Detroit, Michigan, 1966-1970. Certificates of Matriculation: Educational Sciences Institute, 1972; Cranbrook Institute for Advanced Pastoral Studies, 1965
Career: Executive Director, Christian Association for Psychological Studies, International (CAPS), 1974-1988, Emeritus. Founder and Editor in Chief, *Journal of Psychology and Christianity* 1975-1988. Pastor, Pastoral Theologian, Special Ministries, Presbytery of Detroit, Presbyterian Church USA, 1978—. Adjunct Professor of Pastoral Psychology, Drew University D.Min. Extension Program, 1980—. Interim Senior Pastor, Westminister Presybterian Church, 1984-1985. Guest Professor, Princeton Theological Seminary, 1977-1978. Director/Pastor of University Hills Christian Center/Church, 1969-1978. Professor of Communication Psychology, Calvin Seminary, Oakland Community College, Oakland University, 1967-1979. Pastor and Pastoral Counselor, North Hills Church of Troy, Michigan and Newton Christian Reformed Church, Newton, New Jersey, 1961-1969. U.S. Army Chaplain, 1956-1961; U.S. Army, USAR, 1955-1956, 1961-1989. Military Academy Liaison Office, U.S. Military Academy at Westpoint, New York, 1982-1985. Weekly television personality and host of one hour show on three Detroit channels and radio broadcasts, 1970-1975. International research and lecture tours throughout the world 1957-1989

Writings: *Dilemmas of War and Peace* (co-author) 1992. *Christian Perspectives on Human Development* Baker 1992. *Growing Up Holy and Wholly, Understanding and Hope for Adult Children of Evangelicals* (co-author) Wolgemuth and Hyatt 1990. *Gracia e Salud: los Beneficios del Perdon* (Argentina) 1990. *Counseling and the Human Predicament* (co-author) Baker 1989. *Psychotheology: Key Issues* UNISA Press 1987. *Psicoteologia: Aspectos Basicos* (Brazil) 1986. *Stress Management: Self and Ministry* AV Training Module, Academy of Health Sciences 1985. *Research in Mental Health and Religious Behavior* Psychological Studies Institute of Georgia State University (co-author) 1976. *Models of Religious Broadcasting* Eerdmans 1974. *Program Format in Religious Television* Wayne State University 1970. Many others. Over 100 professional

journal articles. Work in Progress: *Psychology in Worship, Practical Theology* and others
Awards or inclusion in other biographical books: *Dictionary of International Biography* 1982—; *International Who's Who of Educators* 1986—; *International Who's Who of Intellectuals* Vol VI—; *Men and Women of Distinction* 1982—; *National Distinguished Service Registry: Counseling and Development* 1989—; *Personalities of America* 1982—; *Personalities of the West and Midwest* 1982—; *Who's Who in America* 1983—; *Who's Who in American Education* 1990—; *Who's Who in Biblical Studies and Archaeology* 1986—; *Who's Who in Religion* 1990—. *Who's Who in Mental Health Professionals* 1986— *Who's Who in the Midwest* 1976—; *Who's Who in Theology and Science* 1990—. Knighted as Knight of Grace, Knights of Malta, 1974. Distinguished lecturer, guest professor, and others

What is the aim or goal of your writing? "To share my world view and sense of the meaning of life, growth, relationship, and hope. To articulate the relationship between religion and social sciences, faith and science, psychology and theology, the perspectives on God's nature and behavior and human growth and function as revealed by science. To explore the linguistic, cultural, historical, anthropological, and hermeneutical factors responsible for the shaping and rise and development of ancient Judaism, early Christianity, and the roots of Western Culture, philosophy, and theology. To leave a thoughtful heritage for my children, should they care to attend to it."
May inquiries be sent to you about doing workshops, readings? Yes

ELLIOTT, MARGARET
Address: 328 E. Saginaw Street, Breckenridge, Michigan 48615
Pseudonym: Ag-Kaa-Noo-Ma-Gaa-Qua
Born: August 31, 1904; Breckenridge, Michigan
Parents: Wilkie M. Drake, Rhoda M. Drake
Education: Albion College, A.B., Albion, Michigan, 1920-1924. University of Michigan, M.S., Ann Arbor, Michigan, 1924-1925. Additional graduate studies: Michigan State University, San Jose State, California, University of Oregon
Career: Freelance writer, retired, Breckenridge, Michigan. Librarian, Muskegon High School, Michigan, 1962-1969. Biology Teacher, Albion College, Albion, Michigan, 1925-1927. Biology Teacher, Bay View University, Petoskey, Michigan, 1927-1941. Biology teacher: Muskegon Community Schools, Revenna Public Schools, Reeths-Puffer Community Schools. Field Naturalist-Freelance Writer-Lecturer on nature, gardening, Native Americans, language subjects. Camp naturalist for DeGraf's Trout Lake Resort, 14 years. Central region chairman of the National Council of Federated State Garden Clubs. Board member, First Vice President for several years, Michigan Audubon Society

Writings: *A Number of Things* Gillette Natural History Association 1988; Dana Printing 1984. *Holy Hills* Workman 1982. Work in Progress: Weekly outdoor column in *Muskegon Chronicle,* 1931—. *ABC of Biblical Herbs. Year of Decision (Diary of Mary Jane Stanton Waggoner)1902.* Over 400 poems, articles for newspapers and magazines
Awards or inclusion in other biographical books: *Michigan Authors,* 2nd ed.; *Michigan Poets.* Distinguished Alumni Award, Albion College. Margaret Drake Elliott Park named in her honor, Muskegon, Michigan. Award, Michigan Audubon Society, 1979. Muskegon County Career Woman of the Year, 1963. Order of the Rose Award, Alpha Xi Delta, 1971. Adopted into the Ottawa Indian Tribe, 1961
What is the aim or goal of your writing? "To present an appreciation of the out-of-doors, in the world around us."

May inquiries be sent to you about doing workshops, readings? No

On the book jacket of *A Number of Things* appeared comment by Robert F. Mainone, Augusta, Michigan, Kellogg Bird Sanctuary's Interpretive Ecologist: "Legion are we whom she has encouraged toward self-realization, toward a spirit of oneness with spring forests, cries of shorebirds, ancient drum songs and the autumn leaves."

ELLISON, JAMES WHITFIELD

Address: 92 Christopher Street, 2nd Floor, New York, New York 10014
Born: May 15, 1931; Lansing, Michigan
Parents: Chester W. Ellison, Clara J. (Waber) Ellison
Children: Owen, Brett
Education: Michigan State College, B.A., East Lansing, Michigan, 1947-1950
Career: Book editor, *American Health* magazine, New York, New York, 1988—. Book editor, *Psychology Today* magazine, New York, New York, 1975-1984. Executive editor, Book-of-the-Month Club, New York, New York, 1967-1975. Senior editor, E.P. Dutton Publishing Company, New York, New York, 1962-1967. Staff screen writer, Columbia Pictures, Hollywood, California, 1955-1958

Writings: *Discovering the Power of Self-Hypnosis* (with Dr. S. Fisher) HarperCollins 1991. *Buddies* Seaview/Putnam 1983. *Proud Rachel* Stein & Day 1976. *The Summer After the War* Dodd, Mead 1972. *Descent* Little, Brown 1970. *Master Prim* Little, Brown 1968. *The Freest Man on Earth* Doubleday 1958. *I'm Owen Harrison Harding* Doubleday 1955. Work in Progress: Novel, *Dark Initiations*
Awards or inclusion in other biographical books: *Michigan Authors,* 2nd ed. Was awarded a lifetime fellowship in the novel at the Bread Loaf Writers' Conference, Middlebury College, 1955
What is the aim or goal of your writing? "To tell the psychological truth as best I can."
May inquiries be sent to you about doing workshops, readings? Yes

ELLISON, MAX (1914-1985)

Born: March 21, 1914; Bellaire, Michigan
Parents: Roy Ellison, Margaret (Fuller) Ellison
Children: Edith, Margaret, John, Roy, Andrew
Education: Bellaire Public Schools
Career: Writer, Poet-Bard

Writings: *The Underbark* Conway House 1969. *The Happenstance* Conway House 1972. *Double Take* Conway House 1973. *The Blue Bird* Conway House 1977. *Poems by Max Ellison* Conway House 1977. Poems included in *The Stone Circle Anthology* Stone Circle Press 1984. Work in Progress at the time of death: *It's Blowing Spring* (a collection of his poetry)
What is the aim or goal of your writing? In the previous edition of *Michigan Authors* he is credited with: "I have read poetry-my own and that of other poets-in college, universities, and public schools in 22 states. This is my way of opening up the world of poetry to students." Michigan poet, Terry Wooten commented about his friend: "Max Ellison was a trail blazer in the current revival of the oral tradition of poetry. His work has inspired a new generation of poets, who like Max strive to revitalize and bring poetry to life. He is still loved, respected and remembered by an amazing number of people from across the country. The 'Rascal Poet' to the end, his final work was sent to hundreds of schools at his request: 'Effective May 2, 1985 Max Ellison cancels all speaking engage-

ments. His Creator called his bluff... He had a pair of deuces against a full house.'" Terry Wooten's *Words Wild With Bloom* is an oral history, poem biography on Max Ellison. Terry relates: "He spent many hours at my kitchen table telling tales and this book is a result of those times. Max knew I was writing it before he died."
Awards or inclusion in other biographical books: *Authors in the News; Contemporary Authors; Michigan Authors,* 2nd ed.

ELLSWORTH, DOROTHEA J.
Address: 5657 Ellsworth Avenue, Stanton, Michigan 48888
Born: August 15, 1923; Six Lakes, Michigan
Parents: William J. Jorgensen, Lena (Wulff) Jorgensen
Children: Sherolyn (deceased), Joseph
Education: Lakeview High School, Michigan, High School Diploma, 1941. Montcalm County Normal, 2 year Teacher's Certificate, Stanton, Michigan, 1941-1942. Summer School, Central Michigan University, Mt. Pleasant, Michigan, 1943
Career: Housewife, Stanton, Michigan, 1944—. Montcalm County Agricultural Office, Stanton, Michigan, 1945-1946. Teacher, Mulholland School, Stanton, Michigan, 1943-1945. Teacher, Mt. Hope School, Carson City, Michigan, 1942-1943

Writings: *The Long Awaited Dream* Anderson Printing 1991. *This Dream is Real* Anderson Printing 1990. *Dreams Do Come True* Anderson Printing 1989. *Give Me My Dream* Anderson Printing 1988. *No Time to Dream* Anderson Printing 1987
What is the aim or goal of your writing? "The aim and reason for writing my books was to tell the story of my aunt's life which turned out to be a history of our family from 1891 to 1937. I wanted it to be a legacy of love to be handed down from generation to generation so the whole family would know the things my aunt shared with me while I was growing up in her home."
May inquiries be sent to you about doing workshops, readings? Yes

EPPS, JACK, JR.
Born: November 3, 1949; Detroit, Michigan
Parents: Jack Epps, Shirley Epps
Children: daughter
Education: Michigan State University, B.F.A., East Lansing, Michigan, 1972
Career: Cinematographer, 1973-1978. Screenwriter

Writings: (Screenplays): *Top Gun* (with Jim Cash) 1986. *Legal Eagles* (with Jim Cash) Zoetrope 1986. *The Secret of My Success* (with Jim Cash). *Izzy and Moe: First Draft, Original Screenplay* 198? *Turner and Hootch* (with Jim Cash) 1989. *Dick Tracy* (with Jim Cash) 1990. "Film Writers Cash and Epps Talk about their Craft and Reminisce about their Days at Michigan State University", sound recording 1986
Awards or inclusion in other biographical books: *Contemporary Authors*

EPSTEIN, HENRIETTA
Address: 17229 New Jersey, Southfield, Michigan 48075
Born: Highland Park, Michigan
Parents: Joseph Reznick, Edith Reznick
Children: Jared Paul, Jonathan Miles, David Benjamin
Education: Wayne State University, B.A., Detroit, Michigan, 1959-1973; Masters Program in English, 1990—.

Career: Instructor in English, Macomb Community College, Warren, Michigan, 1989—
Instructor in Literature, Center for Creative Studies, Detroit, Michigan, 1990—. Writer-in-Residence, Interlochen Academy for the Arts, Interlochen, Michigan, 1987-1988. President, Poetry Resource Center of Michigan, Detroit, Michigan, 1981-1989. Contributing Editor and Poetry/Feature Writer, *Monthly Detroit Magazine,* 1979-1983

Writings: *Contemporary Michigan Poetry: Poems From Third Coast* Wayne State University Press 1988. *The Necessary Pearl* Red Hanrahan Press 1976. Poems in *The Windsor Review, Moving Out, Wayne Review, Notes From the Underground, Passages North, The Denver Quarterly, The Bridge.* Articles in *Monthly Detroit, Detroit News Magazine, Detroit Free Press, American Photographer.* Work in Progress: Poetry, literary criticism

Awards or inclusion in other biographical books: Tomkins Award in Undergraduate Poetry, Wayne State University, 1967. University of Windsor Award for Literature in the Community, 1989

What is the aim or goal of your writing? "To make the best poems I can, while exploring the possibilities of the American language."

May inquiries be sent to you about doing workshops, readings? Yes

ERICKSON, LORENE F.

Address: 6848 Woodlea Road, Oscoda, Michigan 48750
Born: August 17, 1938; Detroit, Michigan
Parents: Leonard D. Billings, Lucy B. (Argabrite) Billings
Children: Lora, Martin, Matthew
Education: Wayne State University, M.E., Detroit, Michigan, 1976
Career: Instructor, Washtenaw Community College, Ann Arbor, Michigan, 1980—.

Writings: *Blood Mother* Ridgeway Press 1990. *Seasons of Small Purpose* Grand River Press 1980. Anthologies: *Contemporary Michigan Poetry: Third Coast; Her Soul Beneath the Bone; Woman Poet: Midwest; Green River Review: Michigan Poets*

What is the aim or goal of your writing? "Enhance, enlighten, entertain".

May inquiries be sent to you about doing workshops, readings? Yes

ERNO, RICHARD BRUCE

Born: May 11, 1923; Boyne City, Michigan
Parents: Richard Gabriel; Edith (Stafford) Erno
Children: Deborah, Bruce, Richard, Christopher, Joanna, Janice
Education: Michigan State University, B.A., East Lansing, Michigan, 1950. University of Denver, M.A., Denver, Colorado, 1951. University of Minnesota, Ph.D., 1953
Career: English Instructor, McCook Jr. College, McCook, Nebraska, 1953-1955. English Instructor, George Washington University, District of Columbia, 1955-1957. Professor, English, Arizona State University, Tempe, Arizona, beginning in 1957

Writings: *My Old Man* Crown Publishers 1955. *The Hunt* Crown Publishers 1959 *The Catwalk, a Novel* Crown Publishers 1965. *Johnny Come Jingle-O, a Novel* Crown Publishers 1967. *Billy Lightfoot* Crown Publishers 1969. *An Ultimate Retreat; a Family's Journey Back to Nature and Self-Renewal* Crown Publishers 1971

Awards or inclusion in other biographical books: *Biography Index; Contemporary Authors; Directory of American Scholars; Michigan Authors,* 2nd ed.; *Writers Directory*

In the 2nd edition of *Michigan Authors* appears: "He says: 'All my books are works of love-

love for the characters, for those characters' struggles, and for the art required to render those people and their lives eternal and unchanging'."

ESKRIDGE, ANN E.
Address: 17217 Fairfield, Detroit, Michigan 48221
Born: July 17, 1949; Chicago, Illinois
Parents: Arnett E.V. Eskridge, Marguerite M. Eskridge
Education: Parker High School, Chicago, Illinois. University of Oklahoma, B.A., Journalism, Norman, Oklahoma, 1968-1971. Michigan State University, M.A., Telecommunications, East Lansing, Michigan, 1978-1981
Career: Freelance writer, Detroit, Michigan, 1990—. Mass Media Teacher, Golightly Vocational Technical Center, Detroit, Michigan, 1983-1989. Public Relations, Administrative Assistant, 1983. Director, Nutrition Commission, Lansing, Michigan, 1982-1983. Television Reporter: WXYZ-TV, Detroit, Michigan, 1972-1976. WBEN-TV, Buffalo, New York, 1971-1972. KWTV, Oklahoma City, Oklahoma, 1970-1971

Writings: *Brother Future* 2 hour feature movie for Public Broadcasting System, aired February, 1991. Work in Progress: *Echoes Across the Prairie,* 3 part mini-series
Awards or inclusion in other biographical books: Michigan Council for the Arts Grant, script *The Shadow Man,* 1987. Chosen one of ten participants in the American Film Institute Summer Dramatic Scriptwriting Program. Michigan Council for the Arts Grant, script *Elmwood,* 1989. Women's Scriptwriters Forum, Grant for Research and Development, 1990. Warner Brothers Comedy Development Workshop Midwest Region, one of thirteen people chosen to attend
What is the aim or goal of your writing? "To combine the qualities of entertainment and education into television scripts."
May inquiries be sent to you about doing workshops, readings? Yes (workshops)

ESTLEMAN, LOREN D.
Born: September 15, 1952; Ann Arbor, Michigan
Parents: Leauvett Charles Estleman, Louise (Milankovich) Estleman
Education: Eastern Michigan University, B.A., Ypsilanti, Michigan, 1974
Career: Writer, *Michigan Fed,* Ann Arbor, Michigan. Cartoonist, *Ypsilanti Press,* 1967-1970. Reporter, *Community Foto-News,* Pinckney, Michigan, 1973; editor in chief, 1975-1976. Special writer, *Ann Arbor News,* Ann Arbor, Michigan 1976-1977. Staff writer, *Dexter Leader,* Dexter, Michigan, 1977-1980. Lecturer, instructor

Writings: *The Oklahoma Punk* Major Books 1976. *Sherlock Holmes vs. Dracula; or, The Adventure of the Sanguinary Count* Doubleday 1978. *Dr. Jekyll and Mr. Holmes* Doubleday 1978. *The Hider* Doubleday 1978. *The High Rocks* Doubleday 1979. *Stamping Ground* Doubleday 1980. *Motor City Blue* Houghton 1980. *Angel Eyes* Houghton 1981. *Aces & Eights* Doubleday 1981. *The Wolfer* Pocket Books 1981. *The Midnight Man* Houghton 1982. *Murdock's Law* Doubleday 1982. *The Glass Highway* Houghton 1983. *Mister St. John* Doubleday 1983. *This Old Bill* Doubleday 1984. *Kill Zone* Mysterious Press 1984. *The Stranglers* Doubleday 1984. *Gun Man* Doubleday 1985. *Roses are Dead* Mysterious Press 1985. *Any Man's Death* Mysterious Press 1986. *Sugartown* Houghton 1984. *Every Brilliant Eye* Houghton 1986. *Lady Yesterday* Houghton 1987. *The Wister Trace: Classic Novels of the American Frontier* Jameson Books 1987. *Lady Yesterday* Houghton 1987. *Red Highway* PaperJacks 1988. *Bloody Season* Bantam 1988. *Downriver* Houghton 1988. *General Murders* Houghton 1988. *Silent Thunder* Houghton 1989.

Peeper Bantam 1989. *Western Story* Doubleday 1989. *Whiskey River* Bantam Books 1990. *Sweet Women Lie* Houghton Mifflin 1990. *Sudden Country* Doubleday 1991. Others. Contributor to such magazines as *Baker Street Journal, TV Guide, Writer, Mystery Magazine, Pulpsmith*. Work appears in anthologies
Awards or inclusion in other biographical books: *Contemporary Authors; Twentieth-Century Crime and Mystery Writers; Twentieth-Century Western Writers*

ETHRIDGE, KENNETH E.
Address: 2900 Shenadoah, Royal Oak, Michigan 48073
Born: November 17, 1950; Ferndale, Michigan
Parents: Troy E. Ethridge, Eleanor M. Ethridge
Children: Christopher, Anna
Education: Oakland University, B.A., M.A., History, Rochester, Michigan, 1968-1978
Career: Webb Junior High School, English and Social Studies Teacher, Hazel Park School District, 1972-1988. Hazel Park High School, American and World History Teacher, Hazel Park School District, Hazel Park, Michigan, 1988—.

Writings: *Viola, Furgy, Bobbi & Me* Holiday House 1988. *Toothpick* Holiday House 1985; Troll Paperback 1988. Work in Progress: *One Sweet Dream. The Little Bird Drop*
Awards or inclusion in other biographical books: *Who's Who Among American High School Teachers,* 1992. *Toothpick*, nominated for Mark Twain Literary Award, 1986. *Viola, Furgy, Bobbi & Me*, a Young Adult Choice, International Reading Association and Children's Book Council, 1991
What is the aim or goal of your writing? "My writing deals with a theme that I believe is timely and important to young people, whether it deals with prejudice, terminal illness, alcohol abuse, or the elderly, I try to focus on it with realism and a sense of humor."
May inquiries be sent to you about doing workshops, readings? Yes

FANKELL, CHRISTINE A.
Address: 719 Novi Street, Northville, Michigan 48167
Born: October 12, 1960; Cedar Rapids, Iowa
Parents: Raymond A. Stephens; Yvonne R. Stephens
Children: Mackenzie, William
Education: Northville High School, Michigan, 1975-1979. University of Iowa, B.S. Elementary Education, Iowa City, Iowa,1980-1983
Career: 4th/5th Grade Teacher-Gifted, Livonia Public Schools, Livonia, Michigan, 1988—. Course Director, Society of Manufacturing Engineers, Dearborn, Michigan, 1988. Project Manager, Michigan Bell Communications, Southfield, Michigan, 1985-1987. Instructional Aide, Northville Public Schools, Northville, Michigan, 1984-1985

Writings: Published in literary journals such as *The Bridge, Red Cedar Review.* Work in Progress: Series of biographical poems based on my husband, Norm Fankell's life
What is the aim or goal of your writing? "My goal is to share the human experience with others through poetry."
May inquiries be sent to you about doing workshops, readings?Yes

FARLEY, CAROL J.
Address: 8574 W. Higgins Lake Drive, Roscommon, Michigan 48653
Born: December 20, 1936; Ludington, Michigan
Parents: Floyd McDole, Thressa O. (Moreen) McDole
Children: Denise, Elise, Roderick, Jeannette
Education: Western Michigan University, Special Teaching Certificate, Kalamazoo, Michigan, 1954-1956. Michigan State University, B.A. Communication, East Lansing, Michigan, 1967-1968. Central Michigan University, Masters in Children's Literature, Mt. Pleasant, Michigan, 1981-1983
Career: Freelance writing, instructor, Institute of Children's Literature, 1983—. English Teacher, Han Yong University, Seoul, Korea, 1977-1979. Various teaching jobs. Many workshops for young writers

Writings: *Korea, Land of the Morning Calm* Dillon 1991. *The Case of the Haunted Health Club* Avon 1991. *2041* (short story in anthology) Delacorte (Yolen) 1991. *The Case of the Lost Lookalike* Avon 1989. *The Case of the Vanishing Villain* Avon 1986. *Mystery of the Fog Man* Avon, Watts (4 books in this series) 1966-1986. *The Garden is Doing Fine* Atheneum 1975. Total of 21 published children's books. Many short stories, articles. Stories in *Children's Playmate, Cricket* 1992. Work in Progress: A new mystery story. Various short stories
Awards or inclusion in other biographical books: *Michigan Authors,* 2nd ed. Best book of the Year, Child Study Association, 1976. The Golden Kite, Society of Children's Book Writers, 1976. Best Juvenile by a Mid-West Writer, Friends of the Writer, 1978. Watts Mystery Medal, 1967. Children's Choice, IRA, 1987
What is the aim or goal of your writing? "To entertain kids and help them see the wonders of life. Also to show kids in other states and countries the beauty of Michigan-two of my books just came out in Japan for Japanese kids."
May inquiries be sent to you about doing workshops, readings? Yes

FARMER, SILAS (1839-1902)
Born: June 6, 1839; Detroit, Michigan
Parents: John F. Farmer
Career: Publisher. Elected City of Detroit Historiographer, 1882.

Writings: *The History of Detroit and Michigan; or,the Metropolis Illustrated; a Chronological Cyclopaedia of the Past and Present, including a Full Record of Territorial Days in Michigan, and the Annals of Wayne County* Silas Farmer & Company 1884, revised, enlarged 1889; revised and enlarged 1890. *History of Detroit and Wayne County and Early Michigan; A Chronological Cyclopedia of the Past and Present* 2 Vols. third edition revised and enlarged, Silas Farmer & Company 1890. *Detroit in 1890 Compared with 1870* Preston National Bank 1890. Map, (scale:1:31,680) "Detroit and its Environs" Silas Farmer & Company 1890. *The Michigan Book: a State Cyclopedia with Sectional County Maps, Alphabetically Arranged* Silas Farmer & Company 1901. Others
Awards or inclusion in other biographical books: *Allibone: A Critical Dictionary of English Literature; Appleton's Cyclopaedia of American Biography; Dictionary of American Authors; Dictionary of North American Authors; Twentienth Century Biographical Dictionary of Notable Americans; Who Was Who in America*

FASQUELLE, ETHEL ROWAN (1867-?)
Born: May 31, 1867; Little Rock, Illinois
Parents: Joseph A. C. Rowan
Education: Could not complete high school but attended University of Michigan, Ann Arbor, Michigan
Career: When eight years old, moved with her parents to Petoskey, Michigan where her father, as a Civil War veteran, took a claim for 160 acres of land. Writer, *Petoskey Evening News*. Freelance writer. Active in Michigan Historical Society, close acquaintance of Native Americans in northern Michigan.

Writings: *Ancient Guardians of the Straits of Michilimackinac* self-published, Petoskey, Michigan 1929. *When Michigan was Young: The Story of Its Beginnings, Early Legends and Folklore* (author was 83 years old at publication) Eerdmans 1950. Historical articles in many newspapers, magazines

FELTNER, CHARLES E.
Address: 166 S. Lafayette, Dearborn, Michigan 48124
Born: June 5, 1936; Raleigh, North Carolina
Parents: Charles E. Feltner, Irene (Robnett) Feltner
Children: Derek, Doug, Mark
Education: University of Illinois, Ph.D., Urbana, Illinois, 1958-1963. North Carolina State University, BSME, Raleigh, North Carolina, 1953-1957.
Career: Director, Ford Motor Company, Dearborn, Michigan, 1988—. Manager, Ford Motor Company, Dearborn, Michigan, 1969-1988. Supervisor, Ford Motor Company, Dearborn, Michigan, 1963-1969

Writings: *Shipwrecks of the Straits of Mackinac* (co-author) Seajay Publications 1991. *Great Lakes Maritime History: Bibliography and Sources of Information* (co-author) Seajay Publications 1982. Work in Progress: *Shipwrecks of Thunder Bay* (Alpena, Michigan)
What is the aim or goal of your writing? "Documenting the history of shipwrecks."
May inquiries be sent to you about doing workshops, readings? Yes

FELTNER, JERI BARON
Address: 166 S. Lafayette, Dearborn, Michigan 48124
Born: May 11, 1943; Detroit, Michigan
Parents: Edward M. Baron, Catherine (Dluski) Baron
Education: Henry Ford Community College, Associate Degree, Dearborn, Michigan, 1972
Career: President, Seajay Publications, Dearborn, Michigan, 1982—. Secretary, Ford Motor Company, Dearborn, Michigan, 1963-1975

Writings: *Shipwrecks of the Straits of Mackinac* (co-author) Seajay Publications 1991. *Great Lakes Maritime History: Bibliography & Sources of Information* (co-author) Seajay Publications 1982
What is the aim or goal of your writing? "Documenting the history of shipwrecks."
May inquiries be sent to you about doing workshops, readings? Yes

FENNER, CAROL B.
Address: 190 Rebecca Road, Battle Creek, Michigan 49015
Born: September 30, 1929; Almond, New York
Parents: Andrew J. Fenner, Esther (Rowe) Fenner. Married Jiles B. Williams-Maj. USAF Ret)
Education: Alfred Almond High School, Almond, New York, 1947-1949. James Madison High School, Brooklyn, New York, 1944-1946. New York University, various courses. New School of Social Research, Spanish. University of the Philippines, Spanish
Career: Public Relations consultant, self employed, 1971—. Copy Director, Battle Creek, Michigan, 1968-1971. Assistant to Public Relations Director, Girl Scout National Headquarters, New York, New York, 1964-1968. Assistant Editor, McCalls Corporation, New York, New York, 1962-1964

Writings: *Randall's Wall* Margaret K. McElderry Books 1991. *A Summer of Horses* Knopf 1989. "Saving Amelia Earhart", short story in *The Third Coast* Wayne State University Press 1982. *The Skates of Uncle Richard* Random House 1978. *Gorilla Gorilla* Random House 1973. "Deer Flight" *Cricket* November 1978. "Cat's Party" *Kalamazoo Collective* April 1985. Author/Illustrator-Juvenile Fiction: *Tigers in the Cellar* Harcourt Brace Jovanovich 1963. *Christmas Tree on the Mountain* Harcourt Brace Jovanovich 1966. *Lagalag, the Wanderer* Harcourt Brace Jovanovich 1968. Work in Progress: *Yolonda's Genius* (juvenile novel). *Running and Dancing* (short story juvenile collection). *Messenger of Jah* (adult short story collection)
Awards or inclusion in other biographical books:
Contemporary Authors; Children & Books; Children's Literature in the Elementary School; A Critical Appraisal of Children's Literature; Dictionary of International Biography; Directory of British and American Writers; Illustrators of Children's Books; International Authors and Writers Who's Who; Something about the Author; The Writer's Directory. Notable Book, American Library Association, 1963. Coretta Scott King Freedom Award, runner-up 1979. Winner, Christopher Award for non-fiction, 1973. Outstanding Science Trade Book For Children, National Science Trade Association, 1973. Notable Book, ALA, Library of Congress Book of the Year, 1973. Proposed for 1974 Newbery Medal. Michigan Council for the Arts Grant, 1982. Member of Michgan Council for the Arts Literature Panel, 1976-1979
What is the aim or goal of your writing? "It is quite selfish: to explore things that bother or excite me in order to clarify or identify or simply illuminate without solving

these things. I am interested in fear and fantasizing and how they serve us. I am concerned about the dreadful educational provisions for our very poor. I never know what will push me into another book (and when)."
May inquiries be sent to you about doing workshops, readings? Yes

FERBER, EDNA (1885-1968)
Born: August 15, 1885; Kalamazoo, Michigan
Parents: Jacob Charles Ferber, Julia (Neuman) Ferber
Education: Ryan High School, Appleton, Wisconsin, graduated in 1902
Career: Reporter, Appleton *Daily Crescent,* 1902-1904, others in Milwaukee, Chicago. Lived in New York after 1912 and served as war correspondent with the U.S. Air Force during World War II

Writings: *Buttered Side Down* Stokes 1912. *Roast Beef, Medium: The Business Adventures of Emma McChesney* Stokes 1913. *Personality Plus: Some Experiences of Emma McChesney and Her Son, Jock* Stokes 1914. *Emma McChesney and Co.* Stokes 1915. *Fanny Herself* Stokes 1917. *Cheerful, By Request* Doubleday 1918. *$1200 a Year* (with Newman Levy) Doubleday 1920. *Half Portions* Doubleday 1920. *The Girls* Doubleday 1921. *Gigolo* Doubleday 1922. *So Big.* Doubleday 1924. *Old Man Minick, a Short Story* Doubleday, Page 1924. *Show Boat* Doubleday 1926. *Mother Knows Best: A Fiction Book* Doubleday 1927. *Cimarron* Doubleday 1930. *American Beauty* Doubleday 1931. *They Brought Their Women: A Book of Short Stories* Doubleday 1933. *Come and Get It* Doubleday 1935. *Nobody's in Town* Doubleday 1938. *A Peculiar Treasure* (autobiography) Doubleday, Doran & Company 1939. *Saratoga Trunk* Doubleday 1941. *Great Son* Doubleday 1945. *One Basket: Thirty-One Short Stories* Simon and Schuster 1947. *Giant* Doubleday 1952. *Ice Palace* Doubleday 1958. *A Kind of Magic* (autobiography) Doubleday 1963. Others. Many novels became musicals, movies. Collaborated with George S. Kaufman in several plays such as *The Royal Family; a Comedy in Three Acts*
Awards or inclusion in other biographical books: *American Books & Authors; American Novelists of Today; American Women Writers; Encyclopedia of World Literature in the 20th Century; Filmgoer's Companion; Modern American Literature; Oxford Campanion to American Literature; Something about the Author; Twentieth Century Authors; Who Was Who among North American Authors; Who Was Who in America; Who's Was Who in the Theatre,* others. Pulitzer Prize 1924. Litt.D., Columbia University, New York and Adelphi College, Garden City, New York

FERGUSON, MARION E.
Address: 297 Lake Breeze, Brighton, Michigan 48116
Born: October 11, 1939; Detroit, Michigan
Parents: Arnold R. Pampreen, Betty A. (Champine) Pampreen
Children: Evert Van Raden, James Van Raden, Michael Van Raden, Donald Van Raden
Education: Brighton High School, Brighton, Michigan, 1976-1977. Washtenaw Community College, Ann Arbor, Michigan, 1987-1988
Career: Rural Mail Carrier, U.S. Postal Service, Brighton, Michigan, 1966—.

Writings: *Mid-Life Cycles* Wilderness Adventure Books 1991.
Work in Progress: Gathering information for family history
What is the aim or goal of your writing? "To share my experiences with those who cannot do the things I've done especially in the mid-life years. To inspire others to try it."
May inquiries be sent to you about doing workshops, readings? Yes

FERRY, CHARLES
Address: 165 Wimpole Drive, Rochester Hills, Michigan 48309
Born: October 8, 1927; Chicago, Illinois
Education: At age 16 joined the U.S. Navy
Career: Forty-three years experience in journalism and related fields-newspapers, radio, television, advertising. Still a professional writer.

Writings: *Binge* Daisy Hill Press 1992. *One More Time!* Houghton Mifflin 1985. *Raspberry One* Houghton Mifflin 1983. *O Zebron Falls!* Houghton Mifflin 1977. *Up in Sister Bay* Houghton Mifflin 1975. Work in Progress: *Royalty in the House* (a young girl becomes queen of the 4-H fair). *The Clarion Kids* (young people working for a weekly newspaper)
Awards or inclusion in other biographical books: *Raspberry One,* a *School Library Journal* Best Book of Year; an American Library Association Best Young Adult Book; Best Juvenile book (First Prize) of 1983 by Friends of American Writers
What is the aim or goal of your writing? "To promote love and friendship."
May inquiries be sent to you about doing workshops, readings? Yes

FETTIG, ARTHUR (ART) J.
Address: 31 East Ave. S, Battle Creek, Michigan 49017
Born: July 5, 1929; Detroit, Michigan
Parents: Arthur J. Fettig; Jenny A. (Sands) Fettig
Children: Nancy, Daniel, Amy, David, Rose Marie (deceased)
Education: University of Detroit High School, Detroit, Michigan, 1943-1947
Career: Clerk-Claim Agent-Employee Communications Officer, Corporate Relations Officer, Grand Trunk Western Railroad, Detroit-Battle Creek, Michigan, 1948-1983. President-CEO, Growth Unlimited Inc., Battle Creek, Michigan, 1983—

Writings: *More Great Safety Meeting Ideas* Growth Unlimited Inc. 1991. *A Declaration of Inter-Dependence for Safety* Growth Unlimited Inc. 1991. *Selling Safety in the 90's* Growth Unlimited Inc. 1990. *World's Greatest Safety Meeting Idea Book* Growth Unlimited Inc. 1990. *Selling Luckier Yet* Growth Unlimited Inc. 1987. *The Pos Activity Book* Growth Unlimited Inc. 1984, 1987. *Como Meterse Al Publico En El Bolsillo* Growth Unlimited Inc. 1982. *The Three Robots* Growth Unlimited Inc. 1981. Others. Booklets by Growth Unlimited Inc. such as: "The Santa Train", "Growth", "This is It", "Anatomy of a Speech", others. Wide range of audio and video selections such as "You Can Sell Your Writing", 17 videos in the Safety Field. Other series. Work in Progress: *Love is the Target,* a book
Awards or inclusion in other biographical books: *Who's Who in Michigan* 1936. Christopher Leadership Award, 1988
What is the aim or goal of your writing? "To bring positive living concepts to people throughout the world."
May inquiries be sent to you about doing workshops, readings? Yes

FIELD, ELLYCE R.
Address: 3311 Parkland, West Bloomfield, Michigan 48322
Born: October 14, 1951; Detroit, Michigan
Parents: Charles Ruben, Belle Ruben
Children: Jordan, Andrew, Garrett
Education: Southfield High School. University of Michigan, Ann Arbor, Michigan, B.A., 1973; M.A., 1976

Career: English Teacher, Hartland High School, Hartland, Michigan, 1973-1977. Columnist, "Kid Stuff", *The Detroit News*, 1987—.

Writings: *Kids Catalog of Michigan Adventures* Wayne State University Press 1993. *Detroit Kids Catalog: The Hometown Tourist* Wayne State University Press 1990. *Kids and Cars: A Parent's Survival Guide to Family Travel* Melius Publishing 1988

What is the aim or goal of your writing? "To help parents enjoy spending time with their children; help them explore Michigan and also increase their ability to plan hassle-free trips. To highlight Michigan's family sites and introduce families to current children's entertainers."

May inquiries be sent to you about doing workshops, readings? Yes

FILKINS, KENN D.

Address: 2160 W. Coleman Road, Farwell, Michigan 48622

Born: August 31, 1957; Flint, Michigan

Parents: Earl J. Filkins, Lucille J. Fiklins

Children: Micaiah, Andrew (wife Carol)

Education: Great Lakes Christian College, Bachelors of Religious Education, 1975-1979. Ferris State College, Big Rapids, Michigan, 1975

Career: Minister, Gilmore Church of Christ, Farwell, Michigan, 1990—. Minister, Fort Dodge Church of Christ, Fort Dodge, Iowa, 1988-1990. Minister, Rolling Prairie, First Christian Church, Rolling Prairie, Indiana, 1981-1988. High School Teacher, LaCrosse Public Schools, LaCrosse, Indiana, 1979-1981. Editor-in-Chief, *The Celebration of Falconry,* anthology of falconry stories

Writings: Articles in such magazines as: *Byline, Michigan Out-of-Doors, Michigan Sportsman, Iowa Game & Fish, Clare County Review, Great Plains Game & Fish, Flyfishing, Christian Standard, Vista, Lookout, Sports Afield, Hawk Chalk.* Work in Progress: *Comfort Those Who Mourn* (book). Book tentatively titled *Wilderness Canoe Camps: A Guide to Leading Christian Adventures in Michigan.* Numerous articles such as "Innkeeper-Villain or Hero?", "Undercover and No Way Out".

Awards or inclusion in other biographical books: *Outstanding Young Men in America,* 1985; *Who's Who of High School Students,* 1975. Drachma Award Winner, Great Lakes Christian College, 1979. Writing Student of the Year, Christian Writer's Institute, 1991

What is the aim or goal of your writing? "I write because I'm a writer. I've written ever since I was a boy, though didn't seek publication until 1981. As a boy mock-dialogue would run through my head, like baseball plays did for other boys. Writing is a catharsis. It keeps my thinking sharp, makes me learn and listen to myself. Writing frees me to grab the fleeting muse and capture it with black letters on white pages. Concretely I aim to become the best writer that I can be. Therefore I write several types of material; magazine articles, short stories, articles, greeting cards, satire and humor pieces. To get better I must write, so I seek 'assignments' from magazines to force me to keep constantly writing. Ultimately, I seek to write several books including some on Christian ministry, fishing, outdoors, falconry, specific Michigan rivers, and some historical novels (one story-line is about the St. Mary's Rapids area in Sault Ste. Marie)."

May inquiries be sent to you about doing workshops, readings? Yes

FILLER, LOUIS
Address: P.O. Box 1, Ovid, Michigan 48866
Born: May 2, 1912; Odessa, Russia
Parents: Pit Filler, Sarah Filler
Children: Emily, Graham
Education: Temple University, A.B., Philadelphia, Pennsylvania, 1929-1934. Columbia University, Ph.D., New York, 1940-1942
Career: Independent Author, Ovid, Michigan, 1977—. Professor, Antioch College, Yellow Springs, Ohio, 1945-1977. Writing, teaching, advising, lecturing, 1939—.

Writings: *Distinguished Shades: Americans Whose Lives Live On* 1992. *The President in the 20th Century* Vol. 2, 1991. *Appointment at Armagaddon: Muckraking and Progressivism in the American Tradition* 1976. *Randolph Bourne* 1965. *The Crusade Against Slavery, 1830-1860* 1960. *A Dictionary of American Social Reform* 1963, 1970. *The Unknown Edwin Markham* 1966. *Muckraking and Progressivism: an Interpretive Bibliography* 1976. Edited Works: *The New Start: Life and Labor in Old Missouri,* Manie Morgan 1949. *Mr. Dooley: Now and Forever,* Finley Peter Dunne 1954. *American Liberalism of the Late Nineteenth Century,* anthology, 1961. *The Removal of the Cherokee Nation: Manifest Destiny or National Dishonor?* 1962. *The World of Mr. Dooley,* 1962. *The Anxious Years,* anthology of the 1930's literature, 1963. *Horace Mann on the Crisis in Education* 1965; Spanish translation, 1972. *Wendell Phillips on Civil Rights and Freedom* 1965. *The Ballad of the Gallows-Bird,* Edwin Markham 1967. *Old Wolfville: the Fiction of A.H. Lewis* 1968. *Slavery in the United States of America* 1972. *Abolition and Social Justice* 1972. Others. Introduction to 13 books such as *Democrats and Republicans* by Harry Thurston Peck 1964. Work in Progress: "I keep up with my subjects, an overview indicating a concern for American traditions, notably in Progressivism and Reform."
Awards or inclusion in other biographical books: Two books received the Ohio Library Association Annual Award
What is the aim or goal of your writing? "Perspective on the American past. Continuity."
May inquiries be sent to you about doing workshops, readings? Yes; but all depends on circumstances and conditions

FISHER, AILEEN L.
Address: 505 College Ave., Boulder, Colorado 80302
Born: September 9, 1906; Iron River, Michigan
Parents: Nelson E. Fisher, Lucia M. Fisher
Education: Iron River High School, Michigan. University of Chicago, 1923-1925. University of Missouri, School of Journalism, B.J., 1925-1927
Career: Women's National Journalistic Register, Director, Chicago, Illinois, 1928-1930. Statistician, Labor Bureau of the Middle West, Chicago, Illinois, 1930-1933. Freelance writer, 1933—.

Writings: *Always Wondering* Harper/Collins 1991. Over 90 books published for children and young adults-plays, verse, fiction, non-fiction (mostly natural history)-biography. Work in Progress: Children's verse
Awards or inclusion in other biographical books: Junior Literary Guild Books: *The Coffee-Pot Face* 1933. *All on a Mountain Day* 1956. *Summer of Little Rain* 1961. *We Dickinsons* 1965. *Feathered Ones and Furry* 1971. Notable Books of the Year, American

Library Association: *My Cousin Abe* 1962. *Listen, Rabbit* 1964. *In the Middle of the Night* 1965. *Valley of the Smallest* 1966. *We Dickinsons* 1965. Western Writers of America, Spur Award: *Valley of the Smallest* 1967. National Council of Teachers of English, Award for Poetry for Children, 1978

May inquiries be sent to you about doing workshops, readings? No workshops

FITTING, JAMES EDWARD

Born: January 18, 1939; Detroit, Michigan
Parents: Edward A. Fitting, Lora (Nunneley) Fitting
Children: Sean, Erik, Christine, Timothy
Education: Michigan State University, B.A., East Lansing, Michigan 1960. University of Michigan, M.A., Ann Arbor, Michigan: M.A., 1962, Ph.D., 1964
Career: Assistant Professor, University of Michigan, Ann Arbor, Michigan, 1964-1968. Associate Professor/Professor, Case Western Reserve University, Cleveland, Ohio, 1968-1972. State Archeologist of Michigan, 1972-1975. Planner and Department Manager, Commonwealth Associates, 1975-1978. Editor, *Michigan Archaeologist,* 1964-1968; *Case Western Reserve University Studies in Anthropology,* 1968-1972, others

Writings: *Late Woodland Cultures of Southeastern Michigan* University of Michigan 1965. *Studies in the Natural Radioactivity of Prehistoric Materials* (co-editor, contributor) University of Michigan 1965. *Contributions to Michigan Archaeology* University of Michigan 1968. *Fred Dustin's Saginaw Valley Archaeology* Michigan Archaeological Society 1968. *Selections from the Michigan Archaeologist* Volumes I-X, (editor) Michigan Archaeological Society 1969. *The Archaeology of Michigan: A Guide to the Prehistory of the Great Lakes Region* Natural History Press 1970. *The Archaeology of Michigan: A Guide to the Prehistory of the Great Lakes Region* Cranbrook Institute of Science 1975. *Archaeological Excavations at the Marquette Mission Site, St. Ignace, Michigan, in 1972* Michigan Archaeological Society 1976. *The Development of North American Archeology* Pennsylvania State University Press 1973. *An Archeological and Historical Survey of the Grass Rope Unit, Lower Brule, South Dakota* The Associates 1978. *Late Woodland Cultures of Southeastern Michigan* University of Michigan 1980. *Prehistoric Projectile Points of Michigan* University of Michigan 1981. *Pioneering the Past: the Development of Archaeology in Michigan* Michigan History Division 1984. Others
Awards or inclusion in other biographical books: *American Men and Women of Science; Contemporary Authors; Directory of American Scholars; Michigan Authors,* 2nd ed.; *Who's Who in the Midwest.* In the 2nd edition of *Michigan Authors* he is credited with: "I am a lifelong resident of Michigan and am fascinated with its past. While I have carried out anthropological and historical research in 22 states and three foreign countries, Michigan is the most exciting of them all."

FITZMAURICE, JOHN W. (1833-?)

Born: May 25, 1833; Cape Breton Island, Gulf of St. Lawrence
Parents: Father an officer, Royal Navy
Education: Niagara, Ontario
Career: Royal Navy, entered at 15 for 3 year hitch. Iron worker, Buffalo, New York. Moved to Richmond Hill, Ontario, decided to prepare for the ministry. 1865, moved to Bedford, Calhoun County, Michigan, was ordained. After preaching in various Michigan communities, he abandoned ministry, 1870. Worked in several newspapers, Saginaw area. Left journalism to work full-time in temperance movement until 1880. Traveled to

lumber camps selling health insurance for Bay City Hospital for 4 years. After moving to Minnesota and Missouri, he came to Cheboygan, Michigan and wrote *The Shanty Boy*. Moved to Saginaw and sold real estate

Writings: *"The Shanty Boy", or, Life in a Lumber Camp: Being Pictures of the Pine Woods in Descriptions, Tales, Songs and Adventures in the Lumbering Shanties of Michigan and Wisconsin* Democrat Steam Print (Cheboygan)1889; Clark Historical Library 1963; Literature House 1970; Hardscrabble Books 1979. *Water Witch of Mackinac: A Tale of the Recollet Fathers in Northern Michigan, 1622* Detroit Sunday News-Tribune 1898. Stories appeared in *Saginaw Daily Republican, Flint Daily Journal,* others

FITZPATRICK, DOYLE C.
Born: March 9, 1908; St. Johns, Michigan
Parents: Rutherford Hayes Fitzpatrick; Jessie Mable (Irving) Fitzpatrick
Children: Leland, Colleen, Susan, Marsha
Education: Michigan State University
Career: Owner, Sales Promotion Company. Vice President, Industrial Display Corporation. Supervisor of Art, General Motors, Olds Division, 1942-1973, retired

Writings: *The King Strang Story; a Vindication of James J. Strang, the Beaver Island Mormon King* National Heritage (Lansing) 1970
Awards or inclusion in other biographical books: *Michigan Authors,* 2nd ed.
In the 2nd edition of *Michigan Authors* appears: "He says: 'I am actively interested in American History, and have devoted years to the study of Strangite Mormon phenomena. We live at Beaver Island all year round on property once owned by 'King Strang'."

FOEHL, HAROLD MAITLAND (1903-1992)
Born: November 10, 1903; Saginaw, Michigan
Parents: Henry E. Foehl, Elizabeth M. Foehl
Education: Saginaw High School, Saginaw, Michigan, 1921. American Academy of Arts and the Chicago Academy of Fine Arts, Warren School of Color, The New York School of Interior Decoration
Career: Supervision of civil engineering projects/product manufacturing, General Motors Corporation. Supervised, planned, City of Saginaw parks construction projects. Advertising agency, self-employed, 25 years

Writings: *The Story of Logging the White Pine in the Saginaw Valley* (with Irene M. Hargreaves) Red Keg Press (Bay City, Michigan) 1964. *McTaggart's Red Keg: Eighteen Sixty-Seven to Eighteen Sixty-Eight: Logging from A-Z on the Tittabawassee in Michigan* (with Irene M. Hargreaves) Red Keg Press (Bay City, Michigan) 1988

FOOTMAN SMOTHERS, ETHEL L.
Address: 441 Adams, S.E., Grand Rapids, Michigan 49507
Born: April 5, 1944; Camillia, Georgia
Parents: Ira L. Footman, Ethel Footman
Children: Delsey, Darla, Dana, Dion
Education: Jewett High School, Winter Haven, Florida, 1963. Grand Rapids Community College, Associate Degree/Liberal Arts, Grand Rapids, Michigan, 1974-1981
Career: Service Specialist, Amway Corporation, Ada, Michigan, 1989—; Telephone Order Processor, 1980-1989

Writings: *Down in the Piney Woods* Knopf 1992. Articles in *Grand Rapids Press, Today's Christian Parent.* Poetry in *Ebony Jr!, Insight, Cat Magazine.* Work in Progress: Children's novel, historical fiction, 1865

What is the aim or goal of your writing? "Above all, the aim of my writing is to produce good literature for children. By introducing them to characters that are 'doers', it is my hope that they will build 'can do' attitudes, and strive to be high achievers."

May inquiries be sent to you about doing workshops, readings? Yes. Readings only.

FORD, RICHARD CLYDE (1870-1951)

Born: May 17, 1870; Calhoun County, Michigan
Parents: Charles A. Ford, Meranda Elizabeth (Floyd) Ford
Children: Ann, Richard
Education: Litchfield High School, Litchfield, Michigan, 1886. Albion College, B.A., Albion, Michigan, 1894, Ph.M. 1897. University of Freiburg, Munich, Ph.D., 1900. University of Mont Pellier, France
Career: Teacher, Methodist Mission School, Singapore, Malaya, two years. Assistant Professor, French and German, Albion College, 1894-1899. Professor of Modern Languages, Northern State Normal School, Marquette, Michigan, 1901-1903. Department Head of Modern Languages, Eastern Michigan University (Michigan State Normal College), 1904-1940. Trustee, State Historical Society; Chairman. Chairman, State Historical Commission. Trustee, Michigan Authors Association; President, 1934-1936. Traveled widely in Europe

Writings: *Scheffel as a Novelist (Scheffel als Romandichter)* Munich, Germany 1900. *Elementary German for Sight Translation* Ginn 1904. *John D. Pierce, Founder of the Michigan School System; a Study of Education in the Northwest* (co-author) The Scharf Tag, Label & Box Company (Ypsilanti) 1905. *De Tocqueville's Voyage en Amerique* D. C. Heath 1909. *Journal of Pontiac's Conspiracy* Speaker-Hines Printing Company 1912. *The Conspiracy of Pontiac* (translation) 1913. *The White Captive: a Tale of the Pontiac War* Rand McNally 1915. *Sandy MacDonald's Man, a Tale of the Mackinaw Fur Trade* Michigan School Service, Inc. 1929. *Heroes and Hero Tales of Michigan* (dedicated to his grandfathers, Daniel Ford and Richard Floyd "who helped carve out Michigan, the state, with their axes") E. M. Hale 1930. *Red Man or White, A Story of Indian Life in the Northwest* Lyons & Carnahan 1931. Edited German, French textbooks

Awards or inclusion in other biographical books: *American Authors & Books; Michigan: A Centennial History of the State and its People*: Michigan Biography Vol. 3; *Michigan Authors,* 1st ed., 2nd ed.; *Who Was Who in America; Who Was Who among North American Authors.* Honorary Degree, Doctor of Letters, Albion College, 1934. Made a member of local Indian tribe

FOSTER, LINDA NEMEC

Address: 2024 Wilshire Dr. SE, Grand Rapids, Michigan 49506
Born: May 29, 1950; Cleveland, Ohio
Parents: John J. Nemec, Helen A. Nemec
Children: Brian, Ellen
Education: Aquinas College, B.A., Grand Rapids, Michigan, 1968-1972. Goddard College, M.F.A., Plainfield, Vermont, 1977-1979
Career: Director of Literature Programming, Urban Institute for Contemporary Arts, Grand Rapids, Michigan, 1991—. Teacher of Poetry Workshops, Summer Institute at

Olivet College, Olivet, Michigan, 1991. Instructor of English, Ferris State University, Big Rapids, 1983-1984. Teacher of Creative Writing Workshops, Michigan Council for the Arts, throughout Michigan, 1980-1990. Poet, writer, 1975—

Writings: *A Modern Fairy Tale: The Baba Yaga Poems* Ridgeway Press 1992. *A History of the Body* Coffee House Press 1987. Over 120 poems published in such publications as: *The Georgia Review, Poetry Now, Nimrod, Hiram Poetry Review, South Florida Poetry Review, Negative Capability, Manhattan Poetry Review, Pennsylvania Review, Wayne Review, University of Windsor Review, Tendril, Blue Buildings, Croton Review, Chowder Review, Contemporary Michigan Poetry* (anthology), *Passages North* and others. Work in Progress: Book of poetry,*The Empty Eye of the Needle* Sun Dog Press. Selection of poems was translated and will be appearing in Poland's leading literary magazine

Awards or inclusion in other biographical books: Creative Artist Grant in Literature, Michigan Council for the Arts, 1984. Creative Artist Grant in Literature, Michigan Council for the Arts, 1990. Pushcart Prize nominations, 1983, 1984, 1989, 1990. Second place winner, contest competition sponsored by *Passages North* and the National Endowment for the Arts, 1988. Nomination for the Anne Sexton Poetry Prize, 1980. Nomination for the First Book Award, 1992. Inclusion in Who's Who Books, 1972, 1984, 1986, 1990, 1991

What is the aim or goal of your writing? "To communicate to the reader/audience poems that speak from our common humanness, our common concerns and fears, our common heart. My poetry (hopefully) does what all true poetry must do: be accessible to the reader by offering a common ground, yet retain a mystery at its core that everyone can relate to in a totally different way. This kind of poetry is a risky balancing act, but it's the most exhilarating kind of writing that I know of. I use extended metaphors, symbolic language, mythology, irony, subtle wit, and cadence to achieve this. Every unwritten poem is a gift waiting to be discovered, ourselves waiting to be met."

May inquiries be sent to you about doing workshops, readings? Yes

FOX, (MRS.) JEAN M.
Address: 33203 Biddlestone, Farmington Hills, Michigan 48334
Born: January 25; Norwood, Ohio
Parents: Floyd W. McGriff, Ruth W. (Edwards) McGriff
Children: John, Jo Anne, Susan
Education: Redford High School, Detroit, Michigan. Indiana University, A.B., cum laude,1933-1937; A.M., History, 1940-1941. Held many offices, received many honors
Career: Oakland County Newspaper Editor and Publisher: *Southfield Sun* 1956-1974; Founder*Farmington Forum* 1967-1974; Founder *Novi Sun-Forum* 1972-1974. Mayor, City of Farmington Hills, 1990. Elected to Farmington Hills City Council, 1987; Board of Zoning Appeals, 1977-1987; Farmington Hills Historic District Commission 1980-1987; Farmington Hills Historical Commission, 1975-1987. Oakland County Parks and Recreation Commission, 1981—. Held numerous other community offices. Served on American Study Commission to the Middle East, 1967; Michigan Partners of the Alliance, Board Member, 1960-1972; Delegate to Conference on Partners of the Alliance, San Jose, Costa Rica, 1970. Others

Writings: *The Windows of Old Mariners* Mariners Church Detroit 1974, 1984. *Farmington's Centennial Families* Farmington Hills Historical Commission 1976. *A Farmington Childhood: The Watercolors of Lillian Drake Avery* Farmington Hills Historical Commission 1985. *More Than a Tavern: 150 Years of Botsford Inn* Farmington Hills Historical

Commission 1986. *Fred M. Warner, A Progressive Governor* Farmington Hills Historical Commission 1988. Edited: *The Natural History of Farmington* 1975; *The Religious History of Farmington* 1976; *Heritage Homes: If Walls Could Talk* 1980. Editor, high school and college student publications

Awards or inclusion in other biographical books: *Michigan Authors,* 2nd ed. Citizen of the Year, Farmington/Farmington Hills Chamber of Commerce, 1985. First Woman Marshal, Farmington Founders' Festival Parade, 1986. Heart of Gold, United Way of Southeastern Michigan, 1992. Historical Society of Michigan, 1987, for *More Than a Tavern: 150 Years of Botsford Inn*

What is the aim or goal of your writing? "To bring to the attention of today's video-vibed generation the accomplishments and difficulties (overcome) of Michigan's wonderful past."

May inquiries be sent to you about doing workshops, readings? Yes

FOX, FRANCES MARGARET (1870-1959)

Born: June 23, 1870; South Farmington, Massachusetts

Parents: James Fox, Frances (Franks) Fox

Education: Michigan Female Seminary, Kalamazoo, Michigan

Career: Secretary, Library of Congress, writer. Primary teacher, Mackinaw City, Michigan; formed Sunshine Club for children while teaching there. Much of her writing was done in Mackinaw City, Michigan, and her ashes were deposited in the Straits of Mackinac after her death. Several books refer to local people and places are dedicated to residents. She and her family resided first at 307 Jamet Street in Mackinac City; then she built cottages at 109 Depeyster Street, then at 512 Huron Street

Writings: *Farmer Brown and the Birds* Page & Company 1900. *Betty of Old Mackinaw* L.C. Page & Company 1901. *What Gladys Saw; A Nature Story of Farm and Forest* W.A. Wilde 1902. *The Little Giant's Neighbours* L.C. Page & Company 1903. *Mother Nature's Little Ones* Page & Company 1904. *Brother Billy* L. C. Page & Company 1904. *The Rainbow Bridge: a Story* W.A. Wilde 1905. *How Christmas Came to the Mulvaneys* L.C. Page & Company 1905. *The Country Christmas* Page & Company 1907. *Mary Anne's Little Indian, and Other True Stories for Children* A. Flanagan 1913. *The Adventures of Blackberry Bear* Moffat, Yard & Company 1918. *Little Bear at Work and at Play* Rand McNally 1920. *Little Bear Stories* Rand McNally 1924. *Janey* Rand McNally 1925. *Uncle Sam's Animals* Century 1927. *Nancy Davenport* Rand McNally 1928. *Washington, D.C., The Nation's Capital* Rand McNally 1929. *Nannette* P.F. Volland 1929. *The Magic Canoe: a Frontier Story of the American Revolution* Laidlaw Brothers 1930. *Flowers and Their Travels* Bobbs Merrill 1936. *Little Toad* Viking 1938. *Little Mossback Amelia* E.P. Dutton 1939; Little Traverse Regional Historical Society 1967. *They Sailed and Sailed* Dutton 1940. Many other books for children. Short stories in *The Woman's Home Companion, Little Folks, Youths Companion, The Christian Register, American Childhood,* others; in school primers

Awards or inclusion in other biographical books: *Michigan Authors,* 1st ed., 2nd ed.; *Who's Who Among North American Authors*

FRANCK, HARRY ALVERSON (1881-1962)
Born: June 29, 1881; Munger, Michigan
Parents: Charles Adolph; Lillie E. (Wilsey) Franck
Children: Harry, Katherine, Patricia, Charles, Peter
Education: University of Michigan, A.B., Ann Arbor, Michigan, 1903. Columbia University, New York, New York. Havard University, Cambridge, Massachusetts. Studies abroad
Career: Teacher, Central High School, Detroit, Michigan, 1903-1904. Traveled, 1904-1905. Teacher, Bellefonte, Pennsylvania, 1906. Teacher, Browning School, New York, New York, 1906-1908. Department Head, Tech High School, Springfield, Massachusetts, 1908-1911. Traveled, taught. Served as both world wars: Lieutenant,1918-1919; Major, 1942-1947

Writings: *Three Hoboes in India* Century 1910. *A Vagabond Journey around the World; a Narrative of Personal Experience* Century 1910. *Four Months Afoot in Spain* Century 1911. *Working North from Patagonia; being the Narrative of a Journey, Earned on the Way, through Southern and Eastern South America* Century 1921. *Wandering in Northern China* Century 1923. *Glimpses of Japan and Formosa* Century 1924. *East of Siam; Ramblings in the Five Divisions of French Indo-China* Century 1926. *I Discover Greece; wherein an Incurable Nomad Sets Forth What Befell Him and an Artist Friend During a Labyrinthine Summer Journey through Modern Hellas* Century 1929. *Foot-Loose in the British Isles; Being a Desultory and Not Too Serious Account of Sixteen Months of Living in England and Peregrinating Hither and Yon throughout Great Britain* Century 1932. *Sky Roaming Above Two Continents; an Aerial Cruise, with Many Landings in the Countries and Islands that Circle the Caribbean* Frederick A. Stokes 1938. *The Lure of Alaska* Frederick A. Stokes 1939. *Pan American Highway from the Rio Grande to the Canal Zone* D. Appleton-Century 1940. *Rediscovering South America* Lippincott 1943
Awards or inclusion in other biographical books: *American Authors and Books; Benet's Reader's Encyclopedia of American Literature; Biography Index; Contemporary Authors; Lincoln Library of Language Arts; Michigan Authors,* 1st ed., 2nd ed.; *Michigan Poets; National Cyclopaedia of American Biography; Reader's Encyclopedia of American Literature; Twentieth Century Authors; Who Was Who among English and European Authors; Who Was Who among North American Authors; Who Was Who in America*

FRANKLIN, DIXIE P.
Address: 972 Valley Road, Marquette, Michigan 49855
Born: July 19, 1927; San Augustine, Texas
Parents: Minor E. Porter, Marby E. (Beard) Porter
Children: Carol, Cynthia
Education: Lufkin Senior High School, High School Diploma, 1938-1942
Career: Freelance writer, self-employed, Marquette, Michigan, 1976—. Contributing editor *Lake Superior Magazine.* Contributing writer, *Midwest Living Magazine.* Dental Assistant/part-time writer, Dr. E.S. Holman, Marquette, Michigan, 1962-1976. Terminal Hostess, Braniff Airlines, 1946-1948. Service Rep, Southwestern Bell Telephone Company, Austin, Texas, 1944-1946

Writings: *Faces of Lake Superior* Atwerger & Mandel Publishing 1991. *Scenic Byways* (Michigan chapters) Falcon Press 1990. *America's Outdoor Wonders* (Midwest chapter) National Geographic Society 1987. *A Place Apart* The Book Concern 1983. *A Most*

Superior Land (four chapters) Two Peninsula Press 1983. Work in Progress: *Michigan Memories* Altwerger & Mandel 1992. *Faces of Lake Michigan*

Awards or inclusion in other biographical books: First Place, Book, Society of American Travel Writers (Central States), 1992. Awards, Michigan Outdoor Writers Association, 1990, 1989, 1988. Awards, Midwest Travel Writers Association, 1989, 1988, 1983, 1979. Award, Society of American Travel Writers (Central States), 1989. Award, Association of Great Lakes Outdoor Writers, 1988. Michigan's U.P. Gold for Tourism, 1988. Award, Travel Industry Association Canada, Discover America, 1987. Ambassador, Michigan Tourism, 1984. Outdoor Writers Association of America, 1983. *Green Bay Press-Gazette,* 1982, 1979. Travel Industry Association Canada, Explore Canada Award, 1978, 1977. Writer of the Year, Upper Peninsula of Michigan Writers, 1976

What is the aim or goal of your writing? "My primary goal is to capture the people and places of my state, nation and world in such a way that others, too, will love them. My secondary goal is to support myself with words."

May inquiries be sent to you about doing workshops, readings? Yes

FRASER, CHELSEA CURTIS (1876-1954)

Born: August 28, 1876; New Sarum, Ontario

Parents: Oliver L. Fraser, Emma M. (Atherton) Fraser

Education: High School, Saginaw, Michigan. Michigan State College, University of Chicago

Career: Messenger, Western Union Telegraph Company, 1892. Musical instruments inlayer, 1893-1899. Montgomery Ward & Company, Chicago, Illinois, 1900-1902. Mandolin, guitar maker, Kalamazoo, Michigan, 1904-1905. Advertising, Saginaw Milling Company, 1906-1907. Furniture Inspector, War Department, 1909-1911. Instructor, Industrial Arts, Grand Rapids Schools, 1913-1931

Writings: *Good Old Chums* 1911. *Heroes of the Wilds* 1923. *Heroes of the Air* Thomas Y. Crowell 1926 1940; German translation 1927; Scandinavian translation 1928. *The Story of Engineering in America* Thomas Y. Crowell 1928. *The Model Aircraft Builder* Thomas Y. Crowell 1931. *The Story of Aircraft* Thomas Y. Crowell 1933, 1939, 1944. *Famous American Flyers* Thomas Y. Crowell 1941. *Silver Strings* 1952. Others. In *Detroit Free Press, Furniture Artisan, American Boy, Youth's Companion, Popular Mechanics, Popular Science*

Awards or inclusion in other biographical books:*American Authors & Books; Who Was Who in Literature; Who's Who in Michigan; Who Was Who in America; Who Was Who among North American Authors*

FRAZIER, NETA (1890-1990)

Born: 1890, Owosso, Michigan

Parents: Emory E. Lohnes, Jennie (Osborn) Lohnes

Children: Lesley, Philip, Richard

Education: Whitman College, B.A., Walla Walla, Washington

Career: Teacher, substitute teacher, Washington. Editor, *Spokane Valley Herald*

Writings: *By-Line Dennie* Crowell 1947. *My Love Is a Gypsy* Longmans, Green 1952. *Little Rhody* Longmans 1953. *Somebody Special* Longmans 1954. *Secret Friend* Longmans 1956. *Magic Ring* Longmans 1959. *Something of My Own* McKay 1960. *One Long Picnic* McKay 1962. *Five Roads to the Pacific* McKay 1964. *The General's Boots* McKay 1965. *Sacajawea, the Girl Nobody Knows* McKay 1967. *Stouthearted Seven* Harcourt 1974. Others

Awards or inclusion in other biographical books: *Authors of Books for Young People; Contemporary Authors; Foremost Women in Communications; Michigan Authors,* 1st ed.; *Something about the Author; Who's Who of American Women; Who's Who among Pacific Northwest Authors; The Writers Directory:1984-1986.* Junior Literary Guild Selections. One of the outstanding Kappa Kappa Gamma alumnae, 1960. Fort Wright College Award, 1968. Governor's Award, l968. Women in Communications Award for Excellence, 1978

FREDERICK, JOHN TOWNER (1893-1975)
Born: February 1, 1893; Corning, Iowa
Parents: Oliver Roberts Frederick, May E. (Towner) Frederick
Children: John, James
Education: Corning High School, Corning, Iowa, 1909. University of Iowa, Iowa City, Iowa, 1915; M.A., 1917
Career: Founder, Editor *The Midland* magazine, begun as college senior, suspended 1933. Teacher, Prescott, Iowa, 1911-1913. Head of English Department, State Teachers College, Moorhead, Minnesota, 2 years. Bought 1,400 acres, near Glennie, Michigan, 1919 which he worked as a farm and built large stone house. Teacher, University of Iowa, University of Pittsburgh, Northwestern University, University of Notre Dame. Regional Director, WPA Writers' Project, 1937-1940. Began weekly book review program 1937 broadcast by CBS radio stations

Writings: *Druida* Knopf 1923. *Stories From the Midland* Knopf 1924. *Green Bush, With 9 Drawings* Knopf 1925. *A Handbook of Short Story Writing* Knopf 1924. *Good Writing* (with Leo L. Ward) 1932. *Reading for Writing* 1935, 1941. *Present-Day Stories* Scribner's Sons 1941. *Out of the Midwest, A Collection of Present-Day Writing* McGraw-Hill 1944. *William Henry Hudson* Twayne 1972. In *Michigan: A State Anthology* Gale 1983
Awards or inclusion in other biographical books: *American Authors and Books: 1640 to the Present Day; Current Biography; Who Was Who in Literature: 1906-1934; Who's Who in America*

FREEDMAN, ERIC
Address: 2698 Linden, East Lansing, Michigan 48823
Born: November 6, 1949; Brookline, Massachusetts
Parents: Morris Freedman, Charlotte L. Freedman
Children: Ian, Cara
Education: Cornell University, B.A., Ithaca, New York, 1967-1971; JD, 1972-1975
Career: Reporter, *Detroit News,* Lansing, Michigan, 1984—. Reporter, *Knickerbocker News,* Albany, New York, 1976-1984. Legislative & Press Aide, U.S. Rep. Charles Rangel, Washington, DC, New York, New York, 1971-1976

Writings: *On the Water, Michigan: Your Comprehensive Guide to Water Recreation in the Great Lake State* Huron-Superior-Michigan Press 1992. *Pioneering Michigan* A&M Publishing 1992
Awards or inclusion in other biographical books: Various awards from State Bar of Michigan, Associated Press, New York State Bar Association, Evening News Association, American Judicature Society and other organizations
What is the aim or goal of your writing? "To bring travel and history alive for readers."
May inquiries be sent to you about doing workshops, readings? Yes

FREISINGER, RANDALL R.

Address: 200 Prospect Street, Houghton, Michigan 49931
Born: February 6, 1942; Kansas City, Missouri
Parents: Earl G. Freisinger, Winifred S. Freisinger
Children: Stepsons: Ian Petersen, Quentin Petersen
Education: University of Missouri-Columbia, B.J., 1959-1963; M.A. and Ph.D., English Literature, 1963-1975
Career: Associate Professor, Michigan Tech University, Houghton, Michigan, 1972—. Assistant Professor, Columbia College, Columbia, Missouri, 1976-1977. Resident Lecturer, University of Maryland-Overseas, Bermuda, Labrador, Iceland, 1975-1976. Instructor, Jefferson Community College, Hillsboro, Missouri, 1964-1968

Writings: Poems in such publications as: *Aspen Leaves, The Chariton Review, Mississippi Valley Review, Passages North, Cottonwood 30, Kansas Quarterly, Stone Country, Milkweed Chronicle, Mickle Street Review, The Panhandler, Interim, Sidewinder, New Letters, The Laurel Review, Great River Review, Poet & Critic,* and others. Several poems published first and soley in chapbooks such as: "Timing" *Running Patterns* Flume Press 1985; "Magic Tricks" *Hand Shadows* GreenTower Press 1988. Poems anthologized in such books as *Passages North Anthology* Milkweed Editions 1990. Work in Progress: Manuscript of poems
Awards or inclusion in other biographical books: *Poets and Writers Directory.* Flume Press National Chapbook Award, 1975
What is the aim or goal of your writing? "To write the best poems I can and to reach a wider audience than is normally associated with poetry."
May inquiries be sent to you about doing workshops, readings? Yes

FROSTIC, GWEN

Address: 5140 River Road, Benzonia, Michigan 49616
Born: April 26, 1906; Sandusky, Michigan
Parents: Fred W. Frostic, Sara A. Frostic
Education: Western Michigan University, Bachelors, Kalamazoo, Micigan, 1928-1930. Eastern Michigan University, Teacher's Certificate, Ypsilanti, Michigan, 1926-1928
Career: Owner and operator, Presscraft Papers, Benzonia, Michigan, 1955—.

Writings: *Abysmal Acuman* Presscraft Papers 1991. *Chaotic Harmony* Presscraft Papers 1989. *Hueristic* Presscraft Papers 1987. *Multiversality* Presscraft Papers 1985. *The Caprice Immensity* Presscraft Papers 1983. *The Evolving Omnity* Presscraft Papers 1981. *The Infinite Destiny* Presscraft Papers 1978. *The Enduring Cosmos* Presscraft Papers 1976. *Contemplate* Presscraft Papers 1973. *Beyond Time* Presscraft Papers 1971. *Wisps of Mist* Presscraft Papers 1969. *Wingborne* Presscraft Papers 1967. *To Those Who See* Presscraft Papers 1965. *A Place on Earth* Presscraft Papers 1962. *These Things Are Ours* Presscraft Papers 1960. *A Walk With Me* Presscraft Papers 1958. *My Michigan* Presscraft Papers 1957
Awards or inclusion in other biographical books: *Michigan Authors,* 2nd ed.; *Michigan Poets.* Inducted into the Michigan Women's Hall of Fame, 1986. Albion College, Doctor of Fine Arts, 1991. Ferris State University, Doctor of Humane Letters, 1985. Alma College, Doctor of Literature, 1977. Michigan State University, Doctor of Fine Arts, 1973. Western Michigan University, Doctor of Humanities, 1971. Eastern Michigan University, Doctor of Laws, 1965
May inquiries be sent to you about doing workshops, readings? No

FULLER, GEORGE NEWMAN (1873-1957)
Born: November 17, 1873; Barry County, Michigan
Parents: Reuben A. Fuller, Delia (Coulter) Fuller
Children: Florence, Margaret
Education: Grand Rapids High School, Michigan, 1894. University of Michigan, A.B., Ann Arbor, Michigan, 1905. Harvard University, Cambridge, Massachusetts; Yale University, New Haven, Connecticut. University of Michigan, Ann Arbor, Michigan, Ph.D., 1912
Career: Teacher, rural schools. Principal, L'Anse Public Schools, L'Anse, Michigan, 1896-1900. Principal, Nashville, Michigan Public Schools, 1900-1901. Department Head, Montana State Normal College, 1908-1909. Organizer, Michigan Historical Commission, Lansing, Michigan, 1913: Director, 1916-1946. Instructor, University of Michigan, 1915

Writings: *Economic and Social Beginning of Michigan* Wynkoop Hallenbeck Crawford 1916. *Democracy and the Great War* Superintendent of Instruction 1918. *Historic Michigan, Land of the Great Lakes* National Historical Association 1924. *Michigan in the World War* (with Charles Hanford Landrum) Michigan Historical Commission 1924. *The Messages of the Governors of Michigan* (editor) The Michigan Historical Commission 1924. *Michigan, A Centennial History of the State and Its People* (Vols. 1-2 edited by author; Vols. 3-5 by staff) Lewis Publishing (sold by subscription) 1939. Series of annual publications known as the *Michigan Historical and Pioneer Collections* which he continued, survives today as the *Michigan History* magazine
Awards or inclusion in other biographical books: *Michigan Authors,* 1st ed.; *Who Was Who among North American Authors; Who Was Who in America*

G

GAERTNER, KENNETH C.

Address: 11447 Weiman Drive, Hell, Michigan 48169
Born: January 18, 1933; Saginaw, Michigan
Parents: Frederick C. Gaertner, Helen M. (Miller) Gaertner
Children: Kurt, Bonnie
Education: St. Peter and Paul High School, Saginaw, Michigan. Attended Bay City Junior College, 1954-1955
Career: Served with USMC, 1951-1954. Youth Specialist VI, W.J. Maxey Boys Training School, Whitmore Lake, Michigan, 1971—.

Writings: Plays: *Seventeen Hoofbeats* 1992. *Koan Bread* 1978. *The Lady and God* 1975. *Moon on Snow* 1978. *Dog's Tooth* 1985. All plays produced. Contributed poetry to *Anthology of American Poetry, Commonweal, New Oxford Review, America, Christian Century, American Poet, Poet Lore, Midwest Quarterly, Generation, Tampa Poetry Journal, Discourse* and others. Short stories to *Voices. Four Quarters:* (libretto) Haiku for chamber orchestra and soprano, 1977. Work in Progress: Various short stories and plays
Awards or inclusion in other biographical books: *Who's Who in U.S. Writers, Editors & Poets*
What is the aim or goal of your writing? "To create a work of art."
May inquiries be sent to you about doing workshops, readings? Yes

GALLUP, LUCY A.

Address: 26408 Banker Road, Sturgis, Michigan 49091
Pseudonym: Amelie. Lucie DeFluent. Amelie DeFluent
Born: July 30, 1911; Dundee, Michigan
Parents: Albert R. DeFluent, Maude N. (Haines) DeFluent
Education: Kalamazoo Central High School, 1929. Western Michigan University, A.B., Kalamazoo, Michigan, 1930-1934; M.L.S., 1957-1958
Career: Librarian, White Pigeon Community Schools, White Pigeon, Michigan, 1958-1960. Librarian, Sturgis Public Library, Sturgis, Michigan, 1951-1957. Assistant, Photostat Department, New York Public Library, New York, New York, 1943-1947. Assistant, Reference, Children's Librarian, Goshen Public Library, Goshen, Indiana, 1938-1942. Part-time work in various parts of the Kalamazoo Public Library System, Kalamazoo, Michigan, 1930-1934, where lived and went to college. First trained in library work in the Kalamazoo Public Library apprentice course.

Writings: *Whispers in the Wind* Green and White Publishing 1992. *The Independent Bluebird* William Morrow 1959. *Spinning Wings* William Morrow 1956. Various poems, articles, a few short stories for children, scattered through the years from the 1930's to the 1980's. Reviews, articles in connection with being a librarian. Work in Progress: Making selections from notebooks for a possible nature study book, interspersed with related poetry. Work on a third bird manuscript based on close actual experience and revealing unexpected sensibility in a very small wild creature.
Awards or inclusion in other biographical books:x *Michigan Authors,* 1st ed., 2nd ed.; *Who's Who of American Women* 1st ed., others

What is the aim or goal of your writing? "As I considered how to answer this, I realized my basic aim in writing is deeply personal. I have kept notebooks and journals all my life, writing in prose and verse, sometimes daily, sometimes sporadically. I write to understand myself and life. An idea, a feeling, a situation set in words is made easier to judge for truth and relevance. Writing of times of delight, beauty, or wonder preserves them for vivid recall. Much as I relish the satisfaction of things published, and hope for more, still I am aware it is this habit of keeping notebooks that has added depth to the experience of being human. Both my 1950's books are based on notebook entries. Travel articles grew from running-comment notebooks during trips. Constant writing sharpens awareness. I value it as a way of life."

May inquiries be sent to you about doing workshops, readings? Possibly-according to the type of occasion

GARTLAND, JOAN W.

Address: 1217 Cherokee, Royal Oak, Michigan 48067
Born: December 24, 1941; Brooklyn, New York
Parents: Frederick Gartland, Nora W. Gartland
Education: Barnard College, B. A., New York, New York, 1959-1963. University of Chicago, M.A. in Egyptology, Chicago, Illinois, 1963-1968. University of Michigan, M.A.L.S., Ann Arbor, Michigan, 1970-1971. University of Detroit and Wayne State University, Detroit, Michigan, post-degree studies
Career: Library for the Blind and Physically Handicapped, Detroit Public Library, Detroit, Michigan, 1989—. Librarian, Detroit Public Library-Main, Detroit, Michigan, 1985-1989. Librarian, Curator, Greenfield Village and Henry Ford Museum, Dearborn, Michigan, 1978-1985. Head of Reference/Librarian, University of Detroit, Detroit, Michigan, 1971-1977

Writings: *A Passionate Distance* Ridgeway Press 1991. Poetry in *Moving Out, Wayne Review, University of Windsor Review, Corridors, Celery, Christian Century, The Bridge.* Work in Progress: Poetry on ancient Egypt; life in U.S. during the eighties
Awards or inclusion in other biographical books: Traveling Fellowship to Egypt, University of Chicago. Woodrow Wilson Fellowship. Phi Beta Kappa. Poet-in-Residence, University of Detroit
What is the aim or goal of your writing? "To capture the feel of memories and give them new life. To speak both for the living and the dead."
May inquiries be sent to you about doing workshops, readings? Yes

GEARHART, CLIFFORD R.

Address: 13866 S. Straits Highway, Wolverine, Michigan 49799
Born: May 6, 1913; West Decatur, Pennsylvania
Parents: Burtis B. Gearhart; Hazel K. Gearhart
Children: Louise, Martha, Jean, Daniel, David
Education: High School, Phillipsburg, Pennsylvania. Night School, Pontiac, Michigan
Career: President, North Star Trees, Inc., Wolverine, Michigan, 1978—. Owner, Gearhart Evergreen, Wolverine, Michigan, 1938—. Director, Wolverine Area Development Advisory Committee, Wolverine, Michigan, 1991—. Vice President, Inland Seas, Hancock, Michigan, 1962-1963. Gearhart Fisheries, Brimley/Escanaba, 1938-1988. Director, Cheboygan Soil Conservation District, Cheboygan, Michigan. Trustee, Free Methodist Church, Wolverine, Michigan, 1970—. Chairman, Wilmot Township Board of

Review, 1965—. President/Board Member, Wolverine School Board, 8 years. President, Michigan Christmas Tree Growers Association, 1959-1960. President, Cheboygan County Christmas Tree Growers Association, 1958-1959

Writings: *Pity the Poor Fish Then Man* Avery Color Studios 1987. *For the Love of Trees* Avery Color Studios 1991. Work in Progress: Recently compiled a 60-page scrapbook regarding Tree Farmer contest headquartered in New York, competing among eight other states in this area
Awards or inclusion in other biographical books: Michigan's Outstanding Tree Farmer Award, 1991. Cheboygan County Outstanding Tree Farmer Award, 1986
What is the aim or goal of your writing? "To make the population aware of what has happened to two important natural resources since man's involvement with both."
May inquiries be sent to you about doing workshops, readings? Yes

GEORGAKAS, DAN
Born: March 1, 1938; Detroit, Michigan
Parents: Xenophon Georgakas, Sophia Georgakas
Education: Wayne State University, B.A., Detroit, Michigan, 1960. University of Michigan, M.A., Ann Arbor, Michigan, 1961
Career: Teacher, Detroit Public Schools, Detroit, Michigan, 1960-1964. Overseas School of Rome, Italy, 1965. Teacher, LaGuardia Community College, Long Island City, New York, 1973-1978. Teacher, New Jersey Council on the Arts, 1972-1978. Guest lecturer at several universities like the University of Michigan, University of Rome. Executive director, Smyrna Press beginning in 1964. Empire State College of State University of New York, Saratoga Springs beginning in 1978. Various script work. Served on different editorial boards

Writings: *Michigan Labor and the Civil War* Civil War Centennial Observance Commission 1964. *Ombre Rosse* Radio-Television Corp. of Italy 1968. Editor, *Z Anthology of Poetry* Smyrna Press 1969. Co-editor, co-translator, *Selected Poems* Quixote Press 1969. *And All Living Things Their Children* Shameless Hussy Press 1972. *Red Shadows; the History of Native Americans from 1600 to 1900, from the Desert to the Pacific Coast* Zenith Books 1973. *The Broken Hoop; the History of Native Americans from 1600-1890, from the Atlantic Coast to the Plains* Zenith Books 1973. Editor, *Prison Poetry* New Jersey Council on the Arts 1973. With Marvin Surkin, *Detroit, I Do Mind Dying: a Study in Urban Revolution* St. Martin 1975. *In Focus: a Guide to Using Films* Zoetrope 1980. *The Methuselah Factors: Strategies for a Long and Vigorous Life* Simon & Schuster 1980. *The Cineaste Interviews: on the Art and Politics of the Cinema* Lake View Press 1983. With others, *Solidarity Forever: An Oral History of the IWW* Lake View Press 1985. Editor with Charles C. Moskos, *New Directions in Greek American Studies* Pella Publishing 1991. *Encyclopedia of the American Left* Garland 1990; University of Illinois Press 1992. Others. Contributed to several other books; wrote reviews, interviews, poetry, essays. In *Chicago Tribune, Village Voice,* others
Awards or inclusion in other biographical books: *Contemporary Authors; Directory of American Poets; International Who's Who in Poetry; Michigan Authors,* 2nd ed.; *Michigan Poets.* Fulbright Research Grant 1963. National Endowment for the Humanities Grant 1983, 1985. Annual Award for Excellence in Scholarship, Empire State College of State University of New York 1986

GERBER, DAN
Born: August 12, 1940; Grand Rapids, Michigan
Parents: Daniel F. Gerber, Dorothy (Scott) Gerber
Children: Wendie, Frank, Tamara
Education: Michigan State University, B.A., East Lansing, Michigan, 1962
Career: Professional racing driver for five years. Teacher, Fremont, Michigan for two years. Poet-in-Residence, Grand Valley State College, Allendale, Michigan, 1969; Michigan State University, 1970. Lecturer in various schools for the National Endowment and Academy of American Poets. Poet, novelist, essayist

Writings: *A Last Bridge Home; Selected and New Poems* Clark City Press 1992. *A Voice from the River* Clark City Press 1990. *The Revenant* Sumac Press 1971. *Grass Fires; Stories* Winn Books 1987. *Snow on the Backs of Animals Poems* Winn Books 1986. *The Chinese Poems; Letters to a Distant Friend* Sumac Press 1978. *Indy, the World's Fastest Carnival Ride* Prentice-Hall 1977. *Out of Control* Prentice-Hall 1974. *American Atlas* Prentice-Hall 1973. *Departure* Sumac Press 1973. *Five Blind Men* (with others) Sumac Press 1969. Contributor to many magazines such as *Stony Brook, New Yorker, Sports Illustrated, Partisan Review, The Nation, The Georgia Review*. Included in many anthologies such as *The Third Coast: Contemporary Michigan Poetry*
Awards or inclusion in other biographical books: *Contemporary Authors; Directory of American Fiction Writers; Directory of American Poets; Michigan Authors,* 2nd ed. Michigan Author Award, Alpena County Library/Michigan Center for the Book, 1992

GESSNER, ROBERT (1907-1968)
Born: October 23, 1907; Escanaba, Michigan
Parents: German Gessner, Anna (Silverman) Gessner
Children: Peter, Stephen
Education: University of Michigan, A.B., Ann Arbor, Michigan, 1929. Columbia University, A.M., New York, New York, 1930
Career: Instructor, New York University, New York, New York, 1930; Assistant Professor, 1941-1943; Associate Professor, 1943-1945; Professor beginning, 1945. Screen playwright, Warner Brothers, 1933. Visiting professor, film adviser, cinema critic, Board of Directors, Motion Picture Foundation for Colleges and Universities. Chairman, Rosenthal Foundation Awards in Cinema, 1962-1964. Founding President, Society of Cinematologists, 1959-1961. Editor, *The Democratic Man*

Writings: *Some of My Best Friends are Jews* Farrar & Rinehart 1936. *Massacre; A Survey of Today's American Indian* Da Capo Press 1931, 1972. *Here is My Home Town* Alliance Book 1941. *Treason* Charles Scribner's Sons 1944. *Youth is the Time* Charles Scribner's Sons 1945. *Behind the Ivy* 1959. *The Art of the Moving Image; A Guide to Cinematic Literacy* Dutton 1968. Others. Script writer, United States Air Force, 1952-1953. Periodical contributions
Awards or inclusion in other biographical books:*American Authors & Books; Who Was Who in America*. New Republic Poetry Prize, 1934. Peabody Radio Writing Award, 1944. Ford Foundation, Traveling Fellow, 1962

GIANAKARIS, CONSTANTINE JOHN
Born: May 2, 1934; Morenci, Michigan
Parents: John George Gianakaris, Anna (Parry) Gianakaris
Children: Elizabeth Ann

Education: University of Michigan, A.B., Ann Arbor, Michigan, 1956, M.A., 1957. University of Wisconsin, Ph.D., 1961

Career: Assistant to Associate Dean, University of Wisconsin, Madison, Wisconsin, 1958-1960. Assistant Professor, Illinois State University, Normal, 1961-1963. Associate Professor, Western Michigan University, Kalamazoo, Michigan, 1966-1972; professor beginning 1972. Visiting professor

Writings: *Antony and Cleopatra* (editor) W.C. Brown 1969. *Plutarch* Twayne 1970. *Foundations of Drama* Houghton 1975. *The Drama of the Middle Ages: Comparative and Critical Essays* (editor) AMS Press 1982. *Drama in the Twentieth Century: Comparative and Critical Essays* AMS Press 1984. *Drama in the Renaissance: Comparative and Critical Essays* AMS Press 1986. *Peter Shaffer: a Casebook* Garland 1991. *Peter Shaffer* Macmillan 1992. Articles in various professional journals. Co-editor, *Comparative Drama*

Awards or inclusion in other biographical books: *Contemporary Authors; Directory of American Scholars; Michigan Authors,* 2nd ed.; *Writers Directory.* Illinois State University Faculty Grant, 1963-1964. Western Michigan University Faculty Research Grants, 1967-1968

GIBSON, ARTHUR HOPKIN (1888-1973)
Born: July 20, 1888; Detroit, Michigan
Parents: Frank B. Gibson, Sophronia A. (Hopkin) Gibson
Children: Colvin
Education: Cass Technical High School, Detroit, Michigan
Career: Errand boy, painter, clerk, accountant, insurance salesman, government auditor, insurance broker, contractor for residential buildings, writer. Retired from business 1961, painter

Writings: *Robert Hopkin, Master Marine and Landscape Painter* self-published 1962. *Artists of Early Michigan: A Biographical Dictionary of Artists Native to or Active in Michigan, 1701-1900* Wayne State University Press 1975. *Index to History of Detroit Society of Women Painters and Sculptors, 1903-1953* 1972. *Letters* 1960. *Robert J. Wickenden: A Biographic Research Report* 1964

Awards or inclusion in other biographical books: *Artists of Early Michigan*

GIDEON, NANCY A.
Address: P.O. Box 526, Kalamazoo, Michigan 49004
Pseudonym: Dana Ransom, Lauren Giddings
Born: May 27, 1955; Kalamazoo, Michigan
Parents: Floyd L. Crumb, Helen L. (Ransom) Crumb
Children: Travis, Andrew
Education: Western Michigan University, major in Journalism, minors in history, communication, cum laude, B.A., Kalamazoo, Michigan, 1973-1977. Michigan State University, Insurance Sales License, East Lansing, Michigan, 1981
Career: Insurance Clerk, Independent Group Service, Kalamazoo, Michigan, 1985. Insurance Sales Person, Farm Bureau Insurance, Kalamazoo, Michigan, 1981. Claims clerk, AAA, Kalamazoo, Michigan 1979-1981. Claims, underwriting, AAA, Battle Creek, Michigan, 1976-1979. Gilmore Brothers, Retail clerk, Kalamazoo, Michigan,1974-1976

Writings: *Dakota Desire* Zebra 1992. *Dakota Dawn* Zebra 1991. *Wild Wyoming Love*

Zebra 1992. *Wild Savage Love* Zebra 1990. *Liar's Promise* Zebra 1990. *Alexandra's Ecstasy* Zebra 1989. *Bartered Bride* Zebra 1989. *Love's Glorious Gamble* Zebra 1988. *Pirate's Captive* Zebra 1987. *Rebel Vixen* Zebra 1987. *Sweet Tempest* Zebra 1987. Work in Progress: *Love's Own Reward, Dakota Destiny, Tempest Waters, Dakota Promises*

Awards or inclusion in other biographical books:*Who's Who Fiction Writers,* 1988, 1989. Industry Award for Self-Promotion, *Romantic Times Magazine,*1988

What is the aim or goal of your writing? "Best-sellerdom (of course), provide continued quality reading enterainment and further the professional image of romance industry."

May inquiries be sent to you about doing workshops, readings? Yes

GILBERT, EDITH W.

Address: 510 Michigan Ave., Charlevoix, Michigan 49720
Born: September 2, 1917; New York, New York
Parents: Oho C. Wiesinger, Ethel L. Wiesinger
Education: Beverly Hills High School, California, High School Diploma. U.C.L.A., Westwood, California, 1937-1938. Sawyer's School of Business, Westwood, California, 1938-1939. Center for Creative Studies, Detroit, Michigan, 1946-1949
Career: Owner of Jet'iquette, a consultation service on modern etiquette. Guest speaker, television, radio, clubs

Writings: *The Complete Wedding Planner* Fell Publisher 1989, 1982; Warner Books 1991, 1984. *Tabletop the Right Way* Jet'iquette 1976, revised edition, Syracuse China Corporation, 1980. *Summer Resort Life: Tango Teas and All* Jet'iquette 1972. *All About Parties* Hearthside Press, 1968. Syndicated newspaper articles in major newspapers through United Features Syndicate; N.E.A.: travel articles for *New York Times, Chicago Tribune.* Magazine articles for *Motor News, Detroit Athletic Club, Cooking for Profit, The Designer, Special Events, Bridal Fair.* Work in Progress: Double slide talk/entertaining lecture on the *Mystery and Romance of Dining Through the Ages*

Awards or inclusion in other biographical books: *Michigan Authors,* 2nd ed. Patron of the Arts, Arts Foundation of Michigan, 1992

What is the aim or goal of your writing? "Informative-'how to' in a pleasant manner."

May inquiries be sent to you about doing workshops, readings? No

GILDNER, GARY

Address: 2915 School Street, Des Moines, Iowa 50311
Born: August 22, 1938; West Branch, Michigan
Parents: Theodore Gildner, Jean Gildner
Children: Gretchen
Education: Holy Redeemer High School, Flint, Michigan, 1952-1956. Michigan State University, B.A., East Lansing, Michigan, 1956-1960; M.A., 1961
Career: Professor of English, Drake University, 1966—. McGee Professor of Writing, Davidson College, 1992. Fulbright Lecturer, University of Warsaw, 1978-1988. Visiting Writer-in-Residence, Michigan State University, 1987; Reed College, 1983-1985. Instructor, Northern Michigan University, 1963-1966

Writings: *Clackamas* Carnegie Mellon 1991. *Blue Like the Heavens: New & Selected Poems* Pittsburgh 1984. *Jabon* Breitenbush 1981. *The Runner* Pittsburgh 1978. *Letters from Vicksburg* Unicorn Press 1976. *Nails* Pittsburgh 1975. *Eight Poems* Bredahl 1973.

Digging for Indians Pittsburgh 1971. *First Practice* Pittsburgh 1969. *The Second Bridge* Algonquin Books of Chapel Hill 1987. *A Week in South Dakota* Algonquin Books of Chapel Hill 1987. *The Crush* Ecco/Norton 1983. *The Warsaw Sparks* University of Iowa Press 1990. Editor, *Out of This World: Poems From the Hawkeye State* Iowa State University 1975. Work in Progress: Novel, a memoir, and a collection of poems

Awards or inclusion in other biographical books: *Contemporary Authors,* 1978, 1984; *Contemporary Poets,* 1985; *World Authors 1985-1990.* National Magazine Award for Fiction, 1986. Pushcart Prize for Fiction, 1986. Stories cited in *The Best American Short Stories,* 1988, 1986, 1985. Helen Bullis Poetry Prize, *Poetry Northwest,* 1979. William Carlos Williams Poetry Prize, *New Letters,* 1977. Theodore Roethke Poetry Prize, *Poetry Northwest,* 1976. National Endowment for the Arts Fellowships, 1976, 1971. Robert Frost Fellowship, Bread Loaf, 1970. Yaddo Fellow, 1978, 1976, 1975, 1973, 1972. MacDowell Colony Fellow, 1974

What is the aim or goal of your writing? "To tell a good story."

May inquiries be sent to you about doing workshops, readings? Yes

GILPIN, ALEC RICHARD

Born: April 23, 1920; Detroit, Michigan

Parents: Archie Gilpin; Clara (Watson) Gilpin

Children: Andrew, Jean

Education: University of Michigan, B.A., Ann Arbor, Michigan, 1941; M.A., 1946; Ph.D., 1950

Career: Instructor to Professor, Michigan State University, East Lansing, Michigan

Writings: *General William Hull and the War on Detroit in 1812* 1949. *The War of 1812 in the Old Northwest* Michigan State University Press 1958. *The Territory of Michigan (1805-1837)* Michigan State University Press 1970

Awards or inclusion in other biographical books: *Directory of American Scholars; Contemporary Authors; Michigan Authors,* 2nd ed.;

In the 2nd edition of *Michigan Authors* appears: "Dr. Gilpin says: 'I am doing research for another book but it will be several years before I finish it'."

GINGRICH, ARNOLD (1903-1976)

Born: December 5, 1903; Grand Rapids, Michigan

Parents: John H. Gingrich, Clara (Speare) Gingrich

Children: Rowe, John, Michael

Education: University of Michigan, A.B., East Lansing, 1925

Career: Began as advertising copywriter, 1925. Associated with *Esquire* 1933, becoming senior vice-president, publisher 1962. Editor, *Coronet,* 1936-1949

Writings: *Cast Down the Laurel* Knopf 1935. *The Well-Tempered Angler* Knopf 1965

Awards or inclusion in other biographical books: *American Authors and Books; Author's and Writer's Who's Who; Celebrity Register; Contemporary Authors; Current Biography; International Authors and Writers Who's Who; International Who's Who; New York Times Biographical Service; Reader's Encyclopedia of American Literature; Who Was Who among North American Authors; Who's Who in America; Who's Who in the World; Writers Directory,* others

GIRARD, HAZEL B. (1901-1989)
Born: December 8, 1901; Glennie, Michigan
Parents: John W. Batten, Johanna A. Batten
Children: Victor, Marvin
Education: Ann Arbor High School, Ann Arbor, Michigan
Career: Freelance writer and photographer, *Michigan Farmer, Detroit Free Press, Detroit Times, American Home, Colliers, Nature Magazine, Outdoors Magazine, Field and Stream, Popular Photography, U.S. Camera.* Many hundreds of photographs syndicated, Freelance Photographers Guild. Has spoken at many engagements. Columnist for *Bay City Times*

Writings: *A Giant Walked Among Them: Half-Tall Tales of Paul Bunyan and His Loggers* Marshall Jones 1977. *Blow for Batten's Crossing!* Glendon Publishing 1979. *Black Loam and Buttermilk: Down-Home Poems* (with Marvin Girard) Golden Quill 1986. In the second edition of *Michigan Authors*, she is credited with saying "I like writing that treks along without the seeming labor pains of creation. I dislike pompous, academical writing as if the author is suffering from the terminal, dread fear of split infinitives. I have been very fortunate in that editors leave my writing intact, exactly as submitted to them. I was once told by Malcolm M. Bingay (venerable editor of the *Detroit Free Press*) that I wrote with cadence, with a proclivity for choosing words with 'ear appeal'. I simply like writing that 'picks up its heels' and get trekking down the printed page."
Awards or inclusion in other biographical books: *Michigan Authors,* 2nd ed.

GIRARD, MARVIN EUGENE
Address: 1217 Pearce Street, Owosso, Michigan 48867
Pseudonym: Mustang Marv, Marv "Slim" Girard
Born: August 3, 1924; Glennie, Michigan
Parents: Joseph Jerome Girard, Hazel (Batten) Girard
Children: Giselle
Education: Owosso High School, Owosso, Michigan, 1943
Career: Circus, wild west show, theatrical performer, poet, non-fiction writer

Writings: *Makin' Circles With a Rope: the Lore of the Lasso Wizards* Marshall Jones 1986. *Black Loam and Buttermilk: Down-Home Poems* (with Hazel B. Girard) Golden Quill 1986. *Rail Fences and Roosters: Poems and Almost Poems* (with Hazel B. Girard) Golden Quill 1976. *These, My Singing Words* Golden Quill 1976
Awards or inclusion in other biographical books: *Michigan Authors,* 2nd ed.
May inquiries be sent to you about doing workshops, readings? Yes

GLAZER, SIDNEY (1905-1983)
Born: November 1, 1905; Quincy, Michigan
Parents: Max Glazer, Mildred (Thal) Glazer
Education: Wayne State University, A.B., Detroit, Michigan, 1927. University of Michigan, Ann Arbor, Michigan, A.M., 1929; Ph.D., 1932
Career: Assistant, Department of History, University of Michigan, 1928-1930. Instructor, Wayne State University, 1930-1938; Assistant Professor, 1938-1948; Associate Professor, 1948-1955; Professor, 1955-1976, retired. Michigan Civil War Centennial Observance Commission, 1963-1966, Adviser to Michigan Constitutional Convention, 1961-1962

Writings: *Michigan: From Primitive Wilderness to Industrial Commonwealth* (co-author) Prentice-Hall 1948. *Industrial Detroit: Men at Work* Wayne State University Press 1951. *Rejected Amendments to the Michigan Constitution, 1910-1961* Michigan Preparatory Committee 1961. *The Middle West* Bookman Associates 1962. *Detroit-A Study in Urban Development* Bookman Associates 1965. *Report of the Michigan Civil War Centennial Observance Commission to the Governor, Legislature and the People of Michigan* Michigan Civil War Centennial Observance Commission 1966
Awards or inclusion in other biographical books: *Michigan Authors,* 1st ed., 2nd ed.; *Who's Who in the Midwest; The Writers Directory: 1982-1984*

GNATKOWSKI, MICHAEL T.
Address: 6934 W. Illinois Street, Ludington, Michigan 49431
Born: June 17, 1956; Saginaw, Michigan
Parents: Thomas C. Gnatkowski, Maxine L. Gnatkowski
Children: Lauren, Matt
Education: Alma College, B.A. Biology/English, Alma, Michigan, 1974-1978
Career: Freelance Outdoor Writer, self-employed, Ludington, Michigan, 1976—. Charterboat Captain/Guide, Gnat's Charters, Ludington, Michigan, 1981—. Wholesale Distributor, Gnat's Custom Flies and Supplies, Ludington, Michigan, 1988—. ACAR, Ford Motor Credit Company, Saginaw, Michigan, 1979-1981

Writings: Articles in *Michigan Out-of-Doors, Michigan Sportsman, Sportsman's Corner.* Work in Progress: Several assignments Michigan, regional, national outdoor periodicals
What is the aim or goal of your writing? "To utilize my educational training in the field of outdoor writing to more fully enjoy hunting and fishing."
May inquiries be sent to you about doing workshops, readings? Yes

GOINES, DONALD (1937?-1974)
Pseudonym: Al C. Clark
Born: December 15, 1937?; Detroit, Michigan
Children: 9
Education: Catholic Schools, Detroit, Michigan
Career: Served in U.S. Air Force, 1951-1954, Korean War. Started writing in prison, found murdered, Highland Park, Michigan, after returning from Los Angeles

Writings: *Dopefiend: The Story of a Black Junkie* Holloway House 1971. *Whoreson: The Story of a Ghetto Pimp* Holloway House 1972. *Black Gangster* Holloway House 1972. *Black Girl Lost* Holloway House 1973. *White Man's Justice, Black Man's Grief* Holloway House 1973. *Criminal Partners* Holloway House 1974. *Daddy Cool* Holloway House 1974. *Death List* Holloway House 1974. *Inner City Hoodlum* Holloway House 1975. *Kenyatta's Last Hit* Holloway House 1975. Others
Awards or inclusion in other biographical books: *Authors in the News; Black American Writers Past and Present; Contemporary Authors, Dictionary of Literary Biography*

GOKAY, NANCY B.
Address: 24010 99th S.W., Vashon, Washington 98070
Born: February 17, 1925; Jackson, Michigan
Parents: Harry M. Hatch, Beulah M. Hatch
Children: Susan, Paul

Education: Battle Creek Central High School. Bay City Junior College, A.A., 1943-1945. Michigan State University, B.A., East Lansing, Michigan, 1950-1952. Masters work finished, 1966, Jackson, Michigan

Career: Teacher, Lansing, Michigan, 1955-1960. Elementary Teacher, Pontiac, Michigan, 1961-1963. Elementary Teacher, Jackson, Michigan, 1963-1966. Elementary Teacher, Kalamazoo, Michigan, 1967-1970. Elementary Teacher, Alburquerque, New Mexico, 1983-1984. Dinner Train Cook, 1990-1991. Counter-Florist and Garden Center, 1991—. Established Day Care Center, served as director and teacher, 1983-1984

Writings: *Sugarbush* Hillsdale Eductional Publications 1980. Work in Progress: Children's novel set in 1845, Fort Wilkins, Michigan

What is the aim or goal of your writing? "To please readers and continue to hone my writing skills."

May inquiries be sent to you about doing workshops, readings? No

GOLDSTEIN, LAURENCE A.

Address: 408 Second Street, Ann Arbor, Michigan 48103
Born: January 5, 1943; Los Angeles, California
Parents: Cecil H. Goldstein, Helen N. Goldstein
Children: Andrew, Jonathan
Education: U.C.L.A., B.A., Los Angeles, California, 1960-1965. Brown University, Ph.D., Providence, Rhode Island, 1965-1970
Career: Professor of English, University of Michigan, Ann Arbor, Michigan, 1970—.

Writings: *The Female Body: Figures, Styles Speculations* (editor) University of Michigan Press 1991. *Writers and Their Craft: Short Stories and Essays on the Narrative* (co-editor) Wayne State University Press 1991. *Seasonal Performances: A Michigan Quarterly Review Reader* (editor) University of Michigan Press 1991. *The Three Gardens* Copper Beech Press 1988. *The Flying Machine and Modern Literture* Indiana University Press 1987. *The Automobile and American Culture* (editor) University of Michigan Press 1983. *Altamira* Abattoir Editors 1978. Poems and short stories in *Poetry, Boulevard, Ontario Review, Iowa Review, Southern Review, Salmagundi, Texas Review.* Op-Ed pieces in *Los Angeles Times, New York Times, Detroit Free Press.* Work in Progress: Third volume of poems. A book on the response of American poets to the movies

Awards or inclusion in other biographical books: Andrew Mellon Fellowship, Horace Rackham Fellowship

What is the aim or goal of your writing? "To help define the contemporary moment in language that continues to interest readers beyond the present. I hope that my own situation in time and place will model for readers how to understand their location too."

May inquiries be sent to you about doing workshops, readings? Yes

GOLDWASSER, JUDY W.

Address: 1776 Maryland, Birmingham, Michigan 48009
Pseudonym: Judy Wax (sometimes for magazine articles)
Born: June 29, 1944; Detroit, Michigan
Parents: Reuben D. Wax; Rena K. Wax
Children: Amy, Lawrence
Education: University of Michigan, B.A., Ann Arbor, Michigan, 1962-1966
Career: President, Wordwatch, Birmingham, Michigan, 1984—. Freelancer, magazine/

newspaper, Birmingham, Michigan, 1971-1984. Reporter, *Detroit Free Press,* Detroit, Michigan, 1966-1970

Writings: *Unstuck for Words: How to Start and Finish Any Writing Project* (with Leon Linderman) Human Resources Press 1993. Hundreds of bylined magazine and newspaper articles in local and national publications
Awards or inclusion in other biographical books: Shared in Pulitzer Prize with *Detroit Free Press Staff,* 1968. Twice placed in top 50 (from 6,000 entries) in *Writer's Digest* National Article Writing Contest, 1980, 1988. Associate editor, *Cranbrook Quarterly* when Council for Advancement and Support of Educators (CASE) named it best independent school publication in the country, 1984; Contributing editor, when CASE named it best independent school publication in the country, 1985, 1986. UNISYS brochure, "Bit by Bit It Helps", took first place, United Foundation writing awards, 1988
What is the aim or goal of your writing? "My writing is diverse-from feature articles and press releases to brochures and books. But my goal is to produce work that is easy to read, clear and grammatically correct. I wrote my book (see above) so that everyone else can do that too!"
May inquiries be sent to you about doing workshops, readings? Yes

GREEN, JAMES J. (1902-1986)
Born: September 19, 1902; Allegan, Michigan
Parents: Frank H. Green, Rhoda (Arnold) Green
Children: James F., Doris Marie
Education: Western State Teachers College, Certificate, 1924
Career: Manager/Owner, City News Stand, Allegan, Michigan, 45 years

Writings: *All Aboard For the Allegan County Fair* Allegan County Historical Society 1975. *Railroads Come and Go in Allegan County* Allegan County Historical Society 1976. *All the World's a Stage* Allegan County Historical Society 1976. *Fire! Fire! Fire!* Allegan County Historical Society 1977. *The Life and Times of B.D. Pritchard* Allegan County Historical Society 1979. *Readin' and 'Ritin' and 'Rithmetic* Allegan County Historical Society 1979. Numerous magazine articles
Awards or inclusion in other biographical books: *Michigan Authors,* 2nd ed. Allegan Community Council Award, 1962. Meritorious Award of the Grand Chapter R.A.M. of Michigan, 1970. Allegan County Liberty Bell Award, 1974

GREEN, JOHN M.
Address: P.O. Box 15364, Detroit, Michigan 48215-0364
Born: May 11, 1932; Lawton, Oklahoma
Parents: Johnny M. McClanahan, Jannie E. (Cheadle) McClanahan
Children: Johnnie, Tiffny
Education: Douglass High School, diploma. Lincoln University, Jefferson City, Missouri. Wayne State University, B.A., Communication Arts, Journalism, Detroit, Michigan, 1972-1976
Career: Secretary of State, State of Michigan, Lansing, Michigan, 1956-1964. Owner, McClanahan, Inc., Detroit, Michigan, 1964-1984. Legal Investigator, Auto Club Michigan, Detroit, Michigan, 1964-1980. Executive Director, Historical Research Repository, Detroit, Michigan, 1984—

Writings: *Negroes in Michigan History* Historical Research Repository 1968, 1985.

International Black Nobel Prize Winners 1993. Work in Progress: *Cake Walk. John Green Looks at John Brown*

Awards or inclusion in other biographical books: Senate Resolution #233 July 24, 1968. House Resolution #81, March 24, 1987. Wayne County Resolution, February 4, 1988. Senate Resolution #459, January 10, 1990

What is the aim or goal of your writing? "The purpose of my efforts is to correct, as much as possible, the misconception about the contributions Black or African American people have made to the history of Michigan & America."

May inquiries be sent to you about doing workshops, readings? Yes

GREENE, MERRITT W. (1897-1972)
Born: April 22, 1897; Buffalo, New York
Parents: William P. Greene, Nora (Smith) Greene
Children: Merritt, L. Page
Education: Jonesville High School, Jonesville, Michigan, 1916. Hillsdale College, Hillsdale, Michigan
Career: Professional Stage Actor, playwright, insurance salesman. Dramatic coach, Hillsdale High School, Hillsdale, Michigan. WCSR Radio News Director. Reporter in Chicago, County Seat Correspondent for United Press International, *The Detroit Free Press, The Jackson Citizen-Patriot, The Toledo Blade*

Writings: *The Land Lies Pretty* Hillsdale Educational Publishers 1959. *Curse of the White Panther* Hillsdale Educational Publishers 1960. *Forgotten Yesterdays* Hillsdale Educational Publishers 1964

Awards or inclusion in other biographical books: *Michigan Authors,* 1st ed., 2nd ed.

GRINGHUIS, RICHARD H. (1918-1974)
Pseudonym: Dirk Gringhuis
Born: September 22, 1918; Grand Rapids, Michigan
Parents: Leonard J. Gringhuis, Ruth (Perry) Gringhuis
Children: Richard
Education: American Academy of Art, Chicago, Illinois, 1940
Career: Freelance illustrator, 1942-1960. Director, Hope College Art Department, 1947-1952. Art editor, *Children's Health,* 1952-1966. Abrams Planetariums, 1963. Muralist, Mackinac Island Park Commission, 1955-1974. Associate Professor and curator of exhibits, museum, Michigan State University, 1964-1974. Writer, producer and teacher, weekly television show, "Open Door to Michigan" from Michigan State University,1965-1974. Murals at Fort Mackinac, Fort Michilmackinac, East Lansing Public Library, Sturgis Public Library (all in Michigan)

Writings: *Hope Haven* Eerdmans 1947. *Here Comes the Bookmobile* Albert Whitman 1948. *Big Mac: The Story of the World's Biggest Bridge* Macmillan 1956. *Tulip Time* Albert Whitman 1951. *The Eagle Pine* Hillsdale Educational Publishers 1958, 1970. *The Big Hunt and the Big Dig* Dial Press 1960. *Rock Oil to Rockets* Macmillan 1960. *Saddle the Storm* Bobbs Merrill 1962. *In Scarlet and Blue; the Story of Military Uniforms in America* Dial Press 1963. *Of Cabbages and Cattle* Dial Press 1962. *Of Ship and Fish and Fisherman* Albert Whitman 1963. *Mystery at Skull Castle* Reilly & Lee 1964. *From Tall Timber* Albert Whitman 1964. *Open Door to the Great Lakes* WKAR-TV Michigan State University 1966. *Stars in the Ceiling* Meredith Press 1967. *Giants, Dragons and Gods*

Meredith Press 1968. *Lore of the Great Turtle; Indian Legends of Mackinac Retold* Mackinac Island State Park Commission 1970. *The Young Voyageur: Trade and Treachery at Michilimackinac* Mackinac Island State Park Commission 1969. *The Great Parade: Tall Tales and True of Michigan's Past* Hillsdale Educational Publishers 1970. *Let's Color Michigan* Hillsdale Educational Publishers 1971. *Werewolves and Will o' the Wisps* Mackinac Island Park Commission 1974. *Michigan's Indians* Hillsdale Educational Publishers 1972. *Moccasin Tracks: A Saga of the Michigan Indian* Michigan State University Museum 1974. Others
Awards or inclusion in other biographical books: *Michigan Authors,* 1st ed., 2nd ed. MEA Award. Governor's Award. Michigan Minuteman Award

GRISSEN, LILLIAN V.
Address: 6721 Leisure Way Dr., S.E., Caledonia, MI 49316
Born: April 23, 1922; Grand Rapids, Michigan
Parents: Henry Velzen, Dina Velzen
Children: Kenneth, Donna, Susan, J. Anita
Education: Grand Rapids Christian High School. Arizona State University, B.A., Tempe, Arizona 1960-1968. Colorado University, M.A., Boulder, Colorado, 1972-1975
Career: Associate Editor, *Banner,* Christian Reformed Church, Grand Rapids, Michigan, 1982-1988. Associate Professor, Sioux Center, Iowa, 1979-1982. Teacher, Denver Christian Schools, Denver, Colorado, 1970-1978. Teacher, Phoenix Christian Schools, Phoenix, Arizona, 1962-1965

Writings: *Managing the Master's Money* CRC 1992. *For Such a Time As This* Eerdmans 1991. *Men and Women: Partners in Service* CRC 1981. Shared in compiling and editing 5 books for junior high literature and accompanying manuals for teachers. Articles in magazines. Work in Progress: *His Way Is In the Sea*
What is the aim or goal of your writing? "1) To promote biblical feminism 2) To help people who suffer depression 3) To provide practical help for junior-high students."
May inquiries be sent to you about doing workshops, readings? Yes

GROSS, STUART D.
Address: 315 Kennely Road, Apt. 22, Saginaw, Michigan 48609
Born: February 2, 1914; Vincennes, Indiana
Parents: Charles A. Gross, Winifred A. (McGillvary) Gross
Children: Amy, Mary
Education: Hope College, B.A., Holland, Michigan, 1932-1936
Career: Assistant to President, Saginaw Valley State University, University Center, Michigan, 1967-1979. City Editor, *The Saginaw News,* Saginaw, Michigan, 1963-1967; Reporter/Photographer, 1936-1967

Writings: *Frankie and the Barons* Wilderness Adventure Books 1991. *Saginaw: History of Land and City* Windsor Publications 1982. *Trouble at the Grass Roots* Pendell Press 1973. *Indians Jacks and Pines* Saginaw Board of Education 1962. *The Stolen Christmas Star* Carlton Press 1975. Work in Progress: *Frankie and the Barons* will be the basis for a motion picture of Michigan's lumber period, 1850-1900
Awards or inclusion in other biographical books: *Michigan Authors,* 2nd ed.
What is the aim or goal of your writing? "Present aim is to awaken in people in Michigan a greater pride in their heritage. Michigan history is not only important; it is fascinating, colorful, brutal, and full of exciting individuals who mined copper, built

automobiles, turned the state's vast brine reserve into chemicals."
May inquiries be sent to you about doing workshops, readings? Yes

GUCK, DOROTHY M.
Address: P.O. Box 115, Nogal, New Mexico 88341
Pseudonym: Dorothy Gray
Born: May 17, 1913; Grand Rapids, Michigan
Parents: Walter E. Gray, Margaret A. Gray
Children: Tom, Mick, Mary
Education: South High, Grand Rapids, Michigan, 1931. University of Wisconsin-Madison, 1931-1934. Western College, New Mexico, 56 credits
Career: Forest Service Clerk at the Smokey Bear Station of Lincoln National Forest, Capitan, New Mexico, 1957-1962. Teacher, Capitan Schools, Capitan, New Mexico, 1950-1957. Freelance writer and Associated Press Reporter in Arizona and New Mexico. Now helps five grandchildren when seek advice in preparing college class papers

Writings: *Danger Rides the Forest* Vanguard Press 1969; self 1990. Wrote and broadcast *Nature Tales* for PBS, Wisconsin. Smokey Bear Pageant, U.S. Forest Service, 1958, distributed to schools throughout the United States. Work in Progress: Preparing copy for the 1994 celebration of the fifty years of the Smokey Bear Fire Prevention Progam. Speaking and writing with the goal of educating children and the public to the need of caring for, yet utilizing natural resources. Autobiography, *The Ranger's Rib.* Novels
Awards or inclusion in other biographical books: *Michigan Authors,* 2nd ed. Tree planted, John Ball Park, Grand Rapids, Michigan in her honor by the South High School Class of 1931; Plaque presented by President Gerald Ford, 1984 recognizing Smokey Bear Conservationist. Memento, U.S. Postal Service, First Day Issuance of the Smokey Bear Stamp, Capitan, New Mexico. Other recognitions by Apache Indians, Ranchmen's Camp Meetings of the Southwest. Zia Award, New Mexico Press Women for Creative Writing, 1965. Special Award, U.S. Forest Service, 1958
What is the aim or goal of your writing? "To promote the enjoyment of reading among children and adults. Composition that is exciting, humorous, mysterious, adventuresome and quick-paced, not cumbersome or dull, is essential to spike the avid interest of readers in turning pages. My elementary and high school schooling in Grand Rapids, Michigan certainly was an excellent preparation for the life I have lived. My enjoyment of reading and wrting started there."

GUEST, EDGAR A. (1881-1959)
Born: August 20, 1881; Birmingham, England
Parents: Edwin Guest, Julia (Wayne) Guest
Children: Janet, Edgar
Education: Central High School, Detroit, Michigan, graduating 1897
Career: Began writing when 14 years old. Newspaperman, *Detroit Free Press,* 1895-1959. Radio presentations. Verse syndicated across the country. President, American Press Humorists

Writings: *Just Glad Things* (Detroit) 1911. *Breakfast Table Chat* (Detroit) 1914. *Every Day a Christmas* Thomas P. Henry 1915. *A Heap o' Livin'* Reilly & Lee 1916. *Just Folks* Reilly & Lee 1917. *A Dozen New Poems* Reilly & Lee 1920. *When Day is Done* Reilly and Lee 1921. *All That Matters* Reilly and Lee 1922. *The Passing Throng* Reilly and Lee 1923. *Rhythms of Childhood* Reilly and Lee 1924. *The Light of Faith* Reilly and Lee 1926.

Harbor Lights of Home Reilly and Lee 1928. *Father* Reilly & Lee 1930. *The Friendly Way* Reilly and Lee 1931. *Faith* Reilly & Lee 1932. *Life's Highway* Reilly and Lee 1933. *Collected Verse* Contemporary Books 1934. *Between You and Me; My Philosophy of Life* Reilly & Lee 1938. *All in a Life Time* Arno 1938. *Today and Tomorrow* Reilly and Lee 1942. *"Letters"* Detroit Free Press 1946. *Living the Years* Reilly and Lee 1949. Others In the 2nd Edition of *Michigan Authors* is noted: "Edgar Guest's family left England and came to Detroit when he was ten years old. During his career with the *Detroit Free Press* he wrote numerous verses and humorous sketches. He was frequently referred to as 'The Poet of the Plain People.'"

Awards or inclusion in other biographical books: *American Authors and Books; Childhood in Poetry; Current Biography; Dictionary of American Biography; Lincoln Library of Language Arts; Michigan: A Centennial History of the State and its People* (Michigan Biography: Vol 4); *Michigan Authors,* 2nd ed.; *Michigan Poets; National Cyclopaedia of American Biography; Oxford Companion to American Literature; Reader's Encyclopedia; Reader's Encyclopedia of American Literature; Who Was Who in America; Who Was Who among North American Authors,* others

GUEST, JUDITH

Born: March 29, 1936; Detroit, Michigan
Parents: Harry Reginald, Marion Aline (Nesbit) Guest, (Great uncle was Edgar Guest)
Children: Larry, John, Richard
Education: University of Michigan, B.A., Ann Arbor, Michigan, 1958
Career: Teacher, Royal Oak, Michigan 1964, Birmingham, Michigan, 1969, Troy, Michigan, 1975. Newspaper Reporter

Writings: *Ordinary People* (Book-of-the-Month Club Selection) Viking 1976; Ballantine Books 1980. *Second Heaven* (Book-of-the-Month Club Selection) Viking 1982; screenplay adaptation of *Second Heaven. Killing Time in St. Cloud* Delacorte Press 1988. Foreign translations in Barcelona, Taipei. Short stories, contributor to periodicals such as *The Writer*. Film *Ordinary People* was 1980 Oscar winner

Awards or inclusion in other biographical books: *Contemporary Authors; Contemporary Literary Criticiticm; Michigan Authors,* 2nd ed.; *Writers Directory; Who's Who in America.* Janet Heidinger Kafka Prize, University of Rochester, 1977. In the 2nd edition of *Michigan Authors* appears: "In an article published by the *Detroit Free Press,* Judith Guest calls writing 'My escape, my terror, my compulsion, my life.' About seven years ago (1972) she began writing seriously and submitted a short story for a *Reader's Digest* contest. There were one hundred prizes and her story received 60th place. Her next short story was the beginning of her highly-acclaimed first novel, *Ordinary People*. She says, 'After I finished my short story, I realized I wasn't ready to put the characters down, that I had more to say about them. So, I thought, I'll write something about what happened to them before and what happened after. And before I knew what I was doing, I was writing a novel.'"

GUSTIN, LAWRENCE ROBERT

Address: 1438 Country View Lane, Flint, Michigan 48532
Born: May 26, 1937; Flint, Michigan
Parents: Robert S. Gustin, Doris M. (Irving) Gustin
Children: Robert, David
Education: Michigan State University, B.A., East Lansing, Michigan, 1955-1959

Career: United Press International, capitol correspondent, Lansing, Michigan, 1959-1960. Sports editor, Detroit, 1960. U. S. Army, 1960, U.S. Air Force Reserve, active duty 1963-1966. Various positions, *Flint Journal,* Flint, Michigan, 1960-1984. Buick Motor Division, Public Relations, 1984-1987; Manager of News Relations, 1987—. Acquisitions Committee, Sloan Museum

Writings: *Billy Durant: Creator of General Motors* Eerdmans 1973; Craneshaw 1980. *The Flint Journal Picture History of Flint* Eerdmans, 1975, 1976, 1978. *The Buick: A Complete History* (with Terry B. Dunham) Automobile Quarterly 1980; 4th edition 1992. Work in Progress: Completing 90th Anniversary Edition of *The Buick: A Complete History.* More research on William C. Durant

Awards or inclusion in other biographical books: *Contemporary Authors; Michigan Authors,* 2nd ed. Certificate of Commendation, American Association for State and Local History, 1974. Award of Merit, Michigan Historical Society, 1974. Thomas McKean Memorial Cup, Antique Automobile Club of America, 1975. Shared Detroit Press Club top news writing award, 1980. Award of Merit, Michigan Historical Society

What is the aim or goal of your writing? "To inform about role of Flint, Buick and W. C. Durant in auto history."

May inquiries be sent to you about doing workshops, readings? Yes

H

HAAN, SHERI D.
Address: 4079 Fruitridge Avenue, N.W., Grand Rapids, Michigan 49504
Born: December 19, 1940
Parents: Glen A. Dunham, Alice S. Dunham
Children: Chad, Keith
Education: Calvin College, A.B., Education, Grand Rapids, Michigan, 1958-1962. Michigan State University, M.A., Reading Instruction, East Lansing, 1962-1965. University of Chicago, Advanced Study
Career: Executive Director, Christian Schools International, Grand Rapids, Michigan, 1989—; Director of Operations, 1984-1989; Elementary Lanuage Arts Consultant, 1966-1984. Instructor, Calvin College, Grand Rapids, Michigan, 1966-1970. Teacher, Oakdale Christian School, Grand Rapids, Michigan, 1962-1965, 1966-1970. Teacher, Battle Creek Christian School, Michigan, 1965-1966

Writings: *God Speaks to a King* Baker Book House 1990. *A World is Born* Baker Book House 1990. *Precious Moments, Stories from the Bible* Baker Book House 1987. *Bible Stories in Rhyme and Rhythm* Baker Book House 1975. *A Child's Storybook of Bible People* Baker Book House 1973. *Good News for Children* Baker Book House 1969. *Reading Rainbow, K-6, Writing Series* Christian Schools International 1981. *Spelling Spectra, 1-6, Spelling Series* Christian Schools International 1979. *Books Worth Reading Aloud, K-6* Christian Schools International 1978. *The Art of Storytelling* Christian Schools International 1977. *Revelation-Response, Grade 4* Christian Schools International 1976. Others printed by Christian Reformed Publishing House as part of the Bible Way Curriculum for Church Education. *Story Hour Program*, Coffee Break Ministries
What is the aim or goal of your writing? "To stimulate children's imaginations, giving their minds both roots and wings."
May inquiries be sent to you about doing workshops, readings? Yes

HACKER, DAVID W.
Address: 1039 W. Long Lake Road, Traverse City, Michigan 49684
Born: June 2, 1928; Fort Wayne, Indiana
Parents: George F. Hacker; Kathryn W. Hacker
Children: Holly, Sandy, Sarah, Jonathan
Education: Roosevelt High School, Wyandotte, Michigan. University of Chicago, 1944-1946. Indiana University, summer 1951. Hanover College, A.B., Hanover, Indiana, 1949-1952. Harvard University, 1952-1953. University of Louisville. University of Oklahoma
Career: U.S. Army, 1946-1948. Sports Editor, *Jonesboro Evening Sun*, Arkansas, 1953. Sports Columnist/Sunday Feature Writer, *Arkansas Gazette,* 1954-1955. Reporter, copy editor, other, *The Louisville Times,* 1955-1962. Various positions, *The National Observer,* Washington DC, 1962-1977. R.M. Seaton Distinguished Visiting Professor, Kansas State University, 1977-1981. Contributing editor, *Flint Weekly News Feature Magazine,*

1978-1980. Editor, *The Manhattan Mercury*, 1981-1986. Writing Coach, Staff Writer, *The Wichita Eagle-Beacon,* 1986-1987. *Detroit Free Press,* Up North Correspondent, 1987–.

Writings: *Leonard Mikowski is Full of Baloney-and Other Michigan Stories* self published 1987. *The Quilted Eye* self published 1986. *Mudbath* self published 1985. *Who Governs Kansas* self published 1986. Stories have appeared or have been reprinted in numerous magazines, textbooks, and collections. Work in Progress: *Nathalie: Her Story.* Untitled biography

Awards or inclusion in other biographical books: International Press Institute Fellowship, Work-Study, South Africa, 1958. *The Observer's,* first nominee for Pulitzer Prize, 1962. Paul Myhre Award University of Missouri Penney for "The Day the Music Stopped", 1981. Co-winner, Pulitzer Prize for local reporting, as writing coach for *Kansas City Times,* 1982. *Manhattan Mercury* named best newspaper in Kansas and Missouri under 50,000 circulation

What is the aim or goal of your writing? "To plumb the mysteries of the human heart."

May inquiries be sent to you about doing workshops, readings? Yes

HAGMAN, HARLAN L.
Address: 1017 Kensington Road, Grosse Pointe Park, Michigan 48230
Born: DeKalb, Illinois
Education: Northern Illinois University, Bachelor, DeKalb, Illinois. Northwestern University, M.A., Ph.D., Evanston, Illinois
Career: Professor, Wayne State University, Detroit, Michigan. Drake University, Des Moines, Iowa. Northwestern University, Evanston, Illinois. Visiting Professor: University of Texas, Western Washington University, Michigan State University

Writings: *Nathan Hale and John Andre: Reluctant Heroes of the American Revolution* Empire State Books 1992. *A Seasonal Present and Other Stories* Green Oak Press 1989. *Second Balcony* (co-author) One-act Plays 1990. *Bright Michigan Morning, the Years of Governor Tom Mason* Green Oak Press 1982. *The Academic Life* Center for Health Education 1983. *September Campus* Kensington Collection 1977. *Administration of American Public Schools* McGraw-Hill 1951. *Administration of Elementary Schools* McGraw-Hill 1956. *Administration in Profile for School Executives* (co-author) Harper 1955. *The School Board Member* School Activities 1941. Work in Progress: *Bloody Moon: the Black Hawk War, The Literary Lives of Washington Irving.* Articles, etc.

Awards or inclusion in other biographical books: *Who's Who in America; Who's Who in the World.* Distinguished Alumnus Award, Northern Illinois University

HAGY, ALYSON
Address: 3616 East Pineview, Dexter, Michigan 48130
Born: August 1, 1960; Springfield, Ohio
Parents: John A. Hagy, Carol L. Hagy
Children: Connor Wroe Southard
Education: Williams College, B.A., Williamstown, Massachusetts, 1978-1982. University of Michigan, M.F.A., Ann Arbor, Michigan, 1983-1985
Career: Lecturer, Department of English, Ann Arbor, Michigan, 1986—. Lecturer, Department of English, University of Virginia, Charlottesville, Virginia, 1985-1986. Summer School Faculty, University of Southern Maine, Gorham, Maine, 1984-1990.

Writings: *Hardware River* Poseidon Press 1991. *Madonna On Her Back* Stuart Wright 1986. Included in anthology, University of Virginia Press 1990. Work in Progress: Novel, *Giving Up Rebecca*
Awards or inclusion in other biographical books: *Dictionary of Literary Biography*, 1992. Hopwood Award in Short Fiction, University of Michigan, 1984
May inquiries be sent to you about doing workshops, readings? Yes

HAIGHT, ROBERT C.

Address: 2138 Oakland Drive, Kalamazoo, Michigan 49008
Born: August 19, 1955; Detroit, Michigan
Parents: Loyal H. Haight, Julia S. Haight
Children: Robert L., Santana
Education: Western Michigan University, Master of Fine Arts, Kalamazoo, Michigan, 1984-1986; Bachelor of Arts, 1973-1977. Michigan State University, East Lansing, Graduate Studies in Education
Career: Instructor of English, Kalamazoo Valley Community College, Kalamazoo, Michigan, 1989—. Instructor, Western Michigan University, Kalamazoo, 1987-1989. Teacher, Kaleva Norman Dickson Schools, Brethren, Michigan, 1977-1984

Writings: Poetry and non-fiction in two anthologies and thirty or so magazines and journals. Work in Progress: A poetry book and a nonfiction/poetry book
Awards or inclusion in other biographical books: *Directory of American Poets & Fiction Writers,* 1991-1993. Grant from Kalamazoo Foundation/Arts Council of Greater Kalamazoo. University Graduate Research and Creation Scholar, Western Michigan University, 1987. Department Research and Creative Scholar, Western Michigan University, 1987. New Voices in Michigan Poetry, 1986
What is the aim or goal of your writing? "My aim or goal is to produce art worthy of a tradition of great artists. Poetry has no commercial value. It is not popular. But it is the form which asks a writer to take language as far as one can take it. The goal of my prose writing is similar, though the non-fiction essay depends more upon the play of content than specifically of language. There is at least a slight utilitarian value to prose. I suppose that as all writers do I write to discover what I think and how I feel."
May inquiries be sent to you about doing workshops, readings? Yes

HAINES, DONAL HAMILTON (1886-1951)

Born: February 28, 1886; Kalamazoo, Michigan
Parents: David Hamilton, Lila Jane (Thayer) Hamilton
Education: Kalamazoo College, Kalamazoo, Michigan; University of Michigan, Ann Arbor, Michigan, A.B. Degree
Career: Editor, *The Michigan Alumnus,* 1921-1925. Instructor in Journalism, University of Michigan, Ann Arbor, Michigan

Writings: *The Return of Pierre* 1912. *Clearing the Seas; or, The Last of the Warships* Harper & Brothers 1915. *The Last Invasion* Harper & Brothers 1914. *The Dragon-Flies* 1918. *Sky-Line Inn* Houghton Mifflin 1923. *Fighting Blood* 1927. *The Transportation Library of the University of Michigan; Its History and Needs* University of Michigan 1929. *The Southpaw* Farrar & Rinehart 1931. *Sporting Chance* Farrar & Rinehart 1935. *Blaine of the Backfield* Farrar & Rinehart 1937. *Langfords Luck* Farrar & Rinehart 1939. *Pro Quarterback* Farrar & Rinehart 1940. *Shadow on the Campus* Farrar &

Rinehart 1942. *The Fortress, a Story of Hillton Academy by Donald Hamilton Haines*
Farrar & Rinehart 1945. Others. Contributor to many magazines
Awards or inclusion in other biographical books: *Michigan Authors,* 2nd ed.;
Science Fiction and Fantasy Literature; Who Was Who Among North American Authors

HALL, CAROLYN VOSBURG
Address: 20730 Kennoway, Birmingham, Michigan 48025
Born: July 22, 1927; Fenton, Michigan
Parents: Guy M. Vosburg, Doris L. (Borns) Vosburg
Children: Randall Ross Hall, Claudia Hall Stroud, Garrett Allan Hall
Education: Cranbrook Academy of Art, B.F.A., 1947-1949; M.F.A., 1950-1951. Olivet
College, Olivet, Michigan, 1945-1946. Michigan State University, East Lansing, 1946-
1947
Career: Art Critic, *Birmingham Eccentric* Newspaper, 1962-1972. Instructor, North
Dakota State College, 1949-1950. Freelance: teaching, art exhibitions/sales, talks,
jurying

Writings: *Friendship Quilts by Hand and Machine* Chilton 1985. *A to Z Soft Animals*
Prentice-Hall 1984. *The Teddy Bear Craft Book* Van Nostrand Reinhold 1981. *Soft
Sculpture* Davis 1980. *The Sewing Machine Craft Book* Van Nostrand Reinhold 1978. *I
Love Popcorn* Doubleday 1976. *I Love Ice Cream* Doubleday 1976. *Stitched and Stuffed
Art* Doubleday 1972. Magazine articles or designs for *Woman's Day, Threads, 1001 Good
Ideas, Creative Living* and others.
Work in Progress: *Pictorial Quilt Art* Chilton. *A Book on Theater Arts* Davis
Awards or inclusion in other biographical books: *Michigan Authors,* 2nd ed.
Awards for painting, soft sculpture, others. Michigan Press Association Award for
newspaper column. Included in various collected works
What is the aim or goal of your writing? "I write to create. Making something (an art
object-a book) that others can experience and enjoy as much as I did in its creation is my
goal."
May inquiries be sent to you about doing workshops, readings? Yes

HAMILTON, FRANKLIN W.
Address: 423 South Franklin Avenue, Flint, Michigan 48503
Born: November 22, 1923; Benton, Illinois
Children: Ann Marla, Douglas, Karen
Education: Southern Illinois University, B.A., M.A., Carbondale, Illinois. Kansas State
University, M.S., Emporia, Kansas. University of Kansas, Ph.D., Lawrence, Kansas
Career: High school teacher, 2 years; Professor, 35 years-in Illinois, Tennessee, Kansas,
Michigan. Editor and founder, Walden Press. Editor and publisher, *Huron Review*

Writings: Poetry books: *Leaf Scar. Love Cry.* Poetry, fiction in dozens of magazines in
the United States and abroad. Work in Progress: Over 200 poems last year
Awards or inclusion in other biographical books: *Michigan Authors,* 2nd ed.
What is the aim or goal of your writing? "The adjustment of the person to his/her
world."

HANCHAR, PEGGY S.
Address: P.O. Box 485, Delton, Michigan 49046
Pseudonym: Peggy Roberts, Jennifer Stevens

Born: January 2, 1940; Jefferson City, Missouri
Parents: Robert L. Smith, Elsie L. Smith
Children: Stephen, James, Robert, Laura
Education: Kellogg Community College, Battle Creek, Michigan, 1975-1977; Western Michigan University, Kalamazoo, Michigan, 1977-1979, Associate Degree
Career: Society Editor, *Berrien County Record,* Buchanan, Michigan, 1965-1966. Bookstore manager, Owl Bookstore, Battle Creek, Michigan, 1971-1972. Owner, manager, Jenny Lynn Fabrics, Delton, Michigan, 1979-1982. Teacher, Berrien County Literacy Council, 1989

Writings: *Where Eagles Soar* Fawcett 1992. *Louisiana Heat* Zebra 1992. *Mrs. Perfect* Zebra 1992. *The Gilded Dove* Fawcett 1991. *Tomorrow's Dream* New American Library 1990. *Tender Betrayal* New American Library 1989. *Golden Promises* New American Library 1988. *Creole Angel* New American Library 1987. *Renegade Heart* New American Library 1986. *Desire's Dream* Pinnacle 1985. Work in Progress: *Cheyenne Dreams* Fawcett
Awards or inclusion in other biographical books: Received Gold 5 Star Review for *Where Eagles Soar.* On Waldenbrooks Bestseller List
What is the aim or goal of your writing? "I try to portray women in an honest, positive manner that will show the importance of their roles in the settling of our country, at the same time I try to entertain."
May inquiries be sent to you about doing workshops, readings? Yes

HANDY, VIRGINIA M.
Address: 3503 Edwards Road, Sodus, Michigan 49126
Born: July 21, 1935; Benton Harbor, Michigan
Parents: Russell Handy, Mary E. Handy
Education: Western Michigan University, B.A. cum laude, Kalamazoo, Michigan, 1954-1956. A. A., Benton Harbor Community College, Benton Harbor, Michigan, 1952-1954
Career: Editor, *Log Cabin News,* Log Cabin Society of Michigan, Sodus, Michigan, 1989—. Medical Records Abstractor, Mercy-Memorial Medical Center, St. Joseph, Michigan, 1972-1991. Cataloger, Sodus Township Library, Sodus, Michigan, 1968-1972. Cataloger, Lakehead University Library, Thunder Bay, Ontario, Canada, 1964-1967. Cataloger, Detroit Public Library, 1956-1962. Founder, Log Cabin Society of Michigan

Writings: Articles, book reviews, *South Bend Tribune, Detroit Free Press, Spin-Off, Log Home Guide,* others. Columnist, *Michigan Magazine.* In various anthologies such as *Talk of the Towns; Stories from Southwest Michigan,* others. Work in Progress: A book on the log cabins of Michigan
Awards or inclusion in other biographical books: Award of Merit, Historical Society of Michigan, 1991
What is the aim or goal of your writing? "A 'voice crying in the wilderness' of rural southwestern Michigan in Berrien County, I feel compelled to communicate my cause to the outside world: the preservation of our historical resources, especially of old log cabins which are in danger of being destroyed. This has a positive side also. By organizing and coordinating the annual Log Cabin Day on the last Sunday of June, the only statewide log cabin festival in the U.S.A., I have learned communication skills which help bring thousands of visitors every year to more than fifty Log Cabin day events in the state, with old-time music, crafts, and historical re-enactments. I also am trying to keep alive

spinning and flax-work in our area, and I probably am the only one in the state now working with flax, with writings and demonstrations."
May inquiries be sent to you about doing workshops, readings? Yes

HARDIN, KENNETH L.
Address: 441 Washington Road, Farwell, Michigan 48622
Born: March 18, 1916; Clinton, Illinois
Parents: Merritt L. Hardin, Bessie P. Hardin
Children: Cheryl Le
Education: Huntington Park High School, California. Ridgedale Theological Seminary, Th.B., Th.M., Chattanooga, Tennessee, 1969-1973. Berean Christian College, D.Min., 1974-1977
Career: Pastoral Ministries, Assemblies of God, 1937—. Dean, Michigan Extension, Ridgedale Theological Seminary, 1970-1974; Vice President, 1975-1977; President, 1977-1978

Writings: *Bluebells Forever* self-published 1984. *Tomorrow's Joy* self-published 1986. *The Fifty Year Trek* self-published 1990. *The Dream Chaser* self-published 1991. Work in Progress: *This Path I Follow*
What is the aim or goal of your writing? "To warm the hearts of readers and leave with them some worthwhile experience."

HARDY, LEE P.
Address: 1325 Hope SE, Grand Rapids, Michigan 49506
Born: May 27, 1950; Ventura, California
Parents: Jess E. Hardy, Anne L. Hardy
Children: Katrina, Andrew, Ian, Grace
Education: Trinity Christian College, B.A. Philosophy, Palos Heights, Illinois, 1972-1976. Duquesne University, M.A., Ph.D., Philosophy, Pittsburgh, Pennsylvania, 1976-1981. University of Pittsburgh, M.A., Philosophy, Pittsburg, Pennsylvania, 1979-1980
Career: Professor of Philosophy, Calvin College, Grand Rapids, Michigan, 1981—. Instructor, Duquesne University, 1980; Teaching Assistant, 1978. Teaching Assistant, University of Pittsburgh, 1979. Chaired sessions, delivered lecture series, papers

Writings: *The Fabric of This World* Eerdmans 1990. Editor, *Phenomenology of Natural Science* Kluwer 1992. Several scholarly publications in *International Studies in Philosophy* and others. Several articles in other publications such as *The Banner*. Work in Progress: Translator: *Husserl's Transcendental Phenomelogy* by Elisabeth Stroker, Stanford University Press, forthcoming
Awards or inclusion in other biographical books: Senior Fellowship in the Lilly Fellows Program in Humanities and the Arts, Valparaiso University, 1992-1993. Calvin Alumni Association Faculty Research Grant, 1990. National Endowment for the Humanities Travel Grant, 1990. Midwest Faculty Seminar Occasional Fellowship, 1982
What is the aim or goal of your writing? "To advance the discipline of philosophy."
May inquiries be sent to you about doing workshops, readings? Yes

HARRIMAN, KARL EDWIN (1875-1935)
Born: December 29, 1875; Ann Arbor, Michigan
Parents: William D. Harriman, Harriett M. (Bliss) Harriman
Education: University of Michigan, A.B., Ann Arbor, Michigan

Career: *Detroit Journal,* 1895, *Detroit Free Press,* 1898-1899. Founding editor *Redbook,* 1903. Editor of various magazines such as *Ladies' Home Journal,* 1912-1919, *Redbook, Blue Book* 1919-1927

Writings: *Ann Arbor Tales* George W. Jacobs & Company 1902; Books for Libraries Press 1969. *Away From the Shore* 1902. *The Homebuilders* George W. Jacobs & Company 1903. *The Girl out there* George W. Jacobs & Company 1906; A. Wessels 1908. *Sadie* 1907. Stories in *Harper's Weekly, Era, Lippincott's,* others
Awards or inclusion in other biographical books: *American Authors and Books; Dictionary of American Authors; Dictionary of North American Authors; National Cyclopaedia of American Biography; Who Was Who in America*

HARRINGTON, STEVE E.
Address: P.O. Box 275, Mason, Michigan 48854
Born: March 13, 1953; Grand Rapids, Michigan
Parents: Donald E. Harrington, Nina R. Harrington
Children: Jason
Education: Michigan State University, B.S., Wildlife Management, 1973-1975. Thomas M. Cooley Law School, J.D., Lansing, Michigan, 1985-1988
Career: President, Maritime Research Associates, Inc., Lansing, Michigan, 1990—. Writer, Editor, *Michigan Lawyers Weekly,* Lansing, Michigan, Michigan, 1988-1990. Reporter, Advance Newspapers, Venison, Michigan, 1983-1984. Teacher, Lowell Area Schools, Lowell, Michigan, 1975-1982

Writings: *Divers Guide to Michigan,* Maritime Press 1990. *Divers Guide to Wisconsin* Maritime Press 1991. *Diving Into St. Ignace Past* (Editor) Maritime Press 1990. *Visitor's Guide to S. Manilou Island* Beagle Publishing 1990
Work in Progress: *Great Lakes Wildflowers. Divers Guide to Ohio*
Awards or inclusion in other biographical books: Benjamin Fine Award for Educational Writing, 1989. Award for Humorous Children's Poetry, American Poetry Association, 1984. School Bell Award, Michigan Education Association, Educational Writing, 1983
What is the aim or goal of your writing? "To facilitate enjoyment of the outdoors."
May inquiries be sent to you about doing workshops, readings? Yes

HARRIS, LEFFIE L.(OUISE)
Address: 7014 Inkster Road, Apt. C110, Dearborn Heights, Michigan 48127
Born: April 20, 1915; Union, Mississippi
Parents: Richmond B. Harris, Ollie S. (Walters) Harris
Education: Wayne State University, Detroit, Michigan: B.S., 1944-1947; M. Ed., 1947-1948; Ed. D., 1949-1957
Career: Teacher, Detroit Public Schools, Detroit, Michigan, 1947-1957; Department Head, 1957-1977. Instructor, Wayne State University School of Business Administration, Detroit, Michigan, 1968-1971. Instructor, Thammasat University, Bangkok, Thailand, 1967-1968. Instructor, Wayne State University College of Education, Detroit, Michigan, 1957-1961

Writings: *Woman in the Christian Church* Green Oak Press 1988. Articles in *Journal of Business Education,* others
What is the aim or goal of your writing? "To search for the truth and to make my findings available to others who are interested in knowing the facts."
May inquiries be sent to you about doing workshops, readings? Yes

HARRISON, JIM (JAMES THOMAS)

Born: December 11, 1937; Grayling, Michigan
Parents: Winfield S. Harrison, Norma Olivia (Wahlgren) Harrison
Children: Jamie, Anna
Education: Michigan State University, B.A., East Lansing, Michigan, 1960. Michigan State University, M.A., East Lansing, Michigan, 1964
Career: Assistant Professor of English, State University of New York at Stony Brook, 1965-1966. Screenwriter for Warner Brothers and other film companies

Writings: *Plain Song* Norton 1965. *Locations* Norton 1968. *Walking Pym* Randall Press 1969. *Outlyer and Ghazals* Simon & Schuster 1971. *Un Bon Jour pour Mourir: Roman* R. Laffont (Paris) 1973. *Letters to Yesinin* Sumac Press 1973. *Farmer* Viking 1976. *Returning to Earth* Ithaca House 1977. *Selected Poems* Delacorte 1982. *Wolf: A False Memoir* Simon & Schuster 1971. Novels: *A Good Day to Die* Simon & Schuster 1973. *Farmer* Viking 1975. *Legends of the Fall* Delacorte 1979. *Warlock* Delacorte 1981. *Natural World: a Bestiary* Open Book 1982. *Sundog* Heinemann 1984, 1985. *Pathways to a Southern Coast* University of South Carolina Press 1986. *Un Buen Dia para Morir* Laia (Barcelona) 1988. *Dalva* E.P. Dutton/Seymour Lawrence 1988; J. Cape 1989. *Just before Dark: Collected Nonfiction* Clark City Press 1991. *The Woman Lit by Fireflies* Houghton Mifflin/Seymour Lawrence 1990; Washington Square 1991. Poems in many anthologies such as *Out of the War Shadow; an Anthology of Current Poetry* War Resisters League 1967; *Fifty Modern American and British Poets* McKay 1973; *Contemporary Michigan Poetry: Poems from the Third Coast* Wayne State University Press 1988. Work has appeared in *Sports Illustrated, American Poetry Review, Nation, Esquire* and others
Awards or inclusion in other biographical books: *American Authors and Books; Contemporary Authors; Contemporary Literary Criticism; Contemporary Poets; A Directory of American Fiction Writers; A Directory of American Poets; International Who's Who in Poetry; Michigan Authors,* 2nd ed.*; The Reader's Adviser; Who's who in America; World Authors; The Writers Directory.* National Endowment for the Arts grants, 1967-1969. Guggenheim fellowship, 1969-1970. Two awards from National Literary Anthology

HARRISON, SUE A.

Address: P.O. Box 6, 18 Mile Road, Pickford, Michigan 49774
Born: August 29, 1950; Lansing, Michigan
Parents: Charles R. McHaney, Jr., Patricia A. (Sawyer) McHaney
Children: Neil, Krystal, Koral (deceased)
Education: Pickford High School, Pickford, Michigan, 1964-1968. Lake Superior State College, B.A., Sault Ste. Marie, Michigan, 1968-1971
Career: Adjunct Faculty, Lake Superior State University, Sault Ste. Marie, Michigan, 1987-1991. Public relations writer, Lake Superior State University, 1985-1988. Co-owner, Pickford Power Sports, Pickford, Michigan, 1974-1981. Cashier, Pickford Meat Company, Pickford, Michigan, 1968-1972

Writings: *My Sister the Moon* Doubleday 1992; Avon, also published in Great Britain. *Mother Earth Father Sky* Doubleday/Avon 1990; also published in Sweden, Great Britain, Italy, Spain, Holland, Germany.
Thorndike published the large print edition in this country. Work in Progress: Untitled third book in *Mother Earth Father Sky* trilogy, option to Doubleday
Awards or inclusion in other biographical books: *Mother Earth Father Sky* selected by American Library Association, Best Books for Young Adults, 1991

What is the aim or goal of your writing? "I want to introduce my readers to the roots of Native American culture. I also want to send an environmental message and to entertain."

May inquiries be sent to you about doing workshops, readings? Yes

HART, ALISON

Address: 1280 Hillandale, Benton Harbor, Michigan 49022
Pseudonym: Jennifer Greene, Jeanne Grant, Jessica Massey
Born: December 9, 1948; Detroit, Michigan
Parents: Frank M. Hart, Lorraine G. (Newkirk) Hart
Children: Jennifer, Ryan
Education: Michigan State University, B.A., East Lansing, Michigan, 1966-1970
Career: Novelist, 1980—. Personnel manager, Modern Plastics, 1971-1975

Writings: *Pink Topaz* Silhouette 1992. *Falconer* Silhouette 1991. *Night Light* Silhouette 1991. *Dancing in the Dark* Silhouette 1989. *Castle Keep* Silhouette 1988. *Dear Reader* Silhouette 1987. *Body and Soul* Silhouette 1986. (About 20 novels published so far by Silhouette). *Tender Loving Care* Berkley 1987. *Sweets to the Sweet* Berkley 1986. *A Daring Proposition* Berkley 1983. (About 15 novels published so far from Berkley) *Stormy Surrender* Dell 1984. Work in Progress: *Just Like Old Times* Silhouette 1992. *It Had to Be You* Silhouette 1992

Awards or inclusion in other biographical books: RITA, Romance Writers of America, 1989. Romantic Times Lifetime Achievement Award, 1988-1989. Romantic Times Best Series Author, 1989. Affaire De Coeur Silver Pen Award, 1987. Silver Medallion, Romance Writers of America, 1984. Others from Romance Writers of America and Romantic Times

What is the aim or goal of your writing? "From the start, I have tried to write about issues of concern to women today."

HART, JOHN E.

Address: 412 Fitch, Albion, Michigan 49224
Born: February 16, 1917; Barnard, Kansas
Parents: Harriss L. Hart, Anna M. Hart
Education: Kansas Wesleyan University, B.A., 1934-1938. Syracuse University, M.A., Syracuse, New York, 1938-1940; Ph.D., 1950-1954
Career: Professor, English Department, Albion College, Albion, Michigan, 1954-1982. Teacher/Scholar, Syracuse University, Syracuse, New York, 1951-1954. Instructor, Odenwaldschule, bei Heppenheim, Germany, 1950. Instructor, University of Cincinnati, Cincinnati, Ohio, 1946-1949. Sgt. U.S. Army, 1942-1945. Instructor, Syracuse University, 1940-1942, Syracuse, New York

Writings: *Heroes and Progresses* Albion Review Press 1985. *Albert Halper* G.K. Hall 1980. *Floyd Dell* Twayne Publishers 1971. Essays on Ring Lardner, Benjamin Appel and others. Entries of writers for *Dictionary of American Biography*. Work in Progress: Critical essay on Carl Van Vechten. Entries for new *Dictionary of American Biography* on James T. Farrell, James Jones

Awards or inclusion in other biographical books: *Contemporary Authors,* around 1973 and update; *Directory of American Scholars* around 1973; *Michigan Authors,* 2nd ed. Scholar of Year, Albion College, 1975

What is the aim or goal of your writing? "To explore the magic and meaning of the written word, especially the artistic and aesthetic creations that man's mind and

imagination are capable of conceiving-in two words: literary criticism."
May inquiries be sent to you about doing workshops, readings? No

HATCHER, HARLAN
Address: 841 Greenhills Drive, Ann Arbor, Michigan 48105
Born: September 9, 1898; Ironton, Ohio
Parents: Robert E. Hatcher, Linda B. Hatcher
Children: Robert Leslie, Anne Linda
Education: Morehead Normal School, Ohio State University, University of Chicago, A.B., M.A., Ph.D., LLD., 1919-1927
Career: President Emeritus, The University of Michigan, 1951-1968. After retirement-private employment, boards and commissions

Writings: *The Western Reserve* Kent State University Press and Western Reserve Historical Society 1991; World Publishing 1966; Bobbs Merrill 1949. *Pictorial History of the Great Lakes* Crown 1963. *The Persistent Quest for Values* (Brick Lectures) University of Missouri 1966. *Giant from the Wilderness* Cleveland 1955. *A Century of Iron and Men* Bobbs Merrill 1950. *Lake Erie* (Lakes Series) Bobbs Merrill 1945. *The Great Lakes* Oxford University Press 1944. *The Buckeye Country: A Pageant of Ohio* Kinsey 1940. *Creating the Modern American Novel* Farrar-Rienhart 1935. *Central Standard Time* Farrar-Rinehart 1937. *Patterns of Wolfpen* Bobbs Merrill 1934. *Tunnel Hill* Bobbs Merrill 1931. *The Versification of Robert Browning* The Ohio State University Press 1928. Editor of books such as *Modern American Dramas* Harcourt 1941, 1949. Contributor of short stories, essays, articles to various magazines and journals. Work in Progress: Memoirs
Awards or inclusion in other biographical books: *The Authors and Writers Who's Who* Burkes Peerage Ltd. London,1960; *Dictionary of International Biography,* 1971; *Michigan Authors,* 1st ed., 2nd ed. Ohioana Award, 1945
What is the aim or goal of your writing? "For the reader to decide."

HATHAWAY, BAXTER L.
Born: December 4, 1909; Cincinnati, Ohio
Parents: William B. Hathaway, Etta (Fee) Hathaway
Children: Hannah, William, James
Education: Kalamazoo College, A.B., Kalamazoo, Michigan, 1935. University of Michigan, M.A., Ann Arbor, Michigan, 1936; Ph.D., 1940
Career: Instructor, Assistant Professor, Montana State College, Missoula, Montana, 1940-1946. Lecturer, University of Wisconsin, Madison, Wisconsin, 1944-1945. Assistant Professor, Professor, Professor Emeritus, Cornell University, Ithaca, New York, 1946-1976—. Became Senior Editor, Ithaca House, 1969; directed workshops. Editor, *Epoch*, 1947-1976; began *Cornell Review*, 1976

Writings: *The Stubborn Way* Macmillan 1937. *Readings for an Air Age* (co-editor) Macmillan 1943. *Expression of Ideas* (co-editor) Heath 1948. *Writers for Tomorrow* Cornell University Press 1952. *Dramatic Essays of the Neoclassic Age* Columbia University Press 1950; B. Blom 1965. *The Age of Criticism: The Late Renaissance in Italy* Cornell University Press 1962. *Marvels and Commonplaces; Renaissance Literary Criticism* Random House 1968. *Transformational Syntax; the Grammar of Modern American English* Ronald Press 1967. *The Petulant Children* Random House 1978. Others. Articles in magazines

Awards or inclusion in other biographical books: *American Authors and Books; Contemporary Authors; Directory of American Scholars; Michigan Authors,* 2nd ed.; *Who's Who in America.* Hopwood Awards, University of Michigan, poetry, fiction. Awarded Fulbright Grants

HAVIGHURST, WALTER (EDWIN)

Born: November 28, 1901; Appleton, Wisconsin
Parents: Freeman A. Havighurst, Winifred Aurelia (Weter) Havighurst
Education: University of Denver, A.B., Denver, Colorado, 1924. King's College, London, England, 1925-1926. Columbia University, A.M., New York, New York, 1928
Career: United States Merchant Marine, 1921-1922, 1925-1926. Assistant Professor, Associate Professor, Professor, Research Professor Emeritus, Miami University, Oxford, Ohio, 1928-?. Ohio Historical Society, Board of Editors, beginning 1956

Writings: *Pier 17: A Novel* Macmillan 1935. *Designs for Writing* (co-editor) Dryden 1939. *Long Ships Passing: The Story of the Great Lakes* Macmillan 1942, 1961, 1975. *Land of Promise: The Story of the Northwest Territory* Macmillan 1946. *Song of the Pines: A Story of Norwegian Lumbering in Wisconsin* (with Marion Havighurst) Winston 1949; Holt 1966. *Wilderness for Sale: The First Western Land Rush* Hastings House 1956. *Life in the Midwest* Fideler 1951; published as *The Midwest* 1965, 1967. *The First Book of Pioneers: Northwest Territory* Franklin Watts 1959. *Voices of the River: The Story of the Mississippi Waterways* Macmillan 1964. *The Great Lakes Reader* (Editor) Macmillan 1966. *Three Flags at the Straits: The Forts of Mackinac* Prentice-Hall 1966. *River to the West: Three Centuries of the Ohio* Putnam 1970. *Men of Old Miami,1809-1873: A Book of Portraits* Putnam 1974. Several others. In *American Heritage, Saturday Review,* others
Awards or inclusion in other biographical books: *Contemporary Authors; Directory of American Scholars; International Authors and Writers Who's Who; Michigan Authors,* 2nd ed.; *Who Was Who among English and European Authors; Who's Who in America; Who's Who in the World; Writers Directory.* Ohioana Library Association Medal, 1946-1950. Friends of American Writers Award, 1947. Honorary Degrees, Lawrence University, Ohio Wesleyan University, Miami University, Marietta College. Ohioana Book Award (with Marion Havighurst) 1949. Association for State and Local History Award, 1956, 1964. History Prize, Society of Midland Authors, 1971. Ohio Hall of Fame, 1981. In the 2nd edition of *Michigan Authors* he is credited with: "As a youthful seaman on Great Lakes freighters I developed an interest in the history of transportation on American waterways. That interest, still continuing, has led to the writing of most of my books. I am especially drawn to Upper Michigan and the entire Lake Superior country. The best literary sources I have found for an understanding of that region are represented in my anthology *The Great Lakes Reader* Macmillan 1966."

HAYDEN, ROBERT EARL (1913-1980)

Born: August 4, 1913; Detroit, Michigan
Parents: Asa Sheffey, Gladys Ruth (Finn) Sheffey. Foster son of William Hayden, Sue Ellen (Westerfield) Hayden
Children: Maia
Education: Wayne State University, B.A., Detroit, Michigan, 1936. University of Michigan, M.A., Ann Arbor, Michigan, 1944.
Career: Researcher for Federal Writers' Project, Detroit, Michigan, 1936-1940. Teaching fellow, University of Michigan, Ann Arbor, 1944-1946. Assistant professor, professor,

Fisk University, Nashville, Tennessee, 1946-1969. Professor of English, University of Michigan, Ann Arbor, Michigan, 1969-1980. Bingham Professor, University of Louisville, Louisville, Kentucky, 1969. Visiting Poet to several universities. Member, Michigan Arts Council, 1975-1976. Consultant in Poetry, Library of Congress, 1976-1978. Book editor

Writings: Editor and author of introduction of *Kaleidoscope: Poems by American Negro Poets* Harcourt 1967. *Collected Prose* University of Michigan Press 1984 (edited by Frederick Glaysher). *Heart-Shape in the Dust* Falcon Press 1940. *Figure of Time: Poems* Hemphill Press 1955. *A Ballad of Remembrance* Paul Breman (London) 1962. *Selected Poems* October House 1966. *Words in the Mourning Time* October House 1970. *The Night-Blooming Cereus* Paul Breman 1972. *Angle of Ascent: New and Selected Poems* Liveright 1975. *American Journal* Effendi Press 1978; Liveright 1982. Contributed to such periodicals as *Atlantic, Negro Digest, Midwest Journal, Michigan Chronicle*
Awards or inclusion in other biographical books: *American Authors and Books; Black American Writers Past and Present; Childhood in Poetry; Contemporary Literary Criticism; Contemporary Poets; Dictionary of Literature in the English Language; Contemporary Authors; Living Black American Authors; Something about the Author; Who's Who in America; World Authors; Writers Directory,* others. Hopwood Poetry Award from the University of Michigan, 1938, 1942. Julius Rosenwald fellow, 1947. Ford Foundation fellow in Mexico, 1954-1955. World Festival of Negro Arts grand prize, 1966. Russell Loines Award, National Institute of Arts and Letters, 1970. National Book Award nomination, 1971. Litt.D., Brown University, 1976; Grand Valley State College, 1976 and others. Academy of American Poets fellow, 1977. Michigan Arts Foundation Award, 1977. National Book Award nomination, 1979. First Black Poet selected as Consultant in Poetry to the Library of Congress

HECK-RABI, LOUISE E.
Address: 1459 Philomene, Lincoln Park, Michigan 48146
Born: Detroit, Michigan
Parents: Andrew M. Heck, Mary V. Heck
Education: University of Michigan, M.A.L.S., Ann Arbor, Michigan, 1956-1960. Wayne State University, M.A., Detroit, Michigan, 1966-1971; Ph.D. in English, 1972-1976
Career: Freelance author, 1980—. Public and special librarian, Wayne County Library, 1955-1972. Assistant Professor-English and Library Science, Wayne State University, 1972-1976. Society of Manufacturing Engineers, 1965-1970

Writings: *Women Filmmakers: A Critical Reception* Scarecrow Press 1984. *The People Pound* Other Stages 1982. *Hier Ist Tobystown* (German Translation) West Germany 1970. Articles on women film directors, articles on films, *International Dictionary of Films and Filmmakers* volumes 1-4, St. James Press, 1986-1990. Poems published in *Peninsula Poets, Driftwind*, others. Plays received staged reading, production, in New York City, Ann Arbor, Michigan, San Antonio, Texas, Southfield, Michigan. Work in Progress: Novel about feminists engaged in struggle for ERA beginning in 1981—. Theatrical video (producer/co-writer) about teen illiteracy
Awards or inclusion in other biographical books: Several prizes for plays in competition and designations as finalist. Winner, Frank Lloyd Wright poetry contest, Poetry Society of Michigan, 1988
What is the aim or goal of your writing? "To publicize and promote the ideals I believe in by excellent and elegant use of the English language, especially in theatrical form."
May inquiries be sent to you about doing workshops, readings? Yes

HEDRICK, ULYSSES PRENTISS (1870-1951)

Born: January 15, 1870; Independence, Iowa
Parents: Benjamin Franklin Hedrick, Mary Catherine (Myers) Hedrick
Children: Catherine, Penelope, Ulysses
Education: Michigan Agricultural College, B.S., East Lansing, Michigan, 1893; M.S., 1895. Hobart College, D.Sc., 1913
Career: Assistant horticulturist, Michigan Agricultural College, 1893-1895. Professor of Botany and Horticulture, Oregon Agricultural College, 1895-1897. Professor of Botany and Horticulture, Utah Agricultural College, 1897-1899. Professor of Horticulture, Michigan Agricultural College, 1899-1905. Horticulturist, 1905-1930; Director, 1928-1937, New York Agricultural Experiment Station

Writings: *Apple Districts of New York with Varieties for Each* (with N. Booth, O. Taylor) New York State Agricultural Experiment Station 1906. *Grapes and Wines from Home Vineyards* Oxford University Press 1945. *The Land of the Crooked Tree* Oxford University Press 1948. *A History of Horticulture in America to 1860* Oxford University Press 1950. Many others on horticulture, 1908-1944. Numerous pamphlets, bulletins on horticultural subjects. *The Land of the Crooked Tree* about the northwestern tip of the lower peninsula of Michigan, according to its author is "...not an autobiography, although it is brazenly personal from beginning to end. It is dedicated "To the memory of my parents, pioneers in the land of the crooked tree".
Awards or inclusion in other biographical books: *Michigan Authors,* 1st ed., 2nd ed.; *National Cyclopaedia of American Biography; Who Was Who among North American Authors; Who Was Who in America.* LL.D. Utah Agricultural College, 1938

HEISE, KENAN JOSEPH

Address: 929 Elmwood, Evanston, Illinois 60202
Born: December 17, 1933; Ferndale, Michigan
Parents: Claude A. Heise, Evelyn C. Heise
Children: Tiger, Dan, Ben
Education: Duns Scotus College, Bachelor of Art, 1951-1955, Southfield, Michigan
Career: Managing editor, *Wage Earner,* Detroit, Michigan, 1959-1961. Reporter, *Chicago American / Chicago Today* , Chicago, Illinois, 1963-1974. Reporter/Writer *Chicago Tribune,* Chicago, Illinois, 1974—.

Writings: *Chicago Originals* (with Ed Baumann) Bonus Books 1991. *Resurrection Mary: A Ghost Story* Chicago Historical Bookworks 1990. *The Chicagoization of America: 1893-1917* Chicago Historical Bookworks 1989. *Hands on Chicago* Bonus Books 1987. *Aunt Ella Stories* Academy Chicago 1985. *Chicago: Center for Enterprise* (with Michael Edgerton) 1982. *The Journey of Silas B. Bigelow* Collage 1981. *How to Survive in Chicago and Enjoy It* Crown 1975. *Is There Only One Chicago* Westover 1973. *The Death of Christmas* Follette 1971. *They Speak for Themselves: Interviews with the Destitute of Chicago* YCW 1965. *Clarence Darrow in Hell: A Play* (with Dan Heise) Performed Talisman Theatre, Chicago 1992. *Alphonse: A One-Man Play About Al Capone*, opened 1986
Awards or inclusion in other biographical books: Vicki Matson Award, Friends of American Literature, 1986
May inquiries be sent to you about doing workshops, readings? Yes

HELBIG, ALTHEA K.
Address: 3640 Eli Road, Ann Arbor, Michigan 48104
Born: June 23, 1928; Ann Arbor, Michgan
Parents: Elmer J. Kuebler, Hilda G. Kuebler
Children: Rick
Education: University of Michigan, A.B., M.A. Ann Arbor, Michigan. Eastern Michigan University, Ypsilanti, Michigan, Kansas State University, others
Career: Professor, Eastern Michigan University, Ypsilanti, Michigan, 1981—; Associate Professor, 1976-1981; Assistant Professor, 1969-1976; Instructor, 1966-1969. Teacher, Ann Arbor Public Schools, Ann Arbor, Michigan, 1966. High School Teacher, Chelsea, Michigan, 1953-1954. High School Teacher, Manchester, Michigan, 1950-1952

Writings: *Dictionary of Children's Fiction from Australia, Canada, New Zealand, India and Selected African Countries* (with Agnes L. Perkins) Greenwood Press 1992. *Dictionary of British Children's Fiction* (with Agnes L. Perkins) Volume I, Volume II Greenwood Press 1989. *Nanabozhoo, Giver of Life* Green Oak Press 1989. *Dictionary of American Children's Fiction, 1960-1984* (with Agnes L. Perkins) Greenwood Press 1986. *Dictionary of American Children's Fiction, 1859-1959* (with Agnes L. Perkins) Greenwood Press 1985. *Dusk to Dawn: Poems of Night* (with Helen Hill, Agnes L. Perkins) Crowell Publishing 1981. *Stranger on Til Morning* (with Helen Hill and Agnes L. Perkins) Crowell 1977. Numerous articles. Work in Progress: A multicutural critical work for Greenwood Press. A supplement to *Dictionary of American Children's Fiction*
Awards or inclusion in other biographical books: Listings in a number of biographical indexes. *Dusk to Dawn* selected for *Saturday Review* list of best books. *Dictionary of American Children's Fiction,* American Library Association's Outstanding Reference of Year. Recipient, Eastern Michigan University Distinguished Faculty Award for Research and Publication. Recipient of Michigan Association of University Governing Boards Outstanding Faculty Award

What is the aim or goal of your writing? "To help people see and appreciate the wealth of good literature available for young readers; to improve the quality of writing for young readers; to help people become aware of the fine multi-cultural materials available, particularly about Native Americans."
May inquiries be sent to you about doing workshops, readings? Yes

HELLER, JANET RUTH
Address: 2719 Pfitzer Avenue, Kalamazoo, Michigan 49002
Born: July 8, 1949; Millwaukee, Wisconsin
Parents: William C. Heller, Jr., Joan R. Heller
Education: Oberlin College, Dean's List, Oberlin, Ohio, 1967-1970, University of Wisconsin-Madison, B.A., M.A., 1970-1973. University of Chicago, Ph.D. in English, Chicago, Illinois, 1973-1975
Career: Assistant Professor of English, Grand Valley State University, Allendale, Michigan, 1990—. Assistant Professor of English, Nazareth College, Kalamazoo, Michigan, 1989-1990. Instructor of English, Northern Illinois University, DeKalb, Illinois, 1982-1988. Lecturer on Creative Writing, University of Chicago, Extention, Chicago, Illinois, 1981-1982. Coordinator of the Writing Tutor Program, University of Chicago, Chicago, Illinois, 1976-1981

Writings: *Coleridge, Lamb, Hazlitt, and the Reader of Drama* University of Missouri

Press 1990. Editor, *Primavera,* a literary magazine, 1974-1982. Published literary criticism in *Poetics, Language and Style, Literature and Psychology, The Eighteenth Century, Shakespeare Bulletin, The Library Quarterly, Theatre Journal, Concerning Poetry.* Published poetry in *The Writer, Anima, Modern Maturity, Light Year, Women, Mothers Today, Organic Gardening, Women Glib, Our Mothers' Daughters.* Work in Progress: Collection of poems about people in the Bible. Study of Coleridge's poetry

Awards or inclusion in other biographical books: *Directory of American Poets and Fiction Writers* since 1979; *International Authors and Writers Who's Who; International Who's Who in Poetry; Personalities of America; Two Thousand Notable American Women; Who's Who in Writers, Editors & Poets; The World Who's Who of Women,* others. Winner, Friends of Poetry Contest, Kalamazoo, 1989; poem displayed on city buses. Poem commissioned by Friends of Poetry for display in public libraries and television broadcast, 1990-1991

What is the aim or goal of your writing? "In poetry, I want to communicate as simply and concisely as possible with a wide audience. I am very interested in psychology, nature, religion, and women's experiences. In literary criticism, I like wrestling with difficult intellectual problems and solving them to illuminate literature and language for others."

May inquiries be sent to you about doing workshops, readings? Yes

HEMANS, LAWTON THOMAS (1864-1916)
Born: November 4, 1864; Collamer, New York
Parents: John A. Hemans; Mrs. Hemans
Children: Charles Sidney
Education: Eaton Rapids High School, Eaton Rapids, 1884. Entered University of Michigan, Law Department, 1887
Career: Teacher, District Schools of Aurelius Township, Michigan. Elected Circuit Court Commissioner, Ingham County, Mason, Michigan. Co-partnership, firm of Corbin & Hemans, 1889-1890. Began practicing law, Mason, Michigan, 1890. Mayor, Mason, Michigan for five terms, city alderman for five terms, other offices. Member of Michigan Legislature, 1901-1902, 1902-1903. Represented Ingham County, Constitutional Convention, 1907. Nominated for governor, 1908, 1910. Railroad Commission, 1910. Delegate-at-large, Democratic conventions

Writings: *History of Michigan* Hammond Publishing, 4th edition, (used in Michigan schools several years) 1910. *Life and Times of Stevens Thomson Mason, the Boy Governor of Michigan* Michigan Historical Commission 1920, 1930. Contributor, "Centennial Souvenir: Commemorating the First Meeting of Michigan's First State Legislature, November 2, 1835", Lansing: Capitol Feature Service, Michigan State Historical Society
Awards or inclusion in other biographical books: *Dictionary of North American Authors; Men of Progress Embracing Biographical Sketches of Representative Michigan Men; Who Was Who in America*

HEMINGWAY, ERNEST MILLER (1899-1961)
Born: July 21, 1899; Oak Park, Illinois
Parents: Clarence E. Hemingway, Grace (Hall) Hemingway
Children: John, Patrick, Gregory
Education: Oak Park High School, High School diploma, 1917
Career: Cub Reporter, *Kansas City Star,* Kansas City, Missouri, 1917-1918. Ambulance driver for Red Cross Ambulance Corps in Italy, 1918-1919. Writer, *Cooperative*

Commonwealth, Chicago, Illinois, 1920-1921. Foreign Corrrespondent, *Toronto Star,* Toronto, Ontario, 1920-1924. Overseas correspondent 1937-1945

Writings: *Three Stories and Ten Poems* Contact (Paris) 1923. *In Our Time* Three Mountain Press (Paris) 1924 Scribner 1930. *The Torrents of Spring* Scribner 1926. *The Sun Also Rises* Scribner 1926. *Men Without Women* Scribner 1927. *A Farewell to Arms* Scribner 1929. *Death in the Afternoon* Scribner 1932. *Winner Take Nothing* Scribner 1933.*The Green Hills of Africa* Scribner 1935. *To Have and Have Not* Scribner 1937. *The Fifth Column and the First Forty-nine Stories* Scribner 1938. *The Short Stories of Ernest Hemingway* Scribner 1938. *For Whom the Bell Tolls* Scribner 1940. *Across the River and into the Trees* Scribner 1950. *The Old Man and the Sea* Scribner 1952. *Short Stories* Scribner 1953. *The Hemingway Reader* Scribner 1961. *The Snows of Kilimanjaro and Other Stories* Scribner 1961. *The Short Happy Life of Francis Macomber and Other Stories* Penguin 1963. *A Moveable Feast* Scribner 1964. *The Fifth Column, and Four Stories of the Spanish Civil War* Scribner 1969. *Hemingway's African Stories: The Stories, Their Sources, Their Critics* Scribner 1969. *Islands in the Stream* Scribner 1970. *The Collected Poems of Ernest Hemingway* Gordon Press 1972. *The Nick Adams Stories* Scribner 1972. *The Garden of Eden* Scribner 1986. *The Complete Short Stories of Ernest Hemingway: The Finca Vigia Edition* Scribner 1987. Others. Only first publishing dates are given as there are so many editions, reprints, foreign translations

Awards or inclusion in other biographical books: *American Authors and Books; American Novelists of Today; American Writers; Contemporary Authors; Dictionary of Literary Biography; Michigan Authors,* 2nd ed.; *Reader's Encyclopedia; Reader's Encyclopedia of American Literature; Twentieth Century Authors; Twentieth Century Writing; Who Was Who in America; Who's Who in Twentieth Century Literature; World Encyclopedia of the Film,* several others. Pulitzer Prize, 1953. Nobel Prize for Literature, 1954. Award of Merit, American Academy of Arts & Letters, 1954

In 1991 Petoskey, Michigan first hosted an annual October tour on foot and bus to places associated with Hemingway when living in the area such as his rooming house where he wrote, the public library where he spoke, the museum exhibiting him, and Walloon Lake where he spent summers as a child. "Windemere", the family summer cottage on Walloon Lake, became a Registered National Historic Landmark of the U.S. Department of the Interior 1968

HENDERSON, KATHY
Address: 2151 Hale Road, Sandusky, Michigan 48471
Born: July 15, 1952; Detroit, Michigan
Parents: Vernon E. Davidson, Peggy A. (Bauman) Davidson
Children: Eric, Amy
Education: Edwin Denby High School, High School Diploma. Northwood institute, Midland, Michigan, 1992—. Institute of Children's Literature, Diploma, 1986
Career: Freelance writer/editor/communications consultant, Echo Communications, Sandusky, Michigan, 1986—. Co-owner/operator, Henderson Dairy Farm, Sandusky, Michigan, 1970—. Executive Director, National Association for Young Writers, 1988-1989. Computer Instructor, Sanilac ISD, Brown City, Michigan, 1991—. Judge for numerous writing competitions, frequent speaker at schools, libraries. Seminar leader, workshop instructor for professional writers' conferences. Former staff editor, regular stringer, *Sanilac County News.* Editorial Advisory Board (current member) *The Writing Notebook.* Book reviewer, Museum of Science and Industry, 1991-1992. Numerous service and professional community organizations helping with public relations, writing

and editing projects, marketing and project planning coordinating. Served as television correspondent

Writings: *I Can Be a Basketball Player* Childrens Press 1991. *I Can Be a Rancher* Childrens Press 1990. *Market Guide for Young Writers* 3rd edition Betterway Publications 1990. *Market Guide for Young Artists and Photographers* Betterway Publications 1990. *What Would We Do Without You? A Guide to Volunteer Activities for Kids* Betterway Publications 1990. *I Can Be a Horse Trainer* Childrens Press 1990. *Great Lakes, A New True Book* Childrens Press 1989. *I Can Be a Farmer* Childrens Press 1989. *Christmas Trees, A New True Book* Childrens Press 1989. *Diary Cows, A New True Book* Childrens Press 1988. Work in Progress: *Spring Training for Young Writers, Giddy-Up Sarah, Practical Wordperfect, Little Immigrants, Help! I Can't Find Time to Write,* and *Strictly for Women, A Guide for Life and Time Management.* Articles in *Detroit News Sunday Magazine, Saginaw Daily News, Successful Farming, Baby Talk, Horseman, Cobblestone, Kinderbook,* and others
Awards or inclusion in other biographical books: *Who's Who in U.S. Writers, Editors and Poets,* since 1988. Cherubim Award, Oklahoma Writer's Federation, 1987. Alternate, Writer's Digest Book Club. New York Public Library, two books selected for annual Best Books for Teens. Book recommended by National Conference of Christians and Jews, 1991
What is the aim or goal of your writing? "To help others be effective communicators. To share important and/or interesting information. To enjoy myself and continually challenge my creative abilities."
May inquiries be sent to you about doing workshops, readings? Yes

HENDRYX, JAMES BEARDSLEY (1880-1963)
Born: December 9, 1880; Sauk Centre, Minnesota
Education: Sauk Centre Public Schools. University of Minnesota, Minneapolis, Minnesota, 2 years
Career: Newspaper work, Springfield, Ohio, 1905-1910. Writer, *Enquirer,* Cincinnati, Ohio, 1915-1920. Other jobs like cowboy, salesman, construction

Writings: *Connie Morgan in the Lumber Camps* Putnam 1919; Jarrolds (London) 1928. *Connie Morgan with the Forest Rangers* Putnam 1925; Jarrolds (London) 1926; eight others in this series for juvenile readers. Dozens in the Western series, Corporal Downey. Halfaday Creek series (four) set on Yukon-Alaska border. Screenplay, *Snowdrift* 1923
Awards or inclusion in other biographical books: *American Authors and Books; Minnesota Writers; Ohio Authors and Their Books; Twentieth-Century Western Writers; Who Was Who in America; Who Was Who among North American Authors*

HENKES, ROBERT J.
Address: 1124 Bretton Drive, Kalamazoo, Michigan 49006
Born: October 28, 1922; Racine, Wisconsin
Parents: Peter J. Henkes, Veronica A. Henkes
Children: Catherine, Anne, Susan, Jane
Education: Washington Park High School, Academic Diploma, Racine, Wisconsin, 1940. Drake University, B.F.A., Des Moines, Iowa, 1944-1948. University of Wisconsin, M.A. Art Education, Madison, Wisconsin, 1949-1950. Post graduate work, Michigan State University, East Lansing, Michigan; University of Michigan, Ann Arbor, Michigan

Career: Art Instructor, Portage Public Schools, Portage, Michigan, 1973-1984, retired. Professor of Art, Nazareth College, Kalamazoo, Michigan, 1966-1973. Art Instructor, Kalamazoo, Michigan, 1961-1966. Art Instructor, Drawing and Painting, Kalamazoo Institute of Arts, 1962-1984

Writings: *Black American Women Artists* McFarland & Company 1993. *New Vision in Painting* International University Press 1992. *Themes in American Painting* McFarland & Company 1992. *American Women Painters* McFarland & Company 1991. *Art Projects Around the Calendar* J. Weston Walch 1991. *Sport in Art* Prentice-Hall Press 1986. *American Art Activity Book* J. Weston Walch 1983. *300 Lessons in Art* J. Weston Walch 1981. *Crucifixion in American Painting* Gordon Press 1980. *Insights in Art & Education* Gordon Press 1979. *Eight American Women Artists* Gordon Press 1977. *Notes on Art & Art Education* Irvington Press 1969. *Orientation to Drawing & Painting* International Textbook 1965. Three filmstrips on art, 1981, 1983, 1985 for J. Weston Walch. *Essay: Great Men* Dial Press 1980. Two hundred twenty four articles in art, education journals, United States and Great Britian. Work in Progress: *Spirit of American Art: The Depression Years. Spirituality of Abraham Rattner. Reflections on the Crucifixion. Christianity in American Art. Modes of Art*

Awards or inclusion in other biographical books: *Contemporary Authors; Dictionary of International Biography; International Authors & Writers Who's Who; International Book of Honor; Personalities of the West and Midwest; Who's Who in International Community Service; Who's Who in the Midwest; Writers Directory*

What is the aim or goal of your writing? "To make a difference in the art educational process; to share with as wide as audience as possible my notions of the creative process as an artist, writer and educator, and to grant credit to those artists whose achievements have been ignored throughout time (American Women Painters of the 1930's and 1940's) and (The Spirit of American Art: The Depression Years). Writing became a product of my teaching and my painting as well as a stimulus for both."

May inquiries be sent to you about doing workshops, readings? No

HENRY, VERA (1909?-1987)
Born: 1909?; Forest, Ontario, Canada
Parents: Hugh T. Johnson, Myrtle (Gammon) Johnson
Children: James, Kevin
Career: Freelance writer, 1942-1975. Teacher, Adult Education, Ferndale, Michigan. Editorial Associate, *Writer's Digest,* 1966-1975. Staff member, Detroit Women Writers-Oakland University Writers Conference, 1962-1974; Sarnia, London, Ontario

Writings: *A Lucky Number* Lippincott 1957. *Mystery of Cedar Valley* Avalon 1964. *Ong, the Wild Gander* Lippincott 1966. *Portrait in Fear* Caravelle 1967. Television, radio scripts, correspondence courses. Numerous short stories, articles in *Redbook, Seventeen, Good Housekeeping,* others. Edited advice column, *Detroit News*

Awards or inclusion in other biographical books: *Contemporary Authors; Michigan Authors,* 1st ed., 2nd ed.; *Writers Directory.* Writer of the Year Award, Detroit Women Writers, 1954, 1957. Headliner Award, Theta Sigma Phi, 1958. Honorary member, Quota International

HERRMANN, JOHN (1900-1959)
Born: November 9, 1900; Lansing, Michigan
Education: Public schools, Lansing, Michigan. University of Michigan, Ann Arbor, Michigan. University of Munich, Munich, Germany.
Career: Newspaper work, Salesman in Michigan. Writer, Paris, France.

Writings: *What Happens* Contact Editions (Paris) 1925. *Summer is Ended* Covici, Friede 1932. *The Salesman, a Novel* Simon and Schuster 1939. In *This Quarter* and other little magazines. Included in *Contact Collection of Contemporary Writers* edited by Robert McAlmon, 1925.
Awards or inclusion in other biographical books: *Contemporary Authors; Dictionary of Literary Biography*. Winner of *Scribner's Magazine* Short Novel Contest, "The Big Short Trip", 1932

HILBERRY, CONRAD A.
Address: 1601 Grand Avenue, Kalamazoo, Michigan 49006
Born: March 1, 1928; Melrose Park, Illinois
Parents: Clarence B. Hilberry, Ruth H. Hilberry
Children: Marilyn, Jane, Ann
Education: Oberlin College, B.A., Oberlin, Ohio, 1946-1949. University of Wisconsin, Ph.D., Madison, Wisconsin, 1951-1954
Career: Professor English, Kalamazoo College, Kalamazoo, Michigan, 1962—. Program Associate, Associated Colleges of the Midwest, Chicago, Illinois, 1961-1962. Assistant Professor of English, DePauw University, Greencastle, Indiana, 1954-1961

Writings: *Sorting the Smoke* University of Iowa Press 1990. *The Lagoon* MelanBerry Press 1989. *Luke Karamazov* Wayne State University Press 1987. *The Moon Seen As a Slice of Pineapple* University of Georgia Press 1984. *Housemarks* Perishable Press 1980. *Man in the Attic* Bits Press 1980. *Rust* Ohio University Press 1974. Anthologies coedited: *Contemporary Michigan Poetry* Wayne State University Press 1988. *The Third Coast* Wayne State University Press 1976
Awards or inclusion in other biographical books: *Dictionary of Literary Biography,* 1992; *Michigan Authors,* 2nd ed. National Endowment for the Arts Fellowship, 1974-1975, 1984-1985. Emily Clark Balch Prize, *Virginia Quarterly Review,* 1984. Michigan Arts Award, Michigan Foundation for the Arts, 1983. Residences: Virginia Center for the Creative Arts, 1991. MacDowell Colony, 1983, 1977. Breadloaf Fellowship in Poetry, Breadloaf Writers Conference, 1970
What is the aim or goal of your writing? "Good poems."
May inquiries be sent to you about doing workshops, readings? Yes

HILL, JACK (1896-1987)
Born: May 25, 1896; Vaasa, Finland
Children: Jack
Education: Self-educated after age 14
Career: Part-time farmer, worked in mines from the early 1920's until retirement. Served as Stambaugh Township Road Commissioner and worked on roads for many years. During that time he became interested in local history and began to write articles for local newspaper; these were compiled into book 1955

Writings: *The History of Iron County* Reporter Publishing 1955; reprinted with photographs and index, Iron County Historical and Museum Society 1976. *Index to the History* *of Iron County, Michigan* Michigan State Library 1957

What is the aim or goal of your writing? In an interview written by Ms. Bernhardt for the *Green Bay Press Gazette* Mr. Hill commented: "History has always been one of my weak points...to combine ideas and express them on paper for the information and enjoyment of others is one of the most satisfying of all hobbies." Adding further, "It was in the early thirties that my interest in history flowered. In time, as the notes and information accumulated, I was struck with the idea of how important it is to learn about local history and the activities of our forebearers and then to compile the material into somewhat chronological order." Ms. Bernhardt adds that information by Hill mounted for over twenty years and ultimately led to *The History of Iron County.* Information on Jack Hill is available from Marcia Bernhardt, curator Iron County Museum, Box 272, Caspian, Michigan 49915

Awards or inclusion in other biographical books: *Michigan Authors,* 2nd ed.

HILLERT, MARGARET
Address: 222 E. ll Mile Road, Royal Oak, Michigan 48067
Born: January 22, 1920; Saginaw, Michigan
Parents: Edward C. Hillert, Lee Hillert
Education: University of Michigan, R.N., Ann Arbor, Michigan, 1941-1944. Wayne State University, A.B., Detroit, Michigan, 1945-1948
Career: Teacher, Royal Oak, Michigan, 1948-1982. Nurse, Woman's Hospital (Now Kutzel) 1945-1948

Writings: *The Three Bears* Follett 1963. *Little Puff* Follett 1973. *Play Ball* Follett 1978. *I Like Things* Follett 1981. *The Boy and the Goats* Follett 1982- over 50 books published by Follett. *The Sleepytime Books* Golden Press 1975. *Who Comes to Your House?* Golden Press 1973. *I Like to Live in the City* Golden Press 1970. *I'm Special...So Are You!* Hallmark 1979. *Let's Take a Break* Continental Press 1981. *Doing Things* Continental Press 1981. *Action Verse in the Primary Classroom* T.S. Denison 1982. *The Three Goats* Ernest Benn 1973. *Go to Sleep, Dear Dragon* Modern Curriculum Press 1985. *A Friend for Dear Dragon* Modern Curriculum Press 1985. *I Need You, Dear Dragon* Modern Curriculum Press 1985. *Come to School, Dear Dragon* Modern Curriculum Press 1985. *Help for Dear Dragon* Modern Curriculm Press 1985. *It's Circus Time, Dear Dragon* Modern Curriculum Press 1985. *Rabbits and Rainbows* Standard Publishing 1985. *Dandelions and Daydreams* Standard Publishing 1987. *Seasons, Holidays, Anytime* Partner Press 1987. *Guess, Guess* Standard Publishing 1988, others from Standard. Hundreds of poems in a variety of periodicals for adults and children. Several books in translation. Numerous anthology inclusions. Poems on posters and cassettes. Work in Progress: Poetry and juvenile books

Awards or inclusion in other biographical books: *Michigan Authors,* 2nd ed.; *Michigan Poets; Something about the Author.* Annual Award of the Children's Reading Round Table of Chicago for outstanding contributions to the field of children's literature, 1991. *The Place My Words Are Looking For-Janeczko,* Bradbury Press

May inquiries be sent to you about doing workshops, readings? Yes

HINRICHSEN, DENNIS
Address: 428 E. Lincoln, Grand Ledge, Michigan 48837
Born: May 10, 1952; Cedar Rapids, Iowa
Parents: William J. Hinrichsen, Deloris L, Hinrichsen
Children: Sophie

Education: Western Michigan University, B.A., Kalamazoo, Michigan, 1970-1974. University of Iowa, Master of Fine Arts, Iowa City, Iowa, 1974-1976
Career: Instructor, Lansing Community College, Lansing, Michigan, 1988—. Technical Writer, Stone & Weber Engineering Corporation, Boston, Massachusetts, 1982-1988. Technical Writer, Raytheon Service Company, Cambridge, Massachusetts, 1978-1982

Writings: *The Rain That Falls This Far* Galileo Press 1992. *The Attraction of Heavenly Bodies* Wesleyan University Press 1983.
Work in Progress: Book of poems as yet untitled
Awards or inclusion in other biographical books: Charles B. Wood Award for Distinguished Writing, for work appearing in *Carolina Quarterly*. Michigan Council for the Arts, Individual Grant, 1989-1990. National Endowment for the Arts, Creative Writing Fellowship, 1984
What is the aim or goal of your writing? "My goals or aims are simply to explore whatever interests me using language. I try to keep two Pound comments in mind-'make it new' and 'listen to the sound it makes' and then move from there to see what happens."
May inquiries be sent to you about doing workshops, readings? Yes

HINSDALE, WILBERT B. (1851-1944)
Born: May 15, 1851; Wadsworth, Ohio
Parents: Albert Hinsdale, Clarinda (Eyles) Hinsdale
Children: Albert
Education: Hiram College, B.S., Hiram, Ohio, 1875; M.S., 1878; A.M., 1897. Cleveland Homeopathic Medical College, M.D., 1887
Career: Teacher, public schools, Ohio. Professor, Department of Medicine and Surgery, Cleveland University. Professor, Internal and Clinical Medicine, Homeopathic Department, University of Michigan, beginning 1895; Dean 1895-1922, Medical Director, College Hospital; retired 1922. Head, Archaeology, University Museum. President, Michigan Academy of Science, Arts and Letters, 1931. Member, President, Michigan State Tuberculosis Board

Writings: *The Indians of Washtenaw County, Michigan* G. Wahr 1927. *Trade and Lines of Overland Travel of the Michigan Indians* 1929. *The First People Of Michigan* G. Wahr 1930. *Archaeological Atlas of Michigan* University of Michigan Press 1931. *Distribution of the Aboriginal Population of Michigan* University of Michigan Press 1932. *Perforated Indian Crania in Michigan* University of Michigan Press 1936. *Primitive Man in Michigan* The University 1925; Avery Color Studios 1983. Medical, scientific papers
Awards or inclusion in other biographical books: *Michigan: A Centennial History of the State and its People:* Michigan Biography Vol. 3; *The Official Who's Who in Michigan*, 1936. Honorary Degree, University of Michigan, 1934

HISCOE, HELEN B.
Address: 1817 Walnut Heights Drive, East Lansing, Michigan 48823
Born: March 10, 1919; Waterford, Connecticut
Parents: Donald L. Brush, Agnes V. Brush
Children: Susan, Elaine, Lenore, Nancy
Education: Vassar College, A.B., Poughkeepsie, New York, 1935-1939. Brown University, M.S., Providence, Rhode Island, 1939-1940. California State University: Los Angeles, Ph.D., 1941-1943

Career: Professor, Department of Natural Sciences, Michigan State University, East Lansing, Michigan, 1959-1986, retired. Research Associate, University of Chicago, Chicago, Illinois, 1946-1947. Instructor, Vassar College, Poughkeepsie, New York, 1940-1941, 1943-1946. Graduate Assistant, University of California: Los Angeles, 1942-1943

Writings: *Appalachian Passage* University of Georgia Press 1992
What is the aim or goal of your writing? "I wanted to share my unique experiences in a tiny mining camp in West Virginia in 1949-1950, based on the diary I kept that year when my husband served as coal company doctor."
May inquiries be sent to you about doing workshops, readings? Yes

HOBBS, J. KLINE
Address: 657 East Michigan Avenue, Battle Creek, Michigan 49017
Born: May 9, 1928; Battle Creek, Michigan
Parents: Joseph W. Hobbs, Elizabeth L. (Kline) Hobbs
Education: Battle Creek Central High School, Michigan, 1946. Michigan State University, B.A., East Lansing, Michigan, 1946-1949. Columbia University, M.A., New York, New York, 1950-1951. Western Michigan University, M.L.S., Kalamazoo, Michigan, 1972-1973
Career: Project Director, Riverlight and Company, Non-profit professional theatre and media, Battle Creek, Michigan, 1981—. Part-time instructor, Kellogg Community College, Battle Creek, Michigan, 1987-1989. Freelance writer/director, Resident artist at Olivet College, Olivet, Michigan; Kalamazoo College, Kalamazoo, Michigan; Kellogg Community College, Battle Creek, Michigan. Freelance director/actor, Off-Broadway theatre, New York, New York, 1952-1963

Writings: *Percy Julian and His Million Dollar Chemistry Business* Riverlight Company 1991. *The First American Diva* Riverlight Company 1985. *Rags to Riches with Scott Joplin* Riverlight Company 1985. *Arrivals and Departures* Expedition Press 1981. *Diary of the Ultimate One Night Stand...and that Other Quest* Expedition Press 1979. Videos such as *Gottschalk and the Romantic Piano* Riverlight Company 1988. *The Fabulous Traveling W.C. Handy Musical Show* (with Arthur R. LaBrew) Riverlight Company 1990, others. Contributions to *Vagaries of Invention* Sidewinder Press 1984. *Undercovers with the Troubadour Poetry Guild* Sidewinder Press 1976. Published in *Green River Review, Sunday New York Times* and others. Broadcast two consecutive Sundays on *Poetry and Others,* WKAR-FM, 1981. Work in Progress: *The Freedom Comers,* narrative theatre piece. *Love on the Way to a Third Millenium*, poetry. *Freakout on Eucalyptus Boulevard: Part 27,* young people's musical
Awards or inclusion in other biographical books: *American Playwrights Directory,* 1976, 1982; *Contemporary Authors,* 1984; *Directory of American Poets,* 1992; *Michigan Authors,* 2nd ed. Calhoun County United Arts Council Special Project Grants, 1991, 1990, 1988. Union Pump Centennial Grant, 1986. Michigan Commerce Outstate Equity Grant, 1985
What is the aim or goal of your writing? "To explore the lives of American cultural pioneers and reflect on my own life and times. In my poetry I deal with my search for a secure sense of identity and self worth. In my narrative dramas and musicals I present other Americans accomplishments in those aspects of their lives."
May inquiries be sent to you about doing workshops, readings? Yes

HOLBROOK, STEWART HALL (1893-1964)
Born: August 22, 1893; Newport, Vermont
Parents: Jesse W. Holbrook, Kate (Stewart) Holbrook
Children: Sibyl, Bonnie
Education: Colebrook Academy, Colebrook, New Hampshire
Career: Various jobs in Canada. Lumber camp work, 1914-1923, New England, Canada. In World War I, 1917-1919. Associate editor, editor, *Lumber News,* 1923-1934. Freelance writer, Portland, Oregon. Lecturer

Writings: *Holy Old Mackinaw: A Natural History of the American Lumberjack* Macmillan 1938, 1956; enlarged edition as *The American Lumberjack* Collier 1962. *Let Them Live* Macmillan 1938. *Iron Brew: A Century of American Ore and Steel* Macmillan 1939. *The Story of American Forest Fires* Macmillan 1943. *America's Ethan Allen* Houghton 1949. *Down on the Farm: A Picture Treasury of Country Life in American in the Good Old Days* Crown 1954. *The Columbia* Rinehart 1956, printed as *The Columbia River* Holt 1965. Several others. Essays, articles in *New Yorker, Saturday Evening Post, American Heritage, New York Herald Tribune,* others
Awards or inclusion in other biographical books: *American Authors and Books; Authors of Books for Young People; Contemporary Authors; Oxford Companion to American Literature; Reader's Encyclopedia of American Literature; Reader's Encyclopedia of the American West; Something about the Author; Twentieth Century Authors; Third Book of Junior Authors; Who Was Who among North American Authors; Who Was Who in America; Who's Who among Pacific Northwest Authors*

HOLLI, MELVIN G.
Address: 1311 Ashland, River Forest, Illinois 60305
Born: February 22, 1933; Ishpeming, Michigan
Parents: Walfred M. Holli, Sylvia Holli
Children: Steven, Susan
Education: Suomi College, Hancock, Michigan. Northern Michigan University, B.A., Marquette, Michigan, 1952-1954. University of Michigan, M.A., Ph.D., Ann Arbor, Michigan, 1954-1957
Career: Teacher, Rock River Township, Michigan, 1957. Flat Rock Public Schools, Michigan, 1958-1959. Professor of History, University of Illinois at Chicago, 1965—

Writings: *Restoration: Chicago Elects a New Daley* Lyceum 1991. *Bashing Chicago Traditions* Eerdmans 1989. *Ethnic Chicago* Eerdmans 1984. *Detroit* Franklin Watts 1975. *Reform in Detroit* Oxford 1969, 1975. Work in Progress: *The American Mayor*
Awards or inclusion in other biographical books: *Michigan Authors,* 2nd ed. Society of Midland Authors, Best Non-Fiction Prize, 1985. Illinois State Historical Society, Book Prize 1986
May inquiries be sent to you about doing workshops, readings? No

HOLLING, HOLLING C. (1900-1973)
Born: Holling Corners, (Jackson County) Michigan
Education: School of the Art Institute of Chicago, 1923. Privately under Dr. Ralph Linton, a noted anthropologist who was at Yale University
Career: Grocery clerk, factory worker, sailor on a Great Lakes Ore boat. Field Museum of Natural History, Chicago, Illinois, 1923-1926. Idea man, artist, copy writer. Traveled widely, studied wildlife to get information for his books. Various film adaptations of *Paddle-to-the-Sea*

Writings: *New Mexico Made Easy* self-illustrated and privately printed 1923. *Sun and Smoke,* self-illustrated and privately printed 1923. *Little Big-Bye-and Bye* self-illustrated Volland 1926. *Roll Away Twins* illustrated by author with wife, Volland 1927. *Rum-Tum-Tummy* Volland 1927. *Claws of the Thunderbird: A Tale of Three Lost Indians* self-illustrated Volland 1928. *Choo-Me-Shoo the Eskimo* illustrated by the author with wife, Volland 1928. *Rocky Billy: The Story of the Bounding Career of a Rocky Mountain Goat* self-illustrated Macmillan 1928. *The Twins Who Flew around the World* self-illustrated, Platt 1931. *The Book of Indians* illustrated by author and his wife Platt 1935, 1962. *The Book of Cowboys* illustrated by author and his wife, Platt 1936, 1962. *Little Buffalo Boy* illustrated by author and his wife, Garden City Publishing 1939. *Paddle-to-the-Sea* self-illustrated, Houghton 1941. *Tree in the Trail* self-illustrated, Houghton 1942. *Seabird* self-illustrated, Houghton 1943. *Minn of the Mississippi* self-illustrated, Houghton 1951. *Pagoo* illustrated by author and his wife, Houghton 1957. Illustrated others

Awards or inclusion in other biographical books: *American Authors and Books; Authors and Illustrators of Children's Books; Authors of Books for Young People; Contemporary Authors; Illustrated Biographical Encyclopedia of Artists of the American West; Illustrators of Children's Books; Junior Book of Authors; Something about the Author; Story and Verse for Children; Twentieth Century Children's Writers.* Runner-up for the Caldecott Medal, 1942. Commonwealth Club of California Literature Award, 1948. Runner-up for the Newbery Medal, 1949, 1952. Southern California Council on Literature for Children Award (awarded jointly to his wife, Lucille Holling), 1961

HOLT, ROBERT E.

Address: 163 S. Wheeling Avenue, Wheeling, Illinois 60090

Born: February 3, 1922; Grand Rapids, Michigan

Parents: Rex E. Holt, Hazel E. (Bird) Holt

Children: James, Sandra, Michael, Patrick

Education: Coopersville High School, Coopersville, Michigan, 1936-1940. Northwestern University, Evanston, Illinois, Real Estate & R.E. Law., 1961-1962. Blackstone Law School, L.L.B., Chicago, Illinois, 1962-1964

Career: Owner, R.E. Holt Realty Company, Wheeling, Illinois, 1962—. Pinkerton's National Detective Agency, 1950-1975. In Sales and Management, Chicago and Minneapolis, 1945-1946. Manufacturer's Representative, R.E. Holt, Grand Rapids, 1946-1950. Selling and management positions. Entered United States Marine Corps 1941, duty included New Zealand, Guadalcanal, British Solomon Islands. President, Wheeling Chamber of Commerce. Teacher, Security and Investigation, Chicago Law Enforcement School. Commander of the Chicago Board of Trade Post No. 304, Chicago, Illinois, 1989. Appeared as an extra in the Gene Hackman movie, *The Package*, 1989. Main character in medical films pertaining to cancer

Writings: *Two Little Devils* Wilderness Adventure Books 1988

Awards or inclusion in other biographical books: *Illinois Lives,* 1969. Golden Gloves champion in the lightweight division of western Michigan

What is the aim or goal of your writing? "To preserve some of the history of that time period (the Depression era of the thirties) in the Michigan area, and of two (2) boys growing into manhood at that time. I have tried to put this into as near a true story as possible and I think that I have and I believe there is a lesson to our young people here in that no matter how hard life was then and now we resorted to good clean fun most of the time. Of course I am also interested in the book selling and believe it has throughout the Middle West area and I trust and hope that persons will enjoy the book and get many laughs out of it."

May inquiries be sent to you about doing workshops, readings? I now live in Illinois, it would not be very convenient to travel out of state

HOLTSCHLAG, MARGARET A.
Address: 5425 Amber Drive, East Lansing, Michigan 48823
Born: January 15, 1953; Chicago, Illinois
Parents: Joseph Prendergast, Margaret Prendergast
Children: Joe, Sarah, Kristen
Education: Northern Illinois University, B.S., Education, DeKalb, Illinois, 1970-1974. Michigan State University, M.A., Reading Instruction, East Lansing, Michigan, 1982-1987
Career: Elementary Teacher, Haslett, Michigan, 1988—. Teacher, Lansing, Michigan, 1986-1988. Teacher, Laingsburg, Michigan, 1976-1982. Teacher, Osseo, Minnesota, 1975-1976

Writings: *Random House Calendar for Kids* Random House 1990-1994. *Celebrate Reading* Michigan Reading Association 1992. *Days and Days* (activity calendar for kids) self-published 1984-1989.
Work in Progress: *Random House Calendar for Kids* (1995). *Celebrate Reading* (1993)
Awards or inclusion in other biographical books: Teacher of the Year, Haslett Public Schools, 1992
What is the aim or goal of your writing? "With co-author Carol Trojanowski, our goal continues to be to write creative activities for children to do with parents."
May inquiries be sent to you about doing workshops, readings? Yes

HOOPER, PATRICIA
Born: May 4, 1941; Saginaw, Michigan
Parents: John Hooper, Edythe (Sharpe) Hooper
Children: John, Katherine
Education: University of Michigan, B.A., Ann Arbor, Michigan, 1962; M.A., 1963
Career: Poet

Writings: *Other Lives* Elizabeth Street Press 1984. *A Bundle of Beasts* Houghton 1987. Published in anthologies. Contributor to such magazines as *Chicago Review, American Poetry Review, American Scholar, Poetry*
Awards or inclusion in other biographical books: *Contemporary Authors.* Five Hopwood Awards, University of Michigan. Farber First Book Award, Poetry Society of America, 1984

HOOVER, BESSIE RAY (1874-?)
Born: September 28, 1874; St. Joseph, Michigan
Parents: Alphonzo V. Hoover, Etta (Mitchell) Hoover
Education: Jamestown High School, New York. Benton Harbor College, Michigan
Career: Teacher, writer

Writings: *Pa Flickinger's Folks* Harper 1909. *Opal* Harper 1910. *Rolling Acres* Small, Maynard 1922

Awards or inclusion in other biographical books: *Who Was Who in America; Who's Who in Michigan*

HOPF, ALICE L(IGHTNER) (1904-1988)

Pseudonym: A. M. Lightner, Alice Hopf, Alice Lightner
Born: October 11, 1904; Detroit, Michigan
Parents: Clarence A. Lightner, Frances (McGraw) Lightner
Children: Christopher
Education: Vassar College, B.A., Poughkeepsie, New York, 1927
Career: Editorial Secretary, Grey Advertising, New York, New York, until 1973

Writings: *Monarch Butterflies* Crowell 1965. *The Galactic Troubadours* Norton 1965. *Doctor to the Galaxy* Norton 1965. *Wild Traveler: The Story of a Coyote* Norton 1967. *Earth's Bug-Eyed Monsters* Norton 1968. *The Space Ark* Putnam 1968. *The Thursday Toads* McGraw 1971. *Biography of a Rhino* Putnam 1972. *Star Dog* McGraw-Hill 1973. *Misunderstood Animals* McGraw 1973. *The Space Gypsies* McGraw 1974. *Wild Cousins of the Cat* Putnam 1975. *Biography of an Armadillo* Putnam 1975. *Misplaced Animals* McGraw 1975. *Biography of An American Reindeer* Putnam 1976. *Animal and Plant Life Spans* Holiday House 1978. *Pigs Wild and Tame* Holiday House 1979. *Biography of a Snowy Owl* Putnam 1979. *Nature's Pretenders* (Junior Literary Guild Selection) Putnam 1979. *Whose House Is It?* Dodd 1980. *Strange Sex Lives in the Animal Kingdom* McGraw 1981. *Chickens and Their Wild Relatives* Dodd 1982. Others. In *New York Daily News, Argosy,* others

Awards or inclusion in other biographical books: *Authors of Books for Young People; Contemporary Authors; Foremost Women in Communications; International Authors and Writers Who's Who; Michigan Authors,* 2nd ed.; *Twentieth-Century Science Fiction Writers; Something about the Author; Who's Who of American Women.* Best Science Award, National Association of Science Teachers, 1972, 1976, 1980

HORAN, KENNETH (O'DONNELL) MRS. (1890-?)

Born: 1890; Jackson, Michigan
Education: University School for Girls, Chicago, Illinois. Vassar College, 1904-1907
Career: Writer, Chicago *Evening Post, Daily Tribune.* Literary editor, Chicago *Journal of Commerce,* 1915. Contributing literary editor, Dallas *Times-Herald*

Writings: *Parnassus en Route: An Anthology of Poems about Places, Not People On the European Continent* Macmillan 1929; Books for Libraries Press 1972. *The Longest Night, A Novel* D.C. Doran 1932. *It's Later Than You Think* R.O. Ballou 1934. *Remember the Day* 1937. *It's Not My Problem* Doubleday, Doran 1938. *Oh, Promise Me* Doubleday Doran 1938. *Night Bell* 1940. *I Give Thee Back* Dutton 1942. *A Bashful Woman* Doubleday 1944. *Papa Went to Congress* Doubleday 1946. *Mama Took Up Travel* Doubleday & Company 1947

Awards or inclusion in other biographical books: *American Authors and Books; American Novelists of Today*

HORVATH, BETTY F.

Address: 2340 Waite Avenue, Kalamazoo, Michigan 49008
Born: May 20, 1927; Jefferson City, Missouri
Parents: Bransford B. Ferguson, Augusta W. (Kapell) Ferguson
Children: Sally, Polly, Jay
Education: Phillips University, Enid, Oklahoma, 3 years

Career: Continuity writer, KWOS in Jefferson City, KCRC in Enid, Oklahoma, WIL in St. Louis, 1946-1952. Advertising Company, St. Louis. Secretary, Private Boys Camp

Writings: *Hooray for Jasper* Franklin Watts. *Jasper Makes Music* Franklin Watts.*Will the Real Tommy Wilson Please Stand Up* Franklin Watts.*The Cheerful Quiet* Franklin Watts. *Be Nice to Josephine* Franklin Watts. *Not Enough Indians* Franklin Watts. *Jasper and the Hero Business* Franklin Watts. *Small Paul and the Bully of Morgan Court* Ginn & Company

Awards or inclusion in other biographical books: *Contemporary Authors; Michigan Authors,* 2nd ed.; *Something about the Author,* others. Child Study Association, Children's Books of the Year, 1966. Three books, Junior Literary Guild selections. Almost, if not all, reprinted in reading textbooks

What is the aim or goal of your writing? "To entertain. Maybe to express my outlook on life. Maybe to present a positive, fun-filled philosophy".

May inquiries be sent to you about doing workshops, readings? No

HOUGHTON, DOUGLASS (1809-1845)

Born: September 21, 1809; Troy, New York
Parents: Jacob Houghton, Mary Lydia (Douglas) Houghton
Education: Fredonia Academy, Fredonia, New York. Studied medicine, qualified as practitioner, 1831. Rensselaer Polytechnic Institute, B.A., Troy, New York, 1829
Children: Two girls
Career: Assistant Professor, lecturer. Appointed surgeon, botanist, Henry R. Schoolcraft expedition to discover sources of the Mississippi, 1831. Physician, surgeon, Detroit, Michigan, 1832-1837. Professor of Geology, Mineralogy, University of Michigan, Ann Arbor, Michigan, 1838-1845. Mayor of Detroit, 1842, 1843. Geological field work begun 1844, but he drowned in Lake Superior storm

Writings: *Geological Reports of Douglass Houghton, First State Geologist of Michigan, 1837-1845* The Michigan Historical Commission 1928. Others. His bibliography is in: J.M. Nickles "Geologic Literature on North America" *U.S. Geological Survey Bulletin 746* 1923

Awards or inclusion in other biographical books: *Allibone: A Critical Dictionary of English Literature; Appleton's Cyclopaedia of American Biography; Biographical Dictionary of American Science; Dictionary of American Biography; Dictionary of Scientific Biography; Drake: Dictionary of American Biography; The National Cyclopaedia of American Biography; The Twentieth Century Biographical Dictionary of Notable Americans; Who Was Who in America.* Honorary member, Academy of Natural Sciences of Philadelphia, Antiquarian Society of Copenhagen. Several Michigan places bear his name

HOUSE, GLORIA A.

Address: 2822 Ewald Circle, Detroit, Michigan 48238
Pseudonym: Aneb Kgositsile
Born: February 14, 1941; Tampa, Florida
Parents: Fred Larry, Rubye M. (Johnson) Larry
Children: Uri
Education: University of Michigan, Ph.D., Ann Arbor, Michigan, 1986. University of California, M.A., Berkeley, California, 1969; California General Secondary Teaching Credential, 1964; B.A., 1961. Monterey Institute of Foreign Studies, Diploma in French Studies, Monterey, California, 1959

Career: Associate Professor of Humanities, Wayne State University, Detroit, Michigan, 1969—. News & Editorial Copy Editor, *Detroit Free Press,* 1969-1971. Administrative Assistant and Staff Writer, Center for Adult Education, Detroit, Michigan, 1968. Teacher, Cass Technical High School, Detroit, Michigan, 1967-1968. Field Secretary, Student Non-Violent Co-ordinating Committee, Lowndes County, Alabama, 1965-1967. French Instructor, San Francisco State College, 1965. Teaching Assistant, University of California, Berkeley, 1964-1965. Graduate Reader, Research Assistant, University of California, Berkeley, 1963-1964. Teacher, Byron House School, Cambridge, England, 1961

Writings: *Tower and Dungeon: A Study of Place and Power in American Culture* Casa de Unidad Press 1991. *Blood River: Poems 1964-1983* Broadside Press 1983. *Rainrituals* Broadside Press 1990. Published in *City Arts Quarterly, Moving Out, Metro Times, Detroit News, Wayne Review,* others. Included in various anthologies such as *Michigan Poetry Sampler, Green River Review: An Anthology of Michigan Poets.* Edited, *Cinders Smoldering: Detroit Since 1967.* Video Documentary Script and Study Guide. *An American Mosaic,* telecourse of 60 half-hour segments, is used in various universities. Numerous other work such as book introductions, translations, book reviews

Awards or inclusion in other biographical books: Wayne State University President's Award for Excellence in Teaching, 1991. Detroit Council of Arts Grant, 1990. Women of Wayne Award, 1990. Keynote Speaker, 25th Anniversary Celebration of Broadside Press, 1990. Invited member, Michigan Delegation to the Middle East, 1990. Project Director, Michigan Council for the Humanities Grant, 1989. Distinguished Award, United Black Artists, 1988. Wayne State University Minority Faculty Research Award, 1987-1988. Award, Michigan Labor Committee, 1987. Wayne State University Educational Development Grant, 1985. Award for Community Service, Black Medical Association, 1984. Distinguished Women of Detroit Award, Women of Wayne Alumni Association, 1983. National Endowment for the Humanities Fellowship, University of Illinois, 1983. Poet-in-Residence, Detroit Public Schools, 1980. Detroit Council of the Arts Grant, 1980. Rackham Graduate Fellowship, University of Michigan, 1980-1986. Center for Continuing Education of Women Scholar Award, University of Michigan, 1979-1980. Levi Straus Fellowship, University of California, Berkeley, 1959-1960. Association of American University Women Scholarship, Sacramento, California, 1958-1959. Delta Sigma Theta Sorority Scholarship, 1958

HOWARD, BRONSON CROCKER (1842-1908)

Born: October 27, 1842; Detroit, Michigan
Parents: Charles Howard, Margaret (Vosburgh) Howard
Education: Detroit, Michigan. Russell's Institute, New Haven, Connecticut
Career: First writing was for *Detroit Free Press.* Left for newspaper work in New York, 1865. First big success came in 1870, with play, *Saratoga.* Founder, first president, American Dramatist's Club-later known as the Society of American Dramatists and Composers. Worked for revision of American laws on international copyright. English versions of plays produced in London

Writings: (dates are when plays were produced) *Saratoga* 1870. *Diamonds* 1872. *The Banker's Daughter* (had an initial run of sixty-eight weeks) 1878. *Old Love Letters* 1878. *Young Mrs. Winthrop* 1882. *One of Our Girls* 1885. *Meet By Chance* 1887. *Shenandoah* 1888. *Aristocracy* 1892. *The Autobiography of a Play* 1914. *The Henrietta: A Comedy in Four Acts* 1887 S. French 1901. *Kate: A Comedy in Four Acts* Harper & Brothers 1906.

Others. Included in *America's Lost Plays* Princeton University Press 1940-1942

Awards or inclusion in other biographical books: *American Authors 1600-1900; American Authors and Books; American Biographies; Dictionary of American Authors; Dictionary of American Biography; Dictionary of Literature in the English Language; Dictionary of North American Authors; National Cyclopaedia of Amerian Biography; Oxford Companion to American Literature; Reader's Encyclopedia of World Drama; Who's Who in America; Who Was Who in America; Who's Who on the Stage,* others

HOWARD, ELLEN

Address: 2011 Waite Avenue, Kalamazoo, Michigan 49008
Born: May 8, 1943; New Bern, North Carolina
Parents: Gerald W. Phillips, Betty J. (Slate) Phillips
Children: Cynthia, Laurie, Anna, Shaley
Education: Franklin High School, Portland, Oregon, 1957-1961. University of Oregon, Eugene, Oregon, 1961-1963. Portland State University, B.A., Portland, Oregon, 1977-1979
Career: Writer, Portland, Oregon, Kalamazoo, Michigan,1979—. Secretary, The Collins Foundation, Portland, Oregon, 1980-1988. Secretary, Oregon Historical Society, Portland, Oregon, 1979-1980. Secretary, Zaik/Miller, Architects, Portland, Oregon, 1977-1978

Writings: *The Cellar* Atheneum 1992. *The Chickenhouse House* Atheneum 1991. *Sister* Atheneum 1990. *Her Own Song* Atheneum 1988. *Edith Herself* Atheneum 1987. *Gillyflower* Atheneum 1986. *When Daylight Comes* Atheneum 1985. *Circle of Giving* Atheneum 1984. *The Big Seed* Simon & Schuster in press. Work in Progress: *The Tower Room*

Awards or inclusion in other biographical books: *Something about the Author, Contempory Authors.* Golden Kite Honor Book, Society of Children's Book Writers, 1984. Notable Children's Trade Books in the Field of Social Studies, 1985, 1986, 1988. Best book of 1987, *School Library Journal.* Children's Middle Grade Fiction Award, International PEN USA Center West, 1989

What is the aim or goal of your writing? "To tell the truth as I know it, in the hope that truth may comfort or teach or at least entertain some children, who are, after all, the most important readership in the world."

May inquiries be sent to you about doing workshops, readings? Yes

HOWARD, HELEN L.

Address: 18120 Woodland Drive, Big Rapids, Michigan 49307
Born: May 4, 1909; Cayuga, Indiana
Parents: William R. Littler, Daisy K. Littler
Children: Roger, James
Education: Northwestern University, B.S., Evanston, Illinois, 1925-1931. Western Michigan University, Correspondence courses, Kalamazoo, Michigan, 1952-1955
Career: Third Grade Teacher, Sturgis, Michigan, 1950-1971, retired; Speech Teacher, Gary, Indiana, 1935-1942. Teacher, Gold Mining Camp, Tiger, Colorado, 1933-1935

Writings: *Hannah's Sod House* Caxton Printers 1947, 1948. Forty-seven stories have been published in children's magazines, three appear in anthologies or reading text books. "Man from Mars" published in *Jack and Jill* was chosen by Scott Foresman and by Ginn & Company for reading textbooks. Forty-eight plays published in *Instructor,*

Highlights for Children, Grade Teacher, Children's Activities and others; ten appear in anthologies and reading text books such as *100 Plays for Children* Burack, Plays Inc., *Thirty Plays for Classroom Reading* Durrel and Crossley. Work in Progress: *Warning in the Wind*, sequel to *Hannah's Sod House* - wind erosion in Colorado, 1914
Awards or inclusion in other biographical books: Selected for exhibit, study conference of Association of Childhood Education International, 1955. Story, "Angel Chimes" selected for Bobbs-Merrill's Best Literature for Children Series
What is the aim or goal of your writing? "To inform and entertain children."
May inquiries be sent to you about doing workshops, readings? Yes

HUBBARD, BELA (1814-1896)
Born: April 23, 1814; Hamilton, New York
Parents: Father a lawyer, served two terms in Congress
Children: Several
Education: Hamilton College, Hamilton, New York, 1834
Career: Corresponding secretary, president, Young Men's Society of Detroit. Farmer, real estate developer. Assistant geologist for state geologist Douglass Houghton, 1837-1841. Founding member, Association of American Geologists. Editor, *Western Farmer*, 1842. Executive committee, Michigan State Agricultural Society, proposed an agricultural school, drafted proposal to Michigan legislature, Michigan Agricultural College (Michigan State University) approved 1855. Vice President, Pioneer Society of the State of Michigan, elected 1874

Writings: *Lake Superior Journal: Bela Hubbard's Account of the 1840 Houghton Expedition* Northern Michigan University Press 1983. *The Climate of Detroit, Michigan* (an essay read before the Detroit Scientific Association Lodge's Pharmacy 1872. *Memorials of a Half-Century in Michigan and the Lake Region* G.P. Putnam's Sons 1888; Gale Research 1978. *Reports of Wm. A. Burt and Bela Hubbard, esqs., on the Geography, Topography and Geology of the U.S. Surveys of the Mineral Region of the South Shore of Lake Superior, for 1845* C. Wilcox 1846
Awards or inclusion in other biographical books: *Allibone: a Critical Dictionary of English Literature; Appleton's Cyclopaedia of American Biography; Dictionary of American Authors; Dictionary of North American Authors; National Cyclopaedia of North American Biography; Twentieth Century Biographical Dictionary of Notable Americans*

HUGGLER, TOM
Address: POB 80320-Delta Branch, Lansing, Michigan 48908
Born: June 19, 1945; Detroit, Michigan
Parents: Eldon A. Huggler, Leona C. (Thompson) Huggler
Children: Brian, Jennifer
Education: University of Michigan-Flint, B.A., Flint, Michigan, 1965-1968. Univesity of Michigan, M.A., Ann Arbor, Michigan, 1968-1972
Career: Freelance writer/Book author, Lansing, Michigan, 1982—. High School English Teacher, Genesee, Michigan, 1968-1982

Writings: *Fish 100 Southern Michigan Lakes* Friede Publications 1991. *Grouse of North America* Northwood Press 1990. *Quail Hunting in America* Stackpole Books 1987. *Cannon's Downrigger Guide* The Century Group 1986. *Fish Michigan-Great Lakes* Friede Publications 1986. *Hunt Michigan* Michigan United Conservation Clubs 1984. *Midwest Meanders* Avery Publishing 1984. *Westwind Woods* Michigan United Conser-

vation Clubs 1978. *Trout Streams of Michigan* volume I editor Michigan United Conservation Clubs 1977. Work in Progress: *Fish 100 Northern Michigan Lakes*
Awards or inclusion in other biographical books: Outdoor Writers Association of America, Best Outdoor Book Award, 1990; Second Place, 1991. Conservation Communicator of the Year Award, Michigan Conservation Clubs, 1978
What is the aim or goal of your writing? "To instill an appreciation for natural resources and to teach readers outdoor ethics, sportsmanship and proper how-to techniques of outdoor sport."
May inquiries be sent to you about doing workshops, readings? Yes

HULBERT, WILLIAM DAVENPORT (1869-1913)
Born: October 12, 1869; Mackinac Island, Michigan
Parents: Frances Robbins Hulbert, Diantha Hulda (Gillett) Hulbert
Career: Teacher, St. Ignace, Michigan area. Writer

Writings: *Forest Neighbors* Row Peterson 1915. *White Pine Days on the Tahquamenon* The Historical Society of Michigan (nine stories were collected, edited by author's brother)1949. Many articles and stories about nature published in such magazines as *McClures Magazine, The Youth's Companion, Frank Leslie's Popular Monthly, The Outlook, Metropolitan Magazine, Outing, American Magazine, Country Life in America, Atlantic Monthly*

HULL, HELEN R(OSE) (1888-1971)
Born: Albion, Michigan
Parents: Warren Charles Hull, Louise (McGill) Hull
Education: Michigan State University, B.A., East Lansing. University of Michigan, M.A. University of Chicago, Ph.B., 1912
Career: Instructor, Wellesley College, Wellesley, Massachusetts, 1912-1914. Instructor, Assistant Professor, Associate Professor, Professor, Columbia University, New York, New York, 1914-1958. Professor emeritus of English, Columbia University, 1958-1971. President, Authors' Guild, 1949-1952 during which she edited, *The Writer's Book* 1950

Writings: *Quest* Macmillan 1922. *Labyrinth* Macmillan 1923. *The Surry Family* Macmillan 1925. *Islanders* Macmillan 1927. *The Asking Price* Coward-McCann 1930. *The Art of Writing Prose* (co-author) R. Smith 1930; Farrar 1936. *Candle Indoors* Coward-McCann 1936. *Heat Lightning* (Book-of-the-Month-Club selection) Coward-McCann 1932. *Hardy Perennial* Coward-McCann 1933. *Morning Shows the Day* Coward-McCann 1934. *Frost Flower* Coward-McCann 1939. *Experiment: Four Short Novels* Coward-McCann 1940. *Through the House Door* Coward-McCann 1940. *A Circle in the Water* Coward-McCann 1943. *Mayling Soong Chiang* Coward-McCann 1943; biography of Madame Chiang Kai-shek, her student at Wellesley). *Hawk's Flight* Coward-McCann 1946. *Octave, a Book of Stories* (editor) Coward-McCann 1947. *Landfall* Coward-McCann 1953. *Writer's Roundtable* (co-editor) Harper 1959. *A Tapping on the Wall* Dodd 1960. *Close Her Pale Blue Eyes* Dodd l963. Others. Contributed short stories, novelettes, serials to various magazines
Awards or inclusion in other biographical books: *American Authors and Books; American Novelists of Today; American Women Writers; Author's and Writer's Who's Who; Current Biography; Dictionary of American Authors; Dictionary of American Biography; Dictionary of North American Authors; Index to Women; Michigan Authors,*

1st ed., 2nd ed.; *National Cyclopedia of American Biography; Twentieth Century Biographical Dictionary of Notable Americans; Who's Who of American Women,* others. Guggenheim Fellowship, 1930. Dodd, Mead Award for the best suspense novel written by a college professor, 1960

HUMPHREYS, JOHN R.

Address: 622 1/2 Canyon Road, Santa Fe, New Mexico 87501
Born: Mancelona, Michigan
Parents: Harold L. Humphreys, Blanch Humphreys
Children: Catherine
Education: University of Michigan, A.B., Ann Arbor, Michigan, 1936-1940
Career: Director Creative Writing Program, Columbia University, New York, New York, 1946-1988

Writings: *Maya Red* Cane Hill Press 1989. *Timeless Towns and Haunted Places* St. Martin's 1989. *The Lost Towns and Roads of America* Doubleday 1967. *Subway to Samarkand* Doubleday 1977. *The Last of the Middlewest* Doubleday 1966. *The Dirty Shame* Dell 1955. *Vandameers Road* Scribners 1941
Awards or inclusion in other biographical books: *Michigan Authors,* 2nd ed. Guggenheim Fellow, Novel, National Endowment for the Arts. Distinguished Teacher Award, Columbia University. Bancroft Award, Distinguished Retiring Professor, Columbia University. Huntington Hartford Fellowship. McDowell Fellowship. Wurlitzer Fellowship. Two Hopwood Awards for Fiction Writing, University of Michigan
May inquiries be sent to you about doing workshops, readings? No

HUYSER-HONIG, JOAN C.

Address: 1016 Oakdale SE, Grand Rapids, Michigan 49507
Born: July 31, 1958; Grand Rapids, Michigan
Parents: Frank Huyser, Wilma C. Huyser
Children: Abram, Joshua
Education: Calvin College, B.A., Grand Rapids, Michigan, 1976-1980
Career: Director of Alternative Program, Calvin College, 1980-1982. Freelance writer and editor, self-employed, 1982—.

Writings: *West Michigan Vacation Saver: A Weatherproof Travel Guide* Altweger and Mandel 1992. *One of a Kind* Christian Reformed Publishing House 1989. *The Church Serves* Christian Reformed Publishing House 1987. Written for corporations, nonprofit agencies, magazines, newspapers. Material sold to *Americana, Cleveland Plain Dealer, Horticulture, Indianapolis News, Lake Michigan Coast, Milwaukee Journal, National Gardening, Organic Gardening, San Francisco Chronicle, Your Health,* Booth Newspapers, and others. Work in Progress: Regular contributor to the home and travel sections of *Grand Rapids Press*
What is the aim or goal of your writing? "God has filled the world with intriguing people, places, and things. I like to discover such subjects and arrange the information in an interesting way for readers. Much of my writing, especially travel and garden subjects, aims to make people care about our common heritage and ties to each other and creation."
May inquiries be sent to you about doing workshops, readings? Yes

HYDE, DAYTON O.
Address: P.O. Box 932, Hot Springs, South Dakota 57747
Born: March 25, 1925; Marquette, Michigan
Parents: Frederick W. Hyde, Rhoda (Williams) Hyde
Children: Dayton, Virginia, Marsha, John, Taylor
Education: Cate School, Carpinteria, California, 1939-1943. University of California, Berkeley, California, B.A., English, 1946-1950
Career: Rancher, writer, conservationist, 1950—

Writings: *Sandy* Dial Press 1968. *Yamsi* Dial Press 1971. *The Last Free Man* Dial Press 1973. *Thunder Down the Track* Macmillan 1985. *One Summer in Montana* Macmillan 1985, Antheneum 1988. *The Mayor, the Poacher, and the Wonderful One Trout River* Macmillan 1985; Antheneum 1987. *Strange Companions* Dutton 1975, 1983. *Island of the Loons* Macmillan 1980; Antheneum 1986. *Don Coyote* Arbor House 1986, 1988. *Raising Wild Water Fowl in Captivity* Dutton 1975. *Brand of a Box* 1975. Work in Progress: *Chimneys. The Pastures of Beyond. Strongholds*
Awards or inclusion in other biographical books: *Michigan Authors,* 2nd ed. *The Mayor, the Poacher,* Northwest Booksellers Award. *Don Coyote,* American Library Association Best Books of Decade. *Strange Companions,* Dutton Award for Nature Writing
What is the aim or goal of your writing? "To make humans aware that instead of dominion over the planet they have responsibility for it."

I

INGERSOLL, ERNEST (1852-1946)
Born: March 13, 1852; Monroe, Michigan
Parents: Timothy Dwight Ingersoll, Eliza (Parkinson) Ingersoll
Children: Helen, Geoffrey
Education: Oberlin College, Oberlin, Ohio. Museum of Comparative Zoology, Harvard University, Cambridge, Massachusetts. Studied with Louis Agassiz, summer of 1873
Career: Naturalist collector on survey, 1873-1879. Member, U.S. Fish Commission, special agent for 10th census of oyster industry. Visited California, Puget Sound area, 1883. Lecturer of zoology, University of Chicago. Co-editor, *Standard Dictionary* and other reference books. Became editor of publications of the Canadian Pacific Railroad 1887. Began lecturing on natural history, travel, 1899. Contributed weekly, *Montreal Star,* 1899-1938

Writings: *The Oyster Industry* Washington Government Printing Office 1881. *The Ice Queen* 1885; Harper & Brothers 1912. *To the Shenandoah and Beyond* Leve & Alden 1885. *Wild Life of Orchard and Field* Harper & Brothers 1902. *Rand McNally & Co.'s Illustrated Guide to the Hudson River and Catskill Mountains* Rand, McNally 1902. *The Raisin Creek Exploring Club* D. Appleton 1919. *Birds in Legend, Fable and Folklore* Longmans, Green 1923. Several others. Contributed scientific descriptive articles, *Tribune* (New York), 1874; *Herald* (New York), 1877. Several serial stories for children
Awards or inclusion in other biographical books: *American Authors and Books; American Literary Yearbook; Bibliophile Dictionary; Biographical Dictionary and Synopsis of Books; Childhood in Poetry; Dictionary of American Authors; Dictionary of North American Authors; Reader's Encyclopedia of American Authors; National Cyclopaedia of American Biography; Twentieth Century Biographical Dictionary of Notable Americans; Who Was Who in America; Who Was Who in North American Authors*, others

ISHAM, FREDERIC STEWART (1866-1922)
Born: March 29, 1866; Detroit, Michigan
Parents: Charles S. Isham, Lucy B. (Mott) Isham
Education: High School, Detroit, Michigan. Royal Academy Music, London, England and Munich, Germany
Career: Editorial staff, *Detroit Free Press,* others

Writings: *The Toy Shop: a Drama for Children* (with Edward Weitzel) T.H. French 1891. *The Strollers* Bowen-Merrill 1902. *Under the Rose* Bowen-Merrill 1903. *Black Friday* Bobbs-Merrill 1904. *The Lady of the Mount* Bobbs-Merrill 1908. *The Thousand and Second Night; a Romantic Comedy* self-published 1911. *This Way Out* Bobbs-Merrill 1917. *The Daisy Pushers* (with Max Marchin) 1919. *Nothing but the Truth* 1915 dramatized at New York and London Theaters, 1916-1919. *Three Live Ghosts; a Comedy in Three Acts* Samuel French 1920
Awards or inclusion in other biographical books: *Allibone: a Critical Dictionary of English Literature; American Authors and Books; Dictionary of American Authors; Dictionary of North American Authors; National Cyclopaedia of American Biography; Who Was Who in America*

IVES, SARAH NOBLE W (1864-1944)
Born: March 10, 1864; Grosse Ile, Michigan
Parents: William Ives, Sarah M. (Hyde) Ives
Education: Port Huron High School, graduated in 1880. Studied three years at the Detroit Training School of Elocution and English Literature. Two years in New York City. Julian School, Paris, three years, studying art
Career: Illustrator, writer of Children and young people's books for 25 years in New York City. Contributor and illustrator of the McClure Newspaper Syndicate, *New York Tribune, Universalist*. Three years in art department, Women's Benefit Association, Port Huron, Michigan. Exhibitions in Detroit, 1892, 1895, 1916, 1922

Writings: (illustrator/author)*Songs of the Shining Way* 1895. *The Story of a Little Bear* 1908. *The Key to Betsy's Heart* 1916. *Dog Heroes of Many Lands* 1922
Awards or inclusion in other biographical books: *American Authors and Books; Childhood in Poetry; Who Was Who among North American Authors; Who Was Who in America; Women's Who's Who of America*

J

JACKSON, C(AARY) PAUL
Pseudonym: Jack Paulson, Colin Lochlons, O.B. Jackson, Caary Jackson
Born: 1902; Urbana, Illinois
Parents: Caary Jackson, Goldie (Harding) Jackson
Children: Mae, Betty, Paul, William
Education: Western Michigan University, A.B., Kalamazoo, Michigan, 1929. University of Michigan, M.A., Ann Arbor, Michigan, 1943
Career: Public School Teacher, Coach, Van Buren County, Michigan, 1922-1927; Kalamazoo, Michigan, 1929-1951. Writer, 1951-?

Writings: *All-Conference Tackle* Crowell 1947. *Rose Bowl All-American* Crowell 1949. *Shorty Makes the First Team* Follett 1950. *Rose Bowl Line Backer* Crowell 1951. *Barney of the Babe Ruth League* Crowell 1954. *Match Point* Westminster 1956. *Bud Plays Junior High Football* Hastings House 1957. *Side Line Victory* Westminster 1957. *Little League Tournament* Hastings House 1959. *The Jamesville Jets* Follett 1959. *Pro Football Rookie* Hastings House 1962. *High School Backstop* (with Orpha B. Jackson) 1963. *Southpaw in the Mighty League* McGraw 1965. *Haunted Halfback* Follett 1969. *The National Baseball Hall of Fame and Museum* Hastings House 1969. *Halfback!* Hastings House 1971. *Eric and Dud's Football Bargain* Hastings House 1972. *Beginner Under the Backboards* Hastings House 1974. *How to Play Better Soccer* Crowell 1978. Many others. Short stories. Magazine articles
Awards or inclusion in other biographical books: *Authors of Books for Young People; Contemporary Authors; Michigan Authors*, 2nd ed.; *Something about the Author*

JACKSON, GEORGE LEROY (1875-?)
Born: May 28, 1875; Springville, New York
Parents: William Jackson, Emma (Knowlton) Jackson
Education: Buffalo State Normal School, 1898. University of Michigan, A.B., Ann Arbor, Michigan, 1906. Columbia University, A.M., New York, New York, 1907, Ph.D. 1909
Career: School principal, North Tonawanda, New York, 1898-1903. Began as instructor and became professor, University of Michigan, 1910-1936, retired

Writings: *The Development of School Support in Colonial Massachusetts* Teachers College, Columbia University 1909. *Outlines of the History of Education* 1911. *The Privilege of Education-a History of its Extension* 1918. *The Development of State Control of Public Instruction in Michigan* Michigan Historical Commission 1926
Awards or inclusion in other biographical books: *Who Was Who in America; Who Was Who among North American Authors*

JACKSON, HAROLD CHARLES LEBARON (1894-1954)
Born: February 18, 1894; North Hatley, Quebec, Canada
Parents: Archibald Jackson, Nellie (LeBaron) Jackson
Children: Harold, Daniel
Education: University of Michigan, B.A., Ann Arbor, Michigan, 1918
Career: Writer, columnist "Listening in on Detroit", *The Detroit News,* 1930-1954

Writings: *Grand Circus Park, U.S.W.* Arnold-Powers 1938. *The Paper Bag and Other Stories* Arnold-Powers 1941. *Longs and Shorts* Arnold-Powers 1942. *Ups and Downs* Arnold-Powers 1943. *Left Hand Up and Other Stories* Arnold-Powers 1944. *'Round Corners* Arnold-Powers 1945. *Back to Vertical, and Other Stories* Arnold-Powers 1946. *It Happened in Detroit* Conjure House 1947. *Dogs, Cats and People* Conjure House 1949
Awards or inclusion in other biographical books: *Michigan Authors,* 2nd ed.

JACOBSON, DANIEL
Address: 1827 Mirabeau Drive, Okemos, Michigan 48864
Born: November 6, 1923; Newark, New Jersey
Parents: Samuel M. Jacobson, Mary Jacobson
Children: Lisa, Darryl, Jerrold Wife: Iris M.
Education: New Jersey State College, B.A., Upper Montclair, New Jersey, 1947. Columbia University, M.A., New York, New York, 1950. Louisiana State University, Ph.D.,1954
Career: Professor, Michigan State University, East Lansing, Michigan, 1967—. Associate Professor, New Jersey State College, Upper Monclair, New Jersey, 1958-1967. Assistant Professor, Brooklyn College, Brooklyn, New York, 1956-1958. Instructor, University of Kentucky, Lexington, Kentucky, 1952-1956

Writings: *The Northwest Ordinance of 1787* Michigan State Alumni Association 1987.*The North Central States* Franklin Watts 1984. *Indians of North America* Franklin Watts 1983. *The Gatherers* Franklin Watts 1977.*The Fishermen* Franklin Watts 1975. *The Hunters* Franklin Watts 1974. *Alabama-Coushatta Indians* Garland Publishing 1974. *Great Indian Tribes* Hammond 1970.*The First Americans* Ginn and Company 1969.*The Story of Man* Home Library Press 1963. Work in Progress:*Ships and Ship-building Among the Ancient Mariners*

Awards or inclusion in other biographical books: *Michigan Authors,* 2nd ed.; *Something about the Author,* Vol. 12, 1977

What is the aim or goal of your writing? "To help young people understand the nature of ethnicity, the American Indian, the urban world and the significance of historical geography."

May inquiries be sent to you about doing workshops, readings? Yes

JAGER, RONALD A.

Address: P.O. Box 292, Washington, New Hampshire 03280
Born: December 2, 1932; McBain, Michigan
Parents: Jess Jager, Kate Jager
Children: Colin
Education: Northern Christian High School. Calvin College, 1951-1955. Harvard University, Cambridge, Massachusetts, 1958-1964
Career: Taught Philosophy, Yale University, Cambridge, Massachusetts, 1965-1977

Writings: *The Development of Bertrand Russell's Philosophy* Muirhead Library of Philosophy Allen & Unwin 1972; Humanities Press 1972. Spanish translation rights 1975. *Essays in Logic from Aristotle to Russell* Prentice-Hall 1963; five reprintings. *Portrait of a Hill Town* (with Grace Jager) Village Press 1977. *Historical Pillsbury* Society for the Protection of New Hampshire Forests 1976. *New Hampshire: An Illustrated History of the Granite State* (with Grace Jager) Windsor Publications, Inc. and New Hampshire Historical Society 1983. *A Sacred Deposit: The Meetinghouse in Washington, New Hampshire* (with Sally Krone) Peter Randall 1989. *Eighty Acres: Elegy for a Family Farm* Beacon Press 1990; excerpted in seven periodicals-about growing up in McBain, Michigan. About fifty essays in *New York Times, Harper's, The Atlantic, Country Journal, Early American Life, Reader's Digest, Natural History, Michigan History* and several others. Work in Progress: A sequel to *Eighty Acres: Elegy for a Family Farm*
Awards or inclusion in other biographical books: Matchette Prize, American Philosophical Association, 1974
May inquiries be sent to you about doing workshops, readings? Yes

JAMISON, JAMES KNOX (1887-1954)

Born: 1887; Mt. Pleasant, Michigan
Children: son, daughter
Education: Graduated from Central State Normal College, Mt. Pleasant, Michigan and University of Michigan, Ann Arbor, Michigan.
Career: Teacher, Ontonagon, Michigan, Detroit, others. Superintendent of Schools, Ontonagon, Michigan, four years. Mananger, large estate as Upper Peninsula agent. Member, Michigan Education Planning Commission. Elected, Michigan House of Representatives, 1934. Deputy Auditor General of Michigan. Journalist

Writings: *This Ontonagon Country: Political Beginnings* Ontonagon Herald 1932. *This Ontonagon Country: Red Men* Ontonagon Herald 1930. *This Ontonagon Country: Red Metal* Ontonagon Herald 1930. *This Ontonagon Country: Silver* Ontonagon Herald 1932. *This Ontonagon Country: Social Life* Ontonagon Herald 1931. *By Cross and Anchor: The Story of Frederic Baraga on Lake Superior* St. Anthony Guild Press 1946; R.W. Drier 1965. *The Mining Ventures of This Ontonagon Country* self-published 1950. *Families of Ontonagon County, Michigan* 1950. *This Ontonagon Country: The Story of An American*

Frontier The Ontonagon Herald Company 1939, 1948, distributed by Hillsdale School Supply; Roy W. Drier 1965. Others

JAY, CHARLES W. (1815-1884)
Pseudonym: O.P. Dildock
Born: 1815; Lamberton, New Jersey
Children: two
Career: Newspaper work, 1840-1871, New Jersey. Farmer, fruit grower, Oceana County, Michigan

Writings: *My New Home in Northern Michigan* printers W.S. & E.W. Sharp (Trenton, New Jersey) 1874; Hardscrabble Books 1979. Numerous letters in *The Great Controversy upon Catholicism and Protestantism* L. F. Whitbeck 1875; originally published in the *Evening Journal* (November 1875)

JEFFERSON, MARK SYLVESTER (1863-1949)
Born: March 1, 1863; Mellrose, Massachusetts
Parents: Daniel Jefferson, Mary Elizabeth (Mantz) Jefferson
Children: Geoggrey, Barbara, Theodore, Phoebe, Hilray, Sally, Thomas, Mary (two marriages)
Education: Harvard University, A.B., Cambridge, Massachusetts, 1897, A.M., 1898
Career: Astronomer, Argentine Republic, 1884-1886. Treasurer and Assistant Manager, Sugar Ingenio "La Providencia" Tucuman, Argentine Republic, 1886-1888. Taught Geography in summer school at Harvard University, University of Michigan, Yale, and others. Chief cartographer, American Peace Commission in Paris, summer 1918. Chairman of City Planning Commission, Ypsilanti, Michigan. Professor and Head of Geography Department, Michigan State Normal College (Eastern Michigan University)

Writings: *Atlantic Tides* Judd & Detweiler 1898. *Material for Geography of Michigan* Scharf Tag, Label & Box Co. 1906. *Commercial Values: Atlas of Raw Materials of Commerce and Commercial Interchanges* Ginn 1912. *Notes on the Geography of Europe* (Ypsilanti, Michigan) 1917. *Recent Colonization in Chile* Oxford University Press 1921. *Man in Europe, Here and There* (Ypsilanti, Michigan)1924. *Peopling the Argentine Pampa* American Geographical Society 1926; Kennikat Press 1971. *Principles of Geography* Harcourt, Brace 1926. *Exercises in Human Geography* (Ypsilanti, Michigan)1930. *Man in Europe* Evans-Starr Printing 1936. *The Mark Jefferson Paris Peace Conference Diary* University Microfilms 1966. Others. Contributing Editor, *Geographical Review*
Awards or inclusion in other biographical books: *Biographical Dictionary of American Educators; Dictionary of American Biography; Who Was Who among North American Authors; Who Was Who in America; Who's Who in Michigan* 1936. American Geographical Society Cullom Gold Medalist, 1931, Culver Gold Medalist, 1932

JENKS, WILLIAM LEE (1856-1936)
Born: December 27, 1856; St. Clair County, Michigan
Parents: Bela W. Jenks, Sarah (Carleton) Jenks
Children: Elizabeth
Education: University of Michigan, classical course, graduated in 1878. Studied law in the office of Brown & Farrand in Port Huron and admitted to the Bar in 1879
Career: Practiced law alone and with various firms. Director and attorney of the city Electric Railway Company of Port Huron, and other corporations, banks. Organized Port

Huron Public Library, 1885. One of the original promoters of the Michigan Historical Commission

Writings: *St. Clair County, Michigan: Its History and its People; a Narrative Account of its Historical Progress and its Principal Interests* Lewis Publishing 1912. *Patrick Sinclair* Wynkoop Hallenbeck Crawford Co. (state printers) 1914. *The First Bank in Michigan, the Detroit Bank* The First National Exchange Bank 1916? Wrote the last chapter of *Life and Times of Stevens Thomson Mason, the Boy Governor of Michigan* Michigan Historical Commission 1920. *First National Exchange Bank: Fifty Years of Banking, 1871-1921* Riverside Printing 1921? Contributed to *Bibliography of the Printed Maps of Michigan, 1804-1880* Michigan Historical Commission 1931, and others. Published in *Michigan Historical Magazine, Michigan Law Review, Mississippi Valley Historical Review*
Awards or inclusion in other biographical books: *Bench and Bar of Michigan* 1897; *Dictionary of North American Authors; National Cyclopaedia of American Biography; Who's Who in Michigan* 1936

JEWELL, EDWARD ALDEN (1888-1947)
Born: March 10, 1888; Grand Rapids, Michigan
Parents: Frank Jewell, Jennie (Osterhout) Jewell
Children: Marcia
Education: High School, Grand Rapids, Michigan. Friends' School, Washington, DC
Career: Lived abroad, 1910-1911. Reporter, *Grand Rapids Herald*, 1911-1914. Secretary to senator, Washington, DC, 1914-1915. *New York Tribune*, 1915. Editor, *World Court Magazine,* 1916. Associate editor, *Everybody's Magazine*, 1916-1917. Sunday editor, *New York Tribune,* 1917-1919. Served in World War I

Writings: *The Charmed Circle* 1921. *The Moth Decides* 1922. *Have We An American Art?* Longman, Green 1939. *Paul Cezanne* Hyperion Press 1944. *Van Gogh* 1946. Others
Awards or inclusion in other biographical books: *American Authors and Books; Dictionary of North American Authors; Twentieth Century Authors; Who Was Who in America*

JEWELL, TERRI L.
Address: 1710 Barritt Street, Apt. 5, Lansing, Michigan 48912
Born: October 4, 1954; Louisville, Kentucky
Parents: Miller L. Jewell, Jr., Mildred Jewell
Education: Montclair State College, B.S., Upper Monclair, New Jersey, 1979. Michigan State University, East Lansing, Michigan, 1988
Career: Freelance writer, 1983—. Writer's residency, Kentucky, 1990. Workshop facilitator, 1984—. Numerous poetry readings in Michigan, several other states. Medicaid Utilization Analyst IV, Michigan Department of Social Services, 1992—. General Office Assistant VI (Administrative) Michigan Department of Corrections, Lansing, Michigan, 1990-1992. Program specialist, Michigan Economics for Human Development, 1986-1989. Medical Claims Adjuster, Provident Accident and Life Insurance Company, 1986. Coordinator, Park Duvalle Meals-on-Wheels Program, 1982-1985. Employment/Training Assistant, Newark Recycling, 1980-1982; Personnel Technician I, 1979-1980. Assistant to Senior Health Planner, Newark Health Planning Agency, 1978-1979

Writings: Work has appeared in over 300 periodicals in the United States and abroad. Poems and short-short fiction has appeared in *Black American Literature Forum, Cottonwood, Off Our Backs, Sing Heavenly Muse, Kalliope, Literati Chicago*, others. Nonfiction in *The Bloomsbury Review, New Directions for Women, The Washington Blade, Women of Power* and others. Book reviews in *Small Press Review, The Black Scholar, Southern Voice* and others. Work included in such anthologies as *Long Journey Home: A Poetry Anthology* Meta Press 1985 and *Sexual Harassment: Women Speak Out* Crossing Press 1992. Guest poetry editor, *Souourner* 1989.

Work in Progress: *Gumbo Ya-Ya: Quotations by Black Women* and personal essays, poetry, fiction

Awards or inclusion in other biographical books: Pushcart nomination for poetry, 1989. Kentucky Poetry Society competition winner, 1983. Bulldog Press poetry competition winner, Texas, 1984. University of Louisville, Kentucky, poetry competition winner, 1984. Michigan New Voices State Poetry competition winner, 1986. American Society for Aging poetry competition winner, California, 1988, Connecticut Poetry Society honorable mention, 1984. Judge for Hispanic Education Writing Contest, 1989. Wolf Pen Women Writers Colony residency, 1990, others

What is the aim or goal of your writing? "When I write, it is the only time I do not lie, demure, go into denial, avoid, or diminish my realities. My aim is to speak the truth; my goal is to assist the reader in learning my world, my 'sight', my life safely...but surely..., to realize the beauty, the strength, the wonder there."

May inquiries be sent to you about doing workshops, readings? Yes

JOHANSON, BRUCE H.

Address: 275 Beck Road, Ontonagon, Michigan 49953
Born: April 29, 1942; Duluth, Minnesota
Parents: John Johanson, Pearl C. (Ellefson) Johanson
Children: Lori Ann, Linda
Education: University of Minnesota, Duluth, Minnesota, B.S. Music, B.S. History
Career: Teacher, Medicine Lake Public Schools, Medicine Lake, Montana, 1965-1966. Teacher, Ontonagon Area Schools, Ontonagon, Michigan 1966—. SNAP negotiator, Michigan Education Association, 1974—.

Writings: *Ontonagon in Days of Yore* Melody Acres Publishers 1992. *This Land, The Ontonagon* Mid Peninsula Library Cooperative 1985; Ontonagon Herald Company 1985. *Victoria, the Gem of Forest Hill* The Lake Superior Miner 1988. Several weekly series, *The Lake Superior Miner;* articles on mining, Native Americans, other topics. Work in Progress: "Confessions of an Angel", humorous recollections of school days of a teacher. Compiling information on homicides in the area

Awards or inclusion in other biographical books: Michigan Council for the Social Studies, Outstanding Social Studies Teacher Award, 1986

What is the aim or goal of your writing? "To teach, to reach, to enlighten. Our area has a unique and fascinating history which has been largely ignored by general American history textbooks. I believe that I owe it to my pupils to give them a sense of pride in the local heritage and the contributions our area has made to the building of the American dream. I also derive a great sense of satisfaction in preserving in words some of the colorful happening of this small town and country area. Recording events as history gives the people here some feeling for the great accomplishments of their forebears. Ontonagon was the hub of the first mineral rush in U.S. history. We have had lumbering, oil drilling, education firsts (Ontonagon schools were the first tax supported schools in the U.P., possibly in the state!), Ontonagon had the first telephone exchange in Michigan in 1877, etc."

May inquiries be sent to you about doing workshops, readings? Yes. On historical subjects only

JOHNSON, ANNA (1860-1943)

Pseudonym: Hope Daring
Born: July 11, 1860; Bradford County, Pennsylvania
Parents: George T. Johnson, L. Jane (Van Vechten) Johnson
Education: Albion College
Career: Teacher in district school, several years

Writings: *Paul Crandal's Charge* American Tract Society 1900. *To the Third Generation* American Tract Society 1901. *Agnes Grant's Education* Jennings & Pye 1902. *Entering into His Own* American Track Society 1903. *The Furniture People* G.W. Jacobs 1903. *An Abundant Harvest* Eaton and Mains 1904; Jennings & Graham 1904. *Madeline, the Island Girl* Abingdon Press 1906. *Father John; or, Ruth Webster's Quest* American Tract Society 1907. *A Virginian Holiday* American Tract Society 1909. *Paying the Price!* American Tract Society 1914. *The Woods in the Home* Whitman 1927. Others
Awards and inclusion in other biographical books: *Michigan Authors,* 2nd ed.; *Who Was Who in America; Women's Who's Who of America*

JOHNSON, WILLIAM A.

Address: 322 S. Drake Avenue, Apt. I-9, Kalamazoo, Michigan 49009
Pseudonym: Arnold Johnston
Born: May 31, 1942; Cambuslang, Scotland
Parents: James R. Johnston, Eliza A. Johnston
Education: Wayne State University, Ph.B., Detroit, Michigan, 1959-1963. University of Delaware, M.A., Ph.D., Newark, Delaware, 1963-1966, 1969-1970
Career: Professor of English, Western Michigan University, Kalamazoo, Michigan, 1966—.

Writings: *Of Earth and Darkness: The Novels of William Golding* University of Missouri Press 1980. *The Witching Voice: A Play About Robert Burns* Western Michigan University Press 1973. Plays produced (full-length): *The Witching Voice; Scrimshaw; The Edge of Running Water; Suitors; Closer to Brel, Automatic Telling* (with Deborah Ann Percy; *But If It Rage* (with Deborah Ann Percy); *A Sheltering Tree* (with D. A. Percy). Head writer/editor for radio series, *Voices from Michigan's Past.* Fiction, poetry, drama, nonfiction widely published in journals. Work in Progress: *The Witching Voice: A Novel About Robert Burns. Deus Ex* (with Deborah Ann Percy) and other screenplays
Awards or inclusion in other biographical books: *Contemporary Authors; International Authors and Writers Who's Who; Who's Who in Entertainment.* Finalist, Embers Poetry Chapbook Competition, 1990. Third Prize, Passages North National Poetry Competition, 1989. Distinguished Service Award, Board of Directors, New Vic Theatricals, Inc., 1988. Resolutions of Recognition for Contributions to the Arts, City of Kalamazoo, County of Kalamazoo; Certificate of Commendation from U.S. Representative Howard Wolpe, 1986. Community Arts Medal, Arts Council of Greater Kalamazoo, 1986. President's Award for Chapter Service, Western Michigan University Chapter, American Association of University Professors, 1979. Resolution of Recognition for University

Service, Michigan State House of Representatives, 1979. Semi-Finalist, Midwest Playwrights Workshop Summer Fellowship Competition, 1979. Victor Award, Best Actor, New Vic Theater, Kalamazoo, 1977; Best Supporting Actor, 1976. Western Michigan University Alumni Teaching Excellence Award, 1990. First Prize (with Deborah Percy), Dogwood National One-Act Competition, 1990. Placed in many other competitions. Received several grants, fellowships

What is the aim or goal of your writing? "To entertain readers and audiences without insulting their intelligence."

May inquiries be sent to you about doing workshops, readings? Yes

JONES, KENSINGER

Address: 425 Pritchardville Road, Hastings, Michigan 49058

Born: October 18, 1919; St. Louis, Missouri

Parents: Walter C. Jones; Anna K. Jones

Children: Jeffrey , Janice (wife, Alice M. Jones)

Education: Washington Univerity, St. Louis, Missouri, 1939-1940. Nadine College of Advertising, St. Louis, Missouri, 1938-1939

Career: Lecturer in Advertising, Michigan State University, East Lansing, Michigan, 1982—. Regional Creative Director, Leo Burnett Advertising, Sydney, Australia, 1973-1977. Senior Vice President, Director, Leo Burnett Advertising, Detroit, Michigan, Chicago, Illinois, 1970-1973. Executive Vice President and Creative Director, Campbell-Ewald Advertising, Detroit, Michigan, 1957-1969. Writer, *Land We Live in* Radio Series, St. Louis, Missouri, 1945-1952. Television copywriter, Leo Burnett, Chicago, Illinois, 1952-1957. Co-author, *Call From the Country,* 1989. Co-author, Cable Television, *New Ways to New Business,* 1986

Writings: *A Call From the Country* Wilderness Adventure Press 1989. *Cable Television-New Ways to New Business* Prentice-Hall 1986. *The Rebellious Colonel Speaks* Prentice-Hall 1964. Articles in *Advertising Age, Journal of Advertising, Detroit Adcrafter, Circumnavigator's Log, Michigan History.* Work in Progress:*Writing for a Living*

Awards or inclusion in other biographical books: In current: *Who's Who in Advertising; Who's Who in America; Who's Who in the Midwest; Who's Who in the World.* Freedom's Foundation Award for Excellence in Economic Education, 1984. Silver Salute, Cooperative Extension, Michigan State University, 1981

What is the aim or goal of your writing? "Hopefully to make a living doing something I thoroughly enjoy. The writing itself may entertain (radio shows and book), instruct (cable text), inform (biography), persuade (ad copy). Aim varies, according to project."

May inquiries be sent to you about doing workshops, readings? Yes

JONES, NETTIE P.

Address: 1511 First Street, Detroit, Michigan 48226

Born: January 1, 1941; Arlington, Georgia

Parents: Benjamin Jones, Delmia (Whorton) Jones

Children: Lynne (Harris)

Education: Wayne State University, B.S., Detroit, Michigan. Marygrove College, M.A., Detroit, Michigan. Graduate Faculty New School for Social Research. Fashion Institute of Technology

Career: Teacher, Detroit, Michigan, 1963-1972. Teacher, Royal George School, Greenfield Park, Quebec, 1966-1968. Teacher, New York Hospital Workers Martin Luther King School, New York, New York, 1971-1972. Lecturer/Visiting Writer, Wayne State

University, Detroit, Michigan 1986-1987. Staff Assistant for Chairman, Wayne county commissioners, Detroit, Michigan 1988. Assistant Professor, Writer-in-Residence, Michigan Technological University, Houghton, Michigan, 1988-1989; Minority Affairs Assistant to the Vice-President, 1989-1990; Educational Consultant to the Dean of the College of Engineering, 1990. Editor of Wayne State University Press series on African-American LIfe, 1987—

Writings: *Fish Tales* Random House, 1984. *Mischief Makers* Weidenfeld and Nicholsen 1989. "When Crack Comes Home", *Detroit Free Press*, 1989. "Nettie Unbound", *Detroit Monthly,* 1989. Numerous reviews, interviews in *Chicago Herald Tribune, Village Voice, New York Times* and others. Work in Progress: *Detroit Beauty in the Beast*, a novel. Essay; autobiography

Awards or inclusion in other biographical books: *Contemporary Authors,* 1985, 1992-1993. *Who's Who in Black America,* 1988. Yaddo Fellow, New York Council of the Arts, 1985. Critics Choice, *Los Angeles Times*, 1989. One of the Most Promising Writers, New Novelists, *New York Times Book Reviews*, 1987. D.H. Lawrence International Writing Competition, 2nd runner up, 1987. Special Recognition Distinguished Service, Michigan Technological University, 1989. Michigan Governor's Art Awards Selection Committee, 1989. National Endowment of the Arts, 1989. Ad Hoc Review Committee, Michigan Council of the Arts, 1990. Benjamin Mays Scholar, University of Chicago, 1991-1992

What is the aim or goal of your writing? "One goal is to become a <u>significant other</u> historically. I want more than anything to have it said of me that I accomplished more than burning the deeds, leases, coupon books of various natures that signify I was a citizen of America. l want scholars to study my work, ministers to reflect and young and old to grow by it."

May inquiries be sent to you about doing workshops, readings? Yes

JORDAN, MILDRED A.

Address: 495 Nellsville Road, Houghton Lake, Michigan 48629
Born: March 18, 1918; Houghton Lake, Michigan
Parents: Truman S. Howe, Maude E. Howe
Children: Neil Alan Carrick, David D. Jordan
Education: High School, Houghton Lake, Michigan, graduated at 15, 1933. Kirtland Community College, Roscommon, Michigan. Famous Writers School, correspondence course
Career: Township Election Chairman, many years. School Election Chairman, many years. Organist, Reorganized Church of Jesus Christ of Latter Day Saints, member ordained Elder, 1986. Organist, funeral home, many years

Writings: *Quiet Walks with Millicent* Vol. III Herald House 1975, 1988. *Quiet Walks with Millicent* Vol. II Herald House 1974, 1988. *Quiet Walks With Millicent* Vol. I Houghton Lake Resorter 1972, 1970. Weekly inspirational column, *Houghton Lake Resorter*, now in 23rd consecutive year. Children's stories. Work in Progress: Worship material, church column

Awards or inclusion in other biographical books: *Michigan Authors,* 2nd ed.

What is the aim or goal of your writing? "To share some of my thoughts with others. I have a need to express myself in this way. I felt it was a God-given gift I should use to uplift and encourage my readers."

May inquiries be sent to you about doing workshops, readings? Yes

JOSEPH, LAWRENCE M.
Born: March 10, 1948; Detroit, Michigan
Education: Cambridge, England, B.A., M.A. University of Michigan, B.A., Ann Arbor, Michigan, 1970; J.D., 1975
Career: Judicial Law Clerk, Michigan State Supreme Court, 1976-1978. Associate Professor of Law, University of Detroit Law School, 1978-1981. Attorney, Private Practice, New York, New York, 1981-1984. Associate Professor, Hofstra University School of Law, New York, New York, 1984-1987. Professor of Law, St. Johns University, Jamacia, New York, 1988—. Poet

Writings: *Curriculum Vitae* University of Pittsburgh Press 1988. *Shouting at No One* University of Pittsburgh Press 1983.
Work in Progress: Poetry book

K

KAHN, WILMA J.

Address: 59 TenBroeck Street, Apartment C, Albany, New York 12210
Born: July 30, 1950; Monroe, Michigan
Parents: Joseph A. Kahn, Edythe A. Kahn
Children: Jennifer
Education: Michigan State University, B.A., East Lansing, Michigan, 1971-1974. Western Michigan University, M.A., M.F.A., Kalamazoo, Michigan, 1985-1988. State University of New York at Albany, Albany, New York, Doctor of Arts, English, 1989—
Career: Presidential Fellow, State University of New York at Albany, Albany, New York, 1989—. Adjunct Faculty, Western Michigan University, Kalamazoo, Michigan, 1988-1989; Graduate Assistant,1987-1988; Graduate College Fellow,1986-1987

Writings: Numerous fiction and poetry publications in literary journals. Work in Progress: *A Week at the Weber*
Awards or inclusion in other biographical books: Presidential Distinguished Dissertion Award, 1992
What is the aim or goal of your writing? "I want to write informative literary fiction."
May inquiries be sent to you about doing workshops, readings? Yes

KAKONIS, TOM E.

Address: 4951 N. Valley Drive, Grand Rapids, Michigan 49505
Born: November 13, 1930; Long Beach, California
Parents: Gus P. Kakonis, Olive M. Kakonis
Children: Thomas, Daniel
Education: University of Iowa, Ph.D., Iowa City, Iowa, 1961-1964. University of Minnesota, B.A., Minneapolis, Minnesota, 1950-1952. South Dakota State University, M.S., 1956-1958
Career: Professor of English, Ferris State University, Big Rapids, Michigan, 1972—. Associate Professor of English, University of Wisconsin-Whitewater, Whitewater, Wisconsin, 1966-1972. Instructor of English, Northern Illinois University, DeKalb, Illinois, 1964-1966. Graduate Assistant, University of Iowa, Iowa City, 1962-1964. Various other college teaching positions. Technical Writer. U.S. Army Officer. Numerous other jobs

Writings: *Double Down* Dutton 1991. *Criss Cross* St. Martin's 1990. *Michigan Roll* St. Martin's 1988. Fourteen college textbooks (12 co-edited, 2 co-authored), 1966-1977. Work in Progress: *Shadow Counter* novel scheduled with Dutton
Awards or inclusion in other biographical books: *Michigan Roll* and *Double Down* were selected by the *New York Times Book Review* as among the top ten crime novels of their respective years. *Criss Cross* was chosen by the *Christian Science Monitor* as among the best mysteries of 1990. *Double Down* was selected by a panel of German critics as the best international crime novel of 1992
What is the aim or goal of your writing? "Beyond the goal of making a living, the aim of my writing, as nearly as I can tell, is to explore the punitive nature of chance in a man's life."
May inquiries be sent to you about doing workshops, readings? Yes

KAMINSKI, MARGARET
Address: 22333 Hanson Court, St. Clair Shores, Michigan 48080
Born: March 16, 1944; Detroit, Michigan
Parents: John J. Kaminski, Gertrude (Malak) Kaminski
Education: Wayne State University, B.F.A., Detroit, Michigan, 1962-1966; Master of Library Science, 1967-1969
Career: First Assistant, Detroit Public Library, Detroit, Michigan, 1985—; Public Relations Librarian, 1974-1976; Reference Librarian, 1969-1973. Co-Editor, *Moving Out; A Feminist Literary & Arts Journal*, 1970—

Writings: *Moving to Antarctica; An Anthology of Women's Writing* (editor) Dustbooks 1975. *A Guatemalan Diary* Cumberland Journal 1980. *El Canon and Other Poems* Rhiannon Press 1979. *La Vida de la Mujer* Fallen Angel 1976. *Martinis* White Light 1973. In *University of Windsor Review, Wayne Review, Corridors, Red Cedar Review, RQ, Library Journal, X, A Journal of the Arts, Quadra Project, Labyris, Artifact, Green River Review, Connections, Wayne Literary Review, South End, Waves, Chomo-Uri, Margins*. Anthologies: *A Change in Weather: Midwest Women Poets*, others. Monograph: *A Short History of the Woman Suffrage Movement in Detroit and Michigan*
Awards or inclusion in other biographical books: *Contemporary Authors; Michigan Authors*, 2nd ed.; *Who's Who of American Women*
What is the aim or goal of your writing? "I am interested in developing journal writing as literature and, in my editing work, exploring the women's feminist aesthetic in literature and art."
May inquiries be sent to you about doing workshops, readings? Yes

KARPINSKI, LOUIS CHARLES (1878-1956)
Born: August 5, 1878; Rochester, New York
Parents: Henry H. Karpinski, Mary Louise (Engesser) Karpinski
Children: Robert, Mary, Louise, Ruth, Joseph, Charles
Education: Cornell University, A.B., Ithaca, New York, 1901. University of Strassburg, Germany, Ph.D., 1903
Career: Faculty, Berea College, Berea, Kentucky, 1897-1899. Faculty, New York higher education institutions, 1903-1910. University of Michigan, Instructor to Professor Emeritus, Ann Arbor, Michigan, 1904-1948. Collector, authority on early American maps

Writings: *The Hindu-Arabic Numerals* (with David E. Smith) Ginn 1911. *Astronomical and Mathematical Rarities in the University of Michigan Library* 1919. *Contributions to the History of Science* University of Michigan 1930. *Bibliography of the Printed Maps of Michigan, 1804-1880, with a Series of over One Hundred Reproductions of Maps Constituting an Historical Atlas of the Great Lakes and Michigan* Michigan Historical Commission 1931. *Historical Atlas of the Great Lakes and Michigan* Michigan Historical Commission 1931. *Bibliography of Mathematical Works Printed in American through 1850* University of Michigan Press; Oxford University Press 1940. *Early Military Books in the University of Michigan Libraries* (with Thomas M. Spaulding) University of Michigan Press 1941. *Maps of Famous Cartographers Depicting North America: an Historical Atlas of the Great Lakes and Michigan, with Bibliography of the Printed Maps of Michigan* Meridian second edition 1977. Others
Awards or inclusion in other biographical books: *American Literary Yearbook; Dictionary of Scientific Biography; Who Was Who among North American Authors; Who Was Who in America*

KAUFFMAN, JANET

Born: June 10, 1945; Lancaster, Pennsylvania
Education: Juniata College, B.A., Huntingdon, Pennsylvania, 1967. University of Chicago, M.A., 1968; Ph.D., 1972
Career: Professor, Jackson Community College, Jackson, Michigan, 1976—. Visiting Associate Professor, University of Michigan, 1984-1985

Writings: *Writing Home* (with Jerome J. McGann) Coldwater Press 1978. *The Weather Book* Texas Tech University Press 1981. *Places in the World: Stories* Knopf 1983. *Places in the World a Woman Could Walk* Knopf 1984. *Collaborators* Knopf 1986. *Obscene Gestures for Women: Stories* Knopf 1989. In *Southern Poetry Review, Beloit Poetry Journal, Antaeus, New Yorker*, others. In *The Third Coast: Contemporary Poetry* Wayne State University Press 1976
Awards or inclusion in other biographical books: *Contemporary Authors*. Special Award, American Academy and Institute of Arts and Letters, 1985

KEARNS, JOSIE A.

Address: 431 Thomson, Flint, Michigan 48503
Born: October 21, 1954; Flint, Michigan
Parents: James V. Kearns, Gladys H. (Randall) Kearns
Education: University of Michigan-Flint, B.A. English and Psychology, Flint, Michigan, 1979-1983
Career: Professor, Baker College, Owosso, Michigan 1992—. Director, Visiting Writer Series, Young Writers Academy, University of Michigan-Flint, Michigan, 1985-1991. Reporter, *The Flint Journal,* Flint, Michigan, 1984—. Visiting Poet/Writer, Creative Writers in the Schools, Michigan, 1986—

Writings: *Life After the Line* Wayne State University Press 1990.
Work in Progress:*Women at Work*, non-fiction. *Agreeing With Everyone*, poetry
Awards or inclusion in other biographical books:*Who's Who in U.S. Poets, Writers, Editors.* Creative Artist Award, Michigan Council for the Arts, 1990, 1986. Fellowship, National Endowment for the Arts, 1989. Hopwood Award, University of Michigan-poetry, 1981, 1982; Major Hopwood Award-poetry, 1983
What is the aim or goal of your writing? "To explore and celebrate and understand the elegance and integrity of everyday people and their lives-what ordinary people contribute."
May inquiries be sent to you about doing workshops, readings? Yes

KEIN, SYBIL

Address: 11211 Woodbridge Drive, Grand Blanc, Michigan 48439
Born: September 29, 1942; New Orleans, Louisiana
Parents: Jules Kein, Rilda B. Kein
Education: Louisiana State University, M.A., Louisiana, 1970-1972. University of Michigan, Ph.D., Ann Arbor, Michigan, 1972-1975
Career: Professor, University of Michigan-Flint, Michigan, 1972—.

Writings: *Delta Dancer* Lotus Press 1984.*Visions From the Rainbow* Hoskins Press 1979. *Gumbo People* Gosserand Press 1981. Cassette of Creole songs, *Serenade Creole* 1986. Work in Progress: *An American South*, publication pending
Awards or inclusion in other biographical books: Best Playwright, Louisiana

State University, 1970. Hopwood Award (Poetry), 1975. Amoco Outstanding Teaching Award, 1979. Michigan Council for the Arts Award, 1981, 1984, 1989

What is the aim or goal of your writing? "To foster knowledge and appreciation for the American Creole culture and language."

May inquiries be sent to you about doing workshops, readings? Yes

KELLAND, CLARENCE BUDDINGTON (1881-1964)

Born: July 11, 1881; Portland, Michigan

Education: Detroit Public Schools. Law Degree, Detroit College of Law, 1902

Career: Writer, political editor for *The Detroit News*. Editor, *American Boy* magazine. One year overseas during World War I as director of publicity Y.M.C.A. Vice-president, director of Phoenix Newspaper, Inc. Executive Director, Republican National Committee

Writings: *Mark Tidd* Harper 1913. *The American Boy's Workshop* McKay 1914. *Mark Tidd, Editor* Harper 1917. *Highflyers* Harper 1919. *Scattergood Baines* Harper 1921. *The Steadfast Heart* Harper 1923. *Gold* Harper 1931. *Roxana* Harper 1936.*Valley of the Sun* Harper 1939. *Scattergood Baines Pulls the Strings* Harper 1941. *Death Keeps a Secret* Harper 1956. Many others-he wrote about 60 novels and over 200 short stories. Serial,*The Saturday Evening Post*. Short stories. *Speaking Easy* and *Mr. Deeds Goes to Town* made into movies

Awards or inclusion in other biographical books: *American Authors and Books; American Novelists of Today; Contemporary Authors; Michigan Authors,* 2nd ed.; *Oxford Companion to American Literature; Reader's Encyclopedia; Reader's Encyclopedia to American Literature; Science Fiction and Fantasy Literature; Twentieth Century Authors; Who Was Who in America; Who's Who among North American Authors*

KELLOGG, JOHN HARVEY (1852-1945)

Born: February 26, 1852; Tyrone, Michigan

Parents: John P. Kellogg, Ann Kellogg

Children: 42 foster children, aided by his wife, Ella

Education: State Normal School. Bellevue Hospital Medical College, New York University, M.D., 1875. European study

Career: Began medical practice, Battle Creek, Michigan, 1875; superintendent, surgeon, Battle Creek Sanitarium, 1876. Member, Michigan State Board of Health, 1878-1890, 1912-1916. Inventor, discoverer in medical field. Founder: health food industries; Battle Creek College; Race Betterment Foundation; Miami-Battle Creek Sanitarium. Editor, *Good Health Magazine*. Organizer and trustee of American Medical Missionary College, Battle Creek College, American Medical Missionary Board. One of his inventions was a vibrating chair with retractable footrest.

Writings: *Diptheria: Its Causes, Prevention, and Proper Treatment* Good Health Publishing 1879. *Plain Facts for Old and Young: Embracing the Natural History and Hygiene of Reproduction* I.F. Segner 1886. *Plain Facts for Old and Young: Embracing the Natural History and Hygiene of Organic Life* I. F. Segner 1890 1892. *Home Book of Modern Medicine* 1880. *Man, the Masterpiece* 1885. *Sanitarium Methods* Good Health Publishing 1893. *The Stomach: Its Disorders and How to Cure Them* Modern Medicine 1896. *The Itinerary of a Breakfast, A Popular Account of the Travels of a Breakfast Through a Food Tube and of the Ten Gates and Several Stations Though Which it Passes* Funk & Wagnall's 1923. *Tobaccoism; or, How Tobacco Kills* Modern Medicine Publishing

1923. *The Natural Diet of Man* 1923. *The New Dietetics; A Guide to Scientific Feeding in Health and Disease* Modern Medicine Publishing 1927. *How to Have Good Health* 1932. Others. Numerous articles, papers
Awards or inclusion in other biographical books: *Allibone: a Critical Dictionary of English Literature; Appleton's Cyclopedia of American Biography; Dictionary of American Authors; Dictionary of North American Authors; Dictionary of American Biography; National Cyclopaedia of American Biography; Twentieth Century Biographical Dictionary of Notable Americans; Who Was Who in America*

KELLY, DAVID M.
Address: P.O. Box 53, Geneseo, New York 14454
Born: June 23, 1938; Grand Rapids, Michigan
Parents: Earl P. Kelly, Margaret W. Kelly
Children: Jordu, Colette, Willow
Education: Michigan State University, B.A. Journalism, M.A., Comparative Literature, East Lansing, Michigan, 1956-1962. University of Iowa, M.F.A., Poetry and Fiction, Iowa City, Iowa, 1965-1966
Career: Associate Professor of English, Director of Creative Writing, State University of New York, Geneseo, New York, 1967—. English Instructor, Eastern Iowa Community College, Muscatine, Iowa, 1966-1967. English Instructor, University of Wisconsin, Menomonie, Wisconsin, 1962-1965

Writings: *Northern Letter* Nebraska Review Press 1981. *Great Lakes Cycle* Steps Inside Press. *Filming Assassinations* Ithaca House 1979. *Poems in Season* Texas Portfolio Editions 1977. *In These Rooms* Red Hill Press 1976. *The Flesh-Eating Horse* Bartholomew's Cobble 1976. *Did You Know They're Beheading Bill Johnson Today?* The Stone Press 1974. *Instructions for Viewing a Solar Eclipse* Wesleyan University Press 1972. *At a Time* Basilisk Press 1972. *All Here Together* Lillabulero Press 1969. *Dear Nate* Hors Commerce Press 1969. *Summer Study* Hors Commerce Press 1960. *The Paris Review Anthology,* 1990 and *The Pushcart Anthology*, 1989. Work in Progress: *Mandelbrot's Beach*, poems
Awards or inclusion in other biographical books: *Michigan Authors,* 2nd ed. National Endowment for the Arts Fellowships, 1992, 1976, 1969. New York Foundation for the Arts Fellowships, 1989, 1980, 1974. Alice Fay di Castagnola Award of the Poetry Society of America, 1990. Pushcart Award in Poetry, 1988. Elliston Foundation Special Distinction for Small Press Book of Poems, 1980. Associated Writing Programs Runner Up in Poetry, Judge's (Robert Penn Warren) selection for special distinction, 1978
What is the aim or goal of your writing? "Not to be stopped."
May inquiries be sent to you about doing workshops, readings? Yes

KELLY, HERRMAN
Address: P.O. Box 14157, Detroit, Michigan 48214
Born: February 25, 1951; Detroit, Michigan
Education: Southeastern High School, Detroit, Michigan, 1965-1969, Diploma
Career: Producer, Afterschool Publishing Company, Detroit, Michigan, 1978—. Artist, R.C.A. Records, International, 1978—.

Writings: *Pyramid Circle* Afterschool 1992. *Amnesty Your Excellency* Afterschool 1991. *Color Blind* Afterschool 1990. Work in Progress: *Musiranma*
What is the aim or goal of your writing? "Educational".
May inquiries be sent to you about doing workshops, readings? Yes

KENNEDY, JOSEPH C.
Address: 4 Fern Way, Bedford, Massachusetts 01730
Pseudonym: X. J. Kennedy
Born: August 21, 1929; Dover, New Jersey
Parents: Joseph F. Kennedy, Agnes J. (Rauter) Kennedy
Children: Kathleen, David, Matthew, Daniel, Joshua. (wife, Dorothy (Mintzlaff) Kennedy)
Education: Seton Hall University, B.Sc., South Orange, New Jersey, 1946-1950. Columbia University, M.A., New York, New York, 1950-1951. University of Michigan, Ann Arbor, Michigan, 1956-1962
Career: Freelance writer, Bedford, Massachusetts, 1978—. Assistant Professor, Professor, Department of English, Tufts University, Medford, Massachusetts, 1963-1978. Lecturer in English, Woman's College, University of North Carolina, Greensboro, North Carolina, 1962-1963. Instructor of English, University of Michigan, Ann Arbor, Michigan, 1960-1962; Teaching Fellow, 1956-1960

Writings: Poetry books: *Dark Horses: New Poems* Johns Hopkins University Press 1992. *Winter Thunder* Robert L. Barth, 1990. *Cross Ties: Selected Poems* University of Georgia Press 1985. *Hangover Mass* Bits Press 1984. *French Leave: Translations* Robert L. Barth 1983. *Three Tenors, One Vehicle* (with James E. Camp and Keith Waldrop) Open Places 1975. *Emily Dickinson in Southern California* David R. Godine 1974. *Celebrations After the Death of John Brennan* Penmaen 1974. *Breaking and Entering* Oxford University Press 1971. *Growing into Love* Doubleday 1969. *Nude Descending a Staircase* Doubleday 1961. For children: *The Beasts of Bethlehem* Macmillan 1992. *Talking Like the Rain: A First Book of Poems* (anthology with Dorothy M. Kennedy) Little, Brown 1992. *The Kite That Braved Old Orchard Beach: Year-Round Poems for Young People* Macmillan 1991. *Ghastlies, Goops and Pincushions: Nonsense Verse* Macmillan 1989. *Brats* Atheneum 1986. *The Forgetful Wishing Well: Poems for Young People* Atheneum 1985. *The Owlstone Crown* Atheneum 1983; Bantam 1985; Troll 1985. *Knock at a Star: a Child's Introduction to Poetry* (with Dorothy M. Kennedy) Little, Brown 1982. *Did Adam Name the Vinegarroon?* David R. Godine 1982. *The Phantom Ice Cream Man* Atheneum 1979. *One Winter Night in August* Atheneum 1975. Anthologies: *Tygers of Wrath: Poems of Hatred, Anger, and Invective* University of Georgia Press 1981. *Pegasus Descending: A Book of the Best Bad Verse* (with James E. Camp and Keith Waldrop) Collier Macmillan 1971. College Textbooks: *An Introduction to Poetry* Little, Brown, 1966; other editions. *Literature* Little, Brown, 1976; HarperCollins 1991. *An Introduction to Fiction* Little, Brown, 1976; HarperCollins 1991. *The Bedford Guide for College Writers* (with Dorothy M. Kennedy) St. Martin's Press 1987, 1990 and others. *Messages: a Thematic Anthology of Poetry* Little, Brown 1973. *Mark Twain's Frontier* (with James E. Camp) Holt Rinehart & Winston 1963. Cassette Recording, Poets' Audio Center, 1985. Work in Progress: Poems, a novel for children

Awards or inclusion in other biographical books: *Who's Who in America, Who's Who in the World, World Authors, Contemporary Authors, Contemporary Authors Autobiographical Series, Contemporary Poets, American Poets Since World War II, Twentieth-Century Children's Writers, Childhood in Poetry: 2nd Supplement, Sixth Book of Junior Authors and Illustrators, Something About the Author, Critical Survey of Poetry.* Guggenheim Fellow, 1973-1974. Hopwood Writing Awards, University of Michigan, First Prizes in Poetry and Essay, 1959. *Los Angeles Times Book Award for Poetry,* 1985. Shelley Memorial Award, 1970. National Endowment for the Arts Grant, 1967-1968. Braude Award of the American Academy and Institute of Arts and Letters, 1989.

Lamont Award of the Academy of American Poets, 1961. Honorary L.H.D. from Lawrence University, 1988. Best of New Books Citation, *Learning 90* magazine. Two Notable Children's Trade Book for the Language Arts. Notable Book, American Library Association, 1985. Nomination for William Allen White Children's Book Award, 1988. Book Award of the Ethical Culture School, Finest Fantasy, 1983. Children's Books of the Year, Library of Congress. NCTE Teacher's Choice Book, 1983. *School Library Journal* Book of the Year, 1983. American Library Association *Booklist* Children's Reviewer's Choice, 1982. New York Public Library, *Children's Books 1990: 100 Titles*

What is the aim or goal of your writing? "To amuse."

May inquiries be sent to you about doing workshops, readings? Yes, readings. No, workshops

KEOWN, ELIZABETH M.

Address: 205 S. Melborn, Dearborn, Michigan 48124

Born: December 23, 1913; Frankfort, Indiana

Parents: John M. Dorner, Mary L. Dorner

Children: Mary, Martha, Arthur

Education: Indiana University, Bloomington, Indiana, 1932-1934. University of Michigan, B.A., Ann Arbor, Michigan, 1934-1936. Wayne State University, Teaching Certification, Detroit, Michigan, 1967-1968

Career: Social Worker, Detroit, Michigan, 1936-1937. Field Representative, Michigan Childrens Aid Society, 1937-1942. Teacher, Detroit Public Pre-School, Detroit, Michigan, 1969-1974

Writings: *Emily's Snowball the World's Biggest* Atheneum 1992.

Work in Progress: *Rhyming George*

What is the aim or goal of your writing? "The enjoyment of young children. Encouraging young children to read."

May inquiries be sent to you about doing workshops, readings? Yes. Readings only

KERMAN, JUDITH

Address: P. O. Box 5473, Saginaw, Michigan 48603

Born: October 5, 1945; Bayside, New York

Parents: Harry Kerman, Betty Z. Kerman

Education: University of Rochester, B.A. with Honors, Rochester, New York, 1963, 1967. State University of New York at Buffalo, 1970-1977, Buffalo, New York

Career: Dean, Arts and Behavioral Sciences, Saginaw Valley State University, University Center, Michigan, 1991—. Associate Vice President for Academic Programs, Edinboro University of Pennsylvania, Edinboro, Pennsylvania, 1989-1991. Assistant Dean for Academic Director-2 Year Technical Programs, Kent State University, Kent, Ohio, 1982-1989. Assistant Director of Management Development Division, Henry Ford Community College, Dearborn, Michigan, 1981-1982. Regional Director, University of Michigan Extension Service, 1978-1981. Assistant to the Dean, SUNY/Buffalo, Office for Credit-Free Programs, 1973-1978

Writings: *Driving for Yellow Cab* Tout Press 1985. *Mothering* Uroboros Books/Allegany 1978. *The Jakoba Poems* White Pine Press 1976. *Obsessions* Intrepid Press 1974. Editor of *Retrofitting Blade Runner: Issues in Ridley Scott's Blade Runner* and *Philip K. Dick's Do Androids Dream of Electric Sheep,* published by Bowling Green State University

Popular Press 1991. Work in Progress: A collection of poems, working title *Choosing Your Own Name*

Awards or inclusion in other biographical books: *Directory of American Poets and Fiction Writers, Contemporary Authors, Index / Directory of Women's Media, Who's Who of American Women, World Who's Who of Women, Who's Who in U.S. Writers, Editors & Poets.* Honorable Mention, Great Lakes Colleges Association New Writers Award in Poetry, 1978

What is the aim or goal of your writing? "This is not something I usually think much about-the poem tells me its goal in the writing of it. However, I think (in retrospect) that I tend to explore the layers of awareness that constantly impact on and underlie (and undercut) everyday consciousness, as well as the underlying realities, whether psychological, political or ecological, of everyday life."

May inquiries be sent to you about doing workshops, readings? Yes

KIBBEY, MARSHA K.

Address: Box 433, South Rockwood, Michigan 48179
Born: August 1, 1940; Muncie, Indiana
Parents: Robert M. Clark, Amelia V. Clark
Children: Todd, Trista
Education: Gaston High School, Gaston, Indiana. Ball State University, B. S., Muncie, Indiana; B.S., 1978; M.L.S., 1983
Career: Wilson Middle School, Media Specialist, Wyandotte Public Schools, 1988—. Librarian, (AIME) Association Indiana Media Education, Muncie, Indiana, 1979-1988. Instructor, Summers, Library/Media classes, Ball State

Writings: *The Helping Place* Carol Rhoda Books 1991. *My Grammy* Carol Rhoda Books 1988. Work in Progress: One non-fiction
What is the aim or goal of your writing? "*My Grammy*-To introduce children to a person who has Alzheimer's disease-to help the child learn to accept such a person, 'just the way they are.' *The Helping Place*-To take a child inside a nursing home via the pages of a book."
May inquiries be sent to you about doing workshops, readings? Yes

KICKNOSWAY, FAYE

Born: December 16, 1936; Detroit, Michigan
Parents: Walter Blair, Louise (Standish) Blair
Children: Kevin, Lauren
Education: University of Michigan, Ann Arbor, Michigan, 1958-1959. Wayne State University, B.A., Detroit, Michigan, 1967. San Francisco State University, M.A., 1969
Career: Instructor, Macomb County Community College, Warren, Michigan, 1967-1968. Instructor, Wayne State University, 1970—. Model for commercial artists, 1958-1969. Poet-in-the-school Program, Michigan Council for the Arts, 1973-1974. Chairperson, Miles Poetry Committee, 1974—. Poetry readings on radio, television, schools

Writings: *O, You Can Walk on the Sky?: Good* Capra Press 1972. *Poem Tree* Red Hanrahan Press 1973. *A Man Is a Hook: Trouble: Poems, 1964-1973* Capra Press 1974. *Second Chance Man: The Cigarette Poems* Alternative Press 1975. *I Search for My Grandfather to Ask the Way* Alternative Press 1975? *The Cat Approaches* Alternative Press 1978. *Asparagus, Asparagus, ah Sweet Asparagus: Poems and Drawings* Toothpaste Press 1981. *Who Shall Know Them?* Penguin 1985. *The Violence of Potatoes*

Ridgeway 1990. Work appears in various anthologies such as *No More Masks!* Doubleday 1973. Published in *Chicago Review, Prairie Schooner, Paris Review, New York Quarterly* and others

Awards or inclusion in other biographical books:
Contemporary Authors; Michigan Authors, 2nd ed.; *Poets and Writers*

KIENZLE, WILLIAM X.

Address: 2465 Middlebelt, Orchard Lake, Michigan 48324
Born: September 11, 1928; Detroit, Michigan
Parents: Alphonse Kienzle, Mary L. (Boyle) Kienzle
Education: St. John's Provincial Seminary, Plymouth, Michigan, 1950-1954. Sacred Heart Seminary, Detroit, Michigan, 1942-1949
Career: Author, 1949—. Director, Center for Contemplative Studies, Dallas, Texas, 1978-1979. Associate Director, Center for Contemplative Studies, Kalamazoo, Michigan, 1976-1978. Magazine Editor-in-Chief, *Minneapolis Magazine*, Minneapolis, Minnesota, 1974-1976. Editor-in-Chief, *The Michigan Catholic*, Detroit, Michigan, 1962-1974. Pastor, St. Anselm Church, Dearborn Heights, Michigan, 1970-1974. Catholic Priest, Archdiocese of Detroit, Detroit, Michigan, 1954-1974

Writings: *Dead Wrong* Andrews & McMeel 1993. *Body Count* Andrews & McMeel 1992. *Chameleon* Andrews & McMeel 1990. *Masquerade* Andrews & McMeel 1989. *Eminence* Andrews & McMeel 1988. *Marked for Murder* Andrews & McMeel 1987. *Deadline for a Critic* Andrews & McMeel 1986. *Deathbed* Andrews & McMeel 1985. *Sudden Death* Andrews & McMeel 1984. *Kill and Tell* Andrews & McMeel 1983. *Shadow of Death* Andrews & McMeel 1982. *Assault with Intent* Andrews & McMeel 1981. *Mind Over Murder* Andrews & McMeel 1980. *Death Wears a Red Hat* Andrews & McMeel 1979. *The Rosary Murders* Bantam 1979. Work in Progress: *For the Care of Souls*
Awards or inclusion in other biographical books: *Contemporary Authors*-Autobiography Series Vol. 1. *Contemporary Authors,* Vol. 93-96. A Cleaver Award, Michigan Mystery Writers, 1983. *Whodunit* 1982. *Murder Ink* 1984. *Mystery Trivia Quiz Book* 1985. *The Mystery Lover's Companion* 1986. Detroit Powers and Personalities, 1989
What is the aim or goal of your writing? 1) Food, clothing, shelter 2) Entertain 3) Instruct
May inquiries be sent to you about doing workshops, readings? Yes

KIMBERLY, GAIL

Address: 5566 Hunter Road, Beaverton, Michigan 48612
Pseudonym: Dayle Courtney, Alix Andre
Born: August 1; New York, New York
Parents: Wilbert R. Kimberly, Evelyn M. (Cox) Kimberly
Children: Leslie, Eric, Michelle, Judi
Education: Ottawa, Ontario, Canada; Windsor, Ontario, Canada; Niagara Falls, Ontario, Canada; Pasadena, California
Career: Fiction writer, Beaverton, Michigan, 1988—. Fiction writer, Concord, California, 1983-1988. Fiction writer, Sierra Madre, California, 1976-1983

Writings: *Nightmare Circus* Cora Verlag 1991. *The Devil's Bride* Cora Verlag 1989. *The Treasure of Pirate's Cove* Standard 1984. *The Trail of Bigfoot* Standard 1983. *Jaws of Terror* Standard 1982. *Escape From Eden* Standard 1981. *Secret at the Abbey* Harlequin Mystique Books 1980. *Star Jewel* Scholastic 1979. *Goodbye is Just the Beginning* Zebra

1979. *Skateboard* Tempo 1979. *Dracula Began* Pyramid Books 1976. *Flyer* Popular Library 1975. Stories appear in such anthologies as *Teen-Age Secret Agent Stories* and *Science Fiction Adventure from Way Out* and others. Stories have appeared in *Gothic Stories, Galaxy, Chiller, Secrets, Alfred Hitchcock's Mystery Magazine* and others. Work in Progress: *Kitling,* a science fiction novel

Awards or inclusion in other biographical books: *The Science Fiction Encyclopedia,* 1991, others. Midnight Zoo, Readers' Favorite Award. "Ice Road" voted third place favorite of all 1990 stories by readers of *Amazing Experiences* magazine

What is the aim or goal of your writing? "Nothing lofty! To tell an entertaining story. I've written stories since childhood and can't imagine doing anything else."

May inquiries be sent to you about doing workshops, readings? Yes

KING, BEN(JAMIN FRANKLIN) (1857-1894)
Born: March 17, 1857; St. Joseph, Michigan
Parents: Father was a leading merchant, postmaster in St. Joseph
Children: Bennett, Spencer
Career: Piano salesman, Chicago, Illinois. Poet, satirist, mimic, humorist, performer. Discovered as entertainer when playing piano at World's Fair, Chicago by humorist, Brick Pomeroy. Dubbed the "Sweet Singer of St. Joe". Died in hotel room, Bowling Green, Kentucky

Writings: *Ben King's Verse* Press Club of Chicago 1894, 1898, 1904, 1905; several printings. *Ben Kings Southland Melodies* Forbes and Company 1911. Best know poem, "If I Should Die Tonight"
Awards or inclusion in other biographical books: *American Authors and Books; Biographical Dictionary of Southern Authors; Childhood in Poetry; Dictionary of North American Authors; Reader's Encyclopedia of American Literataure.* Ben King Memorial Association placed large boulder from banks of the Saint Joe River over his grave. Memorial, Lake Bluff, St. Joseph, Michigan, erected 1924

KINGERY, LIONEL BRUCE
Address: 947 Francis Street, Rochester Hills, Michigan 48307
Born: June 13, 1921; New Albany, Indiana
Parents: Glenda Kingery, Frances E. Kingery
Children: Mary, David, Deborah, Melody
Education: Kokomo High School, 1940. Wayne State University, B.A., 1971; M.A., 1975; Ed.D., 1981, Detroit, Michigan. Graduate, U.S. Army Infantry School: Associate Company Officers School, 1957
Career: Board of Control, Ferris State University, Big Rapids, Michigan, 1985—. International Representative, Education Department, International Union, UAW, 1964-1985. Hourly-rated worker, Delco Electronics Division, GMC, 1940-1985, Kokomo, Indiana. Council-at-Large, Kokomo Common Council, Kokomo, Indiana, 1959-1963. Advisory committees during the 1970's: Michigan Council for the Arts, Michigan Department of Education, Michigan State University, Eastern Michigan University

Writings: *Practical Programming in Continuing Professional Education* American Association for Adults & Continuing Education 1991. *The Role of Labor in Career Education* Florida Career Education 1984. *Eulogy* Young Publications. *Never Have I Seen Paris* Young Publications. *Rivers of Time* Young Publications. *Shadows* Poetry

Parade. *Perspectives* Poetry Parade. *Things* Poetry Parade. *Nietzche on History*... Burro Books Paperback #2, Midwest Poetry, 1972. *Black Lake Legacy* Delco Antenna: UAW Local 292, Shop Paper. *Nestor* Voices International.*Summer Heat* Young Publications. *Tattoos From a Distant Drum* Forever. Others.

Work in Progress: American Legion Bands' recording of 16 marches; Manuscript of labor songs, original words and music. Completion of 46-year manuscript on World War II,*The Mars Triology*

What is the aim or goal of your writing? "1. Publication of my several completed, unpublished manuscripts of verse and prose. 2. Publication and recordings of some of the 800 songs I have written, to date and songwriting contracts for them. 3. Recording and publishing contracts for the 16 marches I have composed, to date"

May inquiries be sent to you about doing workshops, readings? Yes

KIRK, RUSSELL A.

Address: P. O. Box 4, Mecosta, Michigan 49332

Born: October 19, 1918; Plymouth, Michigan

Parents: Russell A. Kirk, Marjorie R. (Pierce) Kirk

Children: Monica, Cecilia, Felicia, Andrea

Education: Michigan State University, B.A., East Lansing, Michigan, 1940. Duke University, M.A., Durham, North Carolina, 1941. St. Andrews University, D. Litt., Scotland, 1952. Only American to hold the highest arts degree (earned) from St. Andrews

Career: U.S. Army, 1941-1945. Professor, Michigan State University, East Lansing, Michigan, 1946-1953. Writer, editor, lecturer, 1953—. Distinguished visiting professor and visiting research professor at numerous colleges and universities, 1953—. Professor, Long Island University, 1957-1961. President, Educational Reviewer Foundation, 1960—. President, Marguerite Eyer Wilbur Foundation, 1979—. Director of social science program, Educational Research Council of America, 1979-1984. Editor of *The University Bookman* 1960—. Founder, first editor of *Modern Age*. Justice of the Peace, Morton Township, Mecosta County, Michigan, 1961-1964. Several public lectures have been broadcast nationally on C-Span. Has debated many such as Hubert Humphrey, Max Lerner, Malcolm X. Editor of The Library of Conservative Though for Transaction Books

Writings: *Randolph of Roanoke* University of Chicago Press 1951, other editions. *The Conservative Mind: From Burke to Santayana* Henry Regnery 1953, other editions. *Old House of Fear* Fleet Press 1961, 1963. *The Surly Sullen Bell* Fleet Press 1962. *Lost Lake: Confessions of a Bohemian Tory* Fleet Press 1963. *Edmund Burke: A Genius Reconsidered* Arlington House 1967; Sherwood Sugden 1985. *Eliot and His Age: T.S. Eliot's Moral Imagination in the Twentieth Century* Random House 1971. *Decadence and Renewal in the Higher Learning* Henry Regnery 1978. *Lord of the Hollow Dark* St. Martin's 1979. *The Roots of American Order* Open Court 1974; Pepperdine University Press 1980. *Reclaiming a Patrimony* Heritage Foundation 1982.*Watchers at the Strait Gate* Arkham 1984. Others. Editor of other books, contributor of introductions/articles to almost fifty books and encyclopedias, dictionaries. Co-founder, columnist, *National Review*, 1956-1983. Columnist, Los Angeles Times syndicate, 1962-1975. Contributed over 500 articles, essays, short stories to periodicals in the United States and abroad such as *New York Times Magazine, Wall Street Journal, Yale Review, Kenyon Review, Fortune, Sewanee Review, Journal of the History of Ideas.* (Work is in *Russell Kirk: A Bibliography* compiled by Charles Brown, Clarke Historical Library, Central Michigan University,

Mt. Pleasant, Michigan). Work in Progress: *Sword of Imagination. Edmund Burke and the Constitution of the United States*

Awards or inclusion in other biographical books: *Contemporary Authors; Directory of American Scholars; International Scholars Directory; Who's Who in America; Who's Who in the Midwest; Who's Who in the World,* others. American Council of Learned Societies senior fellow, 1950-1951. Guggenheim fellow, 1956. Honorary degrees from Boston College, Central Michigan University, Olivet College and several others. Ann Radcliffe Award for Gothic fiction, 1966. Christopher Award, 1972. World Fantasy Award for short fiction, 1977. Weaver Award of Ingersoll Prizes for scholarly humane letters, 1984. Freedom Leadership Award, Hillsdale College, 1985. Constitutional fellowship, National Endowment for the Humanities, 1985. Presidential Citizens Medal, conferred by President Reagan, 1989. For several years a Distinguished Scholar of the Heritage Foundation

KIRKLAND, CAROLINE MATILDA (1801-1864)

Pseudonym: Mrs. Mary Clavers (in Scotch means idle gossip), Caroline M. Stansbury Kirkland, Aminadab Peering

Born: January 11, 1801; New York, New York

Parents: Samuel Stansbury, Eliza (Alexander) Stansbury

Children: Elizabeth, Joseph, Lydia, Sarah, Cordelia Stansbury, William, Charles Pinckney

Education: Quaker school headed by her aunt, Lydia Philadelphia Mott. Could read and speak French, German, Italian, Latin

Career: Came to Michigan 1835 when her husband became the principal of Detroit Female Seminary, the first school for women in the territory in which she taught. Went with husband who founded Pinckney (which she named), Michigan, 1837. Returned to New York state, 1843. Husband drowned and Caroline wrote to make a living; her home attracted Edgar Allan Poe, Ralph Waldo Emerson, others. Later years involved in numerous organizations for social welfare, operated girls school. Went abroad 1848, 1850. Editor, *Union Magazine of Literature and Art,* 1847-1849

Writings: *A New Home-Who'll Follow?: or, Glimpses of Western Life* 1839; C.S. Francis 1841; Putnam 1953; College and University Press 1965; Garrett Press 1969; Rutgers University Press 1990. *Forest Life* C.S. Francis 1842. *Western Clearings* Wiley and Putnam 1846; Garrett Press 1969. *Spenser and the Faery Queen* Wiley and Putnam 1847. *Holidays Abroad; or, Europe from the West* Baker and Scribner 1849. *Sartain's Union Magazine of Literature and Art* John Sartain & Company 1849, 1852. *The Evening Book* Charles Scribner 1852. *Garden Walks with the Poets* Putnam 1852. *The Book of Home Beauty* Putnam 1852. *A Book for the Home Circle* Charles Scribner 1853. *The Helping Hand* Charles Scribner 1853. *A Book for the Home Circle, or, Familiar Thoughts on Various Topics, Literary, Moral and Social: a Companion for the Evening Book* Scribner 1853. *Autumn Hours and Fireside Reading* Charles Scribner 1853, 1854, 1856. *Personal Memoirs of George Washington* D. Appleton 1857. *The School-Girl's Garland* Charles Scribner 1864. *The Story of Chicago* Dibble Publishing 1892-1894. *Some African Highways: a Journey of Two American Women to Uganda and the Transvaal* Duckworth (London) 1908. *Chicago Yesterdays; a Sheaf of Reminiscences* Daughaday 1919. Others. Introduction, *A Plea for Women,* 1845

Award or inclusion in other biographical books: *Allibone: A Critical Dictionary of English Literature; American Authors, 1600-1900; American Authors and Books; Ameri-*

can Women Writers; Dictionary of Literary Biography; Michigan Authors, 1st ed., 2nd ed.; *Index to Women; Michigan Women Firsts and Founders; National Cyclopaedia of American Biography; Notable American Women; Oxford Companion to American Literature; Reader's Encyclopedia; Who Was Who in America,* several others

KLEIN, CLAYTON

Address: P.O. Box 968, Fowlerville, Michigan 48836
Born: February 24, 1919; Fowlerville, Michigan
Parents: George L. Klein, Gertrude E. Klein
Children: Darrell, Deborah
Education: Fowlerville High School, 1933-1936. Michigan State University, East Lansing, 1936-1938
Career: Dairy Technician, Ithaca, Michigan, 1937-1941. Farmer, Fowlerville, Michigan 1941-1950. Owner, Klein Fertilizer Company, Fowlerville, Michigan 1951-1983. Owner, Wilderness Adventure Books, Fowlerville, Michigan, 1984--

Writings: *Challenge the Wilderness* Wilderness Adventure Books 1988. *One Incredible Journey* Wilderness Adventure Books 1987. *A Passion for Wilderness* Wilderness Adventure Books 1986. *Cold Summer Wind* Wilderness Adventure Books 1983
What is the aim or goal of your writing? "To acquaint others with the real hardships and pleasures of wilderness travel and living."
May inquiries be sent to you about doing workshops, readings? Yes

KNAPP, RON

Address: 314 Charlotte Street, Union City, Michigan 49094
Born: February 11, 1952; Battle Creek, Michigan
Parents: Donald L. Knapp, Cecelia Knapp
Children: William, Franklin, Christopher
Education: St. Philip High School, Battle Creek, Michigan, 1966-1970. University of Detroit, B.A., Detroit, Michigan, 1970-1974
Career: Teacher, Union City Community Schools, Union City, Michigan, 1974—. Reporter, *Battle Creek Enquirer*, Battle Creek, Michigan, 1968-1980

Writings: *Sports Great Isiah Thomas* Enslow 1992. *Sports Great Hakeem Olajuwon* Enslow 1992. *Sports Great Bo Jackson* Enslow 1990. *From Prison to the Major Leagues* Messner 1980. *Tutankhamun and the Mysteries of Ancient Egypt* Messner 1979. Work in Progress: *Sports Great Will Clark, Sports Great Barry Sanders,* and other sport figures
What is the aim or goal of your writing? "I write books I hope my middle school students will enjoy. The object is to encourage them to love reading."
May inquiries be sent to you about doing workshops, readings? Yes

KONKLE, JANET E.

Address: 7193 North Cricket Drive, Citrus Springs, Florida 32630
Born: November 5, 1917; Grand Rapids, Michigan
Parents: Charles A. Everest, Minnie (Koegler) Everest
Children: Kraig, Jil-Marie, Dan
Education: Ottawa Hills High School, 1935. Grand Rapids Junior College, 1935-1937. University of Michigan, Ann Arbor, Michigan, 1938. Western Michigan University, B.S., Kalamazoo, Michigan, 1939. Courses at Michigan State University, 1960-1970's

Career: Correspondent/Photographer, *Ocala Star-Banner,* Ocala, Florida, 1987—. Correspondent/Photographer, *Riverland News,* Dunnellon, Florida, 1988-1992. Correspondent/Photographer, *On Track*, Ocala, Florida, 1985. Stringer/Photographer, *Citrus County Chronicle,* Inverness, Florida,1984. Teacher, Hillcrest School, Grand Rapids, Michigan, 1961-1979. Teacher, West Leonard School, Grand Rapids, Michigan, 1953-1960. Teacher, Dickinson School, Grand Rapids, 1952-1953. Teacher, Alexander School, Grand Rapids, Michigan, 1939-1941. President, Michigan Association for Childhood Education, 1976-1977. Leader, Potpourri Poets, Citrus Springs

Writings: (Most illustrated with author's photos)*The Raccoon Twins* Children's Press 1972. *Schoolroom Bunny* Children's Press 1965. *The Sea Cart* Abingdon Press 1961,1964. *Susie Stock Car* Childcraft Encyclopedia in their "Animal Friends and Adventures" book 1961. *J. Hamilton Hamster* Children's Press 1957. *Tabby's Kittens* Children's Press 1956. *Easter Kitten* Children's Press 1955. *Christmas Kitten* Children's Press 1953, 1964. *Kitten and the Parakeet* Children's Press 1952. *Once There was a Kitten* Children's Press 1951,1962. Work in Progress: New Zealand stories: *Moki's Name* and *Peter and the Kea*. Haiku

Awards or inclusion in other biographical books:*Michigan Authors,* 2nd ed.; *Who's Who in the Midwest* 1974-1982; *Writer's Directory,* many years. Ambassador Book Award from English Speaking Union-*J. Hamilton Hamster* was sent overseas with others, 1957. Many national, international prizes in photo contests. Second Prize, Florida State Poets Association, 1991. Manuscripts, photos, books are in the Special Childrens de Grummond Collection, University of Southern Mississippi since 1970

What is the aim or goal of your writing? "I love children and animals and want children to love and care for them, too. I have also traveled overseas many many times and would like to use my memories and photos in future stories."

May inquiries be sent to you about doing workshops, readings? Yes. If up there at the same time

KORFKER, DENA J.

Address: 1720 Plymouth Road, S.E., Grand Rapids, Michigan 49506
Born: April 6, 1908; Grand Rapids, Michigan
Parents: Henry W. Korfker, Dena (DeHaan) Korfker
Education: A.B. in Education, 1984. Two year Teaching Permit. Grand Rapids, Michigan, Kalamazoo, Michigan. Correspondence courses while teaching. Summer classes at Grand Rapids Junior College, Boulder University, Colorado
Career: Teacher, West Side Christian School, Grand Rapids, Michigan, 1927-1933. Teacher, Oakdale Christian, Grand Rapids, Michigan, 1934-1973. Private Course in Photography, Grand Rapids, Michigan, 1945-1947.

Writings: *Can You Tell Me?* Zondervan 1950. *Questions Children Ask* Zondervan 1953. *My Bible ABC Book* Zondervan 1972. *Angie Comes to America* Zondervan 1954. *My Picture Bible Story Book* Zondervan 1960. *My Favorite Bible Story Book* Zondervan 1961. *Mother of Eighty* J.C. Choate 1970. *Good Morning, Lord-Devotions for Children* Baker 1973. *My Bible Story Book* Kregel 1988. Work in Progress: *Shepherd of My People*. Also published in England, Rumania

What is the aim or goal of your writing? "To teach children the importance of their faith in God and Jesus Christ. I have given book reviews (acting out the story) of good Christian books since I retired in 1973."

Awards or inclusion in other biographical books: *Michigan Authors,* 2nd ed.
May inquiries be sent to you about doing workshops, readings? Yes

KORN, CLAIRE V.
Address: 1724 Hermitage, Ann Arbor, Michigan 48104
Born: August 12, 1933; Berkeley, California
Parents: Dmitri N. Vedensky, Helen I. (Montmorency) Vedensky
Children: Alexander
Education: University of California, Berkeley, California, 1951. University of Minnesota, M.A., Minneapolis, Minnesota, 1955-1957. Stanford University, Stanford, California, B.A., 1951-1954, Ph.D., 1964-1968
Career: Freelance writer, self-employed, Ann Arbor, Michigan, 1984—. Open Education Coordinator, Ann Arbor Public Schools, Ann Arbor, Michigan, 1985-1986. Founder and Director, Natural Bridge School, Tallahassee, Florida, 1975-1980. Acting Associate Professor, Assistant Professor, Florida State University, Tallahassee, Florida, 1970-1976. Colleague, Consulting Psychologists Association, Palo Alto, California, 1959-1969. Guidance Consultant, Palo Alto Unified Schools, Palo Alto, California, 1968-1969. Research Associate, Stanford University, Stanford, California, 1958-1960. Instructor, Department of Pediatrics, University of Minnesota Medical School, 1957-1958

Writings: *Free Schools: Reality and Dream* Ikkosha Publishing (Japan) 1984. *Michigan State Parks: Yesterday Through Tomorrow* Michigan State University Press 1989. *Alternative American Schools: Ideals in Action* State University of New York Press 1991. Published in *Michigan Natural Resources Magazine,* Ahoy-the Children's Magazine, *Counseling Psychologist, The Detroit Free Press* (12 feature articles 1985), *The Ann Arbor Observer* (23 contributions), and others. Book contributor. Film (with Paul Elwood) Elizabeth Kenney Institute 1958. Work in Progress: *The End and Beginning of Wally B. Marsh,* novel for 8-11 year olds
What is the aim or goal of your writing? "To move readers to new places, feelings, thoughts".
May inquiries be sent to you about doing workshops, readings? Yes

KRAUSE, FRED K.
Address: 527 LaSalle Avenue, St. Joseph, Michigan 49085
Born: November 1, 1928; St. Joseph, Michigan
Parents: Max Krause, Marie Krause
Children: Gary, Dan, Steve
Education: St. Joseph High School, 1946
Career: Tool Maker, Whirlpool Corporation, St. Joseph Division, St. Joseph, Michigan, 1978-1986, retired

Writings: *Historic Old Saint Joseph, Michigan* G+B Printing (Coloma, Micnigan) 1992. *French Saint Joseph* (co-author) George Johnson. *Le Poste, de la Rieviere 1690-1780* St. Joseph Graphics (Decatur, Michigan) 1986
What is the aim or goal of your writing? "Reveal the history of Saint Joseph, Michigan 1679-1992 Michigan's most historically interesting city."
May inquiries be sent to you about doing workshops, readings? Yes

KUBIAK, WILLIAM J.
Address: 539 Michigan Street, NE, Grand Rapids, Michigan 49503
Born: May 29, 1929; Grand Rapids, Michigan
Parents: Joseph T. Kubiak, Gertrude B. (Zelenski) Kubiak
Children: Heidi, Robin, Joseph, Anthony

Education: Central High School, 1947. Davenport College, 1948-1949
Career: United States Army, 1951-1953. Artist, *Grand Rapids Press,* Grand Rapids, Michigan, 1954-1986

Writings: *Great Lakes Indians* Baker 1970. Work in Progress: Researching and illustrating the American Indian
Awards or inclusion in other biographical books: *Michigan Authors,* 2nd ed.

KUNTZ, LORI A.

Address: 16481 Three Oaks Road, Three Oaks, Michigan 49128
Born: June 12, 1963; St. Joseph, Michigan
Parents: Jim D. Richardson, Bonnie E. (Miller) Richardson
Children: Ryan, Chad, Ashley
Education: River Valley High School, 1981-1986. Lake Michigan College, Associate in Arts, 1990-1991. Indiana University, South Bend, Indiana
Career: Instructor, Montessori School, 1989-1991

Writings: *Kids-Your-Cise* Kid-Business 1991. Work in Progress: Christian themed version to *Kids-Your-Cise. Jump to Spell,* game teaching spelling through movement. Future books include follow along reading books, introducing positive movement and positive self esteem
What is the aim or goal of your writing? "To teach children positive movement, positive self regard, and the joys of education and learning. I want <u>all</u> children to love who they are and find the beauty and originality of every person. A healthy adult begins with a healthy child, and I want to encourage the fitness of mind, soul and body."
May inquiries be sent to you about doing workshops, readings? Yes

L

LAGATTUTA, MARGO E.
Address: 2134 W. Gunn Road, Rochester, Michigan 48306
Born: September 18, 1942; Detroit, Michigan
Parents: Edwin O. Grahn, Elizabeth T. Grahn
Children: Mark, Erik, Adam
Education: Oakland University, B.A., Rochester, Michigan, 1978-1980. Vermont College, M.F.A., Montpelier, Vermont, 1982-1984. Fine Art Studies, Pratt Institute, Brooklyn, New York, 1962-1964
Career: English Instructor, Oakland Community College, Union Lake, Michigan, 1986—. Creative Writing Instructor, Cranbrook, Bloomfield Hills, 1985—. English Tutor, Keller Clinic, Bloomfield Hills, Michigan, 1986-1988. Process Writing Consultant, Inventing the Invisible, Pontiac, Michigan, 1988—. Seminar leader, Oakland Writer's Conference, Midland Writer's Conference, others

Writings: *The Dream Givers* Lake Shore Publishing 1990. *Noedgelines* Earhart Press 1986. *Diversion Road* State Street Press 1983. Published essays or poems in *Passages North, The Women's Yellow Pages, The Bridge, Calliope, Detroit News Anthology of Outstanding Michigan Poets, Odyssey, Moving Out, Green River Review, Earth's Daughters, Waves, The Little Magazine* and others. Audio tape *The Creative Process,* 1990. Work in Progress: *Bride Dust and Other Stories. The Seven Magic Elephants of Creativity*
Awards or inclusion in other biographical books: *Contemporary Authors* 1985--; *Poets and Writers* 1983—. The Gwendolyn Brooks Award in Poetry, Michigan State University,1991. Ohio Poetry Day Award, First Place, 1990. Ragdale Writers Colony Fellowships, 1989, 1992. Departmental Honors in English, Oakland University, 1980
What is the aim or goal of your writing? "I aim to be accessible as well as literary. My poetry is lyrical, metaphoric, and sometimes surreal. I believe in the art of telling stories and the joy of playing with language. I believe that humor is sometimes a way of being very serious. My goal is to connect with my readers on a level of deep image and sound, to share experience of the inner as well as the outer landscape of our lives."
May inquiries be sent to you about doing workshops, readings? Yes

LAGRONE, (CLARENCE) OLIVER
Address: 309 Bauersfeld Street, Hamlet, North Carolina 28345
Born: December 9, 1906; McAlester, Oklahoma
Parents: William L. LaGrone, Lula E. LaGrone
Children: Lotus J.
Education: Howard University, 1928-1930. University of New Mexico, B.A., 1938. Cranbrook Art Academy, Awarded McGregor Fund Grant for advanced study in sculpture with Carl Milles, 1940-1942. Wayne State University, graduate work in art and special education, 1956-1960
Career: International representative, United Auto Workers, 1948-1953. Teacher, Detroit Public Schools, 1956-1957. Pennsylvania State University, 1970-1972; Special Assistant 1972-1974. Board Director, Oliver LaGrone Scholarship Fund, 1974-1985. Has made many television appearances, keynote speeches. Sculpture in bronze, marble,

stone, wood, cast stone, numerous one-man shows. Became Artist-in-Residence to 21 branches of Pennsylvania State University. Artist-in-Residence, Hershey Foundation, Boas Center for Learning, Harrisburg School District. Self-employed sculpting, lecture exhibits. Appointed to many committees, serves on Harrisburg Human Relations Commission. Judge in numerous art and poetry festivals

Writings: *Footfalls* Darel Press (Detroit) 1949.*They Speak of Dawns; A Duo-Poem Written for the Centennial Year of the Emancipation Proclamation: 1863, in 1963* self-published 1963, 1967, 1970. *Dawnfire and Others* Lotus Press-Detroit 1989. In various anthologies such as *The Study of Literature* (high school text) Ginn & Company 1978; *Negro Poetry 1764-1970* by the late Langston Hughes and Arna Bontemps; *Beyond the Blues* Hand and Flower Press (London, England) 1962. Articles have appeared in *Bulletin Negro History* and others

Awards or inclusion in other biographical books: *Arts Source Book; Michigan Authors,* 1st ed., 2nd ed.; *The Poetry of the Negro 1746-1970; Who's Who in Black America.* Scholarship fund named in his honor, Unitarian Church, Harrisburg, Pennsylvania, 1974—. Memorial Plaque Award, Ethelen Jones Crockett American Lung Association, 1981-1982. WPA Competitive Commission Award, 1935. Detroit Chapter Howard University, Alumni of the Year Award, 1965. Advisory Board, Metropolitan Educational and Cultural Activities Association, 1954-1969. Appointed member to Michigan Council for the Arts, 1966. First Prize, Michigan Poetry Society, 1966. Cited with engraved commendation, and later a plaque by Friends of Oliver LaGrone. Award, Detroit Society for Art Culture and Education, 1971. Kappa Alpha Psi Public Service Award, 1981. Honorary membership, Harrisburg Rotary Club, 1980. Nominated for Governor's Award as Outstanding Artist of Pennsylvania, 1980-1981. Award of Recognition, Major and City of Harrisburg, February 3, 1983 declared "Oliver LaGrone Day". Awarded two citations, Eighty Fifth Legislature, State of Michigan, 1990. Poetry and sculpture featured in film produced by the Detroit Board of Education and Wayne State University. Others.

LAHEY, CHRISTINE SUSAN
Address: 1540 Boulan Road, Troy, Michigan 48084
Born: September 7, 1949; Wyandotte, Michigan
Parents: Ignatius Joseph Lahey, Estelle Marie Lahey
Children: Alan, Dana
Education: Wayne State University, B.A., summa cum laude, Detroit, Michigan, 1968-1971; M.A., 1974; course work toward doctorate completed
Career: Adjunct Associate Professor, Center for Creative Studies, College of Art and Design, Detroit, Michigan, 1981—. Instructor (part-time), Wayne State University, Detroit, Michigan, 1975—.

Writings: *American Poets on the Holocaust*, edited by Charles Fishman, Texas Tech University Press, 1991. *Sticks and Stones* Urban Despair Press 1980. Poems included in anthologies. Numerous poems published nationwide. Work in Progress: Work on poetry, photography
Awards or inclusion in other biographical books: Hopwood Award for Poetry, University of Michigan, 1967. Michigan Council for the Arts, Creative Artist Grant, 1991
What is the aim or goal of your writing? "Currently interested in producing interdisciplinary art (poetry/photography) *Black Night Series* (recently finished) is an example. Images from *Black Night Series* have been exhibited at Center Galleries,

Detroit; Detroit Artists Market; and Mt. Clemens Art Center."
May inquiries be sent to you about doing workshops, readings? Yes

LANCE, BETTY RITA (GOMEZ)
Address: 1562 Spruce Drive, Kalamazoo, Michigan 49008
Born: August 28, 1923; San Jose, Costa Rica
Parents: Joaquin Gomez, Blanca (Castillo) Gomez
Children: Edward Theodore, Harold Elliott
Education: Universidad Nacional, Teaching diploma B.S., Heredia, Costa Rica, 1942-1944. Central Missouri State University, M.A., Warrensburg,1944-1947; University of Missouri, Columbia, Missouri. Washington University, Ph.D., St. Louis, Missouri, 1955-1959
Career: Professor, Kalamazoo College, Kalamazoo, Michigan, 1961-1988; Professor Emeritus—. Professor, University of Illinois, Urbana, Illinois, 1959-1961. Instructor, Washington University, St. Louis, Missouri, 1955-1959

Writings: *Alas en el Alba* Compotex 1987. *Hoy Hacen Corro las Ardillas* Editorial Papiro 1985. *Vendimia del Tiempo* Lil 1984. *Bebiendo Luna* Lil 1983. *Vivencias* Trejos Hnos 1981. *La Actitud Picaresca en la Novella Espanola* Costa Amic1969. Numerous publications on literary criticism in journals, periodicals. Work in Progress: Volume of poetry, *Siete Cuerdas*
Awards or inclusion in other biographical books: *Poets and Writers of America. Costa Rican Writers* (Costa Rica). *Academia Iberoamericana de Poesia* (based in Madrid, Dallas Chapter). *Associacion Prometeo de Poesia* (Madrid, Spain)
What is the aim or goal of your writing? "Self expression and to share with my readers feelings, thoughts, experiences"
May inquiries be sent to you about doing workshops, readings? Yes

LANDON, FRED (1880-1969)
Born: November 5, 1880; London, Ontario
Parents: Abram Landon, Hannah H. (Smith) Landon
Children: two sons, one daughter
Education: University of Western Ontario, B.A., 1906; M.A., 1919
Career: Sailor, Great Lakes shipping. Staff, London *Free Press,* 1906-1914. Librarian, London Public Library, 1916-1923. Associate Professor, University Librarian, 1923-1947. Vice-President, Dean of Graduate Studies, 1946-1950, retired. President, London and Middlesex Historical Society, 1918-1920. President, Ontario Library Association, 1926-1927. Others. Chairman, Historic Sites and Monuments Board, 1950. Member, Editorial Boards:*Agricultural History* (Washington),*Northwest Ohio Quarterly* (Toledo)

Writings: *The American Civil War and Canadian Confederation* Printed for the Royal Society of Canada 1927.*The Province of Ontario, a History, 1615-1927* 4 volumes (editor, with J.E. Middleton) Dominion Publishing 1928. *Dalton McCarthy and the Politics of the Later Eighties* F.A. Acland 1932. *Wilberforce, an Experiment in the Colonization of Freed Negroes in Upper Canada* Printed for the Royal Society of Canada 1937. *Western Ontario and the American Frontier* (for the Carnegie Endowment for International Peace) Ryerson Press 1941; McClelland and Stewart 1967; Ryerson Press 1968; Russell & Russell 1970. *Lake Huron* (The American Lakes Series) Bobbs-Merrill 1944. Others. Many articles in historical journals, book introductions. Addresses, such as "The Underground Railway and the Detroit River Border" delivered at Assumption College,

and "When Lincoln Became National Figure" delivered at McMaster University
Awards or inclusion in other biographical books: *Canadian Who's Who; Macmillan Dictionary of Canadian Biography; Oxford Companion to Canadian History and Literature; Who Was Who among English and European Authors; Who Was Who among North American Authors.* Tyrrell Medal, Canadian Historical Association, 1946. Assumption College Alumni Association Award, 1950. Fellow, Royal Society of Canada

LANMAN, CHARLES (1819-1895)
Born: June 14, 1819: Monroe, Michigan
Parents: Charles James Lanman, Marie Jeanne (Guie) Lanman
Career: New York East India mercantile house. Editor: *Gazette*, Monroe, Michigan, *Chronicle,* Cincinnati, Ohio, and others. Various public offices in Washington, DC including Librarian to the War and the Interior departments, the House of Representatives, and the city library. Also served as private secretary to Daniel Webster. Was 11 years secretary of the Japanese legation. Explored many areas by canoe, painted over a thousand landscapes

Writings: *Essays for Summer Hours* 1842, *Letters From a Landscape Painter* 1845. *A Summer in the Wilderness* 1847. *Private Life of Daniel Webster* 1852. *Adventures in the Wilds of America* (London) Longman, Brown, Green, and Longmans 1854. *Bohn's Hand-Book of Washington* C. Bohn 1856. *Dictionary of the United States Congress* J. B. Lippincott 1859; 5th ed. T. Belknap and H.E. Goodwin 1868. *Life of William Woodbridge* 1867. *Red Book of Michigan* 1871. *Biographical Annals of the Civil Government of the United States, During its First Century* J. Anglim 1876. *Landscapes and Nature Studies* Morris Museum of Arts and Sciences 1983. Other books (total of 32). Editor of *Journal of Alfred Ely* 1862; *The Japanese in America* 1872. Work published in numerous periodicals
Awards or inclusion in other biographical books: *Allibone: a Critical Dictionary of English Literature; American Authors 1600-1900; American Authors and Books; American Biographies; Biographical Dictionary and Synopsis of Books; Dictionary of American Authors; Dictionary of American Biography; Dictionary of North American Authors; National Cyclopaedia of American Biography; Reader's Encyclopedia of American Literature; Twentieth Century Biographical Dictionary of Notable Americans,* others. Elected associate of the National Academy of Design,1846

LANMAN, JAMES HENRY (1812-1887)
Born: December 4, 1812; Norwich, Connecticut
Parents: James Lanman, U.S. Senator
Education: Washington College, Hartford, Connecticut. Harvard University, Cambridge, Massachusetts
Career: Practiced law, Norwich and New London, Connecticut, Baltimore, Maryland. Moved to New York, New York, for literary career

Writings: *The American Cotton Trade* Freeman Hunt 1841. *History of Michigan From Its Earliest Colonization to the Present Time* Harper 1841. *The American Fur Trade* (New York)1840. *History of Michigan, Civil and Topographical, in a Compendious Form: With a View of the Surrounding Lakes* E. French 1839. In *Jurist, American Quarterly Review, North American Review,* others
Awards or inclusion in other biographical books: *Allibone: a Critical Dictionary of English Literature; Appleton's Cyclopaedia of American Biography; Dictionary of*

American Authors; Dictionary of North American Authors; Twentieth Century Biographical Dictionary of Notable Americans

LARDNER, RING(GOLD) WILMER (1885-1933)

Pseudonym: Ring Lardner, Ring W. Lardner, Jr.
Born: March 6, 1885; Niles, Michigan
Parents: Henry Lardner, Lena (Phillips) Lardner
Children: John Abbott, James Phillips, Ringgold Wilmer, Jr., David Ellis
Education: Armour Institute of Technology, Chicago, Illinois,1901-1902
Career: Reporter, *South Bend Times,* South Bend, Indiana, 1905-1907. Sports reporter for various Chicago newspapers, 1907-1910. Editor, *Sporting News,* St. Louis, Missouri, 1910-1911. Sportswriter, *Boston American, Chicago Examiner*, until becoming a columnist for *Chicago Tribune,*1913-1919. Writer for Bell Syndicate beginning in 1919. Hosted radio column, 1932-1933

Writings: *Bib Ballads* P.F. Volland 1915. *You Know Me Al: A Busher's Letters* Doran, 1916. *My Four Weeks in France* Bobbs-Merrill 1918. *Treat 'Em Rough* Bobbs-Merrill 1918. *Own Your Own Home* Bobbs-Merrill 1919. *The Real Dope* Bobbs-Merrill 1919. *The Young Immigrunts* Bobbs-Merrill 1920. *The Big Town: How I and the Mrs. Go to New York to See Life and Get Katie a Husband* Bobbs-Merrill 1921. *Symptoms of Being 35* Bobbs-Merrill 1921. *How to Write Short Stories* C. Scribner's Sons 1924. *What of It?* Scribners 1925. *Gullible's Travels, etc.* C. Scribner's Sons 1925. *The Love Nest and Other Stories* Scribners 1926. *Haircut and Other Stories* Scribners 1926. *The Story of a Wonder Man* Scribners 1927. *Round Up, the Stories of Ring W. Lardner* Scribners 1929. *June Moon; a Comedy in a Prologue and Three Acts* (with G.S. Kaufman) Scribners 1930. *Lose with a Smile* Scribners 1933. Others. Several collections of his stories, letters, have been published such as *Ring Around Max: the Correspondence of Ring Lardner & Max Perkins* Northern Illinois University Press 1973. Articles appeared in *Saturday Evening Post* and in many anthologies such as *Modern Essays* Scott, Foresman 1953. Editor, essayist. Wrote song lyrics, plays, comic strip. Radio plays were aired using his work; comedy play first appeared on Broadway 1929. Works went through various editions
Awards or inclusion in other biographical books: *American Authors and Books; American Writers; Contemporary American Authors; Contemporary American Literature; Michigan Authors,* 1st ed., 2nd ed.; *Reader's Encyclopedia; Reader's Adviser; Reader's Encyclopedia of American Literature; Twentieth Century Authors; Twentieth Century Literary Criticism; Twentieth Century Writing; Who Was Who among North American Authors; Who's Who in Twentieth Century Literature,* several others

LARRIE, REGINALD R.

Born: September 5, 1928; Detroit, Michigan
Parents: Robert Reese Larrie, Dora Ramus (Rawlins) Larrie
Children: Debra, Reginald, Raymond
Education: Detroit College of Business, 1970. Wayne County Community College, A.A., Detroit, Michigan, 1974. Upper Iowa University, B.A., Fayette, Iowa, 1977. Marygrove College, M. Ed., Detroit, Michigan, 1983. Pacific Western University, Ph.D., 1988
Career: Instructor, Wayne County Community College, Detroit, Michigan, 1970—. Editor, *Black Sports Magazine,* 1973-1975. Professor, Wayne State University, Detroit, Michigan, 1976

Writings: *Corners of Black History* Vantage 1972; teacher's guide, Olympian King 1986.

Black Experiences in Michigan History Michigan Historical Commission 1975. *Makin' Free: African-Americans in the Northwest Territory* Blaine Ethridge 1981. Columnist, *Michigan Chronicle.* Contributor (with Margaret Larrie) to *Ethnic Groups in the City,* others
Awards or inclusion in other biographical books: *Contemporary Authors; Michigan Authors,* 2nd ed.; *Who's Who Among Black Americans.* 15 Years Award, Boy Scouts of America, 1970. Distinguished Service Award, City of Detroit, 1976. Montgomery Ward Bicentennial Award, 1979. New Detroit Inc., Certificate of Merit, 1980. Wayne County Community College Recognition Award, 1988

LARSON, AMANDA E.
Address: 1103 Northrop Street, Marquette, Michigan 49855
Born: September 17, 1910; Dorsey, Michigan
Parents: John I. Wiljanen, Selma D. Wiljanen
Education: Northern Michigan University, Bachelor of Arts, Marquette, Michigan, 1934-1936. University of Michigan, Master of Arts, Ann Arbor, Michigan, 1950-1953
Career: Teacher, principal, Marquette Public Schools, Marquette, Michigan, 1950-1972. Special Education Teacher, Public Schools, Rhinelander, Wisconsin, 1946-1950. Reading Teacher, Negaunee Public Schools, Negaunee, Michigan, 1939-1946; 1930-1934. Teacher, Owosso Public Schools, Owosso, Michigan, 1936-1939. Teacher, Skandia Township Schools, Skandia, Michigan, 1929-1930

Writings: *Finnish Heritage in America* DKG Society 1975. Book was a Bicentennial Publication of Delta Chapter of the Delta Kappa Gamma Society, prepared as a gift for use in the intermediate grades of the Upper Peninsula Elementary Schools. A kit containing slides, music, puzzles, maps, recipes and 30 copies of the booklet was made available at the seven Intermediate School District Offices. As the public wished to purchase it, an additional 5,000 copies were printed and all profits placed in Scholarship Fund. The fund continues to grow as only the interest is used for scholarships even though the book itself is no longer available. Appears in several bibliographies. "Finnish Immigrants in the Great Lakes States, *Family Trails* magazine, Michigan Department of Education, 1977
Awards or inclusion in other biographical books: *Michigan Authors,* 2nd ed. Award, Marquette PTA Council, 1972. Distinguished Service Award, Michigan Congress of Parents & Teachers, 1972. Life Membership Grant, Michigan Elementary & Middle Schools Principals Association, 1979. Citations, Blind and Physically Handicapped Library of Michigan, reader in the Finnish language, 1973, 1974, 1975, 1977
May inquiries be sent to you about doing workshops, readings? No

LARZELERE, CLAUDE SHELDON (1866-1946)
Born: January 20,1866
Children: had children
Education: Michigan State Normal College, University of Michigan, Harvard University, Oxford University
Career: Professor of history and political science, Head of History Department, Central State Teachers College, Mt. Pleasant, Michigan, 1900-1939. Lecturer at teacher institutes. President of school board, Mt. Pleasant, Michigan, 10 years. Member of City Council and other civic positions

Writings: *Cadillac and the Early Days of Detroit* Michigan Education Company

1924.*The Coming of the White Man* Michigan Education Company 1924. *Government of Michigan* Silver Burdett 1913; Hillsdale School Supply 1932, 1939, 1946, 1951, 1952, 1956, 1961. *The Story of Michigan* Michigan Education Company 1923, 1928, Michigan School Service 1929. *Marquette and Joliet* Michigan Education Company 1924. *The Old Fur Traders* Michigan Education Company 1924. *Pontiac's Conspiracy* Michigan Education Company 1924

Awards or inclusion in other biographical books: *Who Was Who among North American Authors*

LAWDER, DOUGLAS W.

Address: 3430 Delta River Drive, Lansing, Michigan 48906
Born: June 12, 1934; New York, New York
Parents: Douglas W. Lawder, Janice C. Lawder
Children: Leland, Douglas
Education: Kenyon College, B.A., Gambier, Ohio 1953-1957. University of Oregon, M.F.A. with honors, Eugene, Oregon, 1964-1967
Career: Associate Professor, Michigan State University, East Lansing, Michigan, 1969—. Assistant Professor, Earlham College, Richmond, Indiana, 1967-1969

Writings: *Trolling* Little, Brown 1977. *3 Northwest Poets* Quixote Press 1971. Work in Progress: Poetry manuscript, novel
Awards or inclusion in other biographical books: Michigan Council for the Arts Grant. Danford Foundation Grant. Other grants
What is the aim or goal of your writing? "To provoke a sense of existence through the artifice of prose and poetry."
May inquiries be sent to you about doing workshops, readings? Yes

LAWRENCE, ALBERT LATHROP (1865-1924)

Born: November 14, 1865; Coldwater, Michigan
Parents: Henry N. Lathrop, Mary Lathrop
Education: Lansing Public Schools, Lansing, Michigan, 1872-1882
Career: Secretary-treasurer, Lawrence & Van Buren Printing Company, Lansing, Michigan

Writings: *Juell Demming* A.C. McClurg 1901. *The Wolverine: A Romance of Early Michigan* Little, Brown 1904, 1910. Short stories for newspapers, magazines
Awards or inclusion in other biographical books: *Who Was Who in America*

LAWRENCE, JOSEPH

Born: March 10, 1948; Detroit, Michigan
Education: University of Michigan, B.A., Ann Arbor, Michigan, 1970; J.D., 1975. Cambridge, England, B.A., M.A.
Career: Judicial Law Clerk, Michigan State Supreme Court, 1976-1978. Associate Professor of Law, University of Detroit Law School, 1978-1981. Attorney, Private Practice, New York, New York, 1981-1984. Associate Professor, Hofstra University School of Law, New York, New York, 1984-1987. Professor of Law, St. Johns University, Jamaica, New York, 1988—

Writings: *Curriculum Vitae* University of Pittsburgh Press 1988.
Shouting at No One University of Pittsburgh Press 1983. Work in Progress: Third book of poetry

LAWRENCE, MILDRED E.
Address: 1044 Terrace Blvd., Orlando, Florida 52803
Born: November 10, 1907; Charleston, Illinois
Parents: Dewitt Elwood, Gertrude J. (Jefferson) Elwood
Children: Leora
Education: Lawrence College, B.A., Appleton, Wisconsin, 1924-1928. Yale University, M.A., New Haven, Connecticut, 1929-1931
Career: Newspaper society editor, music/art reporter, book reviewer

Writings: *Touchmark* Harcourt Brace 1975, revised edition 1992. *Walk a Rocky Road* Harcourt Brace 1971. *The Shining Moment* Harcourt Brace 1960. *Indigo Magic* Harcourt Brace 1956. *Along Comes Spring* Harcourt Brace 1958. *Inside the Gate* Harcourt Brace 1968. *Crissy at the Wheel* Harcourt Brace 1952. *Sand in Her Shoes* Harcourt Brace 1949. *Peachtree Island* Harcourt Brace 1948. Several others. Some books appear in foreign languages, Braille as talking books. Adult short stories published in the United States and abroad. Work in Progress: Book for adults, short stories
Awards or inclusion in other biographical books: *Michigan Authors,* 2nd ed. *Touchmark*, Junior Literary Guild selection
In the 2nd edition of *Michigan Authors* appears: "I have been especially interested in regional writing, since we have lived and visited a good many fascinating places-a peach orchard on a Lake Erie island, an automobile town (Flint) sprung from a village of wagonmakers, the North Carolina mountains, New Mexico and others."
May inquiries be sent to you about doing workshops, readings? No. Sorry, I used to talk around and about, both to children and adults, but at 84 I can't do it any more.

LAWTON, JAMES FREDERICK (1888-1969)
Born: 1888
Education: University of Michigan, Ann Arbor, Michigan, graduate of the School of Literature, Science, and the Arts, 1911
Career: University of Michigan football star. General Agent, Connecticut Mutual Life Insurance Company. Poet, composer

Writings: *"Hurry Up" Yost in Song and Story* J.W. Edwards 1947. *Roses That Bloomed in the Snow* poetry book. Wrote the words of "Varsity", the University of Michigan football song, the University of Detroit's alma mater, and others. Poems about many Michigan people of note
Awards of inclusion in other biographical books: Poet Laureate, City of Berkley, Michigan, 1946. Title, "Mr. Michigan", bestowed by University of Michigan's Board of Regents and University President, Harlan Hatcher

LEITHAUSER, GLADYS G.
Address: 122 Elm Park, Pleasant Ridge, MI 48069
Born: February 11, 1925; Detroit, Michigan
Parents: Herbert N. Garner, Caroline S. Garner
Education: Wayne State University, B.S., M.A., Ph.D., Detroit, Michigan, 1942-1946, 1965-1977
Career: Lecturer, University of Michigan-Dearborn, Dearborn, Michigan, 1978—.

Writings: *Who Should I Be?* Paulist Press 1991. *The World of Science: An Anthology for Writers* (editor with Marilynn Bell) Holt, Rinehart and Winston 1986. *The Rabbit Is Next* (with Lois Breitmeyer) Western 1978. *The Dinosaur Dilemma* (with Lois Breitmeyer) Golden Gate Junior Books 1964. Work in Progress: *The Old Country* (with Lois Breitmeyer), a children's book. *Stampede* (with Lois Breitmeyer)

What is the aim or goal of your writing? "To create books for children that will enhance their imaginative skills and supply them with sound, substantial materials for mental and emotional growth."

Awards or inclusion in other biographical books: *Michigan Authors,* 2nd ed.

May inquiries be sent to you about doing workshops, readings? Yes

LEITHAUSER, HELEN (PRESCOTT)

Address: 350 Lakeview, Levering, Michigan 49755

Born: October 31, 1951; Beruit, Lebanon

Parents: Miles M. Prescott, Edith R. (Rew) Prescott

Children: Cayce, Rowan

Education: University of Michigan, Bachelor of General Studies, Ann Arbor, Michigan, 1969-1974

Career: Assistant Director, Mackinaw Area Public Library, Mackinaw City, Michigan, 1990—. Freelance Writer, Levering, Michigan, 1980—. Assistant Administrator, Washtenaw County Council for Children, Ann Arbor, Michigan, 1986-1989. Graphic Artist, Prakken Publications, Ann Arbor, Michigan, 1976-1979

Writings: *Turning on Tofu* Bliss Books 1984. *Chettas, A Collection of Women's Writing* (editor, contributor) Cat Anna Press 1978. *Astraea, An Anthology of Women's Works* University of Michigan Women's Studies 1974. *Sistrum* (editor, contributor) University of Michigan Women's Studies 1972. Fiction has appeared in *Women's World, Concierge, North Force, Mother Earth News* and others. Work in Progress: Mystery/romance set in medieval town, Cracow, Poland. Two children's picture books

Awards or inclusion in other biographical books: First Place, Short Story, Thunder Bay Literary Conference, 1991. First Place, Prose, Writer's North Annual Award, 1990. First Place Poetry, Writer's North Annual Award, 1989. Honorable Mention, Short Short Story, University of Florida, 1990. Honorable Mention, Nonfiction, Writer's Digest Annual Contest, 1989

What is the aim or goal of your writing? "I would like to publish the children's books I've completed and the novel I'm writing and then write more! Also, I feel that writing is a wonderful means of self-healing, revelation and expression. I would like to see more creative writing workshops offered to school-age children and made available to older people in the community."

May inquiries be sent to you about doing workshops, readings? Yes

LELAND, CHRISTOPHER T.

Address: Department of English, Wayne State University, Detroit, Michigan, 48202

Born: October 17, 1951; Tulsa, Oklahoma

Parents: Benjamin T. Leland, Julia S. Leland

Education: Marina High School, Huntington Beach, California, 1969. Pomona College, B.A., Claremont, California, 1969-1973. University of California, Ph.D., San Diego, California, 1975-1982

Career: Professor, Wayne State University, Detroit, Michigan, 1990—. Faculty Member, Bennington College, Bennington, Vermont, 1988-1990. Briggs-Copeland Assistant Professor, Harvard University, Cambridge, Massachusetts, 1983-1988

Writings: *The Book of Marvels* Charles Scribners 1990. *Mrs. Randall* Houghton Mifflin 1987. *The Last Happy Men: The Generation of 1922, Fiction + the Argentine Reality* Syracuse University Press 1986. *Mean Time* Random House 1982. *Open Door,* translation of stories.

Work in Progress: *Memory Tapes, The Professor Aesthetics and Other Stories*, and another

Awards or inclusion in other biographical books: Fulbright Fellow (Argentina) 1972, 1984, 1987. USIA American Specialist (Argentina, Uruguay). Massachusetts Artist Fellowship, 1985

What is the aim or goal of your writing? "To write well".

May inquiries be sent to you about doing workshops, readings? Yes

LEO, KATHLEEN RIPLEY

Address: 42185 Baintree Circle, Northville, Michigan 48167

Born: Chicago, Illinois

Parents: Roy Ripley, Jane (Werbowetzki) Ripley

Children: Mark, Joseph

Education: Western Illinois University, B.A., Macomb, Illinois, 1964-1968. University of Pittsburgh, Master of Art, Pittsburgh, Pennsylvania, 1968-1970

Career: Consultant to schools, poet, teacher, presentor, self-Employed, Northville, Michigan, 1975—. Faculty, English Department, Macomb Community College, Warren, Michigan, 1990—. Creative Writing Workshop Instructor, Schoolcraft College, Livonia, Michigan, 1988—. Publisher and co-editor of *Waiting for the Apples,* a K-12 anthology of Young Authors, poetry and prose. Creative Writers in the School Program

Writings: *The Old Ways* Sun Dog Press 1991. *Town One South* Northville Arts Press 1988. Published in literary presses throughout the United States. Work in Progress:*Walking Journal Poems, Glass Poems*, both contracted

Awards or inclusion in other biographical books: Number of grants, Michigan Council for the Arts. Commissioned by Northville Arts Commission, *Town One South*, 1987. Nominated for Pushcart Prize, 1987, 1988

What is the aim or goal of your writing? "In writing: To create art with words; to discover fresh perspectives; to inform my readers of the constantly changing landscape; to catalogue and define the who, what, why and where around us; to infuse readers with enthusiasm for the art of language; to redefine language; to raise the insignificant to the level of the sublime. In teaching: To direct adult students to approach language as art, to acknowledge the emotive and connotative forces of words, and to help them utilize those forces within their own voice; to acquaint elementary students with the possibilities in poems and to help them write poems; to expand middle and high school students' awareness of the strategies of poetry and to help them write poems."

May inquiries be sent to you about doing workshops, readings? Yes

LEONARD, ELMORE

Born: October 11, 1925; New Orleans, Louisiana

Parents: Elmore John Leonard, Flora Amelia (Rive) Leonard

Children: Jane, Peter, Christopher, William, Katherine

Education: University of Detroit, Ph.B., Detroit, Michigan, 1950

Career: U.S. Naval Reserve, 1943-1946. Copywriter for Campbell-Ewald Advertising Agency, Detroit, Michigan, 1950-1961. Freelance copywriter, writer of educational and industrial films, 1961-1963. Head of his own advertising company, 1963-1966

Writings: *Touch* Arbor House 1987. *Bandits* Arbor House 1987. *Glitz* Arbor House 1985. *The Bounty Hunters* Houghton 1953; Bantam 1985. *City Primeval: High Noon in Detroit* Arbor House, 1980. *The Law at Randado* Houghton 1955; Bantam 1985. *Escape from 5 Shadows* Houghton 1956; Bantam 1985. *Fifty-Two Pickup* Delacorte 1974. *Last Stand at Saber River* 1957, Bantam 1985, others. *Gold Coast* Bantam 1980, 1985. *Hombre* Ballantine 1961, 1984. *LaBrava* Arbor House 1983. *Mr. Majestyk* Dell 1974, 1986. *The Moonshine War* Doubleday 1969; Dell 1985. *Valdez is Coming* Gold Medal 1970. *Forty Lashes Less One* Bantam 1972. *Gunsights* Bantam 1979. *Swag* Delacorte 1976; published as *Ryan's Rules* Dell 1976. *Unknown Man, No. 89* Delacorte 1977. *The Hunted* Dell 1977. *Switch* Bantam 1978. *Split Images* Arbor House 1981. *Cat Chaser* Arbor House 1982. *Stick* Arbor House 1983. *Elmore Leonard's Dutch Treat: Three Novels* Arbor House 1985. *Elmore Leonard's Double Dutch Treat: Three Novels* Arbor House 1986. *Detroit, the Renaissance City* Thomasson-Grant 1986. *The Big Bounce* Mysterious Press 1969, 1986; Gold Medal 1969; Armchair Detective 1989. *Elmore Leonard's Bandits* Arbor House 1987. *Freaky Deaky* Arbor House 1988. *Killshot* Arbor House 1989. *Maximum Bob* Delacorte Press 1991. *Raw Punch* Delacorte Press 1992. Screenplays based on novels, collections of works, short stories, novelettes. Published in *Saturday Evening Post, Argosy, Zane Grey's Western Magazine* and others

Awards or inclusion in other biographical books: *Authors in the News; Biography News; Contemporary Authors; Current Biography; International Authors and Writers Who's Who; Michigan Authors,* 2nd ed. Western Writers of America named *Hombre* one of the 25 best western novels written, 1977. Edgar Allan Poe Award, Mystery Writers of America, 1984

LEONARD, JERRY A.

Address: 2214 Miles Avenue, Kalamazoo, Michigan 49001
Born: July 29, 1947; Kalalmazoo, Michigan
Parents: Bud K. Leonard, Faye D. Leonard
Children: Karmen, Sarah (wife: Collette)
Education: Portage Central High School, Portage, Michigan, 1963-1965. Michigan State University, East Lansing, 1965-1967. Western Michigan University, Kalamazoo, Michigan; B.S., M.A., 1967-1985
Career: Elementary teacher, Portage Public Schools, 1970—. Personal racing team sponsored by several manufacturers, travel throughout the Midwest to race large sports car tracks (Mid-Ohio, M.I.S.) 135 mph, working in conjunction with D.A.R.E. anti-drug police program

Writings: *Kart Racing: A Complete Guide* Messner/Simon & Schuster 1980. *An Economic Simulation Program for Classroom Management in the Elementary School* Portage Public Schools 1976. Numerous articles on racing, national magazines
Awards or inclusion in other biographical books: *Who's Who Among America's Teachers,* 1992
What is the aim or goal of your writing? "Obviously that depends upon what I'm writing about. However most of my writing is factual/informational in content so I try to convey (and persuade) the information in an interesting fashion. I try to make it personal so that the reader can relate to what I'm trying to communicate."
May inquiries be sent to you about doing workshops, readings? Yes

LESSTRANG, JACQUES E.

Address: 221 Water Street, Boyne City, Michigan 49712
Born: June 13, 1926; Pittsburgh, Pennsylvania
Parents: Jacques E. LesStrang; Ada M. LesStrang
Children: Christian, David, Michelle, Paul, Steven, Diane, Linda
Education: George Washington University, A.A., Washington, DC, 1948-1949. University of Michigan, B.A., Ann Arbor, Michigan, 1949-1951. University of Hawaii, Fellowship in Sociology
Career: President of international marketing firm. Currently senior editor, publisher, writer

Writings: *Le System Grand Lacs Saint-Laurent* Harbor House 1986. *The Great Lakes St. Lawrence System* Harbor House 1986. *Cargo Carriers of the Great Lakes* Crown 1983; Harbor House, 1983. *Lake Carriers* Superior 1982. *Seaway* Harbor House 1982; Superior 1980. *Michigan U.S.A.* State of Michigan 1969. *Michigan in International Market Place* State of Michigan 1968. Work in Progress:*The Big Boats. Lakes to the Sea. The Great Lakes Fleets*
Awards or inclusion in other biographical books: *Contemporary Authors* 1966–; *English Biography of Authors* 1966—; *Michigan Authors,* 2nd ed.; *Who's Who in the World* 1966—. American Merchant Marine Distinguished Service Award 1985. Maritime Author of the Year 1985
May inquiries be sent to you about doing workshops, readings? Yes

LETHBRIDGE, ALICE G.

Address: 2401 Calumet Avenue, Flint, Michigan 48503
Born: February 14, 1921; Berwyn, Nebraska
Parents: Ted T. Skinner, Mary B. (McEvoy) Skinner
Children: Joan, Hugh Jr., Kevin, Mary, Paul
Education: St. Mary High School, Flint, Michigan, 1938. Mercy College, B.S., Detroit, Michigan, 1944-1946. Nazareth College, Kalamazoo, Michigan, 1938-1940. University of Michigan, Flint, Michigan
Career: Reporter, Feature Writer, *The Flint Journal,* 1945-1984, with times off for family, retired

Writings: *History, St. Cecilia Society* St. Cecilia Society 1990. *...And Fellow Members* Garland Street Literary Club (Occasional Publication Series, UM-Flint) 1988. *Sesquicentennial History* First Presbyterian Church, Flint 1987. *Through the Years in Genesee* Windsor Publications, Inc. 1985. *Well Do I Remember* Privately Published 1976. *Halfway to Yesterday* Genesee County Historical and Museum Society, Flint 1974. Articles in*The Flint Journal Picture History of Flint* 1976, later editions; in *Chronicle.* Work in Progress: Recollections of life in Flint, Michigan, 1925 on, including highlights of career with *The Flint Journal*
Awards or inclusion in other biographical books: *Michigan Authors,* 2nd ed. Award of Merit, Genesee County Historical and Museum Society. Award, Historical Society of Michigan. First Annual Roger VanBolt Heritage Award, Genesee County Historical and Museum Society. Medal for Outstanding Work in History, Genesee Chapter of the Daughters of the American Revolution
What is the aim or goal of your writing? "To present with as much accuracy as possible and in an interesting way the stories of people who made history in Flint and Genesee County especially individuals who received little or no recognition."
May inquiries be sent to you about doing workshops, readings? No

LEVINE, PHILIP
Born: January 10, 1928; Detroit, Michigan
Parents: A. Harry Levine, Esther G. (Priscoll) Levine
Children: Mark, John, Theodore
Education: Wayne State University, B.A., Detroit, Michigan, 1950; M.A., 1954.
University of Iowa, M.F.A., (Writers' Workshop) Iowa City, Iowa, 1957
Career: Detroit Transmission and other jobs, Detroit, Michigan. Faculty, University of Iowa, Iowa City, 1955-1957. Faculty, California State University, Fresno, California, 1958—. Poet-in-residence, visiting professor of poetry. Teacher, writers groups. Read his poetry at Library of Congress, University of Michigan, Stanford University, Guggenheim Museum, Wayne State University, and several others.

Writings: *On the Edge* Stone Wall Press 1961, 1963. *Silent in America: Vivas for Those Who Failed* Shaw Avenue Press 1965. *Not This Pig* Wesleyan University Press 1968. *5 Detroits* Unicorn Press 1970.*Thistles: A Poem Sequence* Turret Books (London) 1970. *Pili's Wall* Unicorn Press 1971, 1980. *7 Years from Somewhere* Atheneum 1979. *Sweet Will* Atheneum 1985. *Selected Poems* Atheneum (several on Detroit)1984. *A Walk with Tom Jefferson* Knopf 1988. *New Selected Poems* Knopf 1991. *What Work Is* Knopf 1991. Others. Also edited, translated, co-edited, wrote introductions, contributed to numerous anthologies
Awards or inclusion in other biographical books: *Contemporary Authors; Contemporary Literary Criticism; Contemporary Poets; Dictionary of Literature in the English Language; Directory of American Poets; Directory of American Scholars; International Authors and Writers Who's Who; International Who's Who in Poetry; Lincoln Library of Language Arts; Who's Who in America; World Authors; Writers Directory.* others. National Book Award for Poetry, 1991. *Los Angeles Times* Book Prize, 1991. Elmer Holmes Bobst Award, New York University, 1990. Ruth Lilly Award, Modern Poetry Association and American Council for the Arts, 1987. Golden Rose Award, New England Poetry Society, 1985. Notable Book Award, American Library Association, 1979. National Book Critics Circle Prize, 1979. American Book Award for Poetry, 1979. Others. Numerous fellowships, grants. Outstanding lecturer, California State University, Fresno, 1971. Outstanding professor, California State University System, 1972

LEWIS, DAVID L.
Address: 2588 Hawthorn, Ann Arbor, Michigan 48104
Born: April 5, 1927; Bethalto, Illinois
Parents: Donald F. Lewis, Edith E. Lewis
Children: Kim, Leilani, Sumi, Lance
Education: University of Michigan, Ph.D., Ann Arbor, Michigan, 1955-1959
Career: Professor of Business History, University of Michigan, Ann Arbor, Michigan, 1965—. Writer, General Motors Corporation, Detroit, Michigan, 1959-1965. Public Relations Staff, Ford Motor Company, Dearborn, Michigan, 1950-1955

Writings: *Ford Chronicle: A Pictorial History From 1893* Publications International Ltd. 1992. *Ford Country* Amos Press 1987. *The Automobile an American Culture* University of Michigan Press 1983. *The Public Image of Henry Ford* Wayne State University Press 1976. Work in Progress: Ford History (1956-1989)
Awards or inclusion in other biographical books: *Michigan Authors,* 2nd ed. Cugnot Award, Society of Automotive Historians, for *The Public Image of Henry Ford*, 1976
May inquiries be sent to you about doing workshops, readings? Yes

LEWIS, FERRIS EVERETT (1904-1981)
Parents: Thomas E. Lewis, Lenora A. Lewis
Children: Virginia, Mary Kathryn
Education: Wayne State University, A.B., Detroit, Michigan, 1927. University of Detroit, M.A., 1931
Career: Teacher, Dearborn Public Schools, 28 years. Chairman, Henry Ford Community College, Dearborn, Michigan. Appointed, Dearborn Historical Commission, 1952.

Writings: *Michigan, A Student's Directive Guide* Hillsdale School Supply 1931. *Our Own State* Hillsdale Educational Publishers 1st edition 1932, 17th edition 1992. *My Government: A Text Book in Michigan Civics* E. M. Hale 1936. *My State and Its Story* Hillsdale Educational Publishers 1st edition 1937, 16th edition 1972. *Then and Now in Michigan* Hillsdale School Supply Company 1944, 1950. *Michigan Yesterday and Today* Hillsdale Educational Publishers 1st edition 1956, 8th edition 1975. *Handbook for the Teaching of Michigan History* Hillsdale Educational Publishers 1st edition 1958, revised 1964. *State and Local Government in Michigan* 1st edition 1960, 16th 1974. *What To See and Where to Find It in Michigan: Tourist Guide for the State of Michigan* Hillsdale School Supply 1958. *Men and Resources, A Study of North American and Its Place in World Geography* Harcourt, Brace 1937, 1943. *A Brief Look at Michigan's New Constitution* Hillsdale School Supply 1963. *Detroit, A Wilderness Outpost of Old France* Wayne University Press 1951. *Michigan Civil Government* Hillsdale Education Publishers 1967. *Michigan Since 1815* Hillsdale Educational Publishers 1973. *A Teaching Guide for Michigan, Yesterday & Today* Hillsdale Educational Publishers 1978. Others. Articles in *Michigan History*
Awards or inclusion in other biographical books: *Michigan Authors,* 1st ed., 2nd ed. Since 1983, Hillsdale Educational Publishers has co-sponsored the Ferris E. Lewis Award with the Historical Society of Michigan. This Award alternates each year between teachers of grades K-6 and teachers of grades 7-12, recognizing excellence in teaching Michigan history

LIEBLER, MICHAEL L.
Address: 31725 Courtland, St. Clair Shores, Michigan 48082
Born: August 24, 1953; Detroit, Michigan
Parents: Vernon S. Liebler, Mabel D. Liebler
Children: Shane, Shelby
Education: Oakland University, M.A., Rochester, Michigan, 1979-1980. Oakland University, B.A., Rochester, Michigan, 1974-1976. Macomb Community College, 1971-1974
Career: Faculty, Wayne State University, Detroit, Michigan, 1980—. Instructor, Macomb Community College, Warren, Michigan, 1989-1991. Instructor, Center for Creative Studies, Detroit, Michigan, 1986-1990. Gives about 100 readings across the country a year. Has done several workshops around the state

Writings: *Deliver Me* Ridgeway Press 1991. *Breaking the Voodoo: Fiction and Poetry* Parkville Publishers 1990. *Measuring Darkness* Ridgeway Press 1980. *Whispers by the Lawn: Volume Two* Ridgeway Press 1986. *Whispers by the Lawn: Volume One* Ridgeway Press 1985. *Unfinished Man in the Perfect Mirror* Casterbridge Press 1976. *Knit Me a Pair of Your Shoes* Ridgeway Press 1975. *The Martyr of Pig* Ridgeway Press 1974. Co-edited, with Frankie Kerouc-Parker, *Save the Frescoes That are Us: A Detroit Tribute to Jack Kerouac* 1982

What is the aim or goal of your writing? "To reach a general audience of potential poetry/fiction lovers. I write much about the common person's experiences and reactions to our contemporary society. I, also, have much work that attempts to interepret the sixties experience."
May inquiries be sent to you about doing workshops, readings? Yes

LIGHTBODY, DONNA MAE (1920-1976)
Born: September 7, 1920; Flint, Michigan
Parents: Don R. Larkin, Edna (Surner) Larkin
Children: Rene
Education: Russell Sage College, Troy, New York, 1937-1940. Wayne State University, B.B.L.S, M.S.L.S., 1965-1969
Career: WAAC and WAC in World War II. Secretary, elementary school librarian. Media Associate, Coronet Films. Helped found International Guild of Craft Journalists

Writings: *Let's Knot, a Macrame Book* Lothrop, Lee & Shepard 1972. *Introducing Needlepoint* Lothrop, Lee & Shepard 1973. *Easy Weaving* Lothrop, Lee & Shepard 1974. *Hooks and Loops* Lothrop, Lee & Shepard 1975. *Braid Craft* Lothrop, Lee & Shepard 1976
Awards or inclusion in other biographical books: *Michigan Authors,* 2nd ed.

LIMBACHER, JAMES L.
Address: 21800 Morley Avenue, Apt. 1201, Dearborn, Michigan 48124
Born: November 30, 1926; Saint Marys, Ohio
Parents: Fritz J. Limbacher, Edith S. Limbacher
Education: Defiance College, School of Music. Bowling Green State University, Bowling Green, Ohio, Bachelor of Arts, 1949; Master of Arts 1954. Indiana University, Master of Science in Education, 1955. Michigan Board of Education, Special Professional Certificate, 1968, 1978. Wayne State University, M.L.S., Detroit, Michigan, 1972
Career: Assistant Director, University News Bureau, Bowling Green State University, 1949-1953. Director, Film Society Project, Film Council of America, 1953. Graduate Assistant in Film Selection and Evaluation, Indiana University, 1954. Script Writer, Indiana University Radio and Television Service, 1954-1955. Audiovisual Librarian, Dearborn Department of Libraries, 1955-1983. Television Producer/Host, Tribune/United Cable Communications, 1984-1985. Television Producer/Host, Cablevision of Dearborn, 1987-1989. Lecturer, speaker, leader, teacher, at many universities, churches, schools, clubs, synagogues. Board member, Chairman of many organizations. Founder, Dearborn Symphony Orchestra, 1959. Founder, Blockbusters Film Series, 1971. President, Detroit Film Society, 1987—. President, Michigan Organization of Visual Instructors and Enthusiasts, 1976-1978, and several others. Several consultantships such as Youth Film Forum, 1968-1989. Many stage appearances

Writings: *Haven't I Seen You Somewhere Before?* Pierian 1992. *Keeping Score* Scarecrow 1992, 1981. *Four Aspects of the Film* Land's End Press 1969; Arno Press, New York Times 1978. *Using Films* Educational Film Library Association 1967. *Film Music: From Violins to Video* Scarecrow Press 1974. *Shadows on the Wall* Henry Ford Centennial Library 1968. *Sexuality in World Cinema* Scarecrow Press 1984. *An Historical Study of Full-Length Plays Presented at Bowling Green State University from 1920-1953* Bowling Green State University Popular Culture Library 1953. *ASCAP Theatrical Productions* ASCAP 1964. *The Song List* Pierian Press 1974. Others. Compiler of several books such

as *Theatrical Events on Records* (3 editions) Henry Ford Centennial Library 1959. Editor of several books such as *Film "Sneaks" Annual* Pierian Press 1972. News stories have appeared in *New York Times, Toledo Blade, Detroit Free Press, Variety* and others. Articles have appeared in many publications such as *Media Spectrum, Detroiter Magazine, Film Library Quarterly, Film News, Variety, Library Journal, Michigan Librarian.* Script writer for various television series. Author of radio series. Many radio and television appearances. Author of plays, opera libretti, musical comedies. Author of several chapters, dictionary entries. Work in Progress: *SICSIC-The Secret Six* Bowling Green University. *A.F.V.A.-Happy Anniversary* American Film and Video Association **Awards or inclusion in other biographical books:** *Contemporary Authors; Dictionary of International Biography; Dictionary of British and American Writers; Dictionary of American Scholars; Directory of Library & Information Professionals; International Authors and Writers' Who's Who; Men of Achievement; Michigan Authors,* 2nd ed.; *Who's Who in American Education; Who's Who in the Midwest; Who's Who in the World; World Who's Who of Authors.* Hometown USA Video Award, Senior Glimpses, National Federation of Local Cable Programmers, 1987, 1988. Michigan Librarian of the Year Award, 1974. Citation, Sons of the Desert, 1964. Gold Medallion Award, Atlanta Film Festival, 1972. Honorary Member, Plan 9 Society, Detroit. Honorary member, Sons of the Desert. Red Balloon Award, Detroit Association of Film Teachers, 1971. Greater Detroit Motion Picture Council Award, 1969. Michigan Top Ten Plays,1960. Honorable Mention, Community Theater Association of Michigan Playwrighting Contest 1960, 1965; Third Prize 1961. Bowling Green State University, Friends of the Library Award, 1991. Others
What is the aim or goal of your writing? "To provide information to researchers and fans."
May inquiries be sent to you about doing workshops, readings? No

LINDBERGH, CHARLES A. 1902-1974
Born: February 4, 1902; Detroit, Michigan
Parents: Charles Augustus Lindbergh, Evangeline (Land) Lindbergh
Children: Charles, Jon, Land, Anne, Reeve, Scott
Education: University of Wisconsin, 1920-1922. Nebraska Aircraft Corporation flying school, 1922
Career: Stunt flier, mechanic, barnstormer, 1922-1924. U.S. Army Air Service Reserve, 1924-1941, 1954-1974. Airmail pilot between Chicago and St. Louis, 1926. Celebrated flight, New York-Paris, 1927. Goodwill ambassador, 1927-1928. Inventor, designer, Rockefeller Institute, 1930-1935. Researcher-inventor, France, 1935-1939. Consultant, Ford Motor Company, Detroit, Michigan and U.S. War Department, 1939-1944. Consultant, United Aircraft Corporation, 1943-1944. Consultant and writer, 1944-1974. Conservationist, helping save whales from extinction

Writings: *We* Putnam 1927. *Culture of Organs* (with Alexis Carrel) Harper 1938. *The Spirit of St. Louis* (Book-of-the-Month Club) Selection Scribner 1953, 1976. *The Wartime Journals of Charles A. Lindbergh* Harcourt 1970. *Boyhood on the Upper Mississippi: A Reminiscent Letter* Minnesota Historical Society 1972. *Banana River* Harcourt 1976. *Autobiography of Values* Harcourt 1978. *Radio Speeches of Charles A. Lindbergh: 1939-1940* Revisionist Press 1982. Foreword, Michael Collins *Carrying the Fire: An Astronaut's Journeys* Farrar, Straus and Giroux, 1974

Awards or inclusion in other biographical books: *American Authors and Books; Contemporary Authors; Current Biography; Encyclopedia of American Biography; International Who's Who; Reader's Encyclopedia; Reader's Encyclopedia of American Literature; Who Was Who in America; Who's Who among North American Authors; Who's Who in America; Who's Who in the World*, several others. Many awards for flying from the United States, foreign countries. Doctor of Laws, Northwestern University, University of Wisconsin, 1928. Master of Science, Princeton University, 1931, Master of Aeronautics, New York University, 1928. Pulitzer Prize in Biography, 1954

LITKOWSKI, O.P., SR. PELAGIA
Address: 10250 N. Maple Island, Fremont, Michigan 49412
Born: November 6, 1911; Saginaw, Michigan
Parents: Peter P. Litkowski, Florence L. Litkowski
Education: St. Joseph High School, Saginaw, Michigan, 1925-1929. Aquinas College, B.A., Grand Rapids, Michigan, 1932-1953 summer sessions. Western Michigan University, M.A. Library Science, Kalamazoo, Michigan, 1953-1961 summer sessions
Career: Volunteer Elementary Librarian, St. Michael Elementary School, Fremont, Michigan, 1991—. Middle School Librarian, Immaculate Conception Middle School, Traverse City, Michigan, 1987-1991. Elementary School Librarian, Traverse City, Michigan, 1982-1984. High School Librarian, St. Mary High School, Saginaw, Michigan, 1972-1980. Volunteer work, Melvindale, Michigan; Gaylord, Michigan

Writings: *Margaret of Catello, Unwanted One* Growth Unlimited, Inc. 1991. *Kateri Tekakwitha, Joyful Lover* Growth Unlimited, Inc. 1989. *Friend To All, St. John Nepomucene Neumann, CSSR* Growth Unlimited, Inc. 1987. Work in Progress: *Father Damien, Loving Neighbor to All*
Awards or inclusion in other biographical books: Annual National Tekakwitha Award, 1991
What is the aim or goal of your writing? "To provide role models for young people and inspiration for all ages."
May inquiries be sent to you about doing workshops, readings? No

LITTLEJOHN, FLAVIUS JOSEPHUS (1804-1880)
Born: 1804; Herkimer County, New York
Education: Hamilton College, 1827, Clinton, New York
Career: Became a lawyer in 1830, setting up practice in Little Falls, New York. Moved to Allegan, Michigan, 1836 and served as surveyor, engineer, geologist. Surveyed the original plat of the City of Allegan. Circuit-riding judge for many years, elected state representative four times, 1842-1855; state senator, 1845-1846. Became expert in Indian lore from job travels

Writings: *The Legends of Michigan and The Old North West; or, a Cluster of Unpublished Waifs, Gleaned Along the Uncertain, Misty Line, Dividing Traditional from Historic Times* Northwestern Bible and Publishing Company (Allegan, Michigan) 1875; reprint Allegan County Historical Society 1956

LITWAK, LEO
Born: May 28, 1924; Detroit, Michigan
Parents: Isaac Litwak, Bessie (Gosman) Litwak
Children: Jessica
Education: University of Michigan, Ann Arbor, Michigan, 1943, 1946. Wayne State University, B.A., Detroit, Michigan, 1948. Columbia University, New York, New York, 1948-1951
Career: United States Army, 1943-1946. Instructor, Washington University, St. Louis, Missouri, 1951-1960. Assistant Professor, San Francisco State University, San Francisco, California, 1961-1964; Professor, beginning in 1964. Visiting lecturer

Writings: *To the Hanging Gardens* World Publishing 1964. *Waiting for the News* Doubleday 1969; Wayne State University Press 1990. *College Days in Earthquake Country: Ordeal at San Francisco State* (co-author) Random House 1971. In *Partisan Review,* others; included in anthologies
Awards or inclusion in other biographical books: *American Authors and Books; Contemporary Authors; Contemporary Novelists; Directory of American Fiction Writers; International Authors and Writers Who's Who; Michigan Authors; Writers Directory.* Longview Foundation Award, 1959. Edward Lewis Wailan Memorial Book Award, 1969. Award, Jewish Book Council of the National Jewish Welfare Board, 1970. Guggenheim Fellowship, 1970. Daroff Memorial Prize,1970

LOBDELL, HELEN B. (1919-deceased)
Born: May 14, 1919; Royal Oak, Michigan
Parents: Walter Lobdell, Vanessa (Perry) Lobdell
Education: Western Michigan University, M.A., Kalamazoo, Michigan
Career: Teacher in Ohio and Michigan, writer. Vickii DeFields, Bridgman High School Media Center, had her as a teacher, and said that she taught history and art in Watervliet, Michigan for many years. She used to read her books aloud to Junior High students and take them on field trips relating to the event.

Writings: *Golden Conquest* Houghton Mifflin 1953. *The King's Snare* Houghton Mifflin 1955. *Captain Bacon's Rebellion* Macrae Smith 1959. *The Fort in the Forest* Houghton Mifflin 1963. *Prisoner of Taos* Abelard-Schuman 1970
Awards or inclusion in other biographical books: *Contemporary Authors; Michigan Authors,* 1st ed., 2nd ed.

LOCKWOOD, WALTER L.
Address: 167 Boltwood NE, Grand Rapids, Michigan 49505
Born: August 2, 1941; St. Joseph, Michigan
Parents: Leon W. Lockwood, Edith E. Lockwood
Children: Ian, Alison, Matthew
Education: Michigan State University, B.A., East Lansing, Michigan, 1959-1963. Indiana University, M.A., Indiana, 1963-1964
Career: Instructor, Grand Rapids Junior College, Grand Rapids, Michigan, 1964—

Writings: *Battling for Baby* CBS Telefilm, Movie of Week) 1992. *The Secret Life of Archie's Wife* CBS Movie of Week 1991. *Indiscreet* CBS Movie of Week 1988. *Finnegan, Begin Again* HBO Film 1985. *Jones Unbound* Prentice-Hall 1973. Work in Progress: Feature film script

Awards or inclusion in other biographical books: *Finnegan, Begin Again*, winner of Locarno Film Festival. Ace Award nomination, writing original script
What is the aim or goal of your writing? "To entertain and occasionally edify."
May inquiries be sent to you about doing workshops, readings? No

LODGE, JOHN CHRISTIAN (1862-1950)
Born: August 12, 1862; Detroit, Michigan
Parents: Edwin Lodge, Christina (Hanson) Lodge
Education: Detroit schools
Career: Reporter, editor, *Detroit Free Press*. Chief clerk, Wayne County Board of Auditors. Employed by Dwight Lumber Company, Chandler Radiator Company. Won senatorial race in his district, 1907. Alderman, first president of the nine-man council of Detroit. Mayor of Detroit, 1927

Writings: *I Remember Detroit* (with Milo Quaife) Wayne State University Press 1949
Awards or inclusion in other biographical books: *Michigan Authors,* 1st ed., 2nd ed.; *National Cyclopaedia of American Biography; Who Was Who in American.* Detroit freeway bears his name

LOOMIS, FRANCES (1896-1981)
Born: March 26, 1896; Lansing, Michigan
Parents: Carrie Loomis
Education: University of Michigan, Library Methods, Ann Arbor, Michigan, 1915
Career: Reference Assistant, Michigan State Library, 1915-1919. Reference Department, Detroit Public Library, 1919-1927; First Assistant, 1929-1949; Rare Books, 1949-1951. Circulation Librarian, U.S. Department of Labor, Washington, DC, 1951-1954. Catalog Librarian, U.S. Bureau of the Budget, Washington DC, 1954-1964

Writings: *Michigan Biography Index* (10 vols.) Detroit Public Library 1958. *The Executive Office Building, Originally the State, War and Navy Building* 1961. Contributed to professional and other periodicals
Awards or inclusion in other biographical books: *Who's Who in Library Service*

LOVE, EDMUND G. (1912-1990)
Born: February 14, 1912; Flushing, Michigan
Parents: Earl D. Love, Muda (Perry) Love
Children: Shannon, Nicholas
Education: University of Michigan, Ann Arbor, Michigan, A.B., 1936; M.A., 1940
Career: Teacher, Flint, Michigan, 1935-1942. Served in U.S. Army, 1942-1946. Historical Division, War Department, Washington, DC, 1946-1949. Columnist, *Flint Journal,* beginning 1979

Writings: *The 27th Infantry Division in World War II* Infantry Journal Press 1949. *The Hourglass: A History of the 7th Infantry Division in World War II* Infantry Journal Press 1950. *Seizure of the Gilberts and Marshals* (with Philip A. Crowl) Office of the Chief of Military History U.S. Department of the Army 1955. *Subways Are for Sleeping* Harcourt 1957. *War is a Private Affair* Harcourt 1959. *The Situation in Flushing* (autobiography) Harper 1965; Wayne State University Press 1987. *A Shipment of Tarts* Doubleday 1967. *Hanging On; Or, How to Get Through a Depression and Enjoy Life* (autobiography) Morrow 1972; Wayne State University Press 1987. *A Small Bequest* Doubleday 1973;

Wayne State University 1987. *Set Up* Doubleday 1980. Film script, articles, stories
Awards or inclusion in other biographical books: *American Authors and Books; Contemporary Authors; Science Fiction and Fantasy Literature*

LOWE, BERENICE JONES (1896-1983)

Pseudonym: Berenice Bryant Lowe
Born: October 26, 1896; Flint, Michigan
Parents: Ralston S. Jones, Jennie Adell (Pierce) Jones
Children: Marjorie, Stewart, Sharon
Education: Hope College, Holland, Michigan, 1914-1917. University of Michigan, A.B., Ann Arbor, Michigan, 1918; M.A., 1927
Career: Teacher, Keene Normal School, Keene, New Hampshire. Came to Battle Creek High School to teach drama, speech, 1919. Married, 1921, moved to Wisconsin, then moved to Ann Arbor, Michigan, became a teaching assistant, University of Michigan. Began studying local history, 1951, donating material to the local Willard Library, University of Michigan, others. Served on Calhoun County Historical Commission, planning committees for Battle Creek's centennial, sesquicentennial celebrations. Trustee, Michigan Historical Society. Newsletter editor, Battle Creek Historical Society. State Fellowship Chairman, American Association of University Women, and the Calhoun County Medical Society Auxiliary. Speaker, play director, promoter of Kimball House Museum

Writings: *Hello, Michigan* L. W. Singer 1939. *Everyday Play in French and English* Banks Upshaw 1960. *Pioneers of Forest and City* Michigan Historical Commission 1985. *Tales of Battle Creek* Albert L. and Louise B. Miller Foundation 1976; she read the book onto cassette tapes for the Regional Library of the Blind and Physically Handicapped in Detroit. *Battle Creek Events By Years* Willard Public Library 1990. Co-author *Battle Creek 150 Sesquincentennial 1831-1991* Embossing Printers 1980. *Sojourner Truth* 1964. Began "Looking Back" column on area history for *Battle Creek Enquirer.* Articles in *Michigan History,* history journals, geneaological magazines
Awards or inclusion in other biographical books: *Michigan Authors,* 1st ed., 2nd ed. Awards: American Association for State and Local History, Historical Society of Michigan, National Organization for Women, Daughters of the American Revolution, Battle Creek Negro Business & Professional Women's Association, Willard Library, Battle Creek Historical Society, *Battle Creek Enquirer*
In the 2nd edition of *Michigan Authors* she is credited with: "In 1951 I decided to 'rock myself into old age,' reading. The first subject to which I was attracted was the lake on whose bank I lived. Inasmuch as I was unable to find easily obtainable material, and felt that much was surely available, I began a search for it. Local history became an obsession and I have indulged in what was dubbed 'attic archeology' every since. Talks and writing have pretty much been along that line these 25+ years. Sojourner Truth, Black 18th century reformer, lived here. Many legends had been accepted about her life that needed clarification, so that delving into her truth also became a pet subject. My findings are in Michigan Historical Collections, U. of M., and on microfilm. Augmented local history is at Willard Library, Battle Creek, Michigan State Library and elsewhere. My collecting philosophy has been not to buy or sell but to beg and give away. This policy strictly adhered to, has greatly contributed to any success I may have had."

LOWE, KENNETH S.

Address: 1037 Blanchette Drive, East Lansing, Michigan 48823
Born: July 18, 1921; St. Paul, Minnesota
Parents: Malcolm Lowe, Irma A. (Henderson) Lowe
Children: Scott, Stuart
Education: University of Michigan, B.A., Ann Arbor, Michigan, 1945-1948
Career: Editor, *Michigan Out-of-Doors* magazine, Lansing, Michigan, 1975—. Various government and private public relations positions, Marquette, Michigan, 1972-1975. Editor, *Daily Mining Journal*, Marquette, Michigan, 1955-1972; Associate Editor, 1952-1955; Telegraph Editor, 1948-1952

Writings: *Michigan Out-of-Doors: An Almanac in Pictures, Prose, and Poetry* (editor) Michigan United Conservation Clubs 1991
Awards or inclusion in other biographical books: *Who's Who in the Midwest.* Award of Merit, Michigan United Conservation Clubs, 1958. Citation, Michigan Outdoor Writers Association, 1952. Special Conservation Award, Michigan United Conservation Clubs, 1987
What is the aim or goal of your writing? "To inform the public about outdoor recreation, conservation, and environmental issues."
May inquiries be sent to you about doing workshops, readings? No

LUGTHART, DOUGLAS W.

Address: 1318 Maude N.E., Grand Rapids, Michigan 49505
Pseudonym: L. Warren Douglas
Born: November 3, 1943; Grand Rapids, Michigan
Parents: Cornell W. Lugthart, Mabel T. Lugthart
Education: The Leelanau School, Diploma, Glen Arbor, Michigan, 1959-1962. Grand Valley State University, B.A., Allendale, Michigan, 1965-1967. Kalamazoo College, 1962-1965. Michigan State University, graduate school,1970-1972
Career: Carpenter, self-employed. Draftsman, designer, artist, woodcarver, archaeologist, assistant professor, stevedore

Writings: *A Plague of Change* Random House 1992, "Del Rey Discoveries" Series. Work in Progress: Sequel to above, working title *Cannon's Crucible. Bright Islands in a Dark Sea*
What is the aim or goal of your writing? "First, of course, to entertain my readers. If they finish my stories with a greater insight into the human condition than they had before, I'll be well-pleased. My stories illustrate, through the magnifying-glass of science fiction, the biochemical, behavioral and evolutionary nature of mankind, womankind and all the rest of us."
May inquiries be sent to you about doing workshops, readings? Yes

LUND, HARRY C.

Address: 1440 Wayne Street, Traverse City, Michigan 49684
Born: December 14, 1914; Muskegon, Michigan
Parents: Oscar A. Lund, Rosa R. Lund
Children: Patricia, David
Education: Muskegon Junior College, B.S., Muskegon, Michigan, 1932-1933. Michigan State University, B.S., East Lansing, Michigan, 1933-1936
Career: Retired, Traverse City, Michigan, 1972—. County Extension Director, Coopera-

tive Extension Service, Midland, Michigan, 1951-1972. Soil Conservationist, Soil Conservation Service, Leelanau County, Midland County, 1943-1951. Forester, Forest Service, Region 4, United States Forest Service, 1937-1943

Writings: *Michigan Wildflowers in Color* A & M Publishing 1992, 1991; self-published 1988, 1985. *Wildflowers of Sleeping Bear* self-published 1978. Work in Progress: *Michigan Wildflower Trails*

What is the aim or goal of your writing? "To encourage a better understanding and appreciation of one of our natural resources, wildflowers, by presenting information in terms understandable to the general public."

May inquiries be sent to you about doing workshops, readings? "The spirit is willing but the flesh may be weak"

LUOTO, M. ETHEL
Address: 200 W. Edgewood Blvd., Apt. 210, Lansing, Michigan 48911
Born: August 8, 1920; Republic, Michigan
Parents: Isaac F. Maki, Hilma (Pietila) Maki
Children: Ethel, Carol, Dorothy
Education: Luther L. Wright High School, Ironwood Michigan, 4 years. Gogebic Community College, Ironwood, Michigan, 1938-1940. Michigan State University, B.A., East Lansing, Michigan, 1956-1959. Western Michigan University, State Certification, 1963-1966. University of Michigan, Ann Arbor, Michigan, Summer of 1973
Career: Tutor, Grace Lutheran Church, Lansing, Michigan. Volunteer Work, 1987-1989. Writer of Michigan and poetry, 1986-1989. Teacher, librarian, Williamston Community Schools, Williamston, Michigan, 1963-1980, retired. Substitute Teacher, Lansing Public Schools, Lansing, Michigan, 1961-1963. Teacher, librarian, Haslett High School, Haslett, Michigan, 1960-1961. Teacher, Leslie High School, 1959-1960

Writings: *Cedarville Saga I* self-published 1990. *Cedarville Saga II* self-published 1990. Work in Progress: Poetry
Awards or inclusion in other biographical books: Invited to be a member in an exclusive 1500 membership International Poetry Association, 1992. Many writings included in the Koret Living Library, San Francisco, California
What is the aim or goal of your writing? "My Michigan writings stress wildlife, waterfront activity and out of doors. Poetry subjects are outdoors and children and family life."
May inquiries be sent to you about doing workshops, readings? Yes

LUTES, DELLA THOMPSON (1869?-1942)
Born: 1869?; Jackson, Michigan
Parents: Elijah Bonnett Thompson, Almira Frances (Bogardus) Thompson
Children: Ralph, Robert
Career: District Teacher, and in Detroit Public Schools. Editor *American Motherhood Magazine,* 1912-1928. Managing editor *Table Talk,* 1917. Editor, *Today's Housewife* 1919. Housekeeping editor, *Modern Priscilla* 1923-1930

Writings: *Just Away* Scott & Parshall 1906. *My Boy in Khaki* Harper 1918. *Table Setting and Service* M. Barrows 1928, 1934. *The Country Kitchen* Little, Brown 1936. *Home Grown* Little, Brown 1937. *Millbrook* Little Brown 1938. *Gabriel's Search* Little, Brown 1940. *The Country Schoolma'am* Little, Brown 1941. *Cousin William* Little, Brown 1942. Contributor to *Atlantic Monthly*, others

Awards or inclusion in other biographical books: *American Authors and Books; American Literary Yearbook; Childhood in Poetry; Current Biography; Dictionary of North American Authors; Index to Women; Michigan Authors,* 1st ed., 2nd ed.; *Who Was Who in America; Who Was Who in North America.* American Booksellers Association, Most Original Book of the Year, 1936

M

MACARO, CATHERINE A.

Address: 4130 St. Anthony Road, Temperance, Michigan 48182
Born: May 16, 1939; Toledo, Ohio
Parents: Chester D. Katafiasz, Leona A. Katafiasz
Children: Anthony, Mary Jo
Education: Siena Heights College, Adrian, Michigan, 1957-1958. University of Toledo, B.A., Toledo, Ohio, 1958-1962
Career: Graphic Artist, Monroe County Library System, Monroe, Michigan, 1988—. Trustee (Chairperson) Bedford Township Library Advisory Board, Temperance, Michigan, 1978-1988. Author/Illustrator, Self-employed, Temperance, Michigan, 1977—. Teacher, St. Luke's School, Lakewood, Ohio, 1964-1969. Teacher, Gary, Indiana, 1961-1964. Cataloging: printing, displays, Toledo Public Library, 1953-1963

Writings: *Santa's Magic Key* (illustrator) Monroe County Library System 1990. *Christmas in Germany* Artic Circle 1992. *Germany: A Book to Color* Artic Circle 1992. *Scotland: A Book to Color* Artic Circle 1989. *Iceland: A Book to Color* Artic Circle 1986. *Christmas in Scandinavia* Artic Circle 1985. *Finland: A Book to Color* Artic Circle 1980. *A Polish-American Book to Color* Artic Circle 1978. *Poland: A Book to Color* Artic Circle 1977, others. Work in Progress: Illustration
What is the aim or goal of your writing? "I try to put things in an interesting format for children and adults. Even though my titles are called coloring books, they all contain information on the geography, history, famous people, customs, costumes and present day life in each country. Each book contains a family tree as well as space for individual research. Each also lists an extensive bibliography. The books have been designed as communication tools to promote ethnicity."
May inquiries be sent to you about doing workshops, readings? Yes

MACULEY, ROBIE M.
Address: P.O. Box 792, South Wellfleet, Massachusetts 02663
Born: May 31, 1919; Grand Rapids, Michigan
Parents: George W. Macauley, Emma A. Macauley
Children: Cameron
Education: South High, Grand Rapids, Grand Rapids, Michigan 1932-1936. Kenyon College, A.B., Gambier, Ohio, 1939-1941. University of Iowa, M.F.A., Iowa City, Iowa, 1947-1950
Career: Editor, *The Kenyon Review*, Kenyon College, Gambier, Ohio, 1959-1966. Fiction Editor, *Playboy*, Chicago, Illinois, 1966-1978. Executive Editor, Houghton Mifflin, Boston, Massachusetts, 1978-1989. Co-Director, Ploughshares International Writing Seminar, Castle Well, The Netherlands, 1990—

Writings: *The Seven Basic Quarrels of Marriage* (with Dr. William Betcher) Villard/Random House 1990. *A Secret History of Time to Come* Alfred A. Knopf 1978. *Technique in Fiction* Harper/revision, St. Martin's Press 1964, 1989. *The End of Pity* McDowell, Obolensky 1957. *The Disguises of Love* Random House 1952. Stories, articles in *Esquire, Cosmopolitan, Playboy, New York Times Book Review, Virginia Quarterly Review, Kenyon Review, Fiction, North American Review, Partisan Review, Southern Review*, others. Work in Progress: A collection of short stories
Awards or inclusion in other biographical books: Benjamin Franklin Award for Fiction, 1950. Massachusetts Arts Council Award for Fiction, 1989. John Train Humor Award, 1991
What is the aim or goal of your writing? "To entertain and edify."
May inquiries be sent to you about doing workshops, readings? No

MADGETT, NAOMI LONG
Address: 16886 Inverness Street, Detroit, Michigan 48221
Born: July 5, 1923; Norfolk, Virginia
Parents: Clarence M. Long, Maude S. (Hilton) Long
Children: Jill
Education: International Institute for Advanced Studies, Greenwich University, Clayton, Missouri, Hilo, Hawaii, Ph.D., 1975-1980. Wayne State University, M.Ed., Detroit, Michigan, 1954-1955. Virginia State University, B.A., Petersburg, Virginia, 1941-1944
Career: Editor, Lotus Press, Inc., Detroit, Michigan, 1972—. Professor Emerita, Eastern Michigan University, Ypsilanti, Michigan, 1984—. Professor, Eastern Michigan University, Ypsilanti, Michigan, 1973-1984; Associate Professor, 1968-1973. Teacher, Detroit Public Schools, Detroit, Michigan, 1955-1965, 1966-1968. Research Associate, Oakland University, Rochester, Michigan, 1965-1966. Recording of poetry for the National Archives, Library of Congress, Washington DC, 1978. Numerous readings, residencies, writers' workshops, locally and nationally. Creative-Writers-in-the Schools Program, Michigan Council for the Arts, from its inception to 1990. Judge in various literary competitions, including grants for state arts councils. Several poems set to music and three publicly performed

Writings: *Octavia and Other Poems* (required reading in Detroit Public Schools-eleventh grade)Third World 1988. *Phantom Nightingale*: *Juvenilia* Lotus 1981. *Exits and Entrances* Lotus 1978. *Pink Ladies in the Afternoon* Lotus 1972, 1990. *Star by Star* Harlo 1965; Evenill 1970; Lotus 1972. *One and the Many* Exposition 1956. *Songs to a Phantom Nightingale* Fortuny 1941. Editor: *Adam of Ife: Black Women in Praise of Black*

Men Lotus 1992; *A Milestone Sampler: 15th Anniversary Anthology* Lotus 1988. *A Student's Guide to Creative Writing* Penway 1980. *Success in Language and Literature / B* (with Ethel Tincher, Henry B. Maloney) Follett 1967. Over a hundred poems included in anthologies, textbooks beginning with *The Poetry of the Negro 1746-1949* edited by Langston Hughes and Arna Bontemps Doubleday 1949; current as 1992. Translations into foreign languages. Published in such magazines and journals as *Callaloo, Essence, Michigan Quarterly Review, Sage, Obsidian*. Work in Progress: A revision and enlargement of *Octavia*. An autobiographical collection of essays

Awards or inclusion in other biographical books:*Black American Writers Past and Present* Vol. II, 1965; *Contemporary Authors; Dictionary of Literary Biography: Afro-American Writers, 1940-1955* Vol. 76, 1988; *Gathering Home: Black Virginia Writers* 1990; *Living Black American Authors* 1973; *Michigan Authors,* 2nd ed.; *Michigan Poets; Who's Who Among Black Americans; Who's Who in America; Who's Who of American Women*. Papers on deposit, Special Collections Library, Fisk University, Nashville, Tennessee. First book of poetry to be designated required reading in Detroit Public Schools. Honorary Doctor of Humane Letters degree, Siena Heights College, 1991. Arts Foundation of Michigan Award (Literature),1990. "In Her Lifetime" Tribute, Afrikan Poetry Theatre, 1989. Creative Achievement Award, College Language Association, 1988. Creative Artist Award, Michigan Council for the Arts, 1987. Robert Hayden Runagate Award, Your Heritage House Writers Series, 1985. Arts Achievement Award, Wayne State University, 1985. Testimonial Resolutions, Detroit City Council, 1982, 1985. Testimonial Resolutions, Michigan State Legislature, 1982, 1984. Citation, National Coalition of 100 Black Women, 1984. Citation, Black Caucus, National Council of Teachers of English, 1984. Induction as honorary member, Stylus Society, Howard University, 1984. Citations, Alpha Kappa Alpha Sorority, Alpha Rho Omega Chapter, 1969, 1984. Citation, Afro-American Museum of Detroit, 1983. Citation, Chesapeake/ Virginia Beach Links, Inc., 1981. Inaugural poem, commissioned by the wife of the governor of Michigan and read at the public ceremony at the State Capitol, January 1, 1975. Josephine Nevins Keal Award, Eastern Michigan University, 1965. Esther R. Beer Memorial Award, National Writers Club, 1957

What is the aim or goal of your writing?"To interpret life as honestly as I can through experience (real, borrowed, or imagined) with the hope that others' experience might be enlightened or broadened by what I write."

May inquiries be sent to you about doing workshops, readings? Yes

MAGNAGHI, RUSSELL M.

Address: 215 E. Michigan St., Marquette, Michigan 49855
Born: October 12, 1943; San Francisco, California
Parents: Mario V. Magnaghi, Grace H. (Mendiara) Magnaghi
Children: Emily
Education: University of San Francisco, B.A., 1961-1965. St. Louis University, Missouri; M.A., 1967; Ph.D., 1970
Career: Professor of History, Northern Michigan University, Marquette, Michigan, 1969—

Writings: *Huron, Ottawa and French Settlement at St.Ignace, Michigan 1670-1715* St.Ignace Downtown Development Authority 1989. *Miners, Merchants and Midwives: Michigan's Upper Peninsula Italians* Belle Fontaine Press 1987. *Immigrants in Marquette County: 1910 Federal Census* Belle Fontaine Press 1984. *A Guide to the Indians*

of Michigan's Upper Peninsula Belle Fontaine Press 1984. *The Way it Happened: Settling Michigan's Upper Peninsula* Mid-Peninsula Library Cooperative 1982
What is the aim or goal of your writing? "To research and write historically accurate histories of little known aspects of Upper Peninsula history."
May inquiries be sent to you about doing workshops, readings? Yes

MAIER, PAUL L.

Address: 8383 West Main Street, Kalamazoo, Michigan 49009
Born: May 31, 1930; St. Louis, Missouri
Parents: Walter A. Maier, Hulda A. (Eickhoff) Maier
Children: Laura, Julie, Krista, Katie
Education: Harvard University, M.A., Cambridge, Massachusetts. Concordia Seminary, St. Louis, 1955. Fulbright Scholarship, post-graduate studies at Universities of Heidelberg, Germany, Basel, Switzerland. University of Basel, Switzerland, Ph.D., summa cum laude, (first American to receive highest honors)
Career: Professor of History, Western Michigan University, Kalamazoo, Michigan, 1959—. Campus Chaplain to Lutheran students, 1958—

Writings: *In the Fullness of Time* Harpers 1991. *Josephus-The Essential Writings* (ed.) Kregel 1988. *Josephus, The Jewish War* (editor) Zondervan 1982. *The Flames of Rome* Doubleday 1981. *First Christians* Harper & Row, 1976. *First Easter* Harper & Row 1973. *First Christmas* Harper & Row 1971. *Pontius Pilate* Doubleday 1968. *A Man Spoke, A World Listened-The Story of Walter A. Maier* McGraw-Hill 1963. *The Best of Walter A. Maier* (ed.) Concordia 1980. Over 200 articles in professional and general journals. Work in Progress: *A Skeleton in God's Closet*
Awards or inclusion in other biographical books: *American Authors Today; Contemporary Authors; Dictionary of International Biography; International Authors and Writers Who's Who; International Scholars Directory; International Who's Who of Contemporary Achievement; Men and Women of Distinction; Men of Achievement; Outstanding Educators of America; The Writers Directory; Who's Who in America; Who's Who in Education; Who's Who in the Midwest; The World Who's Who of Authors; Who's Who in Religion.* Gold Medallion Book Award, Evangelical Christian Publishers Association, 1989. Award Citation, The Michigan Academy of Science, Arts, and Letters, 1985. Professor of the Year Citation, Council for the Advancement and Support of Education, Washington, DC, 1984. Distinguished Faculty Scholar Award, Western Michigan University, 1981. Teaching Excellence Award, Western Michigan University, 1974
What is the aim or goal of your writing? "I am interested in relating the New Testament world to contemporary interests and readership. First-century Roman history is a specialty of mine, and I try to convey that era via fact and fiction."
May inquiries be sent to you about doing workshops, readings? Yes

MAINONE, ROBERT F.

Address: 7431 Pine Lake Road, Delton, Michigan 49046
Born: February 11, 1929; Flint, Michigan
Parents: Robert H. Mainone, Nell C. (Phillips) Mainone
Education: Ravenna High School, Ravenna, Michigan. Michigan State University, B.S., B.S.F., East Lansing, 1947-1952; M.S., 1957-1959
Career: Interpretive Ecologist, Michigan State University's Kellogg Biological Station,

Bird Sanctuary, Hickory Corners, Michigan, 1967-1991, retired. Naturalist, Kalamazoo Nature Center, Kalamazoo, Michigan, 1961-1966. Junior Curator, Detroit Zoological Park, Detroit, Michigan, 1959-1960. Ranger-Naturalist, Rocky Mountains National Park, Estes Park, Colorado; Everglades National Park, Homestead, Florida, 1957, 1958 (seasonal). Weather observer, Utah, California, New York, Illinois, Greenland, U.S. Air Force, 1953-1956

Writings: *The Spring Within* self-published 1989. *The Journey North* self-published 1984. *Moonlight* self-published 1979. *High on the Wind* self-published 1976. *Young Leaves* self-published 1974. *Shadows* self-published 1971. *This Boundless Mist* self-published 1968. *Where Waves Were* self-published 1966. *Parnassus Flowers* self-published 1965. *An American Naturalist's Haiku* self-published 1964. Published in *Michigan Natural Resources Magazine.* Work in Progress: *Memoirs. Haiku Diary*

Awards or inclusion in other biographical books: *International Who's Who in Poetry,* 1970-1971; *Michigan Authors,* 2nd ed.; *Who's Who in the Midwest,* 1976-1981; *The Writer's Directory,* 1976-1978. Harold Henderson Award, Haiku Society of America, 1977, 1980. Japan Air Lines Haiku Contest Finalist (201 of 40,000 entries), 1988, exhibited in Japanese Pavilion, Brisbane Expo.

What is the aim or goal of your writing? "To write to celebrate the wonder of this microcosmos, earth; to rediscover an intrinsic native American spirit that still lives in unspoiled places; to remember thoughts and experiences of happy moments; while passing through the seasons of my life; to create something that pleases me, that is beautiful and lasting."

May inquiries be sent to you about doing workshops, readings? Yes

MAINPRIZE, DONALD C.

Address: 519 W. Higgins Lake Drive, Roscommon, Michigan 48653
Pseudonym: Richard Rock
Born: August 28, 1930; Coleman, Michigan
Parents: James R. Mainprize, Ople B. Mainprize
Children: Daniel, Debra, Susan, Edward
Education: University of Oklahoma, B.A., Norman, Oklahoma, 1960. Central Michigan University, M.A., Mt. Pleasant, Michigan, 1966-1968. Grand Rapids School of the Bible and Music, Grand Rapids, Michigan, Pastor's Diploma
Career: Teacher, Houghton Lake Schools, Houghton Lake, Michigan, 1965—. Editor, Scripture Press, Glen Ellyn, Illinois, 1960-1963. Pastor, First Presbyterian Church, Minco, Oklahoma, 1958-1960. Pastor, Dildine Community Church, Ionia, Michigan, 1953-1956

Writings: *Good Morning, Lord: Meditations for Teachers* 1974. *ABCs for Educators* J.W. Walch 1976. *Stars Stars Stars* 1977. *Stonesville, U.S.A.* 1977. *Christian Heroes of Today* Baker 1966. *Enjoy the Christian Life* Zondervan Key 1966, 1971. *Happy Anniversary* 1975. Poems or articles in *English Journal, Today's Catholic Teacher, Language Arts* and others. Fiction or articles in *Teen Power, Moody Monthly, These 'Times,* others. Work in Progress: *Meditations on Marriage. The Lavender Pit. Anatomy of Christian Joy*

Awards or inclusion in other biographical books: *Community Leaders of America* 1980; *Contemporary Authors; Dictionary of International Biography; International Authors and Writers Who's Who; International Who's Who in Poetry; Men of Achievement* 1975, 1976, 1977; *Michigan Authors,* 2nd ed.; *Notable Americans of the Bicentennial Era; Who's Who in the Midwest; The Writers' Directory*

What is the aim or goal of your writing? "My aim is to entertain the bored, instruct the uneducated, help lift the hopeless, bring joy to the depressed, shake up the apathetic and try to bring order into a nation in chaos."

May inquiries be sent to you about doing workshops, readings? Yes

MALLOCH, DOUGLAS (1877-1938)
Born: May 5, 1877; Muskegon, Michigan
Children: Dorothy, Jean
Education: Muskegon Public Schools
Career: Reporter, editorial staff of *Muskegon Chronicle* until 1903. Staff, editor, *American Lumberman.* President of Press Club of Chicago; Society of Midland Authors; American Press Humorists. Master of the Writers Guild of Chicago. After-Dinner Speaker

Writings: First poem, at the age of 10, published in *Detroit News. In Forest Land* American Lumberman 1906, 1910. *Resawed Fables* American Lumberman 1911. *The Woods* American Lumberman 1913. *The Enchanted Garden* 1915. *Tote-road and Trail, Ballads of the Lumberjack* Bobbs Merrill 1917. *Come on Home* American Lumberman 1923. *The Heart Content* 1926. *Be the Best of Whatever You Are* Scott Dowd 1926. *Little Hop-Skipper* George H. Doran 1926. *The Heart Content, "Lyrics of Life"* Reilly & Lee 1927. *Live Life Today ("Lyrics of Life")* Reilly & Lee 1938. Poems have appeared regularly in many national newspapers and in *Saturday Evening Post, Ladies' Home Journal, National Education Association Journal, Current Opinion*, others. Most famous work, "Michigan, My Michigan", was written in 1902 for the eighth annual convention of the Michigan State Federation of Women's Clubs meeting at Muskegon and became widely used as the Michigan state song
Awards or inclusion in other biographical books: *American Authors and Books; Childhood in Poetry; Dictionary of North American Authors; Michigan Authors,* 2nd ed.; *Michigan Poets; National Cyclopaedia of American Biography; Story and Verse for Children; Who Was Who in America; Who Was Who among North American Authors.* Honorary member of the Forty Club, a Michigan society of Chicago. In 1944, Muskegon dedicated the Douglas Malloch Memorial Forest on U.S. 31 to him. A room in the Muskegon County Museum contains his desk, workshop equipment and part of his library

MALONE, HENRY C.
Address: 23564 Rennselaer, Oak Park, Michigan 48237
Pseudonym: Hank Malone
Born: May 5, 1942; Detroit, Michigan
Parents: Charles J. Malone, Helen M. Malone
Children: Alex
Education: Wayne State University, B.A., Detroit, Michigan, 1960-1964; M.A., 1966-1968
Career: Clinical psychotherapist, Metrotag, PC, Livonia, Michigan, 1987—. Clinical director, Northwestern Guidance Clinic, 1984-1987. Administrative Director, Mental Health, City of Highland Park, Highland Park, Michigan, 1976-1983. Talk Radio Host, WRIF-FM Detroit, Southfield, Michigan, 1972-1976

Writings: *Oranges for Jean Harlow* Pearl Press 1988. *Survival, Evasion, Escape* La Jolla Poets Press 1985. *The Fashion Models and the Astronaut* Detroit River 1982. Three chapbooks-published 1976, 1979, 1981. Work in Progress: Pending publication, book of poetry, *Footstrikes and Spondees*

Awards or inclusion in other biographical books: National Endowments for the Arts Grant, 1967, 1976. American Academy of the Arts Grant, 1968. Inducted as member of Poetry Society of America, 1986; New England Poetry Club, 1987

What is the aim or goal of your writing? "Of course, the Great Mystery."

May inquiries be sent to you about doing workshops, readings? Yes

MANFRED, FREDERICK F.

Address: R.R. 3 Roundwind, Luverne, Minnesota 56156

Pseudonym: Feike Feikema (1944-1953)

Born: January 6, 1912; Doon, Iowa

Parents: Feike Feikes Feikema VI, Aalje (Alice) (Van Engen) Feikema

Children: Freya, Marya, Frederick Jr.

Education: Western Academy, Hull, Iowa, 1924-1928. Calvin College, B.A., Grand Rapids, Michigan, 1930-1934

Career: Reporter, Minneapolis *Journal,* 1937-1939. Interviewer, Minnesota Opinion Poll, St. Paul, 1939-1940. Tuberculosis sanitarium, 1940-1942. Writer, *Modern Medicine,* 1942-1943. Reporter, *East Side Argus,* 1943-1944. Writer-in-Residence, Macalester College, St. Paul, Minnesota, 1949-1952; University of South Dakota, Vermillion, 1968-1982. Chair, Regional Heritage, Augustana College, Sioux Falls, South Dakota, 1983–.

Writings: *The Golden Bowl* Webb 1944; Dobson (London) 1947. *Boy Almighty* Itasca Press 1945; Dobson (London) 1950. *This is the Year* Doubleday 1947. *The Primitive* Doubleday 1949. *The Giant* Doubleday 1951. *Lord Grizzly* McGraw Hill 1954; Corgi (London) 1957. *The Man Who Looked Like the Prince of Wales* Simon and Schuster 1965; as *The Secret Place* Pocket Books 1967. *King of Spades* Simon and Schuster 1966. *Of Lizards and Angels* University of Oklahoma Press 1992. *No Fun on Sunday* University of Oklahoma Press 1990. *Flowers of Desire* Dancing Badger Press 1989. *Winter Count II* Thueson 1987. Others. Short stories in *Fiction 8, Great River Review,* others

Awards or inclusion in other biographical books: *Contemporary Authors; Contemporary Novelists; Dictionary of Literary Biography.* Doctor of Letters, Honorary, Augustana College, Sioux Falls, South Dakota, 1977. Doctor of Humane Letters, Morningside College, Sioux City, Iowa, 1981. Doctor of Humane Letters, Buena Vista College, Storm Lake, Iowa, 1984. Rockefeller Fellowship, 1944, 1945. American Academy Grant, 1945. National Endowment for the Arts Grant, 1976, 1983. Others. Mr. Manfred comments: "Long ago, I 'gave' all my papers to the Manuscript Division, University Libraries, University of Minnesota, Minneapolis, 826 Berry Street in St. Paul. They literally have already tons of all manuscripts to date; and when I die they get the rest. Notes, drafts, proofs, galleys, books, diaries, journals, etc." He stated that *Of Lizards and Angels* "will solidify any reputation I might have" and it was "a book I aimed my whole life to write."

MARTIN, JOHN BARTLOW (1915-1987)

Born: August 4, 1915; Hamilton, Ohio

Parents: John W. Martin, Laura (Bartlow) Martin

Children: Cynthia, Daniel, John

Education: Arsenal Technical High School, Indianapolis, Indiana. De Pauw University, B.A., Greencastle, Indiana, 1937

Career: Military service, 1944-1946. Reporter, *Indianapolis Times.* Consultant, Special

Envoy, U.S. Ambassador, Dominican Republic, Caribbean Affairs, 1961-1965. Senior Fellow, Wesleyan University, 1964-1965. Visiting Fellow, Princeton University, 1966-1967. Other college positions including Professor, Northwestern University for 10 years. Staff member, Adlai Stevenson, 1952-1956, and for John F. Kennedy, Lyndon B. Johnson, Hubert H. Humphrey. Board of Directors, Chicago Institute for Psychoanalysis

Writings: *Call It North Country* Knopf 1944, 1987. *Indiana, an Interpretation* Knopf 1947; Arno 1972. *Butcher's Dozen* Harper 1950. *Break Down the Walls* Ballantine 1954. *Jimmy Hoffa's Hot* Dell 1959. *The Pane of Glass* Harper 1959. *Overtaken by Events* Doubleday 1966. *The Life of Adlai Stevenson* 2 Vols. Doubleday 1976-1977. *The Televising of Heller* Doubleday 1980. Others. In *Harper's, Saturday Evening Post, Redbook, True Detective, Reader's Digest*, others. In the foreword to the 2nd edition of *Call it North Country,* Martin relates that it was written in his twenties and that the caretaker at the camp where he went on his honeymoon to Michigamme, Michigan introduced him to people. He and his wife purchased land for Upper Peninsula summer home

Awards or inclusion in other biographical books: *American Authors and Books; Author's and Writer's Who's Who; Contemporary Authors; Current Biography; International Authors and Writers Who's Who; International Who's Who; Ohio Authors and Their Books; Political Profiles; Who's Who in America.* Sigma Delta Chi Magazine Award, 1950, 1957. Benjamin Franklin Magazine Award, 1954, 1956, 1957, 1958. Indiana Authors' Day Award, Indiana University Writers' Conference, 1967, Ohioana Book Award, 1967

MASON, PHILIP P.
Address: 500 River Place, Apt. 5401, Detroit, Michigan 48207
Born: April 28, 1927; Salem, Massachusetts
Parents: Homer P. Mason, Mildred A. (Trask) Mason
Children: Catherine, Jonathan, Susan, Christopher, Stephen
Education: University of Michigan, Ph.D., Ann Arbor, Michigan, 1951-1956; M.A., 1950-1951. Boston University, B.A., Boston, Massachusetts, 1960. Beverly High School, Beverly, Massachusetts, 1945
Career: Distinguished Professor of History, Wayne State University, Detroit, Michigan, 1958—. Founder and Director, Archives of Labor & Urban Affairs, Walter Reuther Library, Wayne State University, Detroit, Michigan, 1958—. Adjunct Professor of History, University of Windsor, Windsor, Ontario, Canada, 1986—. Distinguished Visiting Lecturer, University of Manitoba, Manitoba, Canada, 1984. Editor, Great Lakes Series, Wayne State University Press, 1986—. Editor, Henry R. Schoolcraft Series, Michigan State University Press, 1991—. Editorial Board Member, Wayne State University Press, 1985—. Editorial Board Member, *Labor History* periodical, 1977—. Board of Editors, *Michigan Historical Review,* 1974—. Numerous papers presented in Michigan and other states and Canada. Seminars and lectures presented at various universities

Writings: *Labor Archives in the United States* Wayne State University Press 1992. *Copper Country Journal* Wayne State University Press and Michigan Bureau of History 1990. *The Ambassador Bridge: A Monument to Progress* Wayne State University Press 1987. *Jewish Archival Institutions* Wayne State University Press 1975. *Prismatic of Detroit* Edwards Brothers 1970. *A History of American Roads* Rand McNally & Company 1967. *Harper of Detroit: the Origin and Growth of a Great Metropolitan Hospital* Wayne State University Press 1964. *After Tippecanoe: Some Aspects of the War of 1812* Michigan State University Press 1963. *Schoolcraft, The Literary Voyager or Muzzeniegun* Michigan State University Press 1962. *From Bull Run to Appomattox: Michigan's Role in the Civil War* Wayne State University Press 1962. *Schoolcraft's Expedition to Lake Itasca: The Discovery of the Source of the Mississippi* Michigan State University Press 1958. Articles in *Michigan History, Labor History, Archivum, The Michigan Connection, The Reference Librarian, The American Archivist* and others. Chapter in *American Issues: Understanding Who We Are.* Work in Progress: *History of Grace Hospital, Detroit, Michigan. Tracy McGregor and Philanthropy in Michigan. Henry R. Schoolcraft Papers. Early American Collectors*

Awards or inclusion in other biographical books: *Contemporary Authors; Dictionary of International Biographies; Directory of American Scholars; Directory of Special Libraries and Information Centers; International Who's Who in Education; Men of Achievement; Michigan Authors,* 1st ed., 2nd ed.; *Who's Who among Writers; Who's Who in the Midwest.* Distinguished Graduate Faculty Award, Wayne State University, 1985. Distinguished Faculty Award, Higher Education Awards Convocation, Michigan Association of Governing Boards, Lansing, Michigan, 1985. Patriotic Award, Detroit Historical Society, 1978. Fellow, The Society of American Archivists, 1970

May inquiries be sent to you about doing workshops, readings? No

MASSIE, LARRY B.

Address: 2109 41st Street, Allegan, Michigan 49010
Born: January 7, 1947; Grand Rapids, Michigan
Parents: Wallace B. Massie; Frieda J. (Miller) Massie
Children: Adam, Wallace, Larry II
Education: Western Michigan University, B.A., summa cum laude, Kalamazoo, Michigan, 1970-1972; M.A., with honor, 1973-1974; Specialist of Arts, 1977
Career: Freelance Michigan Historian, self-employed, Allegan, Michigan, 1983—. Assistant Director, Western Michigan University Archives, Kalamazoo, Michigan, 1978-1983. Regional History Specialist, City of Kalamazoo, Kalamazoo, Michigan, 1976-1978. Co-proprietor, Bicentennial Bookshop, Kalamazoo, Michigan, 1975-1976. United States Army paratrooper, 1964-1967. Paper mill worker, construction laborer, telephone lineman, pickle plant worker, bartender

Writings: *The Romance of Michigan's Past* Priscilla Press 1991. *Pig Boats and River Hogs* Priscilla Press 1990. *Walnut Pickles and Watermelon Cake* (with Priscilla Massie) Wayne State University Press 1990. *Copper Trails and Iron Rails* Avery Color Press 1989. *Warm Friends and Wooden Shoes: History of the Holland Area* Windsor Publications 1988. *Voyages into Michigan's Past* Avery Color Press 1988. *From Frontier Folk to Factory Smoke* Avery Color Press 1987. *Battle Creek: The Place Behind the Product* (with Peter Schmitt) Windsor 1984. *Kalamazoo: The Place Behind the Product* (with Peter Schmitt) Windsor 1981. Work in Progress: *Guardian of the Great Lakes Graveyard: The Heritage of Whitefish Point. The Romance of Michigan's Past* Vol. II

What is the aim or goal of your writing?: "To celebrate the heritage of Michigan, to make others aware of the amazing stories about Michigan's history that I discover in my research, to spread the gospel that Michigan history is fun."

May inquiries be sent to you about doing workshops, readings? Yes

MAY, GEORGE S.

Born: November 17, 1924; Ironwood, Michigan
Parents: Eslie W. May, Louise (Smith) May
Children: Sally
Education: Gogebic Community College, Ironwood, Michigan, 1943-1944. Michigan Technological University, Houghton, Michigan, 1944. University of Michigan, A.B., Ann Arbor, Michigan, 1947; A.M., 1948; Ph.D., 1954
Career: Instructor, Allegheny College, Meadville, Pennsylvania, 1948-1950. Research Associate, State Historical Society of Iowa, Iowa City, Iowa, 1954-1956. Historic sites specialist, Michigan Historical Commission, Lansing, Michigan, 1956-1958; Research Archivist, Editor, 1958-1966. Associate Professor, Eastern Michigan University, Ypsilanti, Michigan, 1966-1968; Professor, beginning in 1968. Editor, *Michigan History*, 1965-1966

Writings: *James Strang's Ancient and Modern Michilimackinac, Including an Account of the Controversy Between Mackinac and the Mormons* (editor) W.S. Woodfill 1959. *Michigan Civil War History: An Annotated Bibliography* (editor) Wayne State University Press 1961. *Michigan and the Civil War Years, 1860-1866* Michigan Civil War Centennial Commission 1964. *Let Their Memories be Cherished: Michigan Civil War Monuments* Michigan Civil War Centennial Commission 1965. *Pictorial History of Michigan: The Early Years* Eerdmans 1967. *Pictorial History of Michigan: The Later Years* Eerdmans 1969. *A Michigan Reader: 11,000 B.C. to A.D. 1865* (with Herbert Brinks) Eerdmans 1974. *A Most Unique Machine: The Michigan Origins of the American Automobile Industry* Eerdmans 1975. *R.E. Olds: Auto Industry Pioneer* Eerdmans 1977. *Michigan: An Illustrated History of the Great Lakes State* Windsor Publications 1987. *The Automobile Industry* Facts on File 1990. Contributor, *Miscellananeous Problems* Michigan Constitutional Convention Preparatory Commission 1961. Pamphlets for Michigan Historical Commission, Mackinac Island State Park Commission. In *New Leader, Michigan State Bar Journal, Michigan Christian Advocate,* others
Awards or inclusion in other biographical books: *Contemporary Authors; Directory of American Scholars; Michigan Authors,* 2nd ed.; *Who's Who in the Midwest.* Award, American Association of State and Local History, 1970

MAZZARO, JEROME

Address: 147 Capen Blvd., Buffalo, New York 14226
Born: November 25, 1934; Detroit, Michigan
Parents: Emmacolato Mazzaro, Maria Carmela (Pedalino) Mazzaro
Education: Wayne State University, Detroit, Michigan, A.B., 1954; Ph.D., 1963. University of Iowa, M.A., Iowa City, Iowa, 1956
Career: Professor, State University of New York at Buffalo, Buffalo, New York, 1964 to date. Assistant Professor, State College at Cortland, Cortland, New York, 1962-1964. Instructor, University of Detroit, Detroit, Michigan, 1958-1961. Specifications/Procedures Writer, General Motors Corporation, Detroit, Michigan, 1955-1956

Writings: *Rubbings* Quiet Hills Farm 1985. *The Caves of Love* Jazz Press 1985. *The Figure of Dante* Princeton University Press 1981. *Postmodern American Poetry* University of Illinois Press 1980. *William Carlos Williams: The Later Poems* Cornell University Press 1973. *Profile of William Carlos Williams* (editor) Charles E. Merrill 1971. *Profile of Robert Lowell* (editor) Charles E. Merrill 1971. *Modern American Poetry* (editor) David McKay 1970. *Transformations in the Renaissance English Lyric* Cornell University

Press 1970. *Changing the Windows* Ohio University Press 1966. *The Poetic Themes of Robert Lowell* University of Michigan Press 1966. *Juvenal's Satires* University of Michigan Press 1965. Work in Progress: Manuscript of poems. Critical study, *Memory and Making*. Study of the sonnet. Study of Pirandello's dramas

Awards or inclusion in other biographical books: Guggenheim Fellowship, 1964. MLA Scholar's Library Selection, 1970

What is the aim or goal of your writing? "To define my (and the culture's) place in the history of culture and ideas."

May inquiries be sent to you about doing workshops, readings? Yes

McARTHUR-WEBERMAN, PATRICIA A.

Address: 25248 Hayes, Taylor, Michigan 48180

Born: December 17, 1946; Detroit, Michigan

Parents: Royal G. Polhamus, Geraldine Polhamus

Children: Patrick Marody, Michelle Marody, Brian Marody

Education: Allen Park High School, Michigan, 1972-1976. A.M.T.A. courses through Health Enrichment Satellites, Certified Massage Therapist, 1985-1987

Career: Health Works Center, A.M.T.A., Neuromuscular Therapy, Taylor, Michigan, 1984—. Creative writing instructor, writing conference speaker

Writings: Booklet, *What Dreams are Made Of* A.R.E. 1984. Nonfiction articles, magazine and newspaper publications. Work in Progress: *The Dreamer Awakens. Adrift in an Alien World*

What is the aim or goal of your writing? "To inspire hope, courage, patience in understanding one's place in the human condition & evolving into one's higher potential. To encourage belief and faith that every individual is unique, highly creative, and has a distinct purpose for life."

May inquiries be sent to you about doing workshops, readings? Yes

McCABE, JOHN

Address: P.O. Box 363, Mackinac Island, Michigan 49757

Born: November 14, 1920; Detroit, Michigan

Parents: Charles J. McCabe, Rosalie T. McCabe

Children: Linard, Deidre, Sean

Education: University of Detroit, Ph. B., Detroit, Michigan, 1943-1947. Fordham University, M.F.A., New York, New York, 1947-1948. The Shakespeare Institute, Ph.D., Stratford-upon-Avon, England, 1954

Career: Child actor, Jessie Bonstelle Stock Company, Detroit, Michigan, 1928-1931; and through other years across English-speaking world. Taught theatre, film, drama: Wayne State University, Detroit, Michigan; City College of New York, New York; Lake Superior State University, Sault Ste. Marie, Michigan; Interlochen Arts Academy, Interlochen, Michigan, Mackinac College, Mackinac Island, Michigan; Chairman, Department of Educational Theatre, New York University, New York, New York, 1948-1985. Lecturer

Writings: *Babe: The Life of Oliver Hardy* Citadel Press 1989. *The High* 38/39 Press 1989. *Grand Hotel: An American Institution* Unicorn Press 1987. *Charlie Chaplin* Doubleday 1978. *Proclaiming the Word* (with G.B. Harrison) Pueblo Press 1977. Ghostwriter of James Cagney's *Cagney by Cagney* 1976. *Laurel & Hardy: Their Films* E.P. Dutton 1975. *The Comedy World of Stan Laurel* Doubleday 1975. *George M. Cohan: The Man Who*

Owned Broadway Doubleday 1973. *Mr. Laurel and Mr. Hardy* Doubleday 1961. Work in Progress: *Player* (novel)
Awards or inclusion in other biographical books: *Who's Who in America*
What is the aim or goal of your writing? "To show humanity part of its face."
May inquiries be sent to you about doing workshops, readings? Yes

McCONNELL, DAVID B.

Address: 2231 Cambria Road, Hillsdale, Michigan 49242
Born: December 20, 1949; Hillsdale, Michigan
Parents: Robert P. McConnell, Stella M. McConnell　(wife: Janice)
Education: Hillsdale High School, 1968. Michigan State University, B.S., East Lansing, Michigan, 1968-1972; Second B.S., 1975-1976
Career: President, Hillsdale Educational Publishers, Hillsdale, Michigan, 1980—. Vice President and Editor, Hillsdale Educational Publishers, Hillsdale, Michigan, 1977-1980. Technical Assistant, Michigan State University, East Lansing, Michigan, 1974-1975. Assistant Editor, Hillsdale Educational Publishers, Hillsdale, Michigan, 1972-1974. Since 1983, Hillsdale Educational Publishers has co-sponsored the Ferris E. Lewis Award with the Historical Society of Michigan. This annual award is presented on Education Day during Michigan Week in May, alternating annually between teachers of grades K-6 and teachers of grades 7-12. Participated in the Norwich Archaeological Survey in 1976 while in England. Advisory Board member, Center for Teaching Michigan History, headquartered at the Historical Society of Michigan. Presentations on Michigan history for the Michigan Council for the Social Studies, elementary and secondary schools (sometimes with my wife), and before civic organizations.

Writings: *Explore Michigan A to Z* Hillsdale Educational Publishers 1993. *Forging the Peninsulas: Michigan is Made* Hillsdale Educational Publishers 1989. *Michigan Activity Masters* Hillsdale Educational Publishers 1985. *A Puzzle Book for Young Michiganians* Hillsdale Educational Publishers 1982. *Discover Michigan* Hillsdale Educational Publishers 1981. *A Little People's Beginning on Michigan* Hillsdale Educational Publishers 1980. Work in Progress: Several ideas under development
Awards or inclusion in other biographical books: Award of Merit from the Historical Society of Michigan for *Forging the Peninsulas*, 1990. Michigan Product of the Year, Greater Michigan Foundation, non-consumer division, for *Discover Michigan,* 1982
What is the aim or goal of your writing? "My goal is to blow a spark into the minds of young readers so their imaginations will glow with all the possibilities of Michigan's exciting history. It is my hope they will develop a lifelong interest in our state!"
May inquiries be sent to you about doing workshops, readings? Yes

McCORMICK, GARY E.

Address: 424 W. Ferry, Berrien Springs, Michigan 49103
Born: September 30, 1933; Dearborn, Michigan
Parents: Melvin C. McCormick, Florence M. McCormick
Children: Theresa, Gary, Berndette, Ann, Paul, Mary Jean (Wife: Jean M.)
Education: Sacred Heart High School, Dearborn, Michigan. University of Detroit, B.A., Detroit, Michigan, 1956-1960
Career: Advertising Representative, *The Herald-Palladium*, St. Joseph, Michigan, 1974—. Account Executive, F.J. Murray Company, Dearborn, Michigan, 1969-1973. Public Relations Executive, Ford Motor Company, 1960-1969

Writings: *One of the Many Roses* Gem Press 1991. Work in Progress: Book of Poetry, entered in competitions. Book of short stories
What is the aim or goal of your writing? "To satisfy my desire to write well and to please my readers."
May inquiries be sent to you about doing workshops, readings? Yes

McCORMICK, JAY
Born: October 1, 1919; Harbor Beach, Michigan
Parents: Jay Cooke McCormick, Alice Lucille (Ryan) McCormick
Children: Twin girls
Education: Detroit Public Schools. University of Michigan, B.A., Ann Arbor, Michigan, 1942
Career: Editor-in-Chief, *Perspectives,* Senior editor, *The Michigan Daily.* Staff, *Detroit News* until 1943. Instructor in creative writing, Wayne State University, Detroit, Michigan, beginning in 1944

Writings: *November Storm* Doubleday, Doran and Company 1943. *Night Shade* Doubleday 1948
Awards or inclusion in other biographical books: *American Authors and Books; American Novelists of Today; Current Biography.* Hopwood Awards, University of Michigan, 1938, 1940, 1941, 1942

McCOY, IOLA FULLER
Pseudonym: Iola Fuller
Born: January 25, 1906; Marcellus, Michigan
Parents: Henry Fuller, Clara (Reynolds) Fuller
Children: Paul Goodspeed
Education: University of Michigan, A.B., Ann Arbor, Michigan, 1935; A.M. in English, 1940; A.M.L.S., 1962
Career: Librarian, U.S. Indian School, Santa Fe, New Mexico. School Librarian, Dexter, Michigan. Ferris State College, associate professor of English, 1964-1969. Traveled a great deal researching for her historical novels

Writings: *The Loon Feather* Harcourt Brace 1940, and several later printings. *The Shining Trail* Duell, Sloan & Pearce 1943. *The Gilded Torch* Putnam 1957. *All the Golden Gifts* Putnam 1966
Awards or inclusion in other biographical books: *Contemporary Authors; Michigan Authors,* 1st ed., 2nd ed.; *Something about the Author.* Hopwood Award for Creative Writing, 1939. University of Michigan Distinguished Alumni Award, 1967

McCUNE, WILLIAM S.
Address: 1134 Charlevoix Avenue, Petoskey, Michigan 49770
Born: June 4, 1909; Petoskey, Michigan
Parents: William G. McCune, Helen S. (Allen) McCune
Children: Carol, Mary, Cynthia, Barbara
Education: Swarthmore College, B.A., Swarthmore, Pennsylvania, 1927-1931. Harvard Medical School, M.D., Boston, Massachusetts, 1931-1935
Career: Clinical Professor Surgery, George Washington University, Washington, DC, 1946-1976. Now retired

Writings: *Ammunition Train* self-published 1989. *A Doctor is Born* self-published 1987. *Blood Against the Moon: The Adventures of a Civil War Surgeon* self-published 1985
What is the aim or goal of your writing? "My own pleasure, and interest in the Civil War and medicine".
May inquiries be sent to you about doing workshops, readings? Yes

McGOVERN, MILNE J.
Address: 5279 Kimball Ave., SE, Grand Rapids, Michigan 49508
Born: December 29, 1911; Jerome, California
Parents: Michael J. McGovern, Elma W. (Allen) McGovern
Children: Sharon, Michael, Patricia
Education: Cadillac High School, Cadillac, Michigan, 1928
Career: Pay master, Mitchell Brothers Company, 1928-1932. Sales Department, Cummer-Diggins Company, Cadillac, Michigan, 1933-1935. Partner, Ensign & McGovern, Cadillac, Michigan, 1935-1940. Secretary, Wood Parts, Inc., Cadillac, Michigan, 1940-1944. Appraiser, City of Cadillac, Cadillac, Michigan, 1944-1945. Purchasing Agent, F.J. McCarthy, Inc., Cadillac, Michigan, 1945-1948. General Manager, Quinn-McGovern, Inc., Grand Rapids, Michigan, 1948-1979

Writings: *The Allegan & Southeastern Railroad* self-published 1992. *Cadillac & Northestern Railway* Michigan Railfan 1987. *Jennings & Northeastern Railway* Michigan Railfan 1988. *Cobbs & Mitchell, Inc.* self-published 1987. *Mitchell Brothers Company* self-published 1987. *Cadillac Chemical Company* self-published 1987. *Cummer Lumber Company* self-published 1988. *Blodgett, Cummer & Diggins* self-published 1988. *Literary Efforts of the Allen Kin* self-published 1986. Others. Work in Progress: R.G. Peters Salt & Lumber Company and Its Manistee & Luther Railway. *Thomas D. Stimson and His Big Rapids & Western Railway. Missaukee County Pictorial History*
What is the aim or goal of your writing? "I research for information pertaining to sawmill, logging and logging operations to satisfy my curiosity and record what I learn for the edification of my peers and posterity."

McGUANE, THOMAS F.
Address: P.O. Box 25, McLeod, Montana 59052
Born: December 21, 1939; Wyandotte, Michigan
Parents: Thomas F. McGuane, Alice T. McGuane
Children: Thomas, Maggie, Heather, Anne
Education: Michigan State University, B.A., East Lansing, Michigan, 1960-1962. Yale University, M.F.A., New Haven, Connecticut, 1962-1965

Writings: *Nothing But Blue Skies* Houghton Mifflin 1992. *Keep the Change* Houghton Mifflin 1989. *To Skin a Cat* Dutton 1986. *Something To Be Desired* Random House 1984. *Nobody's Angel* Random House 1981. *An Outside Chance* Farrar, Straus 1980. *Panama* Farrar, Straus 1978. *Ninety Two In the Shade* Farrar, Straus 1973. *The Bushwhacked Piano* Simon and Schuster 1971. *The Sporting Club* Simon and Schuster 1969
Awards or inclusion in other biographical books: Rosenthal Award, American Academy, 1972. Northwest Bookseller's Award, 1982. Montana Governor's Award, 1989
What is the aim or goal of your writing? "Pleasure, communication, a livelihood".
May inquiries be sent to you about doing workshops, readings? Yes

McGUIGAN, DOROTHY (GIES) (1914-1982)
Born: November 12, 1914; Ann Arbor, Michigan
Parents: Charles Gies, Jennie (Sturman) Gies
Children: Michael, Cathleen
Education: University of Michigan, A.B., cum laude, 1936 Columbia University, M.A., New York, New York, 1939. King's College, London, England, 1937-1938
Career: Sales promotion, Macmillan Publishing, 1938-1943. Feature writer, Jack Starr-Hunt News Agency, 1943-1944. Overseas staff, American Red Cross, 1944-1946. Feature writer, *Stars and Stripes,* Germany, 1946-1949. Instructor, University of Michigan, Ann Arbor, Michigan, 1955-1956. Editor, Program Director, University of Michigan Center for Continuing Education of Women, beginning 1970. Lecturer, University of Michigan. Conference leader. Primary organizer, University Press Services on Women and Culture and the University of Michigan Committee for Gender Research

Writings: *The Habsburgs* Doubleday 1966; also published in England, France and other countries. *A Dangerous Experiment: 100 Years of Women at the University of Michigan* University of Michigan 1970. *A Sampler of Women's Studies* (editor) University of Michigan 1973. *New Research on Women* University of Michigan 1974. *Metternich and the Duchess* Doubleday 1975; (Vienna) 1977. *New Research on Women and Sex Roles* University of Michigan 1976. *The Role of Women in Conflict and Peace* (editor) University of Michigan 1977. *Changing Family, Changing Workplace: New Research* University of Michigan 1980. At her death, she was completing *The Princesses of Courland*
Awards or inclusion in other biographical books: *Contemporary Authors; Dictionary of International Biography; Notable Americans; Michigan Authors,* 2nd ed.; *Who's Who of American Women; World Who's Who of Women.* Hopwood Awards in creative writing, fiction, essay, poetry, 1933, 1934, 1935, 1936. Citation for Distinguished Service, University of Michigan Board of Regents, 1975. International Women's Year Citation, 1975

McKENNY, CHARLES (1860-1933)
Born: September 5, 1860; Dimondale, Michigan
Parents: Albert McKenny, Angeline (Torry) McKenny
Children: Charles, Laurence, Marion
Education: Michigan Agricultural College, B.S., East Lansing, 1881. Olivet College, A.B., Olivet, Michigan, 1889; A.M., 1892; LL. D., 1912. University of Wisconsin, A.M., 1904. Miami University, D. Ed., 1928
Career: Instructor, Olivet Academy, 1889-1895. Professor, Olivet College, 1895-1896. Principal, State Normal School, Mt. Pleasant, Michigan, 1896-1900. President, State Normal College, Ypsilanti, Michigan, beginning 1912. Editor, *American Schoolmaster.* Associate Editor, *Michigan Education Journal.* Lecturer

Writings: *The Personality of the Teacher* Row, Peterson 1910. *The Cycle of the Year, Fugitive Poems* 1934
Awards or inclusion in other biographical books: *Who Was Who among North American Authors; Who Was Who in America*

McMILLAN, TERRY
Born: 1951; Port Huron, Michigan
Children: Solomon
Education: Los Angeles City College, University of California-Berkeley, Columbia University, New York. Harlem Writers Guild

Career: Shelved library books as a teenager. Word processor. Teacher, University of Arizona, Tucson, Arizona

Writings: *Breaking Ice: An Anthology of Contemporary African-American Fiction* Viking 1990. *Disappearing Acts* Viking 1989; Cape 1990; Washington Square Press 1990; In Our Time Arts Media 1992. *Five for Five: the Films of Spike Lee* Stewart, Tabori & Chang (Workman distributor in U.S.) 1991. *Mama* Washington Square Press 1987; Houghton Mifflin 1987; Cape 1987; Pocket Books 1987; Black Swan 1991. *Songs for the Feast* World Library Publications 1978. *Terry McMillan* The Replay Company (spoken recording) 1989. *Waiting to Exhale* Viking 1992; Penguin-Highbridge Audio 1992

Awards or inclusion in other biographical books: Fellow, Yaddo and MacDowell Colony. Grants: PEN American Center, Authors League, Carnegie Fund, New York Foundation for the Arts, National Endowment for the Arts

McMULLEN, RICHARD E.

Address: 128 Marvin Street, Milan, Michigan 48160
Born: March 30, 1926; Ypsilanti, Michigan
Parents: Louis C. McMullen, Myrtle M. McMullen
Children: Christina, Louis, Julie
Education: Alma College, B.A., Alma, Michigan, 1953-1956. University of Michigan, M.A., Ann Arbor, Michigan, 1961
Career: Foundry worker, janitor, payroll clerk, newspaper reporter. Teacher, Fenton Public Schools, Fenton, Michigan, 1956-1960. English Teacher/Creative Writing, Ann Arbor Public Schools, Ann Arbor, Michigan, 1960-1988; retired

Writings: *Trying to Get Out* Crowfoot Press 1981. *Chicken Beacon* Street Fiction Press 1975. Work in Progress: Over 200 poems in over 100 newspapers, periodicals and anthologies such as *California Quarterly, Christian Science Monitor, Commonweal, Epoch, Massachusetts Review, New York Times, Southern Poetry Review, The Hollins Critic*

Awards or inclusion in other biographical books: *Directory of American Poets and Fiction Writers*

What is the aim or goal of your writing? "To explore and perhaps, understand my experiences. To share my experiences with the reader or listener. To, perhaps, give pleasure, instruct in a special way, move intellectually or emotionally, and share mysteries."

May inquiries be sent to you about doing workshops, readings? Yes

McPHERSON, WILLIAM

Born: March 16, 1933; Sault Sainte Marie, Michigan
Parents: Harold A. McPherson, Ruth (Brubaker) McPherson
Children: Jane
Education: University of Michigan, Ann Arbor, Michigan, 1951-1955. Michigan State University, East Lansing, Michigan, 1956-1958. George Washington University, Washington, DC, 1960-1962
Career: Copyperson, *Washington Post,* 1958; Staff writer, editor, 1959-1966. Editor, William Morrow, 1966-1969. Editor, *Washington Post,* 1969-1972. Editor and other positions, *Book World,* 1972-1985. Faculty, American University, Washington, DC, 1971, 1975

Writings: *Testing the Current* Simon and Schuster 1984. *To the Sargasso Sea* Simon and Schuster 1987. Poetry, ghost writer, book reviews, articles, poems. In *Life, Esquire, New Republic* and others
Awards or inclusion in other biographical books: *Contemporary Authors.* Pulitzer Prize for Distinguished Criticism, 1977

McWHIRTER, GLENNA S.
Address: 615 W. LaFayette, Detroit, Michigan 48226
Pseudonym: Nickie McWhirter
Born: June 28, 1929; Peoria, Illinois
Parents: Alfred L. Sotier, Lorene G. (Short) Sotier
Children: Suzanne, Charles, James
Education: Theodore Roosevelt High School, Wyandotte, Michigan, 1947. University of Michigan, B.A., Ann Arbor, Michigan, 1947-1951; graduate work
Career: Columnist, *Detroit News,* Detroit, Michigan, 1989—. Columnist, assorted writing/editing, *Detroit Free Press*, Detroit, Michigan, 1963-1989. Editorial Assistant, McGraw-Hill, Detroit, Michigan, 1951-1955. TV Writer, Campbell-Ewald, Detroit, Michigan, late 1960's

Writings: *Pea Soup* Detroit Free Press, (collection of previously published columns)
Awards or inclusion in other biographical books: *Who's Who in America,* 1986–. Michigan Associate Press (AP) top prize, columns 1981, 1978. Michigan United Press, International (UPI), top prize, columns, 1979. Detroit Press Club Foundation Gold Medallion, 1965; first place, opinion, 1978. WICI, Headliner, 1978
What is the aim or goal of your writing? "Clarity of thought, logic, reasoned persuasion couched in precise language and appealing metaphor. Good stuff."
May inquiries be sent to you about doing workshops, readings? No

MEEK, FORREST B.
Address: 2865 E. Rock Road, Clare, Michigan 48617
Born: June 11, 1928; Tustin, Michigan
Parents: Robert B. Meek, Electa G. Meek
Children: Sally, Thomas, Nancy, Charles
Education: Michigan State University, A.B., East Lansing, Michigan, 1950-1953. Central Michigan University, M.A., Mt. Pleasant, Michigan, 1964-1967. University of Georgia, Athens, Georgia, 1965-1966
Career: Wuhan University, Wuchang, Hubei Province, People's Republic of China, 1986-1987. President, Omega Research Group, Clare, Michigan, 1986—. Senior Researcher, White Pine Historical Society, Clare, Michigan, 1979—. Teacher, Clare Public Schools, Clare, Michigan, 1963-1986. Teacher, Kentwood Public Schools, Kentwood, Michigan, 1961-1963

Writings: *Michigan's Timber Battleground* Edgewood Press 1991. *Lumbering in Eastern Canada* White Pine Historical Society 1991. *The Steam Circular Sawmill* White Pine Historical Society 1989. *One Year in China* Edgewood Press 1988. *Michigan's Heartland* Edgewood Press 1979. *Saginaw Salt* White Pine Historical Society 1978. *Lumbering's Frauds & Thieves* 1990. *White Wings Over Lake Erie* 1987. *Public & Higher Education in China* 1987. Work in Progress: *Logging Railroads of Michigan. Making Lumber the Michigan Way. The Doherty Hotel*

Awards or inclusion in other biographical books: *Contemporary Authors,* 1978, Vol. 110; *Dictionary of International Biography,* 1986; *International Authors & Writer's Who Who,* 1985; *Michigan Authors,* 2nd ed.; *Who's Who in American Education,* 1992-1993

What is the aim or goal of your writing? "The history of a people is a fascinating topic. The United States, Canada and China are fertile fields to cultivate. My focus is upon those forces which propel a nation to greatness. Politicians and generals represent those forces, but they can never reflect the fundamental power of changes and movements. I focus upon those hidden energies and their effects upon communities and nations."

May inquiries be sent to you about doing workshops, readings? Yes

MELLEMA, GREGORY F.

Address: 4834 Curwood S.E., Kentwood, Michigan 49508
Born: June 22, 1948; Chicago, Illinois
Parents: Julius F. Mellema, Alyce G. (Vande Riet) Mellema
Children: Adam Franklin Mellema, Jenna Emily Mellema
Education: Calvin College, B.A., Grand Rapids, Michigan, 1966-1970. University of Massachusetts, Ph.D., Amherst, Massachusetts, 1970-1974. University of Michigan, M.B.A., Ann Arbor, Michigan, 1976-1978
Career: Professor, Calvin College, Grand Rapids, Michigan, 1978—; Assistant Professor, 1975-1976. Instructor, St. Olaf College, Northfield, Minnesota, 1974-1975. Adjunct Professor, Aquinas College, part-time

Writings: *Beyond the Call of Duty* State University of New York Press 1991. *Business: Making Christian Choices* CRC Publications 1990. *Individuals, Groups, and Shared Moral Responsibility* Peter Lang 1988. Over two dozen articles, scholarly journals. Work in Progress: *Collective Responsibility*

Awards or inclusion in other biographical books: Nominated for *Who's Who in the Midwest,* 1992

What is the aim or goal of your writing? "Using the concepts and tools of my discipline to shed light upon problems and concerns of persons in professional or managerial careers."

May inquiries be sent to you about doing workshops, readings? Yes

MERCER, BETTY DEBORAH

Address: 1422 New Street, Muskegon, Michigan 49442
Born: September 10, 1926; New York, New York
Parents: Cecil B. Fishbein, Martha Fishbein
Children: Kenneth, Stephen
Education: Evander Childs High School, 1944. New York University, B.S., New York, New York, 1948. Cornell University, Ithaca, New York, Summer Session, 1951. Queens College, New York, New York, 1954-1955. Hoffman Institute of Electrolysis, Certificate, New York, New York, 1955
Career: Registered Electrologist, self-employed, Muskegon, Michigan, 1966—. Certified Electrologist, self-employed, Sudbury, Ontario, Canada, 1958-1966. Certified Electrologist, self-employed, New York, New York, 1955-1957. Proofreader, various firms, New York, New York, 1950-1955. Book reviewing, baby sitting, selling door-to door, typing, filing, posting, various volunteer jobs. Also poetry writing, piano teaching, private tutoring in English

Writings: *Toward a Brighter Tomorrow!* self-published 1980. Poems in: *New Writers Magazine, Peninsula Poets, The Writers Exchange, Bardic Echoes, Author/Poet, New Earth Review, Poetry Plus,* others. In anthologies such as: *The International Society of Literature* Emeril Publications 1980. Articles. Work in Progress: Collection of poems

Awards or inclusion in other biographical books: *Directory of Active Michigan Poets; International Authors and Writers Who's Who; International Who's Who in Poetry; Who's Who Among Human Services Professionals; Who's Who: Autobiographical Sketches; Who's Who of American Women*

What is the aim or goal of your writing? "Get Published! Get read, get known, and appreciated. Also, I write for my own enjoyment, to record in a manner, moments and scenes, happenings, that I want to pass down to a future generation in my family, hopefully, there'll be one, from my sons."

May inquiries be sent to you about doing workshops, readings? Yes. Readings

METZLER, JOHN G.

Address: P.O. Box 214, Houghton Lake, Michigan 48629
Pseudonym: Jack Metzler
Born: November 30, 1932; Paterson, New Jersey
Parents: Charles H. Metzler, Alice M. Metzler
Children: George, John, Brenda
Education: Passaic Valley High School, Little Falls, New Jersey. Baptist Bible College, Th.M., Clarks Summit, Pennsylvania, Logos Bible College. Mid Michigan Community College, Central Michigan University
Career: Freelance writer and novelist, self-employed, Houghton Lake, Michigan, 1982—. Manager/technician, various cable television companies, 1968-1982. Pastor, conservative Baptist Church, Manitou Beach, Michigan, 1960-1968. Director, Northland Youth Crusade, Houghton Lake, Michigan, 1955-1960

Writings: *Handbook for Deacons* Logos Internation 1992. *River of Joy* Zondervan 1987. *Tachechana* Zondervan 1986. Work in Progress: Novel. Handbook

Awards or inclusion in other biographical books: Author's Citation, 1987. *Tachechana* recommended by the Iowa State Board of Education to be placed in all Iowa High School Libraries because of the cross cultural significance

What is the aim or goal of your writing? "With so many hurting people in the world, I'd like my writing to help heal and make the world a little more beautiful."

May inquiries be sent to you about doing workshops, readings? Yes

MEYERS, HELEN R.

Address: 204 Asbury Drive, Mechanicsburg, Pennsylvania 17055
Born: July 29, 1916; Tsinan, Shantung, North China
Parents: Reuben A. Torrey, Jr., Janet S. (Mallary) Torrey
Children: Janet, Rosalie, Frederick, Jacqueline
Education: High School, Pyengyang, Korea, graduated 1936. Wheaton College, Wheaton, Illinois, 1936-1941
Career: Missionary teacher/speaker, traveled around the world and the United States, 1944-1957. Founder/President, Winning Women Inc., Detroit, Michigan, 1957-1975. Vice President, Living Life Ministries, Montrose, Pennsylvania, 1975-1979; President, 1979—. President, Eastern Winning Women, Montrose, Pennsylvania, 1975—.

Writings: *So You're a Teenage Girl* Zondervan 1966, 1989. *To Have and To Hold* Zondervan 1972. *Did You Marry the Wrong Man* Living Life Ministries 1973, 1979. Four *Between Us Women* Booklets Zondervan 1963. Work in Progress: Enlarge *Did You Marry the Wrong Person. Preventing a Troubled Marriage*
What is the aim or goal of your writing? "To help people to find God's answers to life's troubling situations."
May inquiries be sent to you about doing workshops, readings? Yes

MIKOLOWSKI, KEN
Address: 1207 Henry, Ann Arbor, Michigan 48104
Born: June 22, 1941; Pontiac, Michigan
Children: one
Education: Wayne State University, B.A., Detroit, Michigan, 1964
Career: Lecturer, University of Michigan, Ann Arbor, Michigan, 1977—. Editor, Publisher, Printer, The Alternative Press, Ann Arbor, Michigan, 1969—.

Writings: *Big Enigmas* Past Tents Press 1991. *Little Mysteries* Toothpaste Press 1979. *Thank You Call Again* The Perishable Press 1974. Work in Progress: More poems
Awards or inclusion in other biographical books: *Michigan Authors,* 2nd ed. Michigan Arts Award, Arts Foundation of Michigan, 1982. Creative Artist Grant, Michigan Council for the Arts, 1981, 1989
What is the aim or goal of your writing? "More poems."
May inquiries be sent to you about doing workshops, readings? Yes

MILLER, HELEN (TOPPING) (1884-1960)
Born: December 8, 1884; Fenton, Michigan
Parents: Isaac Wallace Topping, Maria Augusta (Chipman) Topping
Children: John, F. Eugene
Education: Michigan State University, 1905
Career: Began writing for children's magazines when 10 years old; first book published 1931. Teacher

Writings: *Love Comes Last* Triangle Books 1936. *Whispering River* D. Appleton-Century 1936. *Dark Sails: a Tale of Old St. Simons* Bobbs-Merrill 1945. *The Sound of Chariots* People Book Club 1947. *Mirage* Appleton 1949. *Born Strangers: A Chronicle of Two Families* (family history of the author) Bobbs-Merrill 1949. *Cameo* Bobbs-Merrill 1951. *Witch Water* Bobbs-Merrill 1952. *Hollow Silver* Appleton-Century-Crofts 1953. *Rebellion Road* (with John Dewey Topping) Bobbs-Merrill 1954. *April to Remember* Appleton-Century Crofts 1955. *Her Christmas at the Hermitage; a Tale about Rachel and Andrew Jackson* Longmans, Green 1955. *Christmas for Tad; a Story of Mary and Abraham Lincoln* Longmans, Green 1956. *Christmas at Mount Vernon with George and Martha Washington* Longmans, Green 1957. *After the Glory* Appleton-Century-Crofts 1958. *Christmas at Monticello with Thomas Jefferson* Longmans, Green 1959. *Christmas at Sagamore Hill with Theodore Roosevelt* Longmans, Green 1960. Several others; 400 short stories, 11 magazine serials
Awards or inclusion in other biographical books: *American Authors and Books; American Novelists of Today; Authors of Books for Young People; Index to Women; Michigan Authors,* 1st ed., 2nd ed.; *Who Was Who in America; Who Was Who among North American Authors; Who's Who of American Women*

MILNER, RON
Born: May 29, 1938; Detroit, Michigan
Education: Columbia University
Career: Writer-in-residence, 1966-1967. Instructor, Michigan State University, East Lansing, Michigan, 1971-1972. Founder, director, Spirit of Shango Theater Company. Director, workshop leader

Writings: *Don't Get God Started* Longacre Theatre, Broadway, 1987. *Crack Steppin'* first produced, Music Hall, Detroit, Michigan 1981. *Season's Reasons* first produced, Langston Hughes Theatre, Detroit, Michigan 1976. *M(ego) and the Green Ball of Freedom*, first produced, Shango Theatre, Detroit, Michigan 1971; published, *Black World,* April, 1971. *Who's Got His Own* first produced, American Place Theatre, Off-Broadway, 1966. *The Greatest Gift* first produced in Detroit (Michigan) Public Schools. Other plays. *What the Wine-Sellers Buy* French 1974; New Federal Theatre 1973. Contributor to various anthologies such as *Black Short Story Anthology* Columbia University Press, 1972; *Black Drama Anthology* Columbia University Press 1972; New American Library 1986. In *Negro Digest, Black World, Drama Review* and others
Awards or inclusion in other biographical books:*Authors in the News; Biography News; Black American Writers Past and Present; Contemporary Authors; Contemporary Dramatists; Dictionary of Literary Biography; Plays, Players, and Playwrights; Directory of American Poets; Directory of Blacks in the Performing Arts; Living Black American Authors; Selected Black American Authors; Writers Directory.* Rockefeller Grant. John Hay Whitney Fellowship

MINTY, JUDITH
Born: August 5, 1937; Detroit, Michigan
Parents: Karl J. Makinen, Margaret (Hunt) Makinen
Children: Lora, Reed, Ann
Education: Michigan State University, East Lansing, Michigan, 1954-1959. Ithaca College, B.S., Ithaca, New York,1957
Career: Grand Valley State College, English guest lecturer, Allendale, Michigan, 1974-1977. Michigan Council for the Arts Creative Writing Project, 1974-1980. State of Michigan Pilot Project, Muskegon Correctional Facility, 1977. Assistant Professor, poet-in-residence, Central Michigan University, 1977-1978. Lecturer, poet-in-residence at University of California, Santa Cruz, California and others. Associate Professor, poet-in-residence, Humboldt State University, Arcata, California, beginning 1982

Writings: *Lake Songs and Other Fears* University of Pittsburgh Press 1974. *Yellow Dog Journal* Center Publications 1979. *Letters to My Daughters* May Apple Press 1980. *In the Presence of Mothers* University of Pittsburg Press 1981. *Counting the Losses* Jazz 1986. Contributor to several anthologies such as *The Generation of 2000: Thirty Contemporary American Poets* Ontario Review 1984; *Woman Poet: The Midwest* Women in Literature 1985. Contributed articles, short stories, poetry to *Ladies Home Journal, Kansas City Star, New Yorker, Village Advocate, Poetry Northwest* and many others
Awards or inclusion in other biographical books: *Contemporary Authors; Directory of American Poets; International Who's Who in Poetry; Michigan Authors,* 2nd ed. Award, International Poetry Forum, 1973. Breadload Writer's Conference fellowship, 1974. Eunice Tietjens Award, *Poetry* Magazine, 1974. Yaddo Fellowships, 1978, 1979, 1982. Grants, Michigan Council for the Arts, 1981, 1983. PEN Syndicated Fiction Award, 1985

MITCHELL, EDNA I.

Address: 5061 Grand Blanc Road, Swartz Creek, Michigan 48473
Born: March 8, 1900; Flint, Michigan
Parents: Frederick J. Holland, Eva G. (McTaggart) Holland
Children: Erma, Lloyd
Education: Swartz Creek High School, High School Diploma, 1915-1917. Genesee County Normal, 1917-1918
Career: Grade School Teacher, Fletcher and Kline Schools, Swartz Creek, Michigan, 1918-1923. Grand Blanc School, Grand Blanc, Michigan, one year. Housewife, 1923—.

Writings: *Oh For the Life of a Country Girl* Broadblade Press 1985. Work in Progress: Started to collect data for two books, *Goofs and Blunders; Hangups and Phoebias*
What is the aim or goal of your writing? Written for her: "At 80 years old just started to write down a few memoirs then inquired about a few things from a neighbor. Stan Perkins inquired info from the same people a few days later and learned what my mother was doing so came to see what she was writing and encouraged her to continue, thus a 'not intended to write a book' was written and published. She did an excellent and interesting job of it."

MITCHELL, JOHN C.

Address: 301 St. Joseph, Box 361, Suttons Bay, Michigan 49682
Born: May 23, 1951; Detroit, Michigan
Parents: James F. Mitchell, Arleen Mitchell
Children: Matthew, Andrew
Education: Brother Rice High School, Diploma, 1965-1969. University of Michigan, B.A., American Literature, Ann Arbor, Michigan, 1969-1974
Career: Owner, Restoration Specialist, Leelanau Architectural Antiques, Suttons Bay, Michigan, 1977—. Editor, Suttons Bay Publications, Suttons Bay, Michigan, 1987—

Writings: *Great Lakes and Great Ships: An Illustrated History for Children* Suttons Bay Publications 1991. *Michigan: An Illustrated History for Children* Suttons Bay Publications 1987. Work in Progress: *People of the Great Lakes: An Illustrated History for Children*
What is the aim or goal of your writing? "To establish a large body of work which presents our fine midwestern history to children in an enjoyable and historically correct manner."
May inquiries be sent to you about doing workshops, readings? Yes

MITCHELL, NANCY

Address: 221 Neptune Drive, Walled Lake, Michigan 48390
Born: September 24, 1925; Detroit, Michigan
Parents: Charles E. Williamson, Beatrice A. (Ward) Williamson
Children: David, Steven, Laurie
Education: Mackenzie High School, Detroit, Michigan, 1939-1943. Oakland Community College, Rochester, Michigan, 1969-1971
Career: Executive Secretary/Office Manager, Attorneys, Ford Motor Company, Dynapower Corporation, Eaton, Detroit/Farmington/Southfied, Michigan, 1944-1989

Writings: Short stories in *Prime Times, Modern Maturity*. Poems in *Yes, Lord!*, church periodicals. Newsletter editor, Detroit Women Writers. Work in Progress: *The Bachelor*

Company, historical novel currently under consideration at publisher. *Beatrice, Growin' Up*, young adult novel

What is the aim or goal of your writing? "To cause the reader to read on and on, smile, ponder, or whisper, 'Oh, my!' "

May inquiries be sent to you about doing workshops, readings? Yes. (to edit/ critique manuscripts, resumes, brochures, etc.)

MIZNER, ELIZABETH HOWARD

Pseudonym: Elizabeth Howard
Born: August 24, 1907; Detroit, Michigan
Parents: Walter I. Mizner, Agnes (Roy) Mizner
Education: University of Michigan, Ann Arbor, Michigan: A.B., 1930; A.M., 1935. Wayne State University, Detroit, Michigan, 1930-1932
Career: Instructor, Shorter College, Rome, Georgia, 1935-1936

Writings: *Sabina* Lothrop 1941. *Adventure for Alison* Lothrop 1942. *Dorinda* Lothrop 1944. *Summer Under Sail* Morrow 1947. *North Winds Blow Free* Morrow 1949. *Candle in the Night* Morrow 1952. *Peddler's Girl* Morrow 1951. *A Star to Follow* Morrow 1954. *The Road Lies West* Morrow 1955. *Girl of the North Country* Morrow 1957. *The Courage of Bethea* Morrow 1959. *Verity's Voyage* Morrow 1964. *Winter on Her Own* Morrow 1968. *Wilderness Venture* Morrow 1973. *Out of Step With the Dancers* Morrow 1978. In *Story Parade*

Awards or inclusion in other biographical books: *Authors of Books for Young People; Contemporary Authors; Current Biography; Index to Women; International Authors and Writers Who's Who; Michigan Authors*, 1st ed., 2nd ed.; *Something about the Author; Who's Who of American Women*

MONETTE, CLARENCE J.

Address: 942 9th Street, Lake Linden, Michigan 49945
Born: January 13, 1935; Lake Linden, Michigan
Parents: Peter N. Monette, Isabelle M. Monette
Children: Julie Marie
Education: Hubbell High School, Lake Michigan, graduated 1953. Michigan Technological University, Houghton, Michigan, 5 years
Career: retired

Writings: *A Brief List of Publications Pertaining to Copper Country History* 1979. *Upper Peninsula's Wolverine* 1992. *Early Red Jacket and Calumet in Pictures* vol. II 1991. *Trimountain and Its Copper Mines* 1991. *The Copper Range Railroad* 1989. *Freda, Michigan, End of the Road* 1989. *Phoenix, Michigan's History* 1989. *Ojibway, Michigan, A Forgotten Village* 1985. *Laurium, Michigan's Early Days* 1986. *Lake Linden's Disastrous Fire of 1887* 1988. *The Settling of Copper City, Michigan* 1983. *The Keweenaw Waterway* 1980. *Some of the Best From C & H News-Views*, vol. 1 1985; vol. II, 1987. *The History of Eagle River, Michigan* 1978. *The Calumet Theatre* 1979. Others-there are 41 so far in local history series, copyrighted by the author and published, printed (up to 128 pages with illustrations) by Welden H. Curtin. Work in Progress: *Redridge and Its Steel Dam*

What is the aim or goal of your writing? "Hobby only."
May inquiries be sent to you about doing workshops, readings? No

MOORE, CHARLES (1855-1942)
Born: October 20, 1855; Ypsilanti, Michigan
Parents: Charles Moore, Adeline (MacAllaster) Moore
Children: MacAllaster, James
Education: Phillips Academy, Andover, Massachusetts. Harvard, A.B., Cambridge, Massachusetts,1878. George Washington University, Ph.D., Washington, DC,1890
Career: Newspaper positions, Detroit, Michigan, others, 1878-1895. Secretary to U.S. Senator, Clerk to U.S. Senate Committee, 1889-1903. Secretary, Union Trust Company, Detroit, Michigan, 1904-1906. Chairman, Submarine Signal Company, Boston, Massachusetts, 1906-1980. Secretary, Security Trust Company, Detroit, Michigan, 1908-1914. Acting chief, Division of Manuscripts, Library of Congress, 1918-1927. National Commission of Fine Arts, 1910-1937. Helped plan American War Cemetaries in Europe, 1923. Overseer, Harvard College, 1924-1930. President, Detroit Planning Commission, 1912-1919

Writings: *The Ontonagon Boulder in the National Museum at Washington* Charles Moore 1895? *The Northwest Under Three Flags, 1635-1796* Harper & Brothers 1900. *In Memory of Hon. James McMillan, Senator in the Congress of the United States from Michigan* Smith 1903. *The Saint Marys Falls Canal* Semi-Centennial Commission 1907. *History of Michigan* Lewis Publishing 1915. *Daniel H. Burnham, Architect, Planner of Cities* Houghton Mifflin 1921. *The Family Life of George Washington* Houghton Mifflin 1926. *The Life and Times of Charles Follen McKim* Houghton Mifflin 1929. *Wakefield, Birthplace of George Washington* The Wakefield National Memorial Association 1932. Others. Also editor of several books such as *Plan for the Improvement of Washington*
Awards or inclusion in other biographical books: *American Authors and Books; Dictionary of American Authors; Dictionary of American Biography; Dictionary of North American Authors; Who Was Who in America.* Carnegie Corporation Award, 1937. Friedsam Fellowship Gold Medal Award, 1937. Chevalier Legion of Honor, 1928. Others

MOORE, JULIA A. (DAVIS) (1847-1920)
Born: December 1, 1847; Kent County, Michigan

Writings: *The Sentimental Song Book* Loomis 1876, 1877, 1893, 1912; J.F. Ryder 1876, 1877; Platt & Peck 1912. *A Few Choice Words to the Public, With New and Original Poems* Loomis 1878. *The Sweet Singer of Michigan: Later Poems* Eaton, Lyon 1878. *Original Poems* Bartlett 1900. *Sunshine and Shadow: or Paul Burton's Surprise* Cadillac News 1915. *The Sweet Singer of Michigan: Poems* Pascal Covici 1928. Called "The Sweet Singer of Michigan"
Awards or inclusion in other biographical books: *Allibone: a Critical Dictionary of English Literature; Childhood in Poetry; Concise Dictionary of American Literature; Contemporary Authors; Dictionary of North American Authors; Oxford Companion to American Literature; Penguin Companion to American Literature; Reader's Encyclopedia of American Literature*

MORRIS, CAROL L.
Address: 352 Collingwood Drive, East Lansing, Michigan 48823
Born: October 12, 1943; Chester, Pennsylvania
Children: Blythe
Education: Eastern Michigan University, B.S. in Sociology, Ypsilanti, Michigan, 1963-1965. Michigan State University, M.A. in English, East Lansing, Michigan, 1984-1986

Career: Policy analyst, State of Michigan, Department of Social Services, 1965—.

Writings: *Sweet Uprisings* Years Press, Michigan State University 1991. Poems have appeared in *Manhattan Poetry Review, Red Cedar Review, Way Station.* Work in Progress: Hand made books combining collage techniques and fragments of poetry
What is the aim or goal of your writing? "To document those experiences of mine that I think may be of interest to others."
May inquiries be sent to you about doing workshops, readings? Yes

MORRIS, SUSANNE R.
Address: 1230 Fourth Street, SW, Washington DC 20024
Education: Michigan State University, Department of Political Science, Ph.D., 1988
Career: Deputy Director, Management Training and Development Institute, Washington DC, 1987—. Administrator, Masters Program in Public Policy and Administration, Michigan State University, East Lansing, Michigan, 1982-1986; various teaching and research, 1978-1982. Policy Analyst, House Policy Committee, Michigan House of Representatives, Lansing, Michigan, 1975-1976

Writings: *The Legislative Process in Michigan* Hillsdale Educational Publishers 1979. *Making Their Way: Critical Variables Affecting Professional Reintegration of International Students in Their Countries, a Preliminary Study* NAFSA: International Association of Educators 1992. Work in Progress: Articles on the budget cutback process in Michigan
What is the aim or goal of your writing? "Hopefully make a small contribution to our understanding of various public policies and processes."
May inquiries be sent to you about doing workshops, readings? Yes

MORTON, JERRY LEE
Address: 1544 E. Spartan Village, East Lansing, Michigan 48824
Born: May 7, 1943; South Bend, Indiana
Parents: Wade D. Morton, Regina H. (Hosinski) Morton
Education: Michigan State University, East Lansing, Ph.D., 1991. Northwestern University, M.S.J., Evanston, Illinois, 1966. Michigan State University, B.A., East Lansing, Michigan, 1965. Lake Michigan College, A.A., Benton Harbor, Michigan, 1963. Benton Harbor High School, Benton Harbor, Michigan, 1961
Career: Instructor, Michigan State University, East Lansing, Michigan, 1981—; Western Michigan University, 1986-1988. Writer/Reporter, *Akron Beacon*, Akron, Ohio, 1978-1980. Writer, *Enquirer and News,* Battle Creek, Michigan, 1973-1978. VISTA Volunteer, Baltimore, 1966-1968. Staff, National Commission on Causes and Prevention of Violence, 1968. Freelance journalist, Middle East, 1971-1972

Writings: *Back to Algansee-Stories of Now and Then* Jerry Lee Press 1991. *Footprints and Friends-Conversations from Hat Creek to Nirvana* Jerry Lee Press 1988. *Yesterday in Hodunk-Voices from the Michigan Countryside* Jerry Lee Press 1985. Work in Progress: A history of journalism at Michigan State University
Awards or inclusion in other biographical books: McCormick Fellow, Northwestern, 1965-1966. National Endowment for the Humanities Fellowship, University of Michigan, 1976-1977
What is the aim or goal of your writing? "To write about 'ordinary' people...to relate the joy of 'being', of being alive, to express the happiness to be derived in observing brief moments. Simply, looking for humanity's common threads."

May inquiries be sent to you about doing workshops, readings? Yes

MULDER, ARNOLD (1885-1959)
Born: November 12, 1985; Holland Township, Michigan
Parents: Bouke Mulder, Jennie (Snitzler) Mulder
Education: Hope College, Holland, Michigan, 1907; Litt. D. 1923. University of Michigan, Ann Arbor, Michigan, 1909. University of Chicago, A.M., 1910
Career: Managing editor, Holland Daily Sentinel, Holland, Michigan, 1910-1915. Publicity agent, State Board of Health, Michigan, 1915-1917. Director, Michigan Anti-Tuberculosis Association, 1917-1922. Editor, *Holland Sentinel*, 1917-1929. Professor of English, Department Head, Kalamazoo College, 1929-1953. Editor, *Michigan Out-of-Doors,* 1917-1922

Writings: *The Dominie of Harlem* A.C. McClurg 1913. *Bram of the Five Corners* A.C. McClurg 1915. *The Out-Bound Road* Houghton Mifflin 1919. *The Sand Doctor* Houghton Mifflin 1921. *Americans From Holland* J.B. Lippincott 1947. *The Kalamazoo College Story; the First Quarter of the Second Century of Progress, 1933-1958* Kalamazoo College 1958. Contributor to periodicals such as *Michigan History Magazine.* Syndicated feature, "Adventures in the Library"
Awards or inclusion in other biographical books: *American Literary Yearbook; Michigan Authors,* 1st ed., 2nd ed.; *Who Was Who among North American Authors; Who Was Who in America.* Decorated by Government of the Netherlands, named an Officer in the Order of Orange-Nassau

MULLENDORE, WILLIAM J.
Address: 22961 Frederick Street, Farmington, Michigan 48336
Pseudonym: Bill Mullendore
Born: June 26, 1926; Detroit, Michigan
Parents: William E. Mullendore, Lucille G. Mullendore
Children: Mary, Linda
Education: University of Michigan, Bachelor of Arts, Ann Arbor, Michigan, 1943-1946. Columbia University, Master of Science in Journalism, New York, New York, 1946-1947
Career: Retired since 1988 except for occasional free-lancing, Florida, Michigan. Reporter and copy editor, *Lake Wales News*, Florida; *Chelsea Standard*, Michigan, 1982-1988. Public Information Executive, Michigan Department of Natural Resources, Lansing, Michigan, 1964-1981. Correspondent, State Capitol Bureau, Booth Newspapers, Lansing, Michigan, 1963-1964. Assistant Professor of Journalism, University of Montana, Missoula, Montana,1962-1963. Reporter, City Editor, News Editor, Outdoor Editor, *Ann Arbor News*, Michigan, 1946-1962

Writings: Written about fifty articles published in Michigan magazines, mostly on conservation, environmental, travel subjects. Many publications in newspapers. Work in Progress: Magazine articles
Awards or inclusion in other biographical books: Awards: Michigan Outdoor Writers Association and Michigan United Conservation Clubs
What is the aim or goal of your writing? "During my working years my aim in writing was primarily to earn a living, which I did successfully for more than 40 years. My occasional magazine writing in retirement is done to supplement income and also serves to provide a sense of pride in my ability to write up to current commercial standards. Writing is no longer an important part of my life. Frankly, after having written almost

constantly during my working years I am tired of doing it as a steady occupation and write only in response to some occasional urge or whim."

May inquiries be sent to you about doing workshops, readings? Yes

MURRAY, LLOYD W.

Address: P.O. Box 56, Six Lakes, Michigan 48886
Pseudonym: Pat
Born: January 21, 1911; Blanchard, Michigan
Parents: Elon R. Murray, Viola I. (Thornbury) Murray
Children: Yvonne, Karen, Dewey
Education: Blanchard High School, 1927-1930
Career: Retired

Writings: *Aunt Agatha* Pine Crest Publishing 1990. *Adventures of Andy Ayres* Pine Crest Publishing 1982. *The Pick of Pat's Poetry & Prose* Pine Crest Publishing 1983. *Poetry and Prose* Pine Crest Publishing 1983. *Tender Twigs* Pine Crest Publishing 1979. *The Saga of Charlie and Pat. Children's Stories.* Work in Progress: *Christopher. Dr. Nobles*
What is the aim or goal of your writing? "After retirement I began writing as a hobby. This was mainly to fulfill a desire I had to release my thoughts about nature and life. My hope is to provide wholesome entertainment for all ages."
May inquiries be sent to you about doing workshops, readings? No

MYERS, DAVID G.

Address: Hope College, Holland, Michigan 49423
Born: September 20, 1942; Seattle, Washington
Parents: Kenneth G. Myers, Luella N. Myers
Children: Peter, Andrew, Laura
Education: Whitworth College, B.A., Spokane, Washington, 1960-1964. University of Iowa, M.A., Ph.D., Iowa City, Iowa, 1964-1967
Career: Professor of Psychology, Hope College, 1967—. Lectured at various universities, colleges, conventions. Consulting editor, *Journal of Experimental Social Psychology* 1978-1987; *Journal of Personality and Social Psychology* 1986-1990. Reviewer, panelist, and Oversight Review Committee, National Science Foundation

Writings: *The Pursuit of Happiness: Who is Happy-and Why* William Morrow 1992. *Exploring Psychology* Worth Publishers 1990, 1993. *Psychology Through the Eyes of Faith* (with Malcolm Jeeves) Harper & Row 1987; IVP Britain 1992. *Psychology* Worth Publishers 1986, 1989, 1992. *The Human Connection* (with Martin Bolt InterVarsity 1984; Hodder/Stoughton 1985. *Teachers Resource and Test Manual* (with Martin Bolt) McGraw-Hill 1983, 1987. *Social Psychology* McGraw-Hill 1983, 1987, 1990, 1993. *Inflation, Poortalk, and the Gospel* (with Thomas Ludwig, Merold Westphal, Robin Klay) Judson Press 1981. *The Inflated Self: Human Illusions and the Biblical Call to Hope* Seabury 1980; 1981. *The Human Puzzle: Psychological Research and Christian Belief* Harper & Row 1978. Scientific writings have appeared in two dozen periodicals and books, from *Science, American Scientist, Psychological Bulletin, Advances in Experimental Social Psychology.* Articles for the general public include *Saturday Review, Psychology Today, Today's Education, Science Digest, Christianity Today, Christian Century*
Awards or inclusion in other biographical books: Graduate Fellowships: U.S. Public Health Service, 1964-1965; National Science Foundation, 1965-1967. Research Grants from NIMH; four from National Science Foundation. Distinguished Service

Award, Holland Jaycees, 1972. Award, Hope's Outstanding Professor-Educator, 1972. Gordon Allport Prize, APA Division 9. Doctor of Humane Letters, Northwestern College, Whitworth College

May inquiries be sent to you about doing workshops, readings? The demands of my work preclude doing this, except on exceptional cases, I'm afraid.

NAULT, WILLIAM E.
Address: 760 Poplar Street, Ishpeming, Michigan 49849
Pseudonym: Bill Nault, "Old Muskrat"
Born: August 28, 1912; Ishpeming, Michigan
Parents: William J. Nault, Anna T. (Cousineau) Nault
Children: Catherine Anne
Education: Ishpeming High School, Ishpeming, Michigan, 1925-1929. Northern State Teacher College, Marquette, Michigan, 1930-1932
Career: Analytic Chemist, Cleveland Cliffs Iron Company, Ishpeming, Michigan, 1935-1974. Wrote and produced weekly radio outdoor show, Station WJPD.

Writings: Magazine articles in *Sports Afield, Field and Stream, Hiawathan, Michigan Out-of-Doors, Michigan Fisherman*. Weekly outdoors column, The Globe, Ishpeming, Michigan. Work in Progress: *Hunting World, Manual on Wild Flowers in Midwest*
What is the aim or goal of your writing? "Mostly to satisfy desire to make creative use of spare time and to promote constructive and wise use of natural resources."
May inquiries be sent to you about doing workshops, readings? Yes

NEITZEL, SHIRLEY M.
Address: 5060 Sequoia SE, Grand Rapids, Michigan 49512
Born: May 15, 1941; Ewen, Michigan
Parents: Theophilus F. Koehler, Ida A. Koehler
Children: Christine
Education: Ewen High School, 1958. Wayne State University, Detroit, Michigan, part-time, 1958-1962. Eastern Michigan University, A.B., Ypsilanti, Michigan, 1962-1966. Western Michigan University, M.A., Kalamazoo, Michigan, 1979.
Career: Elementary Teacher, Caledonia Community Schools, Caledonia, Michigan, 1969—. Elementary Teacher, Ypsilanti Public Schools, Ypsilanti, Michigan, 1967-1968. Office Clerk, Wayne State University, Detroit, Michigan, 1958-1962

Writings: *The Dress I'll Wear to the Party* Greenwillow Books 1992. *The Jacket I Wear in the Snow* Greenwillow Books 1989
Awards or inclusion in other biographical books: *The Dress I'll Wear to the Party,* Honor Book, Parents' Choice, 1992. To be included in upcoming *Something About the Author*
What is the aim or goal of your writing? "I write to be a better teacher of writing, to model the writing process for my students, and to keep in touch with how it feels to spill my thoughts on paper. My finished drafts are stapled between colorful paper covers and placed on the bookshelf with the work of all the other writers in my classroom. When I'm working on a children's story, I share the work in progress with my students. Their questions and comments help me shape my work. The children who have heard an early draft feel a sense of ownership when they see my name on a book or magazine story."
May inquiries be sent to you about doing workshops, readings? Yes

NELSON, J. RALEIGH (1873-1961)
Born: May 8, 1873; Bement, Illinois
Education: University of Michigan, A.B., Ann Arbor, Michigan, 1894; M.A., 1903
Career: Latin Teacher, Chicago, Illinois. Latin Department Chairman, Lewis Institute, 1900-1908. Faculty, College of Engineering, University of Michigan, 1908-1933; Professor of English, 1936-1943. Produced plays

Writings: *Two Dramatizations from Vergil* University of Chicago Press 1908. *Writing the Technical Report* McGraw-Hill 1940, 1947, 1952. *From Sunny Pastures. Lady Unafraid* (a biography of his mother at the Indian Mission, L'Anse, Michigan) Caxton Printers 1951. *From "Sunny Pastures"* Caxton Printers 1952
Awards or inclusion in other biographical books: *Michigan Authors,* 1st ed., 2nd ed.; *National Cyclopaedia of American Biography*

NEVILL, JOHN T. (1901-1957)
Born: 1901; San Antonio, Texas
Parents: Charles L. Nevill, Sallie Nevill
Children: daughter
Career: Joined the U.S. Marines at 16, traveled widely aboard the *U.S.S. Arizona.* Oil fields, Mexico. Reporter, *Greenville Evening Banner,* Texas, beginning 1922. Scenery construction, New York, New York. Went to sea. *Detroit Free Press,* 1925-1928. Public Service Council, Detroit Street Railways, 1944. Wrote for United Press, Detroit *Times.* Columnist, Feature Writer, *Sault Ste. Marie Evening News*

Writings:*Wanderings: Sketches of Northern Michigan Yesterday and Today* (foreword by Prentiss M. Brown) Exposition Press 1955. *The Bridge That 'Couldn't' Be Built* 1955? *Miracle Bridge at Mackinac* (with David B. Steinman) Eerdmans 1957. In *Aviation Magazine*
Awards or inclusion in other biographical books:*Michigan Authors,* 1st & 2nd ed.

NEWBERRY, PERRY (1870-1938)
Born: October 16, 1870; Union City, Michigan
Parents: Frank D. Newberry, Fannie E. (Stone) Newberry
Education: High School
Career: Insurance business, Chicago, Illinois, 1887-1897. Newspaper work, writer. President, Forest Theatre Society, Carmel, California, 1913-1914

Writings: *Castaway Island* Penn Publishing 1917. Other boys' serials, novelettes, short stories
Awards or inclusion in other biographical books: *American Authors and Books; American Literary Yearbook; Dictionary of North American Authors; Who Was Who in America*

NEWTH, REBECCA
Born: September 21, 1940; Lansing, Michigan
Parents: William A. Newth, Catherine (Messenger) Newth
Children: Gloria, John, Olivia
Education: Michigan State University, B.A., East Lansing, Michigan, 1962
Career: Writer

Writings: *Xeme* Sumac Press 1971. In *The American Literary Anthology Three* Viking 1970. Poetry in *Sumac, Essence, Stony Brook,* others. Short stories
Awards or inclusion in other biographical books: *Contemporary Authors; Directory of American Poets; Michigan Authors,* 2nd ed.

NEWTON, STANLEY (1874-1950)
Born: 1874; Park Hill, Ontario, Canada
Career: Reporter, *Bay City Times.* Bay City Meat Company, 1900-1905. Hammond, Standish & Company, Detroit, 1905. Moved to Sault Ste. Marie, Michigan 1905. Associate Editor, Upper Peninsula Development Bureau. Collected Michigan historical material and active in Chippewa Historical Society

Writings: *Mackinac Island and Sault Ste. Marie* Sault News Printing Company 1909; Black Letter Press 1976.*The Story of Sault Ste. Marie and Chippewa County* Sault News Company 1923; Black Letter Press 1975. *A Souvenir of Sault Ste. Marie, Michigan* A. E. Young 1923? *Paul Bunyan of the Great Lakes* Packard & Company 1946. Many articles on Michigan history
Awards or inclusion in other biographical books: *Michigan Authors,* 2nd ed.

NIEDERMEIER, DONNA M.
Address: 5102 Crump Rd., Cheboygan, Michigan 49721
Born: September 9,1940; Detroit, Michigan
Parents: Oakley D. Seeley, Mary M. Seeley
Children: Diane, Carolyn, Steven

Education: Hallendale High School, Hallendale, Florida, 1954-1958. Lansing Community College, 1967
Career: Songwriter, Nashville Songwriters, Association, ASCAP, 1987—. Songwriter, WCBY Radio Station, Cheboygan, Michigan, 1990—. Freelance writer, columnist, *Cheboygan Daily Tribune*, 1979-1983

Writings: Poems in several anthologies. Collection in Pellston High School Library. Work in Progress: Writing songs about the Catholic churches in Cheboygan and surrounding areas
What is the aim or goal of your writing? "To be the best writer of poetry in Michigan".
May inquiries be sent to you about doing workshops, readings? Yes

NILES, GWENDOLYN A.

Address: 1218 State Street, St. Joseph, Michigan 49085
Born: March 11, 1914; Flynn, Michigan
Parents: Lynn A. Niles, Hazel J. Niles
Education: Eastern Michigan University, B.S., Ypsilanti, Michigan, 1934-1940. University of Michigan, M.A., summer school, Ann Arbor, Michigan, 1942-1946
Career: Teacher, High School, Pickford, Michigan, 1941-1943. Teacher, Plymouth High School, 1943-1947. Teacher, Benton Harbor Community College, 1947-1972

Writings: *Like a Prism* Prairie Poets 1980. *The Silence of the Rose* Branden Press 1970. *The Singing of the Days* Banner Press 1962. *A Changing Sky* Banner Press 1945. Published in *Detroit News, Chicago Tribune, Christian Science Monitor, Denver Post, The Oregonian, Versecraft, The Lyric, Green's Magazine, South and West,* others. Work in Progress: Poems
Awards or inclusion in other biographical books: *Directory of Active Michigan Poets* 1982; *Michigan Authors,* 2nd ed.; *Michigan Poets.* Many poetry prizes from poetry magazines and poetry societies: Poetry Society of Michigan, Alabama Society of Poetry, National Federation of State Poetry Societies
What is the aim or goal of your writing? "To me poetry must be musical and express strong emotion, so I write lyrics. I want to communicate what I feel to other people-so I strive for clarity. I am happy when people respond to what I write-but I must admit I would write, anyway-I need the release! I started as a child."
May inquiries be sent to you about doing workshops, readings? Yes

NIMS, JOHN FREDERICK

Address: 3920 Lake Shore Drive, Chicago, Illinois 60613
Born: November 20, 1913; Muskegon, Michigan
Parents: Frank McReynolds Nims, Anne (McDonald) Nims
Children: deceased: John, George; Frank, Sarah Hoyt, Emily Anne
Education: University of Notre Dame, A.B., Notre Dame, Indiana, 1937; M.A., 1939. University of Chicago, Ph.D., 1945
Career: Faculty, University of Notre Dame, Notre Dame, Indiana, 1939-1945, 1946-1952, 1954-1958. Faculty, University of Toronto, 1945-1946. Faculty, Bocconi University, Milan, Italy, 1952-1953. University of Florence, Italy, 1953-1954. University of Madrid, Spain, 1958-1960. Harvard University, 1964, 1968-1969, summer 1974. University of Illinois-Urbana, 1961-1965. University of Illinois at Chicago, 1965-1985. Member of editorial board, *Poetry Magazine,* 1945-1948. Editor *Ovid's Metamorphoses,* 1965. Editorial adviser, Princeton University Press, 1975-1982. Others

Writings: *The Iron Pastoral* 1947. *A Fountain in Kentucky* 1950. *The Poems of St. John of the Cross* 1959, 1979. *Knowledge of the Evening* 1960. *Of Flesh and Bone* 1967. *Sappho to Valery: Poems in Translation,* 1971, 1980. *Western Mind* 1974, 1983. *The Kiss: A Jambalaya* 1982. *Selected Poems* 1982. *A Local Habitation; Essays on Poetry* 1985. *The Six-Cornered Snowflake* 1990. Others. Contributor to anthologies, magazines
Awards or inclusion in other biographical books: Harriet Monroe Memorial Award, 1942. Guarantors Prize, 1943. Levinson Prize, 1944. Distinguished Fellowship, Academy of American Poets, 1982. Fulbright Grantee, 1952, 1953. Smith Mundt Grantee, 1958, 1959. National Foundation Arts and Humanities Grantee, 1967-1968. Award for Creative Writing, American Adademy of Arts and Letters, 1968. Creative Arts Citation, Brandeis University, 1974. Guggenheim fellow, 1986-1987. Aiken Taylor Award for Modern Poetry, 1991

NOBLE, TRINKA HAKES
Born: October 8, 1944; Albion, Michigan
Parents: Carl M. Hakes; Eva Hakes
Children: Daughter
Education: Michigan State University, B. of Fine Arts, East Lansing, Michigan, 1963-1967. Parson's School of Design, New York, New York. The New School for Social Research, New York, New York. Studied with Caldecott medalist Uri Shulevitz, Greenwich Village Workshop
Career: Art teacher, K-12, Michigan, Virginia, Rhode Island. Settled in New Jersey

Writings: *The Day Jimmy's Boa Ate the Wash* Dial Books for Young Readers 1980. *Hansey's Mermaid* Dial Books for Young Readers 1983. *Jimmy's Boa Bounces Back* Dial Books for Young Readers 1984. *Apple Tree Christmas* Dial Books for Young Readers 1984. *Meanwhile Back at the Ranch* Dial Books for Young Readers 1987. *Jimmy's Boa and the Big Splash Birthday Bash* Dial Books for Young Readers 1989
Awards or inclusion in other biographical books: *American Bookseller* Pick of the List; *Booklist* Children's Editors' Choice for *Jimmy's Boa and the Big Splash Birthday Bash.* American Book Award; Reading Rainbow Featured Selection; *American Bookseller* Pick of the Lists; North Dakota Flicker-Tail Children's Book Award; Arizona Young Reader's Award for *Meanwhile Back at the Ranch.* Child Study Children's Book Committee Books of the Year; Junior Literary Guild Selection for *Apple Tree Christmas.* IRA-CBC Children's Choice for *Jimmy's Boa Bounces Back. American Bookseller* Pick of the Lists for *Hansey's Mermaid.* American Book Award; Reading Rainbow Featured Selection; *Booklist* Children's Editors' Choice; IRA-CBC Children's Choice; *Learning:* The Year's Ten Best; Arizona Young Reader's Award; Junior Literary Guild Selection for *The Day Jimmy's Boa Ate the Wash*
May inquiries be sent to you about doing workshops, readings? No

NORTHUP ALBERT DALE
Address: 1963 Somerset Blvd., Troy, Michigan 48084
Born: April 29, 1941; Highland Park, Michigan
Parents: Everett Northup, Helen (Graves) Northup
Education: Highland Park High School, Highland Park, Michigan. Wayne State University, Detroit, Michigan; B.A., 1966; M.A., 1968. Art Center of Tuscany, Florence, Italy, 1973. Harvard University, Graduate School of Design, 1984
Career: Professor of Art/Art History, St. Clair County Community College, Port Huron, Michigan. Adjunct Professor, Lawrence Technological University. Adjunct Associate

Professor, University of Michigan-Dearborn. Art Chairman and Honorary Trustee, Museum of Arts & History, Port Huron, Michigan, 1973-1978. Member, Museum Advisory Committee, Michigan Council for the Arts, 1976-1977. Art Consultant, Blue Cross/Blue Shield of Michigan, 1972-1973

Writings: *Frank Lloyd Wright in Michigan* Reference Publications 1991. Published in *The Prairie Home Journal*. Work in Progress: Investigating "Rose Terrace", now a demolished structure, in Grosse Pointe, Michigan

Awards or inclusion in other biographical books: National Endowment for the Arts, Summer Institute, 1984. Mini-Grant, Michigan Council for the Arts, 1976, 1978. J.B. Sperry Endowment Fund for the Advancement of Faculty Studies, 1974, 1976

What is the aim or goal of your writing? "To enhance an understanding and appreciation of the built environment for the student and/or layman."

NORTON, MARY B.

Address: 820 Triphammer Road, Ithaca, New York 14850

Born: March 25, 1943; Ann Arbor, Michigan

Parents: Clark F. Norton, Mary E. Norton

Education: University of Michigan, B.A., Ann Arbor, Michigan, 1960-1964. Harvard University, M.A., Ph.D., Cambridge, Massachusetts, 1964-1969

Career: Professor, Cornell University, Ithaca, New York, 1971—. Assistant Professor, University of Connecticut, Storrs, Connecticut, 1969-1971. General editor, *AHA Guide to Historical Literature* 1990; consulting editor, 1987-1990. Chairwoman, member, co-chair, president of many conferences, committees, councils and related professional activities. Served as judge for Society of the Cincinnati Book Prize, others

Writings: *Major Problems in American Women's History* (editor) D.C. Heath 1989. *To Toil the Livelong Day: American's Women at Work, 1790-1980* (co-editor) Cornell University Press 1987. *A People and a Nation* (with others) Houghton Mifflin 1982, 1986, 1990. *Liberty's Daughters: The Revolutionary Experience of American Women, 1750-1800* Little, Brown 1980. *Women of America: A History* (co-editor) Houghton Mifflin 1979. *The British-Americans: The Loyalist Exiles in England, 1774-1789* Little, Brown 1972; Constable and Company 1974. Work in Progress: Books on gender in 17th-Century America

Awards or inclusion in other biographical books: *Directory of American Scholars; Michigan Authors,* 2nd ed.; *Who's Who in America* 1990-1991. Fellowship, Society for the Humanities, Cornell University, 1989-1990. Gender Roles Fellowship, Rockefeller Foundation, 1986-1987. Peterson Fellowship, American Antiquarian Society, 1984. Fellowship, Shelby Cullom Davis Center, Princeton University, 1977-1978. Fellowship, Charles Warren Center, Harvard University, 1974-1975. N.E.H. Younger Humanists Fellowship, 1974-1975. Harvard Prize Fellowship, 1964-1969. Woodrow Wilson Fellowship, 1964. Berkshire Conference Prize for best book by a woman historian, 1981. Allan Nevins Prize for best-written dissertation in American history, 1970

What is the aim or goal of your writing? "To recreate history in an interesting, relevant, and lively manner."

May inquiries be sent to you about doing workshops, readings? No

NYE, RUSSEL B.
Address: 301 Oxford Road, East Lansing, Michigan 48823
Born: February 17, 1913; Viola, Wisconsin
Parents: Charles H. Nye, Zelma (Shimmeyer) Nye
Children: Peter
Education: Oberlin College, A.B., Oberlin, Ohio, 1930-1934. University of Wisconsin, Ph.D., Madison, Wisconsin, 1936-1938; M.A., 1935
Career: Distinguished Professor Emeritus, Michigan State University, East Lansing, Michigan, 1940-1979, retired. Instructor, Adelphi College, Garden City, Long Island, New York, 1939-1940. Instructor, Jordan College, Menonimee, Wisconsin, 1935-1936. Chairman, and other offices, American Studies Association, 1950's and 1960's. Michigan Commission on Culture and the Arts, 1960-1962. Visiting Lecturer. Ferris State College Board of Control 1950-1968. Consultant, editorial adviser, co-editor, editorial board member of several organizations

Writings: *George Bancroft: Brahmin Rebel* Knopf 1945. *Fettered Freedom: Civil Liberties and the Anti-Slavery Controversy* Michigan State University Press 1947. *Midwestern Progressive Politics* Michigan State University Press 1948, 1959. *A Baker's Dozen: Thirteen Unusual Americans* Michigan State University Press 1957. *The Midwest: Myth or Reality* (co-author) Notre Dame 1961. *This Almost Chosen People: Essays in American Ideas* Michigan State University Press 1966. *The Unembarrassed Muse: American Popular Culture* Dial 1970. *Society and Culture in America 1830-69* Harper and Row 1974. Several others. Articles in *Papers of the Michigan Academy, Michigan History, American Speech, Modern Language Notes, Journal of American Culture, Science and Society, Hayes Historical Journal, A Journal of Canadian Culture,* others
Awards or inclusion in other biographical books: *Michigan Authors,* 2nd ed. Knopf Fellowship, 1944. Pulitzer Prize, Biography, 1945. Rockefeller Fellowship, 1947. Newberry Library Fellowship, 1948. Donner Medal, Donner Foundation and the Association for Canadian Studies, 1977. Distinguished Service Award, Society for the Study of Midwestern History and Literature, 1978. Distinguished Service Award, Michigan Council for the Humanities, 1984. Litt.D., Northern Michigan University, 1968; LL.D., Ferris State College, 1968: Bowling Green State University, 1976
May inquiries be sent to you about doing workshops, readings? No

OATES, JOYCE CAROL

Pseudonym: Rosamond Smith
Born: June 16, 1938; Lockport, New York
Parents: Frederic J. Oates, Caroline (Bush) Oates
Education: Syracuse University, B.A., Syracuse, New York, 1960. University of Wisconsin, M.A., 1961
Career: Instructor, University of Detroit, Detroit Michigan, 1961-1965; Assistant Professor, 1965-1967. English Department, University of Windsor, Windsor, Ontario, 1967-1978. Writer in residence, Princeton University, Princeton, New Jersey, beginning in 1978, Roger S. Berlind Distinguished Professor

Writings: *By the North Gate* Vanguard Press 1963; Fawcett 1978. *Upon the Sweeping Flood and Other Stories* Vanguard Press 1966. *A Garden of Earthly Delights* Vanguard Press 1967. *Expensive People* Vanguard Press 1967. *them* Vanguard Press 1969; Fawcett 1986. *The Wheel of Love and Other Stories* Vanguard Press 1970. *Wonderland* Vanguard Press 1971. *Marriages and Infidelities* Vanguard Press 1972. *The Edge of Impossibility: Tragic Forms in Literature* Vanguard Press 1972. *Where Are You Going, Where Have You Been?: Stories of Young America* Fawcett 1974. *The Poisoned Kiss and Other Stories from the Portuguese* Vanguard Press 1975. *Crossing the Border: Fifteen Tales* Vanguard Press 1976. *Night Side: Eighteen Tales* Vanguard Press 1977. *Unholy Loves* Vanguard Press 1979. *The Lamb of Abyssalia* Pomegranate 1980. *Contraries: Essays* Oxford University Press 1981. *A Bloodsmore Romance* Dutton 1982. *The Profane Art: Essays and Reviews* Dutton 1983. *Mysteries of Winterthurn* Dutton 1984. *Raven's Wing: Stories* Dutton 1986. *Lives of the Twins* Simon & Schuster 1987. *On Boxing* Doubleday 1987. *You Must Remember This* Dutton 1987. *(Woman) Writer: Occasions and Opportunities* Dutton 1988. *The Assignation* Ecco Press 1988. *American Appetites* Dutton 1989. *Because it is Bitter, and Because it is My Heart* Dutton 1990. *The Rise of Earth on Earth* New Directions Book 1991. *Black Water* Dutton 1992. Several others. Also several plays, poems, edited or compiled works. Contributor of fiction, poetry, nonfiction to such periodicals as *Michigan Quarterly Review, Vogue, New York Times Book Review, Hudson Review, Paris Review, Esquire, Mademoiselle*
Awards or inclusion in other biographical books: *American Authors and Books; Childhood in Poetry; Contemporary Authors; Contemporary Literary Criticism; Contemporary Novelists; Current Biography; Dictionary of Literary Biography; International Authors and Writers Who's Who; Reader's Adviser; Who's Who in America; Who's Who of American Women; Who's Who in the World,* several more. National Endowment for the Arts grants, 1966, 1968. Guggenheim fellowship, 1967. O. Henry Award, Doubleday, 1967, 1973. Rosenthal Award, National Institute of Arts and Letters, 1968. National Book Award nomination, 1968, 1969. National Book Award, 1970. O. Henry Special Award for Continuing Achievement, 1970, 1986. Lotos Club Award of Merit, 1975. American Library Association Notable Book, 1979. *Los Angeles Times* Book Prize, 1980. St. Louis Literary Award, 1988. Rackham Honors, University of Michigan, 1992
Oates' relationship with Michigan is commented upon in *Michigan Quarterly Review:* "If we had never come to the city of Detroit I would have been a writer (indeed, I had already

written my first two books before coming here, aged twenty-three) but Detroit, my 'great' subject, made me the person I am, consequently the writer I am-for better or worse." Oates made this remark upon receiving honors from the University of Michigan in *Michigan Today* June 1992: "On this celebratory day, however, we need to recall that the life of the mind, the life of art and the life of civilization itself are not decreed by nature, but are the results of human imagination and ceaseless effort."

OHLE, WILLIAM H.
Address: 05081 Lake Street, Boyne City, Michigan 49712
Born: December 6, 1910; St. Louis, Missouri
Parents: Ernest L. Ohle, Margaret H. Ohle
Children: William
Education: Washington University, A.B., St. Louis, Missouri, 1927-1932
Career: Retired, Horton Bay, Boyne City, 1970—. Vice-President, Leo Burnet Company, Chicago, Illinois, 1960-1970. Vice-President, Needham, Louis and Brurby, Inc., Chicago, Illinois, 1942-1960. Various positions,1932-1942

Writings: *How it Was in Horton Bay Charlevoix County, Michigan* self-published 1989. *100 Years in Horton Bay Charlevoix County, Michigan* self-published 1976
Awards or inclusion in other biographical books: *Who's Who in the Midwest, Who's Who in U.S. Advertising, Who's Who in Commerce and Industry*
May inquiries be sent to you about doing workshops, readings? Yes

OIKARINEN, PETER D.
Address: 505 Oak, Calumet, Michigan 49913
Born: January 31, 1950; Hancock, Michigan
Parents: Leonard Oikarinen, Lillian (Wirtanen) Oikarinen
Children: Kacey
Education: Michigan Technological University, B.S., Applied Physics, Houghton, Michigan, 1969-1972
Career: Self-employed, owner satellite sales and service, Antenna Center, Calumet, Michigan, 1982—. Photographer, freelance writer, commercial fisherman, various odd jobs, 1972-1982

Writings: *Armour-A Lake Superior Fisherman* Manitou Books 1991. *Island Folk* Isle Royale History Association 1979. *Blizzard* Manitou Books 1976. *Remembering* 1975. Work in Progress: A collection of short stories
What is the aim or goal of your writing? "What else? To write well; to write honestly, vividly and with passion."
May inquiries be sent to you about doing workshops, readings? Yes

OLDENBURG, E. WILLIAM (1936-1974)
Born: April 4, 1936; Muskegon, Michigan
Parents: William Oldenburg, Thress (Kroes) Oldenburg
Children: Jennifer, William
Education: Calvin College, B.A., Grand Rapids, Michigan, 1958. University of Michigan, M.A., 1960; Ph.D., 1966
Career: Teacher, Kalamazoo Christian High School, 1958-1959. Teacher, Calvin College, 1960-1961. Teacher, Grand Valley State College, 1965-1974

Writings: *Amity Avenue and Other Poems* Metamorphosis Press 1971. *Poems '67 to '72* Pilot Press Books 1973. *Potawatomi Indian Summer* Eerdmans 1975. *William Faulkner's Early Experiments with Narrative Techniques* University of Michigan 1966
Awards or inclusion in other biographical books: *Michigan Authors,* 2nd ed.

OLSON, ELLIS N.
Address: 302 James Street, Cheboygan, Michigan 49721
Born: November 8, 1938; Rochester, Minnesota
Parents: Harold J. Olson; Viola M. (Finley) Olson
Children: Cynthia, Margaret, Susan, Christina, Melanie
Education: Central Michigan University, B.S., Mt. Pleasant, Michigan, 1971; Lifetime Teaching Certificate, 1971-1974. Cheboygan County Normal, County Limited Teaching Certificate, 1956-1957
Career: Junior High Teacher, Cheboygan Area Schools, Cheboygan, Michigan, 1963–. Teacher, Blessed Sacrament, Grand Rapids, Michigan, 1961-1963. Teacher, Ada 8F "Egypt Valley", Kent County, Michigan, 1957-1961. Restaurant cook, "The Hut", "Pierre Room", Cheboygan, Michigan, 1952-1968. Home builder, self-employed, Cheboygan, Michigan, 1963—.

Writings: *1989 Cheboygan Centennial* City of Cheboygan 1989. "Cheboygan Historical Sketches" Cheboygan Chamber of Commerce 1979. "Cheboygan Historical Sketches" Cheboygan Chamber of Commerce 1976. *Wood Butchers of the North* self published 1971; reprint 1989. *Cheboygan Village Centennial 1971* (contributor). Chapter in *Memories of Mackinaw*. Feature article "History of Cheboygan County Schools", *Cheboygan Daily Tribune*. Work in Progress: Untold stories of Cheboygan; pictorial history of Cheboygan; Shadows of the Fort; Duncan City Ghost town
What is the aim or goal of your writing? "My aim is to share the history of Cheboygan and Straits Area with others. I founded the first Cheboygan County Museum and co-founded the first Cheboygan County Historical Society. My research led to my discovery of the Mill Creek site and present State Park."
May inquiries be sent to you about doing workshops, readings? I do not do workshops or readings, but on occasion I do slide presentations or speeches.

ONEAL, ELIZABETH B.
Address: 501 Onondaga Street, Ann Arbor, Michigan 48104
Pseudonym: Zibby Oneal
Born: March 17, 1934; Omaha, Nebraska
Parents: James D. Bisgard, Mary E. Bisgard
Children: Elizabeth, Michael
Education: Stanford University, B.A., Palo Alto, California, 1952-1954. University of Michigan, Ann Arbor, 1968-1970
Career: Lecturer, University of Michigan, Ann Arbor, Michigan, 1972-1989

Writings: *A Long Way to Go* Viking Penguin 1988. *Grandma Moses* Viking Penguin 1986. *In Summer Light* Viking Penguin 1985. *A Formal Feeling* Viking Penguin 1982. *The Language of Goldfish* Viking Penguin 1980. *The Improbable Adventures of Marvelous O'Hara Soapstone* Viking Penguin 1972. *War Work* Viking Penguin 1971. Work in Progress: A novel for adolescents
Awards or inclusion in other biographical books: *Language of Goldfish, A Formal Feeling, In Summer Light:* ALA Notable Books, ALA Best Books for Young Adults, *Booklist* Reviewers Choice. Christopher Award for *A Formal Feeling. Boston Globe/Hornbook* Award

What is the aim or goal of your writing? "To write the best books I can for my intended audience."

May inquiries be sent to you about doing workshops, readings? Yes

ORR, MYRON DAVID (1896-1986)

Born: May 28, 1896; Caro, Michigan

Parents: Fred H. Orr, Katherine (O'Kelly) Orr

Children: Sally

Education: University of Michigan, Columbia University, New York University. Graduated from Detroit College of Law, 1928

Career: Lawyer with his father, Caro, Michigan, until 1942. Served in Marine Corps, World War I, World War II. Taught at Rutgers University, New Jersey and Long Island University, New York. English and History Professor, Alpena Community College, Alpena, Michigan, 1957-1970. Wrote, directed, staged minstrel-musical comedy shows for Catholic Central High School, Alpena, Michigan

Writings: *Rubber Lines; Compensation; and, a Puff of Smoke* The Michigan Farmer 1935. *White Gold: a Mystery Romance of the Great Lakes* Capper Harmon Slocum 1936. *Cathedral in the Pines* Capper Harmon Slocum 1938. *Citadel of the Lakes* (sold over two million copies) Dodd, Mead 1952. *Mission to Mackinac* Dodd, Mead 1956. *The Outlander* Thomas Bouregy 1959; Ryerson Press 1959. *Zeus Speaks* MacGregor Press 1985. Over 200 short stories

The 2nd edition of *Michigan Authors* notes: "Dr. Orr, a 'Fifth Generation Michiganite', has had over two hundred short stories and essays published in American, Canadian, and British publications."

Awards or inclusion in other biographical books: *American Authors and Books; Michigan Authors,* 1st ed., 2nd ed.

OSBORN, CHASE SALMON (1860-1949)

Born: January 22, 1860; Huntington County, Indiana

Parents: George Augustus Osborn, Margaret (Fannon) Osborn

Children: Ethel, George, Lillian, Chase, Emily, Orren, Miriam

Education: Purdue University, B.S., South Bend, Indiana, 1880. Detroit College of Medicine, M.D., 1909. University of Michigan, L.L.D., 1911. Olivet College, Olivet, Michigan, 1911. Wayne University, Sc.D., Detroit, Michigan, l944. Others

Career: Newspaper work *Lafayette, Chicago Tribune, Mining News, Sault Ste. Marie News, Saginaw Courier-Herald*, others. Postmaster, Sault Ste. Marie, Michigan 1889-1893. State Game and Fish Warden, 1895-1899. Commissioner of Railroads for Michigan, 1899-1903. Discoverer of Canadian iron range. Regent, University of Michigan, 1908-1911. Governor of Michigan, 1911-1912; candidate for U.S. Vice-Presidency, U.S. Senate

Writings: *The "Soo": Scenes in and About Sault Ste. Marie, Michigan, with Descriptive Text* King, Fowle & Katz 1887? *The Andean Land (South America)* A.C. McClurg 1909. *The Iron Hunter* (autobiography) Macmillan 1919. *The Law of Divine Concord* Forum 1921. *Madagascar, Land of the Man-Eating Tree* Republic Publishing 1924. *The Earth Upsets (Another Terrestrial Motion)* Waverly Press 1927. *Michigan's One Hundredth Birthday: Centennial Address Delivered at Lansing, Michigan, January 26, 1937, before a Joint Session of the Legislature of Michigan, at the Official Celebration of the One Hundredth Anniversary of the Formal Admission of the State to the Union* 1937? *Father*

Gabriel Richard: an Address Given at a Dinner Commemorating the 169th Anniversary of the Birth of Gabriel Richard, at the Hotel Fort Shelby, Detroit, Michigan, October 15, 1936 1936? *The Conquest of a Continent* (with Stellanova Osborn) Science Press 1939. *Schoolcraft, Longfellow, Hiawatha* (with Stellanova Osborn) Jaques Cattell Press 1942. *"Hiawatha" with its Orginal Indian Legends, Compiled, with Essays on its Authentic Background of Lake Superior Country and Chippewa Indians* (with Stellanova Osborn) Jaques Cattell Press 1944. *Errors in Official U.S. Area Figures* (with Stellanova Osborn) Science Press 1945. *Northwood Sketches* (with Stellanova Osborn) Historical Society of Michigan 1949. Others

Awards or inclusion in other biographical books: *Dictionary of American Biography; Dictionary of North American Authors; Indiana Authors and Their Books; Michigan Authors,* 1st ed., 2nd ed.; *National Cyclopaedia of American Biography; Reader's Encyclopedia of American Biography; Who Was Who in America; Who Was Who among North American Authors; Who Was Who in Literature*

OSBORN, STELLANOVA (BRUNT) (1894-1988)

Born: July 31, 1894; Hamilton, Ontario, Canada
Parents: Edward Brunt, Rosa Lee Brunt
Education: Collegiate Night School, Hamilton, Ontario, Canada. Scott High School, Toledo, Ohio. University of Michigan, A.B., Ann Arbor, Michigan, summa cum laude, 1922; A.M., 1930
Career: Picked berries, clerked in grocery store, stenographer. In college had leading part in founding of magazine *Whimsies,* helped arrange series of lectures for students in Ann Arbor. Teacher, one-room mountain school, Missouri. Staff editor, *New International Yearbook.* Contributing editor, *New International Yearbook,* 1924. Assistant editor, *Good Health* magazine, Battle Creek, Michigan. Editor, University of Michigan, 1925-1930. Secretary for North America, International Movement for Atlantic Union. Lecturer, traveled widely in Europe, North America promoting world government, serving on national council 1950-1951, other offices, established Michigan branch and others

Writings: *The Conquest of a Continent* (with Chase Salmon Osborn) Science Press 1939. *An Accolade for Chase S. Osborn; Home, State, and National Tributes on the Occasion of Chase S. Osborn Day October 4, 1939* (Sault Ste. Marie) 1940. *Eighty and On; the Unending Adventurings of Chase S. Osborn* Sault News Print. Company 1941. *Schoolcraft-Longfellow-Hiawatha* (with Chase Salmon Osborn) Jaques Cattell Press 1942. *Some Sidelights on the Battle of Tippecanoe* 1943. *Hiawatha with its Original Indian Legends, Compiled, with Essays on its Authentic Background of Lake Superior Country and Chippewa Indians* (with Chase Salmon Osborn) Jaques Cattell 1944. *Errors in Official U.S. Area Figures* (with Chase Salmon Osborn) 1945. *A Tale of Possum Poke in Possum Lane* 1946. *Northwood Sketches* (with Chase Salmon Osborn) Historical Society of Michigan 1949. *Balsam Boughs* Torch Press 1949. *Polly Cadotte, a Tale of Duck Island in Verse* Exposition Press 1955. *Iron and Arbutus* 1962. *Summer Songs on the St. Marys* North Star Communications 1982. Pamphlet, "Two Beautiful Peninsulas", widely circulated, supported the need for bridge over Straits of Mackinac
Awards or inclusion in other biographical books: *American Authors and Books; Canadian Who's Who; Foremost Women in Communications; Michigan Authors,* 1st ed., 2nd ed.; *Who's Who in America; Who's Who in the World; Who's Who of American Women.* Phi Beta Kappa, University of Michigan. Citation, National Council Member of the Year, Atlantic Union Committee, 1951

OSBORN, WILLIAM P.

Address: 145 Crestwood Drive, Grand Rapids, Michigan 49504
Born: October 6, 1946; Hastings, Michigan
Parents: Palmer Osborn, Elizabeth G. (Hanna) Osborn
Children: Mark, Samantha
Education: State University of New York at Binghamton, Ph.D., Binghamton, New York, 1983-1986. Bowling Green State University, M.F.A., Bowling Green, Ohio, 1983-1991. University of California, B.A., La Jolla, California, 1979-1981
Career: Assistant Professor, Grand Valley State University, Allendale, Michigan, 1988—. Adjunct Lecturer, California State University, Hayward, California, 1986-1988. Adjunct Lecturer, Santa Clara University, Santa Clara, California, 1986-1988

Writings: Short fiction in *Another Chicago Magazine, Mantucket Review, Mississippi Review, Carolina Quarterly, Kansas Quarterly, Western Humanities Review, Swallow's Tale, Telescope, Santa Clara Review, Sequoia,* and others. Fiction editor of *Mid-American Review*, 1982-1983. Work in Progress: Short fiction, interview, reviews and a novel
Awards or inclusion in other biographical books: S.I. Newhouse Award for Fiction, 1983
What is the aim or goal of your writing? "Though I still write some fiction that challenges the conventions of genre and form, my current impulse is away from such, into a quieter, fuller fiction that examines difficult moments in the lives of characters complex enough (I hope) to seem to be living real lives."
May inquiries be sent to you about doing workshops, readings? Yes

OTIS, CHARLES HERBERT (1886-1979)

Born: January 25, 1886; Raymond, Nebraska
Parents: Willard D. Otis, Louisa M. (Geiger) Otis
Children: Cynthia Jane, James
Education: University of Michigan, Ann Arbor, Michigan; Bachelor Degree, 1910; Ph.D., 1913
Career: Lumberjack, engineer. Curator, Acting Director, Botanical Garden and Arboretum, University of Michigan, 1910-1913. Instructor, Cornell University, Ithaca, New York, until 1915. Assistant Botanist, New Hampshire Experimental Station. Instructor, University of New Hampshire. Assistant Professor, Western Reserve University, University of Wisconsin. Summer, temporary appointments at Pennsylvania State University, University of Vermont, United States Department of Agriculture. Became Chairman, Biology Department, Bowling Green State University, 1936-1947; Professor 1947-1956, retired

Writings: *Michigan Trees: A Handbook of Native and Most Important Introduced Species* University of Michigan Press 1920; many reprints. *Michigan Trees: A Guide to the Trees of Michigan and the Great Lakes Region* University of Michigan Press 1981. Others
Awards or inclusion in other biographical books: *Michigan Authors,* 2nd ed.; *Ohio Authors and Their Books; Who Was Who among North American Authors*

OTTO, SIMON G.
Address: 3267 N. Club Road, Indian River, Michigan 49749
Born: February 19, 1927; Petoskey, Michigan
Parents: Foster J. Otto, Christine M. Otto
Children: Joseph, Simon Jr., Eric, Pat, Pam
Education: University of Washington, B.A., Washington, 1975-1979. Central Michigan University, Mt. Pleasant, Michigan; Northcentral Michigan College, 1972-1974
Career: Executive Coordinator, Little Traverse Bay Band, Petoskey, Michigan, 1990-. Employment Specialist, State of Michigan, Various Offices, 1980-1990. Title IV Counselor, Mt. Pleasant Public Schools, Mt. Pleasant, Michigan, 1976-1980. Director, Tri-County Indian Center, Petoskey, Michigan, 1974-1976. Various positions in landscaping

Writings: *Walk in Peace* Michigan Indian Press 1990. *Aube-Na-bing* (Looking Backward) contributed stories and pictures, Michigan Indian Press 1989. Work in Progress: Book on legends, facts, happenings during my lifetime, mostly pertaining to Indian life
What is the aim or goal of your writing? "Inform and educate".
May inquiries be sent to you about doing workshops, readings? Yes

P

PAANANEN, DONNA M.
Address: 152 Orchard St., East Lansing, Michigan 48823
Born: December 26, 1938; Columbus, Wisconsin
Parents: Oliver W. Jones, Marjorie R. (Earle) Jones
Children: Karl, Neil (husband: Victor N. Paananen)
Education: University of Dubuque, B.A., Dubuque, Iowa, 1957-1961. University of Wisconsin, Master of Science, Madison, Wisconsin, 1963-1964. Brigham Young University, Summer School, Provo, Utah, 1962
Career: Writer/editor (intermittent), USDA Forest Service, East Lansing, 1980—. Partner, Writers' Services, International, East Lansing, Michigan, 1992—. Instructor, Lecturer, Editor, Writer, Michigan State University, East Lansing, Michigan 1977—. Freelance writer/editor, Educational Institute of the American Hotel and Motel Association, East Lansing, Michigan, 1981-1986. Instructor, Berkshire Community College, Williamstown, Massachusetts, 1966-1968. Instructor, Madison Area Technical College, Madison, Wisconsin, 1964-1966. Teacher, Wasatch Academy, Mt. Pleasant, Utah, 1961-1963. National Society of Arts and Letters Literature Chairman

Writings: *Naturally Nutritious* Ideals 1978. *Meatless Meals* Ideals 1979. *Budget Saving Meals* Ideals 1980. *New Mother's Cookbook* American Baby Books 1981. *Successful Credit and Collection Techniques* Educational Institute 1981. *FIREFAMILY: Fire Planning with Historic Weather Data* (co-author) USDA Forest Service 1982. *Condominiums and Timesharing in the Lodging Industry* Educational Institute 1984. *Selling Out* Educational Institute 1985. *Lansing Lifestyles* Educational Institute 1986. *Compendium of Northeastern State Forest Fire Laws* USDA, Forest Service, State & Private Forestry 1989. Others. Articles in *Boston Globe Sunday Magazine, Lady's Circle, Parents', Good Housekeeping, Better Homes and Gardens, Chicago Sun Times, Christian Herald, Canadian Author & Bookman, Michigan Living, Minnesota Volunteer, Midwest Living, Ideals Magazine,* and others. Newsletters. Work in Progress: *Play With Me. Murder Under the Castle*
Awards or inclusion in other biographical books: Michigan Council for the Arts, Writer-in-the-Schools
What is the aim or goal of your writing? "Excellent question! Certainly one of the reasons I write is that I must-it is a deep personal need. Writing gives me pleasure, but it is not always easy and it can be lonely. I began as a writer of fiction and I intend to do more in the future, but I do know that more nonfiction is published than fiction and one can use all one's creativity to make nonfiction interesting and readable. Many of my works have been 'how-to'-I seem to have a talent in this area. I've 'ghosted' a number of works for others to help them get their message across and I truly enjoy motivating writers of all ages to write clearly and in an interesting way."
May inquiries be sent to you about doing workshops, readings? Yes. I can suit my presentation to the needs of the audience

PAANANEN, VICTOR N.
Address: 152 Orchard Street, East Lansing, Michigan 48823
Born: January 31, 1938; Ashtabula, Ohio
Parents: Niles H. Paananen, Anni M. (Iloranta) Paananen
Children: Karl, Neil
Education: Harvard University, A.B., magna cum laude, Cambridge, Massachusetts, 1956-1960. University of Wisconsin, M.A., Ph.D., Madison, Wisconsin, 1962-1966
Career: Professor of English, Michigan State University, East Lansing, 1968-; Chair, English Department, 1986—.
Assistant Professor, Williams College, Williamstown, Massachusetts, 1966-1968. Instructor, Wofford College, Spartanburg, South Carolina, 1962-1963. Fidelity and Surety Bond Underwriter, Continental Insurance Company, Cleveland, Ohio, 1960-1962

Writings: *William Blake* G.K. Hall 1977. Numerous articles. Work in Progress: *British Marxist Criticism* (for Garland)
Awards or inclusion in other biographical books: *Contemporary Authors; Who's Who in America; Who's Who in the Midwest,* others
What is the aim or goal of your writing? "To contribute to an improvement of life and consciousness."
May inquiries be sent to you about doing workshops, readings? Yes

PACOSZ, CHRISTINA V.
Address: P. O. Box 82866, Fairbanks, Alaska 99708
Born: October 12, 1946; Detroit, Michigan
Parents: Walter F. Pacosz, Sophia A. Pacosz
Education: Cass Technical High School, Detroit, Michigan, 1961-1964. Wayne State University, B.S., Detroit, Michigan, 1964-1970. Jagiellonian University, Krakow, Poland, 1986
Career: Approved Artist, Alaska State Council on the Arts, statewide, 1993. Teacher, Learning Disabled, Delta/Greely Schools, Delta Junction, Alaska, 1991-1992. Artist-in-the-Schools, South Carolina Arts Commission, statewide, 1985-1986, 1990-1991. Visiting Artist, North Carolina Arts Council, Charlotte, North Carolina and Asheville, North Carolina, 1986-1990. M.F.A. Creative Writing Program, University of Alaska, Fairbanks, recently accepted

Writings: *This Is Not a Place to Sing* West End Press 1987. *Some Winded Wild Beast* Black and Red 1985. *Notes From the Red Zone* Seal Press 1983. *Shimmy Up to This Fine Mud* Poets' Warehouse 1976. In, *A Gathering of Poets* Kent State University Press, 1992, others. Work in Progress: *A Simple Story,* nonfiction. *Wrestling With the Angel,* nonfiction. *A Dark and Lidded Eye,* poetry
What is the aim or goal of your writing? "Revealing the mystery, whatever that may be."
May inquiries be sent to you about doing workshops, readings? Yes

PARKER, KENNETH C.
Address: 719 E. Orchard, Traverse City, Michigan 49684
Born: August 31, 1914; Lansing, Michigan
Parents: Wilfred E. Parker, Alice O. Parker
Children: Marilyn, Nancy, Robert
Education: Rochester High School, 1931. University of Michigan, B.A., Ann Arbor,

Michigan, 1931-1935; Journalism School, 1935-1936

Career: Retired, Freelance writer, 1980—. PR Director, Traverse City High School, Traverse City, Michigan, 1971-1978. Chief Editorialist, City Editor, *Record-Eagle,* Traverse City, Michigan, 1959-1971. Editor, Publisher, Founder, *Antrim County News,* Bellaire, Michigan, 1947-1959. Apprentice printer, Reporter, *East Tawas News,* East Tawas, Michigan, 1945-1947. U.S. Army, 1943-1945. Chief Correspondent, Michigan Consolidated Gas Company, Detroit, Michigan, 1937-1943

Writings: *Civilian at War* self-published 1984; republication of portion, *Michigan Today,* October, 1986. Short Story,*Yankee Magazine* 1979. Work in Progress: Account of 12 years as publisher and editor of *The Antrim County News*, a self-founded weekly, 1947
What is the aim or goal of your writing? "Illuminate the significant parts of my life as a surviving infantryman in World War II and as a surviving publisher, 1947-1959. Also would like to try fiction."
May inquiries be sent to you about doing workshops, readings? Yes

PASSIC, FRANK JR.
Address: 900 S. Eaton Street, Albion, Michigan 49224
Born: April 19, 1953; Albion, Michigan
Parents: Frank Sr. Passic, Pauline M. (Kulikauskas/Kulikowski) Passic
Education: Albion High School, Diploma, Albion, Michigan. Spring Arbor College, B.A., Spring Arbor, Michigan, 1971-1975
Career: Curator of Local History, Albion Historical Society, Albion, Michigan, 1985–. One of the founders of Lithuanian Numismatic Association, editor of its publication *The Knight.* Volunteer, Numismatic Curator, Balzekas Museum of Lithuanian Culture, Chicago, Illinois

Writings: *History of Albion, Michigan From the Archives* Curtis Media 1991. *A History of Albion Public Schools* Albion Public Schools 1991. *A Comprehensive Guide and Key to Artist Albert Ruger's 1866 Bird's Eye View of Albion, Michigan* Albion Historical Society 1988. *Albion's Banks and Bankers* Albion Historical Society 1985. Over a hundred articles about Albion area, and numismatic topics. Work in Progress: *Lithuanian Numismatics of the 20th Century*
Awards or inclusion in other biographical books: Heath Literary Award, American Numismatic Association, 1983. Literary Awards, Michigan State Numismatic Society; International Bank Note Society
What is the aim or goal of your writing? "To foster appreciation and enjoyment and a sense of community pride for the Albion area. Also, to possibly locate descendants of 19th century Albion residents so I can share with them information we have about their family in our local history archives here at the Gardner House Museum, and to receive additional information in turn."
May inquiries be sent to you about doing workshops, readings? Yes

PAULIN, MARY ANN
Address: 1205 Joliet Road, Marquette, Michigan 49855
Born: February 27, 1943; Bay Port, Michigan
Parents: Ervin F. Strieter, Bertha E. Strieter
Education: Pigeon High School, Pigeon, Michigan, 1956-1960. Western Michigan University, B.A., Kalamazoo, Michigan, 1964; M.A.L.S., 1965, Ed.S., 1971
Career: High School Librarian, Warren Community Schools, Williamsport and Pine

Village, Indiana, 1965-1967. Elementary Media Specialist, Lafayette School Corporation, Lafayette, Indiana, 1967-1970. Middle School Media Specialist, Chelsea School Corporation, Chelsea, Michigan, 1970-1973. High School, Junior High Librarian, Negaunee Public Schools, Negaunee, Michigan, 1973-1983; High School, Media Specialist, 1983—. Adjunct Faculty: Western Michigan University, 1973; Northern Michigan University, 1977-1984. Workshop Presenter in 9 countries,1954

Writings: *Creative Uses of Children's Literature* Library Professional Publications 1982. *Outstanding Books for the College Bound* American Library Association 1983. *More Creative Uses of Children's Literature Vol.1* Libr. Prof. Pubs. 1992. Over a hundred articles, reviews in periodicals, newspapers. *Reading is Life* (video) Marquette-Alger Reading Council 1988. Work in Progress: *More Creative Uses of Children's Literature, Vol 2*

Awards or inclusion in other biographical books: Literacy Award, International Reading Association and Marquette-Alger Reading Council, 1987. Women of Distinction, Delta Kappa Gamma and Delta Chapter, 1987. The Ruby Brown Award for Individual Excellence, Michigan Association for Media in Education, 1988

What is the aim or goal of your writing? "As a library/media specialist, my life's work has been devoted to introducing students of all ages to books in creative ways through music, art, poetry, puppetry, creative dramatics, thinking, listening, storytelling, and multimedia. I have taught workshops, college classes, and given presentations to teachers, librarians, and parents in nine countries as well as throughout the United States so that these adults can also introduce students to books in creative ways. The books that I write reflect the philosophy, techniques, and titles that I share."

May inquiries be sent to you about doing workshops, readings? Yes

PEATTIE, ELIA WILKINSON (1862-1935)
Born: January 15, 1862; Kalamazoo, Michigan
Parents: Frederick Wilkinson, Amanda (Cahill) Wilkinson
Children: Edward, Barbara, Roderick, Donald
Career: Reporter, Chicago newspapers until 1888. Editorial writer, *Omaha World-Herald.* Literary critic, *Chicago Tribune,* 1901-1917

Writings: *Pippins and Cheese: Being the Relation of How a Number of Persons Ate a Number of Dinners at Various Times and Places* Way and Williams 1897. *The Shape of Fear: and Other Ghostly Tales* Macmillan 1899; Books for Libraries Press 1969. *The Beleaguered Forest* Appleton 1901. *Poems You Ought to Know* Fleming H. Revell Company 1903; Books for Libraries Press 1969. *Edda and the Oak* Rand, McNally 1911. *Lotta Embury's Career* 1915. *The Newcomers* 1916. *Painted Windows* George H. Doran Company 1918. *The Wander Weed* 1923. *A Mountain Woman* Books for Libraries Press 1969. Others

Awards or inclusion in other biographical books: *American Authors and Books; American Women; Biographical Dictionary and Synopsis of Books; Childhood in Poetry; Dictionary of American Authors; Dictionary of North American Authors; Twentieth Century Biographical Dictionary of Notable Americans; Who Was Who in America; Women's Who's Who of America*

PECKHAM, HOWARD
Address: 600 Carolina Village Road, Box 361, Hendersonville, North Carolina 28792
Born: July 13, 1910; Lowell, Michigan
Parents: H. Algernon, Harriet (Wilson) Peckham
Children: Stephen, Angela
Education: Olivet College, Olivet, Michigan,1927-1929. University of Michigan, A.B., Ann Arbor, Michigan, 1931; M.A., 1933
Career: Editorialist, *The Grand Rapids Press,* 1935. Curator of Manuscripts, Clements Library, University of Michigan, 1936-1945; Director, 1953-1977. Director, Indiana Historical Bureau, 1945-1953

Writings: *Historical Americana* The University of Michigan Press 1980. *Indiana, A Bicentennial History* W.W. Norton & Company, Inc. 1978. *Sources of American Independence* 2 vols. University of Chicago Press 1978. *The Toll of Independence* University of Chicago Press 1974. *The Making of the University of Michigan* University of Michigan Press 1967. *The Colonial Wars 1689-1762* University of Chicago Press 1964. *Pontiac, Young Ottawa Leader* Bobbs-Merrill 1963. *The War For Independence* University of Chicago Press 1958. *Nathanael Greene, Independent Boy* Bobbs-Merrill 1956. *William Henry Harrison, Young Tippecanoe* Bobbs-Merrill 1951. *Pontiac and the Indian Uprising* Princeton University Press l947; University of Chicago Press 1961; Russel and Russel 1970. *Invitation To Book Collecting* (with C. Storm) R.R. Bowker 1946. Articles
Awards or inclusion in other biographical books: *Michigan Authors,* 1st ed., 2nd ed.; *Who's Who in America*

PEDERSON, MIRIAM E.
Address: 235 Hampton S.E., Grand Rapids, Michigan 49506
Born: January 5, 1948; Windom, Minnesota
Parents: Gordon S. Kling, Regina E. Kling
Children: Benjamin, Madeline
Education: Crystal Lake High School, Crystal Lake, Illinois, 1964-1966. Bethel College, B.A., St. Paul, Minnesota, 1966-1970. Western Michigan University, M.F.A., Kalamazoo, Michigan, 1981-1984
Career: Adjunct Assistant Professor, Aquinas College, Grand Rapids, Michigan, 1983 to date. Artist-in-the-Schools, Forest Hills School District, Grand Rapids, Michigan, 1988-1990. English Teacher, St. Paul, Minneapolis; Grand Rapids, Michigan, 1971-1979

Writings: *Primavera* University of Chicago 1981. Published in *Green River Review, Passages North* and others. Included in such anthologies as *Woman Poet: The Midwest* 1985; *Passages North Anthology* 1990; *The Third Coast: Contemporary Michigan Poets* 1989. Collaborative chapbook, *The Adding We Do In Our Sleep.* Work in Progress: Chapbook tentatively titled *Sleeping in Ireland*
Awards or inclusion in other biographical books: *Directory of Poets and Writers* 1982--. Cranbrook Writers' Conference Scholarship, 1984, 1985. Winner of Kent County Poetry Competition, 1984. Faculty Development Grants, Aquinas College, 1989, 1990
What is the aim or goal of your writing? "To celebrate this time and place in the best way I know how."
May inquiries be sent to you about doing workshops, readings? Yes

PEERADINA, SALEEM
Address: 343 Anthony Court, Adrian, Michigan 49221
Born: October 5, 1944; Bombay, India
Parents: Habib Peeradina, Noorunnisa Peeradina
Children: Shoneizi, Lail
Education: St. Xavier's College, B.A., Bombay, India, 1964-1967. Bombay University, M.A., 1967-1969. Wake Forest University, M.A., North Carolina, 1971-1973
Career: Assistant Professor, Siena Heights College, Adrian, Michigan, 1989—. Copywriter, Hindusthan Thompson Associates, Bombay, India, 1984-1987. Reviews Editor, Indian Express, Bombay, India, 1982-1988. Director, Open Classroom, Sophia College for Women, Bombay, India, 1978-1984

Writings: *Group Portrait* Oxford University Press 1992. *First Offence* Newground, Bombay 1980. *Contemporary Indian Poetry in English* (editor) Macmillan India 1972. Work in Progress: Selected prose, *Private View*. A prose memoir of growing up in Bombay, *The Ocean in My Yard*
Awards or inclusion in other biographical books: *International Who's Who in Poetry* 1982, 1992; *Who's Who in India* 1986, 1988, 1990, 1992. British Council Writer's Grant, 1983. Fulbright Travel Grant, 1971
What is the aim or goal of your writing? "Poetry is first and foremost a means of discovery of self-knowledge. It is a means of showing the relationship between the inner and outer worlds; the individual and the social context inhabited by that individual. Poetry is a stay against time, the preservation of transitory moments, an attempt to seize a brief a duration of time in order to freeze it. It is also the voice of dreams, wild desires that are unacceptable in the everyday prosaic world."
May inquiries be sent to you about doing workshops, readings? Yes. Conducting poetry workshops for the last 12 years. Readings-all over the world, since 1970

PENN, WILLAM S.
Address: 164 Kedzie Street, East Lansing, Michigan 48823
Born: March 21, 1949; Los Angeles, California
Parents: William S. Penn, mother deceased
Children: Rachel
Education: Syracuse University, Doctor of Arts, Syracuse, New York, 1976-1979. University of California, A.B. English, Davis, California, 1966-1971
Career: Associate Professor, Michigan State University, East Lansing, Michigan, 1987—. Assistant Professor, Hostos Community College, Bronx, New York, 1986-1987. Assistant Professor, Pace University, New York, New York, 1984-1986. Assistant Professor, State University of New York, Oswego, New York, 1980-1983. Freelance writer, editor, 1979—. Fiction readings in Canada, United States

Writings: Stories in *The Vanderbilt Review, The Northern Review, Passages, Southern Humanities Review, Port Townsend Journal* and others. Articles, belles lettres, essays in *Spell/binder, Southern Humanities Rreview* and others. Poems in *California Quarterly, Portland Review* and others. Included in *Wayzgoose Anthology of New Canadian-American Writing* . Article, *The Encyclopedia Americana Annual: 1988.* Work in Progress: Novels: *Killing Time With Strangers. The Absence of Angels*
Awards or inclusion in other biographical books: *Directory of American Fiction Writers,* 1983; *Who's Who Directory of Writers, Editors and Publishers,* 1984. Resident Writer, Banff Centre for the Arts, Banff, Alberta, Canada, 1991. Nominated for Pushcart

Prize, 1991. Michigan Council for the Arts Grant, 1990. New York Foundation for the Arts Prize, 1988. All University Research Initiation Grant, Michigan State University, 1988. Finalist, P.E.N. Nelson Algren Awards, 1987. Supporting Grant, Ludwig Vogelstein Foundation, 1985. Finalist, Iowa School of Letters Award for Short Fiction, 1984. Yaddo Fellowship, 1983. Montalvo Center for the Arts Fellowship, 1983. Honorable Mention, James B. Phelan Awards, 1982. Stephan Crane Prize in Fiction, 1979, 1977. Michael Alssid Prize, 1979. University Research Fellowship, 1979. Departmental Citation for Distinguished Work, 1979. Departmental Citation for the Outstanding Undergraduate in English, 1970

What is the aim or goal of your writing? "The pleasure of intelligent readers of novels, stories, narrative essays."

May inquiries be sent to you about doing workshops, readings? Yes. Happy to do them

PERCY, DEBORAH ANN

Address: 2214 Waite Avenue, Kalamazoo, Michigan 49008
Born: December 7, 1944; Kalamazoo, Michigan
Parents: Richard N. Percy, Helen L. Percy
Children: Edward Dzialowski, Andrew Dzialowski
Education: Western Michigan University, B.A., Kalamazoo, Michigan, 1966; M.F.A., 1988
Career: Public School Administrator, Kalamazoo Public Schools, Kalamazoo, Michigan, 1983—. English Teacher, Kalamazoo Public Schools, Kalamazoo, 1974-1983. Creative Writing Teacher, Western Michigan University, Kalamazoo, Michigan, 1988—. Produced several plays

Writings: *But If It Rage* (with Arnie Johnston) Libido 1991. Other plays written with Arnie Johnston. Work in Progress: Screenplay, full-length plays, with Arnie Johnston. Turning *Unseasonable Weather* and *What's for Dinner?* into full-length plays
Awards or inclusion in other biographical books: Five Creative Writing Awards, Western Michigan University, 1985-1988. Graduate Creative Writer/Scholar Award, 1988. Arts Fund of Kalamazoo/NEA Grant. Winner, about 10 national playwriting competitions. Nominated, Susan Smith Blackburn Award, 1992. Samual French Off-Off Broadway Award, 1992. TCG Plays in Progress, 1992. Creative Artist Grant, Michigan Council for the Arts
What is the aim or goal of your writing? "To write intelligent and entertaining plays."
May inquiries be sent to you about doing workshops, readings? Yes

PEREZ-STABLE, MARIA A.

Address: Dwight B. Waldo Library, Western Michigan University, Kalamazoo, Michigan 49008
Born: November 2, 1954; Havanna, Cuba
Parents: Diego J. Perez-Stable, Maria L. (Dominguez) Perez-Stable
Education: Miami University, B.A. in History, Oxford, Ohio, 1972-1976. Case Western Reserve University, M.S.L.S. in Library Science, 1976-1977. Western Michigan University, M.A. in History, Kalamazoo, Michigan, 1980-1986
Career: Social Sciences Reference Librarian, Associate Professor, Dwight B. Waldo Library, Western Michigan University, Kalamazoo, Michigan, 1991—; Education Li-

brarian, Education Library, 1984-1991; Catalog Librarian; 1979-1984. Catalog Librarian, Western Reserve Historical Society, Cleveland, Ohio, 1977-1979

Writings: *Peoples of the American West: Historical Perspectives Through Children's Literature* (with Mary H. Cordier) Scarecrow Press 1989. *Directory of Michigan Academic Libraries, October 1984* (with Judy Brow) Michigan Library Association 1984. In *Education Libraries.* Work in Progress: *America's Story Through Children's Literature: Books and Activities to Enrich the K-8 Curriculum* (with Mary H. Cordier) Oryx Press

Awards or inclusion in other biographical books: *Who's Who among Hispanic Americans,* 1st ed.; *Who's Who in American Education,* 3rd ed.; *Who's Who in the Midwest,* 22nd Edition

What is the aim or goal of your writing? "The object of my writing is to get children enthusiastic about history through the vehicle of children's literature. As a librarian, I have an avid interest in books and the aim of my writing is to expose children to the many wonderful books available to them. Having an advanced degree in American history, I have chosen to write in this area. With the numerous well-written and well-researched fiction and non-fiction historical books currently available, children can learn more about their nation's history using materials outside of the basal textbooks used in the classroom. Both of my books contain learning activities that develop basic concepts and coordinate the children's books with American history."

May inquiries be sent to you about doing workshops, readings? Yes

PERKINS, AGNES REGAN

Address: 2565 W. Ellsworth Road, Ann Arbor, Michigan 48108
Born: April 28, 1926; Helena, Montana
Parents: Thomas P. Regan, Agnes D. Regan
Children: Todd, Aaron, Stuart
Education: University of Montana, B.A., Missoula, Montana, 1943-1947; M.A., 1948-1949
Career: Teaching Fellow, University of Montana, Missoula, Montana, 1948-1949. Professor of English, Eastern Michigan University, Ypsilanti, Michigan, 1961-1986

Writings: *Dictionary of British Children's Fiction* (with Alethea Helbig) Greenwood 1989. *Dictionary of American Children's Fiction, 1960-1984* (with Helbig) Greenwood 1986. *Dictionary of American Children's Fiction, 1859-1959* (with Helbig) Greenwood 1985. *Dusk to Dawn: Poems of Night* (with Helbig, Helen Hill) Crowell 1981. *Straight on Till Morning: Poems of the Imaginary World* (with Hill, Helbig) Crowell 1977. *New Coasts and Strange Harbors: Discovering Poems* (with Hill) Crowell 1974. Work in Progress: *Dictionary of Children's Fiction from Australia, Canada, India, New Zealand, and Selected African Countries* (with Helbig). *Dictionary of American Children's Fiction, 1985-1989* (with Helbig). *Dictionary of American Children's Fiction, 1990-1994* (with Helbig). *Minorities in American Imaginative Literature: Bibliography for School and Public Librarians* (with Helbig)

Awards or inclusion in other biographical books: *Contemporary Authors* Vols. 57-60

What is the aim or goal of your writing? "To introduce children and their teachers and parents to good poems. To provide critical appraisals of fiction for children for researchers, teachers, librarians, and parents."

May inquiries be sent to you about doing workshops, readings? Yes.

PETERS, T. R., SR.

Address: 350 Moselle Place, Grosse Pointe Farms, Michigan 48236
Born: November 14, 1929; Detroit, Michigan
Parents: Norman A. Peters, Eleanor H. (Schneider) Peters
Children: Jennifer, Thomas, Jr., Sarah J. (spouse: Lee Tremonti)
Education: Hillsdale College, B.A., Hillsdale, Michigan, 1950-1954. Wayne State University, M.A., Detroit, Michigan, 1960-1962. University of Iowa, post-degree, Iowa City, Iowa, 1970
Career: Professor of English, Macomb Community College, Warren, Michigan, 1985–. Manager, Communications Department, Blue Cross and Blue Shield of Michigan, Detroit, Michigan, 1972-1985. Education Coordinator,*The Detroit Free Press* , Detroit, Michigan, 1968-1972. High School Teacher, Detroit Public Schools, Detroit, Michigan, 1958-1968. Screen Writer, The Jam Handy Organization, 1954-1958.

Writings: *Two Weeks in the Forties* Xpressway Publishing 1988, 1990. *The Education of Tom Webber* Banner Books 1977. Included in *The Third Coast: Contemporary Michigan Fiction.* Published in *Detroit Monthly Magazine, Detroit News, Detroit Free Press, Bombay Gin.* Others. Work in Progress: A third novel, Wayne State University Campus in 1949, which will complete trilogy
Awards or inclusion in other biographical books:*Michigan Authors,* 2nd ed. Grant from Utica Schools, 1989. International Literary Award, MSS., Inc., 1985. Grant, Grosse Pointe Foundation, 1978
What is the aim or goal of your writing? "To create works of artistic/literary merit from my experiences and convictions which will both entertain and enlighten readers."
May inquiries be sent to you about doing workshops, readings? Yes

PETERSON, WILFERD A.

Address: 2000 Leonard Street, Apt. A., Grand Rapids, Michigan 49505
Born: August 21, 1900; Whitehall, Michigan
Parents: Peter H. Peterson, Elsie (Gilbert) Peterson
Children: Lilian (wife deceased: Ruth Irene (Rector) Peterson
Education: Muskegon High School
Career: Retired. Vice-President, Creative Director, Jaqua Adv., Grand Rapids, Michigan, 1928-1965. Advisory board, *Sunshine Magazine.* Editorial Board, *Science of Mind* magazine. Speaker, service clubs, churches. Appeared on radio, television

Writings: *The Art of Creative Thinking* Hay House 1991. *The Art of Living Treasure Chest* Simon & Schuster 1977; also in Japanese. *The Art of Living Day by Day* Simon & Schuster 1972. *The Art of Living in the World Today* Simon & Schuster 1969. *Adventures in the Art of Living* Simon & Schuster 1968. *More About the Art of Living* Simon & Schuster 1966. *The New Book of the Art of Living* Simon & Schuster 1962-1963. *The Art of Living* Simon & Schuster 1961; in French (Quebec) 1985. *The Art of Getting Along* Harmony Press 1949. Essays for 24 national issues of Sunday supplement, *This Week.* Text, Hallmark Cards/calendars. Excerpts in *Reader's Digest.* Writing in Progress: Writing for *Science of Mind,* monthly (for the past 25-30 years)
Awards or inclusion in other biographical books:*Here's How by Who's Who* 1968; *Michigan Authors,* 2nd ed. Doctorate of Letters, Aquinas College, 1984. George Washington Medal, Freedoms Foundation at Valley Forge. Silver Medal Award, Advertising Federation of America, National Advertising Man of the Year

What is the aim or goal of your writing? "To bring about a better understanding of the American way of life."

May inquiries be sent to you about doing workshops, readings? No. Retired

PHILIPP-PETRICK, MARY, KATHRYN

Address: 2863 Sunnycrest, Kalamazoo, Michigan 49001

Born: March 14, 1951; Kalamazoo, Michigan

Parents: Richard J. Philipp, Zoe I. Philipp

Children: Eric, Emily

Education: Comstock High School, Comstock, Michigan. Kalamazoo College, B.A., Kalamazoo, Michigan, 1969-1973. Western Michigan University, Kalamazoo, Michigan; M.A. Psychology, 1974-1976, M.F.A., 1984

Career: Teacher, Creative Writing for Senior Citizens, Kalamazoo, Michigan, 1992—. Instructor, Western Michigan University, 1987—.
Limited Licensed Psychologist, Borgess Hospital, 1978-1987. Instructor, Kalamazoo Valley Community College, Kalamazoo, Michigan, 1988-1990. Comstock Adult Education. Readings

Writings: Published in *The Small Towner, Passages North, The Great Lakes Review, Farmers Market, The Trial Balloon, Labyris, Permafrost, Currents, The McGuffin, Celery,* others. Work in Progress: Poetry manuscript, *Piecework*

Awards or inclusion in other biographical books: Cranbrook Writer's Conference Scholarships, 1984, 1985, 1986. New Voices in Poetry, Poetry Resource Center of Michigan, 1986. Guild House, Ann Arbor, 1985

What is the aim or goal of your writing? "As a native of Michigan, I hope that is reflected in my appreciation for the nature in this state. I often write about nature and people-I aim to reveal their critical connection."

May inquiries be sent to you about doing workshops, readings? Yes

PIERCY, MARGE

Address: Box 1473, Wellfleet, Massachusetts 02667

Born: March 31, 1936; Detroit, Michigan

Parents: Bob Piercy, Bert Piercy

Education: University of Michigan, A.B., Ann Arbor, Michigan, 1957. Northwestern University, Evanston, Illinois, 1958

Career: Taught various classes at Gary Extension of Indiana University, 1960-1962. Novelist, poet, essayist, reviewer, 1963—. Poet-in-Residence, University of Kansas, Lawrence, Spring, 1971. Poetry workshop, Distinguished Visiting Lecturer, 1975. Staff, Fine Arts Work Center, Provincetown, Massachusetts, 1976-1977. Visiting Faculty, Women's Writers Conference, Cazenovia College, Cazenovia, New York, 1976, 1978, 1980. Fiction Writer-in-Residence, Holy Cross University, Worcester, Massachusetts, 1976. Poetry and fiction workshops at Writers Conference, University of Indiana, Bloomington, 1977-1980. Butler Chair of Letters, Summer Writer-In-Residence, 1977. Poetry workshop, visiting faculty, fiction lecturer, 1979, 1981, 1984, such as Lake Superior Writers Conference. Various workshops, classes, to the present. Has given readings, workshops, lectured at over 250 institutions in several countries such as the City University of London, Library of Congress. Given numerous benefits to raise money for: The Women's Bail Fund, Feminist Writer's Guide, Detroit Women's Community Health Project, Mobilization for Survival, The Boston and San Francisco Rape Crisis Centers and many more. Consultant, judge, board member, advisor, panelist, and related positions on many occasions since 1971, such as being a judge at the Avery Hopwood contest, University of Michigan, 1983, 1988. DeRoy Distinguished Visiting Professorship at the University of Michigan Honors Program, 1992

Writings: *Breaking Camp* Wesleyan University Press 1968. *Hard Loving* Wesleyan University Press 1969. *Going Down Fast* Trident 1969. *4-Telling* (with others) Crossing Press 1971. *Dance the Eagle to Sleep* Doubleday 1971. *Small Changes* Doubleday 1973. *To Be of Use* Doubleday 1973. *Living in the Open* Knopf 1976. *The Twelve-Spoked Wheel Flashing* Knopf 1978. *Woman on the Edge of Time* Knopf 1976; Fawcett Crest 1983. *The High Cost of Living* Harper 1978. *Vida* Summit 1980. *Circles on the Water: Selected Poems of Marge Piercy* Knopf 1982. *The Moon is Always Female* Knopf 1980. *Stone, Paper, Knife* Knopf 1983. *Available Light* Knopf 1988. *Braided Lives* (autobiographical novel) Summit 1982. *Fly Away Home* Summit 1984. *He, She and It* Knopf 1991. *Gone to Soldiers: a Novel* Summit Books 1987. *Mars and Her Children* Knopf 1992. Several others. Work is in many anthologies and has been translated into foreign languages. Contributor of essays, poetry, fiction, reviews to such periodicals as *Paris Review, Village Voice, New Republic*. With Ira Wood: *The Last White Class: A Play about Neighborhood Terror* Crossing Press 1979. *Parti-Colored Blocks for a Quilt* University of Michigan Press 1982
Awards or inclusion in other biographical books: *Michigan Authors,* 2nd ed. Phi Beta Kappa. Phi Kappa Phi. James B. Angell Scholar. Lucinda Goodrich Downs Scholar. Orion Scott Award in Humanities. Major and minor awards in poetry and fiction, Avery Hopwood contest. Borestone Mountain Poetry Award (Twice). Literature Award from the governor's commission on the Status of Women (Massachusetts). National Endowment for the Arts. Rhode Island School of Design Faculty Association medal. Carolyn Kizer Poetry Prize from *Calapooya Collage* 1986, 1990. Shaffer/PEN/New England Award for Literary Excellence. Honorary Doctor of Letters, Bridgewater State College. The Golden Rose Poetry Prize, New England Poetry Club, 1990. May Sarton Award, New England Poetry Club, 1991 In an article by Joan Oleck, "The Present is a Very Hard Place" *Michigan Today* (June 1992): "When Piercy appraises her own writings, she finds that a dominant theme is that: 'beings have a right to live, a right to their own consciousness, and must acknowledge that they're a part of the web of all living things, in history and in community.' "

PIERSON, CLARA ELEANOR (DILLINGHAM) (1868-1952)
Born: March, 1868; Coldwater, Michigan
Parents: Father from Vermont, mother from Massachusetts
Children: Son died in infancy, adopted Harold, John Howard
Career: Faculty, Alma College. Moved to Stanton, Michigan when married. Housewife, Children's author. The Pierson's Stanton home, built in 1904, became Trinity Evangelical Free Church, 1952

Writings: *Among the Meadow People* E. P. Dutton 1897. *Among the Forest People* E.P. Dutton 1898; J. Murray 1899. *Plow Stories* E.P. Dutton 1923. *The Plucky Allens* E.P. Dutton l925. *The Allens and Aunt Hannah* E. P. Dutton l927. Others, published by E. P. Dutton. Books published by Chambers and Murrays in England
Awards or inclusion in other biographical books: *Carolyn Sherwin Bailey Historical Collection of Children's Books*

PITRONE, JEAN MADDERN

Address: 3878 Pare Lane, Trenton, Michigan 48183
Born: Ishpeming, Michigan
Parents: William C. Maddern, Gladys M. (Beer) Maddern
Children: Joseph, Jill, Anthony Jr., Joyce, John, Janet, Julie, Jane, Cheryl
Education: Ishpeming High School, Latin Course, Ishpeming, Michigan, 1934-1938
Career: Short Story Writing Instructor, Writer's Digest School, Cincinnati, Ohio, 1967-1988. Music Director, St. Alfred Church, Taylor, Michigan, 1974-1980. Organist, Our Lady of Grace Church, Dearborn Hts., Michigan, 1958-1966. Freelance writer for past 30 years. Past president, Detroit Women Writers. Staff member, speaker, Oakland University Writer's Conference, 12 years

Writings: *Hudson's: Hub of America's Heartland* A & M Publishing 1991. *Tangled Web: Legacy of Auto Pioneer John F. Dodge* A & M Publishing 1989. *Jean Hoxie: The Robin Hood of Tennis* Avenue Publishing 1985. *The Dodges: the Auto Family Fortune & Misfortune* Icarus Press 1981. *Myra: The Life and Times of Myra Wolfgang, Trade Union Leader* Calibre Books1980. *Chavez: Man of the Migrants* Pyramid 1972. *The Touch of His Hand* Alba House 1970. *Trailblazer: Negro Nurse in the American Red Cross* Harcourt Brace & World 1969. *The Great Black Robe* St. Paul Press 1963. Hundreds of short stories and articles in such publications as *Detroit News Sunday Magazine, Family Digest, Redbook, Chicago Tribune, New York Mirror, Catholic Digest* and others. Work in Progress: Historical novel set in Detroit, *Victoria: A Woman of Means*
Awards or inclusion in other biographical books: *Who's Who of American Women.* Book of Distinction Award, International Society of Automotive Historians, 1990. Books Across the Sea Selection, 1982. First Place Award, Friends of American Writers, 1970
What is the aim or goal of your writing? "The goal of my writing is to satisfy my own needs to write—I cannot imagine my life without this creative outlet. I find the historical aspects of my writings most satisfying."
May inquiries be sent to you about doing workshops, readings? Yes

PITTMAN, PHILIP MCMILLAN

Address: P.O. Box 187, Les Cheneaux Club, Cedarville, Michigan 49719
Born: April 6, 1941; Detroit, Michigan
Parents: Lansing M. Pittman, Sally B. Pittman
Children: Philip McMillan III, Mary Christine, Noel,
Education: Kenyon College, A.B., Gambier, Ohio, 1959-1963. Vanderbilt University, B.A., Ph.D., Nashville, Tennessee, 1963-1967
Career: Author, editor, publisher, self-employed, Les Cheneaux Ventures, Inc., 1980–. Associate Professor, Marshall University, Huntington, West Virginia, 1968-1980. Assistant Professor, University of Victoria, Victoria, British Columbia, 1967-1968. Instructor, Vanderbilt University, Nashville, Tennessee, 1966-1967

Writings: *Fishing the King Salmon in Michigan's Northern Waters* A & M 1992. *Don't Blame the Treaties: Native American Rights and the Michigan Indian Treaties* A & M 1992. *The Portrayal of Life Stages in English Literature 1500-1800* Edwin Mellen Press1989. *Ripples From the Breezes: A Les Cheneaux Anthology* Les Cheneaux Ventures 1988. *The Les Cheneaux Chronicles: Anatomy of a Community* Les Cheneaux Ventures 1984. Work in Progress: *American Apartheid: Where it is and How It Works*
Awards or inclusion in other biographical books: *Who's Who in the Midwest* 1990–; *Who's Who in the World* 1991—. AASLH Award, 1986

What is the aim or goal of your writing? "To teach and to delight".
May inquiries be sent to you about doing workshops, readings? Yes

POKAGON, SIMON (1830-1899)
Born: 1830; Indian village on St. Joseph River, near or on Indiana border, Berrien County, Michigan
Parents: Leopold Pokagon, famous Potawatomi chief; Elizabeth Pokagon
Education: At 14, entered Notre Dame University, Indiana, where he studied 3 years. Oberlin College, Ohio, 1 year. Twinsburg, Ohio, 2 years
Career: Tribal chief of eastern Potawatomi Indians. Tried many years to obtain payment for sale of Indian land to the government, lectured widely; while at Columbian Exposition in Chicago, he represented his people as owners of Chicago area. Translated several hundred sermons into Indian language

Writings: *Birch Bark Booklets* (Hartford, Michigan)1893-1901. *O-Gi-Maw-Kwe Mit-I-Gwa-Ki* (*Queen of the Woods*). *Also Brief sketch of the Algaic Language.* (autobiographical novel) C.H. Engle (Hartford, Michigan) l899, 1901; Hardscrabble 1972. Articles in magazines such as *Chicago Inter-Ocean, Harper's, The Arena, Review of Reviews, The Chautauquan,* others. Poem, "The Red Man's Greeting", circulated at the 1893 Columbian Exposition
Awards or inclusion in other biographical books: *Dictionary of Indians of North America; Indiana Authors and Their Books*

PORTER, PHIL
Address: 995 Duncan Avenue, Cheboygan, Michigan 49721
Born: January 29, 1953; Grosse Pointe, Michigan
Parents: William C. Porter, Lorone S. Porter
Children: William, Joseph, Susanna, Katherine, Elizabeth
Education: Kenyon College, B.A., Gambier, Ohio, 1970-1974. State University of New York, M.A., History Museum Studies, Cooperstown Graduate Program of History, Cooperstown, New York, 1974-1975
Career: Curator of Collections, Mackinac Island State Park Commission, Mackinac Island, Michigan, 1976-1982; Curator of Interpretation, 1982—.

Writings: *The Eagle at Mackinac, the Establishment of United States Military and Civilian Authority on Mackinac Island, 1796-1802* Mackinac Island State Park Commission 1991. *The Wonder of Mackinac, A Guide to the Natural History of Mackinac Island* Mackinac Island State Park Commission 1984. *View From the Veranda, the History and Architecture of the Summer Cottages on Mackinac Island* Mackinac Island State Park Commission 1981. Articles in *Michigan History Magazine* and *The Historical Society of Michigan Newsletter, House Beautiful.* Contributor to *Mackinac, the Gathering Place*
What is the aim or goal of your writing? "Interpretation and presentation of the history of the Straits of Mackinac, Michigan."
May inquiries be sent to you about doing workshops, readings? Yes

POUND, ARTHUR (1884-1966)
Born: June 1, 1884; Pontiac, Michigan
Education: University of Michigan, B.A., Ann Arbor, Michigan
Career: Associate editor, editor of *Atlantic Monthly*. Other positions at *The New York Evening Post, New York Herald*. Associate editor, *The Independent,* 1924-1927. Official

Historian for the state or New York for four years, founder and first president of the Society for Colonial History

Writings: *The Iron Man in Industry* Atlantic Monthly 1922. *Johnson of the Mohawks* Macmillan 1930. *Building on Faith in Flint* Union Industries 1930. *Native Stock* Macmillan1931. *Mountain Morning, and Other Poems* Argus Press 1932. *Washington, Freeman of Albany* Albany Institute 1932. *Around the Corner* Sears Publishing 1933. *Once a Wilderness* Reynal & Hitch, 1934. *The Turning Wheel; The Story* Doubleday 1934. *The Golden Earth* Macmillan 1935. *Hawk of Detroit, a Novel* Reynal & Hitch 1939. *Salt of the Earth; The Story* Atlantic Monthly 1940. *Detroit: Dynamic City* D. Appleton 1940. *Lake Ontario* Bobbs-Merril 1945.*The Only Thing Worth Finding* Wayne State University 1964. Several others; many books had more than one printing, publisher
Awards or inclusion in other biographical books: *American Authors and Books: 1640 to the Present Day; Contemporary Authors; Michigan Authors,* 1st ed.; *Who Was Who among North American Authors; Who Was Who in America.* Honorary degrees from University of Michigan, Ann Arbor, Michigan; Union College, Schenectady, New York

POYER, JOSEPH JOHN
Pseudonym: Joe Poyer
Born: November 30, 1939; Battle Creek, Michigan
Parents: Joseph Poyer, Eileen (Powell) Poyer
Children: Joseph, Geoffrey
Education: Kellogg Community College, A.A., Battle Creek, Michigan, 1959. Michigan State University, B.A., East Lansing, Michigan, 1961
Career: Assistant Director of Public Information, Michigan Tuberculosis and Respiratory Disease Association, Lansing, Michigan, 1961-1962. Proposals Writer, Pratt & Whitney Aircraft, East Hartford, Connecticut, 1963-1965. Proposals Writer, Beckman Instruments, Fullerton, California, 1965-1967. Manager of Interdisciplinary Communications, Bioscience Planning, Anaheim, California, 1967-1968. Senior Project Manager, Research Administrator, Allergan Pharmaceuticals, Irvine, California, 1968-1977. Full-time writer, 1977—. Teacher, Golden West College, 1974-1976. Field editor

Writings: *Operation Malacca* Doubleday 1968. *North Cape* (Book-of-the-Month Club Selection, England) Doubleday 1969. *The Chinese Agenda* (Junior Literary Guild Selection; Book-of-the-Month Selection, Sweden) Doubleday 1972. *Vengeance 10* Atheneum 1980. *Devoted Friends* Atheneum 1982. *A Time of War: The Transgressors* Sphere 1983. *Devoted Friends* Sphere 1985. *Milspeak: a Dictionary of International Military Acronyms & Abbreviations* North Cape Publications 1986. *The Complete Book of Top Gun: American's Flying Aces* Publications International 1990. *The Complete Book of U. S. Fighting Power* Publications International 1990. *The Illustrated History of Helicopters* Publications International 1990. *The .45-70 Springfield* North Cape Publications 1991. Others. Editor of medical books. Short stories, articles
Awards or inclusion in other biographical books: *Contemporary Authors; Michigan Authors,* 2nd ed.; *Writers Directory*

PRESS, SIMONE N.
Address: 2215 Chaucer Ct., Ann Arbor, Michigan 48103
Pseudonym: Simone Juda Press
Born: April 12, 1943; Cambridge, Massachusetts
Parents: Walter Juda, Renee Molino

Children: Corinna Nicole, Valerie Gabriella

Education: Lexington High School, Diploma. Bennington College, B.A., Bennington, Vermont, 1965-1967. Columbia University, M.A., New York, New York, 1962-1965. University of Michigan, Ann Arbor, Michigan, 1989-1990

Career: Associate Professor of English, Siena Heights College, Adrian, Michigan, 1973—. Artistic Director, Ann Arbor Repertory Theatre, Ann Arbor, Michigan, 1986-1990. Artistic Director, Young People's Theater, Ann Arbor, Michigan, 1985-1988. Playwright in Residence, New Playwrights Forum Coordinator, Arts Education Director, Detroit, Michigan, 1982-1986. Michigan Council for the Arts, Participant in Creative Writers in the Schools Program

Writings: *Lifting Water* Crowfoot Press 1974. *Thaw* Inward Horizons 1969. Play in two acts, produced at Attic Theatre, Equity Showcase. Work in Progress: *The Deal With Claire Brooke,* a screenplay

Awards or inclusion in other biographical books: *Michigan Authors,* 2nd ed.; *Who's Who in American Poets and Fiction Writers.* Michigan Council for the Arts Creative Artist Award, 1983

What is the aim or goal of your writing? "To say what I need to say to as many people as possible in an imaginative, memorable and enlightening fashion. In teaching creative writing, to allow and encourage others to tap their 'inner voices'."

May inquiries be sent to you about doing workshops, readings? Yes

QUAIFE, MILO MILTON (1880-1959)
Born: October 6, 1880; Nashua, Iowa
Parents: Albert Edward Quaife, Barbara S. (Hine) Quaife
Children: Helen, Donald, Dorothy, Mary
Education: Grinnell College, Ph.B., Grinnell, Iowa, 1903. University of Missouri, A.M., 1905. University of Chicago, Ph.D. Wayne State University, Litt.D., 1951
Career: Historian. Secretary, Burton Historical Collection, Detroit, Michigan. Co-founder, The Algonquin Club, for men interested in the history of the Detroit-Windsor area, 1934. Lecturer of history, Wayne State University, University of Detroit

Writings: *The Indian Captivity of O.M. Spencer* R. R. Donnelley 1917. *Alexander Henry's Travels and Adventures in the Years 1760-1776* (edited with historical introduction and notes) R. R. Donnelley & Sons 1921. *Fort Wayne in 1790* William Mitchell Printing 1921. Edited *Papers* (of John Askin) Detroit Library Commission 1928-1931. *The Kingdom of St. James; a Narrative of the Mormons* Yale University Press (Amasa Stone Mather Memorial Publication Fund) 1930. *Alexander Mackenzie's Voyage to the Pacific Ocean in 1793* R. R. Donnelley & Sons 1931. *Chiccagou; from Indian Wigwam to Modern City, 1673-1835* University of Chicago Press 1933. *The Bark Covered House; or, Back in the Woods Again* Lakeside Press R. R. Donnelley & Sons 1937. *Condensed Historical Sketches for Each of Michigan's Counties* J.L. Hudson Company 1940. *Sixty Years: Six Decades in Growth & Development of Detroit and It's Environs, 1881-1941* J.L. Hudson Company 1941. *The Flag of the United States* Grosset & Dunlap 1942. Editor of 10 Volumes, The American Lake Series, Bobbs-Merrill, 1942-1949 that included such books as: *Lake Michigan. Michigan: From Primitive Wilderness to Industrial Commonwealth* (co-authored with Sidney Glazer) Prentice-Hall 1948. *I Remember Detroit* (with John C. Lodge) Wayne State University Press 1949. *This is Detroit: 1701-1951, Two Hundred & Fifty Years in Pictures* Wayne State University Press 1951. *Detroit's 250th Anniversary, Hudson's 70th Year* J.L. Hudson Company 1951? *The Siege of Detroit in 1763: the Journal of Pontiac's Conspiracy, and John Rutherfurd's Narrative of a Captivity* R.R. Donnelley 1958. Several others
Other biographical books: Honorary President for Life: The Algonquin Club. Tribute of a published bibliography; *46 Years: The Published Writings of M.M. Quaife, 1910-1955*, Algonquin Club 1956

QUIMBY, GEORGE IRVING,
Address: Burke Museum, University of Washington, Seattle, Washington 98195
Born: May 4, 1913; Grand Rapids, Michigan
Parents: George Irving Quimby, Ethelwyn S. Quimby
Children: Sedna, Edward, John, Robert
Education: University of Michigan, B.A. Anthropology, Ann Arbor, Michigan, 1932-1936; M.A., 1936-1937. University of Chicago, 1938-1939
Career: Professor Emeritus, Director Emeritus, University of Washington, Seattle, Washington, 1984—. Curator, Professor, Museum Director, University of Washington, Seattle, Washington, 1965-1984. Curator-Anthropology, Field Museum, Chicago, Illi-

nois, 1952-1965. Director, Muskegon Museum, Museum Board, Muskegon, Michigan, 1941-1942

Writings: *Edward Curtis in the Land of the War Canoes* (co-author) University of Washington Press 1980. *Indian Life in the Upper Great Lakes* University of Chicago 1960. *Indian Culture and Trade Goods in the Western Great Lakes* University of Wisconsin Press 1966. *Indians Before Columbus* (co-author) University of Chicago Press 1947. Monographs, scholarly articles, over 150 chapters. Work in Progress: Autobiography, Society for American Archaeology, publisher

Awards or inclusion in other biographical books: *Who's Who in America, Who's Who in the World.* Sigmapsi, Harrington Medal, Society for Historical Archaeology. Distinguished Service Award, Society for American Archaeology, 1989. Honorary Degree, Grand Valley State University. Fellow, American Anthropology. Fellow, American Association for the Advance of Science. Honorary Life Member, Council of Michigan Archaeologists

May inquiries be sent to you about doing workshops, readings? No

R

RAMET, CARLOS
Address: 2621 Adams Blvd., Saginaw, Michigan 48602
Born: March 30, 1955; London, England
Parents: Sebastian M. Ramet, Ida M. Ramet
Education: University of Southern California, B.A., Los Angeles, California, 1973-1977. San Francisco State University, M.A., San Francisco, California, 1978-1980. University of Illinois, Ph.D., Chicago, Illinois, 1983-1988
Career: Assistant Professor of English and Creative Writing, Saginaw Valley State University, Saginaw, Michigan, 1991—. Assistant Professor in English, Indiana University in Malaysia, Shah Alam, Malaysia, 1988-1990. Instructor in English, Columbia Arts College, Chicago, Illinois, 1987-1988. Teaching Assistant in English, University of Illinois-Chicago, Chicago, Illinois, 1983-1988. Play productions, staged reading, film aired

Writings: Short stories in *Alchemy, Red Shoes Review, Body Electric, Perigraph, Kola, RAFALE: Revue Litteraire*. Work in Progress: A collection of short stories. Two finished novels currently with literary agency in New York
Awards or inclusion in other biographical books: California State Scholar, 1974, 1976, 1977. Phi Beta Kappa, 1977. UIC Campus Programs Award, 1987
What is the aim or goal of your writing? "In my writing, I attempt to meet the demands of modernism and realism, regionalism and internationalism; in other words, my writing is set amidst the conflicts of contemporary literature and culture."
May inquiries be sent to you about doing workshops, readings? Yes

RANDALL, DUDLEY
Born: January 14, 1914; Washington, DC
Parents: Arthur George Clyde Randall, Ada Viola (Bradley) Randall
Children: Phyllis
Education: Wayne State University, B.A., Detroit, Michigan, 1949. University of Michigan, M.A.L.S., Ann Arbor, Michigan, 1951. University of Ghana 1970
Career: Foundry worker, Ford Motor Company, River Rouge, Michigan, 1932-1937. U.S. Army, 1942-1946. Carrier, clerk, U.S. Post Office, Detroit, Michigan, 1938-1951. Librarian, Lincoln University, Jefferson City, Missouri, 1951-1954. Associate Librarian, Morgan State College, Baltimore, Maryland, 1954-1956. Assistant Branch Librarian, Branch Librarian, Head, Reference Interloan department, Wayne County Federated Library System, Wayne, Michigan. Reference librarian, poet-in-residence, University of Detroit, Detroit, Michigan, 1969-1975. Visiting lecturer, University of Michigan, 1969. Founder and general editor, Broadside Press, Detroit, Michigan, 1965-1977, consultant, 1977—. Founded Broadside Poets Theater, Broadside Poetry Workshop, 1980. Member, Advisory Panel, Michigan Council for the Arts, New Detroit, 1970. Seminars, festivals in poetry, translator of Russian poetry

Writings: *Poem Counterpoem* (with Margaret Danner) Broadside Press 1966. *Cities Burning* Broadside Press 1968. *Black Poetry: A Supplement to Anthologies Which*

Exclude Black Poets (editor) Broadside Press 1969. *For Malcolm: Poems on the Life and Death of Malcolm X* (editor and contributor with Margaret G. Burroughs) Broadside Press 1967, 1969. *Love You* Paul Breman (London)1970, 1971; Broadside Press 1970. *More to Remember: Poems of Four Decades* Third World Press 1971. *The Black Poets* Bantam Books 1971, 1972. *After the Killing* Third World Press 1973. *A Capsule Course in Black Poetry Writing* (with others) Broadside Press 1975. *Broadside Memories: Poets I Have Known* Broadside Press 1975. *A Litany of Friends: New and Selected Poems* Lotus Press 1981, 1983. *Homage to Hoyt Fuller* Broadside Press 1984. *Golden Song: The Fiftieth Anniversary Anthology of the Poetry Society of Michigan* (editor with Louis J. Cantoni) Harlo 1985. Compiled *The Black Poets* Bantam 1971. Contributed to others. Work is in various anthologies and in such publications as *Wayne Review, Journal of Black Poetry, Midwest Journal, Black World.* Poems first published in *Detroit Free Press* when 13

Awards or inclusion in other biographical books: *Biographical Directory of Librarians in the United States and Canada; Black American Writers Past and Present; Contemporary Authors; Contemporary Literary Criticism; Contemporary Poets; Dictionary of Literature in the English Language; Directory of American Poets; Living Black Authors; Michigan Authors,* 2nd ed.; *Who's Who among Black Americans; Who's Who in America; Who's Who in the Midwest; Writers Directory,* others. Tompkins Award, Wayne State University, 1962, 1966. Kuumba Liberation Award, 1973. Arts Award in Literature, Michigan Foundation for the Arts, 1975. D. Litt., University of Detroit, 1978. Creative Artist Award in Literature, Michigan Council for the Arts, 1981; Senior fellowship, 1986. Appointed First Poet Laureate of the City of Detroit, 1981

RANKIN, CARROLL (WATSON) (1864-1945)
Born: May 11, 1864; Marquette, Michigan
Parents: Jonas William, Emily (Wood) Watson
Children: Florence, Ernest, Eleanor, Phyllis
Education: Taylor's Academy, Greenoch, Scotland, 1 year. Kemper Hall, Kenosha, Wisconsin, 2 years. Chicago Female College, Morgan Park, Illinois, 1 year
Career: Writer. First short story appeared in print when she was eleven years old. By the time she was 15 she had stories published in various Sunday School papers and in *Waverly's Magazine.* Became Society Editor at 16 for *Mining Journal.* Gave drawing and painting lessons to private pupils before marriage

Writings: *Dandelion Cottage* Holt 1904, 1923, 1931, 1946, 1951; Marquette County Historical Society 1977. *The Girls of Gardenville* Holt 1906. *The Adoption of Rose Marie* Holt 1908, 1936, 1943. *The Castaways of Pete's Patch* Holt 1911. *The Cinder Pond* Holt 1915. *Girls of Highland Hall; further Adventures of the Dandelion Cottagers* Holt 1921. *Gypsy Nan* Holt 1926. *Finders Keepers* Holt 1930. *Wolf Rock: a Sequel to The Cinder Pond* Holt 1933. *Stump Village* Holt 1935. Skits and short stories published in *Youth's Companion, Harper's Monthly, Life, St. Nicholas, Century, Bookman, Garden, Critic, Delineator, Leslie's, Lippincott's, Metropolitan, Everybody's, Munsey's.*
In the 2nd edition of *Michigan Authors,* her daughter, Phyllis, is credited with saying "She loved gardening. She had an artist's keen observation and delight in minute detail of form, color, and design in anything she encountered."
Awards or inclusion in other biographical books: *Michigan Authors,* 1st ed., 2nd ed.; *Who Was Who in America*

RANKIN, ERNEST HARVEY (1888-1979)
Born: January 6, 1888; Marquette, Michigan
Parents: Ernest Rankin, Caroline (Watson) Rankin
Children: Ernest Harvey, Jr., Mary Carol, John Breslin, Eleanor Ann
Education: Marquette High School, Marquette, Michigan, 1907. School Railway Signaling, 1910-1911
Career: Railroad signal engineering, mostly in Cleveland, Ohio with the New York Central Railroad, 1909-1954, retired. Genealogist, secretary/treasurer and executive secretary, Marquette County Historical Society, 1955-1969. Founder/editor, *Harlow's Wooded Man*

Writings: *A Brief History of the Marquette Iron Range* Marquette County Historical Society 1965, 1966. *The Indians of Gitchi Gumee* Marquette County Historical Society 1966. *North to Lake Superior: the Journal of Charles W. Penny 1840* (co-editor) John M. Longyear Research Library 1970. Numerous articles, book reviews. In *Michigan History,* newspapers. Provided a chapter in Walter Havinghurst's *Great Lakes Reader* 1968.
In the 2nd edition of *Michigan Authors* he is credited with: " 'Do not be afraid of work and keep the mind active.' He has recently completed *A Rankin Family History* for the benefit of Rankin descendants, a task which spanned thirty years of research and writing. His grandfather, Edward Peter Rankin, brought his name and bride to Pontiac in 1844 and his family of eight was raised and lived in the Detroit area. His father left the family hearthside in 1885 and moved to Marquette."
Awards or inclusion in other biographical books: *Michigan Authors,* 2nd ed.

RAPHAEL, LEV
Address: 4695 Chippewa Drive, Okemos, Michigan 48864
Born: May 19, 1954; New York, New York
Parents: Alex Steinberg, Helen Steinberg
Education: Fordham University, B.A., New York, New York, 1971-1975. University of Massachusetts, M.F.A., Amherst, Massachusetts, 1976-1978. Michigan State University, Ph.D., East Lansing, Michigan, 1981-1986
Career: Full-time Writer, 1988—. Assistant Professor of American Thought and Language, Michigan State University, East Lansing, Michigan, 1986-1988

Writings: *Winter Eyes* St. Martin's Press 1992. *Edith Wharton's Prisoners of Shame* St. Martin's Press 1991. *Dynamics of Power* (co-author) Schenkman 1991. *Stick Up for Yourself!* (co-author) Free Spirit 1991. *Dancing on Tisha B'Av* St. Martin's Press 1990
Awards or inclusion in other biographical books: Lambda Literary Award, 1990. Harvey Swados Fiction Prize, 1978. Reed Smith Fiction Prize, *Amelia* Magazine
What is the aim or goal of your writing? "To build bridges between various communities. To keep the legacy of the Holocaust alive."
May inquiries be sent to you about doing workshops, readings? Yes

RATIGAN, ELEANOR (ELDRIDGE) (1916-1981)
Pseudonym: Virginia Wharton
Born: May 23, 1916; Denver, Colorado
Parents: William T. Eldridge, Ida (Strickler) Eldridge
Children: Patricia, Anne, Shannon
Education: University of Tennessee at Chattanooga, 1934-1935. Professional Writers College, Hollywood, California, 1940-1944

Career: Writer, editor, "Musical Magazine", KOA Radio, Denver, Colorado, 1937-1939. Teacher, adult education, Charlevoix, Michigan, 1955-1956. Assistant dramatic coach, Charlevoix High School beginning1960

Writings: *Deep Water* Lothrop, Lee & Shepard 1961. *Coming of Flame* Dell 1963. *Son of Flame* Dell 1963. *Flame, Son of Silver Cloud* Dell 1964. *The Adventurers of Trudy* (series) Dell. Hundreds of articles, stories, *Family Circle, Co-Ed, Vogue, Chatelaine,* others

Awards or inclusion in other biographical books: *Contemporary Authors; Michigan Authors,* 2nd ed.; *Who's Who in America* In the 2nd edition, her husband, William Ratigan, comments: "Like many who were forced by illness to 'lay abed' (Robert Louis Stevenson, for instance) in childhood, Eleanor developed a love for books and music. She had a sharp ear and eye and could mimic the sound of any language without knowing the words. She could imitate anyone. In later school years she fancied herself an opera prima donna and drove her sisters somewhat wild. She loved to dance, especially with her handsome Tennessee father, she was his girl to his death. She collected stamps during her illness, began a collection of famous signatures (now quite unusual) and carried away her first prize in poetry in her senior year of high school. Meanwhile, she and some bright girfriends had formed a 'very sophisticated' poetry club which tended toward writing imitations of Dorothy Parker, Gibron et al. She still loves to recite *Gunga Din.*"

RATIGAN, WILLIAM O. (1910-1984)
Born: November 7, 1910; Detroit, Michigan
Parents: B. J. Ratigan, Bertie (Laing) Ratigan
Children: Patricia, Anne, Shannon
Education: University of Detroit, Detroit, Michigan, 1931-1933. University of Tennessee at Chattanooga, A.B., Chattanooga, Tennessee, 1935. Michigan State University, M.A., East Lansing, Michigan; Ph.D., 1963
Career: Continuity Director and Producer, National Broadcasting Company, 1937-1940, Supervisor of the Far East listening post on the West Coast,1940-1942, Managing News Editor of the Western Division, Supervisor of Commentators and Correspondents in the Pacific Theatre of Operation, 1942-1945, News Editor and Scriptwriter at the United Nations Conference, 1945. Came to Charlevoix, Michigan in 1946 where he continued writing for Curtis Publishing Company and other magazines. Became part of the Advisory Council, Naval Affairs, 1957. Became chief of the Ottawa tribe, Opwananian Kanotong (Interpreter of Dreams), 1957. Consultant to the Smithsonian Institution on the technical development of Great Lakes craft, 1959. Founder/Proprietor of The Dockside Press. In 1965 he became Charlevoix High School's first counselor, retiring 1975. Taught a Michigan State University extension course at Northwestern Michigan College, Traverse City, Michigan; University of Miami and University of Wisconsin

Writings: *NBC War Poems* 1945. *Great Lakes Sea Chanteys* 1948-1956. *Soo Canal* (with foreward by Gen. Douglas MacArthur) 1954, 2nd Edition Eerdmans 1968. *Young Mr. Big* Eerdmans 1955. *Hiawatha and America's Mightiest Mile* Eerdmans 1955. Editor of *Song of Hiawatha* Centennial Facsimile Edition. *The Adventures of Captain McCargo* Random House 1956. *Straits of Mackinac* Eerdmans 1957. *The Blue Snow, Tiny Tim Pine, Adventures of Paul Bunyan and Babe* Eerdmans 1958. *The Long Crossing* Eerdmans 1959. *Highways Over Broad Waters* Eerdmans 1959. *Conflicts With Counseling* University Microfilms 1964. *School Counseling, a View from Within* American School Counselor Association 1967. *Great Lakes Shipwrecks and Survivals* Eerdmans Bradley Edition,

Lake Michigan1960; Morrell Edition, Lake Huron1969; Edmund Fitzgerald Edition, Lake Superior 1977.*Theories of Counseling* 2nd Edition McGraw-Hill 1972

Awards or inclusion in other biographical books: *American Authors and Books; Contemporary Authors; Michigan Authors,* 1st ed., 2nd ed.; *Who's Who in America; Who's Who in the Midwest; Who's Who in the World.* Intercollegiate Odes to Horace Award, 1935. California Chaparral Poetry Prize, 1944

In the 2nd Edition of *Michigan Authors,* he is credited with: "There is a joy in writing that I have never found in any other occupation." His obituary in *Petoskey News-Review* (Petoskey, Michigan), October 22, 1984, stated "Ratigan was a true spinner of tales", and his family suggested memorials go to the William O. Ratigan Memorial Fund at Charlevoix Public Library, Charlevoix, Michigan

REED, J.(AMES) D.

Born: October 7, 1940; Jackson, Michigan
Parents: Clair Samuel Reed, Esther (Bryden) Reed
Children: Phoebe Christina
Education: Albion College, Albion, Michigan, 1958-1960. Michigan State University, B.A., East Lansing, Michigan, 1962. State University of New York, Stony Brook, 1967-1969
Career: Assistant Professor, University of Massachusetts, Amherst, Massachusetts, beginning in 1971

Writings: *Expressways: Poems* Simon and Schuster 1969. *Five Blind Men* (with others) Sumac Press 1969. *Whiskey Profiles* Baleen Press 1971. *Fatback Odes* Sumac Press 1972. *Free Fall: A Novel* Delacorte Press 1980. In anthologies, *New Yorker, McCall's,* others
Awards or inclusion in other biographical books: *Contemporary Authors; Directory of American Poets; Michigan Authors,* 2nd ed. Guggenheim Fellowship, 1969-1971. Discovery Prize, Young Men's Hebrew Association/Poetry Center of New York, 1969

REED, JOHN R.

Address: 17320 Wildemere, Detroit, Michigan 48221
Born: January 24, 1938; Duluth, Minnesota
Parents: John S. Reed; Josephine F. Reed
Education: University of Minnesota at Duluth, Minnesota, 1955-1959. University of Rochester, Rochester, New York, 1959-1963
Career: Professor of English, Wayne State University, Detroit, Michigan, 1971—. Associate Professor of English, Wayne State University, Detroit, Michigan, 1968-1971; Assistant Professor of English, 1965-1968; Assistant Professor of English, University of Connecticut, Storrs, Connecticut, 1964-1965. University of Cincinnati. University of Warwick, Coventry, England

Writings: *Stations of the Cross* Ridgeway Press 1992. *A Gallery of Spiders* Ontario Review Press 1980. *Hercules* Fiddlehead Poetry Books 1973. Poems in *Poetry East, Michigan Quarterly Review.* Work in Progress: Collection of poems associated with Lake Huron
Awards or inclusion in other biographical books: Named Distinguished Professor, Wayne State University
What is the aim or goal of your writing? "In my poetry and fiction I am interested in exploring what might be called the gravity of ordinary experience even when I use a comic approach."

May inquiries be sent to you about doing workshops, readings? Yes

REESE, LESLIE A.
Address: c/o 1526 Chandler Road, Huntsville, Alabama 35801
Born: October 23, 1961; Detroit, Michigan
Parents: Claude Reese, Patricia D. Reese
Education: Cass Technical High School, Detroit, Michigan, 1979. Spelman College, Atlanta, Georgia, 1979-1981. Alabama A & M University, Normal, Alabama, 1991—
Career: Volunteer Drama Instructor, "College of Discovery", Children ages 9-12, Huntsville Housing Authority, Huntsville, Alabama, 1992—. New Volunteer Docent, Huntsville Museum of Art, Huntsville, Alabama, 1992—. Poetry Consultant/Performer, Detroit Dance Collective, Oakland Community College, Royal Oak, Michigan, 1991—. Scriptwriter/Consultant, SafeTimes Software Project, Wayne State University Health Center, Detroit, Michigan, 1990-1991. Artist/Youth Coordinator, Boniface Community Action Corporation/Taylor Teen Health Center, Taylor, Michigan, 1990. Guest Artist, invited to perform, lecture, exchange ideas, values, knowledge, experiences: Detroit Public Schools, Detroit Public Libraries, Detroit Council of the Arts, Detroit Festival of the Arts, Detroit Institute of Arts, Museum of African-American History in Detroit, Public Radio WDET, Western Wayne Correctional Facility (ARTS-GROWTH Opportunities), University of Michigan-Ann Arbor, Oakland Community College, Wayne State University, Marygrove College, others

Writings: *Upside Down Tapestry Mosaic History* Broadside Press 1987. Included in: *Adam of Efe'* (edited by Naomi Long Madgett) Lotus Press 1992. *HIPology* (edited by Stella Crews, Ron Allen) Broadside Press 1990. *Anthology 1990* Poetry Society of Michigan 1990. *Nostalgia For the Present: An Anthology of Detroit Writing* (edited by Kofi Natambu) Post Aesthetic Press 1985. Work in Progress: *Prodigal Daughter Spiritworks*
Awards or inclusion in other biographical books: Rising Star Award, Renaissance Chapter of The Links, Inc., 1991 "Women of Excellence" Benefit Luncheon
What is the aim or goal of your writing? "To express my joy in the experience of living. To witness my connection to The Creator. To support myself and service my community."
May inquiries be sent to you about doing workshops, readings? Yes

REID, DORIS E.
Address: 10785 E.W. Resort Road, Burt Lake, Michigan 49717
Born: June 6, 1913; Burt Lake, Michigan
Parents: Frank C. Reid, Ella E. (Waldron) Reid
Education: Alanson High School, Alanson, Michigan. Northwestern Michigan College, R.N., Traverse City, Michigan, 1933-1936. Frontier Graduate School of Midwifery, C.M., 1943. Other credits in public health nursing
Career: Surgical and general nursing, Little Traverse Hospital, Petoskey, Michigan, 1936-1941. Public Health Nursing and Midwifing, Kentucky, 1942-1949. Nurse, Petoskey, Michigan, 1940-1951. Nurse, District Health Department, Cheboygan, Michigan, 1951-1966. Nurse Coordinator, Supervisor, District Health Department, Rogers City, Michigan, 1966-1968; Nursing Supervisor 1968-1973, retired. Doris E. Reid Center named in her honor, Cheboygan, Michigan

Writings: *Saddlebags Full of Memories* Straits Area Printing Inc. 1992
May inquiries be sent to you about doing workshops, readings? Yes

REIMANN, LEWIS C. (1890-1961)
Born: September 22, 1890; Stambaugh, Michigan
Children: Mrs. Lawrence F. Smith
Education: University of Michigan, B.A., Ann Arbor, Michigan, 1916
Career: When at University of Michigan he was tackle on the Fielding Yost's "Point-a-Minute" football team, 1914-1915, and the Big Ten Wrestling Champion, heavyweight division, 1915. YMCA, 3 years. Director, Presbyterian Students activities, University of Michigan, 1920-1927. Organizer and Director, University of Michigan Fresh Air Camp. Director, Canadian Canoe Treks. Owner, Northwoods Publishing Company. Democratic candidate for 33rd District Michigan Senator, 1954

Writings: *Between the Iron and the Pine* Northwoods Publishing (Ann Arbor) 1951. *When Pine was King* Northwoods Publishing 1952. *Incredible Seney* Northwoods Publishing 1953. *Hurley-Still No Angel* Northwoods Publishing 1954. *The Lake Poinsett Story* Arlington, South Dakota 1957. *The Successful Camp* University of Michigan Press 1958. *The Game Warden and the Poachers* Northwoods Publishing 1959
Awards or inclusion in other biographical books: *Michigan Authors,* 1st ed., 2nd ed.

RENDLELMAN, DANNY L.
Address: 942 E. 7th Street, Flint, Michigan 48503
Born: November 25, 1945; Flint, Michigan
Parents: William F. Rendleman, Beatrice J. Rendleman
Children: Eliot
Education: Flint Northern High School, 1960-1963. University of Michigan-Flint, B.G.S., Flint, Michigan, 1970-1974. Goddard College, M.F.A., Plainfield, Vermont, 1976-1978
Career: Lecturer, English Department, University of Michigan-Flint, Flint, Michigan, 1986—; Sr. Instructional Associate/Lecturer 1978-1986; Instructional Associate 1975-1978; Secretary 1974-1975

Writings: *Skilled Trades* Ridgeway Press 1989. *Asylum* Red Hill Press 1977. *The Winter Rooms* Ithaca House 1975. *Signals to the Blind* Ithaca House 1972. Various anthologies. Work in Progress: Manuscript of poetry, *Inadequate Praise*
Awards or inclusion in other biographical books: *Michigan Authors,* 2nd ed. Michigan Council for the Arts Grants, 1986, 1990. Two P.E.N. Syndicated Fiction Awards
May inquiries be sent to you about doing workshops, readings? Yes

RENKER, FRED W., JR.
Address: 608 Hillcrest, Midland, Michigan 48640
Pseudonym: Skip Renker
Born: February 14, 1945; Cheyenne, Wyoming
Parents: Fred W. Renker, Sarah H. Renker
Children: Chris, Corey
Education: University of Notre Dame, B.A., Notre Dame, Indiana, 1962-1966. Duke University, M.A.T., Durham, North Carolina, 1966-1967. Sonoma State University, M.A., Rohnert Park, California, 1972-1974
Career: Honors Director, Delta College, University Center, Michigan. University of Notre Dame Food Service, Notre Dame, Indiana. English Professor, Delta College.

English Teacher, Armstrong High School, Richmond, Virginia. Desk Clerk/Bellhop, Colonial Inn, Harbor Springs, Michigan

Writings: *Birds of Passage* Delta Press 1990. About 20 small press poetry publications, including *Garfield Lake Review, Dreamworks, Passages North.* Work in Progress: A full-length poetry manuscript. Several prose pieces. Included in *Passages North Anthology* 1991

Awards or inclusion in other biographical books: First Place, Florida Poetry Contest, 1979. First Place, New Voice in Michigan Poetry, 1983. First Place, Abbie M. Copps Poetry Award, 1990. First Place, University of Michigan Writing Award, 1991

What is the aim or goal of your writing? "To please my audience and myself. To discover meaning. To satisfy an inner need to communicate."

May inquiries be sent to you about doing workshops, readings? Yes

RENKO, DOROTHY M.

Address: 23211 Lawrence, Dearborn, Michigan 48128

Pseudonym: Kristi Andrews, Barbara Hilton

Born: October 18, 1923; Hamtramck, Michigan

Parents: Stanley J. Goralczyk, Mary A. Goralczyk

Children: Marian, Harry, John, Barbara

Education: Michigan State University, B.S., East Lansing, Michigan, 1941-1945. Wayne State University, M.S., Detroit, Michigan, 1964-1965. University of Michigan, P.D.D., Ann Arbor, Michigan, 1978-1979

Career: Professional Writer, Creative Writing Teacher, self-employed, Dearborn, Michigan, 1981—. School Media Specialist, Dearborn Schools, Dearborn, Michigan, 1965-1980; teacher, 1947-1963. Columnist, *Rave Reviews* magazine, 1989-1990

Writings: *Love Lights* Bantam 1988. Published 6 articles,12 book reviews, an essay, a short story. Work in Progress: Western historical novel being considered by Zebra Books. Victorian historical novel, with agent. Science fiction novel, *Looking for Melyssar*

Awards or inclusion in other biographical books: Golden Medallion Award (runner-up), Romance Writers of America, Best Young Adult Novel for *Love Lights*

What is the aim or goal of your writing? "To fulfill my life-long love affair with books and reading, by writing novels of my own and then teaching others to do the same."

May inquiries be sent to you about doing workshops, readings? Yes

REYNOLDS, MOIRA D.

Address: 225 East Michigan St., Marquette, Michigan 49855

Pseudonym: Marna Moore

Born: June 22, 1915; Bangor, Northern Ireland (Parents were American citizens)

Parents: Asa F. Davison, Marjorie R. (Bolton) Davison

Children: Ronald

Education: Dalhousie University, B.A., Halifax, Nova Scotia, 1932-1936. Boston University, A.M., Ph.D., Boston, Massachusetts, 1948-1952

Career: Freelance writer, Marquette, Michigan, 1968—. Head, Laboratory Department, Porter Hospital, Middlebury, Vermont, 1963-1968. Cancer Research Team, Boston University, Boston, Massachusetts, 1952-1962. Research Technologist, Wayne University, Detroit, Michigan, 1946-1948. Held various positions as a medical technologist, 1939-1946

Writings: *Coping With an Immigrant Parent* Rosen 1992. *Women Champions of Human Rights* McFarland 1991. *Nine American Women of the 19th Century* McFarland 1988. *Uncle Tom's Cabin & Mid-19th Century U.S.* McFarland 1985. *Margaret Sanger, Birth Control Pioneer* Story House 1981. *The Outstretched Hand: Modern Medical Discoveries* Rosen 1980. *Aim for a Job in the Medical Laboratory* Rosen 1972, 1982. *Clinical Chemistry for the Small Hospital Laboratory* Thomas 1969. Contributor to magazines, newspapers. Work in Progress: Contributor to magazines and newspapers. Book on women advocates of reproductive freedom, contract from McFarland. *Use and Abuse of the Telephone* Rosen (Young Adult)
Awards of inclusion in other biographical books: *Contemporary Authors* vol. 105. *Who's Who in the Midwest* 23rd edition
What is the aim or goal of your writing? "To make science and also history understandable and interesting to the educated lay person."
May inquiries be sent to you about doing workshops, readings? Yes

RICE, CATHERINE A.
Address: P.O. Box 3, Alden, Michigan 49612
Born: October 10, 1953; Bellaire, Michigan
Parents: Richard A. Potrafke, Blanch Y. Potrafke
Children: Carrie, Shannon
Education: Mancelona High School, Diploma, Mancelona, Michigan, 1970. Traverse City, Michigan, certification, 1986
Career: Therapeutic Masseuse, self-employed, Alden, Michigan, 1986—. Pianist, Mancelona High School, Alden Community Choir, 1980—. Cosmotologist Assistant, Joyce's Hair Fashions, Alden, Michigan, 1988-1991. Poetry Writers Workshop, Shanty Creek Lodge, Bellaire, Michigan, 1989—. Catering for dinners, weddings, self-employed. Co-manager of Higgins Store, 1970-1972. Slimnastics Instructor, 1983-1985. Odyssey of the Mind Coach, 1992

Writings: *Through the Eyes of Life* Parta Printers, Inc. 1989. Several works published in area news media. Several poems have been used by permission at various conventions, seminars, workshops. Work in Progress: Negotiations with several card companies
Awards or inclusion in other biographical books: *Who's Who in Poetry,* 1989, 1990, 1991. Golden Poet Award, World Book of Poetry, 1989. Silver Poet Award, World Book of Poetry 1990, 1991
What is the aim or goal of your writing? "Full time contract with a card company. Possibly publication of a second book of poetry." (My maternal grandmother's great, great, great uncle was Ralph Waldo Emerson)
May inquiries be sent to you about doing workshops, readings? Yes

RICHARDSON, ARLETA
Address: 5736 Lomitas Drive, Los Angeles, California 90042
Born: March 9, 1923; Flint, Michigan
Parents: Clarence A. Wright, Alma P. (Richardson) Wright
Education: Spring Arbor College, A.A., Spring Arbor, Michigan, 1942-1944. Western Michigan University, B.S., Kalamazoo, Michigan, 1947-1949. Immaculate Heart College, M.S., Los Angeles, California, 1962-1963
Career: Teacher, Private School, Los Angeles, California, 1963-1969. College Teacher/ Librarian, Los Angeles Pacific College, Los Angeles, California, 1953-1963. College

Teacher/Librarian, Spring Arbor College, Michigan, 1949-1953. Teacher, Beecher School District, Flint, Michigan, 1945-1947. Self-employed writer—.

Writings: *Christmas Stories From Grandma's Attic* David C. Cook 1991. *Stories From the Growing Years* David C. Cook 1991. *New Faces, New Friends* David C. Cook 1989. *At Home in North Branch* David C. Cook 1988. *Nineteen and Wedding Bells Ahead* David C. Cook 1987. *Eighteen and On Her Own* David C. Cook 1986. *Sixteen and Away From Home* David C. Cook 1985. *Treasures From Grandma* David C. Cook 1984. *Still More Stories From Grandma's Attic* David C. Cook 1980. *More Stories From Grandma's Attic* David C. Cook 1979. *In Grandma's Attic* David C. Cook 1974. *Double Trouble in Puerto Rico* Light and Life Press 1991. *Double Trouble in Mexico* Light and LIfe Press 1991. *The Shiny Black Shoes* Light and Life Press 1991. *A New Heart for Carmela* Light and Life Press 1990, and others. Work in Progress: A new series on the orphan train children. Grandma's cook book

Awards or inclusion in other biographical books: Writer of the Year Award, Mt. Hermon Christian Writer's Conference, 1986

What is the aim or goal of your writing? "To emphasize moral and Christian values to children in an entertaining, non-preaching way."

May inquiries be sent to you about doing workshops, readings? Yes

RICHEY, DAVID J.

Address: P.O. Box 192, Grawn, Michigan 49637

Pseudonym: Richard Johnson, John Davey

Born: July 22, 1939; Flint, Michigan

Parents: Lawrence D. Richey, Helen Richey

Children: Kimberly, Stacey, David Jr., Guy

Education: Clio High School, Clio, Michigan, graduated 1957

Career: Staff outdoor writer,*The Detroit News*, Detroit Michigan, 1980—. Freelance outdoor writer, 1967-1980. Barber, self-employed, Flint, Michigan, 1961-1970

Writings: *Hunting Michigan Whitetails* SOE, Inc. 1991. *Hunting Fringeland Bear* Outdoor Life Book Club 1986. *Steelheading in North America* Stackpole 1983. *Trout of Michigan* SOE, Inc. 1982. *Complete Guide to Lake Fishing* Outdoor Life Book Club 1981. *The Fly Hatches* Hawthorn Books 1980. *Great Lakes Steel Head Flies* SOE, Inc. 1979. *How to Catch Trophy Fresh Water Gamefish* Outdoor Life Book Club 1979. *The Small-Boat Handbook* Crowell 1979. *Dardevle's Guide to Fishing* Dardevle (Eppinger Co.) 1978. *Brown Trout Fisherman's Guide* Hawthorn Books 1978. *Trout Fisherman's Digest* D.B.I.Books 1976. *Steelheading for Everybody* Stackpole 1976. *A Child's Introduction to the Outdoors* Pagurian Press 1976. *Getting Hooked on Fishing* (with J. Knap) Pagurian Press 1974. Over 6,600 published outdoor magazine articles and thousands of published newspaper columns. Work in Progress: Two books

Awards or inclusion in other biographical books: *Michigan Authors,* 2nd ed.

What is the aim or goal of your writing? "To educate and entertain others about the outdoors, and to make a living."

May inquiries be sent to you about doing workshops, readings? Yes

RICHEY, KAY L.
Address: P. O. Box 192, Grawn, Michigan 49620
Born: March 25, 1936; Frankfort, Michigan
Parents: Oliver E. Doane, Dorothy E. Bosselman
Children: Nancy, Dan
Education: High School
Career: Freelance writer, self-employed, Grawn, Michigan, 1977—. Craftsman, self-employed, Honor, Michigan, 1962-1976

Writings: *Fish and Game Menu Cookbook: Meal Planning for Sportsmen* SOE, Inc. 1987. *My 10 Favorite Walleye Recipes* SOE, Inc. 1985. *My 10 Favorite Salmon-Trout Recipes* SOE, Inc. 1985. *My 10 Favorite Venison Recipes* SOE, Inc. 1985. *My 10 Favorite Gamebird Recipes* SOE, Inc. 1985. *My Favorite Game Animal Recipes* SOE, Inc. 1985. *Savor the Wild* SOE, Inc. 1981. Many outdoor magazine articles. Unpublished book
May inquiries be sent to you about doing workshops, readings? Yes

RICKARD, GLEN L.
Address: 901 Brookside Drive, Apt. 215, Lansing, Michigan 48917
Pseudonym: Glen L. (Lucky) Rickard
Born: July 3, 1918; Dimondale, Michigan
Parents: Delbert A. Rickard, Alice A. (Becker) Rickard
Children: K, J
Education: Jackson High School, G.E.D., 1933-1934
Career: Factory worker, Macklin Grinding Wheel, Jackson, Michigan, 1939-1966. Industrial Safety Inspector, Michigan Department of Labor, Lansing, Michigan, 1966-1974. Variance Officer, Michigan Labor Department, Lansing, Michigan, 1974-1982, retired

Writings: *Saint Or Slaver* self-published 1990. Work in Progress: Novels: *Forever Your Own. You Walk But Once.* Several poems and songs
What is the aim or goal of your writing? "Produce entertaining prose poems and songs".
May inquiries be sent to you about doing workshops, readings? Yes

RIDL, JACK R.
Address: 2309 Auburn Ave., Holland, Michigan 49424
Born: April 10, 1944; Sewickley, Pennsylvania
Parents: Charles G. Ridl, Elizabeth R. Ridl
Children: Meridith
Education: Westminster College, B.A., New Wilmington, Pennsylvania, 1962-1967
Career: Professor English, Hope College, Holland, Michigan, 1971—. Assistant Dean-Admissions, University of Pittsburgh, Pittsburgh, Pennsylvania, 1968-1971

Writings: *The Same Ghost* Dawn Valley Press 1985. *Between* Dawn Valley Press 1989. *After School* Samisdat Press 1988. Work in Progress: *Losing Season*
Awards or inclusion in other biographical books: Nominated three times for Pushcart Prize. *Between* reviewed in *American Book Review* as one of two best books of 1989 from a small or university press
What is the aim or goal of your writing? "To connect."
May inquiries be sent to you about doing workshops, readings? Yes

RIENSTRA, MARCHIENE VROON

Address: 66 Lakeshore Drive, Douglas, Michigan 49406
Born: November 12, 1941; Rangoon, Burma
Parents: John Vroon, Theresa (Oppenhuizen) Vroon
Children: Jonathan, Ronald, Janelle, Rachel
Education: Calvin College, B.A., Grand Rapids, Michigan, 1958-1962; Seminary, Master of Divinity, 1972-1978
Career: Pastor, Lakeshore Community Church, West Olive, Michigan, 1992—. Pastor, Hope Church, RCA, Holland, Michigan, 1984-1989. Pastor, Port Sheldon Presb. Church, Port Sheldon, Michigan, 1979-1984. Adjunct Professor, Western Theological Seminary, Holland, Michigan, 1981-1992

Writings: *Knowing the Lord* Reformed Church Press 1990. *Swallow's Nest* Eerdmans 1993. Work in Progress: Novel, children's story, and a book on personality and spirituality
What is the aim or goal of your writing? "To delight, deepen, and stimulate people of all ages with truth, beauty, and the magic and mystery of life."
May inquiries be sent to you about doing workshops, readings? No

ROBBINS, LOIS B.

Address: 2050 Pontiac Drive, Sylvan Lake, Michigan 48320
Born: June 11, 1929; Detroit, Michigan
Parents: Stanley H. Burton, Mildred C. Burton
Children: Janet, Jeffrey, Sarah, William
Education: Michigan State University, East Lansing, Michigan, 1946-1948. Marygrove College, Detroit, Michigan, B.A., 1980-1981. Mundelien College, M.A., Chicago, Illinois, 1981-1982
Career: Semi-Retired. Editor, *Ecologic*, Upland Hills Ecological Awareness Center. Creative Process, Self-employed, Consultant, Sylvan Lake, Michigan, 1988—. Teacher, adjunct faculty, University of Detroit, Detroit, Michigan, 1986-1988. Founder, former director, Kairos Institute, Birmingham, Michigan, 1983-1987. Administrative Associate, Institute for Advanced Pastoral Studies, Bloomfield Hills, Michigan, 1976-1980. Mom, Family, West Bloomfield, Michigan, 1956-1988

Writings: *Waking Up in the Age of Creativity* Bear and Company 1985. Articles in *Creation Spirituality* Magazine, *Haelon;* ongoing ones in *Eco Logic*. Work in Progress: *Clara and Eleanore*, a play. *Tilandsia Sprouts*, collection of poems. *Wake Me at Midnight,* book of personal essays
What is the aim or goal of your writing? "I want to raise consciousness about ecological issues and the crisis of the human spirit these issues represent. My orientation is feminist, earth-based and paradigm-shifty."
May inquiries be sent to you about doing workshops, readings? Yes. I give "re-enchantment" workshops around the country (also workshops on creative process and creation spirituality)

ROBERTS, REBECCA S.

Address: 3170 Clipper Court, Oxford, Michigan 48371
Pseudonym: Rebecca Emlinger Roberts
Born: November 3, 1942; Alma, Michigan
Parents: Merlin F. Emlinger, Vivian E. Emlinger

Children: Michael, Adam Roberts
Education: Mott Community College, Flint, Michigan, 1974-1978. Oakland University, Rochester, Michigan, 1990—
Career: Newsletter Editor (freelance contract), Center for Independent Living for Oakland/Macomb, Troy, Michigan, 1991—. Public Relations project for Michigan Department of Mental Health-freelance, 1988-1989. Freelance journalist, poet, writer, self-employed, Oxford, Michigan, 1983—. President of theatre group, Brandon S.T.A.G.E.

Writings: Published columnist and journalist in Michigan newspapers, including *The Detroit News, The Detroit Free Press*. Poetry in *Beloit Poetry Journal* and others. Included in *Passages North Anthology* and others. Work in Progress: Several short stories, poems. Major theatre project
Awards or inclusion in other biographical books: Annual Student Achievement Award, Mott Community College, 1974, 1975. First Place Journalism Award, ACT/ Developmental Disabilities, 1986. Overall Print Media Award for Feature Journalism, Association for Retarded Citizens, 1987. State Fair Cash Award, 1976. Others from Mott Community College
What is the aim or goal of your writing? "To write as well as I can. To be involved in the world to the extent that my writing and my life come together to reflect what I believe to be a writer's second obligation, and that is to the world in which she writes. The first obligation, as other writers (John Barth, and others) have said, is to write as well as one can. I am active in the disability movement and vocal too about women's rights, education, and the political in our lives."
May inquiries be sent to you about doing workshops, readings? Yes

ROBERTS, WILLO DAVIS
Address: 12020 W. Engebretsen Road, Granite Falls, Washington 98252
Born: May 29, 1928; Grand Rapids, Michigan
Parents: Clayton Davis (Bill), Lealah (Gleason) Davis
Children: Kathleen, David, Larrilyn, Christopher
Education: Pontiac Senior High School, graduated 1946, Pontiac, Michigan
Career: Doctors' offices, hospitals, California. U.S. Postal Department, Drayton Plains, Michigan, 1946-1947. Founder, Regional Vice President, Seattle Chapter of Mystery Writers of America and member of the national board. Board member of Pacific Northwest Writers Conference, leader of workshops. Heads book writers' workshop, Seannchae. Lectures across the country at colleges, schools, conferences

Writings: *Murder at Grand Bay* Arcadia House 1955. *Nurse At Mystery Villa* Ace Books 1967. *Becca's Child* Lancer Books 1972. *The Minden Curse* Atheneum 1978. *The Gresham Ghost* Popular Library 1980. *Jo and the Bandit* Atheneum 1992. *Dark Secrets* Fawcett 1991. *Scared Stiff* Antheneum 1991. *To Grandmother's House We Go* Antheneum 1990. *Destiny's Women* Popular Library 1980. *The View From the Cherry Tree* Atheneum 1975. *Don't Hurt Laurie!* Atheneum 1977. *More Minden Curses* Atheneum 1980. *The Girl with the Silver Eyes* Atheneum 1980. *A Long Time to Hate* Avon 1982. *The Pet Sitting Peril* Atheneum 1983. *No Monsters in the Closet* Atheneum 1983. *Eddie and the Fairy God Puppy* Atheneum 1984. *Caroline* Scholastic 1984. *Baby Sitting is a Dangerous Job* Atheneum 1985. *The Magic Book* Atheneum 1986. *To Share a Dream* Worldwide Library 1986. *Megan's Island* Atheneum 1988. *What Could Go Wrong?* Atheneum 1989. *Nightmare* Atheneum 1989. *What Are we Going to Do About David?* Atheneum 1993. Others. Sold 85 books in the fields of mystery, suspense, medical background, Gothic, juvenile, young adult, historical and contemporary fiction. Work in Progress: Adult historical novel

Awards or inclusion in other biographical books: *Contemporary Authors,* Vols. 49-52; *International Authors and Writers Who's Who; Something about the Author* Vol. 21, Autobiographical Series Vol. 8; others. Numerous Awards in the juvenile field, including the Mark Twain Award and California Young Readers Medal. Young Hoosier Award. Evansville Book Award. Georgia Children's Book Award. Young Readers of Western Australia Award. Children's Choice Awards in Indiana, Missouri, South Carolina, Nevada. Edgar Allen Poe Award for Best Juvenile Mystery, 1988; nominee 1991, 1989, 1980. Nominee for numerous Children's Choice Awards, 1990-1991. Honor Book, West Virginia Children's Book Award, 1984. *What Could Go Wrong?* is currently on a number of Children's Choice reading lists. *Sugar Isn't Everything* recommended by diabetes research specialist, and it was nominee for 1990 Young Hoosier Award. Pacific Northwest Writers Association Achievement Award, 1986. Children's Books of the Year, Library of Congress, 1975, 1980, 1983, 1986. Many Junior Library Guild Books. First Prize, American Diabetes Association, 1987. Texas Lone Star List, 1990-1991. Nominee, Volunteer State Book Award (Tennessee), 1991-1992. Governor's Award, State of Washington. Nominee, runner-up, winner of dozens of others

What is the aim or goal of your writing? "To entertain (first) myself, and (second) fiction readers, particular young people, to inform and encourage and support young readers, and to earn a living."

May inquiries be sent to you about doing workshops, readings? Yes

ROBERTSON, MARY ELLEN

Address: 1959 Shorewood, Muskegon, Michigan 49441
Pseudonym: Rose Francis (for work in progress only)
Born: November 30, 1942; Detroit, Michigan
Parents: Frank J. Schaden, Sara J. Schaden
Children: Cynthia, Connie, Karen (husband: John H. Robertson)
Education: Immaculata High School, graduate, Detroit, Michigan, 1956-1960. Providence Hospital, R.N., Detroit, Michigan, 1960-1963
Career: Owner/Manager, Seaway Motel, Muskegon, Michigan, 1978—. Medical Personnel Pool, Southfield, Michigan, 1976-1978. St. Joseph Hosptial, Pontiac, Michigan, 1973-1974. Cottage Hospital, Grosse Pointe Farms, Michigan, 1972-1973. Georgian Bloomfield Nursing Home, 1972. Providence Hospital, 1963-1968

Writings: *Meditations for Working Men* Rose Enterprises 1988. *Meditations for Working Women* Rose Enterprises 1987, 1988, 1989. In *The Anniversary-The Writers Anthology* 1992. Articles in *Lifeglow Magazine, The Forum Magazine, Lifeline Magazine, Between the Sheets.* Freelance, *Western Michigan Catholic,* 1978-1980. Editor (ongoing) of seven newsletters. Work in Progress: *Meditations for Incest Survivors*

What is the aim or goal of your writing? "My writing of my meditation books is to help others discover that prayer is not complex or wordy but simple communication from the heart connecting to the divine within. I appreciate my gift of writing and respond to the call by sharing the words that come."

May inquiries be sent to you about doing workshops, readings? Yes

ROCHE, GEORGE CHARLES

Address: 189 Hillsdale Street, Hillsdale, Michigan 49242
Born: May 16, 1935; Denver, Colorado
Parents: George and Margaret Stewart Roche
Children: George, Muriel, Maggie, Jacob
Education: B.S. from Denver's Regis College in 1956; MA in 1961 and Ph.D. in 1965 from the University of Colorado
Career: Taught at the University of Colorado 1963-64 and at the Colorado School of Mines 1964-66. Director of seminars at the Foundation for Economic Education in Irving on Hudson, New York 1966-71. President of Hillsdale College 1971–.

Writings: *Education in America* (1969) Foundation for Economic Education. *Legacy of Freedom* (1969), Arlington House. *Frederic Bastiat: A Man Alone* (1971) Arlington House. *The Bewildered Society* (1972) Arlington House. *The Balancing Act: Quota Hiring in Higher Education* (1974) Open Court. *America by the Throat: The Stranglehold of Federal Bureaucracy* (1983) Devin-Adair. *Going Home* (1986) Greenhill Press. *A World Without Hereos: The Modern Tragedy* (1987) Hillsdale College Press. *A Reason for Living* (1989) Regnery Gateway. *One by One: Preserving Values and Freedom in Heartland America* (1990) Hillsdale College Press. Also contributed many articles to national journals and magazines.
Awards or inclusion in other biographical books: Freedoms Foundation Awards, including Freedom Leadership Award (1972): Honorary Doctor of Public Service, Regis College (1978); Honorary Doctor of Social Science, Universidad Francisco Marroquin, Guatemala (1980). Who's Who in America
What is the aim of goal of your writing? "The defense of traditional values in American society."
May inquiries be sent to you about doing workshops, readings? Yes, schedule permitting.

ROETHKE, THEODORE (1908-1963)

Pseudonym: Winterset Rothberg
Born: May 25, 1908; Saginaw, Michigan
Parents: Otto Theodore Roethke, Helen Marie (Huebner) Roethke
Education: University of Michigan, A.B., Ann Arbor, Michigan, 1929. University of Michigan, M.A., Ann Arbor, Michigan, 1936. Harvard University, 1930-1931
Career: Worked in a pickle factory several seasons, college tennis coach. English Department, Lafayette College, Easton, Pennsylvania, 1931-1935. Pennsylvania State University, University Park, Pennsylvania, 1936-1943. Bennington College, Bennington, Vermont, 1943-1946. University of Washington, Seattle, Washington, 1947-1962, Poet in Residence, 1962

Writings: *Open House* Knopf 1941. *The Lost Son, and Other Poems* Doubleday 1948. *Praise to the End!* Doubleday 1951. *The Waking: Poems, 1933-1953* Doubleday 1954. *Words for the Wind* Doubleday 1958. *I Am! Says the Lamb* Doubleday 1961. *Sequence, Sometimes Metaphysical, Poems* Stonewall Press 1963. *Party at the Zoo* Doubleday 1963. *Far Field* Doubleday 1964. *On the Poet and His Craft; Selected Prose of Theodore Roethke* (editor Ralph J. Mills, Jr.) University of Washington Press 1965. *The Achievement of Theodore Roethke; a Comprehensive Selection of His Poems* Scott, Foresman 1966. *Dirty Dinky and Other Creatures: Poems for Children* Doubleday 1973. *Collected Poems* Doubleday 1966. *Selected Letters* University of Washington Press 1968. *Straw for the*

Fire, from the Notebooks of Theodore Roethke, 1943-63 Doubleday 1972. Others. His work has appeared in many foreign languages, in sound recordings

Awards or inclusion in other biographical books: *American Authors and Books; American Writers; Childhood in Poetry; Contemporary Authors; Contemporary Literary Criticism; Contemporary Poets; Dictionary of Literature in the English Language; Michigan Authors,* 2nd ed.; *Michigan Poets; Reader's Adviser; Reader's Encyclopedia; Twentieth Century Authors; Who Was Who in America; Who's Who in Twentieth Century Literature,* several others. Guggenheim Fellowship, 1945, 1950. Tietjens Prize, 1947. Levinson Award, 1951. Ford Foundation Fellowship, 1952. The National Institute of Arts & Letters, 1952. Honorary Membership in the International Mark Twain Society. Pulitzer Prize for Poetry, 1954. Fulbright Grant, 1955. Borestone Mountain Awards, 1958. Edna St. Vincent Millay Award, 1959. Bollingen Award, 1959. Longview Award, 1959. Pacific Northwest Writers Award, 1959. National Book Award, 1959. Shelley Award Winner, 1962. Honorary Doctorate of Letters Degree, University of Michigan, 1962. Phi Beta Kappa

ROMANACK, MARK C.

Address: 110 Franke Lane, Cadillac, Michigan 49601
Born: March 3, 1960; Clio, Michigan
Parents: Pete Romanack, Mildred Romanack
Education: Northern Michigan University, B.S., Fisheries and Wildlife Management, Marquette, Michigan, 1978-1982
Career: Freelance, Self-employed, Cadillac, Michigan, 1987—. Field Editor, *Michigan Hunting and Fishing,* 1986—. Field Editor, *Walleye Magazine,* 1987—. Environmental Educator, Green Point Nature Center, Saginaw, Michigan, 1982-1987

Writings: *Advance Walleye Tactics* North American Fishing Club 1992. *Big Walleye Secrets* In Fisherman, Inc. 1991
What is the aim or goal of your writing? "Educate and entertain sport fishermen."
May inquiries be sent to you about doing workshops, readings? Yes

ROMANOWSKI, WILLIAM D.

Address: 720 Griswold, S.E., Grand Rapids, Michigan 49507
Born: August 2, 1954; Edwardsville, Pennsylvania
Parents: William A. Romanowski, Mary Romanowski
Children: Michael, Tara
Education: Bowling Green State University, Ph.D., Bowling Green, Ohio, 1986-1990. Youngstown State University, M.A., Youngstown, Ohio, 1979-1982. Indiana University of Pennsylvania, B.A., Indiana, Pennsylvania, 1972-1976
Career: Assistant Professor of Communication Arts and Sciences, Calvin College, Grand Rapids, Michigan, 1989—; Visiting Faculty Fellow, Calvin Center for Christian Scholarship, 1988-1989. Graduate Assistant, Bowling Green State University, Bowling Green, Ohio, 1986-1988. Resource Specialist, Coalition for Christian Outreach, 1982-1988; Regional Director, 1979-1982; Campus Minister, 1976-1979

Writings: *Risky Business: Rock in Film* (with R. Serge Denisoff) Transaction Books 1991. *Dancing in the Dark: Youth, Popular Culture and the Electronic Media* (et al.) Eerdmans 1990. *At Work and Play: Biblical Insight for Daily Obedience* (et al.) Paideia Press 1986. *All of Life Redeemed: Biblical Insight For Daily Obedience* (et al.) Paideia Press 1983

Awards or inclusion in other biographical books: *Dancing in the Dark: Youth, Popular Culture and the Electronic Media,* first runner-up, *Christianity Today* Critic's Choice Award, Contemporary Issues Division 1992
What is the aim or goal of your writing? "To contribute to our understanding of American culture and the entertainment industry."
May inquiries be sent to you about doing workshops, readings? Yes

ROMIG, WALTER (1905-1977)
Born: December 29, 1905; New York, New York
Parents: Arthur J. Romig, Phobie (Lawrence) Romig
Children: Mary, Thomas, Teresa
Education: Sacred Heart Seminary, A.B., Detroit, Michigan, 1927. Mt. St. Mary Seminary, Norwood, Ohio. Post graduate
Career: Writer, religious editor

Writings: *The Man in the Mirror* Walter Romig 1928. *Who's Who in Detroit* Walter Romig & Company 1935-1936. *The American Catholic Who's Who* Walter Romig & Company 1937-1971. *The Catholic Bookman* 1937-1940. *The Guide to Catholic Literature* 6 vols. Walter Romig & Company 1940-1960. *The Book of Catholic Authors* 5 vols., Walter Romig & Company 1942. *Negro Catholic Writers* Walter Romig & Company 1945. *Josephine Van Dyke Brownson* Gabriel Richard Press 1955. *Michigan Place Names: the History of the Founding and the Naming of More than Five Thousand Past and Present Michigan Communities* Walter Romig (Grosse Pointe)1973; Wayne State University Press (foreword by Larry B. Massie) 1986
Awards or inclusion in other biographical books: *Michigan Authors,* 2nd ed. Catholic Library Association, Honorary Membership, 1957. Honorary Degree, St. Bonaventure University, Olean, New York; L.H.D. 1960. Award of Merit, Historical Society of Michigan, 1973. First Annual Walter Romig Award conferred posthumously by Sacred Heart Seminary College, Detroit, Michigan, December 11, 1977

RORKE, MARGARET L.
Address: 1882 Lathrup Road, Saginaw, Michigan 48603
Born: November 1, 1915; Ann Arbor, Michigan
Parents: Robert J. Curry, Anna K. (Ludolph) Curry
Children: Robert Craig, Margaret Ann
Education: University of Michigan, B.A., Ann Arbor, Michigan, 1934-1938; J.D., 1939-1942
Career: Law practice, Curry & Curry, beginning 1942, with father; sole practicioner, 1959-1976, retired

Writings: *Christmas Could-Be Tales* (and other verses) Northwood Press 1984. *An Old Cracked Cup* Northwood Press 1980. *My Ego Trip* Exposition Press 1976. Poetry (over 2500) column, *Saginaw News,* 1950-1972. Poetry (about 400) for column of Judd Arnett, *Detroit Free Press,* 1975-1990. Verses in many magazines and anthologies including *Guideposts, Better Homes & Gardens, Peo Record, Ideals, Reader's Digest.* Work in Progress: Contemplating a fourth collection of verse
Awards or inclusion in other biographical books: *Michigan Authors,* 2nd ed. *Ideals* Best Loved Poet, 1981. Honorary Doctor of Letters Degree, Saginaw Valley State University, 1985. Woman of the Year Award, Saginaw Zonta Club, 1989-1990. John J. Hensel Award, Michigan State Bar Association, 1987-given to a lawyer who has contributed to the arts

What is the aim or goal of your writing? "This hobby has been most rewarding. I believe nearly 4000 poems have been published in some form. Subject matter is everyday life with an upbeat approach, and (I hope) a clear recognition of the Source from which all talent comes. My greatest joy is the use by others in their writings and programs."
May inquiries be sent to you about doing workshops, readings? No. I am no longer offering programs, readings, etc. I have done a great many in my day.

ROURKE, CONSTANCE (1885-1941)
Born: November 14, 1885; Cleveland, Ohio
Parents: H. B. Rourke, Constance E. (Davis) Rouke
Education: Vassar College, A.B., Poughkeepsie, New York, 1907. Sorbonne, University of Paris, 1908-1909
Career: English Instructor, Vassar College, Poughkeepsie, New York, 1910-1915. Cultural historian

Writings: *Trumpets of Jubilee: Henry Ward Beecher, Harriet Beecher Stowe, Lyman Beecher, Horace Greeley, P.T. Barnum* Harcourt 1927, 1963. *Troupers of the Gold Coast: The Rise of Lotta Crabtree* Harcourt 1928. *American Humor: A Study of the National Character* Harcourt 1931, 1971. *Davy Crockett* Harcourt 1934, 1962; Junior Deluxe Editions 1956. *Charles Sheeler: Artist in the American Tradition* Harcourt 1938; Kennedy Galleries, 1969. *Audubon* Harcourt 1938; F. Watts 1964. *The Roots of American Culture and Other Essays* (Van Wyck Brooks edited incomplete manuscript) Harcourt 1942; Kennikat 1965. Contributor, editor of others. Movies, filmstrips, records, television made of *Davy Crockett*. Published in numerous journals, magazines
Awards or inclusion in other biographical books: *American Authors and Books; Contemporary American Authors; Contemporary Authors; A Critical Survey and 219 Bio-Bibliographies; Current Biography; Dictionary of North American Authors; National Cyclopaedia of American Biography; Reader's Encyclopedia; Twentieth Century Authors; Twentieth-Century Literary Criticism; Who Was Who in America; Yesterday's Authors of Books for Children,* several others. Borden Fund for Foreign Travel and Study. Runner-up, Newbery Medal, 1935

ROUT, KATHLEEN K.
Address: 836 Huntington Road, East Lansing, Michigan 48823
Born: July 16, 1942; Syracuse, New York
Parents: Joseph P. Kinsella, Elizabeth J. (Tindall) Kinsella
Children: Deidre, Brennan
Education: LeMoyne College, B.S., Syracuse, New York, 1959-1963; Ph.D., 1963-1967. Stanford University, Palo Alto, California
Career: Professor, Michigan State University, East Lansing, Michigan, 1967—

Writings: *Eldridge Cleaver* Twayne (MacMillan) 1991. Work in Progress: Biography, Huey Newton
What is the aim or goal of your writing? "Clarify the contributions of women and minorities to American culture."
May inquiries be sent to you about doing workshops, readings? Yes

ROUTSONG, ALMA
Pseudonym: Isabel Miller
Born: November 26, 1924; Traverse City, Michigan
Parents: Carl John Routsong, Esther (Miller) Routsong
Children: Natalie, Joyce, Charlotte, Louise
Education: Western Michigan University, Kalamazoo, Michigan, 1942-1944. Michigan State University, B.A., East Lansing, Michigan, 1949
Career: U.S. Navy, Hospital Apprentice, 1945-1946. Editor, Columbia University, New York, 1968-1971

Writings: *A Gradual Joy* Houghton Mifflin 1953. *A Round Shape* Houghton 1959. *A Place for Us* Bleeker Street Press 1969; republished as *Patience and Sarah* McGraw-Hill 1972
Awards or inclusion in other biographical books: *Contemporary Authors; Michigan Authors,* 1st ed., 2nd ed.

RUBEN, DOUGLAS H.
Address: 4211 Okemos Road, Suite 22, Okemos, Michigan 48864
Born: June 30, 1958; Detroit, Michigan
Parents: Charles Ruben, Bella Ruben
Children: Michael, Jennifer
Education: Western Michigan University, Kalamazoo, Michigan, B.A., 1979; M.A., 1983. Pacific Western University, Ph.D., Los Angeles, California, 1986
Career: Private Practice/Consulting Firm, Best Impressions International Inc., Okemos, Michigan, 1984—. Adjunct Teacher, local colleges/universities. Consulted on infomercials regarding smoking, appears regularly on television and radio talk shows. Workshop leader

Writings: Author of 30 books. *Drug Abuse and the Elderly: An Annotated Bibliography* Scarecrow Press 1984. *Readings in Anorexia Nervosa and Eating Disorders* Special Learning Corporation 1984. *Philosophy Journals and Serials: An Analytical Guide* Greenwood Press 1985. *Progress in Assertiveness, 1973-1983: An Analytical Bibliography* Scarecrow Press 1985. *Self-Control: A Programmed Text* Best Impressions International 1986. *Behavorial Handbook: Rapid Solutions to Difficult Behavior* Best Impressions International 1988. *Aging and Drug Effects: A Planning Manual for Medication and Alcohol Abuse Treatment of the Elderly* McFarland 1990. *Tips to Success* Best Impressions 1989. *Avoidance Syndrome: Doing Things Out of Fear* Warren H. Green 1992. *Family Addiction: An Analytical Guide* Garland Press 1992. *Bratbusters: Say Good-bye to Tantrums and Disobedience* Skidmore-Roth 1992. *After War: Overcoming Post-Traumatic Stress Syndrome* (booklet-with J. Mayor) Best Impressions International 1991. *Your Public Image: Using TV, Radio, and Print Media in Clinical Practice* Professional Resource Exchange 1992. Others. Over 100 articles. Feature-length screenplay under contract. Educational script. Work in Progress: *Transitions: Effective Passage from Inpatient to Outpatient Treatment* (et al) Praeger Press. *No More Guilt: A 10 Step Guide for Adult Children of Alcoholic Families and Troubled Families* Mills & Sanderson. *Mother, Mistress or Manager: Beating the Game of Office Stereotypes* (with M.J. Ruben). Others
What is the aim or goal of your writing? "To distill down technical ideas about human behavior and self-improvement into simple, ready-to-use, practical information for public consumption."
May inquiries be sent to you about doing workshops, readings? Yes

307

RUBIN, GAY

Address: 1560 Indianwood Court, Bloomfield Hills, Michigan 48302
Born: Detroit, Michigan
Children: Jessica, Rebecca
Education: Mumford High School, Seaholm High School, 1960. Michigan State University, Bachelor of Arts, East Lansing, Michigan, 1961-1965. Wayne State University, Master of Arts, Detroit, Michigan, 1968-1971. Columbia University, New York, New York, Creative Writing Workshop 1985; Private Class, 1986. University of Michigan, M.F.A., Ann Arbor, 1988-1990
Career: Creative Writing Teacher, University of Michigan, 1989. President, Detroit Women Writers, 1985-1987. Co-chaired, Oakland University, Conference, 1983-1984, 1985-1987. Contest judge, many public readings, speaking engagements, in southern Michigan area

Writings: *On a Good Day* Ridgeway Press 1992. Short stories published in *The Bridge, Metro Times Summer Fiction Issue. If It's a Good Day, One Thing,* to be performed, Reader's Theatre. Work in Progress: Stories, novel
What is the aim or goal of your writing? "To give the reader an experience he/she had not had before and could have in no other way but by reading my story."
May inquiries be sent to you about doing workshops, readings? Yes

RUITER, EMMA

Address: 2121 Raybrook Manor, Apt. 141, Grand Rapids, Michigan 49546
Born: January 8, 1908; Grand Rapids, Michigan
Parents: Ralph Ruiter, Elizabeth Ruiter
Education: Grand Rapids Christian High School, 1921-1925. Calvin College, Grand Rapids, Michigan, 1925-1926. Western Michigan University, Kalamazoo, Michigan, 1926-1927. University of Michigan, A.B., M.A., Ann Arbor, Michigan. Syracuse University, Syracuse, New York
Career: Teacher, Southwest Christian School, Grand Rapids, Michigan, 1927-1942. Remedial Reading Teacher, Calvin Christian School Association, Grand Rapids, Michigan, 1942-1973

Writings: Centennial hymn for church's 100th anniversary. Centennial hymn, Raybrook Manor. Hymns published in *Grandville Avenue Christian Reformed Church* paper, Christian Reformed churches, Grand Rapids, Michigan. Poems and short stories in church publications
What is the aim or goal of your writing? "To thank and glorify the Lord and for the enjoyment and enrichment of myself and others."

RUSSELL, ANNE D.

Address: P.O. Box 430063, Pontiac, Michigan 48343
Born: January 7, 1931; Daleville, Alabama
Parents: Curtis G. Roberson, Bertha I. Roberson
Children: John, Shirley
Education: University of Michigan, Master of Education, Ann Arbor, Michigan, 1964-1969; part-time doctoral studies 1971-1979. Alabama State College, Bachelor of Science, Montgomery, Alabama,1955-1958. Northwestern University, Evanston, Illinois, summers 1961, 1962. Wayne State University, Detroit, Michigan, summer 1967

Career: Assistant Principal, Pontiac School District, 1971-1988, teacher, 1965-1971; substitute teacher 1962-1963. Director, Health-Welfare and Housing, Pontiac Urban League, Pontiac, Michigan, 1964-1965. Secretary, University of Michigan, 1963-1964. Business/English teacher, Enterprise, Alabama, 1958-1962. Part-time Instructor, Wayne Community College, Detroit, Michigan, 1979-1982. Part-time Associate Professor, Oakland Community College, Bloomfield Hills, Michigan, 1982-1983

Writings: *Builders of Detroit* self-published 1979. *Blacks in Pontiac* revised self-published 1977. *Blacks in Pontiac* Vol.1 self-published 1975. *The Michigan Chronicle Newspaper*, weekly. Articles also been published in *Pontiac Citizens Metro Post Newspaper, The Alabama State Teachers Association Journal, The Crisis Magazine, Epoch Magazine*. Work in Progress: *Rosa! A Pictorial Biography*

Awards or inclusion in other biographical books:*Michigan Authors,* 2nd ed.; *Who's Who of American Women,* 1985-1986; *Who's Who in the Midwest,* 1982-1983

What is the aim or goal of your writing? "The goal of my writing is to introduce readers to Blacks in Michigan who are in leadership positions, and to provide role models for young people".

May inquiries be sent to you about doing workshops, readings? Yes

RYDHOLM C. (CHARLES) FRED

Address: 221 Lakewood Lane, Marquette, Michigan 49855
Born: March 11, 1924; Marquette, Michigan
Parents: Eber F. Rydholm, Louise H. Rydholm
Children: Frederick Kim, Danial Charles
Education: Albion College, A.B., Albion, Michigan, 1942-1948
Career: United States Navy, 1942-1946. Huron Mountain Club (summers),1941-1970. Republic High School, Republic, Michigan, 1948-1950. Clear Lake Camp, Battle Creek Public Schools, Battle Creek, Michigan, 1950-1951. Vermontville Rural Agriculture Schools, 1951-1953. Marquette Public Schools, 1953-1982, retired. Marquette County History Workshops, Northern Michigan University, 1976-1982. Elderhostle Programs, Northern Michigan University, 1983-1991. Appointed by Michigan Governor Romney to Michigan Higher Education Assistance Authority; appointed by Governor Millikin to Michigan Loan Authority, 1969-1982. Board of Directors, Marquette Foundation, and others 1989—. Member of Executive Committee, Burrows Cave, State of Illinois, 1990–. Board of Directors, Institute for the Study of American Cultures, 1990. Mayor of the city of Marquette, Michigan, 1959-1960, 1963-1964, 1968-1969. State Policy Commission of Michigan Education Association committee member, 1967-1969. Others

Writings: *Superior Heartland,* (four books in two volumes)1989. *Mystery Cave of Many Faces* (with Russell Borrows)1991

Awards or inclusion in other biographical books: Award of Merit, Historical Society of Michigan, 1990. Citizen of the Year, Marquette Chamber of Commerce, 1989. Meritorious Award, Native Americans of Marquette County, 1989. Helen Longyear Paul Memorial Award, Marquette County Historical Society, 1989. Distinguished Service Award, Michigan Association of Retired School Personnel, 1987. Award of Appreciation, Northern Michigan University, 1968. Outstanding Young Man of the Year Award, City of Marquette, Michigan, 1959. Louis G. Kaufman Character Award, Marquette High School, 1941. Others

S

SABINO, OSVALDO R.
Address: 1301 Orleans, Apt. 1701 E, Detroit, Michigan, 48207
Born: December 26, 1950; Caseros Pra. de Buenos Aires, Argentina
Parents: Horacio H. Sabino, Carolina (Schipani de) Sabino
Education: University of California: San Diego, M.A., 1982-1985, La Jolla, California. Boston University, Ph.D., Boston, Massachusetts, 1986-1992
Career: Teacher, Boston City Schools, Boston, Massachusetts, 1986-1990. Teaching Assistant, University of California, La Jolla, California, 1982-1984

Writings: Book of poetry, published in Argentina, 1990. Critical study, published in Argentina, 1987. Published in *Human Rights Quarterly*. Work in Progress: Novel. Critical study
Awards or inclusion in other biographical books: Massachusetts Artists Fellowship, 1985

May inquiries be sent to you about doing workshops, readings? Yes

SACHS, HARLEY L.
Address: 113 W. Houghton Avenue, Houghton, Michigan 49931
Born: January 1, 1931; Chicago, Illinois
Parents: Jack S. Sachs, Miriam B. Sachs
Children: Anna-Lena, Belinda, Cynthia
Education: Indiana University, M.A.T., 1955-1956; B.A., 1949-1953. University of Stockholm, Sweden,1957-1960. University of Copenhagen, Denmark, 1962
Career: Author, freelance, Houghton, Michigan, 1957—. Assistant Professor, Aalborg University, Aalborg, Denmark, 1986-1987. Associate Professor, Michigan Technological University, Houghton, Michigan, 1965-1986, retired. Instructor, Southern Illinois University, Alton, Illinois, 1963-1965

Writings: *Irma Quarterdeck Reports* Westcott Cove 1991. *Freelance Nonfiction Articles* Society for Technical Communication 1987. *How to Write the Technical Article and Get it Published* Society for Technical Communication 1976. *Threads of the Covenant* recorded for the Michigan Blind and Disabled, available now on tape. Short stories have apeared in *Hadassah, Tailings, Passages North, Woods Runner* and others. Many articles, poetry, plays, essays. Work in Progress: Novel in the thriller genre, book of cartoons, collection of ethnic short stories, revision of a literary novel
Awards or inclusion in other biographical books:*Directory of American Scholars; Who's Who in Community Service; Who's Who in the Midwest,* and others. First prize for essay, H.G. Roberts Foundation, 1988. Ed Powers Humor Award, Upper Peninsula of Michigan Writers, 1990. Society for Technical Communication Award for Excellence, 1989
What is the aim or goal of your writing? "That's a tough question. Writing is a compulsion, a discipline, a habit, a joy. It's also a way to earn some money to supplement my pension. It's a means of communication of ideas beyond the grave. It's an ego trip. It's a way to entertain, amuse, and educate audiences."
May inquiries be sent to you about doing workshops, readings? Yes

SAGENDORPH, KENT (1902-1958)
Born: April 23, 1902; Jackson, Michigan
Parents: William Kent Sagendorph, Ethel May (Abbott) Sagendorph
Children: Mary Lou, Wallace
Education: University of Michigan, Air Corps Flying School, 1922
Career: Lecturer, author for the U.S. Air Force. Technical material for aviation trade magazines. Published more than 300 articles. President, Veteran's Flying Association. Lt. Colonel, World War II. Editor, *Inside Michigan*

Writings: *Radium Island* Cupples & Leon 1938. *Beyond the Amazon* Cupples & Leon 1938. *Sin-Kiang Castle* Cupplies & Leon 1938. *Thunder Aloft: U.S. Air Power Today...Tomorrow* Reilly & Lee 1942. *Stevens Thomson Mason: Misunderstood Patriot* Dutton 1947. *Michigan: The Story of the University* Dutton 1948. *Charles Edward Wilson American Industrialist* General Electric 1949
Awards or inclusion in other biographical books: *Michigan Authors,* 1st ed., 2nd ed.

SAGER, ROBERT CLAY
Address: 8976 King Road, Box 66, Alanson, Michigan 49706
Born: January 7, 1918; Burt Lake, Michigan
Parents: William K. Sager, Jane P. (Parke) Sager
Children: Scott, Pamela
Education: Ann Arbor High School, Ann Arbor, Michigan, 1932-1937. Eastern Michigan University, B.S., Ypsilanti, Michigan, 1937-1941
Career: Defense-Intelligence Agency, Pentagon, Washington, DC, 1949-1973, retired. Captain, Army Air Corps, 1941-1949, retired, a Lt. Col. in the Reserve

Writings: *Supplement to The Pageant of Tuscarora* Helen Boyd Higgins Memorial Library of Burt Lake Christian Church 1985. *The Pageant of Tuscarora* Helen Boyd Higgins Memorial Library of Burt Lake Christian Church 1975. *Photogrammetric Engineering* The American Society of Photogrammetry 1951. *Photo Interpretations of Artic Territories* 1949
Awards or inclusion in other biographical books: The Legion of Merit Award, United States Air Force. The Patriot Award, Pentagon, upon retirement. Many other awards from manuals
What is the aim or goal of your writing? "Personal histories"
May inquiries be sent to you about doing workshops, readings? No

SANDBURG, HELGA
Address: 2060 Kent Road, Cleveland Heights, Ohio 44106
(Lived much of her childhood at Harbert in Michigan dune country, used setting in *Blueberry*, etc.)
Born: November 1918; Maywood, Illinois
Parents: Carl Sandburg, Lilian (Steichen) Sandburg
Children: John Carl Steichen, Paula Steichen Polega
Education: Michigan State College, East Lansing, Michigan, 1939-1940. The University of Chicago, 1940
Career: Secretary to her father, Carl Sandburg, as adolescent and adult. Dairy goat breeder with her mother, 1944-1951. Secretary in Manuscripts Division and for The Keeper of the Collections, Library of Congress, Washington, DC, 1952-1956. Administra-

tive Assistant for The Papers of Woodrow Wilson, Woodrow Wilson Foundation, Washington, DC, 1958-1959. Conducted seminars in Great Britain, Europe, as an American specialist under the State Department's Bureau of Cultural and Educational Affairs. Lecturer

Writings: *The Wheel of Earth* McDowell, Obolensky 1958. *Measure My Love* McDowell, Obolensky 1959. *The Owl's Roost* The Dial Press 1962. *The Wizard's Child* The Dial Press 1967. *Sweet Music* The Dial Press 1963. *Above and Below* (with George Crile, Jr.) McGraw-Hill American Wilderness Series 1969. *A Great and Glorious Romance: The Story of Carl Sandburg and Lilian Steichen* Harcourt Brace Jovanovich 1978. *"...Where Love Begins"* Donald I. Fine 1989. *The Unicorns* Dial Press 1965. *To a New Husband* World Publishing Company 1970. *Blueberry* The Dial Press 1963. *Gingerbread* The Dial Press 1964. *Joel and the Wild Goose* The Dial Press 1963. *Bo and the Old Donkey* The Dial Press 1965. *Anna and the Baby Buzzard* Dutton 1970. *Children and Lovers: 15 Stories by Helga Sandburg* Harcourt Brace Jovanovich 1976. Short stories, poems, articles in *The New Yorker, The New York Times, The Saturday Evening Post, Harpers, Good Housekeeping, Ladies Home Journal, Seventeen, Redbook* and others. Included in anthologies. Several translations. Work in Progress: *Why Go to Mexico,* non-fiction. *Child,* poems for children. *74—Poems by Helga Sandburg,* for adults
Awards or inclusion in other biographical books: *Michigan Authors,* 2nd ed. Florence Roberts Head Ohioama Book Award, 1990. Short story, "Witch Chicken", *Virginia Quarterly Review,* 1958-Best Articles and Stories, 1958. O. Henry Prize Stories, 1959. *Virginia Quarterly Review First Prize,* Best Story, 1959. Poem awards: Borestone Mountain Poetry Second Prize, 1962; *Chicago Tribune* Poetry Third Prize, 1970; Honorable Mention, Kansas Poetry Contest, 1974, Second Prize, 1974; Honorable Mention, Utah State Poetry Contest, 1975; Medal, Triton College "All Nations" Poetry Contest, 1976. Grant, Finnish American Society and Svenska Institutet, 1961

SANFORD, CAROL L.
Address: 1030 S. Drive, Mt. Pleasant, Michigan 48858
Born: November 22, 1940; Clare, Michigan
Parents: Lorence E. Acker, Effie M. Acker
Children: Keven, Renee. Kirk (recently deceased)
Education: Central Michigan University, Bachelor of Arts, English, Mt. Pleasant, Michigan, 1958-1962; Master, Creative Writing, 1973-1976
Career: Instructor of English, Central Michigan University, Mt. Pleasant, Michigan, 1988—. Associate Professor, Northwood Institute, Midland, Michigan, 1980-1988. Teacher, Librarian, Meridian Public Schools, Sanford, Michigan, 1962-1977

Writings: Poems in *Moving Out, Spirit, The Windless Orchard, Huron Review, Happiness Holding Tank, Calliope, Review Magazine, Verve, Plainsongs* and others. Included in *Anthology of Magazine Verse & Yearbook of American Poetry* 1980. Others pending. Work in Progress: Book of poems, *First Grace*
What is the aim or goal of your writing? "As a poet, I am primarily interested in telling the truth about life in a fresh way, so that the reader is both startled and satisfied <u>and</u> convinced that words/expression are a criterion for a meaningful existence."
May inquiries be sent to you about doing workshops, readings? Yes

SARETT, LEW (1888-1954)
Born: May 16, 1888; Chicago, Illinois
Parents: Rudolph Sarett, Jeanette (Block) Sarett
Children: Lewis, Helen
Education: University of Michigan, 1907-1908. Beloit College, A.B., Beloit, Wisconsin, 1911. Harvard University, Cambridge, Massachusetts, 1911-1912. University of Illinois, LL.B., 1916. Litt.D., Baylor University, Waco, Texas, 1926
Career: Forest ranger, woodsman, wilderness guide. Professor, University of Illinois, 1914-1920. Professor, Northwestern University, 1920-1953. Poet, writer, lecturer. Visiting Professor, University of Florida, 1951-1954

Writings: *Many, Many Moons* Holt 1920. *The Box of God* Holt 1922. *Slow Smoke* Holt 1925. *Wings Against the Moon* Holt 1931. *Collected Poems* Holt 1941. *Covenant with Earth* (edited by Alma Sarett) University of Florida Press 1956. *Basic Principles of Speech* Houghton Mifflin 1936, 1946, 1958, 1966. *Modern Speeches on Basic Issues* Houghton Mifflin 1939. *Speech: a High School Course* (with James H. McBurney) Houghton Mifflin 1943, 1947, 1951, 1956
Awards or inclusion in other biographical books: *American Authors and Books; Childhood in Poetry; Contemporary American Authors; Concise Dictionary of American Literature; Contemporary American Literature; Michigan Authors,* 2nd ed.; *Michigan Poets; Oxford Companion to American Literature; Reader's Encyclopedia; Reader's Encyclopedia of American Literature; Twentieth Century Authors; Who Was Who among English and European Authors; Who Was Who among North American Authors; Who Was Who in America,* others. Helen Haire Levinson Prize, 1921. Poetry Society of America Award, 1925. Honorary Litt. D., Baylor University, 1926. Chicago Foundation for Literature Award, 1934. Honorary L.H. D., Beloit College, 1945. Lew Sarett Collection, Library Archives, Northwestern University, 1956. Lew Sarett Wildlife Sanctuary and Nature Center, Benton Harbor, Michigan, 1965

SCANLON, MARION STEPHANY (?-1977)
Born: Lanesboro, Minnesota
Parents: Cornelius Scanlon, Margaret (Rafferty) Scanlon
Education: Ripon College, B., Ph., Ripon, Wisconsin. University of Minnesota. Graduate study in Medical School. University of Wisconsin, M.S.; postgraduate study. University of Michigan, postgraduate study
Career: Professor of Health Education, Marygrove College, Detroit, Michigan, 1936-1970.

Writings: *Wiggley Nell* Edwards 1949. *Calm and Cool was Penguin Row, a Ferry-Boat I'd Like to Ride* Edwards 1953. *Seven Frisky Lambs* Edwards 1954. *Trails of the French Explorers* Naylor 1956. *Pudgie Pat's Pets* Edwards 1958. *Freddie the Froggie* Edwards 1959. *Three Little Clouds* Denison 1959. *Mister Roberto R. Robot* Edwards 1960. *Little Johnnie Trout* Denison 1962. *Hygiene for College Freshman* Edwards 1963. *Sports and Ballroom Dancing for College Freshman* Edwards 1963. *White Beaver* 1974
Awards or inclusion in biographical books: *Contemporary Authors; Foremost Women in Communications; Michigan Authors,* 2nd ed.; *Minnesota Writers; Something about the Author; Who's Who of American Women; Writers Directory.* Hopwood Award for drama, University of Michigan, 1943. Award, National League of American Pen Women, 1961

SCANNELL, FRANCIS P. (1915-1988)

Born: 1915; Royal Oak, Michigan
Children: Suzanne, Stasia, Stephen, Shawn, Sharla
Education: University of California, Los Angeles, California, 1940
Career: Served in U.S. Army, World War II, as cryptographer in South Pacific. Scriptwriter, including "The Lone Ranger" series, MGM Studios. Moved to Detroit area 1955, automotive accounts, Jam Handy. Freelance writer

Writings: *In Line of Duty* Harper 1946. *Ready or Not* 1968.
Awards or inclusion in other biographical books: *Contemporary Authors*

SCHABECK, TIMOTHY A.

Address: 543 Jener, Plymouth, Michigan 48170
Born: April 3, 1945; Toledo, Ohio
Parents: Frank J. Schabeck, Dorothy R. Schabeck
Children: Todd, Wendy, Rebecca
Education: St. John's University, Ph.D., Criminal Justice, New Orleans, Louisiana, 1980. Indiana Northern Graduate School of Professional Management, M.P.M.-Management, Fort Wayne, Indiana, 1977-1979. University of Detroit, Michigan. University of Toledo, Ohio
Career: Self-employed, Schabeck Consulting, Plymouth, Michigan, 1988—. Author/Technical Manager, Chantico, Publishing, Dallas, Texas (only in 1987), 1983-1987. Manager of Customer Support, Computer Solutions, Troy, Michigan, 1978-1983 (intermittent). Senior Management Consultant, Seidman & Seidman, CPA, Troy, Michigan, 1977-1978. Senior Analyst, Criminal Justice Institute, Detroit, Michigan, 1974-1975. Lead analyst, Blue Cross/Blue Shield, Detroit, Michigan and Toledo, Ohio, 1965-1974. Appeared on television talk shows, special news segments. Lectured throughout the United States. Currently Chaplain Coordinator, Wayne County Emergency Management Division; Police Chaplain, Plymouth Township Police Department

Writings: *EDP Security* (update author) 3 vols. FTP Publications 1984-1987. *EDP Disaster Recovery* (update author 3 vols. FTP Publications 1984-1987. *Management and Benefits Reporting* (technical editor) Chantico Publishing 1987. *Chargeback* (technical editor) Chantico Publishing 1987. *Managing Change* (technical editor) Chantico Publishing 1987. *Desktop Publishing* Chantico Publishing 1987. *Managing Microcomputer Security* FTP Publications 1986. *Emergency Planning Guide for Data Processing Centers* Assets Protection/The Territorial Imperative, Inc. 1979. *Computer Crime Investigation* Assets Protection/Territorial Imperative, Inc. 1979. Contributing editor *Assets Protection Journal.* International newsletters: *Computer Security Digest,* 1983-1986; *ICI Forum,* 1987. Over thirty articles. Work in Progress: *Police Chaplain's Reference Manual*
What is the aim or goal of your writing? "To share information."
May inquiries be sent to you about doing workshops, readings? Yes

SCHABERG, JANE D.

Address: 18202 Fairfield, Detroit, Michigan 48221
Born: February 20, 1938; St. Louis, Missouri
Parents: Kenneth D. Schaberg, Helen (Walsh) Schaberg
Education: Manhattanville College, B.A., Purchase, New York, 1956-1960. Columbia University, M.A., New York, New York, 1968-1970. Union Theological Seminary, Ph.D., New York, New York, 1972-1980

Career: Professor, University of Detroit, Detroit, Michigan, 1977—

Writings:*The Illegitimacy of Jesus: A Feminist Theological Interpretation of the N.T.Infancy Narratives* Harper and Row 1987; Crossroad 1990. *The Father, the Son and the Holy Spirit: Matthew 28:19* Scholars Press 1982. Work in Progress: *Thinking Back Through the Magdalene,* Crossroad Press

What is the aim or goal of your writing? "To bring a feminist consciousness and a woman's experience to bear on interpretation of biblical texts and their traditions."

May inquiries be sent to you about doing workshops, readings? Yes

SCHARFENBERG, DORIS A.

Address: 35949 Quakertown, Farmington Hills, Michigan 48331

Born: August 2, 1925; Detroit, Michigan

Parents: Leroy K. Fleming, Muriel (Keenan) Fleming

Children: Bruce, Douglas, Jane, Gretchen

Education: Mackenzie High School, Detroit, Michigan. Hillsdale College, B.S., Hillsdale, Michigan, 1943-1947

Career: Housewife

Writings: *Long Blue Edge of Summer: Vacation Guide to Michigan Coasts* Eerdmans 1982; revised, enlarged Momentum Books 1992. *Long Blue Edge of Ontario: Guide to Ontario's Great Lakes Coast* Eerdmans 1983. *Michigan Country Roads* Country Roads Press 1992. Two chapters, *Rand McNally National Parks Campground Guide.* Many travel articles. Work in Progress: Book on courthouses of the United States. Children's books

Awards or inclusion in other biographical books: First place, Society of American Travel Writers-Central States, 1982. Mark Twain Award, Midwest Travel Writers Association

What is the aim or goal of your writing? "To inform and entertain."

May inquiries be sent to you about doing workshops, readings? Yes

SCHEMM, MILDRED WALKER

Pseudonym: Mildred Walker

Born: May 2, 1905; Philadelphia, Pennsylvania

Parents: Walter M. Walker, Harriet (Merrifield) Walker

Children: Margaret, George

Education: Wells College, B.A., Aurora, New York, 1926. University of Michigan, M.A., Ann Arbor, Michigan, 1934

Career: Copy writer, John Wanamaker Company, Philadelphia, Pennsylvania, 1926-1927. Professor, Wells College, Aurora, New York, 1955-1968. Lecturer, writers conference staff member

Writings: *Fireweed* Harcourt, Brace 1934. *Light from Arcturus* Harcourt, Brace 1935. *Dr. Norton's Wife* Sun Dial Press 1938. *The Brewers' Big Horses* Harcourt, Brace 1940. *Unless the Wind Turns* Harcourt, Brace 1941.*Winter Wheat* Harcourt, Brace & World 1944; Harcourt, Brace, Jovanovich 1972. *The Quarry* Harcourt, Brace 1947. *Medical Meeting* Harcourt, Brace 1949. *The Southwest Corner* Harcourt, Brace 1951.*The Curlew's Cry* Harcourt, Brace 1955. *The Body of a Young Man* Harcourt, Brace 1960.*If a Lion Could Talk* Harcourt, Brace, Jovanovich 1970. *A Piece of the World* Atheneum 1972

Awards or inclusion in other biographical books: *American Authors and Books;*

American Novelists of Today; Author's and Writer's Who's Who; Benet's Reader's Encyclopedia of American Literature; Biography Index; Index to Women; Michigan Poets; Michigan Authors, 2nd ed.; *Reader's Encyclopedia of American Literature; Twentieth Century Authors; Who's Who of American Women; Who's Who in America; Writers Directory.* Avery Hopwood Award, University of Michigan, for *Fireweed.* Awarded Fulbright Scholarship. In the 2nd edition of *Michigan Authors* appears: "Born in a parsonage in Philadelphia, Mildred Walker came to Michigan 1927 when she married Dr. F.R. Schemm, a young surgeon. It was here in a lumber town on Lake Superior that she wrote short stories, verse, and novels, most of which she burned. Her first novel, *Fireweed*, with its background of a Lake Superior mill town, reflects a Michigan influence."

SCHINKEL, RICHARD E.
Address: P.O. Box 316, Berrien Springs, Michigan 49103
Born: July 16, 1943; Benton Harbor, Michigan
Parents: Edmund Schinkel, Edith R. Schinkel
Children: Jennifer, Marna, Cara
Education: Berrien Springs High School. Western Michigan University, B.A., M.A., Kalamazoo, Michigan, 1964-1970
Career: Teacher, Niles Community Schools, Niles, Michigan,1966-1967. Naturalist, Michigan Audubon Society, Sarett Nature Center, Benton Harbor, Michigan, 1977—

Writings: *Suburban Nature Guide* Stackpole 1991. *Building for Birds* Generations 1988. Work in Progress: *The Birds of Michigan* Indiana University Press
What is the aim or goal of your writing? "Impart natural history to children and adults."
May inquiries be sent to you about doing workshops, readings? Yes

SCHLIEHTER, VIRGINIA S.
Address: 122 Walnut Court, Mason, Michigan 48854
Born: February 24, 1919; Cheboygan, Michigan
Parents: William C. Norton, Lillian A. (Bryce) Norton
Children: Linda, Mark, Susan, Kathy
Education: Michigan State University, East Lansing, Michigan; Eastern Michigan University, Ypsilanti, Michigan, B.A., 1937-1942. Michigan State University, Counseling Certificate, 1963-1966
Career: Secondary teacher, Napoleon, Michigan, 1942-1946. Secondary teacher, counselor, Mason, Michigan, 1955-1979

Writings: *The Pink School* self-published 1990. In *Lansing State Journal, Mature Michiganians*
What is the aim or goal of your writing? "To preserve history and make it come alive for present generation."
May inquiries be sent to you about doing workshops, readings? No

SCHNEIDER, REX
Address: 26829 37th Street, Gobles, Michigan 49055
Born: February 22, 1937; Butler, Pennsylvania
Parents: Cyril L. Schneider, Alice E. (Jewell) Schneider
Education: Ball State University, B.S., Muncie, Indiana, 1955-1959

Career: Self Employed Artist, Blue Mouse Studio, Baltimore, Maryland; Union, Michigan; Gobles, Michigan, 1972—. Art Editor, *Performance*, weekly paper, 1971-1973. Manager/Owner, General Eclectic, Crafts and Antique Store, 1971-1973, Baltimore, Maryland. Employment Counselor, Baltimore Association for Retarded Adults, 1964-1971. Set Designer, WNIT PBS Station, Elkhart, Indiana. Filmstrips for Nystrom/ Eyegate, 1990; Encyclopedia Britannica, 1985; Clearview, 1988; SVE, 1982. Hundreds of spot/full page illustrations for work/text books. Animation, bookplates, greeting cards, books, posters, and other illustration formats

Writings: *Dinosaurs Galore* Educational Book Fair 1993. *The Wide-Mouthed Frog* Stemmer House 1980. *That's Not All* Schoolzone 1984. *Ain't We Got Fun?* Blue Mouse Studio 1982. Work in Progress: *I Declare*, book of tongue-twisting rhyme about hares, chairs, stairs, bears, and a pear bearing mare

Awards or inclusion in other biographical books: Hidden Picture of the Year Award, 1988. Silver Medal Award, Atlanta International Film Festival, 1969, 1986. Children's Choice Award, 1980. Book of the Month Club Selection, for illustrating *Poems of Emily Dickinson for Children,* 1978

What is the aim or goal of your writing? "(And or illustration.) To bring enjoyment to children (or adults) through books. Learning something of the world and universally helpful values would be most desirable but the goal is 'fun'."

May inquiries be sent to you about doing workshops, readings? Yes

SCHOOLCRAFT, HENRY ROWE (1793-1864)

Pseudonym: Damoetas

Born: March 28, 1793; Albany County, New York

Parents: Lawrence Schoolcraft, Margaret Anne Barbara (Rowe) Schoolcraft

Children: William Henry, Jane Susan Anne, John, Alice

Education: Union College, Middleberry College

Career: At 16 began literary society for young men, edited its magazine,*The Cricket* or*Whispers from a Voice in the Corner.* Went into glass-making industry, 1809, 4 years later was managing a glass factory in Vermont. Explored Missouri and Arkansas, 1817. Expedition with Lewis Cass, 1820. Explored western Lake Superior, established the source of Mississippi River, 1831-1832. Indian Agent, Lake Superior tribes, 1822. Served in Michigan Territorial Legislature, 1828-1832. Secured through treaties a large portion of Michigan. Superintendent of Indian Affairs for Michigan, 1836-1841. Helped to found: State Historical Society of Michigan, 1828; Michigan Territorial Library, 1828; Algic Research Society, 1832, American Ethnological Society, 1842. Regent, University of Michigan, 1837-1841. Went to Washington, DC, 1846, petitioning Congress on Indian affairs

Writings:*A View of the Lead Mines of Missouri* Charles Wiley 1819. *Alhalla, or the Lord of Talladega* Wiley and Putnam 1843. *An Address Delivered Before the Was-ah Ho-de-no-son-ne, or, New Confederacy of the Iroquois* Jerome & Bro. 1846. *Scenes and Adventures in the Semi-Alpine Region of the Ozark Mountains.* 1853. *Narrative Journal of Travels Through the Northwestern Regions of the United States* Gisford 1821.*Travels in the Central Portions of the Mississippi Valley* Collins & Hanney 1825.*The Rise of the West* (poem)Whitney 1830. *A Discource Delivered on the Anniversary of the Historical Society of Michigan, June 4, 1830* G.L. Whitney 1830.*Narrative of an Expedition through the Upper Mississippi to Itasca Lake* Harper 1834. *Algic Researches, Comprising Inquiries Respecting the Mental Characteristics of the North American Indians* Harper

& Brothers 1839. *Oneonta, or the Red Race of America* Burgess, Stringer 1844-1845. *Notes on the Iroquois* Pease 1847. *The Indian in His Wigwam: or, Characteristics of the Red Race of America* Graham 1847. *A Bibliographical Catalogue of Books, Translations of the Scriptures, and Other Publications in the Indian Tongues of the United States, with Brief Critical Notices* C. Alexander 1849. *Personal Memoirs of a Residence of Thirty Years with the Indian Tribes on the American Frontiers* Lippincott, Grambo 1851. *The American Indians. Their History, Condition and Prospects, From Original Notes and Manuscripts* new revised edition Wanzer, Foot and Company 1851. *Western Scenes and Reminiscenes* Derby & Miller 1853. *Historical and Statistical Information Respecting the History, Condition and Prospects of the Indian Tribes of the United States* (8 vols.) Lippincott, Grambo 1851-1857. *The Indian Fairy Book. From the Original Legends* Leavitt & Allen 1868. Many others. Various editions of many of his works have been printed such as: *Schoolcraft's Indian Legends* (editor, Mentor L. Williams) Michigan State University Press 1956. Sound cassettes. Published verse in *Detroit Gazette* newspaper

Awards or inclusion in other biographical books: *American Authors; American Authors and Books; American Biographies; Dictionary of American Authors; Dictionary of American Biography; Dictionary of North American Authors; Encyclopedia of American Biography; Michigan Authors,* 1st ed., 2nd ed.; *National Cyclopaedia of American Biography; Oxford Companion to American Literature; Reader's Encyclopedia; Reader's Encyclopedia of American Literature; Twentieth Century Biographical Dictionary of Notable Americans,* several others

SCHOOLLAND, MARIAN M. (1902-1984)

Born: March 6, 1902; Grand Rapids, Michigan
Parents: Klaas Schoolland, Nellie (Heyboer) Schoolland
Education: Calvin College, A.B., Grand Rapids, Michigan, 1934. University of Michigan, A.M., Ann Arbor, Michigan, 1943
Career: Teacher, Grand Rapids, Michigan, 1919-1929. Instructor, Calvin College, Grand Rapids, Michigan, 1939-1947. Editor, *Bible Light*

Writings: *Marian's Book of Bible Stories* Eerdmans 1947. *A Land I Will Show Thee* Eerdmans 1949, 1954. *The Story of Van Raalte, "a Man Strong and of Good Courage"* W. B. Eerdmans 1951. *Forest Folk Tales* Eerdmans 1953. *The Wide, Wide World* (editor) Eerdmans 1955. *De Kolonie: The Church That God Transplanted* Board of Publication of the Christian Reformed Church 1974. Others. In *Banner, Key*
Awards or inclusion in other biographical books: *Contemporary Authors; The Writers Directory 1976-1978.* Distinguished Alumni Award, Calvin College, 1980

SCHORER, CALVIN E.

Address: 770 Bedford, Grosse Pointe Park, Michigan 48230
Born: June 29, 1919
Parents: William C. Schorer, Anna E. Schorer
Children: Anna, Joseph, John, Mary
Education: University of Wisconsin, Madison, Wisconsin, B.A., 1935-1939; M.D., 1950-1955. University of Chicago, Chicago, Illinois, M.A., 1940-1942; Ph.D., 1946-1948
Career: Director of Medical Staff Services and Director of Training, Lafayette Clinic, Detroit, Michigan, 1959—. Assistant Professor of English, Northern Michigan College of Education, Marquette, Michigan,1948-1950

Writings: *Indian Tales of C. C. Trowbridge* Green Oaks Press 1988.
Published in *American Speech, Western Folklore, Michigan History, Mississippi Valley Historical Review, Midwest Journal, American Literature, Midwest Folklore, Southern Folklore, American Journal of Psychiatry, Exceptional Child, Comparative Psychiatry, British Journal of Criminology* and others. Work in Progress: Aspects of 19th Century Indian culture. Medical student stress and coping styles

What is the aim or goal of your writing? "My work has almost all been in the form of articles in two fields-American Literature and Psychiatry. The aim of my writing in American literature has been primarily to bring to light previously unpublished or unrecognized contributions such as manuscript material located in the Burton Collection, Detroit Public Library. The aim of my writing in psychiatry has been in several directions 1) publishing results of research 2) translating relevant articles from German and French 3) book reviews. I trust that in all cases my aim has been to contribute to knowledge."

May inquiries be sent to you about doing workshops, readings? Yes

SCHRADER, PAUL JOSEPH

Born: July 22, 1946; Grand Rapids, Michigan
Parents: Charles A. Schrader, Joan (Fisher) Schrader
Education: Calvin College, B.A., Grand Rapids, Michigan, 1968. University of California, M.A., Los Angeles, California, 1970
Career: Film critic, *Free Press*, Los Angeles, California, 1968-1969. Film critic, editor for others. Writer of screenplays, director, essayist. Teacher, Columbia University

Writings: *Transcendental Style in Film* University of California Press 1972. *The Yakuza* (with Leonard Schrader) Warner Brothers 1972. *Taxi Driver* Columbia 1976; Faber and Faber 1990. *Blue Collar* (with Leonard Schrader, Universal 1977. *Hardcore* Columbia 1979. *Raging Bull* (with Mardik Martin) United Artists 1980. *American Gigolo* Paramount 1980. *Mishima* (with Leonard Schrader) Zoetrope 1985. *Schrader on Schrader* Faber and Faber 1990. *Light Sleeper* Faber and Faber 1992. Others. In *Film Quarterly, Academy Leader, Film Comment,* others

Awards or inclusion in other biographical books: *Contemporary Authors; Dictionary of Literary Biography; Michigan Authors,* 2nd ed. First Place Essay, *Atlantic,* 1968. First Place Essay, *The Magazine of Discovery,* 1968

SCHULTZ, GERARD (1902-1974)

Born: February 11, 1902; near Herman, Missouri
Parents: George C. Schultz, Helene (Meier) Schultz
Children: John, Gerard, Dan
Education: Elmhurst Academy, 1921. Knox College, A.B., Galesburg, Illinois, 1925. University of Minnesota, M.A., 1928
Career: History Department, University of Minnesota, 1925-1928. Teacher, writer, 30 years

Writings: *A History of Miller County* 1933. *The Early History of the Northern Ozarks* 1937. *History of Warren County, Iowa* 1953. *History of Marshall County, Iowa* 1955. *A History of Michigan's Thumb* 1964; revised as: *The New History of Michigan's Thumb* 1969. *Walls of Flame* 1972. *Treasure Map of the Great Lakes Region*
Awards or inclusion in other biographical books: *Michigan Authors,* 2nd ed.

SCHULTZE, QUENTIN J.
Address: Department of Communication, Calvin College, 3201 Burton SE, Grand Rapids, Michigan 49546
Born: September 22, 1952; Chicago, Illinois
Parents: Theodore L. Schultze, Agnes C. (Dopke) Schultze
Children: Stephen, Bethany
Education: Maine West High School, 1966-1970. University of Illinois, B.S., M.S., Ph.D., 1970-1978
Career: Instructor, University of Illinois, Urbana-Champaign, Illinois, 1977-1978. Assistant/Associate Professor, Drake University, Des Moines, Iowa, 1978-1982. Associate Professor/Professor, Calvin College, Grand Rapids, Michigan, 1982—. Workshop leader

Writings: *Redeeming Television* InterVarsity Press 1992. *Televanagelism and American Culture: The Business of Popular Religion* Baker 1991. *Dancing in the Dark: Youth, Popular Culture and the Electronic Media* (first author) Eerdmans 1991. *American Evangelicals and the Mass Media* Academie/Zondervan 1991. *Television: Manna from Hollywood?* Zondervan 1986. Several dozen scholarly essays, numerous book chapters. Seventy articles for magazines, newspapers. Work in Progress: Several books on the role of narratives in contemporary culture
Awards or inclusion in other biographical books: Finalist, *Christianity Today* Reader's Choice Award, 1992. First runner up, *Christianity Today,* Critic's Choice Award, 1992. Religious Speech Communication Association Annual Award, 1988. Nominated, Newcommen Society of North America, 1982
What is the aim or goal of your writing? "My major aim is to analyze and interpret the impact of the electronic media on traditional cultures anchored in ethnicity, race, community, and religious faith. My supporting aim is to encourage traditional authority figures, including educators and parents, to work with youth on ways to maintain and improve cultural life."
May inquiries be sent to you about doing workshops, readings? Yes

SCIESZKA, JON
Born: Flint, Michigan; September 8, 1954
Parents: Louis Scieszka, Shirley Scieszka
Children: Casey, Jake
Education: Albion College, B.A., Albion, Michigan, 1976. Columbia University, M.F.A., New York, New York, 1980
Career: Teacher, 1980—. Various jobs

Writings: *The True Story of the Three Little Pigs* Viking Kestrel 1989. *The Frog Prince, Continued* Viking Children's 1991. *Knights of the Kitchen Table* Viking Children's 1991. *The Not-So-Jolly Roger* Viking Children's 1991. *The Good, the Bad, and the Goofy* Viking Children's 1992. *The Stinky Cheeseman and Other Fairly Stupid Tales* Viking Children's 1992
Awards or inclusion in other biographical books: *Contemporary Authors*

SCOTT, HERBERT
Born: February 8, 1931; Norman, Oklahoma
Parents: Herbert Hicks, Betty (Pickard) Scott
Children: Herbert, Megan, Rannah, Erin, Kyla
Education: Fresno State College, B.A., 1964. University of Iowa, MFA, 1966. Studied at others

Career: Worked in grocery business, 1953-1964. Instructor in English, Southeast Missouri State College, 1966-1968. Assistant Professor of English, Western Michigan University, 1968—1972; Associate Professor beginning 1972

Writings: *Disguises* University of Pittsburgh Press 1974. *The Shoplifters' Handbook* Blue Mountain Press 1974. *Groceries* University of Pittsburgh Press 1976. *The Third Coast: Contemporary Michigan Poetry* (co-editor) Wayne State University Press 1976. *Dinosaurs* W. D. Hofstadt & Sons 1978. *The Ceremony of the Ducks* Persimmon Tree Press 1981. *As She Enters Her Seventieth Year She Dreams of Milk* Bits Press 1982. *Contemporary Michigan Poetry: Poems From the Third Coast* Wayne State University Press 1988. *Our Appetites in Our Eyes* 30 minute color video tape, Western Michigan University, 1977. Poems in *North American Review, Harper's, Epoch,* others
Awards or inclusion in other biographical books: *Contemporary Authors; Directory of American Poets; Michigan Authors,* 2nd ed. Creative Writing Fellowship, University of Iowa, 1964-1966. National Endowment for the Humanities Fellow at Boston University, 1976. Poet in Residence on the American Wind Symphony's Bicentennial Tour, 1976

SCOTT, RANDALL W.
Address: 1708 N. Fairview, Lansing, Michigan 48912
Born: June 2, 1947; Alpena, Michigan
Parents: William F. Scott, Bernice J. (Nordstrom) Scott
Children: Sara, Ziba, Margaret
Education: Alcona High School, 1961-1965. Michigan State University, B.A., East Lansing, Michigan, 1965-1972. Columbia University, M.S., New York, New York, 1976-1977
Career: Catalog Librarian, Michigan State University Libraries, East Lansing, Michigan, 1977—

Writings: *Comics Librarianship* McFarland 1990. *Comic Books and Strips* Oryx 1988
What is the aim or goal of your writing? "To advance and encourage research and study of comic books and strips."
May inquiries be sent to you about doing workshops and readings? No

SCOTT, VIRGIL J.
Born: August 1, 1914; Vancouver, Washington
Parents: Charles E. Scott, Elda T. (Swift) Scott
Children: Nancy, Catherine, David, Mrs. Gary Miller
Education: Ohio State University, A.B., M.A., Ph.D., 1935-1945
Career: English Teacher, Franklin High School, Franklin, Ohio, 1937-1941. Instructor, Ohio State University, 1941-1945. Instructor, University of Minnesota, 1945-1947. Professor, Michigan State University, 1947-1977, retired

Writings: *The Dead Tree Gives No Shelter* Swallow Press 1947. *The Hickory Stick* Swallow Press 1948. *The Savage Affair* Harcourt Brace 1958. *I, John Mordaunt* Harcourt Brace 1964. *The Kreutaman Formula* Simon & Schuster 1974. *Walk-In* Simon & Schuster 1976. *Studies in the Short Story* Holt 1949, 1960, 1968, 1970, 1976. Others
Awards or inclusion in other biographical books: *American Authors and Books; American Novelists of Today; Author's and Writer's Who's Who; Contemporary Authors; Directory of American Scholars; International Authors and Writers Who's Who; Michigan*

Authors, 2nd ed.; *Ohio Authors and Their Books.* Ohioanna Award, 1948. Nominated, Edgar Award, Mystery Writers of America

SCRIPPS, JAMES EDMUND (1835-1906)
Born: March 19, 1835; London, England
Parents: James Mogg Scripps, Ellen Mary (Saunders) Scripps
Children: Three daughters, one son
Education: District School, Rushville, Illinois. Business College, Chicago, Illinois
Career: Bookkeeper, Chicago, Illinois. Reporter, *Democratic Press,* Chicago, Illinois, 1857. Commercial Editor, *Detroit Daily Advertiser,* 1859; part owner, business manager, editor. Began *Evening News* (later known as *Detroit News*)1873. Started *Penny Press,* 1878, Cleveland, Ohio; others in St. Louis, Cincinnati. These jointly owned daily newspapers (with brothers and sister) were first chain of daily newspapers in the country. Purchased *Detroit Tribune* 1891. Elected, Michigan Senator, 1902. On commission, Detroit Museum of Art, contributed paintings from visits abroad. Donated park to Detroit

Writings: *An Outline History of Michigan* Tribune Book and Job Office 1873. *Five Months Abroad, or, the Observations and Experiences of an Editor in Europe* F. B. Dickerson & Company 1882. *History of the Scripps Family* (Detroit: for private circulation) J. F. Eby & Company 1882. *Catalogue of the Scripps Collection of Old Masters, Designed to Illustrate the History of the Art of Painting from the Thirteenth to the Eighteenth Century* J. F. Eby & Company 1889. *Trinity Church, Detroit* Detroit? 189-? *An Attempt to Establish the Descent of the Scripps Family from Anthony Pearson* J. E. Scripps 1900. *A Genealogical History of the Scripps Family and Its Various Alliances* (Detroit: for private circulation) R. L. Polk 1903. Many pamphlets
Awards or inclusion in other biographical books: *American Authors and Books; American Authors, 1600-1900; Appleton's Cyclopaedia of American Biography; Dictionary of American Authors; Dictionary of American Biography; A Dictionary of North American Authors; The National Cyclopaedia of American Biography; Webster's American Biographies; Who Was Who in America; Who's Who in America*

SEAGER, ALLAN (1906-1968)
Born: February 5, 1906; Adrian, Michigan
Parents: Arch Seager, Emma (Allan) Seager
Children: Mary, Laura
Education: University of Michigan, A.B., Ann Arbor, Michigan, 1930. Oriel College, Oxford, B.A., 1933; M.A., 1947
Career: Assistant Editor, *Vanity Fair.* Teacher, Bennington College, Bennington, Vermont. Professor, English Department, University of Michigan, 1945-1968

Writings: *They Worked for a Better World* MacMillan 1939. *Equinox* Simon & Schuster 1943.*The Inheritance, a Novel* Simon & Schuster 1948.*The Old Man of the Mountain, and Seventeen Other Stories* Simon & Schuster 1950. *Amos Berry, a Novel* Simon & Schuster 1953. *Hilda Manning, a Novel* Simon & Schuster 1956. *Death of Anger* McDowell-Obolensky 1960. Translator of Stendhal's *Memoirs of a Tourist* Northwestern University Press 1962.*A Frieze of Girls; Memoirs as Fiction* McGraw 1964. *The Glass House: the Life of Theodore Roethke* McGraw 1968; University of Michigan Press 1991. About 80 stories in magazines like *Atlantic, New Yorker, Saturday Evening Post, Esquire, Cosmopolitan.* Writing has appeared in various foreign languages

Awards or inclusion in other biographical books: *American Authors and Books; American Novelists of Today; Concise Dictionary of American Literature; Contemporary Authors; Michigan Authors,* 2nd ed.; *Oxford Companion to American Literature; Twentieth Century Authors; Who Was Who in America; Who Was Who among English and European Authors.* Guggenheim Fellowship. National Foundation on the Arts and the Humanities, 1966

SECRIST, MARGARET C.
Address: P.O. Box 185, Andover, Ohio 44003
Born: October 29, 1905; West Andover, Ohio
Parents: Lyle S. Peck, Eva C. (Howe) Peck
Education: Oberlin College, B.A., Andover, Ohio, 1923-1927. Wayne State University, M.A., Detroit, Michigan, 1957-1959. Post Graduate, University of Michigan, Ann Arbor, Michigan
Career: Teacher, Napoleon, Ohio, 1927-1931. Teacher Detroit Public Schools, 10 years. Organist at First Congregational Church, Andover, Ohio, 7 years

Writings: *The Trumpet Time* Mountain Press 1958. *Before Flight* Branden Press 1965. *Ville Detroit* Penman Publications 1967. *All These* Branden Press 1972. *Women of the Revolution* Spoon River Press 1976. *My Town* Citizen Printing 1978. *Graceful Mischief* Avonelle Associates 1979. *Above a Whisper* Vimach Associates 1985. Inclusion in 12 anthologies, 1935-1990 such as *Contemporary Women Poets, National Poetry Anthology.* Work in Progress: Poetry for magazines and local papers
Awards or inclusion in other biographical books: *Michigan Authors,* 2nd ed.; *Michigan Poets.* Detroit Women Writer's Award, 1959, 1968
What is the aim or goal of your writing? "Nothing but satisfaction-now. My voice was a small one. I belong to Ohio Verse Writers."
May inquiries be sent to you about doing workshops, readings? No. My age forbids.

SEESE, ETHEL GRAY
Address: P.O. 90, Lake Ann, Michigan 49650
Born: September 13, 1903; Brandenburg, Kentucky
Parents: David C. Gray, Mary E. (Bruner) Gray
Children: Carol Seese Parker, Dr. Perry Seese, Dr. Chas. S. Roberts. David H. Roberts-deceased
Education: Meade County High School, Kentucky, 1917-1922. Laboratory and x-ray training, Dr. McNeal. Kentucky College, Rolling Green, Kentucky, 6 week extension course for teaching at Brandenburg, Kentucky. Night class in creative writing, Wayne State University
Career: Teacher, Meade County, 1922-1923. Housewife, 1923-1932. Through the Depression sold door to door, ironed for 25 cents an hour, sewed evening gowns, cookie factory. X-ray technician, Louisville, Kentucky, 1934-1936. Detroit Health Department, 25 years. Worked at Herman Kiefer, Maybury Sanitarium. Foster Grandmother, R.S.V.P.,1974—. Served as Vice-President, President, poetry societies, 1950's-1960's

Writings: *Psychic Hinge* Golden Quill 1974. *Sojourner* Golden Quill 1981.*The Listener* Golden Quill 1987. *Many Loves* Golden Quill 1990. *Through the Childs Eye* Encore Performance Publishing 1989
Awards or inclusion in other biographical books: *Michigan Authors,* 2nd ed.

SEMONES, TERRY G.
Address: 6447 East Dunbar, Lot 60, Monroe, Michigan 48161
Born: October 7, 1938; Portsmouth, Ohio
Parents: Howard Semones, Glenna E. Semones
Children: Michelle, Daniel, Sherry, Terry Jr., Bethany, Michelle, Kelly
Education: Portsmouth High School, Portsmouth, Ohio, 1952-1956. University of Toledo, B.S., Toledo, Ohio, 1956-1960; M.A., 1967
Career: Principal, South Monroe Townsite Elementary School, Monroe, Michigan. Director of Federal Programs, Monroe Public Schools, Monroe, Michigan, 1985—. Director, Special Education, Monroe Public Schools, Monroe, Michigan, 1967-1985. Junior High English Teacher, Sylvania Public Schools, Sylvania, Ohio, 1965-1967. Junior High English Teacher, Washington Local Schools, Toledo, Ohio, 1960-1965

Writings: *Santa's Magic Key* Monroe County Library 1990. Work in Progress: *What If Words Were Things to Eat*, a poetry book for young children who don't like poetry
Awards or inclusion in other biographical books: Named the Outstanding Educational Administrator in Monroe County, 1986
What is the aim or goal of your writing? "To entertain and encourage students to be the best they can be."
May inquiries be sent to you about doing workshops, readings? Yes

SEVERANCE, HENRY ORMAL (1867-1942)
Born: February 19, 1867; St. Johns, Michigan
Parents: Charles L. Severance, Louisa (Forbush) Severance
Children: Philip, Esther
Education: Michigan Normal School, 1891; B. Pd., 1894. Michigan Agricultural College, East Lansing, Michigan, 1892, 1893. University of Michigan, A.B., Ann Arbor, Michigan, 1897; A.M., 1899. Central College, Litt. D., Fayette, Missouri,1929
Career: Superintendent, Lakeview Schools, Lakeview, Michigan, 1891-1893. Student Assistant, Librarian, University of Michigan, senior year (1899)-1906. Organized, first president, Ann Arbor (Michigan) Library Club, 1903. Librarian, University of Missouri, 1907-1937, retired. Founder, president, Columbia (Missouri) Library Club, 1907, Book Review Club, 1931. Leadership positions in many associations like American Library Association

Writings: *Books for Journalism Students* University of Missouri 1914. *Michigan Trailmakers* George Wahr 1930. *The Story of a Village Community* G.E. Stechert 1931. *Palmer Hartsough: Singing School Teacher, Michigan Song Writer, and Minister* private printing 1937. Several others. Articles in *The Huron County Tribune, Michigan Normal College News, Library Journal, University of Michigan Monthly Bulletin, American Library Association Bulletin, The Grail,* others
Awards or inclusion in other biographical books: *American Literary Yearbook; Who Was Who among North American Authors; Who Was Who in America.* Honorary member of the Eugene Field Society, the Kiwanis Club of Columbia, Missouri. Honorary President of Columbia Library Club. Honorary consultant, Library of Congress. Honorary Degree, Master of Pedagogy, Michigan Normal School, 1911

SHACKETT, MARYL
Address: 323 Jefferson, Marine City, Michigan 48039
Born: April 30, 1929; Marine City, Michigan

Parents: Frank L. Merrill, Dora B. (Noel) Merrill
Children: Lawrence II, Timothy, Julie
Education: Holy Cross High School, graduate, Marine City, Michigan, 1943-1947. Writing and literature courses, continuing education
Career: Freelance writer, Marine City, 1980—. Board of Directors, United Nations of Michigan, Lansing, Michigan,1968-1980. Board of Directors, Visiting Nurse Association, Port Huron, St. Clair Counties, Michigan, 1963-1969. Staff Writer, *Marine City Independent*, Marine City, Michigan, 1957-1959

Writings: *Seasons of Us* Riverside Print 1980. *Lovesounds* Riverside Print 1979. *From Love Comes* Riverside Print 1978. Several short stories, poems in *The South Hill Gazette, Sylvan Quarterly, Papyrus*. Work in Progress: Three novels. Book of poetry
Awards or inclusion in other biographical books: *Directory of American Poets and Fiction Writers*, 1991-1992
What is the aim or goal of your writing? "Writing fills emotional needs of others unable to express themselves. I think that's what I give other people in my work."
May inquiries be sent to you about doing workshops, readings? No

SHARPSTEEN, ERNEST JACK (1880-1976)
Pseudonym: Ernest Jack Sharpe
Born: July 8, 1880; Wyoming, Michigan
Parents: Washington Irving Sharpsteen, Amelia Adelaid (Anderson) Sharpsteen
Education: Grand Rapids Public Schools
Career: Circus Performer, Clown. Vaudeville Actor, Director, Playwright. Founder, Jugville and Newt Publications

Writings: *Red Thread of Guilt: a Mystery Drama in Four Acts* T.S. Dennison & Company 1927. *A Rural Belle: a One-Act Comedy* T.S. Dennison & Company 1927. *His Wife's First Husband: a One-Act Comedy* T.S. Dennison & Company 1928. *The Rat* Central Play Company 1924. *Adventures of Windy* Patterson Printing 1944. *Bugle, the Smart Dog* Patterson Printing 1944. *One Life-Autobiography and Verse* Dean Hicks Company 1950. *Narratives of Nature* Adams Press 1960. *Memories of Yesteryear* Adams Press 1960. *Tall Tales of Newago Newt: Over 500 Narratives of the North Woods Selected From Mr. Sharpe's Published Writings of the Past 30 Years* Pyramid 1962. *Verse to Live By* Pyramid 1963. *Jack Squires, a Scout with Kit Carson; a True Historical Narrative of the Early West* Newt 1965. *Century Wit and Humor* Patterson Printing 1966. *Remembering* Newt Publications 1966. *Some Look But Do Not See the Wonders of Nature: a Book of Verse* Adams Press 1972. *Michigan: Its Emblem and Environments: Descriptive Narrative Rhythm* Adams Press 1973. Others
Awards or inclusion in biographical books: *Michigan Authors*, 2nd ed.; *Michigan Poets*. Outstanding Friend to Libraries, Michigan Library Association, 1972. He willed his estate to the White Cloud Public Library which renamed it the E. Jack Sharpe Public Library

SHEEHAN, MARC J.
Address: 226 S. Hayford, Lansing, Michigan 48912
Born: October 28, 1954; Grand Rapids, Michigan
Parents: Michael E. Sheehan, Elvis M. Sheehan
Education: Western Michigan University, B.S., Kalamazoo, Michigan, 1973-1977. University of Michigan, M.F.A., Ann Arbor, Michigan, 1984-1986

Career: Secretary, American Red Cross, Lansing, Michigan, 1991—. Bookkeeper, Shaman Drum Bookshop, Ann Arbor, Michigan, 1990-1991. Secretarial, Kelley Services, Lansing, Michigan, 1989-1990. Instructor, University of Michigan, Ann Arbor, Michigan, 1987-1989. Staff Writer, *Capital Times,* 1990—

Writings: *The Cursive World* Ridgeway Press 1991. Poems in *New York Quarterly, Michigan Quarterly Review, Passages North, Pennsylvania Review,* over 40 others

Awards or inclusion in other biographical books: National Endowment for the Arts Grant, 1984. Major Hopwood Award, Poetry, 1985. Michigan Council for the Arts Grant, 1990

What is the aim or goal of your writing? "I'll agree with Harrison and say 'awareness'."

May inquiries be sent to you about doing workshops, readings? Yes

SHOVALD, ARLENE E.

Address: 1124 D Street, Salida, Colorado 81201

Born: April 14, 1940; Stambaugh, Michigan

Parents: William L.A. Mellstrom and Dorothy M. (Scott) Mellstron

Children: Robert W., Terri, Rick, Anne

Education: Iron River High School, 1955-58. Colorado Mountain College, Associate in Arts, 1989-1992

Career: Freelance Writer, Salida, Colorado. Reporter/Photographer, *The Pueblo Chieftain,* Pueblo, Colorado, 1987-1989. *The Mountain Mail*, Salida, Colorado 1981—. Nurse Aide, Salida Hospital, Salida, Colorado, 1979-1981. Editor, *The Reporter,* Iron River, MI, 1974-1979

Writings: *Kill the Competition*. Cliffhanger Press, 1987. Others with agent

Awards or inclusion in other biographical books: *Who's Who of American Women,* 1986-1987. *Who's Who in the Midwest, 1980-1981. Who's Who in Writers, Editors, & Poets, 1989-1992. Who's Who among Students in American Junior Colleges,* 1991. Upper Peninsula of Michigan Writers, Writer of the Year Award, 1977. Colorado Domestic Violence Coallition Award, Community Member Award of Appreciation, 1991

What is the aim or goal of your writing? "I am concerned about social injustice and the themes of my novels generally involved the 'underdog' getting back in some way. If I had to condense this into a 'theme' I guess I would say my theme is to call people's attention to social injustices in an entertaining, non-preaching way and at the same time give them something to think about."

May inquiries be sent to you about doing work-shops, readings? Yes

SIBLEY, FREDERIC M.

Address: 230 Vendome Road, Grosse Pointe, Michigan 48236

Born: October 8, 1911; Detroit, Michigan

Parents: Frederic M. Sibley, Mabel M. (Bessenger) Sibley

Children: Frederic III, Jeffrey, Julie, Lorraine

Education: Hotchkiss High School, Diploma, Lakeville, Connecticut, 1930-1934. Princeton University, B.A., Princeton, New Jersey, 1935-1936. University of Paris (Sorbonne), Ecole de Preparation des Professurs de Fransais a l'Ettanger, France

Career: Managing Partner, Sawtooth Lumber Company, Mt. Home, Idaho, 1946-1985. President, F.M. Sibley Lumber Company, Detroit, Michigan, 1946-1965. U.S. Navy, Pacific Fleet, Lieut. Commander, 1941-1945. Teacher, Hotchkiss School, Lakeville, Connecticut, 1934-1935. Poet Laureate, Past President, Witenagemote Literary Society

Writings: *An Iambic Odyssey* Carlton Press 1982. Poems, stories, papers presented before literary society. Poems in: *Nassau Literary Magazine Alumni Edition,* 1974; *Mullett Lake Village,* 1975. Princeton 1934 Class Reunion requested poems as did *Grosse Pointe News* for their 50th year

What is the aim or goal of your writing? "To teach young people to write <u>clearly</u> and <u>concisely</u> and with <u>emotion</u>."

May inquiries be sent to you about doing workshops, readings? Yes

SIKKENGA, RAYMOND R.

Address: 242 Briarhill Drive, Battle Creek, Michigan 49015
Born: August 16, 1934; Kalamazoo, Michigan
Parents: Henry L. Sikkenga, Hellen P. Sikkenga
Children: David, Steven, Paul
Education: Western Michigan University, Masters, Kalamazoo, Michigan, 1954-1958
Career: Teacher, Lakeview School District, Battle Creek, Michigan, 1958-1989. Student Teacher Coordinator, Western Michigan University, Kalamazoo, Michigan, 1990—

Writings: *Doers and Dreamers: Governors of Michigan* River Road Publishers 1987. *American & Michigan Activities* Lakeview School District 1986

Awards or inclusion in other biographical books: Freedoms Foundation at Valley Forge, Teacher of the Year, 1972

What is the aim or goal of your writing? "I have no interest in writing anything else."

May inquiries be sent to you about doing workshops, readings? Yes

SMALLWOOD, CAROL

Address: 1359 Michigami Drive, Cheboygan, Michigan 49721
Born: May 3, 1939; Cheboygan, Michigan
Parents: Lloyd B. Gouine, Lucille M. (Drozdowiski) Gouine
Children: Michael, Ann
Education: Cheboygan High School, Cheboygan, Michigan, 1957. Eastern Michigan University, B.S., Ypsilanti, Michigan, 1957-1961; M.A., History, 1962-1963. Western Michigan University, M.L.S., Kalamazoo, Michigan,1975-1976
Career: Michigan Water Resources Commission, Civil Service Clerk/Typist, summers 1956-1957. Teacher, Public Schools, Michigan, 1961-1964. Founder, Cheboygan County Humane Society, 1972; President, Publicity Chairman, 1972-1975. Publicity Chairman, helped found, Cheboygan Area Arts Council, 1971-1975. Graduate Assistant, Social Sciences Dept. of Waldo Library, Western Michigan University, 1975-1976. Title I Library Consultant, Grand Traverse/Northland Library Cooperatives, Alpena, Michigan,1976-1977. Media Director, Pellston Public Schools, Pellston, Michigan 1977—.

Writings: *Michigan Authors* (editor) 3rd ed. Hillsdale Educational Publishers 1993. *Helpful Hints for the School Librarian* McFarland 1993. *Reference Puzzles and Word Games for Grades 7-12* McFarland 1991. *Library Puzzles and Word Games for Grades 7-12* McFarland 1990. *An Educational Guide to the National Park System* (in Brodart's *Elementary School Library Collection* 17th ed.) Scarecrow Press 1989. *Current Issues Builder* McFarland 1989. *Health Resource Builder* McFarland 1988. *A Guide to Selected Federal Agency Programs and Publications for Librarians and Teachers* Libraries Unlimited 1986. *Free Resource Builder for Librarians and Teachers* McFarland 1985; 2nd ed. 1992. *Free Michigan Materials for Educators* Hillsdale Educational Publishers 1980, 1986. Others. Columnist: *Detroit News* 1983-1985; *Catch: The Entertainment*

News 1988-1989; *Library PR News* 1990—*Educational Oasis* 1990—, others. Software. Articles in *Instructor, School Library Media Activities Monthly, The Book Report,* others. Work in Progress: Magazine columns, articles; manuscripts with publisher

Awards or inclusion in other biographical books: *Community Leaders of America; Contemporary Authors; Dictionary of International Biography* 1988—; *Directory of Library & Information Professionals; 5,000 Personalities of the World; International Authors and Writers Who's Who; International Directory of Distinguished Leadership; International Leaders in Achievement; International Who's Who of Professional and Business Women; 2,000 Notable American Women; Who's Who in American Education* 1987—;*Who's Who in the Midwest* 1988—; *Who's Who in U.S. Writers, Editors & Poets* 1988—;*Who's Who of American Women* 1989—; *The World Who's Who of Women*, others. *Michigan Woman* magazine cover May/June 1990

What is the aim or goal of your writing? "Connect people with information they hopefully can use. Putting words down helps me think but I wish I could do fiction. To contribute earnings to animal rights, population stabilization, the environment, and women's rights- really one aren't they?"

May inquiries be sent to you about doing workshops, readings? No

SMITH, FRED T.

Address: 30765 Woodgate Drive, Southfield, Michigan 48076
Born: April 12, 1917; Detroit, Michigan
Parents: Ernest L. Smith, Charlotte E. Smith
Children: Tina Marie, Virginia Theresa
Education: Holy Name High School, Detroit, Michigan, 1930-1934
Career: Group Sales, Detroit Tigers, Detroit, Michigan, 1974-1983. AAA Sales, 1953-1974

Writings: *Tiger Stats* Momentum Books 1991. *Tiger Tales and Trivia* self-published 1988. *Tiger Facts* self-published 1986. *Fifty Years With the Tigers* self-published 1984. *Tiger Trivia* (with Ernie Harwell) self-published 1976

What is the aim or goal of your writing? "To have people enjoy baseball more."

May inquiries be sent to you about doing workshops, readings? Yes

SMITH, MARK (RICHARD)

Born: November 19, 1935; Charlevoix, Michigan
Parents: Marcus Smith, Nellie (Van Eeuwen) Smith
Children: Heidi, Matje, Maida, Gudrun
Education: Northwestern University, B.A., Evanston, Illinois,1960
Career: Professor, University of New Hampshire, Durham, New Hampshire. Advisor, Rockefeller Foundation, 1967-1969

Writings: *Toyland* Little, Brown 1965. *The Middleman* Little, Brown 1967. *The Death of the Detective* Knopf 1974. *The Moon Lamp* Knopf 1976. *The Delphinium Girl* Harper 1980. *Doctor Blues* Morrow 1983. Others

Awards or inclusion in other biographical books:

Contemporary Authors; Directory of American Fiction Writers; Directory of American Scholars; International Authors and Writers Who's Who; Writers Directory. Rockefeller Foundation Grant, 1965-1966, Guggenheim Fellowship, 1968. Nomination, National Book Award, 1974. Ingram Merrill Foundation Grant, 1976-1978. National Endowment for the Arts Grant, 1978

SMITH, NORMAN FOSTER

Address: 522 Orchard Street, East Lansing, Michigan 48823
Born: May 8, 1914; Ann Arbor, Michigan
Parents: Carl H. Smith, Ada B. (Rust) Smith
Children: Gaylord, Janet, Martha
Education: University of Michigan, A.B., B.S.F., M.F., Ann Arbor, Michigan, 1932-1937
Career: Chief, Office of Planning Services, Michigan Department of Natural Resources, 1964-1976, retired. Staff Forester, Planning and Development, Michigan Department of Conservation, Lansing, Michigan, 1949-1962. Regional forester, Northern Lower Peninsula, Lansing, Michigan, 1946-1949. Forest Technician, Lansing, Michigan,1937-1946

Writings: *Michigan Trees Worth Knowing* Michigan Department of Natural Resources fifth edition 1986; Hillsdale Educational Publishers 1978; fourth edition 1970; third edition, Michigan Department of Conservation 1961; second edition 1952; first edition 1948
What is the aim or goal of your writing? "To provide a non-technical reference book which describes Michigan trees in easy-to-read text and pictures. The text covers tree characteristics, history of use, present importance, where found, growth patterns and shapes, insect and disease problems, wood qualities, and values to wildlife and the landscape. Photographs show typical tree shapes, leaves, flowers and fruit, and the bark."

SMITH, THOMAS HUGH

Address: Drawer 337, Munising, Michigan 49862
Pseudonym: T. Kilgore Splake
Born: December 8, 1936; Three Rivers, Michigan
Parents: Emery C. Smith, Margaret L. Smith
Education: Three Rivers High School, Three Rivers, Michigan. Western Michigan University, Kalamazoo, Michigan, B.A., 1956-1959; M.A., 1959-1961. Michigan State University, 1963. University of Maine, 1970
Career: Teacher, Comstock High School, Comstock, Michigan, 1959-1963. Teacher, Lansing Public Schools, Lansing, Michigan, 1963-1964. Teacher, Western Michigan University, Kalamazoo, Michigan, 1973-1974. Teacher, Kellogg Community College, Battle Creek, Michigan, 1964-1989. Judge for poetry contests

Writings: *Superior Land Lights. Pictured Rocks Memories. Keweenaw: Copper Country. Pictured Rocks Poetry. Reststop. Blue Book of Silent Tides. Moon Shadows. Dark Musings. Mute Whispers. October Softly. Beyond The Fire. Alaskan Letters. Paris Express. Ghost Soundings. Notes From the Cave. Soul Whispers. A Hole In Reality. The Reunion and Other Poems. Springtime Musings for Brautigan and Oona. A Loving Enemy My Muse. Keweenaw Love Story.* Over 1,000 poems in literary journals and small magazines. Articles such as "The Passion of Poetry", "Cure For Writer's Block". In *Hammers, Shockbox, Marquette Mining Journal, Ajax Poetry Review, In Your Face, Gaia, New York Quarterly, Wired, Pearl, Backwoods,* others. Work in Progress: Poetry chapbook, *Soft Echoes Behind the Waterfall,* other chapbooks. Manuscript, "Sadness of Backwater Women"
Awards or inclusion in other biographical books: Nominated for Pushcart Award, 1991-1992. First Place, *Sisyphus,* 1991. First Place, Michigan Poetry Society, 1992. First Place, *Zephyr Magazine,* 1992. Several second, third place finishes and honorable mention awards. *Hemingway Puttin' On The Ritz* by Hank Marksbury dedicated to him.

First poet/writer to take part in the "Q and Arts" interviews conducted by Mark Anthony Rosse, Los Angeles writer /reviewer

What is the aim or goal of your writing? "I am presently retired and living in Munising in Michigan's Upper Peninsula. As long as I live within the small retirement benefits sent monthly from Lansing, Michigan, I am basically a free man. I hope to use this small stipend and days of my solitude to press the boundaries of literary art as far as I can in the time I have remaining. As I grow in my writing I succeed in learning more about myself and societal surroundings. Also, I hope as a frustrated teacher of a sorts to be able to leave something behind after I am gone that others will find beneficial. In short, I want to leave a small literary legacy that will say later, 'I was here!' "

SMITH-KNIGHT, SHARON

Address: 102 Church Street, Highland Park, Michigan 48203
Born: June 6, 1943; Detroit, Michigan
Parents: James W. Smith, Betty R. (Milas) Smith
Children: Deborah
Education: Inkster High School, diploma, 1961. University of Michigan, B.S. of Education, Ann Arbor, Michigan, 1978
Career: Instructor, Highland Park Adult Education, Highland Park, Michigan, 1980–. Instructor, Shaw College at Detroit, Detroit, Michigan, 1973-1976. Instructor, Wayne County Community College, summer 1978-1979. Instructor, Redford Union Schools, Redford, Michigan, 1976-1980

Writings: *Winesip (And Other Delicious Poems)* Broadside Press 1991. *Hipology* Broadside Press 1990
What is the aim or goal of your writing? "Share poetry with as many people as possible."
May inquiries be sent to you about doing workshops, readings? Yes

SNEIDER, VERN (1916-1981)

Born: October 6, 1916; Monroe, Michigan
Parents: Fred Sneider, Matilda (Althaver) Sneider
Children: Timothy S. Clark
Education: Notre Dame, A.B., 1940. Princeton University, Graduate Studies, 1942
Career: Assistant Credit Manager, Credit Manager, Sears, Roebuck & Co., 1940-1941. U.S. Army, Private to Captain, 1941-1946. Writer beginning in 1946

Writings: *The Teahouse of the August Moon* Putnam 1951. *A Pail of Oysters* Putnam 1953. *A Long Way From Home, and Other Stories* Putnam 1956. *The King From Ashtabula* Putnam 1960. *West of the North Star* Putnam 1972. In *Four Complete Modern Novels* (Lilian M. Popp, editor) Globe Book Company 1962. Published in such magazines as *Saturday Evening Post, The Writer, Antioch Review, Holiday* and others. Work appeared on television, stage
Awards or inclusion in other biographical books: *Contemporary Authors; Current Biography; International Authors and Writers Who's Who; Michigan Authors,* 2nd ed. Friends of American Writers Award, 1952

SNODGRASS, EARL R.

Address: P.O. Box 223, Okemos, Michigan 48864
Born: June 17, 1927; Monroe, Michigan

Parents: Andrew V. Snodgrass, Dorothy M. Snodgrass
Education: High School graduate, Monroe, Michigan. University of Toledo, Ohio, 1949--1951. University of Michigan, M.A., Ann Arbor, Michigan, 1968-1969
Career: Freelance writer/editor, 1987—. Media specialist, Haslett High School, Haslett, Michigan and Roseville, Michigan, 1971-1987. English teacher, Department of Defense Schools, Okinawa, Japan, Germany, England, Puerto Rico, 1961-1969

Writings: *East-West Encounters* Japanophile Press 1991. Work in Progress: Nonfiction book on Japanese culture and influence in United States
What is the aim or goal of your writing? "Writing on Japan is neither to praise nor blame, but to promote understanding. The fiction is meant to entertain as well. My travel column is to help active travelers and to entertain armchair travelers."
May inquiries be sent to you about doing workshops, readings? Yes

SODDERS, BETTY J.
Address: P.O. Box 5, Gulliver, Michigan 49840
Born: August 26, 1928; Ironwood, Michigan
Parents: William J. Bier, Ida R. (Basko) Bier
Children: Terry, Bruce, Bonnie, Billie
Education: Gogebic Junior College, Ironwood, Michigan; University of Michigan, Ann Arbor, Michigan, 1946-1948
Career: Freelance writer and book author, Gulliver, Michigan, 1983—. Regional/States Editor, *Louisiana Mounds Society Newsletter,* Shreveport, Louisiana, 1991—. Contributing Editor, *The Varmint Hunter Magazine*, Lone Grove Oklahoma, 1992—. Lecturer, Wildlife photographer

Writings: *Michigan Prehistory Mysteries II* Avery Color Studios 1991. *Getting To Know Our Wildlife, Book I* Avery Color Studios 1991. *Getting to Know Our Wildlife, Book II* Avery Color Studios 1991. *Michigan Prehistory Mysteries I* Avery Color Studios 1990. Institute for the Study of American Cultures uses the two *Michigan Prehistory Mysteries,* making them available through computer for scientists in this country and other countries researching prehistory Michigan artifacts. Regular contributor to *Michigan Out-of-Doors* since 1983, about 50 articles and columns. Also regular contributor/columnist to *Peninsula People, North American Bear Hunter, The Varmint Hunter, Peninsula.* Published in *The Turkey Hunter, Above the Bridge, Fate, Dog Fancy, Whitetails Unlimited, Trapper & Predator Caller.* Progress: Under contract for historic book dealing with devastating forest fires of Michigan between 1871 and 1922, *Michigan on Fire.* Possibly *Getting To Know Our Wildlife, Book III*
What is the aim or goal of your writing? "My goal in writing is to present my material, albeit historical or naturalist material, to my public in an interesting, easy to read style that will make my readers want to learn more about the subjects I've presented. Example: When *Michigan Prehistory Mysteries I* was published, I received over 300 phone calls and letters from complete strangers who just either wished to state that they enjoyed reading the book or else were academic people requesting further research information. My wildlife books have also generated this same type of reaction. It was through these two books that I am now on staff of this national magazine which is indeed an honor for very few women are Contributing Editors of a national hunting publication...perhaps none, I am not sure." (See book review in July 1992 issue of *The Varmint Hunter.*)
May inquiries be sent to you about doing workshops, readings? Yes

SOMMER, KAREN J.
Address: 1871 Maplewood Drive, Owosso, Michigan 48867
Born: June 28, 1947; Windsor, Canada
Parents: Bruce C. Nash, Jean L. Nash
Children: Jason, Jeffrey
Education: Central Michigan University, Bachelor of Science, Mt. Pleasant, Michigan, 1965-1969. Michigan State University, Master of Arts, East Lansing, Michigan, 1969-1971
Career: Teacher, Owosso Public Schools, Owosso, Michigan, 1969—

Writings: *Satch and the Motormouth* D.C. Cook 1987. *New Kid on the Block* D.C. Cook 1985. Work in Progress: Continuation of "Satch" series
What is the aim or goal of your writing? "Kids should enjoy reading and writing activities. Actually, I never set out to become an author. I was creating stories as examples for children to see what might be done. The kids loved the stories and encouraged me to turn the stories into a book-and it really happened."
May inquiries be sent to you about doing workshops, readings? Yes

SOULE, MARIS A.
Address: Route 1, Box 173B, Fulton, Michigan 49052
Born: June 19, 1939; Oakland, California
Parents: Mario L. Chirone, Thelma W. Chirone
Children: Deryk, Mia
Education: University of California at Berkeley, Secondary Teaching Credential, 1962-1963. University of California at Davis, Bachelor of Arts, 1957-1961. University of Santa Barbara
Career: Teacher, Kellogg Community College, Battle Creek, Michigan, 1990—. Teacher, Galesburg-Augusta High School, Galesburg, Michigan, 1970-1972. Teacher, La Cumbre Junior High School, Santa Barbara, California, 1968-1970. Art Department Chairperson, Rio Americano High School, Carmichael, California, 1963-1967

Writings: *Missy's Proposition* Silhouette/Romance 1992. *Jared's Lady* Bantam/Loveswept 1992. *Storybook Hero* Harlequin/Temptation 1989. *The Law of Nature* Harlequin/Temptation 1988. *The Best of Everything* Harlequin/Temptation 1988. *A Winning Combination* Harlequin/Temptation 1987. *Sound Like Love* Harlequin/Temptation 1986. *Lost and Found* Harlequin/Temptation 1985. *No Room for Love* Harlequin/Temptation 1984. *First Impressions* Harlequin/Temptation 1983. Books translated into eleven languages, sold in over 21 countries. Work in Progress: *Lyon's Pride, Con Man, No Strings Attached*
Awards or inclusion in other biographical books: *International Writers and Authors Who's Who,* last 3 editions. Finalist, Romance Writers of American's Golden Medallion Award, 1988
What is the aim or goal of your writing? "To entertain. To write stories of men and women falling in love. To leave the reader with knowledge of an occupation, sport or location that the reader may or may not have known about before. And my goal is to make each book better than the last."
May inquiries be sent to you about doing workshops, readings? Yes

SOUTHWOOD, LORELEI L.
Address: 09985 Maple Grove, Charlevoix, Michigan 49720
Born: September 23, 1969; Petoskey, Michigan
Parents: George B. Southwood, Jr., Leanna R. Southwood
Education: Charlevoix High School, Charlevoix, Michigan, 1983-1987. North Central Michigan College, Petoskey, Michigan, 1987-1989; Central Michigan University, Mt. Pleasant, Michigan, 1989-1992, B.A.
Career: Cashier, Carter's Food Center, Petoskey, Michigan, 1991

Writings: In: *The National Library of Poetry* 1992; *Poetry: An American Heritage* 1993. Work in Progress: Work of fiction: *Did You Ever Dance with the Devil by the Pale Moonlight?*
What is the aim or goal of your writing? "To entertain but to also reveal a part of <u>myself</u>-my hopes, my thoughts, my fears, my convictions. I just want to <u>write</u>!"
May inquiries be sent to you about doing workshops, readings? Yes

SPOONER, ELLA BROWN (JACKSON) (1880-1963)
Born: December 3, 1880; Denver, Colorado
Parents: S.M. Jackson, Rachel Moriah (Brown) Jackson
Education: Presbyterian Academy. Northern Michigan College, 1911
Career: Music teacher, organist, author

Writings: *Clark and Tabitha Brown; the First Part of Their Adventures and Those of their Three Children in New England, Washington, and Maryland* privately published 1927; 2nd edition Exposition Press 1957. *The Brown Family History: Tracing the Clark Brown Line* The Laurel Outlook 1929. *This Broad Land, Poems* Exposition Press 1949. *From Mountain to Shore: a Sequel* Exposition Press 1951. *Way Back When; Ideas Wise and Otherwise, and Memories about American Furniture* Exposition Press 1953. *A Lullaby of Names; Meditations for Walking on Air* Exposition Press 1956. *Tabitha Brown's Western Adventures* Exposition Press 1958
Awards or inclusion in other biographical books: *Michigan Authors,* 1st ed., 2nd ed. Honorary member of the International Mark Twain Society, 1952

SPROSS, PATRICIA McNITT
Address: 4773 Ardmore, Okemos, Michigan 48864
Born: April 24, 1913; Nashville, Michigan
Parents: Ralph V. McNitt, Lynde D. McNitt
Children: Harold
Education: Nashville High School, Nashville, Michigan. Michigan State University, B.A., M.A., Ed. D., East Lansing, Michigan, 1951-1962. University of Michigan
Career: Teacher, Administrator at local and national levels. Pioneered supplementary materials in space-age mathematics. Director of Elementary Science and Mathematics, Lansing Schools, Lansing, Michigan. Television teacher, workshop leader, speaker

Writings: Curriculum material in space-age mathematics, self-help for teachers in arithmetic. *Sundogs and Sunsets* Wilderness Adventure Books 1990, used at University of Northern Illinois School of Nursing to make aging more real. Work in Progress: *Linnie Your Water's Boiling!. The Rooster Crows and Away She Goes!*
What is the aim or goal of your writing? "To offer humor as therapy for problems of aging."
May inquiries be sent to you about doing workshops, readings? Yes

SPYKMAN, GORDON J.
Address: 1715 Griggs Street SE, Grand Rapids, Michigan 49506
Born: March 25, 1926; Holland, Michigan
Parents: Albert Spykman, Dina (Klompmaker) Spykman
Children: Steven, Erik, Donald, Gary, EveLynn
Education: Calvin College, B.A., Grand Rapids, Michigan, 1945-1949. Calvin Theological Seminary, Th.M., Grand Rapids, Michigan, 1949-1952. Free University of Amsterdam, D. Th., Amsterdam, The Netherlands, 1952-1955
Career: Professor of Religion and Theology, Calvin College, Grand Rapids, Michigan, 1959-1991. Minister, Christian Reformed Church, Blenheim, Ontario, Canada, 1955-1959

Writings: *Attrition and Contrition at the Council of Trent* Kok, Kampen 1955. *Never on Your Own* CRC Publishing House 1969. *Christian Faith in Focus* Baker Book House 1971. *Pioneer Preacher* CRC Publishing House 1976. *Society, State, and Schools* Eerdmans 1980. *Testimony on Human Rights* Ref. Ecumenical Synod 1981. *Men and Women: Partners in Service* CRC Publishing House 1982. *Spectacles* Potchefstroom University, Republic of South Africa 1984. *Let My People Live: Faith and Crisis in Central America* Eerdmans 1988. *Reformational Theology: A New Paradigm for Doing Theology* Eerdmans 1992
What is the aim or goal of your writing? "To contribute to Christian faith, life, and scholarship."
May inquiries be sent to you about doing workshops, readings? Yes

STADTFELD, CURTIS K.
Address: 41434 Coolidge, Belleville, Michigan 48111
Born: April 9, 1935; Remus, Michigan
Parents: Lawrence R. Stadtfeld, Dorothy J. Stadtfeld
Children: Chris, Peter
Education: Michigan State University, B.A., East Lansing, Michigan, 1953-1957, 1958-1959. Eastern Michigan University, M.A., Ypsilanti, Michigan, 1961-1962
Career: Reporter, *Marquette Mining Journal*, Marquette, Michigan, 1957-1958. Reporter, *Jackson Citizen Patriot*, Jackson, Michigan, 1959-1962. Reporter, *St. Louis Post Dispatch*, 1962-1965. Professor, Eastern Michigan University, Ypsilanti, Michigan, 1965—

Writings: *Whitetail Deer-A Year's Cycle* Dial 1972. *From the Land and Back* Scribners 1970. Fiction, essays, articles in national magazines. "Linefence" included in a *Yankee* anthology as one of the best New England stories
Awards or inclusion in other biographical books: *Michigan Authors,* 2nd ed. Magazine Award for Excellence in Reporting
What is the aim or goal of your writing? "To illuminate facts and feelings of humanity."
May inquiries be sent to you about doing workshops, readings? Yes

STAHL, HILDA A.
Address: 5891 Wood School Road, Freeport, Michigan 49325
Born: September 13, 1938; Chadron, Nebraska
Parents: Jay Clements, Zelma I. (Fehrenholz) Clements
Children: Jeffrey, Laurie, Bradley, Mark, Sonya, Evangelynn, Joshua
Education: Wayne State College, Normal, Wayne, Nebraska, 1956

Career: Country School Teacher, Winnebago, Nebraska, 1956-1957. Pre School Teacher, Hastings, Michigan, 1970-1972. Writer, 1967—

Writings: About 100 books, hundreds of short stories. Best Friends Series:*Chelsea and the Outrageous Phone Bill* Crossway 1992; others. Sadie Rose Adventure Series: *Daring Escape* Crossway 1989; others. Elizabeth Gail series 1979-1988: *The Hidden Key Mystery* Tyndale House Publisher 1992; others. Wren House Mystery Series: *The Mystery at the Wheeler Place* David C. Cook 1984; others. Teddy Jo Series 1983-1988: Tyler Twins Series 1985-1990. Sandi Lee Mason Adventure Series, Daisy Punkin Series, Kayla O'Brien Adventure Series, Amber Ainslie Detective Series 1990-1991.*The Covenant* Thomas Nelson 1991. *The Inheritance* Thomas Nelson 1992. Books published in several languages, video. Work in Progress: *Well Mannered Murder*
Awards or inclusion in other biographical books: *Foremost Women of the 20th Century; International Authors and Writers Who's Who; The World's Who's Who of Women.* Silver Angel Award, 1989
What is the aim or goal of your writing? "To write books people will read and enjoy and to have my books made in movies on video."
May inquiries be sent to you about doing workshops, readings? Yes

STARK, GEORGE WASHINGTON (1884-1966)
Born: February 22, 1884; Detroit, Michigan
Parents: Nicolas Stark, Isabelle (Wharry) Stark
Children: George, Alison Jean, Richard, Harry
Education: Eastern High School, Detroit, Michigan, 1903. University of Michigan, Ann Arbor, Michigan, class member of 1907
Career: Copy desk, *Republic,* St. Louis, 2 years. Columnist, *The Detroit Free Press* 1905-1914. *The Detroit News* 1914-1958. Managing editor, *Detroit Athletic Club News.* Publicity, Maxwell Motor Car Company. Managing Director, Detroit Historical Society (first and only president). Pushed for erection of Detroit Historical Museum. Official Historiographer, City of Detroit 1943-1966

Writings: *In Old Detroit* Arnold-Powers 1939. *City of Destiny* Arnold-Powers 1943. *Two Heads are Better, George W. Stark and Anne Campbell* (co-authored with wife, poet Anne Campbell) Alved 1947. *Seventy-Five Years in Public Service: Detroit News* The Detroit News 1948. *Detroit at the Century's Turn, as Remembered by George W. Stark* Wayne University Press 1951. *Detroit: An Industrial Miracle* 1951. *The Huron Heritage; Fifty Years of Concrete Achievement by the Huron Portland Cement Company, 1907-1957* Denman and Baker 1957. *Made in Detroit* (co-authored with Norman Beasley) Putnam 1957. *The Best Policy; the Story of Standard Accident Insurance Company* Powers 1959
Awards or inclusion in other biographical books: *Contemporary Authors; Michigan Authors,* 1st ed., 2nd ed.; *Michigan Through the Centuries: Family and Personal History,* Vol 3;*Who Was Who in America.* Honorary Degree, Wayne State University, Detroit, Michigan, 1946
In the 2nd edition of *Michigan Authors* appears: "In his 'Town Talk' column in *The Detroit News*, Mr. Stark became reccognized as almost the official voice of Old Detroit. His encyclopedic knowledge and love of the city had been recognized in 1947 when he was named city historiographer, a title Mr. Stark described many times as his proudest distinction."

STCHUR, JR., JOHN W.
Address: 5245 Berwyck, Troy, Michigan 48098
Born: March 21,1947; Detroit, Michigan
Parents: John W. Stchur, Inez Stchur
Children: John, Robert, David, Katie
Education: Michigan State University, B.S., East Lansing, Michigan, 1965-1969
Career: Physical Education Teacher, Troy Public Schools, 1969—

Writings: *Down on the Farm* St. Martin's Press 1987. *Paddywhack* St. Martin's Press 1989. Work in Progress: *Something Unnatural,* horror. *The Strongman Obsession,* mainstream/action adventure
What is the aim or goal of your writing? "To scare people with my horror, to cause them to 'reaffirm their own normalcy' through reading how other normal, everyday people react in extraordinary circumstances."
May inquiries be sent to you about doing workshops, readings? Yes

STEELE, JEFFERY E.
Address: 865 McClelland Ave., Route 1, White Cloud, Michigan 49349
Born: May 1, 1940; Frankfort, Michigan (Pt. Betsie Lighthouse)
Parents: Bob H. Steele, Ruth (Wolf) Steele
Children: Jeffery Jr., Kirsten
Education: Lansing Eastern High School, Diploma, Lansing, Michigan, 1954-1958. U.S. Armed Forces Institute, Madison, Wisconsin, 1960
Career: Freelance Writer/Photographer, self-employed. President, Arkay Services, Inc., White Cloud, Michigan, 1986-1990. Sales Representative, Zee Medical Services, Detroit, Michigan, 1985-1986

Writings: *Fur-Fish-Game Magazine, Michigan Out-of-Doors, Michigan Fisherman Magazine, Woods-N-Waters News, Midwest Outdoors, Times-Indicator, Muskegon Chronicle, Bay City Times, Photo Digest, Sportsman's Corner,* Booth Newspaper Syndicate, regular columnist for *Shutterbug Magazine.* Work in Progress: Two articles selected for *The Best of Shutterbug*
Awards or inclusion in other biographical books: Nominated for membership, Outdoor Writers of America
What is the aim or goal of your writing? "To inform readers of the many special aspects of life in Michigan outdoors and to find and write about special people in west Michigan."
May inquiries be sent to you about doing workshops, readings? Yes

STEINBERG, MICHAEL J.
Address: P. O. Box 6293, East Lansing, Michigan 48826
Born: July 9, 1940; New York, New York
Parents: Jack Steinberg, Estelle M. Steinberg
Education: Hofstra University, B.A., Hempstead, New York, 1960-1964. Michigan State University, M.A., Ph.D., East Lansing, Michigan, 1964-1974
Career: Professor, Michigan State University, East Lansing, Michigan, 1970—

Writings: *I'm Almost Famous* stage play, co-authored with Bob Baldori, produced at Michigan's Boarshead Theater 1982, Chicago's Apollo Theater 1984. *The Writer's Way* (co-authored with Clinton Burhans Jr.) Spring Publishing 1982. Several years writing feature articles/columns for*Detroit Free Press Sunday Magazine*. Essays, poems published in small literary magazines. Articles in education journals. Work in Progress: *City Kid: Growing Up in New York City in the 50's*, a collection of stories, poems, essays. *Men Who Love Women Who Love Men*, a collection of stories, poems, essays. Included in *Writers in the Classroom* and *Baseball Diamonds*

Awards or inclusion in other biographical books: The Roberts Writing Awards Annual, 4th prize, 1991

What is the aim or goal of your writing? "The aim of my writing is to discover and express my ideas, to find out what's on my mind and to shape those thoughts for readers in as graceful and reasonable way as possible."

May inquiries be sent to you about doing workshops, readings? Yes

STEINHARDT, HERSCHEL S.

Born: May 21, 1910; Zambrow, Poland

Parents: Abraham Steinhardt, Zelda (Shafran) Steinhardt

Children: Joyce, Judie

Education: Wayne State University, Detroit, Michigan, 1930-1931; New School for Social Research, 1938-1940. Hunter College, 1946-1947

Career: Theater usher, newsboy, Detroit, Michigan. Writer, Federal Theater Project, New York, New York, 1938-1940. Press Representative, Displaced Persons Program, New York, New York, 1944-1952

Writings: Plays: *No One Walks Alone* American Jewish Committee (first on radio) 1946. *Sons of Men* Bookman Associates 1959. *A Star in Heaven* New Voices (originally produced in Detroit) 1967. Unpublished play, student theater, Wayne State University, 1955 and others in New York. Plays in *Young Israel Viewpoint, Impresario*

Awards or inclusion in other biographical books: *Contemporary Authors; Michigan Authors,* 2nd ed.; *National Playwrights Directory*

STEINMAN, DAVID B(ARNARD)   (1886-1960)

Born: June 11, 1886; New York, New York

Parents: Louis K. Steinman, Eva (Scollard) Steinman

Children: John Francis, Alberta, David

Education: City College of New York, B.S., summa cum laude, 1906. Columbia University, New York; C.E., 1909; A.M., 1909; Ph.D. 1911

Career: Instructor, University of Idaho, Moscow, Idaho, 1910-1914. Professor, College of the City of New York, 1917-1920. Partner, Holton D. Robinson, bridge builder, until 1945. Involved in reconstruction, Brooklyn Bridge, 1948-1954. Designed over 400 bridges in the United States and other countries including Mackinac Straits Bridge, 1953-1957. Developed improvements in bridge design, system of loading for railway bridges, others. Founder: National Society of Professional Engineers; David B. Steinman Foundation

Writings: *Fifty Years of Progress in Bridge Engineering* American Institute of Steel Construction 1929? *The Builders of the Bridge; The Story of John Roebling and His Son* Harcourt, Brace 1945; Arno Press 1950, 1972. *Famous Bridges of the World* Random House 1953; Dover 1961. *Mackinac Straits Bridge* 1954. *Suspension Bridges: The Aerodynamic Problem and Its Solution* American Soc. C.E. 1954. *Bridges and Their Builders* G.P. Putnam's Sons 1941; revised, Dover Press 1957. *Miracle Bridge at Mackinac* Eerdmans 1957. *Songs of a Bridgebuilder* Eerdmans 1959. Others. Contributor, various encyclopedias

Awards or inclusion in other biographical books: *American Authors and Books; Current Biography; Dictionary of American Biography; Webster's American Biographies; Who Was Who among English and European Authors; Who Was Who among North American Authors; Who Was Who in America.* Over 150 awards for engineering, poetry, citizenship. Columbia University, Medal for Excellence, 1947. French Legion d'Honneur, other foreign prizes. Several honorary degrees such as Doctor of Science from: City College of New York, 1947 and Columbia College, 1953

STERLING, PHILLIP D.
Address: 20600 Edgewood Drive, Big Rapids, Michigan 49307
Born: November 10, 1950; Pontiac, Michigan
Parents: James F. Sterling, Barbara J. Sterling
Children: Matthew, Rachel, Sarah, Andrew
Education: Bowling Green State University, Ph.D., Bowling Green, Ohio, 1976-1979. Central Michigan University, M.A., Mt. Pleasant, Michigan, 1974. Centre College of Kentucky, B.A., Danville, Kentucky, 1972. Traverse City High School, Traverse City, Michigan, 1968
Career: Associate Professor of English, Ferris State University, Big Rapids, Michigan, 1987—. Associate Professor of English, Keuka College, Keuka Park, New York, 1979-1987

Writings: Poems, stories, essays in dozens of journals and magazines such as *The Detroit Free Press Magazine, West Michigan Magazine, Michigan Country Lines, Upstate New York, New York Alive, Mike Shayne Mystery Magazine, The MacGuffin, Hayden's Ferry Review, Seneca Review, Boston Literary Review, Sucarnochee Review.* Work in Progress: *The Discoveries of the Voice,* a sequence of poems. *We Find Our Lives,* collection of stories. Memoirs, essays of a Michigan childhood
Awards or inclusion in other biographical books: Poetry Society of America, runner up for Robert Winner Memorial Award, 1992. Fulbright Lecturer in Belgium, 1992-1993. Michigan Association of Governing Boards Distinguished Faculty Award, 1992. PEN Syndicated Fiction Award, 1991. National Endowment for the Arts Fellowship, 1990. Poet Hunt, First Place, 1989, 1991. Bay de Noc Writers' Conference Emerging Writer Assistantship, 1989. National Poetry Series Finalist, 1987
What is the aim or goal of your writing? "To teach and delight."
May inquiries be sent to you about doing workshops, readings? Yes

STEVENS, JAMES FLOYD (1892-1971)
Born: November 15, 1892; Albia, Iowa
Parents: Hague A. Stevens, Octavia (Turner) Stevens
Education: Public Schools
Career: Served in World War I, United States Army, 1917-1919. Began writing for publication, 1924. Public relations counsel, West Coast Lumbermen's Association. Board Member of Trustees, Keep Washington Green Association. Held other positions.

Writings: *Paul Bunyan* Knopf 1925; Ballantine 1947, 1975. *Brawnyman* Knopf 1926. *Mattock* Knopf 1927. *Homer in the Sagebrush* 1928. *Saginaw Paul Bunyan* 1932. *Green Power; the Story of Public Law 273* Superior Publishing 1958
Awards or inclusion in other biographical books: *American Authors and Books; American Novelists of Today; Concise Dictionary of American Literature; Contemporary American Literature; Contemporary Authors; Cyclopaedia of World Authors; Oxford*

Companion to American Literature; Reader's Encyclopedia of American Literature; Twentieth Century Authors; Who Was Who in America; Who Was Who in Literature. Honorary Degree, Litt. D., Pacific University, 1958. Honorary Life Member, University of Washington Foresters Alumni Association

STILES, MARTHA BENNETT
Born: March 30, 1933; Manila, Phillippine Islands
Parents: Forrest Hampton Wells, Jane (McClintock) Wells
Children: John Martin
Education: College of William and Mary, Williamsburg, Virginia. University of Michigan, B.S., Ann Arbor, Michigan, 1954
Career: Taught writing at Ann Arbor, Michigan, YMCA

Writings: First children's story, *Humpty Dumpty's Magazine,* November, 1957. First short story, *Virginia Quarterly Review*, January, 1959. *One Among the Indians* Dial Press 1962. *The Strange House at Newburyport* Dial Press 1963. *Darkness Over the Land* Dial Press 1966. *Dougal Looks for Birds* Four Winds Press 1972. *James the Vine Puller: a Brazilian Folktale* Carolrhoda 1974. *Sarah, the Dragon Lady* Macmillan 1986. *Kate of Still Waters* Macmillan 1990. Reviewer for various Michigan newspapers such as *The Ann Arbor News, The Detroit Free Press.* Articles, poetry, short stories in various magazines such as: *Green's Magazine, Esquire, Seventeen, Stereo Review, Perspectives in Biology & Medicine, Georgia Review*
Awards or inclusion in other biographical books: *Contemporary Authors; Michigan Authors,* 2nd ed.; *Something about the Author; Who's Who of American Women.* Hopwood Award, University of Michigan, 1956, 1958. Notable Books of 1966, *Hornbook*

STOCKING, KATHLEEN J.
Address: P. O. Box 132, Lake Leelanau, Michigan 49653
Born: August 21, 1945; Petoskey, Michigan
Parents: Pierce Stocking, Eleanore E. Stocking
Children: Jesse, Lilah, Gaia
Education: University of Michigan, B.A., Ann Arbor, Michigan, 1963-1968
Career: Writer, self-employed, Lake Leelanau, Michigan, 1979—. Contributing editor, *Detroit Monthly*, 1979-1987. Reporter, *Traverse City Record-Eagle,* Traverse City, Michigan, 1977-1979. Writer, *Woman's Day,* 1975

Writings: *Letters From the Leelanau* University of Michigan Press 1990. Work in Progress: *Lake Country*
Awards or inclusion in other biographical books: Best Emerging Writer, Bay de Noc Writers' Conference, 1989. Michigan Council for the Arts, Creative Artist Award, 1989. Biederman Foundation Award, Non Fiction, 1991. Thunder Bay Literary Conference Award, Short Fiction, 1992
What is the aim or goal of your writing? "Reach people."
May inquiries be sent to you about doing workshops, readings? Yes

STONE, NANCY Y.
Address: 337 Hillview Road, Venice, Florida 34293
Born: December 15, 1925; Crawfordsville, Indiana
Parents: William F. Young, Mary Emma E. Young
Children: John, Emily
Education: Antioch College, B.A., Yellow Springs, Ohio, 1943-1948. Western Michigan University, M.A., Kalamazoo, Michigan, 1965-1970
Career: Associate Professor of English, Western Michigan University, Kalamazoo, Michigan, 1970-1988, retired. Part-time secretary, assistant, writer, Sequoia Press, Kalamazoo, Michigan, 1950—. Clerk, Upjohn Company, Kalamazoo, Michigan, 1951-1952. *The Cleveland Press, Washington Courthouse Record Herald*

Writings: *Dune Shadow* Houghton Mifflin 1980. *The Wooden River* Eerdmans 1973. *Whistle Up the Bay* Eerdmans 1967. Articles, newspaper stories, advertising copy. Work in Progress: Rewrite of a novel to follow *Dune Shadow.* Two other juvenile novels
Awards or inclusion in other biographical books: *Contemporary Authors* Vols. 49-52; *Michigan Authors,* 2nd ed.
What is the aim or goal of your writing? "To entertain young people, to broaden their view of the world and the people in it, to help them see through another's eyes events that might have happened in the past."
May inquiries be sent to you about doing workshops, readings? Yes. (But it should be noted that I now live a long way from Michigan !!!)

STONEHOUSE, FREDERICK
Address: 531 Luce Avenue, Flushing, Michigan 48433
Born: August 21, 1948; New Brunswick, New Jersey
Parents: Frederick Stonehouse, Jr., Martina (Mortensen) Stonehouse
Children: Brandon Frederick
Education: Northern Michigan University, Marquette, Michigan, B.S., 1966-1970; M.A., 1974-1977. Phi Kappa Phi Honor Society member
Career: Executive Officer, 46th Engineer group, Michigan Army National Guard, Flint, Michigan, 1990—; Operations Officer (S-3), 1988-1990. Executive Officer, 107th Engineer Battalion, Michigan Army National Guard, Ishpeming, Michigan, 1987-1988; Operations Officer (S-3), 1985-1987. Directed special history field surveys for Parks Canada, 1978, 1989. Project director for shipwreck survey of Lake Superior's Isle Royale National Park, Northern Michigan University in cooperation with Isle Royale National Park, 1978, 1979. Lecturer. Past president of the Board of Directors, Marquette Maritime Museum. Participated in 1989 EDMUND FITZGERALD Great Lake Shipwreck Historical Society/National Geographic remote operated vehicle survey. Licensed Coast Guard vessel operator. Special consultant, Cousteau Great Lakes Expedition, 1980

Writings: *Shipwreck of the MESQUITE, Death of a Coast Guard Cutter,* Lake Superior Magazine 1991. *Keweenaw Shipwrecks, A Survey of Maritime Accidents From Big Bay Point, West to Ontonagon* Avery Studios 1988. *A Short Guide to the Shipwrecks of Thunder Bay* B & L Watery World 1986. *Lake Superior's "Shipwreck Coast", Maritime Accidents From Whitefish Bay to Grand Marais* Avery Studios 1985. *Went Missing II* Avery Studios 1984. *Combat Engineer, The History of the 107th Combat Engineering Battalion* Engineer Battalion Association 1981. *Munising Shipwrecks* Shipwrecks Unlimited 1980; Avery Studios, 1983. *Historic Resource Study, Pictured Rocks National Lakeshore* Mark F. Pfaller Associates 1981. *The Wreck of the Edmund Fitzgerald* Avery

Studios 1977-revised and expanded editions through 1991. *Went Missing, Fifteen Vessels That Disappeared on Lake Superior* Avery Studios 1977. *Marquette Shipwrecks* Harboridge Press 1974, Avery Studios 1977. *Isle Royale Shipwrecks* Harboridge Press 1974, Avery Studios 1977, 1983. *Historic Resources Study* of the Pictured Rocks National Lakeshore, for the United States National Park Service, historical research, underwater photography, field site location. Work in Progress: *Wreck Ashore, A History of the United States Life-Saving Service on the Great Lakes*
Awards or inclusion in other biographical books: *Michigan Authors,* 2nd ed.; Distinguished Service Award, Alger Underwater Preserve Committee, 1989. Ancient Mariner's Award, Marquette Maritime Museum, 1986. Rogue's Gallery Award, Ontario Underwater Council, 1986. Service Award, Our World Underwater, 1985
What is the aim or goal of your writing? "To provide a better appreciation for the tremendous maritime history of the Great Lakes."
May inquiries be sent to you about doing workshops, readings? Yes

STROSCHIN, JANE H.
Address: 7340 Lake Drive, Fremont, Michigan 49412
Born: September 27, 1946; Milwaukee, Wisconsin
Parents: Robert A. Vogel, Helen B. Vogel
Children: Lauren, Brian
Education: Pulaski High School, 1961-1964. University of Wisconsin-Milwaukee, B.S., Art Education, 1964-1968
Career: Teacher, Painting/Drawing, Community Education, Fremont, Michigan, 1974–. Children's Librarian, Fremont Public Library, Fremont, Michigan, 1969, 1972-1974. Author/illustrator of children's books. Young Authors Programs, Author-In-Residence. Teacher workshops on creativity in the classroom. Assemblies for elementary students and teachers

Writings: *Young at Art-20 Drawing Lessons* Mooy/Stroschin 1992. *A Unicorn Named Beulah Mae* Mooy/Stroschin 1990. *Sidney-The Story of a Kingfisher* Mooy/Stroschin 1985. *The Tale of Boris, A Fable of the Red-Tailed Hawk* Mooy/Stroschin 1984. *The Cloudy Day* Regnery Gateway 1979, revised edition Mooy/Stroschin 1991
What is the aim or goal of your writing? "To stir the imagination. To help readers be aware of the beauty in Nature. To reinforce concepts of self-esteem."
May inquiries be sent to you about doing workshops, readings? Yes

STURTZEL, JANE LEVINGTON
Pseudonym: Jane Annixter, Jane Levington Comfort
Born: June 22, 1903; Detroit, Michigan
Parents: Will Levington Comfort, Ada (Duffy) Comfort
Career: Writer

Writings: All with husband, Howard Allison Sturtzel: *The Runner* Holiday House 1958. *Peace Comes to Castle Oak* Longmans, Green 1961. *Trouble at Paintrock* Golden Press 1962. *The Great White* Holiday House 1966. *Ahmeek* Holiday House 1970. *White Shell Horse* Holiday House 1971. *Trumpeter: The Story of a Swan* Holiday House 1973. *Wapootin* Coward 1976. *Brown Rats, Black Rats* Prentice-Hall 1977. *The Year of the She-Grizzly* Coward 1978. *The Last Monster* Harcourt 1980. Others. Short stories in magazines
Awards or inclusion in other biographical books: *Contemporary Authors; Michigan Authors,* 2nd ed.; *Something about the Author*

SULLIVAN, THOMAS W.
Address: 17376 Catalpa, Lathrup Village, Michigan 48076
Born: November 20, 1940; Highland Park, Michigan
Parents: Wilson H. Sullivan, Maud E. Sullivan
Children: Colleen, Sean
Education: Michigan State University, East Lansing, Michigan; Wayne State University, Detroit, Michigan and others, B.A., 1960-1964. Wayne State University, B.A., Detroit, Michigan, 1964-1967
Career: High School Teacher, Dearborn Fordson, Dearborn, Michigan, 1968—. Various other types of jobs

Writings: *Born Burning* E.P. Dutton 1989. *The Phases of Harry Moon* E. P. Dutton 1988. *Diapason* E.P. Dutton 1978. Foreign edtions of novels. Over fifty short stories, journalism in newspapers, magazines such as *Omni, Michigan Magazine, Detroit Free Press, Fantasy & SF*. In anthologies such as *The Science Fictional Olympics* NAL 1984, several others. Work in Progress: *Drummers on Glass. H.E.R.S. & H.I.M.S.*
Awards or inclusion in other biographical books: *Contemporary Authors; Dictionary of International Biography; Men of Distinction.* Pulitzer Prize nomination, 1989. D.A.D.A. Literary Cash Awards, 1985, 1987. Hemingway Days Literary Cash Award, 1985. Nebula Award nomination, 1987. Listed in all-time top 10 horror stories, *Writer's Digest*
What is the aim or goal of your writing? "I'm told that I am a 'writer's writer', and that I often write of families. My goal, as I see it, is to hold a mirror up to life-sometimes a fun-house mirror, sometimes a darkened one-and to find within it a little beauty, a little truth, a little wisdom. If in that process I make peace with the muses who drive me, so much the better. My writing runs the gamut of categories and styles, and that too is by design."
May inquiries be sent to you about doing workshops, readings? Yes

SUMERIX, GRETCHEN A. (1908-1989)
Born: May 13, 1908; Wolverine, Michigan (Haakwood Lumber Camp)
Parents: Frank Goddard, Minnie (Winne) Goddard
Children: Delores, Sharol, Patricia, Elon Jr., Elden, G. Jean, Darrel
Education: Eighth grade graduation, 1921. Learned writing from her mother, a poet
Career: Freelance writer, Wolverine, Michigan, 1930-1988. Business Owner, Grocery Store, Wolverine, Michigan, 1965-1981. Business Owner, drug store, Wolverine, Michigan, 1954-1962. Business Owner, Service Station, Lansing, Michigan, 1941-1954. Assistant editor, *Wolverine Courier Newspaper*, 1930-1941

Writings: "Our Yesterday" Series: *Bay City Times, Cheboygan Daily Tribune* 1954-1975. *Our Yesterdays I* Voyager Press 1978. *Our Yesterdays II* Cheboygan Observer Printing 1981. *Our Yesterdays III* Southwell Printing 1982. Published in *Detroit Free Press, The Lansing State Journal, The Cheboygan Observer, The Straitsland Resorter.* Her daughter, Jeanne Sumerix-Poupard, kindly supplied: "The author Gretchen Sumerix had one thing in mind when she wrote her historical articles and later her books; to keep the history alive for our youth. She was proud of her heritage and wanted others to carry the torch."

SUMPTER, JERRY L.

Address: P. O. Box 286, Cheboygan, Michigan 49721
Born: August 13, 1942; Detroit, Michigan
Parents: Joseph E. Sumpter, Telcie (Crager) Sumpter
Children: Alicia, JL, Shaundra
Education: Ball State University, B.S., Muncie, Indiana, 1963-1966. Detroit College of Law, J.D., Detroit, Michigan, 1967-1970
Career: Instructor, Alpena Community College, 1971. Prosecuting Attorney, Cheboygan County, Michigan, 1972-1974. Law Firm of Sumpter & Perry, P.C., 1970—. Lecturer

Writings: *Civil Trial Strategy & Technique Notebook* 2 vols. Carnegie Press 1982. *Personal Injury: Discovery &Trial* James Publishing 1986. Supplements. Others. Published in *Michigan State Bar Journal, American Trial Lawyers Association Bar News, Trial Lawyers Quarterly, Detroit News, Case & Comment, Petoskey News-Review, Michigan Lawyers Weekly* and others. Contributor: Melvin Belli, *Modern Trials* 1982; MTLA *Complaint Book* 1991. Work in Progress: Supplements to *Personal Injury: Discovery & Trial*
Awards or inclusion in other biographical books: *Who's Who in American Education; Who's Who in American Law; Who's Who in Society; Who's Who in the World,* others. Honorarium, Northern Football League. Honorarium, Executive Reports Corporation. Golden Poet Award-World of Poetry, 1991
What is the aim or goal of your writing? "Educate lawyers in the specialty field of trial practice and technique."
May inquiries be sent to you about doing workshops, readings? Yes

SUNDAHL, DANIEL J.

Address: 2220 North Lake Wilson, Hillsdale, Michigan 49242
Born: February 14, 1951; Windom, Minnesota
Parents: Jesse C. Sundahl, Eileen A. Sundahl
Education: The University of Utah, M.A., Ph.D., 1975-1982. Gustavus Adolphus College, B.A., St. Peter, Minnesota, 1968-1972
Career: Professor of English, Hillsdale College, Hillsdale, Michigan, 1983—. Assistant Professor, College of the Ozarks, Clarksville, Arkansas, 1979-1982

Writings: About 350 poems published, about 12 articles, 24 or so book reviews. Work in Progress: Two collections of poems: *Hiroshima Maidens: Imaginary Translations from the Japanese. Loss of Habitat*
Awards or inclusion in other biographical books: Numerous writing awards
What is the aim or goal of your writing? "To speak of accepting one's individual history, of learning to love, of knowing that all that one loves perishes, to understand the limits of life."
May inquiries be sent to you about doing workshops, readings? Yes

SWARTHOUT, GLENDON F.
Address: 4800 N. 68th Street, Apt. A-115, Scottsdale, Arizona 85251
Born: April 8, 1918; Pinckney, Michigan
Parents: Fred H. Swarthout, Lila (Chubb) Swarthout
Children: Miles
Education: University of Michigan, Ann Arbor, Michigan, A.B.,1935-1939; M.A., 1945-1948. Michigan State University, Ph.D., East Lansing, Michigan, 1952-1955
Career: Writer

Writings: *Willow Run* Thomas Y. Crowell 1943. *They Came to Cordura* Random House 1958. *Where the Boys Are* Random House 1960. *Welcome to Thebes* Random House 1962. *The Cadillac Cowboys* Random House 1964. *The Eagle and the Iron Cross* New American Library 1966. *Loveland* Doubleday 1968. *Bless the Beasts and Children* Doubleday 1970. *The Tin Lizzie Troop* Doubleday 1972. *Luck and Pluck* Doubleday 1973. *The Shootist* Doubleday 1975. *The Melodeon* Doubleday 1977. *Skeletons* Doubleday 1979. *The Old Colts* Donald I. Fine 1985. *The Homesman* Weidenfeld & Nicolson 1988. Six juvenile books with Kathryn Swarthout: *The Ghost and the Magic Saber, Whichaway, The Button Boat, TV Thompson, Whales to See the, Cadbury's Coffin.* Popular film and song made based on *Where the Boys Are*
Awards or inclusion in other biographical books: *Contemporary Authors; Contemporary Novelists; Magill's Survey of American Literature; Michigan Authors,* 2nd ed.; *Who's Who in America.* Playwriting Award, Theatre Guild, 1947. Hopwood Award in Fiction, 1948. O. Henry Prize Short Stories, 1960. Gold Medal, National Society of Arts & Letters, 1972. Spur Award, Best Novel Western Writers of America, 1975, 1988. Wrangler Award, Outstanding Western Novel, Western Heritage Foundation, 1988. Lifetime Achievement Award, Western Writers of America, 1991
May inquiries be sent to you about doing workshops, readings? No

SWARTHOUT, KATHRYN B.
Address: 4800 N. 68th Street, Apt. A-115, Scottsdale, Arizona 85251
Pseudonym: Kate Swarthout
Born: January 8, 1919; Columbus, Montana
Parents: Lige H. Vaughn, Blair C. Vaughn
Children: Miles H.
Education: Ward-Belmont, Junior College Degree, Nashville, Tennessee. University of Michigan, B.A., English, Ann Arbor, Michigan, 1938-1940. Michigan State University, M.A., Education, East Lansing, Michigan, 1954-1956
Career: Elementary Teacher, Red Cedar School, East Lansing, Michigan, 1954-1958

Writings: *Cadbury's Coffin* (with Glendon Swarthout) Doubleday 1982. *Whales to See the* (with Glendon Swarthout) Doubleday 1975. *TV Thompson* Doubleday (with Glendon Swarthout) 1972. *The Button Boat* Doubleday (with Glendon Swarthout) 1969. *Whichaway* (with Glendon Swarthout) Random House 1966; Knopf 1992. *The Ghost and the Magic Saber* (with Glendon Swarthout) Random House 1963. *Life Savors* Doubleday 1982. Work in Progress: Fifteen years of continuing columns of *Life Savors* for *Woman's Day*
Awards or inclusion in other biographical books: *Michigan Authors,* 2nd ed.
What is the aim or goal of your writing? "To use my educational skills in various ways of creative writing."
May inquiries be sent to you about doing workshops, readings? No

SWIFT, IVAN (1873-1945)
Born: June 24, 1873; Wayne County, Michigan
Parents: John Swift, Jennie (Birge) Swift
Education: Harbor Springs High School, Harbor Springs, Michigan, 1892. Petoskey Normal Academy, Petoskey, Michigan, 1895. Art Institute, Chicago, Illinois. Pupil of various masters in New York
Career: Served in Spanish American War, First World War. Landscape paintings exhibited, New York, Pennsylvania, Detroit Public Library, Detroit Institute of Arts, Library of Michigan, others. Served on Executive Council, Society of Michigan Authors

Writings: *Fagots of Cedar* self designed and printed at To-morrow Press (Chicago) 1907; The Lizzard Shop (Harbor Springs, Michigan) 1909; The Willows Shop (Harbor Springs, Michigan) 1909; Bookfellow Edition, The Torch Press, Cedar Rapids, Iowa, by the Bookfellows, printed (limited edition) for The Lofts, Chippewa Cove Woods (Good Hart, Michigan) 1926. *Blue Crane and Shore Songs* James T. White (New York) 1918. *Green Bench Writs and Opinions* (Harbor Springs, Michigan) 1929. Several articles in *Michigan History Magazine* such as "The House of Autobiography", describing his Harbor Springs summer home (Spring, 1930). In *New Michigan Verse* 1940. Poems in *The Independent, The Outlook, Poetry, Recreation, Outers' Book, Smart Set, Midland, All the Arts, American Lumberman, The Transcript, Chicago American*
Awards or inclusion in other biographical books: *American Authors and Books; American Literary Yearbook; Anthology of Magazine Verse; Who Was Who among North American Authors; Who Was Who in America; Who's Who in America.* Honorary member, Eugene Field Society. In his introduction to *Fagots of Cedar*, Swift credited Carl Sandburg with describing his work as "inevitable and autobiographical."

TALBOT, FANNIE SPRAGUE (1873-1957)

Born: May 4, 1873; East Leroy, Michigan
Parents: Elliott Sprague, Marie Hannah Sprague
Education: High School, Battle Creek, Michigan
Career: Newspaper work. Involved with DAR, Women's League, Federation of Women's Clubs, Poetry Society of Michigan

Writings: *Poems* R.G. Badger 1910. *Nosegay* Torch Press 1946. "Old Days and Old Ways at Meadowbrook", series of articles on Michigan
Awards or inclusion in other biographical books: *Childhood in Poetry; Michigan Authors,* 2nd ed.; *Women's Who's Who of America*

TAPPAN, HENRY PHILIP (1805-1881)

Born: April 18, 1805; Rhinebeck, New York
Parents: Peter Tappan, Ann (DeWitt) Tappan
Children: Son, four daughters
Education: Union College, Schenectady, New York, B.A., 1825. Auburn Theological Seminary, graduated 1827
Career: Minister, Congregational Church, 1828. Professor, University of the City of New York, 1832. First President, University of Michigan, Ann Arbor, Michigan, 1852-1863; committee chairman, recruiting for Civil War. Founded Detroit Astronomical Observatory. Went to live in Europe where he died

Writings: *The Doctrine of the Will, Determined by an Appeal to Consciousness* Wiley and Putnam 1840. *An Essay on the Expression of Passion in Oratory* C. W. Benedict 1848. *University Education* Putnam 1851. *A Step from the New World to the Old, and Back Again; with Thoughts on the Good and Evil in Both* D. Appleton 1852. *A Discourse* Advertiser Power Presses (Detroit) 1852. *Illustrious Personages of the Nineteenth Century* Stringer & Townsend 1853. *The Progress of Educational Development* E.B. Pond 1855. *Elements of Logic* D. Appleton 1856. *The Mutual Responsibilities of Physicians and the Community, Being an Address to the Graduating Class of the Medical College of the University of Michigan. Delivered March 27th, 1856* Peninsular Journal of Medicine (Detroit) 1856. *Public Education: an Address; Delivered in the Hall of the House of Representatives, in the Capitol at Lansing, on the Evening of January 28th, 1857* H. Barns 1857. *The University; its Constitution. A Discourse Delivered June 22d, 1858* S. B. McCracken 1858. *Elements of Logic; Together with an Introductory View of Philosophy in General, and a Preliminary View of the Reason* D. Appleton 1860. *President Tappan's Annual Message to the Second Moot Congress of the Law Department of the University of Michigan. Delivered 6th December, 1862* C.G. Clark, Jr., 1862. *Review by Rev. Dr. H. P. Tappan of His Connection With the University of Michigan* Detroit Free Press Steam Book and Job Printing Establishment 1864. Others
Awards or inclusion in other biographical books: *Allibone: A Critical Dictionary of English Language; American Authors, 1600-1900; Biographical Dictionary of American Educators; Cyclopaedia of American Literature; Dictionary of American Authors; Dictionary of American Biography; Dictionary of North American Authors; Drake:*

Dictionary of American Biography; National Cyclopaedia of American Biography; Twentieth Century Biographical Dictionary of Notable Americans; Who Was Who in America

TAYLOR, DONNA (DOWLING) (1921-1990)
Born: July 12, 1921; Detroit, Michigan
Parents: Francis (Frank) J. Dowling, Melba C. (Cavill) Dowling
Children: Brian Keven, Kim Eric
Education: Wayne State University, Detroit, Michigan, B.A., 1940-1944; M.Ed., 1962-1964; working on doctoral dissertation at time of death
Career: Wayne State University, Professor, Library Science, Detroit, Michigan, 1974-1978. South Redford School District, Consultant, Media Center Development, Redford Township, Michigan, 1974-1978; School Librarian, 1964-1965; Substitute Librarian, 1962-1963. Oakland Schools, Consultant, Title III, Social Studies Project, Pontiac, Michigan, 1973-1978? (intermittently). Professor, Library Science, Eastern Michigan University, Ypsilanti, Michigan, 1970-1972. Instructor, Library Science, Wayne State University, Detroit, Michigan, 1965-1970. Librarian, Detroit Board of Education, 1944-1949, 1953-1955. Partner-owner (with husband), Green Oak Press, 1977-1990. Participant in USOE Institute on Modern Publishing

Writings: *Yesteryears of Green Oak, 1830-1930* Green Oak Township Historical Society 1981. Editor, *The Great Lakes Region in Children's Books* Green Oak Press 1980. Book Review, "Media Review" column, *School Media Quarterly* 1974. Published in *Elementary English, Motor News, Motor Travel* and others. Chairperson, Editorial Committee, Second Edition *Michigan Authors* 1980. Work in Progress: Book on Kensington, Michigan interrupted by illness and death
Awards or inclusion in other biographical books: *Who's Who in Library Service; Who's Who of American Women* 7th edtion. Pi Lambda Theta, Alpha Pi Chapter, Wayne State University. Awarded Life Membership, Green Oak Township Historical Society
What is the aim or goal of your writing? Kindly supplied by her husband, James E. Taylor: "To author, edit, publish worthwhile books which need to be published-those which large publishers ignore."

TAYLOR, KEITH
Address: 1715 Dexter Avenue, Ann Arbor, Michigan 48103
Born: June 4, 1952; Kelowna, British Columbia, Canada
Parents: Donald M. Taylor, Joyce M. Taylor
Children: Faith
Education: Bethel College, B.A., Mishawaka, Indiana, 1975. Central Michigan University, M.A., Mt. Pleasant, Michigan, 1982
Career: Adjunct Lecturer, English Department, University of Michigan, Ann Arbor, Michigan, 1991—. Trade Manager, Shanan Drum Bookshop, Ann Arbor, Michigan, 1989—. Bookseller, Borders Book Shop, Ann Arbor, Michigan, 1981-1989

Writings: *Dream of the Black Wolf* Ridgeway Press 1992. *Weather Report* Ridgeway Press 1988. *Learning to Dance* Falling Water Press 1985. Poems in *The Michigan Quarterly Review, New Letters, Caliban, Witness, The Beloit Poetry Journal, The Alternative Press, The Great Lakes Review, Passages North* and others. Work in Progress: A collection of prose poems, *Behind the Green Wall*
Awards or inclusion in other biographical books: Fellow in Creative Writing,

National Endowment for the Arts, 1991. Artist in Residence, Isle Royale National Park, 1991

What is the aim or goal of your writing? "To find my place in the world."

May inquiries be sent to you about doing workshops, readings? Yes

TAYLOR, MARK (1927-1992)

Born: August 15, 1927; Linden, Michigan

Parents: Wilton Huebler, Constance (Page) Huebler Chinery

Education: Tufts College, 1945-1947. University of Michigan, B.A., Ann Arbor Michigan, 1950; M.A.L.S., 1952. University of Southern California, M.S., 1970, Ph.D., 1976

Career: Children's librarian, University of Michigan Elementary School, Ann Arbor, Michigan, 1950-1956. University of Michigan Broadcasting Service, Ann Arbor, radio producer and performer, 1950-1956. Head of Youth Adult Services, Dayton and Montgomery County Public Library, Dayton, Ohio, 1957-1960. Assistant Professor, Graduate School of Library Science, University of Southern California, 1960-1969. Television producer and performer, Columbia Broadcasting System, 1962-1964. Children's book columnist, *Los Angeles Times,* 1962-1969. Freelance writer, lecturer, consultant, 1970–. Storyteller, balladeer, 1950–. Guest lecturer, instructor at San Francisco State University, University of Nebraska, many others. Conducted workshops and seminars for many associations such as The Children's Book Council. Author-in-residence for many schools across the country

Writings: *Henry, the Explorer* Atheneum 1966. *The Bold Fisherman* Golden Gate Junior Books 1967. *A Time for Flowers* Golden Gate Junior Books 1967. *Henry Explores the Jungle* Atheneum 1968. *Composition Through Literature: Understanding Your Language* (3 vols.) American Book Company 1968. *The Old Woman and the Peddler* Golden Gate Junior Books 1969. *Bobby Shafto's Gone to Sea* Golden Gate Junior Books 1970. *Old Blue, You Good Dog, You* Golden Gate Junior Books 1970. Compiler with May H. Arbuthnot, *Time for Old Magic* Scott, Foresman 1970. *Wind in My Hand* Golden Gate Junior Books 1970. *The Fisherman and the Goblet: A Vietnamese Folk Talk* Golden Gate Junior Books 1971. *Lamb, Said the Lion, I Am Here* Golden Gate Junior Books 1971. *Henry, the Castaway* Atheneum 1972. *The Wind's Child* Atheneum 1973. *Henry Explores the Mountains* Atheneum 1975. *Jennie Jenkins* Little, Brown 1975. *The Case of the Missing Kittens* Atheneum 1978. *Young Melvin and the Bulger* Doubleday 1981. Many are Junior Literary Guild Selections. Several other books. Educational filmstrip and television scripts. Articles and reviews, *Library Journal, Book Talk, The Reading Teacher* and others

Awards or inclusion in other biographical books: *Authors of Books for Young People; Something about the Author.* Dutton-Macrae Award, 1956. National Association for Better Radio and Television, best children's television series of 1963-1964. *Library Journal,* selected *The Bold Fisherman* one of best books of the year, 1967. National Defense Education Act Fellowship, graduate study in media, 1969-1971. Newbery Award consideration, 1975. Southern California Council on Literature for Children and Young People, recognition of excellence, 1976

TCHUDI, STEPHEN N.

Name before legally changed: Stephen Judy, Stephen N. Judy

Born: January 31, 1942; Waterbury, Connecticut

Parents: John Judy, Anna (May) Judy

Children: Stephen, Emily, Michael, Christopher

Education: Hamilton College, B.A., Clinton, New York, 1963. Northwestern University, M.A., 1964; Ph.D., Evanston, Illinois, 1967
Career: Assistant professor, Northwestern University, Evanston, Illinois, 1967-1969. Assistant professor, Michigan State University, East Lansing, Michigan 1969-1971; associate professor, 1971-1976; professor, 1976—. Visiting professor. Editor, *English Journal*, beginning 1973

Writings: *Gifts of Writing: Creative Projects with Words and Art* (with Susan J. Judy) Scribner 1980. *Putting on a Play: A Guide to Writing and Producing Neighborhood Drama* (with Susan J. Judy) Scribner 1982. *Publishing in English Education* (editor) Boynton Cook 1982. *Teaching Writing in the Content Areas: Elementary School* (with Susan J. Tchudi) National Education Association 1983. *Teaching Writing in the Content Areas: Middle School/Junior High* (with Margie C. Huerta) National Education Association 1983. *Teaching Writing in the Content Areas: Senior High School* (with Joanne Yates) National Education Association 1983. *The Burg-O-Rama Man* Delacorte 1983. *Language, Schooling, and Society* (editor) Boynton Cook 1985. *The History of Soft Drinks in America* Scribner 1986. *The Green Machine* Delacorte 1987. *The Young Learner's Handbook* Scribner 1987. Others
Awards or inclusion in other biographical books: *Contemporary Authors.* Charles Carpenter Fries Award, Michigan Council of Teachers of English, 1978. Several awards, Educational Press Association

TEBBEL, JOHN WILLIAM
Born: November 16, 1912; Boyne City, Michigan
Parents: William Farr Tebbel, Edna Mae Tebbel
Children: Judith
Education: Central Michigan University, A.B., Mt. Pleasant, Michigan, 1935. Columbia University, M.S., New York, New York, 1937
Career: City Editor, *Times-News*, Mt. Pleasant, Michigan, 1935-1936. Reporter, *Detroit Free Press,* 1937-1939. Feature Writer, Sunday Music Editor, *Providence Journal*, 1939--1941. Managing Editor, *American Mercury,* 1941-1943. Other newspaper work. Part-time, Instructor, Columbia University, New York, New York, 1941-1946. Associate Editor, E.P. Dutton, 1943-1946. Assistant Professor, New York University, 1949-1952; Associate Professor, 1952-1954; Professor, 1954-1976; Department Head 1954-1965; Director of Graduate Institute of Book Publishing, 1958-1962. Consultant, Ford Foundation

Writings: *An American Dynasty: The Story of the McCormicks, Medills, and Pattersons* Doubleday 1947; Greenwood Press 1968. *The Marshall Fields* Dutton 1947. *The Inheritors: A Study of America's Great Fortunes and What Happened to Them* Putnam 1962. *George Washington's America* Dutton 1954. *Paperback Books: A Pocket History* Pocket Books 1963. *Red Runs the River: The Rebellion of Chief Pontiac* Hawthorn 1963; 1969. *The Battle of Fallen Timbers, August 20, 1794: President Washington Secures the Ohio Valley* F. Watts 1972. *A History of Book Publishing in the United States* Bowker (14 volumes) 1972-1980. *The Media in America: A Social and Political History* Crowell 1974. *Opportunities in Book Publishing* National Textbook 1986. *A Certain Club: 100 Years of The Players* Weiser 1989. *The Magazine in America, 1741-1991* Oxford University Press 1990. Several others. Ghost writer of about 40 books. Over 500 articles in magazines
Awards or inclusion in other biographical books: *American Authors and Books; Contemporary Authors; Current Biography; Directory of American Scholars; Something*

about the Author; Who's Who in America. Alumni Award, Journalism Alumni Association, Columbia University, New York, New York, 1975. Litt.D., Central Michigan University, Mt. Pleasant, Michigan, 1948

TEFFT, BESS H. (1913-1977)
Born: October 6, 1915; Hillsdale, Michigan
Parents: Elmer B. Hagaman, Violetta (Greenshaw) Hagaman
Children: William, Robert
Education: Hillsdale College, 1937
Career: Editor, Washtenaw County Farm Bureau News. Teacher, Ann Arbor Public Schools. Member, Saline School Board, 1956-1965. Helped found the University of Michigan's International Hospitality Program

Writings: *Ken of Centennial Farm* Follett 1959. *Merrie Maple* Dutton 1958
Awards or inclusion in other biographical books: *Michigan Authors,* 1st ed., 2nd ed.

TEICHMAN, DENNIS B.
Address: 3168 Trowbridge, Hamtramck, Michigan 48212
Born: April 15, 1949; Detroit, Michigan
Parents: Louis B. Teichman, Lillian K. (Suinka) Teichman
Children: Jason, Liberty, Fielding
Education: Wayne State University, B.A., Detroit, Michigan, 1970-1974
Career: Refrigeration Operator, Difco Labs, Detroit, Michigan, 1984—. Boiler Operator, Deaconess Hospital, Detroit, Michigan, 1975-1984

Writings: *Edge to Edge* Past Tents Press 1985. *V-8* Past Tents Press 1989. Work in Progress: Yes
What is the aim or goal of your writing? "To decode the language behind the statements and functions of the ruling powers, and pass along my findings."
May inquiries be sent to you about doing workshops, readings? Yes

TENNIS HAMLIN, ROSE V.
Address: 16025 Herrington Road, Webberville, Michigan 48892
Born: July 25, 1912; Webberville, Michigan
Parents: Bert Brimley, Emilie (Schmitt) Brimley
Education: Livingston County Normal, 3 Year Certificate, 1930-1931. Eastern Michigan University, B.S., Ypsilanti, Michigan, 1933-1952. Michigan State University, Masters, East Lansing, Michigan, 1952-1961
Career: Junior High Science Teacher, Fowlerville Community Schools, Fowlerville, Michigan, 1960-1967. High School Science Teacher, Perry High School, Perry, Michigan, 1958-1960. Elementary Teacher, Fowlerville, Michigan, 1948-1956. Rural School Teacher, 1931-1948, Livingston and Shiawasee Counties

Writings: *The School That Was a School Marm's Tale* Wilderness Adventure Books 1990
What is the aim or goal of your writing? "I wanted a record of the organization, daily program and activities, and the learning and good teaching that went on in the rural schools."
May inquiries be sent to you about doing workshops, readings? Yes

THACKER, SHELLY
Address: P.O. Box 1022, Novi, Michigan 48376
Born: August 4, 1963; Livonia, Michigan
Parents: Robert D. Thacker, Sylvia A. Thacker
Education: Albion College, B.A., Phi Beta Kappa, summa cum laude, Albion, Michigan, 1981-1985
Career: Novelist, self-employed, Bedford, Michigan, 1990—. Freelance writer, self-employed, Walled Lake, Michigan, 1986—. Public Relations Assistant, Crittenton Hospital, Rochester, Michigan, 1985-1986. Romance Writers of America President, Newsletter Editor, Conference Co-Chair, Membership Chair. Judge in numerous writing contests. Speaker

Writings: *Midnight Raider* Avon Books 1992. *Falcon on the Wind* Avon Books 1992. Articles in *Country Living, Entrepreneur, Writer's Digest, American Bookseller, Romance Writers' Report,* others. Work in Progress: *Silver and Sapphire*
Awards or inclusion in other biographical books: Nominee, *Romantic Times* Reviewer's Choice Award 1991. Winner, Seattle Valentine Love Scene Contest, 1990. Winner, Ontario Golden Opportunity Synopsis Contest, 1989. Winner, Delaware Diamond Synopsis Contest, 1988. Winner, Texas Heartland Historical Contest, 1988. Finalist, Romance Writers of America Golden Heart, 1989. Finalist, Georgia Maggie Awards, 1988
What is the aim or goal of your writing? "To write fast-paced, entertaining historical romances that touch the hearts of readers."
May inquiries be sent to you about doing workshops, readings? Yes

THOMAS, F. RICHARD
Address: 145 Kenberry Drive, East Lansing, Michigan 48823
Born: August 1, 1940; Evansville, Indiana
Parents: Franklin A. Thomas, Lydia K. Thomas
Children: Severn, Caerllion
Education: Purdue University, A.B., M.A., West Lafayette, Indiana, 1958-1964. Indiana University, Ph.D., 1965-1970
Career: Professor of American Thought and Language, Michigan State University, East Lansing, Michigan, 1971—. Assistant Professor of English, Purdue University-Calumet, Hammond, Indiana, 1969-1971. Editor/Publisher, Years Press poetry chapbooks, 1973—

Writings: *Prism: The Journal of John Fish* Canoe Press 1992. *Americans in Denmark* Southern Illinois University Press 1990. *The Whole Mustery of the Bregn* Canoe Press 1989. *Heart Climbing Stairs,* Odense University 1986. *Corolla, Stamen, and Style* Odense University 1986. *Literary Admirers of Alfred Stieglitz* Southern Illinois University Press 1983. *Frog Praises Night: Poems With Commentary* Southern University Press 1980. *Alive With You This Day* The Raintree Press 1980. *Fat Grass* Nosferato Press 1970. Work in Progress:*Travel and the Art of Learning*
Awards or inclusion in other biographical books: *Contemporary Authors,* 1978, 1990;*Who's Who in Writers, Editors, and Poets,* 1986, 1991. Fulbright Teacher 1974-1975; Lecturer 1985-1986, Denmark. Michigan Council for the Arts Creative Artist Grant, 1990
What is the aim or goal of your writing? "To communicate by evoking a physical and intellectual response in an audience."
May inquiries be sent to you about doing workshops, readings? Yes

THOMAS, STEVEN L.

Address: 2143 Raleigh Drive, Okemos, Michigan 48864
Born: November 4, 1945; Muskegon, Michigan
Parents: Frank A. Thomas, Ann (Dollslager) Thomas
Children: Patrick
Education: Muskegon Catholic Central High School. Muskegon Community College, Associates Degree, 1964-1966. Central Michigan University, B.A., Mt. Pleasant, Michigan, 1963-1967; M.A., 1967-1968. Michigan State University, M.A., East Lansing, Michigan, 1970.
Career: Teacher, Social Studies Department Head, Okemos High School, Okemos, Michigan, 1968—. Supervisor, Meridian Township, Okemos, Michigan, 1988—. Instructor, Michigan State University, East Lansing, Michigan, 1986-1990. Instructor, Lansing Community College, Lansing, Michigan, 1986. County Commissioner, Ingham County, 1977-1988

Writings: *Michigan Government and You* Hillsdale Educational Publishers 1991. *State and Local Government in Michigan* (ed.) Hillsdale Educational Publishers 1984
What is the aim or goal of your writing? "To assist Michiganians in better understanding the Michigan political process and to encourage their active involvement in that process."
May inquiries be sent to you about doing workshops, readings? Yes

THOMAS, VONNIE E.

Address: 8757 Berridge Road, Greenville, Michigan 48838
Born: April 10, 1917; Montcalm County, Michigan
Parents: Earl J. Wilcox, Myrtle B. (Berridge) Wilcox
Children: Mary Kathleen, Michael. Robert (deceased)
Education: Greenville High School, graduated 1933. Central Michigan University, Mt. Pleasant, Michigan, 1933-1935; extension and summer school after
Career: Floor Inspector, Federal Mogul Corporation, Greenville, Michigan, 1947-1977, retired. Service representative, Michigan Bell Telephone Company, Ypsilanti, Michigan, 1943-1945. Teacher, Montcalm, Kent Counties; 1935-1943, 1945-1947

Writings: *Changing View A Book of Sonnets* Belding Printing 1991. *View Beyond the Tree* Greenville Printing 1981. Over 135 poems published in *Lyric, Inkling, New England Writers/Vt., Connecticut Review, Pennsylvania Prize Poems, Tennessee Prize Poems, Kentucky Prize Poems, Alura, Arizona Prize Poems, Ohio Prize Poems, Encore* and others. Work in Progress: *The Gift of Time. They Do Not Answer*
Awards or inclusion in other biographical books: *Michigan Poets,* Poetry Society of Michigan; *Poets and Writers Directory.* First Honorable Mention, Arkansas Writers' Conference, 1992
What is the aim or goal of your writing? "To improve my work. I have hundreds of books of poetry and I enjoy them. I have books to increase my writing skills. I study them all. I have favorite writers: Shakespeare, Milton, Bronte Sisters, Byron, Keats, Robert Lowell, Yeats, Frost, Maxine Kumin, Elizabeth Bishop, Robert Penn Warren, Dave Smith, Seamus Heaney and many others."
May inquiries be sent to you about doing workshops, readings? Yes

THOMPSON, IONE M.

Address: 600 Michigan Street, Ontonagon, Michigan 49953
Born: June 28, 1921; Metamora, Ohio
Parents: Carey A. Clark, Pearl E. (Gleckler) Clark
Children: Patrick, Molly, Bridget, Timothy, Terrence. Michael deceased
Education: Ohio Northern University, Ada, Ohio, 1938-1941. Northern Michigan University, B.S., Marquette, Michigan, 1967-1968
Career: Teacher, Whitefish Township School, Paradise, Michigan, 1960-1973. Teacher, Tahquamenon Area Schools, Newberry, Michigan, 1969-1971. Co-owner, Manager, Cloud Nine Resort, Paradise, Michigan, 1958-1991

Writings: *Amik!* Bookmasters 1991. *The Anonymous Dead* Carlton Press 1972. Work in Progress: *Rebecca and Daniel Boone*
What is the aim or goal of your writing? "To prove the ongoing, everlasting value of the written, printed word."

THORN, BERRIEN

Address: P.O. Box 455, Suttons Bay, Michigan 49682
Pseudonym: Berrien Fragos
Born: November 16, 1948; New Rochelle, New York
Parents: George Phrangos, Carol June (Thorn) Phrangos
Education: New York Phoenix School of Design, Degree in Fine Art, 1968-1972. Private Study, Richard Coe, Painter for the Brooklyn Botanical Gardens, 2 years. Harvard Divinity School, Storytelling. Ukulele Master Class, Roy Smeck, 1982-1984. Tibetan teachers, Buddhism. Others
Career: Elevator operator, various other jobs. Performing, Open Arts Grant, Westchester Arts Council, New York, 1979. Writing projects; singing in prisons, 1975-1983. S.U.N.Y. Migrant Farm Worker Literacy Projects, rural upstate New York, 1979-1988. Performances in Migrant Camps; Festivals, including working with folk singer Pete Seeger; other activist work, 1980-1983

Writings: *Berrien, Utility Music,* Album Recording, 1985. Literary, fine art reviews, column "Easy Street", *Traverse City Record-Eagle,* 1989—. Work in Progress: *The Wooing of the North*
What is the aim or goal of your writing? "I believe the salvation of all of us is as little as the most obscure destiny. There are moments in the long spaces of every existence where time flows together. In that slight infinity being grows big as the world or little as death. We are all responsible to pay attention. That's it."
May inquiries be sent to you about doing workshops, readings? Yes. I love to do readings. Sometimes they verge on singings.

THORPE, ROSE HARTWICK (1850-1939)

Born: July 19, 1850; Mishawaka, Indiana
Parents: William Morris Hartwick, Louisa (Wight) Hartwick
Children: Lulo May, Lillie Maud
Education: Litchfield High School, Litchfield, Michigan, 1868
Career: Verse for publication, editor and writer for such monthlies as *Temperance Tales, Words of Life.* Active in woman suffrage and Y.M.C.A.

Writings: Frequent contributor to *Detroit Free Press, Youth's Company* and others.

Children's fiction books such as *Fred's Dark Days* 1881. *The Curfew Shall Not Ring Tonight* Lee and Shepard 1882; C.T. Dillingham 1883. *As Others See Us, or, the Rules and Customs of Refined Homes and Polite Society..: Also Complete Self Instruction in Physical Culture for Both Ladies and Gentlemen* F.B. Dickerson 1896. *The White Lady of La Jolla* Grandier & Company 1904. *The Poetical Works of Rose Hartwick Thorpe* 1912. Her most famous poem "The Curfew Shall Not Ring Tonight" appeared in 1870 in Detroit newspaper, *Commercial Advertiser*. This poem, written when she was 17 years old, was printed throughout the nation, translated abroad. A monument to the poem, topped by a cast-iron bell, was erected in 1934 in Litchfield, Michigan at the centennial of the town's founding. Also wrote the popular poem, "Remember the Alamo"

Awards or inclusion in other biographical books: *American Authors and Books; Childhood in Poetry; Dictionary of American Biography; Dictionary of North American Authors; Index to Women; Michigan Women Firsts and Founders; National Cyclopaedia of American Biography; Reader's Encyclopaedia of American Literature; Twentieth Century Biographical Dictionary of Notable Americans; Who Was Who among North American Authors; Who Was Who in America; Woman's Who's Who of America,* several others

THWAITES, REUBEN GOLD (1853-1913)
Born: May 15, 1853; Dorchester, Massachusetts
Parents: William George Thwaites, Sarah (Bibbs) Thwaites
Education: Self-instructed, college. Yale University, post-graduate work, 1874-1875
Career: Managing editor, *Wisconsin State Journal*, 1876-1886. Secretary, Superintendent, State Historical Society of Wisconsin, 1886. President, American Library Association, 1900; on executive council. Lecturer, University of Wisconsin

Writings: *Biographical Sketches of Lyman C. Draper* D. Atwood 1887. *Biographical Sketch of David Atwood* David Atwood 1887. *The Colonies, 1492-1750* Longmans, Green 1890, 4th edition 1893. *The Jesuit Relations and Allied Documents; Travels and Explorations of the Jesuit Missionaries in New France, 1610-1791; the Original French, Latin, and Italian Texts, with English Translations and Notes* (editor) 73 volumes Burrows Brothers Company 1896-1901. *Afloat on the Ohio; an Historical Pilgrimage of a Thousand Miles in a Skiff, from Redstone to Cairo* Way & Williams 1897. *Father Marquette* D. Appleton 1902. *A Brief History of Rocky Mountain Exploration, with Especial Reference to the Expedition of Lewis and Clark* D. Appleton 1904. *Cyrus Hall McCormick and the Reaper* The Society (Madison) 1909. *Frontier Defenses on the Upper Ohio* 1911. *The Jesuit Relations and Allied Documents; Travels and Explorations of the Jesuit Missionaries in North America (1610-1791)* A. & C. Boni 1925. *The Jesuit Relations and Allied Documents; Travels and Explorations of the Jesuit Missionaries in New France, 1610-1791* Pageant Book Company 1959. *France in America, 1497-1763* Haskell House 1969. *The Revolution on the upper Ohio, 1775, 1777* Kennikat Press 1970. Others. Many monographs on history of New France, Middle West

Awards or inclusion in other biographical books: *American Authors and Books; American Biographies; Dictionary of American Authors; Dictionary of American Biography; Dictionary of American Literary Biography; Dictionary of North American Authors; National Cyclopaedia of American Biography; Oxford Companion to American Literature; Reader's Encyclopaedia of American Literature; Twentieth Century Authors; Twentieth Century Biographical Dictionary of Notable Americans; Who Was Who in America,* several others. LL.D., University of Wisconsin, 1904

TIMMERMAN, JOHN H.
Address: 2668 Union, Grand Rapids, Michigan 49507
Born: January 19, 1945; Grand Rapids, Michigan
Parents: John J. Timmerman, Carolyn J. Timmerman
Children: Jeffrey, Betsy, Tamara, Joel
Education: Calvin College, A.B., Grand Rapids, Michigan, 1963-1967. Ohio University, Ph.D., 1968-1973
Career: Professor of English, Calvin College, Grand Rapids, Michigan, 1977—. Assistant Professor of Philosophy, Grove City College, Grove City, Pennsylvania, 1973-1977

Writings: *The Dramatic Landscape of Steinbeck's Short Stories* Oklahoma University 1990. *A Season of Suffering* Multnomah 1988. *The Way of Christian Living* Eerdmans 1987. *In the World* Baker 1987. *John Steinbeck's Fiction* Oklahoma 1986. *A Layman Looks at the Names of Jesus* Tyndale 1985. *Other Worlds: The Fantasy Genre* Bowling Green State University 1983. *Shaper* Chosen Books 1983. *Frederick Manfred: A Bibliography and Publishing History* Center for Western Studies 1981. Short stories in*Western Humanities Review, Texas Review, Negative Capability, Cimarron Review* and others. Work in Progress: *T.S. Eliot's Ariel Poems: The Poetics of Recovery. Children Green and Golden: Short Stories*
Awards or inclusion in other biographical books: Steinbeck Scholar of the Year, 1989. Michigan Council of Fine Arts Award for fiction, 1989
What is the aim or goal of your writing? "In fiction-writing stories that are historically rooted in actual events. In scholarship-the study of works of Steinbeck and Eliot."
May inquiries be sent to you about doing workshops, readings? Yes

TIPTON, JAMES
Born: January 18, 1942; Ashland, Ohio
Parents: J. Robert Tipton, Ruth (Burcher) Tipton
Children: Jennifer, James
Education: Purdue University, B.A., Indiana, 1968
Career: Writer-in-Residence, Kalamazoo College, Kalamazoo, Michigan, 1969-1970. English Professor, Alma College, Alma, Michigan, 1970—

Writings: *Bittersweet* Cold Mountain Press 1975. *The Third Coast: Contemporary Michigan Poetry* (editor with Herbert Scott, Conrad Hilberry, contributor) Wayne State University Press 1976. *The Third Coast: Contemporary Michigan Fiction* (co-editor with Robert Wegner) Wayne State University Press 1982. In various anthologies such as *Heartland II: Poets of the Midwest* Northern Illinois University Press 1975. Poems, stories, reviews, translations in various literary journals and magazines such as *Southern Humanities Review, Esquire, Carolina Quarterly*
Awards or inclusion in other biographical books: *Contemporary Authors; Directory of American Fiction Writers; Directory of American Poets; International Who's Who in Poetry; Michigan Authors,* 2nd ed. National Endowment for the Humanities, 1972. First Prize, Festival of the Arts, Birmingham, Alabama, 1973

TITUS, HAROLD (1888-?)
Born: February 20, 1888; Traverse City, Michigan
Parents: Dorr B. Titus, F. Josephine (Smith) Titus
Children: Elizabeth, John

Education: University of Michigan, Ann Arbor, Michigan, 1907-1911
Career: Reporter, *Detroit News,* 1907-1910. Fruit grower, Grand Traverse County, Michigan, beginning 1911. Served in World War I. Chairman, Michigan Conservation Commission, several years, after being named by Governor Green, 1927

Writings: *I Conquered* A.L. Burt 1916. *Bruce of the Circle A* A. L. Burt 1918. *The Last Straw* A.L. Burt 1920. *Timber* Small, Maynard 1922; several editions; movie version. *The Beloved Pawn* A.L. Burt 1923. *Spindrift* Doubleday 1924. *Below Zero* A. L. Burt 1932. *Code of the North* A.L. Burt 1933. *Flame in the Forest* A. L. Burt 1933. *The Man from Yonder* A.L. Burt 1934. *Black Feather* Macrae Smith 1936. *The Land Nobody Wanted: The Story of Michigan's Public Domain* Michigan State College, Agricultural Experiment Station, (Special Bulletin: 332) 1945. Hundreds of short stories. In *Ladies' Home Journal, Red Book, Pictorial Review, Metropolitan, Field and Stream, Saturday Evening Post, Collier's Weekly,* others
Awards or inclusion in other biographical books: *American Authors and Books:1640 to the Present Day; Who's Who among North American Authors; Who's Who in America.* Honorary Degree, University of Michigan, 1931

TOMEY, INGRID H.
Address: 7565 Lilac Court, West Bloomfield, Michigan 48324
Born: May 25, 1943; Port Huron, Michigan
Parents: Frank V. Goff, Georgena R. (Carter) Goff
Children: Paul M., Kristin
Education: Michigan State University, B.A., East Lansing, Michigan, 1963-1965. University of Michigan, M.F.A. Creative Writing, Ann Arbor, Michigan, 1983-1985
Career: Freelance writer, travel writer, stringer, children's book author, 1981—

Writings: *Savage Carrot* Boyds Mills Press 1993. *Grandfather's Day* Boyds Mills Press 1992. *Neptune Princess* Bradbury Press 1992. Work in Progress: *Loss Events,* adult novel. *Dreams Unlimited*, Young Adult novel
Awards or inclusion in other biographical books: Tyson Award, Most Promising Novel at University of Michigan, *Loss Events,* 1985. American Poets Prize, "Baby in a Tree" and "Where the Skies are Not Cloudy", University of Michigan, 1984
What is the aim or goal of your writing? "To reveal life's simple truths-that the world is a safe place, a place where love, if given, is returned; that those who live with integrity, prosper and, above all, that we should enjoy the trip."
May inquiries be sent to you about doing workshops, readings? Yes

TOMPERT, ANN
Address: 2905 12th Avenue, Apt. A., Port Huron, Michigan 48060
Born: January 11, 1918; Detroit, Michigan
Parents: Joseph Bakeman, Florence (Pollitt) Bakeman
Education: Siena Heights College, A.B., Adrian, Michigan, 1934-1938
Career: Teacher, various schools in Michigan, 1938-1959

Writings: *Savina the Gypsy Dancer* Macmillan 1991. *The Tzar's Bird* Macmillan 1990. *Grandfather Tang's Story* Crown 1990. *Sue Patch and the Crazy Clocks* Dial 1989. *The Silver Whistle* Macmillan 1988. *The Greatest Showman on Earth* Dillon 1987. *Nothing Sticks Like a Shadow* Houghton 1984. *Charlotte and Charles* Crown 1979. *Three Foolish Tales* Crown 1979. *Badger On His Own* Crown 1978. *It May Come in Handy Someday*

McGraw 1975. *Little Otter Remembers* Crown 1977. *The Clever Princess* Lollipop Power 1977. *Little Fox Goes to the End of the World* Crown 1976. *Hyacinth, The Reluctant Duck* Steck 1972. *Fun for Ozzie* Steck 1971. *The Crow, the Kite and the Golden Umbrella* Abelard 1971. *A Horse for Charlie* Whitman 1969. *The Big Whistle* Whitman 1968. *What Makes My Cat Purr?* Whitman 1965. Others. Work in Progress: Several Japanese folktales

Awards or inclusion in other biographical books: *Contemporary Authors; Michigan Authors,* 2nd ed.; *Something about the Author;* Wilson's Biographical Series. *Little Fox Goes to the End of the World:* ALA Notable Book, 1976; Best of the Best 1966-1978,*School Library Journal;* Honors, Children's Reading Round Table of Chicago. *Little Otter Remembers:* Classroom Choice, International Reading Association. *Charlotte and Charles,* runner-up, Irma Simonton Black Award, 1980; Woodward Park School Annual Award, 1980. *The Silver Whistle:* Notable Children's Trade Books in the Field of Social Studies, Children's Book Council, 1988. *Grandfather Tang's Story:* Notable Children's Trade Books in the Field of Social Studies, 1990; Nominated for Golden Sower Award, 1990. *Savina, The Gypsy Dancer* Pick of the List, American Booksellers Association, 1991

What is the aim or goal of your writing? "My main aim in writing is to tell a good story, to entertain. And, if, by chance, the reader learns a little, grows a little, gains a little insight and becomes a better person, that will be an added bonus."

May inquiries be sent to you about doing workshops, readings? Yes

TREBILCOCK, DOROTHY E.

Address: 109 N. Gaylord Ave., Ludington, Michigan 49431

Born: July 8, 1926; Lansing, Michigan

Parents: Harold H. Warner, Grace H. Warner

Children: Amy, Robert (Husband: James, deceased)

Education: Sexton High School, Lansing, Michigan, 1944. Oberlin Conservatory of Music, Oberlin, Ohio, 1944-1946. Michigan State University, East Lansing, Michigan, B.A., 1946-1948, M.A.,1971-1973

Career: Professor, Department of English, Yonsei University, Seoul, Korea, 1990—. Writer in the Schools, Michigan Council for the Arts, Michigan, 1975-1990. Part-time teacher: Michigan State University (off campus), West Shore Community College, Saginaw Valley State University, Delta College. Advisor to *Korea: Land of the Morning Calm*

Writings: *Shield of Innocence* Major Books 1978. Various sociological studies, published in Sociology Department, Michigan State University, 1974-1976. Short fiction, articles, poetry. In *Jack and Jill, Korea Times Newspaper, Instructor, Far East Traveler, Sailing,* others. About 400 pieces. Work in Progress: *All My Mr. Kims*, Korean students at Yonsei University

What is the aim or goal of your writing? "I think basically the goal of my writing is to share-ideas, exeriences, hopes, dreams-etc. with others. In writing workshops and classes I try to show students how valid writing comes from themselves-their <u>individual</u> response to the world and the people around them."

May inquiries be sent to you about doing workshops, readings? Yes

TRIPLETT, DAWN E.
Address: 306 S. Spruce, P.O. Box 822, Kalkaska, Michigan 49646
Born: September 10, 1951; Grayling, Michigan
Parents: Donald B. DePeel, Katherine F. (Bluer) DePeel
Children: Jennifer, Michael, Brandy
Education: Kalkaska Public Schools, Kalkaska, Michigan, graduated 1969. Northwestern Michigan College, Traverse City, Michigan, 1987-1989
Career: Secretary, Erb Lumber Company, Kalkaska, Michigan, 1991—. Secretary, First Christian Church, Traverse City, Michigan, 1988-1990. Secretary (Marketing), Cherryland Mall, Traverse City, Michigan, 1988. Bakery Worker, Northland Foods, Kalkaska, Michigan, 1986-1988

Writings: *Church of Christ at Barker Creek and Rapid City, Michigan* Kinseeker Publications 1990. Work in Progress: *Barker Creek, Michigan: A Ghost Town*
What is the aim or goal of your writing? "My goal in this kind of writing is to preserve family and area history. I have had articles published in Christian magazines. The purpose of those articles was to inspire people to either live a better life or to encourage them to keep on amid life's difficulties."
May inquiries be sent to you about doing workshops, readings? No

TROJANOWSKI, CAROL H.
Address: 5653 Ventura Place, Haslett, Michigan 48840
Born: May 29, 1950; Grand Rapids, Michigan
Parents: Joseph V. Trojanowski, Lee Trojanowski
Education: Michigan State University, East Lansing, Michigan: M.A., 1978; B.A, 1972
Career: Fifth Grade Teacher, Laingsburg Community Schools, Laingsburg, Michigan, 1992—; Third Grade, Second Grade, Reading Consultant. Fourth Grade, private school, Saginaw, Michigan

Writings: *Random House Calendar for Kids: 1993* Random House 1993. *Random House Calendar for Kids: 1992* Random House 1992. *Random House Calendar for Kids: 1991* Random House 1991. *Random House Calendar for Kids 1990* Random House 1990. *Grolier Calendar for Kids 1991-1993* Book Club version of Random House Calendar. Work in Progress: *Random House Calendar for Kids: 1994. Random House Calendar for Kids: 1995*
What is the aim or goal of your writing? "Enrich parents and/or children's lives with fun, stimulating facts and activities to celebrate every day of the year."
May inquiries be sent to you about doing workshops, readings? Yes

TROUTMAN, JACQUELYN D.
Address: 48075 Colony Farm Circle, Plymouth, Michigan 48170
Pseudonym: Jackie Dalton
Born: September 10, 1928; Detroit, Michigan
Parents: John J. Dalton, Lucille E. Dalton
Children: David, Matthew, Margaret, Anne (surname, Johnson)
Education: Michigan State University, B.S., East Lansing, Michigan, 1946-1950. Wayne State University, M.Ed., Detroit, Michigan, 1975-1976
Career: Freelance writer, self-employed, Plymouth, Michigan, 1983—. Owner-partner,

Nutrition Know-How, Plymouth, Michigan, 1978-1983. Teacher, Plymouth/Canton Schools, Plymouth, Michigan, 1967-1970, 1971-1978. State Program Coordinator, Dairy Council of Michigan, Detroit, Michigan, 1970-1971. Home Service Advisor, Consumers Power Company, Freelance Corporate Trainer, Training Materials Designer

Writings: *Forbidden Treasure* Thomas Bouregy and Company 1989. *Dark Lullaby* Lynx Books 1988. Nutrition education learning activity packets. Nutrition education filmstrips. Travel articles. Work in Progress: *Puanani*, suspense novel
What is the aim or goal of your writing? "Entertainment".
May inquiries be sent to you about doing workshops, readings? Yes

TROWBRIDGE, CHARLES CHESTER (1800-1883)
Born: December 29, 1800; Albany, New York
Parents: Father was a volunteer at the Battle of Lexington
Career: Came to Detroit, 1819 becoming prominent in business affairs of Michigan as a Territory and State. Private secretary, General Cass. Secretary of the Board of Regents, University of Michigan. Took census of Michigan, 1820. Early connected with first Protestant Church in Detroit. Whig candidate for governor of Michigan, 1837. President, Oakland Railroad Company, and then the Detroit and St. Joseph Railroad Company

Writings: *Detroit, Past and Present, in Relation to Its Social and Physical Condition* (Paper read before Historical Society of Michigan) 1864. *Indian Tales of C.C. Trowbridge: Collected from Wyandots, Miamis, and Shawanoes* Green Oak Press 1986. *Meearmeear Traditions* University of Michigan Press 1938. *Shawnese Traditions* University of Michigan Press; AMS Press 1980. *With Cass in the Northwest in 1820* 1942. Others

TRUITT, GLORIA A.
Address: 332 E. Ohio Street, Marquette, Michigan 49855
Born: August 26, 1939; Laurium, Michigan
Parents: Earl E. Smith, Ellen M. (Makolin) Smith
Children: John, Laura
Education: Northern Michigan University, Marquette, Michigan, 1957-1960
Career: Promotion Manager, Public Relations Director, WLUC-TV (CBS), Marquette, Michigan, 1960-1965

Writings: *Peter Set Free* Concordia 1991. *The Raising of Jairus' Daughter* Concordia 1990. *People of the Bible and Their Prayers* Concorida 1987. *Cheerful Chad* Concordia 1985. *Noah and God's Promise* Concordia 1985. *Events of the Bible* Concordia 1984. *Places of the Bible* Concordia 1984. *People of the New Testament* Concordia 1983. *People in the Old Testament* Concordia 1983. *Nature Riddle Coloring Book: Creatures* Standard 1982. *Nature Riddle Coloring Book: Animals* Standard 1982. *Nature Riddle Coloring Book: Birds* Standard 1982. Others. Forty-eight stories and poems in several anthologies such as *The Hopeless Hen and Other Animal Tails* Victor Books 1989. Work in Progress: Several activity books under contract for Concordia. Writing for numerous children's periodicals
Awards or inclusion in other biographical books: *Contemporary Authors* Vol. 111, others. Two books selected as Best Children's Books, 1984. Numerous awards, organizations and schools
What is the aim or goal of your writing? "I try to reflect my appreciation of life. I see beauty in a lacy spider web and in the violence of a nor'wester blowing in from across Lake

Superior. I love to make-believe! 'Once Upon a Rainy Morning' I navigated a ship in the form of a laundry basket to a mysterious isle. Though I was 30 at the time, I was just as delighted with the voyage as my 3-year-old passenger. To overcome a case of writer's block at 38, I left my typewriter to shinny up a rope and sit in my son's tree house. From there I composed the 15 stories and poems that appeared in *The Peanut Butter Hamster*. In brief, I try to invoke creative imagination and a sense of discovery! For instance, so many 'big people' don't take the time to stop and think and realize what kids are doing. When a small child holds a few grains of sand to the sunlight, I understand. It isn't sand, but tiny jewels. My two E's...Entertain and Educate!"

May inquiries be sent to you about doing workshops, readings? Yes

TURNER, ARNELLA K.

Address: 4331 Hulett Road, Okemos, Michigan 48864
Born: May 22, 1917; Milwaukee, Wisconsin
Parents: Arnold L. Klug, Ella E. (Kronenberger) Klug
Children: Richard, Georgia, John
Education: Milwaukee-Downer College, B.A., Milwaukee, Wisconsin, 1934-1938. University of Wisconsin, M.A., 1938-1939. Michigan State University, East Lansing, Michigan
Career: Assistant Professor, Michigan State University, East Lansing, Michigan, 1964-1981, retired. Assistant Professor, University of Maryland Overseas Program, Taipei, Taiwan. Taipei American School, English Teacher, Taipei, Tawan, 1963-1964. College, Taipei, Taiwan, 1963-1964. Instructor, Saigon American School, Saigon, Vietnam, 1959-1961

Writings: *Victorian Criticism of American Writers, 1824-1900* Borgo Press 1990. *American Thought: The Consistency of Change* (co-editor) Michigan State University 1973. Articles in *Early American Life, Journal for Study of Midwestern Literature*
What is the aim or goal of your writing? "That it be both useful to colleagues, etc., and it be interesting to the general public."
May inquiries be sent to you about doing workshops, readings? Yes

TURNER, GORDON J.

Address: 211 S. Bailey St., Cheboygan, Michigan 49721
Born: March 18, 1906; Chatham, Ontario, Canada
Parents: Seth R. Turner, Gwendolin (Keever) Turner
Education: College of City of Detroit, Bachelor of Arts, Detroit, Michigan, 1923-1927
Career: Correspondent of *Detroit News, Detroit Free Press, Bay City Times, Grand Rapids Press, United Press, Associated Press*. Reporter, Sports Editor, City Editor, News Editor, *Cheboygan Daily Tribune*, Cheboygan, Michigan, 1927—.

Writings: *Pioneering North* Cheboygan Daily Tribune 1987
Awards or inclusion in other biographical books: Boy Scouts, Northern District Award of Merit, 1974, 1988; Northern District Troop Committeeman of the Year. Cystic Fibrosis, Greater Michigan Foundation, Volunteer of the Year, 1991. Rotary Club Boosters Award, 1991. Red Cross, for conducting program of water safety instruction at beaches throughout the county, 1951. Kiwanis Club Plaque for outstanding service in scouting, 1963. Cheboygan Sports Hall of Fame, First Inductee, 1980. Cheboygan High School Hall of Fame, 1975. Cheboygan Catholic Schools Athletic Award of Appreciation, 1986. Dads Club, Plaque of Appreciation, support to

Cheboygan Sports Program, 1978. Jaycees selectee for Citizen of Year, honorary membership. Many other awards from School Board, Kiwanis Club, Salvation Army, City Council. Municipal Bathing Beach Park named the Gordon Turner Park in his honor by the City Council
What is the aim or goal of your writing? "Book is collection of about 30 of my weekly historical articles about the Northern Michigan area."
May inquiries be sent to you about doing workshops, readings? Yes

TURRILL, DAVID A.
Address: 6194 Long Lake Road, Belding, Michigan 48809
Born: January 25, 1946; Saginaw, Michigan
Parents: Victor R. Turrill, Marjorie E. Turrill
Children: Amy, David Jr.
Education: Arthur Hill High School, Saginaw, Michigan. Saginaw Valley State University, Saginaw, Michigan, B.A.,1970-1972; M.A., 1974-1976
Career: Teacher/Director of Theatre, Belding High School, Belding, Michigan, 1991–. Teacher, Adjunct Faculty, Saginaw Valley State University, Saginaw, Michigan, 1991. Teacher/Theatre/Coach, Valley Lutheran High School, 1978-1991. St. Stephen's High School, Saginaw, Michigan, 1972-1978. United States Air Force, 1966-1970. Several workshops, lectures throughout Michigan

Writings: *Michilimackinac, A Tale of the Straits* Wilderness Publishing 1989. Work in Progress: *Noble Zealot, A Novel of LaSalle. White Death*, modern murder mystery set in Michigan
What is the aim or goal of your writing? "I would like to become a full-time writer. It is my intent to increase national awareness of the rich history and bountiful natural beauty of my native state."
May inquiries be sent to you about doing workshops, readings? Yes

TYMAN, DEBORAH
Address: 613 Fountain, Ann Arbor, Michigan 48103
Pseudonym: Deborah Bayer
Born: June 21, 1951; Memphis, Tennessee
Parents: George M. Bayer, Jeanette M. Bayer
Education: Michigan State University, East Lansing, Michigan, B.A., 1969-1973; M.A., 1976-1978
Career: Instructor, Washtenaw Community College, Ann Arbor, Michigan, 1989—. Teacher, Bloomfield Hills Schools, Bloomfield Hills, Michigan, 1976-1988. Teacher, Escondido Schools, San Diego, California, 1973-1975

Writings: Stories, profile in *Iris, Paragraph Magazine, Short Fiction by Women, Greensboro Review, Hayden's Ferry Review, Special Report: Fiction, The Sacred Octagon, Women's Artist News.* Work in Progress: A novella. Collection of prose poems
Awards or inclusion in other biographical books: National Endowment for Humanities Fellowship, 1988
What is the aim or goal of your writing? "If my fiction moves a reader, even in some small way, I am grateful."
May inquiries be sent to you about doing workshops, readings? Yes

TYSH, CHRIS
Address: 2371 Pulaski, Hamtramck, Michigan 48212
Born: November 18, 1945; Paris, France
Parents: Alexandre Grodzicki, Klara (Kopilewicz) Grodzicki
Children: Julian, Bruno
Education: Lycee Victor Hugo, B.A., Paris, France, 1959-1966. Sorbonne, M.A., Paris, France, 1966-1969
Career: Lecturer, Wayne State University, Detroit, Michigan, 1989—. Instructor, Center for Creative Studies, Detroit, Michigan, 1981-1989. Instructor, Weekend College, Wayne State University, Detroit, Michigan, 1974-1976

Writings: *In the Name* Past Tents 1992. *Coat of Arms* Station Hill 1992. *Porne* In Camera 1984. *Secrets of Elegance* Detroit River Press 1981. *Allen Ginsberg* Pierre Sechers (France) 1974. *Julie or the Rose,* French translation1979, Transgravity Press (England). Included in anthologies such as *Hipology* Broadside Press 1990. Work in Progress: *Francois/e*
Awards or inclusion in other biographical books: Michigan Council for the Arts Grant, 1987
What is the aim or goal of your writing? "For me, writing is linked with a certain inevitable sedition, an incitement to resistance, something that seduces, arouses, leads astray from the docile flowers, softening bones of communication. The unlawful (incite) becomes erotic (excite). I travel in and out, I separate, I refuse to gather my skirts. A poem, then? Yes, already treason and punishment, ravishing; a haunted place from which, insatiable and troping judas, I stage and police the ceaseless comings and goings of my desires. But who am I? What is my ideological situation (place of work, conditions of production, my status as a woman)? It would be utterly foolish to imagine that my desires and poems live in a state of grace, sealed off from history, economy and the cultural cross-hatchings of gender. Writing, understood as a gendered textual practice cuts through this hypothetical hymen. Its encounter (read its contamination) with the ideological body generates a new object, inscribed and already erased, disfiguring both bodies yet neither, only different, disturbing the mania to assemble, put under the sign of mimesis; the bearded plot of identity and memory."
May inquiries be sent to you about doing workshops, readings? Yes

TYSH, GEORGE K.
Address: 2371 Pulaski, Hamtramck, Michigan 48212
Born: September 9, 1942; Passaic, New Jersey
Parents: Walter Tysh, Helen Tysh
Children: Julian, Bruno
Education: Wayne State University, Detroit, Michigan, B.A., 1960-1965; M.A., 1988-1991
Career: Lecturer, Wayne State University, Detroit, Michigan, 1992—. Assistant Curator of Education, Detroit Institute of Arts, Detroit, Michigan, 1980-1991. Poet in the Schools, Colorado Council on the Arts and Humanities, Denver, Colorado, 1976-1979. Lecturer in Humanities, Wayne State University, College of Lifelong Learning, Detroit, Michigan, 1974-1976

Writings: *Echolalia* United Artists Books 1992. *Ovals* In Camera 1985. *Tea* Burning Deck 1979. *Shop/Posh* Burning Deck 1973. *Mecanorgane* Burning Deck 1971. *Cheapness Means Forgiveness* Sand Project Press (France)1970. *Sit Up Straight* Artists

Workshop Press 1965. *Julie or the Rose* translated from the French of Guilloume Apollinaire, with Chris Tysh, Transgravity Press (England) 1979.

Work in Progress: Collection (untitled yet) of poetry

Awards or inclusion in other biographical books: National Endowment for the Arts, Creative Writing Fellowship Grant, 1979

What is the aim or goal of your writing? "To explore the connections between the formal and the lyrical on the one hand and the visible and the unconscious on the other; to write the music of the libido."

May inquiries be sent to you about doing workshops, readings? Yes

U

UMSCHEID, CHRISTINE M.
Address: 149 Washington Street, Petoskey, Michigan 49770
Pseudonym: Christina-Marie
Born: January 28, 1946; Weiden, West Germany
Parents: Alfred T. Hoffman, Barbara B. Hoffman
Children: Joyelle, Heidi
Education: Notre Dame High School, diploma, St. Louis, Missouri. Meramac Junior College, Associate, St. Louis, Missouri, 1969. North Central Michigan College, Associate in Liberal Arts, with high honors, Petoskey, Michigan, 1984
Career: Registered Nurse, Petoskey, Michigan, 1976—. Visiting Poet, Lake Linden-Hubbell, Michigan. Guest Poet, North Central Michigan College, 1976-1989. Visiting Poet, Houghton High School. Creative Writers in the Schools, 1990-1992

Writings: *Portraits* Snow Owl Press 1977. In *The Small Pond Magazine, Sou'wester, Huron Review, Passages North, Great Lakes Review, Negative Capability, The Poetry Review, Odyssey, Caliban, Chicago Review, MacGuffin.* Work in Progress: *Rituals. From the Belly of Jonah's Whale. From Where We Come/To Where We Go*
Awards or inclusion in other biographical books: *A Directory of American Poets and Fiction Writers* 1980-1981, 1984, 1985, 1986, 1990. *Directory of Active Michigan Poets* Poetry Society of Michigan 1982. *International Authors and Writers Who's Who* 1982. Scholarship, Cranbrook Writer's Conference, 1984. Residency, Ragdale Foundation, 1991
What is the aim or goal of your writing? "Over all, my goal with poetry has been to write poems that have power and meaning in as few words as possible. My poems do not ramble. They reflect my belief in seeking meanings beyond the first impression. *From the Belly of Jonah's Whale* deals with death and dying issues. *From Where We Come* deals with inner peace and strength."
May inquiries be sent to you about doing workshops, readings? Yes

URIST, RACHELLE Z.
Address: 310 Awixa, Ann Arbor, Michigan 48104
Pseudonym: Rachel Feldbin Urist
Born: March 22, 1949; Brooklyn, New York
Parents: Abraham Feldbin, Betty Feldbin
Education: University of Michigan, M.A., Ann Arbor, Michigan, 1968-1969; Ph.D. Candidate in Comparative Literature, 1991. Queens College of The City of New York, B.A.,1966-1968
Career: Freelance writer. Theatre critic for *The Ann Arbor News,* 1981-1984. Theatre critic/commentator, WUOM/WVGR, FM radio, 1977-1981. Resident theatre critic for "Ann Arbor Tonight", Ann Arbor cable television, 1981. Instructor, University of Michigan, 1972-1975. Artist in residence, Midrasha College for Jewish Studies, 1986. Writer in residence, Brooklyn, Michigan, public schools, 1990. Commissioned by various groups. Play Director

Writings: *Shtetl Tales,* a play published in *Playwrights Companion* Feedback Theatrebooks 1986. Plays written: *The Talking Cure. A Pound of Feathers* (musical adaptation of *Shtetl Tales* in collaboration with Andrew Lippa, Tom Greenwald. *Off and Running. Going Up. Thin Ice. Oral Hygiene. Blueprints. The Whipping Boy. The Three Wishes. Just Friends. Worlds Torn Asunder. Tales of Wit and Wisdom. Solomon Williams. Consequences. Collaborations.* Work in Progress: A screenplay. *The Sentimental Father,* a play
Awards or inclusion in other biographical books: Finalist, 5th Annual City Lights Theatre Playwriting Contest, 1990. Finalist, IUPUI Playwriting Contest, 1989. Finalist, Jacksonville University Playwriting competition, 1987; winner 1984. U-M Flint, Playwriting competition, 1981. First prize, John Gassner Memorial Playwriting competition, 1982-1983. Individual Creative Artist Award, Michigan Council for the Arts, 1984, 1990. Grant, Michigan Council for the Humanities, 1985. F S Drama Award with publication in *The Playwrights Companion,* 1986. Individual Creative Artist Award, Michigan Council for the Arts, 1987.
What is the aim or goal of your writing? "Production-stage or screen".
May inquiries be sent to you about doing workshops, readings? Yes

UTLEY, HENRY MUNSON (1836-1917)
Born: August 5, 1836; Plymouth, Michigan
Parents: Hiran Utley, Jane (Sands) Utley
Education: University of Michigan, Ann Arbor, Michigan, A.B., 1861; A.M., 1870
Career: Staff, *Detroit Free Press,* 1861-1866. City editor, *Detroit Post, Post-Tribune,* 1866-1881. Secretary, Detroit Board of Education, 1881-1885. City Librarian, 1885-1913, Detroit, Michigan

Writings: *General Catalogue of the Books, Except Fiction, French, and German, in the Public Library of Detroit, Michigan 1888* O.S. Gulley, Bornman & Company 1889. *The Class of Sixty-One, University of Michigan and Something about What 'the Boys' have been Doing During Forty Years from 1861 to 1901* J. Bornman & Son 1902. *Wildcat Banking in Michigan* 1875. *The First President of Michigan University* 1882. *Michigan as a Province, Territory and State, the Twenty-Sixth Member of the Federal Union* The Publishing Society of Michigan 1906
Awards or inclusion in other biographical books: *Who Was Who in America*

V

VACHON, JENNY M.
Address: P.O. Box 42A, Toivola, Michigan 49965
Pseudonym: Jingo Viitala Vachon
Born: May 29, 1918; Toivola, Michigan
Parents: Erick Viitala, Elina (Makinen) Viitala
Children: Erik, Clara, John, Phillip, Pamela, Victor, Helmi
Education: Eighth grade diploma, one room grade school, Misery Bay area, Toivola, Michigan, 1931. Eight weeks typing course, St. Ignace High School, St. Ignace, Michigan
Career: Upper Peninsula correspondent/columnist, *Lapeer County Press,* Lapeer, Michigan, 1965-1970. Columnist/Cartoonist/Reporter, *Weekly Wave,* Hessel, Michigan, 1960—. Columnist/Cartoonist/Reporter *Republican News,* St. Ignace, Michigan, 1960's-1970's. Columnist/Cartoonist *L'Anse Sentinel,* L'Anse, Michigan. Columnist/cartoonist, *Amerikan Uutiset* (Finnish language weekly). *Chugiak Eagle River Star*

Writings: *Finnish Fibbles, The L'Anse Sentinel* 1979. *Sagas From Sisula, The L'Anse Sentinel* 1975. *Tall Timber Tales, The L'Anse Sentinel* 1973. Poetry in *The Anthology of Verse of the U.P.* First poetry,*Wild West Weekly* a nationwide magazine, in 1932. Stories in foreign publications. Work in Progress: Historical novel
Awards or inclusion in other biographical books: *Michigan Authors,* 2nd ed. Several awards
What is the aim or goal of your writing? "I wanted the country to see the heart and soul of the poor hard working immigrant Finns who carved homes out of the U.P. wilderness, and because I was a little fed up with always reading about some rich famous high-nose cultured educated mogul. I wanted others to see that we weren't dumb, stupid, and ignorant just because we lived far back in the woods. And we did have loads of fun between hard work! It's exactly why I am back here after living all over the country for almost 40 years."
May inquiries be sent to you about doing workshops, readings? No

VAN ALLSBURG, CHRIS
Born: June 18, 1949; Grand Rapids, Michigan
Parents: Richard Van Allsburg, Chris Van Allsburg
Education: University of Michigan, B.F.A., Ann Arbor, Michigan, 1972. Rhode Island School of Design, M. F. A., Providence, Rhode Island, 1975
Career: Teacher, Rhode Island School of Design, 1977—. Works exhibited at: Whitney Museum of American Art, New York, New York; Museum of Modern Art, New York, New York; Grand Rapids Art Museum, Grand Rapids, Michigan; Alan Stone Gallery, New York, New York, others

Writings: (self-illustrated) *The Garden of Abdul Gasazi* Houghton Mifflin 1979; L'Ecole des Loisirs 1982; Division 1988; Random House 1988. *Jumanji* Houghton Mifflin 1981; Random House 1988; Scholastic 1988. *Ben's Dream* Houghton Mifflin 1982; Made-to-Order 1990. *The Wreck of the Zephyr* Houghton Mifflin 1983. *The Mysteries of Harris Burdick* Houghton Mifflin 1984; L'Ecole des Loisirs 1985; Spoken Arts 1988. *The Polar Express* Houghton Mifflin 1985, 1989; National Braille 1991; Listening Library 1989;

Random House 1988; others. *The Stranger* Houghton Mifflin 1986. *The Alphabet Theatre Proudly Presents the Z Was Zapped: A Play in Twenty-Six Acts* Houghton Mifflin 1987; Spoken Arts 1988. *Two Bad Ants* Houghton Mifflin 1988. *Swan Lake* Houghton Mifflin 1989. *El Expreso Polar* Edicones Ekar 1990, 1991. *The Wretched Stone* Houghton Mifflin 1991. *Just a Dream* Houghton Mifflin 1990; Scholastic 1992. *The Widow's Broom* Houghton Mifflin 1992. *4 Strange Stories* Houghton Mifflin 1992. Many adaptations on cassettes, filmstrips

Awards or inclusion in other biographical books:*Fifth Book of Junior Authors and Illustrators; Newbery and Caldecott Medal Books; Something about the Author.* Caldecott Medal, 1982, 1986. Several ALA Notable Books. Several *Horn Book* Honor List Books. New York Public Library's Children's Books, 1983, 1985. Awards from: Child Study Association, Northern Kentucky University, Parents' Choice Foundation, International Board on Books, Bank Street College of Education, *New York Times*, *Redbook*, many others

VAN EVERY, DALE (1896-1976)
Born: July 23, 1896; Levering, Michigan
Parents: Wilbert Maurice, Estella (Palmer)Van Every
Children: David, Joan
Education: Stanford University, A.B., Stanford, California, 1920
Career: United Press International, New York, New York and Washington, DC, correspondent and editor, 1920-1928. Writer and producer for various motion picture studios in Hollywood, California, 1928-1943. Freelance writer, 1943-1976. Served in U.S. Army Ambulance Service, 1917-1919

Writings: *The A.E.F.in Battle* Appleton 1928.*Westward the River* Putnam 1945. *The Shining Mountains* Messner 1948. *Bridal Journey* Messner 1950, Bantam 1976. *The Captive Witch* Messner 1951.*The Trembling Earth* Messner 1953, Popular Library 1975. *Men of the Western Waters* Houghton 1954. *The Voyagers* Holt 1957. *Our Country Then* (anthology) Holt 1958.*The Scarlet Feather* Holt 1959. Frontier People of America Series, 4 vols: *Forth to the Wilderness: The First American Frontier1754-1774* Morrow 1961; New American Library 1962; Arno 1977. *A Company of Heroes: The First American Frontier 1775-1783* Morrow 1962; New American Library 1963; Arno 1977. *Ark of Empire: The American Frontier 1784-1803* Morrow 1963; New American Library 1964. *The Final Challenge: The American Frontier 1804-1845* Morrow 1964; New American Library, 1965. *Disinherited: The Lost Birthright of the American Indian* Morrow 1966.*The Day the Sun Died* Little, Brown 1971. Editor of *The First American Frontier*
Awards or inclusion in other biographical books: *American Authors and Books; American Novelists of Today; Contemporary Authors; Reader's Encyclopedia of the American West; Who's Who in America.* Commonwealth Club of California Awards for 5 books. Colonial Dames of America Award for contribution of outstanding excellence to the field of American colonial history, 1962

VAN HOOSEN, BERTHA (1863-1952)
Born: March 26, 1863; Rochester, Michigan
Parents: Joshua Van Hoosen, Sarah Ann (Taylor) Van Hoosen
Education: University of Michigan, B.A., Ann Arbor, Michigan, 1884; M.D., 1888
Career: Founder, First President of American Medical Women's Association. Women's and Children's Hospital, Chicago, Illinois. Practiced medicine and surgery, 1892-1951.

Professor of Medicine at the Women's Medical College at Northwestern University, The University of Illinois, Loyola University of Chigago. Started a human breast-milk bank in Chicago, pioneer in prenatal care, sought cure for breast cancer. Set up her own practice in Chicago, 1892. Named Emergency Physician for the Columbian World's Fair of 1893 in Chicago. First woman to head a department of medicine in Loyola University. One of the founders, La Leche League. Pioneer in the use of scopolamine morphine anesthesia during childbirth

Writings: *Twilight Sleep* 1909. *Petticoat Surgeon* Pellegrini & Cudahy 1947; People's Book Club 1947; Edwards Brothers 1968; Arno Press 1980. Assistant editor, *Narcotic Review*

Awards or inclusion in other biographical books: *Index to Women; Who Was Who in America.* Inducted into Michigan Women's Hall of Fame, 1984. Many honorary doctorates from various universities. Named honorary member of the International Association of Medical Women

VAN OOYEN, AMY JOY

Address: 13508 N. Partridge Lane, Ironwood, Michigan 49938
Born: May 13, 1921; Netherlands
Parents: Jacob J. Hoekstra, Catherine A. (Vanderwall) Hoekstra
Children: Catherine, Anne, Janice, Peter, Judith, Eleanor, Amy, Calvin, Alvin, John
Education: Zuidhorn Leeuwarden, Registered Nurse, Netherlands, 1940-1944. Wisconsin University Extension Course. Gogebic College, Ironwood, Michigan
Career: Writer. Beekeeper. Lecturing demonstrator for students, Future Farmers of America, teachers, conferences, clubs. Traveled extensively in adoption work, Japan, Korea, Philippines, Thailand, Burma, Scandinavia, France, Italy, Holland. Board member of Holt International

Writings: *Live it U.P.* Anundsen 1991. Work in Progress: *Live it U.P. Now and Then. Concert of Life.* Appears regularly in *Above the Bridge, Peninsula People, Superior Magazine*
Awards or inclusion in other biographical books: First Place, U.P. Writers Award, 1989, 1991
What is the aim or goal of your writing? "To publish *Concert of Life* next winter 1992--1993 and *Live it U.P. Now and Then* before Christmas. Write a children's book, *BEE Funny*, ages 5-8 years old. "Write about Nature" column or articles on the outdoors."
May inquiries be sent to you about doing workshops, readings? Yes

VAN REKEN, DONALD

Address: 44 E. 15th Street, Holland, Michigan 49423
Born: May 17, 1920; Clifton, New Jersey
Parents: Henry Van Reken, Louise W. DeWaal Malefyt Van Reken
Children: Mary, Judith, Donna, Mark, Margaret
Education: Calvin College, A.B., Grand Rapids, Michigan, 1940-1948. University of Chicago, Chicago, Illinois. University of Michigan, Ann Arbor, Michigan
Career: Librarian, Holland Christian High School, Holland, Michigan, 1965-1985, retired. Teacher, Timothy Christian School, Cicero, Illinois, 1958-1965. Missionary Teacher, Christian Reformed World Missions, M Karvia Makurdi, Nigeria, 1950-1958

Writings: *Macatawa Park: A Chronicle* self-published 1991. *A Window to the Past* self-

published 1988. *Ottawa Beach and Waukangoo* self-published 1987. *Changing Footprints (Holland Christian Schools)* self-published 1987. *The Farm That was a Zoo (Getz Farm)* self-published 1983. *The Holland Fire of October 8, 1871* self-published 1982. *The Interurban Era in Holland, Michigan* self-published 1981. *Macatawa, An Historic View* self-published 1979. *A Brief History of Holland, Michigan* self-published 1977, 1973. *32nd Troop Carrier Squadron (WWII)* self-published 1989
What is the aim or goal of your writing? "To preserve and enhance the local history of Holland, Michigan."

VAN RIPER, CHARLES G.
Address: 3821 W. Milham, Kalamazoo, Michigan 49002
Pseudonym: Cully Gage
Born: December 1, 1905
Education: University of Iowa, Ph.D., Iowa City, Iowa, 1934
Career: Professor, Speech Pathology, Western Michigan University, Kalamazoo, Michigan, 1936-1976

Writings: *Old Bones and Northern Memories* Avery 1991. *And Still Another* Avery 1989. *A Love Affair With the U.P.* Avery 1988. *What? Another Northwoods Reader* Avery 1987. *The Last Northwoods Reader* Avery 1984. *Heads and Tales* Avery 1982. *Tales of the Old U.P.* Avery 1981. *The Northwoods Reader* Avery 1979. *My Father, Dr. Van* Marquette Historical Society 1982. Thirty textbooks on speech pathology
What is the aim or goal of your writing? "Fun and money."
May inquiries be sent to you about doing workshops, readings? No

VANDE ZANDE, JOHN M.
ADDRESS: 823 Grove Street, Marquette, Michigan 49855
Born: January 26, 1938; Big Bay, Michigan
Parents: Charles W. Vande Zande, Thelma B. Vande Zande
Children: John, Audrey, Jeffrey
Education: Northern Michigan University, B.A., Marquette, Michigan, 1957-1962. Michigan State University, M.A., East Lansing, Michigan, 1963-1964
Career: Professor of English, Northern Michigan University, Marquette, Michigan, 1964—.

Writings: *Night Driving: Stories* William Morrow 1990. Work in Progress: Novel in circulation by agent
Awards or inclusion in other biographical books: Chautauqua Literary award and prize, 1990. Award for best fiction, *Michigan Quarterly Review,* University of Michigan and story reprinted in *The Third Coast: Contemporary Michigan Fiction*
What is the aim or goal of your writing? "To write as well as I am able."
May inquiries be sent to you about doing workshops, readings? Yes

VANDENBERG, ARTHUR H. (1884-1951)
Born: March 22, 1884; Grand Rapids, Michigan
Parents: Aaron Vandenberg, Alpha (Hendrick) Vandenberg
Children: Barbara, Elizabeth, Arthur Hendrick
Education: Grand Rapids High School, 1900. Attended University of Michigan
Career: Cracker factory work, copy boy, reporter, editor, publisher, Grand Rapids, Michigan, *Herald.* Staff, *Collier's,* New York. Member: Grand Rapids Charter Commission, Michigan Republican Central Committee. United States Senator, 1928-1951

Writings: *Alexander Hamilton, the Greatest American; an Historical Analysis of His Life and Works Together with a Symposium of Opinions by Distinguished Americans* G.P. Putnam's Sons 1921. *If Hamilton Were Here Today; American Fundamentals Applied to Modern Problems* G.P. Putnam's Sons 1923. *The Trail of a Tradition* G.P. Putnam's Sons 1925. *The Private Papers of Senator Vandenberg* Houghton Mifflin 1952. Short stories appeared in *Lippincott's, Pearson's* magazines
Awards or inclusion in other biographical books: *Current Biography; International Who's Who; Who's Who in America; World Biography.* Collier's Award for Distinguished Congressional Service, 1946. Freedom Award, Freedom House, 1948. Roosevelt Medal of Honor, 1948. Honorary LL.D., Columbia University, 1948

VIRCH, PATRICIA D.
Address: 1506 Lynn Ave., Marquette, Michigan 49855
Pseudonym: Pat Virch
Born: September 29, 1926; Murdo, South Dakota
Parents: William H. Draeger, Laura T. (Larsen) Draeger
Children: Margaret Conover, Rosemary Michelin, William Virch, Julie Dupras
Education: Oconto (Wisconsin) High School. Seven years of seminars, Norwegian American Museum, Decorah, Iowa
Career: Writer. Artist

Writings: *Swedish Folk Painting of Dalarna* Nordic Publishers 1981. *Rosemaling Norwegian Folk Art Fun* Nordic Publishers 1983. *Traditional Rosemaling Telemark Techniques* Nordic Publishers 1979. *Decorated Tinware An Early American Folk Art* Nordic Publishers 1977. *Rosemaling in the Round* Nordic Publishers 1976
Awards or inclusion in other biographical books: *Michigan Authors,* 2nd ed. Gold medal of honor for techniques of Norwegian rosemaling, Norwegian American Museum, 1974 (currently 23 people have achieved this level of excellence in the United States). Biographical sketches in *Norwegian Rosemaling in America* 1986; *Treasury of Decorative Painting* 1986; *Celebrity Sampler of Decorative Painting* 1987; *Family Creative Workshop* 1975
What is the aim or goal of your writing? "I write instruction books about the folk arts to enable others to try their hand at painting these charming forms of decorations. I always give the history of the origins of these folk arts."
May inquiries be sent to you about doing workshops, readings? Yes

VIS, WILLIAM RYERSON (1886-1969)
Born: August 17, 1886; Drenthe, Michigan
Parents: Ryer Vis, Nancy Vis
Children: Vincent
Education: University of Michigan, M.D., 1916
Career: Practicing physician, Internal Medicine, 52 years, Grand Rapids, Michigan

Writings: *Saddlebag Doctor* Eerdmans 1964
Awards or inclusion in other biographical books: *Michigan Authors,* 2nd ed. *National Cyclopaedia of American Biography*

VLASOPOLOS, ANCA

Address: 820 Notre Dame, Grosse Pointe, Michigan 48230
Born: October 14, 1948; Bucharest, Rumania
Parents: Paul Vlasopolos, Hermina (Grunberg) Vlasopolos
Children: Olivia
Education: Wayne State University, B.A., with high distinction and honors in English, Detroit, Michigan, 1966-1970. University of Michigan, Ann Arbor, Michigan, M.A., Ph.D., in comparative literature, 1970-1977
Career: Instructor of English, Wayne State University, Detroit, Michigan, 1974-1977; Assistant Professor, 1977-1983; Associate Professor of English, 1983—. Director, Women's Studies Program, 1991—. Co-editor, *Moving Out* (oldest continuing feminist literary magazine)

Writings: *Missing Members* Corridors Press 1990. *Evidence of Spring* Ridgeway Press 1989. *Symbolic Method of Coleridge, Baudelaire, and Yeats* Wayne State University Press 1983. Over forty poems in such magazines as *Seneca Review, Interim, Wascana Review, Spoon River Quarterly.* Work in Progress: *Oral Transgressions: A Memoir. A Little Elf Won't Hurt You: Sequel to Missing Members. Cracking Masks: Violence and Anti-Generic Theater*
Awards or inclusion in other biographical books: *Michigan Council of the Arts Directory of Scholars; Who's Who among Writers in the Midwest*
What is the aim or goal of your writing? "To make people reflect about their views and possibly to change them: to give readers pleasure through the art of writing."
May inquiries be sent to you about doing workshops, readings? Yes

VOELKER, JOHN DONALDSON (1903-1991)

Pseudonym: Robert Traver
Born: June 29, 1903; Ishpeming, Michigan
Parents: George Oliver, Annie (Traver) Voelker
Children: Elizabeth, Julie, Grace
Education: Northern Michigan College, Marquette, Michigan, 1922-1924. University of Michigan, L.L.B., Ann Arbor, Michigan, 1928
Career: Prosecuting Attorney, Marquette County, Michigan, 1934-1952. Supeme Court Justice, State of Michigan, 1957-1960

Writings: *Trouble Shooter* Viking 1943. *Danny and the Boys; Being Some Legends of Hungry Hollow* World Publishing 1951; Wayne State University Press 1987. *Small Town D.A.* Dutton 1954. *Anatomy of a Murder* St. Martins Press 1957, 1958, 1983; Dell 1959; Ullstein (Berlin) 1959; was Book-of-the-Month-Club; as a film it won seven Academy Awards).*Trout Madness* St. Martins Press 1960. *Horstein's Boy* St. Martins Press 1962. *Anatomy of Fisherman* McGraw 1964. *Laughing Whitefish* McGraw-Hill 1965.*The Jealous Mistress* Little, Brown 1967, 1968.*Trout Magic* Crown 1974. *People versus Kirk* 1981. Stories in *Story, Prairie Schooner, Hinterland.* Articles, essays, book reviews
Awards or inclusion in biographical books:*American Authors and Books; Contemporary Authors; International Authors and Writers Who's Who; Michigan Authors,* 1st ed., 2nd ed.,*Who's Who in America; World Authors; Writers Directory.* Mark Twain Award for Distinguished Contributions to Mid-Western Literature, Society for the Study of Midwestern Literature, 1983

WAGNER-MARTIN, LINDA

Born: August 18, 1936; St. Marys, Ohio
Parents: Sam A. Wagner, Esther (Scheffler) Welshimer
Children: Paul, Thomas, Andrea
Education: Bowling Green State University, B.A., magna cum laude, Bowling Green, Ohio, 1957; M.A., 1959; Ph.D., 1963
Career: English teacher, Michigan and Ohio. Instructor, Bowling Green State University, Bowling Green, Ohio, 1960-1964. Wayne State University, Detroit, Michigan, 1966-1968. Michigan State University, East Lansing, 1968-1971; Associate Dean, College of Arts and Letters, 1979—

Writings: *The Poems of William Carlos Williams: A Critical Study* Wesleyan University Press 1964. *Intaglios: Poems* South & West 1967. *The Prose of William Carlos Williams* Wesleyan University 1970. *Phyllis McGinley* Twayne 1970. *William Faulkner: Four Decades of Criticism* Michigan State University Press 1973. *Ernest Hemingway: Five Decades of Criticism* Michigan State University Press 1974. *T.S. Eliot: a Collection of Criticism* McGraw-Hill 1974. *Introducing Poems* (with C. David Mead) Harper 1976. *"Speaking Straight Ahead": Interviews with William Carlos Williams* New Directions 1976. *Ernest Hemingway: A Reference Guide* G.K. Hall 1977. *Robert Frost: The Critical Heritage* Burt Franklin 1977. *Hemingway and Faulkner: Inventors / Masters* Scarecrow 1975. *Critical Essays on Joyce Carol Oates* G.K. Hall 1979. *Dos Passos: Artist as American* University of Texas Press 1979. *American Modern Selected Essays in Poetry and Fiction* Kennikat Press 1980. *Critical Essays on Sylvia Plath* G.K. Hall 1984. *Critical Essays on Anne Sexton* G.K. Hall 1989. *Critical Essays on Denise Levertov* G. K. Hall 1990. Others. Several essays, poems in *Kenyon Review, Shakespeare Quarterly, Minnesota Review,* others
Awards or inclusion in other biographical books: *Contemporary Authors; Michigan Authors,* 2nd ed. In the 2nd Edition of *Michigan Authors* appears: "I teach writing, criticism, and literature classes at Michigan State, believing that all three are inter-related-must be inter-related-and the same conviction shows in my own writing."

WAKEFIELD, LAWRENCE M.

Address: Box 7930 W. Bay Shore Road, Traverse City, Michigan 49684
Pseudonym: Larry Wakefield
Born: May 5, 1914; Grand Rapids, Michigan
Parents: Earle M. Wakefield, Nell E. (Ball) Wakefield
Children: Philip, James
Education: Oberlin College, 1932-1935, Oberlin, Ohio
Career: Chief copy writer, Mason-Warner Ad Agency, Chicago, Illinois, 1936-1937. Reporter, *Pontiac News*, Pontiac, Michigan, 1938-1939. Advertising Manager, *Traverse City Bay News,* Traverse City, Michigan, 1974-1975. Freelance writer, Traverse City, Michigan, 1976—. Editor,*Grand Traverse Business,* 1989—

Writings: *Traverse City Postcard History* Grand Traverse Pioneer Society 1992. *Butcher's Dozen, 13 Famous Michigan Murders* Atwerger & Mandel 1991. *Queen City of the North* Village Press 1988. *Elmwood Township History* Elmwood Township 1987. *Cherry Festival History* Wayne O'Connell & Assoc. 1987. *Sail & Rail* Empire National Bank 1980. *Historic Traverse City Houses* Empire National Bank 1978. *Mystery of the Missing Nun* Wakefield 1977. *All Our Yesterdays* Empire National Bank 1977. Work in Progress: *Leelanau County Postcard History. Ghost Towns of Michigan*

What is the aim or goal of your writing? "I want to write at least two more books on various Michigan history subjects. I sold my first short story to *Esquire* magazine and was named "Esquire Discovery of the Month" in September 1936. Recently I've returned to short story writing, and my goal is to write a short story as good as James Joyce's "The Dead" or Tolstoy's "Death of Ivan Ilych". This may not happen-probably won't-because I consider these the two best short stories ever written, but it's my goal."

May inquiries be sent to you about doing workshops, readings? Yes

WAKOSKI, DIANE

Address: 607 Division Street, East Lansing, Michigan 48823
Born: August 3, 1937; Whittier, California
Parents: John J. Wakoski, Marie E. Wakoski
Education: University of California: Berkeley, B.A., Berkeley, California, 1956-1960
Career: University Distinguished Professor, Michigan State University, East Lansing, Michigan, 1976—. Visiting writer to several colleges and universities

Writings: *Medea the Sorceress* (volume I, *The Archaeology of Movies & Books*) Black Sparrow Press 1991. *Emerald Ice: Selected Poems 1962-1987* Black Sparrow Press. *The Rings of Saturn* Black Sparrow Press 1986. *The Collected Greed: Parts I-XIII* Black Sparrow Press 1984. *The Magician's Feastletters* Black Sparrow Press 1982. *Cap of Darkness* Black Sparrow Press 1980. *The Man Who Shook Hands* Doubleday 1978. *Waiting for the King of Spain* Black Sparrow Press 1976. *Virtuoso Literature for Two and Four Hands* Doubleday 1975. *Smudging* Black Sparrow Press 1972. *The Motorcycle Betrayal Poems* Simon & Schuster 1971. *The Magellanic Clouds* Black Sparrow Press 1970. *Inside the Blood Factory* Doubleday 1968. *The George Washington Poems* Riverrun Press 1967. *Discrepancies & Apparitions* Doubleday 1966. *Coins & Coffins* Hawk's Well Press 1962. *Toward a New Poetry* University of Michigan (Poets On Poetry Series) 1980. Poems translated into Romanian by Liliana Ursu in *Norii Magelanici* Editura Univers Bucharest 1982. Others. Included in several anthologies and reference works such as *The Norton Anthology of Modern Poetry* and *The Practical Imagination: An Introduction to Poetry*. Work in Progress: *Jason the Sailor* (book II of *The Archaeology of Movies and Books* to be published by Black Sparrow Press. Over twenty-five volumes published by small presses in limited, signed editions

Awards or inclusion in other biographical books: In several, including *Who's Who in America*. Winner, William Carlos Williams Prize, PSA. Dorothy Churchill Cappon Essay Award, Runner Up, *New Letters* Literary Awards. Michigan Arts Foundation Distinguished Artist Award, 1989. Michigan State University Distinguished Faculty Award, 1989. Michigan Arts Council Grant, 1988. Writer's Fulbright Award, Yugoslavia, 1984. USIA Tour, Romania, Yugoslavia, Hungary, 1976. CAPS Grant, New York State, 1974. National Endowment for the Arts Grant, 1973. Guggenheim Foundation Grant, 1972. Cassandra Foundation Grant, 1970

What is the aim or goal of your writing? "The quest for beauty."

May inquiries be sent to you about doing workshops, readings? Yes

WALDMEIR, JOSEPH J.

Address:1377 Biscayne, Haslett, Michigan 48840
Born: December 12, 1923; Detroit, Michigan
Parents: Joseph J. Waldmeir, Helen S. (Seurynck) Waldmeir
Children: John
Education: Wayne State University, B.A., Detroit, Michigan, 1946-1948. University of Michigan, M.A., Ann Arbor, Michigan, 1948-1949. Michigan State University, Ph.D., East Lansing, Michigan, 1953-1959
Career: Professor Emeritus, Michigan State University, 1990—; Professor of English, 1965-1990. Instructor, English Department, University of Detroit, Detroit, Michigan, 1950-1953

Writings: *American Novels of the Second World War* Mouton 1968. *Recent American Fiction: Some Critical Views* (editor) Houghton, Mifflin 1963. *Essays in Honor of Russel B. Nye* (editor) Michigan State University Press 1978. *Up in Michigan: Papers of the National Conference of the Hemingway Society* (editor) East Lansing 1984.
Articles in *The Nation, Modern Fiction Studies, Wisconsin Studies in Contemporary Literature*, others. Numerous papers at scholarly conferences: "And the Wench Was Faith and Value", second International Conference of the Hemingway Society, Lignano, Italy-to be included in collection of essays edited by Jackson Blenson, Duke University Press. Essay, "Confiteor Hominem: Ernest Hemingway's Religion of Man", multiple reprints. Work in Progress: *Hemingway: Up in Michigan II* (editor) Michigan State University Press. *Critical Essays of Truman Capote* (co-editor) G.K. Hall
Awards or inclusion in other biographical books: Fulbright Professor, University of Helsinki, 1963-1964. Fulbright Professor, University of Copenhagen, 1967-1968
What is the aim or goal of your writing? "To share the results of my scholarship and research."
May inquiries be sent to you about doing workshops, readings? Yes

WALDRON, WEBB (1882-1945)

Born: September 8, 1882; Vergennes, Michigan
Parents: William A. Waldron, Alice (Hubbs) Waldron
Children: Patricia
Education: University of Michigan, A.B., Ann Arbor, Michigan, 1905
Career: Teaching, travel, ranching, western states, 1905-1911. Advertising writer, New York, 1911-1916. Associate Editor, *Collier's Weekly,* 1917-1918; European Editor, 1918-1920. Staff Writer, *Reader's Digest*

Writings: *The Road to the World* Century 1922. *We Explore the Great Lakes* Century 1923. *Blue Glamor; Ports and People of the Mediterranean* J. Day 1929. *Shanklin* Bobbs-Merrill 1925. *The Tale of an Island and a Ship* Greystone Press 1936. *A New Star in the Union?* Crowell 1937. *Changing the Skyline; An Autobiography* (with Paul Starrett) McGraw-Hill; Whittlesey House (London) 1938. *Americans* Greystone Press 1941. Others. In *Woman's Home Companion, Harper's Bazaar, Collier's,* others
Awards or inclusion in other biographical books: *American Authors and Books; Dictionary of North American Authors; National Cyclopaedia of American Biography; Who Was Who among North American Authors; Who Was Who in America.* Honorary member, Michigan Authors Association

WALKER, LINDA ROBINSON

Address: 1516 Brooklyn, Ann Arbor, Michigan 48104
Born: October 26, 1941; Peoria, Illinois
Parents: Ralph A. Robinson, Nadine L. Robinson
Children: Max, Samuel
Education: University of Iowa, B.A., Iowa City, Iowa, 1959-1963. University of Michigan, M.S.W., Ann Arbor, Michigan, 1964-1966
Career: Freelance writer, 1990—. Intern, *Michigan Today,* University of Michigan, Ann Arbor, Michigan, 1990

Writings: *My Lady's Deception* Zebra 1990. Many articles in *The Washington Post* and others. Work in Progress: *Earth Bound*, a novel. Two novels with agent: *A Perfect Rose. Thief of Love*
May inquiries be sent to you about doing workshops, readings? Yes

WALKER, LOUISE JEAN (1891-1976)

Born: February 10, 1891; Jackson, Michigan
Parents: Quinton Smith Walker
Education: Albion College, A.B., Albion, Michigan, 1917. Columbia University, M.A., New York, New York, 1924. Studies at University of Michigan, Ann Arbor, Michigan; University of Colorado; Miami University
Career: Teacher of high school English in Indiana, Michigan. Associate Professor of English, Western Michigan University, Kalamazoo, Michigan, 37 years retiring 1961. Visiting professor

Writings: *Legends of Sky Hill* Eerdmans (foreword by E.C. Beck) 1959. *Red Indian Legends* Odhams Press Limited, (London) 1961. *Woodland Wigwams* Hillsdale Educational Publishers 1964. *Beneath the Singing Pines* Hillsdale Educational Publishers 1967. *Daisy Strikes on Saturday Night* Eerdmans 1968. Over 160 articles and stories for such magazines as *Children's Activities, Highlights for Children, Journal of American Folklore, American Nature Magazine, Your Personality, Out Dumb Animals, The English Journal* and others. While living in Charlevoix, Michigan she became interested in Chippewa Indian legends and felt they should be preserved
Awards or inclusion in other biographical books: *Directory of American Scholars; Michigan Authors,* 1st ed., 2nd ed.; *Who's Who of American Women*

WALKINSHAW, LAWRENCE HARVEY

Pseudonym: Larry
Born: February 25, 1904; Calhoun County, near Battle Creek, Michigan
Parents: Beatson Charles Walkinshaw, Eva Marie (Grinnell) Walkinshaw
Children: James Richard, Wendy Anne
Education: Olivet College, Olivet, Michigan, 1924-1925. University of Michigan, D.D.S., Ann Arbor, Michigan, 1929
Career: Dentist, Battle Creek, Michigan, 1929-1968. Co-editor, *Jack-Pine Warbler*, 1939-1948

Writings: *The Sandhill Cranes* Cranbrook Institute 1949. *Cranes of the World* Winchester Press 1973. *Birds of the Battle Creek, Calhoun County, Michigan Area* 1981. *Kirtland's Warbler: the Natural History of an Endangered Species* Cranbrook Institute of Science 1983. *Life History of the Eastern Field Sparrow in Calhoun County, Michigan* 1978. *Nest Observations of the Kirtland's Warbler: A Half Century Quest* University Microfilms International 1988. *A Number of Things: The Year With Nature* (editor) Gillette Natural History Association 1988. *Some American Descendants of Clotworthy Walkinshaw* University Microfilms International 1989. About 200 articles on birds, animals

Awards or inclusion in other biographical books: *Contemporary Authors; International Authors and Writers Who's Who; Michigan Authors,* 2nd ed. Awards: Michigan Academy of Sciences; Detroit Audubon Society. In the 2nd edition of *Michigan Authors* appears: "I believe in God and Jesus Christ. Our world, its inhabitants, its perfect and complete organization, could have been produced only by God. I believe in work, in accomplishing things and completing them. I believe in people and their ability. I feel there are times we need to help those less fortunate than we, that we can serve them at times, and we can aid the young. I thus worked with Boy Scouts for 40 years and with the Battle Creek Lions Club of which I was president. I have also worked with the S.W. Michigan Dental Society, Wilson Ornithological Society and the Ridge Audubon Society at Wales, Florida. I am happy to see boys like two of my grandsons and prior to that, my son, become Eagle Scouts-they finished something they started."

WALLER, RAYFIELD A.
Address: 4465 Garland, Detroit, Michigan 48214
Born: March 15, 1960; Detroit, Michigan
Parents: Schofield W. Waller II, Bessie L. Waller
Children: Lena Julia Cintron-Waller
Education: Finney Senior High. Wayne State University, B.A., Detroit, Michigan, 1987. Cornell University, Ithaca, New York, M.A., M.F.A.; Ph.D, 1988—1993
Career: Instructor/Minority Fellow, Cornell University, Department of English, Ithaca, New York, 1989—1992. Staff Writer *The Ithaca Times*, Ithaca, New York, 1990—1992. Newspaper Columnist *The Ithaca Journal*, Ithaca, New York, 1992. Teacher, Detroit Department of Recreation, Detroit, Michigan, 1988. Truck driver in Detroit, tutor of English/Spanish, Wayne County Community College. King/Parks/Chavez Visiting Scholar, Wayne State University, Detroit, Michigan, summer of 1990. Guest Lecturer at others. Editor, *The Wayne Review*. Editorial board of *Epoch*

Writings: *Abstract Blues* Broadside Press 1988. *Third Coast Anthology of Michigan Poets* Wayne State University Press 1989. Fiction, poetry, journalism, articles, essays, scholarly criticism in *Solid Ground: A New World Journal, Obsidian, Black American Literature Forum, Black Scholar, Metro Times,* and others. Work in Progress: *Zero,* a novel. *Death By Hanging*, feature-length play

Awards or inclusion in other biographical books: Eleven Tompkins and Bruenton Prizes for fiction, poetry, and essay, Wayne State University. The John Clare Prize, Academy of American Poets. The Judith Seagal Peirson Award for Fiction. The Forbes Heermans and George S. McCalmon Award for playwriting, Cornell's Department of Theatre Arts. The Tompkins Country League of Human Rights Award, New York State. Honorable mention, New York Press Association's Better Newspaper Competition. Professional Recognition Award, Syracuse Press Club

What is the aim or goal of your writing? "To examine the human condition; to expose the existence of inhumanity and oppression/dehumanization in all its forms; to relate the political and social realities of dehumanization to historical and material reality."

May inquiries be sent to you about doing workshops, readings? Yes

WARSAW, IRENE

Address: 888 N. Scheurmann Rd., Apt. D-20, Essexville, Michigan 48732
Born: November 26, 1908; Kawkawlin Township, Bay County, Michigan
Parents: Herman A. Warsaw, Auguste (Malzahn) Warsaw
Education: Bay City Central High School, graduated 1925. College extension courses, writers' conferences such as Bread Loaf Writers' Conference
Career: Vice-President, Trust Officer (administration of trusts and estates), Peoples National Bank and Trust Company, Bay City, Michigan,1957-1974, retired. Secretary to Trust Officer, Bay Trust Company , Bay City, Michigan, 1932-1957. Office Secretary, State Office, Federal Life Insurance Company of Chicago, at Bay City, Michigan Office, 1925-1932. Judge for various contests. Convention workshops, others. Speaker

Writings: *Warily We Roll Along* Golden Quill 1979; third printing 1992. *A Word in Edgewise* Golden Quill 1964; eighth printing 1989; taping for blind under production. Poems published in about a hundred magazines and papers, United States, Canada, reprints abroad.   Recent poems in *Good Housekeeping.* Poems included in many anthologies. Work in Progress: Submission to magazines, contests
Awards or inclusion in other biographical books: *Michigan Authors,* 2nd ed.; *Michigan Poets.* Honorable mentions, Poetry Society of Michigan, Utah State Poetry Society, Poets' Study Club of Terre Haute, Poets of the Palm Beaches (Florida) and others. Honorary Degree, Doctor of Letters, Saginaw Valley State University, 1980. Bay Central High School Hall of Fame, 1976. Bay Area Chamber of Commerce, Certificate of Superior Community Service, 1979
What is the aim or goal of your writing? "To keep on writing poetry (and some prose) in the hope of getting it published and of giving people pleasure-the latter also through speaking to groups."
May inquiries be sent to you about doing workshops, readings? Yes. (I would welcome inquiries about speaking and conducting workshops-with one proviso. Since I have never taught, have had no children, have never worked with them, and have written NOTHING for children, I avoid speaking to children because I feel I'm inadequate for their interests.)

WATANABE, SYLVIA A.

Address: 145 Crestwood, NW, Grand Rapids, Michigan 49504
Born: January 13, 1952; Wailuku, Maui, Hawaii
Parents: Walter H. Watanabe, Betty C. Watanabe
Education: University of Hawaii, B.A., 1973-1977. State University of New York at Binghamton, M.A., Binghamton, New York, 1983-1985
Career: Author, Editor, self-employed, presently under contract to Doubleday

Writings: *Talking to the Dead* Doubleday 1992. *Home to Stay* (co-edited with Carol Bruchac) Greenfield Review Press 1989. Work in Progress: A novel
Awards or inclusion in other biographical books: JACL National Literary Award, 1985. NEA Fellowship in Fiction, 1989-1990. O. Henry Prize Story, 1991. PEN Syndicated Fiction Project, 1992-1993
What is the aim or goal of your writing? "To explore the coming together of cultures in contemporary American life."
May inquiries be sent to you about doing workshops, readings? Yes

WATERLOO, STANLEY (1846-1913)
Born: May 21, 1846; St. Clair County, Michigan
Parents: Charles H. Waterloo, Mary Jane Waterloo
Education: University of Michigan, Ann Arbor, 1869
Career: Reporter in Chicago, 1870-1871. Worked on various newspapers such as *Chicago Tribune*, editor-in-chief for the *Chicago Mail,* other editorial positions. Began *St. Paul Day,* 1884

Writings: *A Man and a Woman* F.J. Schulte 1892. *An Odd Situation* Morrill, Higgins 1893. *A Michigan Romance* Neely Printing 1896. *The Parties and the Men; or, Political Issues of 1896; A History of Our Great Parties From the Beginning of the Government to the Present Day* W.B. Conkey 1896. *Armageddon; A Tale of Love,War, and Invention* Rand, McNally 1898. *The Seekers* H.S. Stone 1899. *The Story of Ab: a Tale of the Time of the Cave Man* 1897 (16 editions through 1934). *The Launching of a Man* Rand, McNally 1899. *The Wolf's Long Howl* 1899. *These Are My Jewels* 1902. *The Story of a Strange Career* 1902. *The Cassoway* 1906. *A Son of the Ages, the Reincarnations and Adventures of Scar, the Link; A Story of Man From the Beginning* Doubleday, Page 1914. Others
Awards or inclusion in other biographical books: *Allibone: a Critical Dictionary of English Literature; American Authors and Books; Biographical Dictionary and Synopsis of Books; Dictionary of American Authors; Dictionary of North Amerian Authors; Encyclopedia of Science Fiction; Science Fiction and Fantasy Literature; Twentieth Century Biographical Dictionary of Notable Americans; Who Was Who in America.* Honorary master's degree from the University of Michigan, 1898

WATSON (LOIS) ELAINE
Address: 1205 Island Drive, Apt. 102, Ann Arbor, Michigan 48105
Born: October 13, 1921; Jackson, Michigan
Parents: William J. Reno, Elsie O. (Feldkamp) Reno
Children: David, Douglas, Diane
Education: Manchester High School, 1939. University of Michigan, Ann Arbor, Michigan, A.B., 1943; M.A., 1950; graduate work
Career: Instructor, Henry Ford Community College, Dearborn, Michigan, 1958-1960; 1966-1986. English Teacher, Dearborn High School, Dearborn, Michigan, 1946-1956. English Teacher, Milan High School, 1943-1946

Writings: *To Dwell in the Land* Zondervan 1985. *Anna's Rocking Chair* Zondervan 1984. *Scraps of History* Reno Press 1985. Numerous articles in journals and newspapers such as *Michigan History.* Verse, mostly in small press publications, anthologies. Work in Progress: Young Adult historical novel. Adult historical novel. Both with Michigan settings
Awards or inclusion in other biographical books: *Contemporary Authors* Vol.115
What is the aim or goal of your writing? "I write verse, articles, and fiction. Mostly, I just want to write well, illuminating concerns of our time and concerns of people who lived in the past, too."
May inquiries be sent to you about doing workshops, readings? Yes

WAY, JOHN H.
Address: 903 North Powell Road, Essexville, Michigan 48732
Pseudonym: John David Connor
Born: December 24, 1932; Galesburg, Illinois
Parents: Harold E. Way, Fern R. Way
Children: Jeffrey, Kathleen, Ellen, Douglas, Brian
Education: Nott Terrace High School, Schenectady, New York, 1950. Allegheny College, B.A., Meadville, Pennsylvania, 1950-1954. Albany Medical College, M.D., Albany, New York, 1954-1958
Career: Self-employed, physician-internal medicine, Bay City, Michigan, 1970—. Physician, U.S. Army, U.S. Army Hospital, Camp Kue, Okinawa, Japan, 1967-1970. Self-employed, physician, internal medicine, Bay City, Michigan, 1963-1967. Physician, Department of medicine-hypertension, Henry Ford Hospital, Detroit, Michigan, 1962-1963; resident, 1959-1962. Internship, Blodgett Memorial Hospital, Grand Rapids, Michigan, 1958-1959

Writings: *Contagion* Diamond Books (Berkley Publishing Group) 1992. *Cardiac Arrest* Charter Books (Berkley Publishing Group)1988. *Blood-Link* Charter Books (Berkley Publishing Group) 1986. *Dreamwatch* Playboy Paperbacks 1981. Work in Progress: Novel set in Oman, with Jeffrey C. Way
What is the aim or goal of your writing? "To write a fine novel!"
May inquiries be sent to you about doing workshops, readings? No

WEATHERWAX, WILMA M.
Address: 401 Maple Street, Owosso, Michigan 48867
Born: May 4, 1914; Bancroft, Michigan
Parents: Joseph G. Hunt, Olive M. Hunt
Children: Judith
Education: High School studies interrupted by illness. Home Study, College Course in English, History, Journalism, Library Science, Philosophy, 1944
Career: Legal Secretary, Owosso, Michigan, 1959-1962. Writer/editor, *Argus Press,* Owosso, Michigan, 1957-1959. Inspector, Universal Electric, Owosso, Michigan, 1951-1957. Piecegoods Department Manager, Montgomery Wards, Owosso, Michigan, 1946-1951

Writings: *The Blue-Eyed Chippewa* Broadblade Press 1986. Work in Progress: Compiling book of poetry. Fiction, entitled *Fantasy*
What is the aim or goal of your writing? "My only aim is to write authentic material that has been well researched, and to write <u>clean</u> literature."
May inquiries be sent to you about doing workshops, readings? Yes

WEBBER, GEORGE (1912-1986)
Born: October 25, 1912; Linden, Michigan
Parents: Roy Webber, Dorothea (Boyd) Webber
Children: Jacqueline, Dorothea, Laura
Education: Jamestown College, A.B., Jamestown, North Dakota, 1933. University of Michigan, M.A., Ann Arbor, Michigan, 1936
Career: Writer, editor, National Broadcasting Company, New York, New York, 1938-1940. Served in World War II,1942-1945. Copywriter, associate creative director, head of creative group, Benton & Bowles, New York, New York, 1948-1969; administrative

positions, 1970-1975. Instructor, writer, Parsons School of Design, New York, New York, 1975-1976. Film producer, 1970-1971. Co-chairperson of Rye Council on Human Rights, 1963-1964. Lecturer

Writings: *Years of Eden* Little, Brown 1951. *The Far Shore* Little, Brown 1954; Bantam 1955; Victor Gollanz (London) 1955. *What End but Love* Little, Brown 1959. *The Great Buffalo Hotel* Little, Brown 1979. *Our Kind of People: The Story of the First Fifty Years at Benton & Bowles* Riverside Press 1979. Television series 1950-1955, *I Remember Mama.* Magazine writer

Awards or inclusion in other biographical books:
American Authors and Books; Contemporary Authors; Michigan Authors, 1st ed., 2nd ed.; *Who's Who in America; Who's Who in the World.* Film which he produced/directed, *The Jogger,* won CINE Golden Eagle and Edinburgh Film Festival Certificates

WEDELL, ROBERT F.
Address: 3350 Lakeshore Drive, Muskegon, Michigan 49441
Born: May 9, 1925; Boston, Massachusetts
Parents: Victor Wedell, Lillian Wedell
Children: David, Thomas, Steven, Shirley (wife: Mildred Edith)
Education: Plymouth High School, Plymouth, Massachusetts, 1943. Western Michigan University, Bachelor of Music, Kalamazoo, Michigan, 1946-1950; M.A., Elementary Education, 1959-1962
Career: Elementary Teacher, Orchard View Schools, Muskegon, Michigan, 1962-1985, retired. Elementary Teacher, Kalamazoo Public Schools, Kalamazoo, Michigan, 1958-1962. High School Music Director, Richland Public Schools, Richland, Michigan, 1956-1958. High School Band/Chorus/Speech, Reed City Public Schools, Reed City, Michigan, 1950-1956

Writings: *Rolf the Green Ghost Leans a Lesson* Milrob Press 1992. *Rolf in Save the Haunted House* Milrob Press 1991. *Rolf and the Rainbow Christmas* Milrob Press 1989. *Rolf the Green Ghost* Milrob Press 1988. "Read Along with the Author" tape. Work in Progress: *Rolf Learns About the First Thanksgiving*
What is the aim or goal of your writing? "I write to entertain <u>and</u> teach my young readers how important it is to learn to 'be what you are' and to 'learn all you can <u>all</u> your life'-and to make the world around you a better place."
May inquiries be sent to you about doing workshops, readings? Yes

WEEKS, GEORGE C.
Address: Sleeping Bear Pt., Glen Arbor, Michigan 49636
Born: August 1, 1932; Traverse City, Michigan
Parents: Donald C. Weeks, Juanita M. (Magdanz) Weeks
Children: Julie, Don
Education: Michigan State University, B.A. in Journalism, East Lansing, Michigan, 1950-1954
Career: Columnist, *Detroit News,* Detroit, Michigan, 1984—. Chief of Staff, Governor William G. Milliken, Lansing, Michigan, 1975-1982. Press Secretary/Special Counsel for Programs, State Affairs and Public Affairs, Governor William G. Milliken, 1969-1975. Foreign Editor in Washington, previously Bureau Chief in Lansing, United Press International, 1957-1969. U.S. Army, 1955-1957. UPI, 1954-1955

Writings: *Mem-ka-weh: Dawning of the Grand Traverse Band of Ottawa and Chippewa Indians* GTB 1992. *Stewards of the State: The Governors of Michigan* Detroit News & Historical Society of Michigan 1987,1991. *Sleeping Bear: Yesterday and Today* A&M 1991. *Sleeping Bear: Its Lore, Legends and First People* Cottage Book Shop of Glen Arbor & Historical Society of Michigan 1988. *The Milliken Years: A Pictorial Reflection* (co-author) Village Press & Traverse City Record-Eagle 1988. *Michigan: Visions of Our Past* (contributing author) Michigan State University Press 1989. *A Handbook of African Affairs* (contributing author) Praeger 1964

Awards or inclusion in other biographical books: *Who's Who in America.* Michigan Small Press Book of the Year, 1987. Michigan Week selection by the Great Lakes Booksellers Association, 1991,1992

May inquiries be sent to you about doing workshops, readings? Yes

WEESNER, THEODORE

Born: July 31, 1935; Flint, Michigan
Parents: William Weesner, Margaret (McInnes) Weesner
Children: Ted, Anna, Steve
Education: Michigan State University, B.A., East Lansing, Michigan, 1959. University of Iowa, M.F.A., Iowa City, Iowa, 1965
Career: Army, 3 years. Novelist, short story writer

Writings: *The Car Thief* Random House 1972. *A German Affair* Random House 1977. *The True Detective* Summit Books 1987. *Winning the City* Summit Books 1990. *Children's Hearts: Stories* Summit Books 1992. In *The New Yorker, Esquire, Saturday Evening Post, Atlantic Monthly*

Awards or inclusion in other biographical books: *Contemporary Authors; Michigan Authors,* 2nd ed. Great Lakes Colleges Award, 1972. In the 2nd edition of *Michigan Authors* he is credited with: "I am a realist. There is something in the term 'neorealism' which implies an intense realism, and as both writer and reader this is where my interest lies. Stated otherwise, while some writers write about what might or could happen, I write about what has happened. But I am not a reporter."

WEIGER, DEAN P.

Address: P. O. Box 172, L'Anse, Michigan 49946
Born: September 25, 1949; Merrill, Wisconsin
Parents: Walter R. Weiger, Lauretta J. Weiger
Children: Sarah, Luke
Education: Marquette Senior High School, 1967. Northern Michigan University, Marquette, Michigan, Michigan State University, East Lansing, Michigan, B.A., M.S., 1967-1973
Career: Instructor and Alternative Education, L'Anse-Baraga Community Schools, Baraga, Michigan, 1986—. Instructor and faculty assistant, Michigan Technological University, Houghton, Michigan, 1979-1986. Instructor, Gogebic Community College, Ironwood, Michigan, 1991—. Instructor, Suomi College, Hancock, Michigan, 1982-1983. L'Anse High School, Gladstone High School, Delta County Probate Court Juvenile Officer. Teaching Graduate Assistant, Northern Michigan University

Writings: *The Bay Prospector* (contributing editor) Copper Country Intermediate School District 1991. Work in Progress: *His Lives*
What is the aim or goal of your writing? "To lead us to a deeper understanding of our common humanity."

May inquiries be sent to you about doing workshops, readings? Yes

WEXSTAFF, BERNICE (1898-1987)
Born: June 28, 1898; Charlevoix, Michigan
Parents: Loren Eugene Crandell, Mary (Ward) Crandell
Children: Robert Eugene
Education: Charlevoix High School, Charlevoix, Michigan. Alma College, Alma, Michigan
Career: Writer, part-time musician, and business woman

Writings: *The Black Panther of the Great Lakes* Eerdmans 1957. *Haunt of High Island* Eerdmans 1958. *Belvedere Club* private publication. *Church of God* private publication In the 2nd edition of *Michigan Authors* she is credited with: "I do historical research on many topics including the old Dixie from Canada to Key West. Rex Beach, author, was born in northern Michigan but never recognized there until this year, 1977,when I represented his credentials on the occasion of his 100th birthday anniversary September 1st. I am also interested in politics on both the local and national level and work on grass-roots opinions on national legislation for the Monitor Poll based in Washington, DC. I am a member of the Daughters of the American Revolution and concerned about the future of our American Republic and the democratic processes inasfar as my family has been here since 1634."
Awards or inclusion in other biographical books: *Michigan Authors,* 2nd ed.

WHELAN, GLORIA A.
Address: 9797 N. Twin Lake Road N.E., Mancelona, Michigan 49659
Born: November 23, 1923; Detroit, Michigan
Parents: William J. Rewoldt, Hildegarde Rewoldt
Children: Joseph, Jennifer
Education: University of Michigan, B.A., M.S.W., Ann Arbor, Michigan, 1942-1948

Writings: *Goodby, Vietnam* Knopf 1992. *Bringing the Farmhouse Home* Simon & Schuster 1992. *Hannah* Knopf 1991. *The Secret Keeper* Knopf 1990. *Silver* Random House 1988. *Playing With Shadows* University of Illinois Press 1988. *A Week of Raccoons* Knopf 1988. *Next Spring an Oriole* Random House 1987. *The Pathless Woods* Lippincott 1981. *A Time to Keep Silent* Putnam's 1979. *A Clearing in the Forest* Putnam's 1977. Anthologies: *The Third Coast,* Wayne State University Press and others
Awards or inclusion in other biographical books: Nomination for an Edgar, Mystery Writers of America. Four Pushcart Prize nominations. O. Henry Award. Master List Finalist, Florida Sunshine State Young Reader's Award. Juvenile Book Award, Friends of American Writers. Baker & Taylor School Selection Guide Book. Two nominations, Notable Children's Trade Book in the Field of Social Studies. Two nominations, IRA Children's Choices List. Dorothy Canfield Fisher Master List. California Reading Iniative. Creative Artist Award. Michigan Council for the Arts
What is the aim or goal of your writing? "To write the very best most honest book I can."
May inquiries be sent to you about doing workshops, readings? Yes

WHITE, CAROLYN
Address: 1661 Mt. Vernon Avenue, East Lansing, Michigan 48823
Born: March 27, 1948; Brooklyn, New York
Parents: Aaron White, Sylvia White
Education: Michigan State University, East Lansing, Michigan, M.A., Ph.D., 1969-1974. State University of New York at Binghamton, B.A., Binghamton, New York, 1965-1969. University de Dijon, Diplome d'e'tude, Dijon, France, 1967-1968
Career: Self-employed writer, 1974—

Writings: *The Children Who Lived in a Tree House* Simon & Schuster 1993. *A History of Irish Fairies* Mercier Press (Ireland) 1976. Many poems, stories in *Parabola, Magical Blend, Poet Lore, Studia Mystica, Earth's Daughters, Kansas Quarterly, Michigan Quarterly Review, Negative Capability* and others. Work in Progress: *Good Looking*, adult novel. *Into the Forest of Chanteloube*, children's novel. Revisions of a number of children's picture books using folklore motifs
Awards or inclusion in other biographical books: Michigan Council for the Arts Grant, 1987. Chosen New Voice of Michigan, Poetry Resource Center, 1984
What is the aim or goal of your writing? "Writing is my entire life. It is my way to explore my passions, my hopes and fears, as well as working out a good story. What I most want is for some one to read my work and say: 'Ah, that's right.' Writing is a means of self-exploration."
May inquiries be sent to you about doing workshops, readings? Yes

WHITE, PAULETTE CHILDRESS
Born: December 1, 1948; Hamtramck, Michigan
Parents: Norris Childress, Effie (Storey) Childress
Children: Pierre, Oronde, Kojo, Kala, Paul
Education: High School, Ecorse, Michigan
Career: Poet, story writer, painter

Writings: *Love Poem to a Black Junkie* Lotus Press (Detroit) 1975. *Blacksongs, Series 1: Four Poetry Broadsides by Black Women* Lotus Press 1977? *The Watermelon Dress: Portrait of a Woman* Lotus Press 1984. In anthologies such as *Midnight Birds* Doubleday 1980. In *Redbook, Essence,* others
Awards or inclusion in other biographical books: *Contemporary Authors; Michigan Authors,* 2nd ed.

WHITE, STEWART EDWARD (1873-1946)
Born: March 12, 1873; Grand Rapids, Michigan
Parents: T. Stewart White, Mary E. (Daniell) White
Education: Grand Rapids High School, Grand Rapids, Michigan. University of Michigan, Ann Arbor, Michigan, Ph.B., 1895; M.A., 1903. Columbia Law School, 1896-1897
Career: Served in World War I, 1917-1918. Gold seeker, Black Hills. Writer

Writings: *The Westerners* McClure, Phillips 1901. *Blazed Trail* Grosset and Dunlap 1902, several editions. *The Forest* Outlook 1903. *Conjuror's House: A Romance of the Free Forest* McClure, Phillips 1903. *Blazed Trail Stories* 1904. *The Pass* Outing Publishing 1906. *The Riverman* McClure 1908. *Adventures of Bobby Orde* Grosset and Dunlap 1911. *The Cabin* Doubleday, Page 1911. *Gold* Doubleday, Page 1913. *African Camp Fires*

Doubleday, Page 1913.*The Last Frontier* Yale University Press 1918.*The Forty-Niners; A Chronicle of the California Trail and El Dorado* Yale University Press 1921. *Across the Unknown* (with Harwood White) E.P. Dutton 1939. *Wild Geese Calling* Literary Guild of America 1940. *The Unobstructed Universe* E.P. Dutton 1940. *Call of the North* Triangle Books 1941. *Anchors to Windward; Stability and Personal Peace-Here and Now* E.P. Dutton 1943. *The Story of California* 1940; AMS Press 1975. Several others. Short Stories in *McClure's*

Awards or inclusion in other biographical books: *American Authors and Books; Contemporary American Authors; Contemporary American Literature; Dictionary of American Authors; Dictionary of American Biography; Dictionary of North American Authors; National Cyclopaedia of American Biography; Reader's Encyclopedia of American Literature; Reader's Encyclopedia of American West; Twentieth Century Authors; Who Was Who among North American Authors; Who Was Who in America,* several others

WIDDER, KEITH R.
Address: 126 Centerlawn, East Lansing, Michigan 48823
Born: August 16, 1943; Sheboygan, Wisconsin
Parents: Hugo A. Widder, Marie E. (LeMahieu) Widder
Education: Wheaton College, A.B., Wheaton, Illinois, 1961-1965. University of Wisconsin-Milwaukee, M.A, Milwaukee, Wisconsin, 1965-1968. Michigan State University, Ph.D., East Lansing, Michigan, 1982-1989
Career: Curator of History, Mackinac Island State Park Commission, Mackinac Island, Michigan, 1971—. Teacher (American History), Librarian, Brookfield East High School, Brookfield, Wisconsin, 1968-1971

Writings: *At the Crossroads: Michilimackinac During the American Revolution* (with David A. Armour) Mackinac Island State Park Commission 1978. *Reveille Til Taps: Soldier Life at Fort Mackinac, 1780-1895* Mackinac Island State Park Commission 1972. Articles in *Michigan History Magazine,* others. Contributor to *Historic Women of Michigan: A Sesquicentennial Celebration* 1987. Work in Progress: British intrusion into the western Great Lakes region, 1760-1783
Awards or inclusion in other biographical books: *Michigan Authors,* 2nd ed.
What is the aim or goal of your writing? "Through my writing I hope to interpret for readers meaningful segments of the human experience in eighteenth and nineteenth-century North America. I believe that we can only comprehend the present if we understand the truth of our past. I hope that, in some small measure, my writing may help achieve that end."
May inquiries be sent to you about doing workshops, readings? Yes

WIDICK, B. J.
Born: October 25, 1910; Yugoslavia
Parents: Joseph Widick, Angelina Widick
Children: Marshall, Brian
Education: University of Akron, B.A., Akron, Ohio, 1933. Wayne State University, M.A., Detroit, Michigan, 1963
Career: Newspaper work, 1933-1937. Military service, 1942-1945. Union official, research economist, United Autoworkers Union, 1947-1961. Labor correspondent, *The National Magazine,* 1958-1978. Professor of industrial relations, Columbia University, New York, New York, beginning in 1972. Research director, United Rubberworkers Union, 1930's. Faculty, Wayne State University, Detroit, Michigan, 1962, 1968-1969.

Lectured, United States and abroad. Advisory Council, Industrial Relations Research Association, 1960-1961

Writings: *UAW and Walter Reuther* (with Irving Howe) Random House 1949; Da Capo Press 1973. *A New Focus on Detroit and Michigan's Economy* Wayne State University Press 1963. *Labor Today: Triumphs and Failures of Unionism* Houghton-Mifflin 1964. *Detroit: City of Race and Class Violence* Quadrangle Books 1972; Wayne State University Press 1989; R. R. Bowker, 1987, 1991. *Auto Work and Its Discontents* Johns Hopkins University Press 1976; reprinted by Books on Demand. In *Monthly Labor Review, New Republic, Nation,* others

Awards or inclusion in other biographical books: *Contemporary Authors; Michigan Authors,* 2nd ed. Distinguished Teaching Award, Graduate School of Business, Columbia University. In the 2nd edition of *Michigan Authors* he is credited with: "As a social critic, I conceive of my function as a writer to ask the tough questions. So few people do that today. This is not the road to financial or other success, but it is rewarding for such a function does assist people to come up with better answers than the old cliches."

WIEGAND, WILLIAM
Born: June 11, 1928; Detroit, Michigan
Parents: Jack J. Wiegand; Kathryn (Diener) Wiegand
Education: University of Michigan, A.B., Ann Arbor, Michigan, 1945; A.M., 1950. Stanford University, Stanford, California, Ph.D., 1960
Career: Instructor, Harvard University, Cambridge, Massachusetts, 1960-1962. Assistant Professor to Professor of English and Creative Writing, San Francisco State University, beginning in 1962

Writings: *At Last, Mr. Tolliver* Rinehart 1950. *The Treatment Man* McGraw-Hill 1959. *The School of Soft Knocks* Lippincott 1968. *Student's Choice* (anthology-with R. Kraus) Merrill 1970. *The Chester A. Arthur Conspiracy* Dial Press 1983. Introduction, to reprint of the novel, *In War Time* College & University Press 1978

Awards or inclusion in other biographical books: *Directory of American Poets and Fiction Writers*; *Michigan Authors,* 2nd ed.; *Twentieth-Century Crime and Mystery Writers; Writers Directory*

WILLARD, NANCY
Address: 133 College Avenue, Poughkeepsie, New York 12603
Born: Ann Arbor, Michigan

Writings: *In His Country: Poems* Generation 1966. *Skin of Grace* University of Missouri Press 1967. *A New Herbball: Poems* Ferinand-Roter Gallerias 1968. *Nineteen Masks for a Naked Poet: Poems* Story Lines 1971; Harcourt Brace 1984. *The Carpenter of the Sun: Poems* Liveright 1974. *Water Walker* Knopf 1989. *The Ballad of Biddy Early* Knopf 1989. *Lively Anatomy of God* Eakins 1968. *Childhood of the Magician* Liveright 1973. *Angel in the Parlor* Harcourt, Brace 1983. *Household Tales of Moon and Water* Harcourt Junior 1982, 1987. *The Merry History of Christmas Pie: With a Delicious Description of a Christmas Soup* Putnam 1975. *All on a May Morning* Putnam 1975. *The Snow Rabbit* Putnam 1975. *Shoes Without Leather* Putnam 1976. *The Well-Mannered Balloon* Harcourt 1976. *Strangers' Bread* Harcourt 1977. *Simple Pictures Are Best* Harcourt 1977; Harcourt Junior 1978, 1984, 1987, 1988. *The Highest Hit* Harcourt Junior 1978; Scholastic 1983. *Papa's Panda* Harcourt Junior 1979. *The Marzipan Moon* Harcourt

Junior 1981. *A Visit to William Blake's Inn: Poems for Innocent and Experienced Travelers* Harcourt, Brace 1981; Harcourt Junior 1982, 1988. *The Nightgown of the Sullen Moon* Harcourt 1983; Harcourt Junior 1987, 1988. *Night Story* Harcourt Junior 1986. *The Mountains of Quilt* Harcourt Junior 1987. *The Voyage of the Ludgate Hill: A Journey with Robert Louis Stevenson* Harcourt 1987. *Firebrat* Knopf 1987. *East of the Sun, West of the Moon* Harcourt 1989. *Things Invisible to See* Knopf 1985. *Beauty and the Beast,* Harcourt, Brace 1992. Children's fantasy trilogy, others. Work in Progress: *Sister Water,* a novel
Awards or inclusion in other biographical books: John Newbery Award
May inquiries be sent to you about doing workshops, readings? Yes

WILLEY, MARGARET M.

Address: 431 Grant Street, Grand Haven, Michigan 49417
Born: November 5, 1950; Chicago, Illinois
Parents: Foster L. Willey, Barbara R. Willey
Children: Chloe Joanisse
Education: Thomas Jefferson College, B.Ph., B.A., Allendale, Michigan, 1973-1975. Bowling Green State University, M.F.A., Bowling Green, Ohio, 1978-1980. Michigan State University, East Lansing, Michigan, 1968-1971
Career: Full-time writer

Writings: *The Melinda Zone* Bantam 1993. *Saving Lenny* Bantam 1990. *If Not for You* Harper & Row 1988. *Finding David Dolores* Harper & Row 1986. *The Bigger Book of Lydia* Harper & Row 1983. Fiction, poetry, essays in literary and commercial magazines. Young adult novels translated into many languages. Work in Progress: *Metallurgy,* adult novel. *The Thanksgiving Uncles,* children's picture book. *Belle-Mere,* short story collection
Awards or inclusion in other biographical books: Three ALA Best Books for Young Adult Awards, 1990, 1986, 1983. Two ALA Best Books for Reluctant Readers Awards, 1970, 1988. Two IRA Young Adult Choices Awards, 1986, 1990. Three New York Library Books for the Teen Age Awards, 1990, 1988, 1986. Two Michigan Council for the Arts Creative Artist Grants, 1988, 1984
What is the aim or goal of your writing? "I have many goals, but my main goal is to be both truthful and hopeful in my depictions of coming-of-age in today's world."
May inquiries be sent to you about doing workshops, readings? Yes

WILLIAMS, JOHN H.

Address: 1205 Best Road, Metamora, Michigan 48455
Born: June 1, 1946; Rochester, New York
Parents: Walter M. Robert (stepfather), Margaret M. Robert
Children: Kimberly, John Jr., Acacia, Shawn (stepson), Eric (stepson)
Education: University of Michigan, B.S., Ann Arbor, Michigan, 1964-1968. Oakland University, B.A., Rochester, Michigan, 1969-1971; M.B.A., 1979-1981
Career: Hospital Supervisor, Fairlawn Center, Pontiac, Michigan, 1966—. Registered Nurse, Avondale Convalescent Home, Rochester, Michigan 1981-1991. Teacher, Huron Valley Schools, Milford, Michigan, 1970-1972. Chemist, Price Brothers, White Lake, Michigan, 1972-1974

Writings: *The Deer Hunter's Field Guide-Pursuing Michigan's Whitetail* Momentum Books Ltd. 1990. Published more than 250 regional and national magazine and newspaper articles over the past 20 years. Also contributing author to *Outdoor Life's, Deer Hunting Annual,* 1978, 1987, 1988, 1989, 1990. Work in Progress: Three year field study on the daily habits and life cycles of the Whitetail Deer for a book on the natural history of the Whitetail

What is the aim or goal of your writing? "I've had an incurable fascination with animals and the outdoors all my life. I truly enjoy being able to share that with others."
May inquiries be sent to you about doing workshops, readings? Yes

WILLIAMSON, ANN L.
Address: 3334 Valley View, St. Joseph, Michigan 49085
Born: January 8, 1943; Cincinnati, Ohio
Parents: Herbert E. Williams, Rose V. Williams
Children: Chuck, Tom, Dan
Education: Western Michigan University, B.A., Kalamazoo, Michigan, 1976-1982. The Christ Hospital School of Nursing, Graduate Nurse, Cincinnati, Ohio, 1960-1963
Career: Staff, R.N., Mercy Memorial Medical Center, St. Joseph, Michigan, 1975—. Staff, R.N., Miami Valley Hospital, Dayton, Ohio, 1967. Staff, R.N., The Christ Hospital, Cincinnati, Ohio, 1963-1967. Readings, Annual Poetry Festival, Michigan State Poet Series, Lake Michigan College; Krasl Art Center, St. Joseph, Michigan

Writings: In small magazines such as *Blue Unicorn, The Mickle Street Review, Earth Daughters. Wild Rumors* Lakeshore Publishing 1992. In *The Third Coast:Contemporary Michigan Poetry* 1988. Work in progress: Poems, no general theme at present

Awards or inclusion in other biographical books: Abbie M. Copps Award, Olivet College, 1991. Michigan Council for the Arts, Creative Artist Grant, 1987
What is the aim or goal of your writing? "I see every being, thing, and abstraction as connected, I write nature poems about quarks and electrons. I write about my dear old sofa (as a woman I worry over or as Mother Nature) impersonal and doling out life and death. I love the image, the event. I write poetry because poetry lets me shuffle the cards, deal the hands, and, <u>then</u>, decide if I'm playing Canasta or Old Maid or Poker."
May inquiries be sent to you about doing workshops, readings? Yes

WILOCH, THOMAS
Address: 43672 Emrick Drive, Canton, Michigan 48187
Born: February 3, 1953; Detroit, Michigan
Education: Wayne State University, B.A., Detroit, Michigan, 1978
Career: Associate editor, Gale Research Inc., Detroit, Michigan, 1989—; senior writer, 1985-1989; senior assistant editor, 1981-1985; assistant editor, 1978-1981

Writings: *Narcotic Signature* Burning Books 1992. *Decoded Factories of the Heart* Trombone Press 1991. *Night Rain* Runaway Spoon Press 1991. *Tales of Lord Shantih* Unicorn Press 1990. *The Mannikin Cypher* Bomb Shelter Props 1989. *Paper Mask* Stride 1988. *Stigmata Junction* Stride 1985. Co-editor with Leonard Kniffel, *Directory of Michigan Literary Publishers*, Poetry Resource Center, 1982. Work in Progress: "Always."
Awards or inclusion in other biographical books: *Contemporary SF; Directory of American Poets and Fiction Writers; Fantasy and Horror Poetry; International Authors and Writers Who's Who; International Who's Who in Poetry; Small Press Register; Who's*

Who in U.S. Writers, Editors & Poets. Poet Hunt Award, Schoolcraft College, 1985. Scantle Magazine Prize, 1986. Pushcart Prize nomination, 1988, 1990. Rhysling Award nomination, 1992
What is the aim or goal of your writing? "Revelatory moments."
May inquiries be sent to you about doing workshops, readings? Yes

WILSON, HELEN ANN (FINNEGAN) (?-1980)
Pseudonym: Holly Wilson
Born: Duluth, Minnesota
Children: Mary, Ann
Education: University of Michigan, Ann Arbor, Michigan
Career: Moved to Marquette, Michigan, after the death of her father; after marriage lived in Topeka, Kansas, and Clifton Springs, New York; in 1959 moved to Traverse City, Michigan

Writings: *The King Pin* Macmillan 1939. *Deborah Todd* Messner 1955. *Caroline, the Unconquered* Messner 1956. *Always Anne* J. Messner 1957. *Snowbound in Hidden Valley* Messner 1957; Scholastic Book Services 1957. *The Hundred Steps* J. Messner 1958. *Stranger in Singamon* Messner 1959. *Maggie of Barnaby Bay* J. Messner 1963
Awards or inclusion in biographical books: Hopwood Award, University of Michigan, *The King Pin*

WILSON, JAMES R.
Address: P.O. Box 717, Bellaire, Michigan 49615
Born: July 31, 1928; Warsaw, Poland
Parents: J. Ryley Wilson, Florence C. Wilson
Education: Cooley High School, graduated 1946. General Motors Institute, B.A., Flint, Michigan, 1946-1950
Career: United States Marines, 1951-1953. General Motors Corporation, 1954-1988

Writings: *No Ordinary Crime* Broadblade Press 1989. Articles in magazines, newspaper editorials, poetry. Work in Progress: Family history/Civil War history, untitled yet
What is the aim or goal of your writing? " 1.) Current goal-for *No Ordinary Crime* to become screenplay; 2.) Long term-lecturer/instructor at college, seminars-lectures etc.-WWII History, Michigan in WWII."
May inquiries be sent to you about doing workshops, readings? Yes

WILSON, SUZANNE
Address: P.O. Box 22, Glen Arbor, Michigan 49630
Born: May 6, 1940; Iron Mountain, Michigan
Parents: Raymond Uhlinger, Virginia Uhlinger
Children: Allison, Amy, Andrea
Education: John D. Pierce High School. Northern Michigan University, Marquette, Michigan, 1958-1960. Central Michigan University, B.A., Mt. Pleasant, Michigan, 1979-1981
Career: Self-employed artist, Glen Arbor, Michigan, 1987—. Artist-in-Residence, Leelanau Center for Education, Glen Arbor, Michigan, 1981-1987. Art Consultant, Traverse Bay Area Intermediate School District, Traverse City, Michigan, 1975-1981

Writings: *Donut Days* A & M Publishing 1992. *A Sketchbook of Leelanau County* self-published 1989. Work in Progress: Several children's stories

What is the aim or goal of your writing? "To integrate my interests in children, painting-the part of Michigan (the north) that I love. Both of my books use my own illustrations, and I would hope to continue that as well."
May inquiries be sent to you about doing workshops, readings? Yes

WINTERS, DONNA M.
Address: P.O. Box 177, Caledonia, Michigan 49316
Born: November 19, 1949; Rochester, New York
Parents: Donald W. Rogers, Frances P. Rogers
Education: Potsdam State College, B.S. Music Education, Potsdam, New York, 1967-1971. Aquinas College, Grand Rapids, Michigan. University of Oklahoma, Norman, Oklahoma
Career: Writer/Publisher, Bigwater Publishing, Caledonia, Michigan; Freelance writer, self-employed, Caledonia, Michigan, 1984-1988. Proofreader, Lear/Siegler, Inc., Grand Rapids, Michigan, 1978-1984. Kelly Temporary, Kelly Services, Grand Rapids, Michigan, 1977-1978. Public school music teacher, New York

Writings: *Charlotte of South Manitou Island* Bigwater 1992. *Sweethearts of Sleeping Bear Bay* Bigwater 1991. *The Captain and the Widow* Bigwater 1990. *Mackinac* Bigwater 1989. *Jenny of L'Anse Bay* Zondervan 1988. *Elizabeth of Saginaw Bay* Zondervan 1986. *For the Love of Roses* Thomas Nelson 1985. Editor and wrote introduction for *Sweet Clover: A Romance of the White City* Bigwater 1992, a reprint of 1894 by Clara Louise Burnham. Work in Progress: *Aurora of North Manitou Island* Bigwater 1993. *Bridget of Cat's Head Point* Bigwater 1994
What is the aim or goal of your writing? "I strive to create wholesome fiction which portrays Michigan's history both accurately, and in a positive light. My focus from 1989 to present is the 1890's."
May inquiries be sent to you about doing workshops, readings? Yes

WOIWODE, LARRY
Born: October 30, 1941; Carrington, North Dakota
Parents: Everett Woiwode, Audrey (Johnston) Woiwode
Children: Newlyn, Joseph, Ruth, Laurel
Education: University of Illinois at Urbana-Champaign, 1959-1964
Career: Writer, 1964—. Visiting Professor, State University of New York at Binghamton, 1983-1985, Professor, 1985—. Writer-in-residence, University of Wisconsin-Madison, 1973-1974. Professor, Wheaton College, Norton, Massachusetts, summers, 1981, 1984. Workshop director, panel member, reader at many colleges such as Northwestern University, Dartmouth College. Judge for National Book Awards, 1972, others

Writings: *What I'm Going to Do, I Think* Farrar, Straus 1969. *Mietin Mita Minun Pitaisi* Tammi (Helsinki) 1970. *Beyond the Bedroom Wall: A Family Album* Farrar, Straus 1975. *Even Tide* Farrar, Straus 1975. *Pappa John* Farrar, Straus 1981. *Born Brothers* Farrar, Straus and Giroux 1988. *The Neumiller Stories* Farrar, Straus and Giroux 1989. *Indian Affairs: A Novel* Atheneum; Maxwell Macmillan Canada; Maxwell Macmillan International 1992. Contributor to many anthologies such as *Best American Short Stories*, Houghton Mifflin 1983. Published reviews, poems, short stories in such periodicals as *McCall's, New Yorker, Esquire, Harper's, Partisan Review, New American Review*,
Awards or inclusion in other biographical books: *Contemporary Authors; Contemporary Literary Criticism; Current Biography; Dictionary of Literary Biography; Direc-*

tory of American Fiction Writers; Directory of American Poets; Who's Who in America; Writers Directory

WOLF, SARAH
Address: 15570 Ingram, Livonia, Michigan 48154
Born: October 9, 1936; Winona, Minnesota
Parents: Wilmert H. Wolf, Sarah E. (Staffeld) Wolf
Children: Sarah, Laurel, Daniel
Education: University of Michigan, A.M.L.S., Ann Arbor, Michigan, 1982-1983. Nebraska State College, B.A., Kearney, Nebraska, 1960-1961
Career: Full-time writer, 1988—. Librarian, University of Michigan, Ann Arbor, Michigan, 1983-1987. Teacher, Ballard Community Schools, Huxley, Iowa, 1964-1965. Teacher, Alma Public Schools, Alma, Nebraska, 1961-1962

Writings: *MacKinnon's Machine* Simon & Schuster 1991. *The Harbinger Effect* Simon & Schuster 1989. *Long Chain of Death* Walker & Company 1987. Work in Progress: *Blowback*
Awards or inclusion in other biographical books: *Contemporary Authors*
What is the aim or goal of your writing? "To tell good stories".
May inquiries be sent to you about doing workshops, readings? Yes

WOLF-TAYLOR, MELINDA S.
Address: 1761 Oxford Road S.E., Grand Rapids, Michigan 49506
Pseudonym: Mindy Wolf
Born: April 5, 1958; Grand Rapids, Michigan
Parents: Stanford H. Wolf, Marianne R. (Thrall) Wolf
Children: Rachel, Matthew
Education: Olivet College, B.A., Olivet, Michigan, 1977-1980. Miami University, M.A., Oxford, Ohio, 1980-1982. Columbia University, New York, New York, 1982-1983
Career: Adjunct Instructor, Grand Valley State University, Allendale, Michigan, 1983—. Teaching Assistant, Columbia University, New York, New York, 1982-1983. Adjunct Instructor, Jersey City State College, Jersey City, New Jersey, 1982-1983. Teaching Assistant, Miami University, Oxford, Ohio, 1980-1982. Tutor, Grand Rapids Community College, Grand Rapids, Michigan—

Writings: Poems in *American Literary Review, New York Quarterly, Mudfish, South Coast Poetry Journal, Anthology of Magazine Verse and Yearbook of American Poetry, Kalliope, Outerbridge, Pig Iron Press, AWP, The Cape Rock.* Others. Work in Progress: Completing first volume of poems, *Making Our Way*
Awards or inclusion in other biographical books: Individual Artist Award, Michigan Council for the Arts, 1990-1991
What is the aim or goal of your writing? "I'm not sure I set out to write with a specific goal in mind; rather, my aim is discovery. I write in order to discover what makes us act as we do and what keeps us hopeful despite the many difficult circumstances of our lives. In many of my poems, however, I have come to the same discovery-the necessity for compassion and love in all human relationships."
May inquiries be sent to you about doing workshops, readings? Yes

WOLF-MORGAN, LOIS L.
Address: P.O. Box 404, Plymouth, Michigan 48170
Born: February 6, 1948; Flint, Michigan
Parents: Lawrence D. Lyden, Muriel E. Lyden
Children: Scott C. Morgan, Erin S. Morgan
Education: Oakland Community College, Oakland University, California Pacific University, Bachelor Degree, Master Degree
Career: Director and owner, Wolfe Associates, Plymouth, Michigan, 1985—. Program Director, Executive Managerial Development, U.S. Army Tank Auto Command, 1981-1985; Administrative positions, 1975-1981; Secretarial positions, 1966-1975. Former Owner/Director, Academic Funding Institute, Plymouth, Michigan

Writings: *Build Your Own Road* New Executive Press 1990; Berkley 1992. Work in Progress: *Breaking the Negativity Roadblock*
What is the aim or goal of your writing? "Encourage people to recognize that there is always a choice. Today's choices are tomorrow's reality!"
May inquiries be sent to you about doing workshops, readings? Yes

WOLFF, MARITTA M.
Address: 11622 Exposition Blvd., Apt. 1, Los Angeles, California 90064
Born: December 25, 1918; Sharon Township, Washtenaw County, Michigan
Parents: John W. Martin, Ivy G. (Ellis) Martin
Children: Hugh Stegman
Education: Grass Lake High School, Michigan. University of Michigan, B.A., Ann Arbor, Michigan, 1936-1940

Writings: *Button Wood* Random House 1962. *The Big Nickelodeon* Random House 1956. *Back of Town* Random House 1952. *About Lyddy Thomas* Random House 1947. *Night Shift* Random House 1942. *Whistle Stop* Random House 1941
Awards or inclusion in other biographical books: *Current Biography; Michigan Authors,* 1st ed., 2nd ed.; *Twentieth Century Authors,* others. Hopwood Awards, University of Michigan, 1938, 1939, 1940. Metro-Goldwyn-Mayer Novel Contest, 1947
What is the aim or goal of your writing? "I do not like to intellectualize about my work."
May inquiries be sent to you about doing workshops, readings? Yes

WOOD, IVAN L.
Address: 437 West Ridge Street, Marquette, Michigan 49855
Pseudonym: Ike Wood
Born: August 12, 1915; Manistique, Michigan
Parents: James E. Wood, Mayme Wood
Children: Mary-Margaret, James, Mariann
Education: Manistique High School, Graduate G.E.D., 1930-1933. Institute of Applied Science, Forensic Studies, Graduated cum laude, Chicago, Illinois, 1956-1958. Northern Michigan University, Marquette, Michigan, 1978-1979
Career: Retired, Author, Marquette, Michigan, 1982—. Forensic Studies Instructor, Criminal Justice Department, Northern Michigan University, Marquette, Michigan, 1978-1982. Director of Identification, Michigan Department of Corrections, Marquette State Prison, Marquette, Michigan, 1956-1978. Prison Guard, Prison Officer, Marquette State Prison, Marquette, Michigan, 1943-1956. Timber

Cruiser, Logging Scaler, Burrell Logging Company, Munising, Michigan, 1941-1943

Writings: *100 Years at Hard Labor* KA-ED Publishing Company 1985. *Criminal Identification Procedures* NMU Publishing 1972

Awards or inclusion in other biographical books: Michigan Corrections Association, Publication of the Year, 1986. State of Michigan Corrections Commission, Resolution, 1986. MCO Service Employees' International Union AFL-CIO, 1986. Criminal Justice Department of Northern Michigan University, Distinguished Fellowship Award, 1989

What is the aim or goal of your writing? "To compile authentic historical facts in the field of corrections and local history. Also, to further the study of forensic procedures in criminal investigation."

May inquiries be sent to you about doing workshops, readings? No

WOODFORD, ARTHUR MACKINNON

Born: November 23, 1940; Detroit, Michigan
Parents: Frank B. Woodford, Mary-Kirk (MacKinnon) Woodford
Children: Mark, Amy
Education: University of Wisconsin, 1958-1960. Wayne State University, B.A., Detroit, Michigan, 1963. University of Michigan, A.M.L.S., Ann Arbor, Michigan, 1964
Career: Librarian, Detroit Public Library, 1964-1972; Personnel director, 1972-1974. Assistant director, Grosse Pointe Public Library, 1974-1977. Director, St. Clair Shores Public Library, 1977—

Writings: *All Our Yesterdays: A Brief History of Detroit* (with father, Frank B. Woodford) Wayne State University 1969. *Detroit and Its Banks: The Story of Detroit Bank & Trust* Wayne State University 1974. *Substitute Currency of Early Detroit* Geneve Libraire Droz 1978. *Detroit: American Urban Renaissance* Continental Heritage 1979. *Charting the Inland Seas: A History of the U.S. Lake Survey* U.S. Army Corps of Engineers, Detroit District 1991

Awards or inclusion in other biographical books: *Biographical Directory of Librarians in the United States and Canada; Contemporary Authors; Michigan Authors,* 2nd ed.

WOODFORD, FRANK BURY (1903-1967)

Born: February 27, 1903; Detroit, Michigan
Parents: Fred V. Woodford, Florence (Bury) Woodford
Children: Susan, Arthur
Education: Hillsdale College, Hillsdale, Michigan, 1921-1923. Wharton School, University of Pennsylvania, B.S., 1925
Career: Reporter, Chief Editorial Writer, *Detroit Free Press,* 1931-1962. Deputy City Treasurer, Detroit, Michigan, 1962-1967

Writings: *A Telescope on Mars* privately printed 1925. *Lewis Cass, the Last Jeffersonian* Rutgers University 1950; Octagon Books 1973. *Yankees in Wonderland* Wayne State University 1951. *Mr. Jefferson's Disciple; a Life of Justice Woodward* Michigan State University 1953. *Gabriel Richard, Frontier Ambassador* (co-author with Alfred Hyma) Wayne State University 1958; Catholic Family Book Club 1959. *Introduction to Mighty Mac* Wayne State University 1958. *Law Day U.S.A.* State Bar of Michigan 1961. *We Never Drive Alone: the Story of the Automobile Club of Michigan* (Detroit) 1958, 1961?

Father Abraham's Children; Michigan Episodes in the Civil War Wayne State University 1961. *Alexander J. Grosebeck: Portrait of a Public Man* Wayne State University 1962. *Harper of Detroit; the Origin and Growth of a Great Metropolitan Hospital* (co-author with Philip P. Mason) Wayne State University 1964. *Parnassus on Main Street: A History of the Detroit Public Library* Wayne State University 1965. *All Our Yesterdays: A Brief History of Detroit* (co-authored with his son) Wayne State University 1969
Awards or inclusion in other biographical books: *Contemporary Authors; Who Was Who in America*

WOODS, JOHN

Born: July 12, 1926; Martinsville, Indiana
Parents: Jefferson Woods, Doris (Underwood) Woods
Children: David, Richard
Education: Indiana University, B.S., 1949; M.A., 1954. University of Iowa, 1957-1958
Career: U. S. Military Service, 1944-1946. Assistant professor, Western Michigan University, Kalamazoo, Michigan, 1955-1961; Associate professor, 1961-1965; professor, 1965-1992, retired. Visiting professor, University of California at Irvine, 1967-1968. Visiting professor, poet-in-residence, Purdue University, 1975. Workshops, judged contests, read poetry at hundreds of colleges and universities. Recorded his poetry for Library of Congress, Aural Press

Writings: *The Deaths at Paragon* Indiana University Press 1955. *On the Morning of Color* Indiana University Press 1961. *The Cutting Edge* Indiana University Press 1966. *Keeping Out of Trouble* Indiana University Press 1968. *The Knees of Windows* Westigan Review 1971. *Turning to Look Back: Poems, 1955-1970* Indiana University Press 1972. *Voyages to the Inland Sea* (with others) Wisconsin State University at LaCrosse 1972. *Alcohol* Pilot Press 1973. *Bone Flicker* Juniper Books 1974. *Striking the Earth* Indiana University Press 1976. *Thirty Years on the Force* Juniper Press 1977. *The Night of the Game* Raintree Press 1982. *The Valley of Minor Animals* Dragon Gate 1982. *The Salt Stone: Selected Poems* Dragon Gate 1985. In various anthologies such as *A Geography of Poets* Bantam 1979. Poems, stories, plays, reviews in numerous magazines such as *Saturday Review, Kenyon Review, Calliope*. Radio dramas broadcasted
Awards or inclusion in other biographical books: *Contemporary Authors; Contemporary Poets; Directory of American Poets; Indiana Authors and Their Books; International Who's Who in Poetry; Lincoln Library of Language Arts; Michigan Authors,* 2nd ed.; *Penguin Companion to American Literature; Who's Who in the Midwest; World Authors; Writers Directory.* Theodore Roethke Award, *Poetry Northwest,* 1969. Award, National Endowment for the Arts, 1970. First Distinguished Faculty Scholar Award given by Western Michigan University, 1978. First poet-in-residence at Western Michigan University, 1991. Distinguished Michigan Artist Award, 1978. Michigan Individual Artist Grant, 1981. National Endowment for the Arts Fellowship, 1982. In an April 22, 1992 article in the *Kalamazoo Gazette,* he comments: "It's a part of my nature to deal with life in plain and simple terms. Its accessiblity is also what some critics don't like about my writing. They think poets should deal with the eternal verities instead of various images of popular culture. I can't resist it."

WOOLSON, CONSTANCE FENIMORE (1840-1894)

Pseudonym: Anne March
Born: March 5, 1840; Claremont, New Hampshire
Parents: Charles Jarvis Woolson, Hannah Cooper (Pomeroy) Woolson. (Niece of James Fenimore Cooper)
Education: Schooling in Cleveland, Ohio. Madame Chegary's School in New York City, graduating in 1858, head of her class
Career: Summers spent at family cottage until 1869 on Mackinac Island, Michigan. Travel, United States, England, Italy, Egypt. Pioneer in regional American fiction

Writings: *The Old Stone House* Lothrop 1873. *Castle Nowhere: Lake-Country Sketches* Harper 1875. *Rodman the Keeper: Southern Sketches* Harper 1880; Garrett Press 1969. *Anne* Harper 1882; Arno 1977. *For the Major* Harper 1883. *East Angels* Harper 1886. *Jupiter Lights; A Novel* Harper 1889. *Horace Chase* Harper 1894; Literature House 1970. *The Front Yard and Other Italian Stories* Harper 1895. *Dorothy and Other Italian Stories* Harper 1896; Books for Library Press 1969. *Mentone, Cairo, and Corfu* Harper 1895, 1896. Others. Short stories in *Harper's Monthly, Atlantic Monthly, Lippincott's,* others. A monument, named Anne's Tablet after the heroine of one of her novels, is located on Mackinac Island, Michigan. Stone benches at the site also have titles of her works chiseled on them.

Awards and inclusion of other biographical books: *American Authors and Books; American Authors 1600-1900; American Biographies; American Women Writers; Childhood in Poetry; Dictionary of American Authors; Dictionary of American Biography; Dictionary of Literature in the English Language; Dictionary of North American Authors; Reader's Encyclopedia; Reader's Encyclopedia of American Literature; Twentieth Century Biographical Dictionary of Notable Americans,* several others

WOOTEN, TERRY

Address: Stone Circle Dr., Kewadin, Michigan 49648
Born: November 20, 1948; Cadillac, Michigan
Parents: Dale Wooten, Mona (Bugbee) Wooten
Children: Ezra, Ablaisia
Education: Marion High School, H.S. Diploma. Western Michigan University, 1967-1970, Kalamazoo, Michigan, worked toward a degree in education. Apprenticed with poet-bard, Max Ellison, 1980-1985
Career: Builder and host poet of the Stone Circle, a triple ring of large boulders forming a natural amphitheater. The Stone Circle hosts other poets, storytellers and folk musicians who perform to audiences up to 300 in the summer. Self-employed poet who has made his living for the past 7 years performing and conducting writing workshops in schools K-College level. Has been keynote speaker for many Young Author celebrations, performer for the Michigan Council for the Humanities' programs. Included in the Directory of Michigan Touring Arts Attractions and the Creative Writers in the Schools. Presenter for: 28th Annual Detroit Women's Writers' Conference, 1988 State MAME Conference, 1987 Michigan Oral History Conference, 1990 State Conference of Michigan English Teachers, 1991 Jackson Storyfest, Flint Institute of Arts, Thunder Bay Writers Conference, 1992 Michigan Reading Association Conference, and others. Oral repertoire of over seven hours includes Michigan folklore, American classics, children's poems, Native American, and others. Film: *Poets of the Stone Circle* (an educational video by Paradigm Video) 1988

Writings: *Jutting Out Into the Water* Stone Circle Press 1991. *Boulders in Exile* Stone Circle Press 1989. *Words Wild with Bloom* (about his friend, Max Ellison) Stone Circle Press 1987. *The 45th Parallel* (a limited handbound edition)1983. *Okeh* Stone Circle Press 1984. *Got in an Argument with Harmony* Stone Circle Press 1978. Poems included in: *Contemporary Michigan Poetry: Poems from The Third Coast* Wayne State University Press 1988. *The Stone Circle Anthology* Stone Circle Press 1984. Work in Progress: Book of children's poetry with author-illustrator, Jane Stroschin. Numerous contributions in magazines and newspapers

Awards or inclusion in other biographical books: Creative Artist Award Finalist, Michigan Council for the Arts, 1988

What is the aim or goal of your writing? "Through my work I try to show how the written and oral traditions of literature enhance each other. When people talk there are ideas and lines of poems going off in the air like firecrackers. It is the poet's job to catch and store these moments, borrowing and building off of earlier voices, until you become an oracle of voices past and present, as well as your own. It is these voices, condensed into poetry, that provide us with a unique and valuable way to preserve our personal or community myths for the examination and enjoyment of contemporary and future generations."

May inquiries be sent to you about doing workshops, readings? Yes

WORST, JOHN W.

Address: 3301 Midland Drive S.E., Grand Rapids, Michigan 49546
Born: July 13, 1940; Grand Rapids, Michigan
Parents: William A. Worst, Frances J. (Vander Mole) Worst
Children: Laura, Sarah
Education: Calvin College, A.B., Grand Rapids, Michigan, 1958-1962. Ohio State University, M.A., Columbus, Ohio, 1962-1964. University of Michigan, Ph.D., Ann Arbor, Michigan, 1967-1974
Career: Professor of Music, Calvin College, Grand Rapids, Michigan, 1966—. Professor of Music, Dordt College, Sioux Center, Iowa, 1964-1966. Instructor in Music, University of Michigan, Ann Arbor, Michigan, 1967-1968

Writings: *Dancing in the Dark* (co-author) Eerdmans 1991. *Songs of Rejoicing* Selah 1988. *Hymns of the Month* Christian Schools International 1978-1982
May inquiries be sent to you about doing workshops, readings? Yes

WORTH, JANICE M.

Address: 942 E. 7th Street, Flint, Michigan 48503
Born: November 14, 1949; Canton, Ohio
Parents: Everett K. Worth, Carol L. Worth
Education: Wooster High School, Wooster, Ohio. Kent State University, B.A., Journalism, Kent, Ohio, 1967-1971. University of Michigan, M.S.W., Ann Arbor, Michigan, 1979-1981. Warren Wilson College, Swannanoa, North Carolina, M.F.A., 1992
Career: Coordinator, Adult Resource Center and Women's Center, University of Michigan-Flint, Flint, Michigan, 1987—. Director, Payee/Guardianship Program, Family Service Agency, Flint, Michigan, 1984-1987; Family Counselor, 1981-1984. Peace Corps Volunteer, U.S. Government, Nukualofa, Tonga, South Pacific, 1976-1978. Reporter, *Orange Coast Daily Pilot*, Costa Mesa, California, 1973-1976

Writings: *Home During a Dry Spell* Ridgeway Press 1989. Work in Progress: *Blissfield,* full-length collection of poems
Awards or inclusion in other biographical books: Creative Artist Award, State of Michigan, 1989
What is the aim or goal of your writing? "To use language passionately and with originality, respect and heart. To be honest, to pay attention, to celebrate and elegize the beauty and brevity of life."
May inquiries be sent to you about doing workshops, readings? Yes

WRIGHT, JAMES NORTH (1838-1910)
Born: 1838; Middletown, Connecticut
Career: Clerk, Minnesota Mine; Clerk, Agent, Quincy Mine. General Superintendent, Calumet, Hecla Mines, Keweenaw Peninsula, Michigan

Writings: *Where Copper Was King* Small, Maynard & Company 1905
Awards or inclusion in other biographical books: *Dictionary of North American Authors*

WRIGHT, JOHN COUCHOIS (1874-?)
Born: April 14, 1874; Harbor Springs, Michigan
Parents: John B. Wright, Roseine (Graveraet) Wright
Education: Harbor Springs High School. Petoskey Normal School, Petoskey, Michigan. Bay View Summer School, Bay View, Michigan
Career: Publisher, *Standard*, Harbor Springs, Michigan

Writings: *Pe-tah-se-ga and Other Poems* 1908? *Stories of the Crooked Tree* Lakeside Press 1915. *The Crooked Tree: Indian Legends and a Short History of the Little Traverse Bay Region* Matthew A. Erwin 1917. *The Great Myth* The Michigan Education Company 1922. *Chicago-Jig: Legend of the Indian Paradise* Babcock & Babcock 1934, self-published 1935. *Chicago-Jig: The Authentic Indian Tradition of the Happy Hunting Ground* self-published 1934. *Scenic Michigan in Verse* The Gratiot County Herald 1939
Awards or inclusion in other biographical books: *Childhood in Poetry. Detroit Times* contest winner. Commendation, President Franklin D. Roosevelt, for work in behalf of Indians and Conservation

WROBEL, JANUSZ, K.
Address: 1508 Dulong, Madison Heights, Michigan 48071
Born: July 5, 1953; Cieszyn, Poland
Parents: Wladyslaw Wrobel, Anna Wrobel
Children: Agata, Olga, Mikolaj
Education: Jagiellonian University, Cracow, Poland, M.A., 1973-1978; Ph.D., 1984
Career: Chairman, Foreign Languages Department, St. Mary's College, Orchard Lake, Michigan, 1992—. Lecturer, The Summer University of Polish Culture, Instituto Polacco Di Cultura Cristiana, Fondazione Giovanni Paolo II, Rome, Italy, 1992. Lecturer, International Studies, Oakland University, Rochester, Michigan, 1990—. Associate Professor, Chairman, Polish Studies Department, St. Mary's College, Orchard Lake, Michigan, 1989—; Assistant Professor 1986-1989. Visiting Lecturer, Slavic Department, Wayne State University, Detroit, Michigan, 1984-1986. Director of Polish Language Program for Foreigners, summer school of Polish Language and Culture, The Jagiellonian University, Cracow, 1984; others

Writings:*Language and Schizophrenia* John Benjamins (Amsterdam-Philadelphia)1990. *Poland in Polish: A Polish Language Handbook for Beginners* (with W. Miodunka) 2 vols. 3 tapes Warszawa Interpress 1986. *Papers from the Second Congress of the Scholars of Polish Origin* (editor) Warszawa-Krakow Ossolineum 1984. *People's Poland Through the Eyes of the Younger Generation* (editor) with Frank Corliss, Slavica Publishers, in press. In *Journal of Interdisciplinary Studies, Studium Paper, Polish Daily News*, others. Work in Progress: *New Poland-Old Obstacles*, book with B. Misztal

What is the aim or goal of your writing? "1) Psycholinguistic analysis of the language of schizophrenics 2) Situation in Poland after the collapse of communism."

May inquiries be sent to you about doing workshops, readings? Yes

WUNSCH, JOSEPHINE M.

Address: 830 Bishop Road, Grosse Pointe Park, Michigan 48230
Pseudonym: J. Sloan McLean (adult suspense in collaboration with Virginia Gillette)
Born: February 3, 1914; Detroit, Michigan
Parents: John F. McLean, (Sarah) Georgiana (Grant) McLean
Children: Katherine, Elizabeth, Edward, Jr.
Education: University of Michigan, B.A., Ann Arbor, Michigan, 1932-1936. Night classes, Wayne State University
Career: Writer-housewife, freelance, Grosse Pointe, Michigan, 1941—. Reporter, Women's Department, *The Detroit Free Press,* Detroit, Michigan, 1938-1941; Freelance, 1937-1938. Public relations, Jack Goehrin, New York, New York, 1936-1937. Speaker. Board member, Detroit Women Writers

Writings: *Flying Skis* David McKay 1962. *Passport to Russia* David McKay 1965. *Summer of Decision* David McKay 1968. *Girl in the Rough* First Love-Silhouette 1981. *Class Ring* Wildfire-Scholastic 1983. *Free As a Bird* First Love-Silhouette 1984. *Breaking Away* First Love-Silhouette 1985. *The Perfect 10* First Love-Silhouette 1986. *Lucky in Love* Crosswinds-Harlequin 1987. *Between Us* Crosswinds-Harlequin 1989. *The Aerie* (with Viginia Gillette) Nash 1974. Several reprinted in foreign languages. *Breaking Away* in closed circuit radio broadcast for blind. In *McCall's, Canadian Home Journal, Ford Times, Modern Bride, Yachting, Ski, Lakeland Yachting, Toronto Star Weekly.* Chapter in *Voices on Writing Fiction*

Awards or inclusion in other biographical books: *Michigan Authors,* 2nd ed.; *Something about the Author* Vol. 64; *Who's Who in the Midwest* 1984-1985. Work in Progress: Young adult book; adult suspense book

What is the aim or goal of your writing? "Goal??? At the height of the Great Depression-1936-upon graduating from the U of M my goal was simple enough. Landing a job. I was fortunate in that my experience as women editor of the *Michigan Daily* led to public relations and newspaper work. Following my marriage, I continued writing– my first sale was to the Dye-dee Wash magazine. From articles, I graduated to short fiction to books. My greatest satisfaction in the young adult field– the fan letters from young people identifying with my fictional characters, and the fact that an unknown someone in a faraway country is reading something I wrote right here in Michigan."

May inquiries be sent to you about doing workshops, readings? No

Y

YOUNG, ALBERT JAMES
Born: May 31, 1939; Ocean Springs, Mississippi
Parents: Albert James Young, Mary (Campbell) Young
Children: Michael
Education: University of Michigan, Ann Arbor, Michigan, 1957-1961. University of California, B.A., Berkeley, California, 1969
Career: Touring musician, 1957-1964. Disc jockey, KJAZ-FM, Alameda, California, 1961-1965. Instructor, San Francisco Museum of Art, 1967-1969. Instructor, Berkeley Neighborhood Youth Corps, California, 1968-1969. Lecturer, Stanford University, Stanford, California, 1969-1974. Screenwriter, Laser Films, 1972, Universal Studios, 1979, others. Writer-in- Residence, University of Washington, Seattle, Washington, 1981-1982. Speaker, lecturer. Founding editor, *Loveletter*, 1966-1968; co-editor, contributing editor of others

Writings: *Dancing: Poems* Corinth 1969, 1973. *New Directions in Prose and Poetry 22* New Directions 1970. *Snakes: A Novel* Holt 1970. *The Song Turning Back into Itself* Holt 1971. *Some Recent Fiction* San Francisco Book Company 1974. *Who is Angelina?* Holt 1975. *Geography of the Near Past* Holt 1976. *Sitting Pretty* Holt 1976. *Yardbird Lives!* Grove Press, distributed by Random House 1978. *Ask Me Now* McGraw-Hill 1980. *Bodies & Soul: Musical Memoirs* Creative Arts 1981. *The Blues Don't Change: New and Selected Poems* Louisiana State University Press 1982. *Kinds of Blue: Musical Memoirs*

D.S. Ellis, distributed by Creative Arts Book Company 1984. *Things Ain't What They Used to Be: Musical Memoirs* Creative Arts Book Company 1987. *Seduction by Light* Delta Books/Seymour Lawrence 1988. Others. Screenplays: *Nigger*; *Sparkle* 1972. In *Rolling Stone, New Times, Audience, Journal of Black Poetry*, others

Awards or inclusion in other biographical books: *A Biographical and Bibliographical Dictionary; Black American Writers Past and Present; Contemporary Authors; Dictionary of Literary Biography; International Who's Who in Poetry; Michigan Authors*, 2nd ed.; *Who's Who among Black Americans; Who's Who in the West.* Fellowship, Stanford University, 1966-1967. National Endowment for the Arts grants, 1968, 1969, 1975. San Francisco Foundation, Award, 1969. National Arts Council awards, 1968-1970. Citation, *New York Times*, 1980. Pushcart Prize, 1980. Before Columbus Foundation award, 1982. Others

YOUNG, DAVID E.

Address: 402 Houghton Street, Ontonagon, Michigan 49953
Born: February 11, 1947; Flint, Michigan
Parents: Eugene J.C. Young, Angeline M. Young
Children: Jonathan, Amy, David, Thomas
Education: Michigan State University, B.S., East Lansing, Michigan, 1969-1972. Flint Community Junior College, A.S., Flint, Michigan, 1966-1969. Flint Southwestern High School
Career: Park Ranger, Michigan Department of Natural Resources, State Parks Division, Porcupine Mountains Wilderness State Park, Ontonagon, Michigan, 1974—; Fort Wilkins State Park, Copper Harbor, Michigan, 1971-1974

Writings: *The Origin of the Second Amendment: A Documentary History in Commentaries on Liberty, Free Government and an Armed Populace During the Formation of the Bill of Rights* (editor) Golden Oak Books 1991. *True Bear Tales* Golden Oak Books 1987. Work in Progress: Revision of *True Bear Tales* for a second edition
What is the aim or goal of your writing? "To provide important factual information."
May inquiries be sent to you about doing workshops, readings? No

YOUNGS, ANNE C.

Address: 5171 Highway M35, Escanaba, Michigan 49829
Pseudonym: Anne Ohman Youngs
Born: June 25, 1939; Marquette, Michigan
Parents: Clifford F. Long, Ann I. (Hurskainen) Long
Children: Jeffrey Ohman, James Ohman, Neil Youngs
Education: Northern Michigan University, Marquette, Michigan, B.S., 1979-1981; M.A., 1985-1986. Vermont College of Norwich University Program for Writers
Career: English Instructor, Northern Michigan University, Marquette, Michigan, 1987—. English Instructor, Bay de Noc Community College, Escanaba, Michigan, 1981-1985

Writings: *Markers* Andrew Mountain Press 1988. In *Passages North Anthology* 1990, *The Third Coast: Comtemporary Michigan Poetry* 1988. *Patchwork-Selected Work by U.P. Writers*, 1989. *Anthology of Magazine Verse and Yearbook of American Poetry*, 1986-1987. Work in Progress: Book length poetry book, *Primary Colors*. Poetry chapbook, *Reminding Each Other*

Awards or inclusion in other biographical books: *Poets and Writers Directory,* 1989—. Prize winning entry, National Poetry Chapbook Competition. Chester H. Jones Foundation Anthology of National Poetry Competition Winners, 1987

What is the aim or goal of your writing? "To share experience, to present the 'ordinary' in a unique way, to touch other's lives through poetry."

May inquiries be sent to you about doing workshops, readings? Yes

Z

ZARIF, MARGARET MIN'IMAH (?-1983)

Pseudonym: Margaret Boone Jones

Born: Detroit, Michigan

Parents: William E. Boone, Manie (Bascome) Boone

Children: Michael

Education: Hillsdale College, 1940-1942; Wayne State University, B.A., Detroit, Michigan, 1944. Oberlin College, M.A., Oberlin, Ohio, 1947. Graduate work in Wayne State University and others

Career: District Field Director, African Methodist Episcopal Church, 1947-1949. Director of Religious Education, St. James AME Church, Cleveland, Ohio, 1949-1950. Teacher, rural Virginia, 1950-1963. Teacher, Toledo, Ohio, 1963-1966. Teacher, Detroit, Michigan, 1966-1981. Director, Salaam Travel Agency, Detroit, Michigan, 1981. Trustee Board Member, Afro-American Museum of Detroit. Member of founding committee, Your Heritage House. Board member of Fire Commissioners, Detroit Fire Department, 1974-1981. Newsletter editor, Muslim business organization

Writings: *Martin Luther King, Jr.: A Picture Story* Childrens Press 1968. *To Be Somebody: Portraits of Nineteen Detroiters* Vantage 1976. Wrote pamphlets for National Association of Sickle Cell Disease. In *World Muslim News, American Muslim Journal.* Articles for *Detroit Tribune*

Awards or inclusion in other biographical books: *Michigan Authors,* 2nd ed.; *Something about the Author; Who's Who of American Women.* National Association of Negro Business and Professional Women's Clubs, Detroit Chapter Award, 1969. Afro-American Museum of Detroit Award, 1976. Sojourner Truth, Toledo Chapter Award, 1976

ZEMAN, HENRY F.
Address: 768 Westview NW, Grand Rapids, Michigan 49504
Born: April 29, 1923; Grand Rapids, Michigan
Parents: Frank Zeman, Apolinia (Stygar) Zeman
Children: James, William, Theresa, Paul
Education: Davis Tech High School, Diploma, Grand Rapids, Michigan, 1939-1942
Career: Freelance outdoor writer, retired. Outdoor editor/staff photographer, *Grand Rapids Press,* 1952-1987

Writings: Magazine writer primarily outdoor writing, hunting, fishing, related subjects. Field editor, *Michigan Hunting & Fishing, Great Lakes Fisherman*
What is the aim or goal of your writing? "Continue to write to supplement Social Security and pension to degree to which I have become accustomed."
May inquiries be sent to you about doing workshops, readings? Yes

ZERLER, KATHRYN S.
Address: 548 Ridgeway, St. Joseph, Michigan 49085
Born: June 16, 1950; Benton Harbor, Michigan
Parents: Louis C. Schultz, Ardys J. Schultz
Education: Benton Harbor High School, Benton Harbor, Michigan. Western Michigan University, B.A., Kalamazoo, Michigan, 1968-71. Michigan State University, M.A., East Lansing, Michigan, 1973-1978. Continuing education workshops, writer's workshops
Career: Director, St. Joseph Today, St. Joseph, Michigan, 1984—. Reading Consultant, Lake Michigan College, Benton Harbor, 1983-1984; Lead Research Consultant, 1982-1983; Research Consultant, 1981-1982. Reading Consultant, Ingham Intermediate School District, Mason, Michigan, 1977-1981

Writings: *Talk of the Towns* St. Joseph Today 1991. *On the Banks of the Ole St. Joe* St. Joseph Today 1990. *Serving Business in Berrien County* Lake Michigan College 1982. *Directory of Training & Placement Resources for Berrien County* Lake Michigan College 1981. *Blended Pleasures* vols. 1, 2 The Sleeping Cat Press 1980. *Love Poems for Dreamers* The Sleeping Cat Press 1979. In *Lakeland Boating, South Bend Tribune, Showcase, Our Town Michiana, Actionline, Tri-State Vistas, West Michigan.* Work in Progress: *A Slip in Time* (working title) fiction
Awards or inclusion in other biographical books: *Who's Who in the Midwest,*1984
What is the aim or goal of your writing? "I want to write fiction".
May inquiries be sent to you about doing workshops, readings? Yes

ZLOTNIK, DONALD E.
Address: 2549 Coolidge Highway, Troy, Michigan 48084
Born: December 25, 1941; Saginaw, Michigan
Parents: Paul J. Zlotnik, Linda L. Zlotnik
Children: Michael, Nicole

Education: Saginaw High School, GED. Methodist College, B.S., Fayetteville, North Carolina, 1974. University of Southern California, MSED, 1976-1977. Officers Candidate School, Airborne School, 1965; Special Forces School 1965-1966
Career: Novelist/Columnist, Troy, Michigan, 1986—. Executive Manager, General Dynamics, Troy, Michigan, 1983-1986. U.S. Army Major, International, 1960-1981

Writings: *The Bronze Star* Signet/NAL 1992. *The Soldier's Medal* Signet/NAL 1991. *The Silver Star* Signet/NAL 1991. *The Distinguished Service Cross* Signet/NAL 1991. *The Medal of Honor* Signet/Nal 1991. *Court-Marshal* Warner Books 1989. *Black-Market* Warner Books 1989. *Prisoner of War* Warner Books 1989. *Baptism* Warner Books 1988. *Eagles Cry Blood* Zebra Books 1986. *Reclamas* Exposition Press 1972. Weekly columns, *Troy-Somerset* and *Northwest Gazettes.* Over a hundred columns published under the byline: *Thoughts From the Right.* Work in Progress: *Myk of the Dark Woods*, trilogy based on 2nd century southern Poland. *David's Child,* boy survial during Holocaust. *Amerasians,* children left in Vietnam. *War Sins*, murder mystery. *Luke,* about child pornography
Awards or inclusion in other biographical books: "I do not solicit awards, I judge the quality of my publications based on my readership. I write novels for the pure enjoyment of writing a story and not for personal recognition or gain."
What is the aim or goal of your writing? "To tell stories and hopefully, entertain my readership if only for a couple of hours."
May inquiries be sent to you about doing workshops, readings? Yes

ZUCKER, HELEN
Address: 14050 Vernon Street, Oak Park, Michigan 48237
Born: January 19, 1937; Manhattan, New York
Parents: Jack Goldberg, Anna Goldberg
Children: Laurie, Elizabeth
Education: Oakland University, Rochester, Michigan, B.A., 1977-1981; M.A., English, 1981-1983. Radcliffe Institute for Advanced Studies/Ruth Whitman Workshop, Cambridge, Massachusetts, 1992
Career: Fiction Editor, *The Bridge: A Journal of Fiction and Poetry,* Oak Park, Michigan, 1990—. Writing Instructor, Oakland University, Rochester, Michigan, 1984-Art Critic, *Observer,* Eccentric Newspapers, Birmingham, Michigan, 1977-1989; Theatre Reviewer, 1979-1981. Art Critic, *Detroit Monthly,* Detroit, Michigan, 1979-1982. Library Public Relations Writer, Bloomfield Hills, Michigan and Birmingham, Michigan

Writings: Short stories in *Wayne Review.* Hundreds of newspaper, magazine articles, 1968—. Work in Progress: *Honel: Girl with an Orange*
Awards or inclusion in other biographical books: Council of Literary Magazines and Small Presses New Magazine Award, 1991. Recommended, *Library Journal*, 1992. Runner up, Nimrod Award, 1981. Fellowship to MacDowell Colony, 1975. Fellowship, Mont Chateau. Fellowship Fiction Award, 1968. Fellowship to Suffield Writer/Reader Conference, 1965
What is the aim or goal of your writing? "To be honest-in an attempt to illuminate often impossible difficulties between generations. (As an editor, to find authoritative, lively writing-the pulse behind a voice)."
May inquiries be sent to you about doing workshops, readings? Yes

ZUIDERVAART, LAMBERT P.

Address: 515 Norwood Avenue SE, Grand Rapids, Michigan 49506
Born: August 1, 1950; Modesto, California
Parents: Martin Zuidervaart, Tena (Beliving) Zuidervaart
Education: Institute for Christian Studies, Ph.D., Toronto, Canada; Free University of Amsterdam, Netherlands, 1972-1981. Dordt College, B.A., Sioux Center, Iowa, 1968-1972
Career: Chairperson, Department of Philosophy, Calvin College, Grand Rapids, Michigan, 1991—; Professor of Philosophy, 1985—. Assistant Professor of Philosophy and Interdisciplinary Studies, The King's College, Edmonton, Alberta, Canada, 1981-1985. President, Board of Directors, Inn Roads Housing Cooperative, Ltd., Edmonton, Alberta, Canada, 1982-1985

Writings: *Adorno's Aesthetic Theory: the Redemption of Illusion* MIT Press 1991. *Dancing in the Dark: Youth, Popular Culture, and the Electronic Media* (co-author) Eerdmans 1991. *Kant's Critique of Beauty and Taste* Institute for Christian Studies 1977. Work in Progress: *Cultural Politics and Artistic Truth: Aesthetics After Heidegger*
What is the aim or goal of your writing? "To study the philosophical underpinnings of contemporary art and culture in order to promote social transformation."
May inquiries be sent to you about doing workshops, readings? Yes

ZWAANSTRA, HENRY

Address: 1707 Morningside S.E., Grand Rapids, Michigan 49506
Born: January 1, 1936; Grangeville, Idaho
Parents: John Zwaanstra, Gertrude Zwaanstra
Children: Karl, Kerrie, Matthew
Education: Calvin College, A.B., Grand Rapids, Michigan, 1954-1958. Calvin Seminary, B.D., 1958-1961. Free University of Amsterdam, Th.D., 1973
Career: Professor, Historical Theology, Calvin Theological Seminary, Grand Rapids, Michigan, 1963—

Writings: *Catholicity and Secession* Eerdmans 1991. *Reformed Thought and Experience in a New World* J.H. Kok, Kampen, The Netherlands 1973. Work in Progress: Study of World Council of Churches Programme to Combat Racism
Awards or inclusion in other biographical books: Association of Theological Schools, Faculty Scholarship and Research Grant, 1989
What is the aim or goal of your writing? "Increase knowledge of the historical life of the Christian Church."
May inquiries be sent to you about doing workshops, readings? Yes

(Page left blank for future expansion)

Sources Consulted

Adams, Oscar Fay., ed. *A Dictionary of American Authors.* Detroit: Gale Research, 1969.

"All about Chris Van Allsburg" (Student Page) *Learning 93*, (April/May 1993): 44.

Allegan County News & Gazette. (Allegan, Michigan), "Obituaries". February 27, 1986: 5.

Alpena News. (Alpena, Michigan), "Obituaries", December 18, 1986.

American Authors and Books. New York: Crown Publishers, 1972.

Anderson, David D., ed. *Michigan: A State Anthology.* Detroit: Gale Research Company, 1983.

Andrews, Clarence. "A Bibliography of the Literature and Lore Together With Historical Materials, of the Upper Peninsula of Michigan". *The Great Lakes Review* Vol. 3, No. 1 (Summer, 1976): 37-66.

Andrews, Clarence. *Michigan in Literature.* Detroit: Wayne State University Press, 1992.

Andrews, Clarence. "A Bibliography of Fiction and Drama By Women from Iowa and Michigan." *The Great Lakes Review,* Vol. VI, No. 1, (Summer, 1979): 56-68.

Andrews, Clarence. "A Bibliography of the Literature and Lore, Together With Historical Materials, of the Upper Peninsula of Michigan". *The Great Lakes Review* Vol. 3, No. 1 (Summer, 1976): 37-66.

ANSWER. Online Public Catalog, Library of Michigan. Lansing, Michigan.

Associations Directory of Michigan. Dearborn, Michigan: Primary Publications, 1993.

The Author's and Writer's Who's Who. Darien, Connecticut: Hafner, 1971.

"Awards To Be Given At Sojourner Truth Luncheon". *Battle Creek Enquirer*, (Battle Creek, Michigan), May 17, 1984, B-1, B-2.

Bader, Barbara. *American Picturebooks from Noah's Ark to the Beast Within.* New York: Macmillan Publishing Company, 1976.

Baker, Patricia J. "Henry Rowe Schoolcraft", Lansing: Michigan History Division, (Series 1, Number 6: Famous Michiganians): 1-4.

Banta, Richard Elwell, ed. *Indiana Authors and Their Books, 1816-1916; Biographical Sketches of Authors Who Published during the First Century of Indiana Statehood, with Lists of their Books.* Crawfordsville, Indiana: Wabash College, 1949.

Barnstone, Alike; Barnstone, Willis, eds. *A Book of Women Poets from Antiquity to Now.* New York: Schocken Books, 1987.

Battle Creek Sesquicentennial Committee. *Battle Creek Sesquicentennial 1831-1981.*

Beacham, Walton, ed. Vol. 3, *Beacham's Popular Fiction in America.* Washington, DC: Beacham Publishing, 1986.

Beacham, Walton, ed.; Niemeyer, Suzanne, ed. Vol. 1 *Popular World Fiction 1900-Present*. Washington, DC: Beacham Publishing, 1987.

Beetz, Kirk H.; Niemeyer, Suzanne; eds. Vol. 2, *Beacham's Guide to Literature for Young Adults*. Washington, DC: Beacham Publishing, Inc., 1990.

"The Bentley Library Annual Report 1973-1974". The Bentley Historical Library, Michigan Historical Collections, University of Michigan, Ann Arbor, Michigan: 33-45.

"Berkley's Lawton, 'Mr. Mich.,' Has Big Role in 'M' Celebration". *The Daily Tribune* (Royal Oak, Michigan), March 4, 1967: 7.

Bernagozzi, Tom. "Curriculum Adventures with Chris Van Allsburg", *Learning 93,* (April/May 1993): 42-43.

"Bibliography of Sources Relating to Women". Michigan History Division, Michigan Department of State. 2nd ed., rev. 1978.

The Bibliophile Dictionary; a Biographical Record of the Great Authors, with Bibliographical Notices of their Principal Works from the Beginning of History. Detroit: Gale Research, 1966.

Bigelow, Martha M. "Michigan's Pioneering Role in Education", Lansing: Michigan History Division, (Series 2, Number 3: Topics in History): 1-4.

Bishop, Bette, ed. "Count Your Blessings: Inspirational Verse by Edgar A. Guest". Treasures, Hallmark Cards, Inc.

Black, Albert G. *Michigan Novels: An Annotated Bibliography*. Ann Arbor: Michigan Council of Teachers of English, 1963.

Blayton, Zada A. "Nun Pens Novel Account of 'Blessed' Indian." *Saginaw News* (Saginaw, Michigan), August 3, 1991: A-4.

Bogater, Jillian. "Poet Paints With Words", *Cheboygan Daily Tribune*, (Cheboygan, Michigan), February 18, 1993: 1.

Books in Print. New York: R. R. Bowker.

Bradbury, Malcolm; Mottram, Eric; Franco, Jean; eds. *The Penguin Companion to American Literature*. New York: McGraw-Hill, 1971.

Brelin, Christa, ed. *Who's Who Among Black Americans 1992-1993*. Northbrook, Illinois: Who's Who Among Black Americans, Inc. Publishing Company, 7th ed.

Bugeja, Michael J. "Easy Writers: Three Prominent Poets Discuss the Quality That Sets Them Apart: Discipline". *Writer's Digest*. May 1993): 12-15.

Bulger, William T. Introduction to the Michigan Heritage edition of *The Shanty Boy*. Berrien Springs, Michigan: Hardscrabble Books, 1979.

Bureau of History, Michigan Department of State. "150 Years Worth Celebrating". (An introduction to Michigan's sesquicentennial sponsored by the McDonald's Restaurants of Michigan and the Detroit Free Press: an educational services special)

Bureau of Library Services, Michigan Department of Education. "Michigan Media: a Selected List of Learning Materials Useful in Elementary Schools." Lansing: 1971.

Cappel, Constance (Montgomery). *Hemingway in Michigan.* Vermont Crossroads Press, 1977.

Carter, Merton. "Who's Bruce Catton?" *Graphic,* (Petoskey, Michigan), July 21, 1977.

Case, Herbert Spaulding, ed. *The Official Who's Who in Michigan.* Vol.1, Munising: 1936 ed.

Catalog of Credentials: Michigan Authors' Association, 1911-1912. Detroit: 1912.

Catton, Bruce. *Waiting for the Morning Train.* New York: Doubleday, 1972.

Cemetery Records. Forest Hill, Stanton, Michigan.

Chambers, Robert. *Chamber's Cyclopedia of English Literature.* Volume VII, New York: American Book Exchange, 1881.

Chmielewski, Tom. "Paranoia of Cold War Years Inspires Local Novelist", *Kalamazoo Gazette,* (Kalamazoo, Michigan), November 8, 1992, Books Section.

Commire, Anne. *Yesterday's Authors for Children.* Detroit: Gale Research Company, 1977.

Compton's MultiMedia Encyclopedia. Compton's Learning Company, Britannica Software, 1990.

Conrad, Lawrence H. "Michigan Authors and Their Books". *Michigan Library Bulletin,* (XXVII, No. 2:71), 1926.

Contemporary Authors. Detroit: Gale Research Company. Various volumes, permanent, new rev. series.

Contemporary Novelists. London: St. James Press, 1991.

"Cordier Book Chronicles Lives of School Teachers of the Midwestern Plains". November 19, 1992. *Western News.* Kalamazoo: Western Michigan University.

Coyle, William, ed. *Ohio Authors and Their Books.* Cleveland: World Publishing Company, 1962.

Current Biography Yearbook. 1940, 1948, 1951, 1957, 1960, 1971, 1985, 1988, 1989. New York: H.W. Wilson Company.

Czuchna-Curl, Ardyce. "Hometown Author Will Sign Books", *Kalamazoo Gazette,* (June 7, 1992): B6.

The Daily Mining Gazette, (Houghton, Michigan), August 21, 1992: 18.

Detroit Public Library. *Michigan in Books,* 1956.

DeWeese, June LaFollette. *The History of the Library, University of Missouri-Columbia.* Columbia: University of Missouri, 1980.

DIALOG Online. Palo Alto: Dialog Information Services, Inc., 1991.

Dammann, Tom. "Hemingway Enjoyed His Time in North", *Petoskey News-Review,* (Oct. 19, 1990): 32-33.

Dictionary of American Biography. 20 Vols. New York: Charles Scribner's Sons, 1928-1936.

Dictionary of Indians of North America. Vol. 2, St. Clair Shores, Michigan: Scholarly Press, Inc.

Directory of American Scholars. Vol. 1: History. New York: Bowker, 1982.

"'Dollmaker' Author Buried in Kentucky". *Ann Arbor News,* (May 19, 1986).

Doud, Katherine. "Changes Afoot at Passages North Magazine". *Kalamazoo Gazette,* September 13, 1992: (Book Marks page)

Dunbar, Willis Frederick. *Michigan Through the Centuries.* Vols. 1, 2. New York: Lewis Historical Publishing Company, 1955.

Dictionary of Literary Biography. Vols. 4, 38, Detroit: Gale Research Company, 1985.

Dunbar, Willis Frederick. *Michigan Historical Markers.* Lansing: Michigan Historical Commission, 1967.

Edwin, Carl, ed. *New Michigan Verse.* Ann Arbor: University of Michigan Press, 1940.

Ehrlich, Eugene; Carruth, Gorton. *The Oxford Illustrated Literary Guide To the United States.* New York: Oxford University Press, 1982.

"Ernest Hemingway", *Sports Illustrated,* (May 5, 1986): 58-72.

Faust, Langdon Lynne, ed. *American Women Writers.* 2 Vols., New York: Frederick Ungar Publishing, 1983.

Feltner, Charles E.; Feltner, Jeri Baron. *Great Lakes Maritime History: Bibliography and Sources of Information.* 1st ed. Dearborn: Seajay Publications, 1982.

Foremost Women in Communications. New York: Foremost Americans, 1970.

Foster, Bernice M. *Michigan Novelists.* Ann Arbor: George Wahr, 1928.

Fourth Book of Junior Authors and Illustrators. New York: H.W. Wilson Company, 1985.

Fuller, George N., ed. "Centennial Souvenir: Commemorating the First Meeting of Michigan's First State Legislature, November 2, 1835." Lansing: Capitol Feature Service, State Historical Society: 11-12.

Fuller, George N., ed. *Michigan A Centennial History of the State and Its People.* 5 Vols. Chicago: The Lewis Publishing Company, 1939.

Fuller, Muriel, ed. *More Junior Authors.* New York: H.W. Wilson Company, 1963.

Gibson, Arthur Hopkin. *Artists of Early Michigan: A Biographical Dictionary of Artists Native To or Active in Michigan 1701-1900.* Detroit: Wayne State University Press, 1975.

Gilbar, Steven. "The Skyline is Detroit, and the Story Line is: Here's How Our City Looks Between the Covers of an Expatriate's Home Library", *Michigan: The Magazine of The Detroit News* (December 4, 1983): 36-40.

Goldstein, Laurence. "The Image of Detroit in Twentieth Century Literature." *Michigan Quarterly Review.* Vol. 25, (Spring, 1986): 269-291.

Goodrich, Madge Knevels, *A Bibliography of Michigan Authors*. Richmond: Richmond Press, Inc., Printers, 1928.

Graff, George P. "The People of Michigan", (State Library Occasional Paper No. 1), Michigan Department of Education, Bureau of Library Services, 1970: 5, 56.

Green, Andrew J. "A Centennial History of Michigan". *New York Times Book Review,* September 1, 1940.

"Gridiron Star Will Do His 'Stuff'." "Life Underwriter". (September, 1927): 1.

Grimm, Joe. "Michigan: A Sampler of the Lore of Great Lakes State." *Detroit Free Press,* December 4, 1988: H-7.

Halliwell, Leslie. *The Filmgoer's Companion.* New York: Hill and Wang, 1977.

Harley, Rachel Brett; MacDowell, Betty. *Michigan Women Firsts and Founders.* Lansing: Michigan Women's Studies Association, Inc., 1992.

Harris, Fran. *Focus: Michigan Women 1701-1977.* Michigan Coordinating Committee of the National Commission of the Observance of Women's Year, 1977.

Hart, James D., ed. *Oxford Companion to American Literature.* 5th ed. New York: Oxford University Press, 1983.

"Hemingway Weekend Set for Oct. 19-21", *Petoskey News-Review ,* (Petoskey, Michigan), October 5, 1990.

"Hemingway's Old Man and His Movie Epic". *Life.* (September 1, 1952): 124-129.

Henderson, James W. "Saginaw Poet's Works are 'of the People'." *The Saginaw News* (Saginaw, Michigan), December 5, 1986: C-2.

Herbert, Miranda C., ed; McNeil, Barbara, ed. *Biography and Genealogy Master Index.* Detroit: Gale Research, 2nd ed.

Herzberg, Max J. and staff of the Thomas Y. Crowell Company. *The Reader's Encyclopedia of American Literature.* New York: Thomas Y. Crowell, 1962.

Hilbert, Rachel M., ed. *Michigan Authors.* Ann Arbor, Michigan: Michigan Association of School Librarians, 1960.

Hilbert, Rachel M., ed. *Michigan Poets With Supplement to Michigan Authors 1960.* Ann Arbor: Michigan Association of School Librarians, 1964.

"Historic Women of Michigan: A Sesquicentennial Celebration". Lansing: Michigan Women's Studies Association, Inc., 1988.

"Historic Women of Michigan Theme Trail", Michigan Women's Historical Center and Hall of Fame, 3-fold, n.d.

"The History of Kellogg's". Battle Creek, Michigan: Kellogg Company, 1982.

Hoffman, Mark S., ed. *The World Almanac and Book of Facts.* New York: Pharos Books, 1992.

Hughes, Lanston; Bontemps, Arna, ed. *The Poetry of the Negro 1746-1970.* Garden City, New York: Doubleday, 1970.

Hulbert, William Davenport. *White Pine Days on the Taquamenon.* Lansing: The Historical Society of Michigan, 1949.

International Who's Who in Poetry. Cambridge, England: International Biographical Centre, 1977.

Introduction, *History of the Ottawa and Chippewa Indians of Michigan.* (Reprint of 1887 Ypsilanti edition of Chief Blackbird) Petoskey, Michigan: Little Traverse Regional Historical Society, 1977.

Ireland, Norma Olin. *Index to Women of the World.* Westwood: F.W. Faxon, 1970.

James, Edward T., ed. *Notable American Women 1607-1950* Vols. 2, 3. The Belknap Press of Howard University Press 1971.

Jarvis, Nancy H., ed. *Historical Glimpses-Petoskey.* Petoskey, Michigan: Little Traverse Historical Society, 1986.

Johnson, Allen; Malone, Dumas. *Dictionary of American Biography.* Vol. 4, New York: Charles Scribner's Sons, 1930.

Johnson, Curt, ed. *Who's Who in Writers, Editors & Poets: 1989-1990.* Highland Park: December Press.

Johnson, Rossiter. *Twentieth Century Biographical Dictionary of Notable Americans.* 10 Vols. Boston: The Biographical Society, 1904; Reprint Detroit: Gale Research, 1968.

Kaplan, Justin. Review of *Hemingway in Love and War* by Henry Serrano Villard, James Nagel Northwestern University Press in*The New York Times Book Review* (October 22, 1989): 7.

"Kellogg: Barney Brought Home Our Most Distinguished Citizen". *Petoskey News-Review,* (Petoskey, Michigan), February 14, 1968.

Kern, John. "A Short History of Michigan". Michigan History Division, Michigan Department of State, 1977.

Kibler, James E., Jr., ed. *American Novelists Since World War II.* Second Series. Detroit: Gale Research Company, 1980.

Kirk, John Foster, ed. *Allibone: A Critical Dictionary of English Literature.* 2 Vols. Philadelphia: J.B. Lippincott, 1891; reprint, Detroit: Gale Research, 1965.

Kirkpatrick, D.L., ed. *Reference Guide to American Literature.* Chicago: St. James Press, 1987.

Kotlowitz, Alex. "At 75, Full Speed Ahead: For Author Harriette Arnow, Life Begins at the End of the Road", *Michigan: The Magazine of the Detroit News,* (December 4, 1983): 14-28.

Krohe, James Jr. "Come Home, Papa, All is Forgiven", *The New York Times Book Review,* (July 8, 1990): 7, 23-26.

Kunitz, Stanley J.; Haycraft, Howard, ed. *American Authors 1600-1900.* New York: H.W. Wilson Company, 1938.

Kunitz, Stanley J.; Haycraft, Howard, ed. *American Authors 1600-1900.* New York: H.W. Wilson Company, 1938.

Kunitz, Stanley J.; Haycraft, Howard, ed. *The Junior Book of Authors.* New York: H.W. Wilson Company, 1951.

Kunitz, Stanley J.; Haycraft, Howard, ed. *Twentieth Century Authors.* New York: H.W. Wilson Company, 1942.

Kunitz, Stanley J., ed; Colby, Vineta, asst. ed., *Twentieth Century Authors.* first supplement. New York: H.W. Wilson Company, 1955.

Lamport, Warren W. *Michigan Poets and Poetry.* Leslie: Michigan Publishing Company, 1904.

Legislative Service Bureau. *Michigan Manual* 1991-1992.

Library of Michigan. *Directory of Michigan Libraries,* 1991-1992. Lansing.

Library of Michigan. *Michigan Directory of Humanities Scholars.* Lansing, 1990.

Library Staff. *Henry Ormal Severance, Librarian 1907-1937.* Columbia: University of Missouri, 1937.

Literary Michigan: A Sense of Place, A Sense of Time. The Michigan Council for the Humanities, 1988.

Little Traverse Historical Society. "The Passenger Pigeon". (Vol. 2: Issue 3). Petoskey, Michigan: Summer 1991: 3.

The Lincoln Library of Essential Information. Vol. 2. Buffalo, New York: The Frontier Press Company, 1969.

The Lincoln Library of Social Studies. Vol. 3. Buffalo, New York: Frontier Press, 1969.

"Lives of the Authors." *Esquire,* (July, 1988): 100-103.

Lovell, Susan, senior ed. *The College Handbook.* New York: College Entrance Examination Board, 23rd ed.

"Lowes Look Back 50 Years", *Battle Creek Enquirer* (Battle Creek, Michigan) July 15, 1971: A-10.

Magill, Frank N., ed. *Cyclopedia of World Authors.* New York: Harper & Row, 1958.

Main Library Reference Departments. *Michigan Readings.* Detroit Public Library, 1987.

Mainiero, Lina, ed. *American Women Writers.* New York: Frederick Ungar, 1979-1982.

"Man in an Apron". *Newsweek,* (March 17, 1947): 70.

Manassah, Sallie M., ed. *A Year to Remember* Albert L. and Louise B. Miller Foundation 1982.

A Manual of Style. The University of Chicago Press. Chicago: 10th ed.

Marguerite de Angeli Library. "Marguerite de Angeli Centennial Celebration 1889-1989". Lapeer, Michigan.

Marowski, Daniel G.; Matuz, Roger, ed. *Contemporary Literary Criticism.* Vol. 42, Detroit: Gale Research Company, 1987.

Martineau, Janet I. "Author! Author! Meow! Meow!" *The Saginaw News*, (Saginaw, Michigan) July 27, 1991: A-1, A-2.

Martineau, Janet I. "Writing Cures Anxiety Over the Cat Who Died." *The Saginaw News*, (Saginaw, Michigan), July 27, 1991: B-1, B-2.

Massie, Larry. *From Frontier Folk to Factory Smoke: Michigan's First Century of Historical Fiction.* Au Train: Avery Color Studios, 1987.

Matlaw, Myron, ed. *Modern World Drama; An Encyclopedia.* New York: Dutton, 1972.

Mattson, Steven J., ed. Michigan Council for the Humanities. *Celebrate! Great Lakes.* East Lansing:1989.

Max, Daniel. "McMillan's Millions." *New York Times Magazine,* (August 9, 1992): 20+.

Magill, Frank N., ed. *American Literature Realisism to 1945.* Pasadena: Salem Press, 1981.

McGraw-Hill Encyclopedia of World Drama. Vol. 2, New York: McGraw-Hill, 1972.

Membership Directory. Michigan Association for Media in Education. 1992.

Men of Progress Embracing Biographical Sketches of Representative Michigan Men. Detroit: Evening News Association, 1900.

Michigan Association of Educational Representatives, Inc. 1991-1992 Directory. Remus: M.A.E.R., 1991.

Michigan Council for the Arts. *Creative Writers in Schools.* 1990-1992.

Michigan Council for the Humanities. *Directory of Michigan Humanities Scholars.* East Lansing: 1st ed.

Michigan Department of Transportation Map. 1992.

"Michigan Heritage Library Reprint, 'The Shanty Boy' Now Available". *The Historical Society of Michigan Newsletter*, Vol. 5/No. 3 (September-October, 1979): 1.

Michigan History Division, Michigan Department of State. "Michigan's Historic Attractions": Lansing, 1973, 1976.

Michigan History Magazine. Vols. 1, 6, 8, 11, 12, 13, 14, 16, 20, 24, 25, 27, 28, 30, 33, 35, 41, 48.

Michigan Librarian. Vol. 42 No. 7. (Fall 1976): 12-13.

Michigan Librarian. Vol. 58 No. 10. (November/December 1992): 1-3.

Michigan Official Directory and Legislative Manual 1935-1936.

Michigan Pioneer and Historical Collections. Lansing: Michigan Pioneer and Historical Society, various volumes, 1874-1912.

"Michigan Poetry Sampler". (Supplement to the PRC Newsletter and Calendar) Poetry Resource Center of Michigan. Detroit: Summer 1983.

"Michigan Readings". Main Library Reference Departments, Detroit Public Library. Detroit: 1987.

Michigan State Library. "Library Tools" (5: A Selected List of Basic and Recent Books and Pamphlets about the Wolverine State): Lansing, 1966.

Michigan Today. Ann Arbor: University of Michigan, December 1990, February 1991, May 1991, December 1991, June 1992.

"Michigan Women: A History of Achievement", *Detroit Free Press*, (special school supplement project): 24.

Michigan Writers' Program. *Michigan: A Guide to the Wolverine State.* New York: Oxford University Press, 1941.

MichNet. Online Computer Network, Ann Arbor, Michigan, providing access to Michigan University Library Systems online card catalogs: Central Michigan University, Eastern Michigan University, Michigan State University, Michigan Technological University, Kalamazoo College, University of Michigan, University of Michigan Law Library, University of Michigan at Dearborn, Western Michigan University, Wayne State University, Oakland University, Detroit Public Library, others.

Miel, Carol, ed. *Stanton Centennial 1863-1963.* Stanton: Stanton Centennial, Inc., 1963.

Miles, William. Introduction, Charles W. Jay's *My New Home in Northern Michigan and Other Tales.* Berrien Springs: Hardscrabble Books, 1979.

Miller, Madelaine Hemingway. *Ernie.* New York: Crown, 1975.

Moran, Neil. "For Best-Selling Author, Pickford (pop. 600) is Still Home", Presque Isle Electric: *Michigan Country Lines* (January/February 1992): 10-11.

Morrill, Claire. "Author Led in Fight to Save the Waning Land of the Pine." *Detroit Free Press*, (Detroit, Michigan) July 5, 1936.

Mosher, Edith R.; Williams, Nella Dietrich. *From Indian Legends to the Modern Book-Shelf.* Ann Arbor: George Wahr, 1931.

Mulder, Arnold. "Authors and Wolverines." *Saturday Review of Literature.* Vol. 19, (March 4, 1939): 3-4, 16.

Mulder, Arnold. "Michigan as a Field for the Novelist", *Michigan History*, Vol. 6: No. 1, (1922):142-155.

Nemanic, Gerald, ed. *A Bibliographical Guide to Midwestern Literature.* Iowa City: University of Iowa Press, 1981.

Nerber, John. Introduction to Kirkland, Caroline *A New Home or Life in the Clearings* New York: G.P. Putnam 1953.

Norton, Karen. "Dormant Ideas Ripen With Thought". *Traverse City Record-Eagle,* (Traverse City, Michigan), August 2, 1992: 1E, 3E.

Ohle, William H. *How it was in Horton Bay.* Boyne City: Lake Street, 1989.

"Our First Poetry Contest Winners". *Michigan: The Magazine of the Detroit News* (April 22, 1984): 10-11, 15, 17-21.

Petoskey News-Review, (Petoskey, Michigan), "Obituaries", October 22, 1984: 2.

Preston, Wheeler. *American Biographies.* Detroit: Gale Research, 1974.

Ranville, Judy; Campbell, Nancy A. *Memories of Mackinaw.* Petoskey: Little Traverse Printing, 1976.

Readers' Guide to Periodical Literature. Various volumes. New York: H.W. Wilson.

Reginald, R., ed. *Science Fiction and Fantasy Literature.* Detroit: Gale Research, 1979.

Richardson, Kenneth, ed. *Twentieth Century Writing.* Levittown, New York: Transatlantic Arts, Inc., 1971.

Saginaw News, (Saginaw, Michigan), "Obituaries", May 31, 1992.

Samudio, Josephine, ed. *Book Review Digest.* New York: H.W. Wilson Company, 1975.

Scheer, Luke. "Michigan and the Old Northwest: From the Ice Age to the End of French Rule". Great Lakes Greyhound Lines, Inc., 1945.

Scherman, David E.; Redlich, Rosemarie. *Literary America.* New York: Dodd, Mead & Company, 1952.

Siepmann, Katherine Baker, ed. *Benet's Reader's Encyclopedia.* 3rd ed. New York: Harper & Row, 1987.

"Sept. 22 Reading by Kalamazoo Writers to Benefit the Homeless as Part of National Fund-Raiser", *Western News.* (Kalamazoo, Michigan) Western Michigan University, September 17, 1992.

Severance, Henry O. *The Story of a Village Community.* New York: Stechert & Co., 1931.

Seymour-Smith, Martin. *Novels and Novelists.* New York: St. Martin's Press, 1980.

Sharp, Robert Farquharson, ed. *A Dictionary of English Authors.* London: Kegan Paul, Trench, Trubner, 1904; reprinted, Detroit: Gale Research, 1978.

Shaw, John MacKay. *Childhood in Poetry* 1st Supplement. Detroit: Gale Research, 1967.

Siepmann, Katherine Baker, ed. *Benet's Reader's Encyclopedia.* New York: Harper & Row, 1987.

Silberman, Eve. "Michigan in Fiction", *Michigan Today.* (Ann Arbor, Michigan) University of Michigan, Vol. 20, No. 6, (December, 1988): 1-5.

Skora, Lois. "17 Women Chosen for Hall of Fame", *Detroit Free Press,* (October 19, 1983):?-2B.

Something about the Author. Vols. 15, 28, Detroit: Gale Research Inc.

State Library Services. "Read About Michigan." Michigan Department of Education, n.d.

Taylor, Donna, Editorial Chairperson. *Michigan Authors.* Ann Arbor: Michigan Association for Media in Education, 1980.

Taylor, Donna, ed. *The Great Lakes Region in Children's Books.* Brighton, Michigan: Green Oak Press, 1980.

Telephone Directories.

Third Book of Junior Authors. New York: H.W. Wilson Company, 1972.

Thomas, Craig A. "Woods' Words" *Kalamazoo Gazette,* (Kalamazoo, Michigan), April 22, 1992: B-1, B-8.

Tinling, Marion. *Women Remembered– A Guide to Landmarks of Women's History in the United States.* New York: GreenWood Press, 1986.

Tipton, James; Wegner, Robert E., ed. *The Third Coast: Contemporary Michigan Fiction.* Detroit: Wayne State University Press, 1982.

"Trinity Evangelical Free Church Bulletin". Stanton: April, 1985.

Troester, Rosalie Riegle, ed. *Historic Women of Michigan: A Sesquicentennial Celebration.* Lansing: Michigan Women's Studies Association, 1987.

Turabian, Kate L. *A Manual for Writers of Term Papers, Theses, and Dissertations.* Chicago: The University of Chicago Press, 1987.

The 20th Century Biographical Dictionary of Notable Americans, Detroit: Gale Research, 1968.

20th Century Literary Criticism. Vol. 12, Detroit: Gale Research, 1984.

Unger, Leonard, ed. Vol. 2, *American Writers.* New York: Charles Scribner's Sons, 1972.

"U.S. Census-1900". Montcalm, Michigan, June 9, 1900, Sheets 3B, 4B.

Vernoff, Edward; Shore, Rima, eds. *The International Dictionary of 20th Century Biography.* New York: New American Library, 1987.

Vincent, Hal. *The World's So Full of Things.* Detroit: Harlo Press, 1966.

Vinson, James, ed. *Contemporary Novelists.* New York: St. Martin's Press, 1972.

Vinson, James; Kirkpatrick, D.L., eds. *Twentieth-Century Western Writers.* Detroit: Gale Research Company, 1982.

Wallace, William Stewart, ed. *A Dictionary of North American Authors.* Detroit: Gale Research, 1968.

Walz, Grace. *Andrew Jackson Blackbird of L'Arbre Croche.* Thesis, Western Michigan University, Kalamazoo, Michigan, 1964.

Ward, Jeff. "Author Encourages Cheboygan Students", *Cheboygan Daily Tribune,* (May 14, 1992): 1, 14.

Ward, Martha E., et al. *Authors of Books for Young People.* Metuchen, New Jersey: Scarecrow Press, 1971.

Warfel, Harry R. *American Novelists of Today.* New York: American Book Company, 1951.

Warner, Robert M.; Vander Hill, C. Warren, ed. *A Michigan Reader 1865 to the Present.* Grand Rapids: Eerdmans, 1974.

"Wayne County Census-1900". Detroit, Michigan, E.D. 6, sheet 9, line 70.

Wellisch, Hans H. *Indexing From A to Z.* New York: H.W. Wilson, 1991.

Westener. "The Book Nook". September, 1992. Kalamazoo: Western Michigan University.

White, Sue. "Delta Prof's Book Digs up 'Buried' Lumbermen, Laborers." *Saginaw News*, (Saginaw, Michigan), October 6, 1990: B-3.

Who Was Who among English and European Authors. Detroit: Gale Research, 1978.

Who Was Who among North American Authors. Detroit: Gale Research, 1976.

Who Was Who in America. Vols. 1, 2, 3, 4, 5, 7, 9, Chicago: Marquis.

Who's Who in American Art 1973. New York: Jaques Cattell Press/R.R. Bowker Company.

Who's Who in Library Service. 3rd, 4th ed. New York: The Grolier Society, 1955, 1966.

Who's Who in the World. 2nd. ed.; 4th ed. Wilmette, Illinois: Marquis, 1974-1975; 1978-1979.

Willard, Frances Elizabeth; Livermore, Mary A., eds. *American Women: Fifteen Hundred Biographies with over 1,400 Portraits; a Comprehensive Encyclopedia of the Lives and Achievements of American Women during the Nineteenth Century.* Detroit: Gale Research, 1973 (c1897).

The Writers Directory. New York: St. Martin's Press. 3rd, 4th eds.

Yesterday's Authors of Books for Children. Detroit: Gale Research

Zip Code Directories.

Author Index

Names followed by an* indicate authors willing to do workshops or readings. Names printed in itallics are pseudonyms. These authors are are found in the text under their real names.

Geographical Index of Authors

The entries in this index are selected using the following criteria:
1. If an author lives in a Michigan city, he or she is referenced to that city.
2. If the author does not live in Michigan, but was born in the state, reference is given to the birthplace.
3. Should an author's career relate to a particular Michigan location and there is no information available about the current address or birthplace, then the city which relates to the career is used.
4. If the author's only association with Michigan is through writings, then an attempt was made to reference a prominent location used in his or her writing.

As a point of interest, the populations of most cities are listed according to the 1990 census. This number is printed to the right of the city name. Those towns listed without populations are usually very small.

Author Index

St. Joseph
    Krause, F.
    Niles, G.
    Williamson, A.
    Zerler, K.
Stambaugh 1,281
    Carli, A.
    Hill, J.
    Reimann, L.
    Shovald, A.
Stanton 1,504
    Ellsworth, D.
Sturgis 10,130
    Gallup, L.
Suttons Bay 561
    Mitchell, J.
    Thorn, B.
Swartz Creek 4,851
    Mitchell, E.
Sylvan Lake 1,884
    Robbins, L.

T

Taylor 70,811
    McArthur-Weberman, P.
Temperance
    Chorzempka, R.
    Macaro, C.
Three Oaks 1,786
    Kuntz, L.
Toivola
    Vachon, J.
Traverse City 15,155
    Barnes, H.
    Hacker, D.
    Lund, H.
    Parker, K.
    Routsong, A.
    Titus, H.
    Wakefield, L.
Trenton 20,586
    Pitrone, J.
Troy 72,884
    Lahey, C.
    Northup, A.

Stchur, J.
Zlotnik, D.

U

Union City 1,767
    Knapp, R.
    Newberry, P.

V

Vulcan
    Armstrong, C.

W

Walled Lake 6,278
    Mitchell, N.
Walloon Lake
    Hemingway, E.
Warren 144,864
    Binkowski, D.
    Kicknosway, F.
Washington
    Buzzelli, E.
Watervliet 1,867
    Lobdell, H.
Webberville 1,698
    Tennis Hamlin, R.
West Bloomfield
    Field, E.
    Tomey, I.
West Branch 1,914
    Gildner, G.
White Cloud 1,147
    Burkland, C.
    Steele, J.
Williamston 2,922
    Cleland, C.
Wolverine 283
    Gearhart, C.
    Sumerix, G.
Wyandotte 30,938
    McGuane, T.
Wyoming 63,891
    Sharpsteen, E.

Author Index

Y

Ypsilanti 24,846
    Jefferson, M.
    Moore, C.

Z

Zeeland 5,417
    DeKruif, P.